Governance and Politics of China

COMPARATIVE GOVERNMENT AND POLITICS

Founding Series Editor: The late **Vincent Wright**

Published

Rudy Andeweg and Galen A. Irwin
Governance and Politics of the Netherlands

Nigel Bowles
Government and Politics of the United States (2nd edition)

Paul Brooker
Non-Democratic Regimes: Theory, Government and Politics

Robert Elgie
Political Leadership in Liberal Democracies

Rod Hague and Martin Harrop
Comparative Government and Politics (6th edition)

Paul Heywood
The Government and Politics of Spain

B. Guy Peters
Comparative Politics: Theories and Methods
[Rights: World excluding North America]

Tony Saich
Governance and Politics of China (2nd edition)

Anne Stevens
Government and Politics of France (3rd edition)

Ramesh Thakur
The Government and Politics of India

Forthcoming

Judy Batt
Government and Politics in Eastern Europe

Robert Leonardi
Government and Politics in Italy

Comparative Government and Politics
Series Standing Order
ISBN 0–333–71693–0 hardcover
ISBN 0–333–69335–3 paperback
(outside North America only)

You can receive future titles in this series as they are published by placing a standing order. Please contact your bookseller or, in the case of difficulty, write to us at the address below with your name and address, the title of the series and the ISBN quoted above.

Customer Services Department, Macmillan Distribution Ltd
Houndmills, Basingstoke, Hampshire RG21 6XS, England

Governance and Politics of China

Second Edition

Tony Saich

First edition 2001
Reprinted twice
Second edition 2004

Published by
PALGRAVE MACMILLAN
Houndmills, Basingstoke, Hampshire RG21 6XS and
175 Fifth Avenue, New York, N.Y. 10010
Companies and representatives throughout the world

PALGRAVE MACMILLAN is the global academic imprint of the Palgrave
Macmillan division of St. Martin's Press, LLC and of Palgrave Macmillan Ltd.
Macmillan® is a registered trademark in the United States, United Kingdom
and other countries. Palgrave is a registered trademark in the European
Union and other countries.

ISBN 1–4039–2184–9 hardback
ISBN 1–4039–2185–7 paperback

This book is printed on paper suitable for recycling and made from fully
managed and sustained forest sources.

A catalogue record for this book is available from the British Library.

A catalog record for this book is available from the Library of Congress.

Saich, Tony.
    Governance and politics of China / Tony Saich — 2nd ed.
        p.   cm. — (Comparative government and politics)
    Includes bibliographical references and index.
    ISBN 1–4039–2184–9 (cloth) — ISBN 1–4039–2185–7 (pbk.)
    1. China—Politics and government—1949– 2. China—Economic policy—
    1949– I. Title. II. Comparative government and politics (Palgrave (Firm))

JQ1510.S26 2004
951.05—dc22   2003063272

10   9   8   7   6   5   4   3
13   12   11   10   09   08   07   06   05

Printed in China

To Yinyin, Alex and Amanda

Contents

List of Maps, Boxes and Figures

Map

Boxes

Figures

Preface to the Second Edition

Over the winter and spring of 2002–03, the Chinese Communist Party (CCP) appointed a new General Secretary, Hu Jintao and a new Premier, Wen Jiabao, to oversee China's future development. This completed a major leadership transition from what is commonly referred to as the 'Third Generation' of leaders to the 'Fourth', a group of technocrats trained during the late 1950s and 1960s. Given the multitude of challenges China faces, it probably never occurred to them that their first major challenge would be in the health sector let alone with a sickness (Severe Acute Respiratory Syndrome, SARS) that would let loose a global concern. Their response to the disease reveals interesting signs about their approach to and the remaining problems with governance in China. After the initial attempts at a cover-up, international pressure and domestic information flows made it impossible for the Chinese leadership to remain in denial. Certainly, if the spread of the disease is brought under control effectively, the prestige of the new leadership will be greatly enhanced. Unlike outgoing President Jiang Zemin and his supporters, they have appeared business-like, open and willing to adopt modern management techniques. Yet 'old politics' has also reasserted itself. We see different factions trying to position themselves to take credit for the 'victory' while the party as a whole is extolling its virtues in taming the viral beast. The traditional propaganda system has also kicked in with little ditties such as 'Angels in White Coats' that pay homage to the nurses and doctors of China who, moved by love of the party and concern for the people, have worked tirelessly. However, it is clear that fundamental shortcomings in China's system of management and governance exacerbated the problem and got the CCP into the mess in the first place. It should help the leadership realize that in a 'wired' world it is not so easy to screen and control information as effectively as in the past nor is it possible in a global world to maintain an open system for business investment but close off flows of information and deny transparency.

However, in some ways the fact that this leadership transition took place at all is remarkable as when the Soviet Union collapsed in 1991 many thought that it would not be long before the People's Republic of China followed. The CCP had just survived the massive student-led demonstrations of 1989 that protested against official corruption and authoritarian political rule. These demonstrations by millions of urban Chinese exposed deep divisions within the senior leadership about the way forward and considerable disillusionment and distrust among society. The regime was saved only by the intervention of the People's Liberation Army (PLA) and it faced a major task to restore its tarnished image and authority, an authority that was weakened further by the subsequent economic recession. By 1992, senior leader Deng Xiaoping saw that any attempt to return to a more traditional, centrally planned economy was doomed to failure and would undermine the party's remaining legitimacy. He recognized that the only way forward was for the CCP to deliver economic benefits to China's citizens and he set in train an economic free-for-all that ignited growth rates of 12–14 per cent and encouraged huge numbers of citizens and party, state and military officials to get involved in business. This clearly saved the regime but it also set off the highest inflation levels since the early years of the People's Republic of China (PRC), gave a boost to the rising corruption, and further loosened party control over state and society. During the 1990s as Jiang Zemin consolidated his power as party general secretary and Zhu Rongji took greater control over economic issues, they wrestled to address these negative legacies by setting economic growth on a firmer footing while strengthening the authoritarian power structure. The new general secretary, Hu Jintao (appointed in November 2002) and Premier Wen Jiabao (in March 2003) are still grappling with these legacies, especially how to extend the fruits of reform to those who have not benefited so well to date. The problems of governance and social equity provide a major test for China's new leadership and how well they deal with them will determine the future and longevity of CCP rule.

At the same time, the leadership is grappling with the deeper legacies of its Soviet inheritance while trying to ready the nation for the shock of World Trade Organization (WTO) entry. It is no easy task and the challenges are complex for policy-makers. At the same time, they must provide policy responses and priorities for its industry and financial sector to compete internationally; transform its state-owned sector without encountering major social unrest; provide a new framework for urban social welfare and rebuild the rural system; legislate for a growing private economy; while dealing with de-industrialization in the cities they must accommodate industrialization of the countryside; and find employment for some 200 million surplus labourers in the countryside. Any one of these policy challenges could overwhelm a government's capacity, yet the CCP leaders must deal with all of them at the same time.

To do justice to this complexity in an introductory text is no easy matter. In the chapters below I have tried to present some of the complexities of governing the most populous country in the world. The danger is that almost anything one writes seems too simple but too many qualifications tend to confuse as much as clarify. It is a difficult line to tread. I hope that the book will be of interest not only to those beginning to thread their way through the maze of Chinese politics, but also to those who already know the basics as well as to students of comparative politics, transitional regimes, communist and post-communist politics and the politics of development.

There are a number of specific problems with writing an introduction to Chinese politics. First, few have knowledge of the country before starting a university or other programme. China barely figures as a subject on the syllabus at secondary school. In addition, the general assumption that the institutions, theories and practices developed within Europe and the United States are the norm of politics means that the study of countries such as China are often pushed to the periphery of the syllabus.

Second, China is changing so fast that it is difficult to keep abreast of developments. It sets a challenge to highlight what is significant and enduring and to ignore what is irrelevant and ephemeral. China is a maze of intricacies, complexities and contradictions. In 2002 and 2003 the Sixteenth Party Congress and the Tenth National People's Congress (NPC) met and subsequently a number of new policy initiatives have been launched, others will certainly follow. Updates to this book in light of major developments will be posted on the Palgrave website at http://www.palgrave.com/politics/saich/.

Third, all political systems experience a disjuncture between political practice and rhetoric and between social reality and the desires of the political centre. This disjuncture is even greater in China. When Prime Minister Blair or President Bush makes a speech about their vision for their respective countries, no one believes that this reflects entirely political and social reality. Such pronouncements provide a policy blueprint or political aspiration that is contested within the bureaucracy and by the local political authorities and society. Such visions represent an ideal type of the kind of society that the leaders would like to see. In the past some observers of the Chinese political scene took what leaders said to represent social reality and saw the political system as geared to implementing the pronouncements of the CCP's General Secretary. Perhaps the fact that China's ruling party still calls itself a *communist party* conjures up visions of a totalitarian political system that really does function with one heart and mind from top to bottom. Reality is quite different. Contrary to much press reporting and general perceptions, the political centre does not control the system throughout and there is significant deviation from central policy across bureaucracies and at the local level. In some senses, real politics in China is local politics. It is at the local level that problems have to be solved concerning economic policy and social equity. Policy implementation can vary enormously even within one province in accordance with the local distribution of power. This pluralism of policy outcome has led to different analyses of the Chinese state as being essentially predatory, corporatist, clientelist, or bureaucratic–authoritarian. Making sense of this seemingly contradictory country is what makes the study of its politics and society so endlessly fascinating.

This complexity is one of the main themes that runs through the book together with the notion that history and institutions matter. Reform did not begin with a blank slate in 1978 and even the best macroeconomists have to deal with the fact that policy implementation is predicated on responses drawn from historical and cultural repertoires and mediated through political institutions that have been inherited from the Maoist years. The focus is on the politics and governance of China during this process of transition. The use of the term 'governance' moves us beyond the functioning of government institutions and administrative departments to the broader issues of how individual citizens, groups and communities relate to the state. It includes processes and institutions, both formal and informal, which guide and restrain the policy challenges. Included are issues of accountability and transparency and the potential role of actors within civil society and the international community.

Three main themes emerge from the chapters below. First, the economic reform programme has been more consistently successful than many outside observers have predicted over the years, but it is now facing more significant challenges. The CCP has shown a remarkable capacity to adapt to the rapidly changing environment, and its performance has looked particularly impressive when compared to developments in post-Soviet Russia. However, the question now arises as to whether the limits of the current development strategy have been reached. Many of the problems now confronting China's leaders are those of delayed reform. Much of the initial success and popular support stemmed from the fact that there were relatively few losers and those who did lose out were politically marginalized. It is now apparent that as reform moves to the next stage and China integrates further into the world economy, there will be significant losers, including those workers and institutions that have formed the core of the CCP socialist system. The easy reforms have been completed and China has benefited enormously from a process of catching up with its East Asian neighbours. As one eminent Peking University professor said to me in the summer of 1999, 'reform' is no longer a popular word.

Time is no longer on the side of China's leaders, and with the requirements of WTO compliance applying external pressure the pace of change will accelerate. Muddling through might no longer be sufficient. At the end of the 1990s, deflation was a new problem and it was clear that the massive state-led investment programme has not stimulated the economy as expected and in any event cannot be a long-term solution. Future reform must get to grips with the problems of the financial sector to provide a sound environment for state-owned enterprise (SOE) restructuring, further investment and the optimal use of savings. It must set as a priority expansion of the service sector that can provide a major source of future employment. However, this can take place only with a significant shift of investment resources to education. Without this, China will suffer from a continual shortage of skilled labour that will leave much of the country on the lower rungs of the production chain and it will not be able to follow the development strategies of Japan, South Korea and Taiwan. While most analysts focus on the question of state enterprise reform, this is a temporary problem and a political problem for the CCP given its traditional power base and privileging of an urban proletarian elite over other workers and farmers. The real challenge for the CCP remains as always in the countryside, and further reform of marketing and distribution needs to be pursued.

Second, China, like many transitional economies, has not been able to deal well with the social transition and the development of social policy has lagged badly behind economic development. In major part, this derives from the CCP's bias towards what it sees as productive forces and the health and education level of its population are not factored in sufficiently. Yet failure to tackle social policy effectively could also lead to undermining the progress made with economic reforms. For example, the demographics of China while currently favourable will begin to turn over the next 10–15 years. Unless China's leaders are able to get to grips with pension and other welfare reforms the economic advancement for many in this generation could be undone in the next by an unaffordable welfare burden. The fears that SARS might spread into the rural areas highlighted the weakness of the health infrastructure for this section of the population.

China's new leaders must also deal with the distribution of the benefits of the reforms. One distinctive feature of China's development in comparison with other East Asian politics is its toleration and even encouragement of inequality as a driving force for change. The current development strategy favours the coast over the inland areas, the urban over the rural, and male over female. The inability to develop the hinterland will act as a brake on economic growth as it will limit the size of the domestic market. It will also provide the potential for social conflict as the politics of resentment may arise. The urban bias of current policy needs to be changed and the structural impediments that block rural dwellers from benefiting fully from the reforms need to be removed. While women have enjoyed the general benefits of reform, more freedom of choice and rising prosperity, they have been disfavoured by comparison with men. They have been encouraged to retire early, are the first to be laid off from SOEs, bear the brunt of the family-planning programme, and shoulder a disproportionate amount of the rural labour. It is not surprising that women have no effective representation in the political system.

The third theme is that while there has been substantial adaptation of institutions, there has been insufficient genuine political reform. New institutions have been set up to manage the new economy and a legal system has been revived and extended to preside over it. Social organizations with varying degrees of autonomy have been established to meet people's material and leisure needs and, to a much lesser extent, their spiritual ones. However, with the exception of the village election programme, little has been done to make the system more accountable. The CCP still rules as an autocratic elite often out of touch with the consequences of its own economic policies. As good Marxists they should recognize that substantive change in the economic base must impact on the political superstructure. The truth is that Marx is irrelevant to their visions of the political future and those who may read more liberal tracts on the need for checks, balances and accountability keep quiet for fear of being branded a 'bourgeois liberal'. By default, theories of authoritarianism hold sway. At the local level, at its worst this system can lead to rule by corrupt, despotic cabals who see the local population merely as a source of revenue. It is hard to see such a system providing the kind of stability that will produce long-term economic growth.

TONY SAICH

Update material for this title is available on the publisher's website at http://www.palgrave.com/politics/saich/.

Acknowledgements

First and foremost I should thank Steven Kennedy, my publisher at Palgrave. His persistence and good humour overcame my reservations about writing an introduction to Chinese politics. He was always helpful with creative advice and suggestions. He must have the patience to test a saint.

I am grateful to the students and staff of the Sinologisch Instituut, Leiden University, the Netherlands who provided a good environment for teaching and research. I would particularly like to thank my new academic home, the Kennedy School of Government, Harvard University, and the students in my courses since 1999 in which tried out many of the ideas in this book. My understanding of contemporary China has been shaped by a number of teachers and friends, of whom David S. G. Goodman, Stuart R. Schram, and the late Gordon White deserve special mention. I trust that the references in the text do justice to the influence of the work of other colleagues. I would like to thank two anonymous referees for their comments. I did not agree with all they wrote but they saved me from making a number of mistakes and caused me to amend some judgements.

My formative experience of China was spent in Beijing and Nanjing at the end of the Cultural Revolution (1976–77). This experience opened my eyes to the complexity of Chinese reality and to take nothing at face value. Many of the ideas expressed in the book were shaped by this early experience and by my five years as Representative of the Ford Foundation in China (1994–99). I learned an enormous amount from our Chinese grantees and staff at the Beijing Office. I enjoyed wrestling policy issues with Mary Ann Burris, Phyllis Chang, James Harkness, Joan Kaufman, Stephen McGurk and Nick Menzies. In addition, Pieter Bottelier and Arthur Holcombe were always a source of advice. However, it is to my Chinese colleagues too numerous to mention that I owe my greatest debt.

Nancy Hearst did a terrific job with the bibliography and picked up a number of errors that saved me from embarrassing myself even further. I would like to thank Nancy for all her help to the family and myself over the last 15 years or so.

Last I would like to thank Yinyin, Alex and Amanda – to whom this book is dedicated.

TONY SAICH

Romanization and Chinese Measures

The system of romanization for Chinese characters used in this book is the *Pinyin* system, as used by the PRC and scholars in the West. It may be adopted by Taiwan, which has traditionally used the Wade–Giles system. Students will come across this system not only in publications from Taiwan but also in most of the works written before 1979. Also, there are numerous names with familiar spellings in English that belong to neither of these two systems. Two names have been used in their more familiar spelling – Chiang Kai-shek and Sun Yat-sen.

Chinese measures

jin   Weight measure equal to 0.5 of a kilogram.
mu   Measure for land equal to one-sixth of an acre. Often spelt *mou*.
yuan Chinese currency unit. The value varies but in the year 2003 there were 8.3 *yuan* to the US dollar and 11.7 to the pound sterling.

List of Abbreviations

ABC	Agricultural Bank of China
ACFTU	All-China Federation of Trade Unions
ADB	Agricultural Development Bank
ADB	Asian Development Bank
AFP	*Agence France Presse*
APC	Agricultural Producers' Cooperative
APEC	Asia-Pacific Economic Cooperation Forum
ARF	ASEAN Regional Forum
ASEAN	Association of Southeast Asian Nations
CC	Central Committee
CCP	Chinese Communist Party
CDIC	Central Discipline Inspection Committee
CEC	Central Executive Committee
CMAC	Central Military Affairs Commission
CNN	Cable News Network
CPPCC	Chinese People's Political Consultative Conference
CPSU	Communist Party of the Soviet Union
EBF	Extra budgetary funds
FBIS-CHI	*Foreign Broadcast Information Service – China*
FDI	Foreign direct investment
FEER	*Far Eastern Economic Review*
GDP	Gross domestic product
GLF	Great Leap Forward
GMD	Guomindang (Kuomintang, National Party)
GNP	Gross national product
GONGO	Government-Organized NGO
ILO	International Labour Organisation
IMF	International Monetary Fund
IPO	Initial public offering
ISP	Internet Service Provider
Jin-Cha-Ji	Shanxi–Chahar–Hebei
Jin-Ji-Yu-Lu	Shanxi–Hebei–Shandong–Henan
MFA	Multi-Fiber Agreement
MFN	Most-Favoured Nation
MOCA	Ministry of Civil Affairs
NATO	North Atlantic Treaty Organization

NGO	Non-governmental organization
NPC	National People's Congress
NPL	Non-performing loan
PLA	People's Liberation Army
Politburo	Political Bureau
PPP	Purchasing power parity
PRC	People's Republic of China
SAR	Special Administrative Region
SARS	Severe Acute Respiratory Syndrome
SCMP	*South China Morning Post*
SETC	State Economic and Trade Commission
SEZ	Special Economic Zone
SFPC	State Family-Planning Commission
Shaan-Gan-Ning	Shaanxi–Gansu–Ningxia
SME	Small- and medium-sized enterprise
SOE	State-owned enterprise
SWB: FE	*Summary of World Broadcasts: The Far East*
TVE	Township and village enterprises
UN	United Nations
UNDP	United Nations Development Programme
UPI	*United Press International*
US	United States
VAT	Value-added tax
WHO	World Health Organization
WTO	World Trade Organization

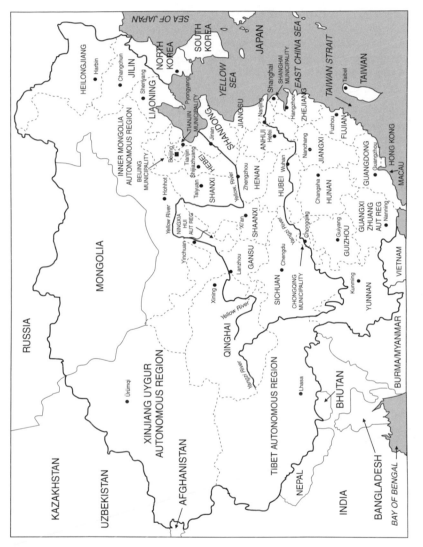

The People's Republic of China

1

Introduction

Some years ago, I was in a jeep driving down a mountain road in rural Sichuan and was held up by a long queue of traffic meandering down the hill to a new bridge that was being dedicated. Getting out of the jeep I wandered down to the bridge to witness an elaborate ceremony complete with the lighting of incense and various actions to ward off evil spirits. Somewhat facetiously, I began to ask those waiting what the Communist Party must think about this ceremony as it clearly represented an example of 'superstitious practice' so soundly denounced during the Cultural Revolution (1966–76) and still denounced today, albeit with less severity. I was greeted with puzzled faces before one person replied that the man in the exotic robes leading the ceremony *was* the party secretary. As the most important person in the village, he had no choice but to dedicate a new bridge that would link it to the world outside and bring greater wealth.

The event set me thinking about the relationship between the party, the state and society and between China's tradition and modernity. Did the party secretary believe in the ceremony and its power to conjure up good spirits to protect the bridge or was he simply going through the motions to increase credibility among the local population? Was the party secretary importing the power of the party into the village community or bringing heterodox beliefs into the party or both? The traditional nature of the ceremony contrasted with the objective of building the bridge that would integrate the local community with the world outside. The bridge provided the link to the market that is the driving force for development in the post-Mao years. Such small events are daily occurrences throughout rural and urban China and they cause us to question any notion of China as a monolith. China comprises a patchwork of local cultures and histories that the Chinese Communist Party (CCP) and its nationalist and imperial predecessors have tried to weld into a unitary entity. While the CCP may have tried to penetrate society more thoroughly than its predecessors, the last 20 years have revealed the residual power of local cultures.

More recently, in 1998 I was walking out of the tranquillity of the cradle of the communist revolution in Yan'an, where Mao had moved his red army in the late 1930s, only to be besieged by the trinket sellers who are the products of China's economic reform. From Mao Zedong's China to Deng Xiaoping's

1

in a few paces. The market responds to the desires of consumers rather than to those of communist ideologues, something clearly seen by the books on sale. While those sold inside Yan'an, such as *Mao Zedong Enters Yan'an*, tell the official story of the revolution, the books on sale outside, often under the counter, tell a different tale. They range from Mao Zedong's notorious womanizing, through the inner-secrets of who destroyed whom in the party's new headquarters (Zhongnanhai in Beijing), the corruption of a former mayor of Beijing, to unofficial biographies of former general secretaries, Hu Yaobang and Zhao Ziyang. These are the CCP's hidden histories, those the conservative party veterans do not want their people to know about, but they are the ones that the people with interest and money want to buy. Rather than a revolutionary world full of selfless heroes, they tell stories of betrayal, corruption and greed. Whose history, whose politics? This warns us not to take official pronouncements at face value and to peer behind the public façade to discover the reality of how the Chinese polity really works.

This chapter seeks to introduce the reader to the diversity of China, its land and its peoples, and how CCP policy since 1949 has affected them.

A Land of Diversity

As the two anecdotes reveal, China is a very complex land where multiple realities are operating beneath a façade of a unitary nation-state. However, this does not mean as some have claimed that China may fall apart into its regional components as a result of the reforms (Segal, 1994) or that a *de facto* federalist structure is emerging (Wang, 1995). Rather, we should be careful about any generalization we make and be aware that the same policy will impact on different areas and different groups in China in a variety of ways, sometimes with unexpected results.

China's land, climate and peoples exhibit a wide range of diversity. The land mass is roughly equal to that of the United States (9.6 million square kilometres) but is home to a population of around 1.26 billion (about five times that of the United States), meaning that every fifth child is born in China. However, this population is not spread evenly across the land and while the images of teeming cities full to bursting are correct, there are massive expanses of China where one can roam the hills or desert for days and barely see a soul. While the population density is 126 sq. km for the country as a whole, the figure is 383 sq. km for the eastern coastal regions and only 51 sq. km for the western provinces (Benewick and Donald, 1999, p. 14).

This population spread has always been the case with the predominantly peasant population concentrated along the river deltas and basins of the east, providing the bodies for the development of the mega-cities of Shanghai, Tianjin, Beijing and further west, Chongqing (see map, p. xxiii). By contrast the high Tibetan-Qinghai plateau is home to a sparse, scattered population engaged in pastoral activities. The plateau lies some 4,000 metres above sea level and occupies a full 20 per cent of China's land mass. Radiating out from the plateau are the major rivers of China, Southeast Asia and the Asian sub-continent. The Yangzi, Yellow, Mekong, Red, Ganges and the Brahmaputra all find their source here on this desolate plateau. Beyond the plateau there is a series of smaller descending plateaus and basins that eventually give way to the major plains of the east such as the Yangzi Delta, the North China Plain and the Northeast (Manchuria) Plain.

The huge oceans to the east, the plateau to the west and the surrounding mountain ranges have protected China throughout its history. This, combined with the continuation of some form of the Chinese state over two millennia, contributed to an insular attitude to alternative modes of thought and an ethnocentrism that the dominant Han Chinese felt was justified by the heritage to which they were the unique heirs. This insularity is reflected by the name of China itself, *Zhongguo*, which literally means the middle or 'central' king-dom. Yet even here there have been variations. China has witnessed periods of extensive dealings with foreigners such as in the Han (205 BC–AD 220) and the Tang (AD 618–907) dynasties. These were periods of extensive trading when foreign products were well received in China and when Chinese goods reached far-flung corners of the globe. This trade was even accompanied by the influx of foreign systems of thought. Most noticeable was the increasing influence of Buddhism, which arrived from India from the late Han period onwards. The later Qing period (AD 1644–1911), despite some attempts to keep foreigners out, and the Republican period (1911–49), were both influ-enced by foreign trade and the influx of new ideas. The Taiping Rebellion (1850–64) with its strange mix of half-baked Christianity, iconoclasm and traditional notions of peasant rebellion mounted a major challenge to Confucian orthodoxy (Spence, 1996). The May Fourth Movement (1915–19), in part a response to the decision to cede the German concession of Shandong to Japan following the First World War, also witnessed a major attack on the Confucian tradition and revealed an intellectual fascination with a whole host of foreign ideas ranging from liberalism to Marxism to anarchism (Chow, 1960). Indeed, during the reforms, the CCP has tried to make use of the more cosmopolitan trading of China's coastal regions as a key element in its economic programmes. Policy has favoured a development strategy that relies heavily on coastal trade and investment by revitalizing historic links with the overseas Chinese communities in Southeast Asia and beyond.

Given that China has such an expansive and varied land-mass, it will come as no surprise that there is enormous climatic variation, much more so for the winters rather than the summers. While most of the country lies in the temperate zone, there are wide variations of climate. The northeast freezes with temperatures dropping as low as minus 25–30 degrees centigrade, and even the capital Beijing can still get the occasional winter day of minus 10–15 degrees, although the average temperature for January hovers just a few degrees below zero. By contrast, Kunming in the southwest province of

Yunnan is known as the city of eternal spring, Guangzhou (Guangdong) enjoys winters with around 15 degrees and the island of Hainan has a balmy tropical climate. This north–south climatic divide led the CCP to decree that south of the Yangzi River public buildings would not be heated in winter. I have never been so cold in my life as in the winter of 1976–77 when studying at Nanjing University just south of the Yangzi river. We used to look forward to occasional trips across the Yangzi by ferry to sit in the local post office north of the river that was allowed heating.

The forces of nature have not been tamed as fully as in more advanced countries, and this has resulted in different problems. Rainfall is variable and each summer one is treated to the news that while certain areas have been subjected to flooding (Jiangxi, Zhejiang, Hunan, Jiangsu), other areas are suffering from severe drought (Hebei, Henan, Shanxi). South China depends on the vagaries of the monsoon for its rainfall whereas most of the north and west of China does not receive its effects. Thus, while almost 6 million hectares were affected by flooding in 1997, 20 million were affected by drought (Benewick and Donald, 1999, p. 87). The severity and diversity of these problems may be illustrated by the fact that in 1981 millions of people in north-central China faced quite severe food shortages because of extensive drought; in the western province of Sichuan, 1.5 million people lost their homes because of floods. The water shortages of the north have been exaggerated by the industrial development and urbanization of recent years and the watertable of the North China Plain has been dropping precipitously. This has led to the ambitious government programme to divert water from the abundant rivers of the south to the north.

These climatic and topographic variations have caused a rather varied environment for agricultural production. It is only in the areas around the Yangzi River and the south that the flooded paddy fields are commonplace. In fact, most of China is dependent on dry-field cropping of wheat and millet. The staple for most in the north is noodles and steamed bread rather than the rice that many associate with being Chinese. This dependence on staple grains has meant that traditionally the overwhelming majority of China's population has settled along the fertile plains and basins that provide suitable arable land. By contrast, the grasslands of Inner Mongolia and Ningxia, the far northwest and Tibet are the home to livestock with vast stretches of land for grazing. The periphery in the northeast and southwest is home to China's main remaining forest cover. This forestry cover has been declining rapidly, it now covers only 14 per cent of the land mass and perhaps as much as 90 per cent of the remaining coverage is threatened. The current coverage is considered insufficient for economic needs and for everyday use (Xu and Pei, 1997). While the government often blames local practices such as swidden (slash and burn) agriculture in southwest China for the decline in the remaining forests and the subsequent soil erosion and flooding, it is clear that the major culprit in recent times has been the government itself through its massive forestry industry. With the decline of forest cover and the expansion of arable land and urbanization, there has been a decline in China's great biodiversity and wildlife. Animals such as elephants, tigers and the golden monkey are to be found only in small parts of remote Yunnan, while the giant panda can only be found in declining numbers in a few Sichuan reserves.

These more remote areas are home to most of China's 55 recognized national minorities (there were 400–500 applications to be recognized, Blum, 2000, p. 74). While these minorities comprise less than 10 per cent of China's total population (still almost 100 million), the remainder being the Han Chinese, they occupy over 60 per cent of the total land mass. This includes the very sensitive border areas of China including the Xinjiang, Tibet, Inner Mongolia, and Guangxi Zhuang Autonomous Regions that touch against Russia, Mongolia, Kazakhstan, Kyrgyzstan, Tajikistan, Afghanistan, Pakistan, India, Nepal, Bhutan, Myanmar and Vietnam. Yunnan, home to 25 minorities, borders on Myanmar, Laos and Vietnam. China has had difficult relations with virtually all of these countries over time. These peripheral areas have always been important to Chinese security concerns and provide a buffer zone to protect the 'Han-core' from possible invaders. Beijing's concern about these areas is increased by the fact that they possess enormous natural resources and they are the last areas into which China's growing population can expand (Grunfeld, 1985).

This concern with security from external threat explains in part why Beijing is so concerned with consolidating its rule over the border areas and has adopted various policies to encourage more Han to move into them so that they form the majority population group in many such areas. However, regions such as Tibet and Xinjiang have also been the site of considerable domestic opposition to CCP rule, and tensions have increased because of the settlement policies. Both have experienced sporadic resistance to Beijing's rule and both are viewed with suspicion by the Centre. In Tibet, many still pledge their allegiance to the exiled Dalai Lama, who fled to India in 1959 after the PLA crushed the Tibetan revolt. In Xinjiang, Beijing fears that people might forge links with radical Islamic groups that have been more active since the breakup of the Soviet Union. However, the Tibetans (7 million) and the Uighurs (8 million), the main ethnic group in Xinjiang, are not united groups internally. With respect to Tibet, the CCP has had some success in trying to circumvent the authority of the Dalai Lama by developing local Buddhist leaders more sympathetic to Beijing. The Panchen Lama, the second most important religious leader, did not flee to India and was used by Beijing to mediate with Buddhist groups domestically. However, the former Panchen's death in 1989 and the débâcle of finding a successor combined with the heavy hand of repression from the late 1980s, seem to have undermined Beijing's attempts to build Tibetan loyalty. A further blow to Beijing came in December 1999 when the young religious leader the CCP was grooming to mediate on its behalf with the Tibetan community fled to join the Dalai Lama in India. In Xinjiang, Uighur nationalists carried out various violent attacks in the 1990s, inspired to recreate a pan-Islamic state by the newly independent Central Asian states after the fall of the Soviet Union. However, the Uighurs are a far from homogeneous group.

The tension between Han and non-Han peoples is a legitimate topic for discussion in China, indeed it was legitimated by Mao in 1956 when he referred to it as one of the Ten Great Relationships that marked the post-1949 political landscape. However, in some cases it is the tensions between the different minorities that have their own cultural and historical origins that are more important. In the border areas of Yunnan, some villagers will never have come across Han Chinese. In fact, many minorities in Yunnan such as the Bai (2 million), Miao (10 million) and Hani (1.5 million) are more likely to complain about the way the Yi (7.3 million) dominate the ethnic minorities' administrative networks in the province. This they feel enables the Yi to dispense a disproportionate amount of largesse to their own group.

Many of the ethnic groups living in the Yunnan border region are closely related to groups in Myanmar, Laos and Vietnam and indeed the border is quite porous and seems to have become more so since the reforms began. Cross-border trade and work is common. While the main roads have border posts and each village has a border office, there is little attempt to stop this casual movement. In the village of Mengla you can see the hills of Myanmar across the fields and the border is secondary to economic activity for many. The local head of the village had a four-wheel drive Toyota jeep with Thai number-plates, indicating the extent of his business travels. When asked about whether he needed to affix Yunnan plates to the car, he replied that as he had been head of the border patrols and knew the local police, he could drive wherever he needed to go in Yunnan with the Thai plates and besides much of his work was over the border. His optimism was not entirely justi-fied as at least once he was stopped by the police on his way to the provincial capital of Kunming. Yet even in such a remote point, decisions made far away in Beijing can exert an enormous impact on the local economy (see Box 1.1).

Many of the minorities, despite their special status, are for all intents and purposes assimilated. This is the case with China's two largest minorities, the Zhuang (18.7 million) and the Manchu (11.5 million) and to a lesser extent with the Muslim Hui (9.3 million). The Zhuang live primarily in the Guangxi Zhuang Autonomous Region that borders on Vietnam. Despite their dis-tinctive Dai language, a language common to a number of other groups in the southwest, they have effectively adopted a Han lifestyle. It was the Manchus who established the Qing dynasty (AD 1644–1911) and were the last imperial rulers before the Republic was established in 1911. Many have suggested that their survival as imperial rulers derived from the Sinification of their practices. While a Manchu language survives, it is used by very few. The Hui are an interesting group with the largest concentration in the

---

BOX 1.1

Decisions Taken on High Can Reach the Farthest Corners

A walk up the mountains to the remote regions above Yunnan province's Mengla is like travelling back in time. A bumpy dirt road gives way to narrow, slippery paths that wind up the steep inclines. Life in these villages – among the 200,000 across China that still lack roads – has changed little over the past 50 years. These hills are inhabited by the Hani, a minority people bypassed by reforms. Yet, in the mid-1990s, the main village had experienced a mini-economic boom when it became a main transit point for the shipment for Bauxite brought over the border from Myanmar for refining on the Chinese side. This had led to a widening of the village square, the setting up of a number of roadside restaurants, a Karaoke bar and a brothel as well as a couple of places to stay. It looked as if this business would finally bring the village out of poverty. However, after a couple of years, Beijing decided that such economic activities entailing cross-border movements might endanger its security concerns. As a result the shipments stopped, the road emptied, the restaurant customers dwindled, and the prostitutes had to limit themselves to serving the needs of the local border patrol.

---

northwest (the Ningxia-Hui Autonomous Region) but they also live in many cities such as Xi'an (Shaanxi), Kunming (Yunnan) and even in Beijing. They speak the national language (Mandarin or *guoyu*) and are indistinguishable from their Han neighbours except for their cuisine and worship at the mosque.

Last but not least, we should note that the broad classification of Han Chinese conceals great diversity within the group itself. Even the national language is a fairly recent construct and many of the Han Chinese actually speak other languages. These are more commonly referred to as dialects as the written script is the same. In reality they can be as different as English and German. The national language is derived from the language spoken around Beijing. The CCP as a part of its drive to bring unity and to increase literacy both simplified the written characters and promoted the use of the national language in schools and through radio and television. As a result, those who have enjoyed basic schooling can speak some of the national language. Whenever I am in non-Han villages one of the easiest ways for communication is to seek out school-age children and to ask them to act as interpreters for their parents and grandparents, many of whom may only speak a few words of the national language at best. In one village a couple of hours' bike ride from the tourist destination of Yangshuo, I chatted with one of the village elders through his grandson as interpreter. He was particularly interested in trying foreign cigarettes. My colleague offered him one that he finished in one puff and dismissively discarded. Not a patch on his home-grown tobacco, a whiff of which would seriously damage your health. He seemed blasé in the presence of foreigners, unusual for the mid-1980s. I asked him if many foreigners came to the village. He thought for a second, drew on his cigarette and replied in a matter of fact tone 'Oh yes, one came here about forty years ago'.

The home language even for many Han is quite distinct, with about 30 per cent (some 350 million) speaking something other than the national language at home. In Guangdong the language is Cantonese (*yue*) while *Minnan* is spoken in various dialects throughout Fujian, *Gan* is spoken in Jiangxi and *Wu* in Shanghai. Before communications improved it is said that travelling up the Yangzi Valley one would have to change languages at each county town. This may be apocryphal but it indicates how fragmented local Chinese society was until the twentieth century. An important part of the nation-building process for the CCP has therefore been to build a common language. In this it has been fairly successful with, at least, the written script understood by all those who are literate. The official figures claim that 83.5 per cent of the population is literate, with Beijing leading the way at 92.5 per cent and Tibet bringing up the rear at 45.9 per cent. For those who cannot read there has been a continual bombardment of officially approved news through radio and television. In the Cultural Revolution, there were even the communal loudspeakers that dictated the pace of one's life from when one woke up until one went to sleep. I remember lying in bed one morning trying to work out what was different and why I felt so relaxed before I realized that someone had cut the wires on the campus speakers. It was bliss to lie in bed and not listen to the blare of early morning wake-up routines.

So long as the leadership speaks with one voice this system has been remarkably successful in providing acceptance for the official narrative. In 1991 I was visiting relatives in Shashi, a town of some 3 million inhabitants a few hours up the Yangzi from Wuhan. They were considered free-thinking liberals in Shashi and thus I was surprised when we talked of the 1989 student-led demonstrations in Beijing and they referred to them as chaos and a counterrevolutionary uprising rather than using the milder phrases used by liberals in Beijing. When I asked them how they knew this, they replied that it was true because they had read about it in the *People's Daily*, the CCP's official media organ, and seen it on Central Television. In the same way, the CCP was successful in getting most of its citizens to believe that the NATO bombing of the Chinese Embassy in Yugoslavia in May 1999 had been a deliberate act of provocation by the United States.

The aforementioned linguistic affiliations and local ties have, if anything, strengthened with the reforms. Within the locality these ties are reinforced by various local festivities and deities and even for many by the local cuisine. There is a clear cultural divide between the north of the country and the south. The southern parts of China were only effectively integrated into China in the later part of the Song Dynasty (AD 960–1279, Blum, 2000, p. 82). The north is the political capital and operates under a more bureaucratic culture, while the south represents the more open and cosmopolitan trading culture. The rise of a nationalist discourse in the mid-1990s and anti-American tracts such as *The China That Can Say No* (Song *et al.*, 1996) and *Behind the Scenes of Demonizing China* (Li *et al.*, 1996) also led to a rise in publications that stressed local identity and cultural essence. Books appeared on what it is to be Shanghainese or Sichuanese and even related local cooking to identity. The spicy food of Sichuan and the chilly taste of Hunan cooking contrasts markedly with the fish and steamed food of Guangdong or Shanghai, or the noodle soups of Shaanxi. Hunan even had the phrase patronized by Mao Zedong that you could not be a revolutionary if you could not eat peppery food.

It is also in the south that lineage and clan play an important role in rural life, much more important than in the north. In many villages I have visited in the south, large lineage halls have been restored or built anew and clearly form the most important organizing point for political and socio-economic exchange. This reemergence of more overt traditional power structures has made the implementation of party rule more difficult. In such villages the party group is often ineffective and often where effective the party secretary and lineage head are one and the same. A number of officials involved with the programme to introduce direct elections into China's villages complained that the election was decided by the most important lineage and there was little the party or the higher level administrative authorities could do to alter this.

These local identities are reinforced by religious practice and customs. While China is officially an atheist country, the CCP has had no choice but to tolerate religious practice so long as it is not seen as a challenge to state power. The CCP has adopted a series of secular official celebrations that mark key dates of the revolution or communist tradition (such as 1 October – National Day, or 1 May – International Labour Day) but the most important festivals have to do with Chinese tradition (Chinese New Year – a week in January or February, or Qing Ming, grave sweeping – early April) and local custom. Local religious worship and traditional practices have blossomed since the reforms began but organized religion that stresses an allegiance beyond the CCP is viewed with suspicion and usually repressed. This is the case not only with Tibetan Buddhism because of the presence of the Tibetan government-in-exile under the leadership of the Dalai Lama, but also with Christianity. Not surprisingly it is difficult to get a number of how many people practise these religions but official estimates suggest there to be 15 million Protestants and 4 million Catholics (Benewick and Donald, 1999, p. 76). The Vatican believes the number of followers to be closer to 12 million (see Madsen, 1998). The CCP refuses to recognize the authority of the Catholic Church and cracks down hard on those who profess allegiance, often arresting priests who accept the Vatican's authority. Instead, practising Catholics are required to belong to the Chinese Catholic Patriotic Association, an organization that follows the ranks and salary scales of the state administrative system. CCP suspicion of Christianity is compounded by the association of the missionaries with imperialism before 1949. As a result, all missionary activity is banned in China but it is not very hard to find active missionaries in both the cities and the countryside. The number may exceed 10,000 and there is a large underground trade in bibles. Some missionaries have been involved in rural development projects and the local authorities have tolerated their work as long as they do not become too public with their beliefs.

Buddhism is widespread with anywhere between 70 and 100 million practitioners. There are three main variants: Tibetan Buddhism (with four major sects), Theravada Buddhism and a mixture of Chinese folk traditions and Buddhism. However, practitioners may also follow another religion, such as Daoism, thus making it difficult to assess the true numbers (Blum, 2000, p. 88). Figures are similarly inexact concerning followers of Daoism and folk religion but are in the realm of 250 million (Benewick and Donald, 1999, p. 76). The CCP attitude toward local religion is also ambivalent. It denounces what it sees as 'superstitious' practices and in the Cultural Revolution it destroyed not only places of worship but also sought to stamp out practices such as ancestor worship and fortune-telling. However, unless there is a perceived political threat, it now tolerates a wide range of locally based religious worship.

Some of these practices can be quite striking. In Yunnan, I have watched a video of the exorcism of spirits that had possessed the body of a young female researcher from the Yunnan Academy of Social Sciences, and have witnessed ceremonies to welcome young men into manhood (see Box 1.2). The young anthropologist had been carrying out research in a remote mountain area and the village elder took pity on her when she was about to return to the city possessed by a bad spirit. Normally, he did not care about city folk and did not mind them carrying evil spirits away. He felt that she was a good person and as a result was willing personally to oversee the lengthy process to excise the evil spirits before allowing her to return.

The local party has to make accommodation to these religious practices. Perhaps this is seen best in those areas where overseas Chinese investment has been vital to local economic health and where these investors have allied with the local population to demand the restoration of local lineage houses or temples. In Wuxi, overseas Chinese have donated money to erect an enormous gold leaf Buddha that looks over the local lake. It is the dominant site of the locality. However, it was not constructed without controversy. The local propaganda bureau set the building of the Buddha as one of the three great tasks for completion in 1997, one of the other tasks being to strive to ensure the successful return of Hong Kong to Chinese sovereignty. This caused uproar when reported to the Propaganda Department in Beijing, that claimed that the erection of a Buddha representing a backward superstition could in no way be equated with the 'glorious task' of regaining

BOX 1.2

The Party, Religion and Worship

In one mountain village, I witnessed the performance of a traditional ceremony to welcome a young man into adulthood. At the entrance to the village I was met by a middle-aged man who introduced himself as the local party secretary and he guided me to where the performance would take place before exiting. Shortly, the ritual began with an elaborate demonstration in front of the boy who was about to be initiated. The ritual was led by a man draped in a tiger skin and wearing a crucifix and who occasionally slipped into a language that none could understand. The fact that only he could speak this language added to his power among the village community. After a few minutes, I recognized the man as the village party secretary who had greeted me. A clear example of the fusion of religious and political power at the local level. I also slowly recognized that the strange language into which he occasionally lapsed resembled Latin and was later informed that in the past Jesuits had been active in the village, although they had now gone and not returned. Indeed, while Jesuits have been active in some villages in rural Yunnan, the Protestants seem to have been more successful among non-Han groups in recent years. We then joined a parade to where the young boy would complete his ritual. At one point, all passers were challenged at spear point to make a gift. The final part of the ceremony entailed the boy climbing onto a small tower perhaps some 10 feet high. Once on the tower he had to clasp his hands together and fall backward off the tower to be caught by his colleagues in a large blanket. When unwrapped, if his hands were still clasped, he had passed into manhood. Fortunately they were. We were told that in the past the fall had been much more arduous with the young men rolling backwards down a hill that was a couple of hundred feet high. This sanitized version was much safer.

sovereignty over Hong Kong. The Wuxi party authorities were forced to withdraw it from the glorious three tasks for 1997, but the Buddha was finished the next year!

Should, however, traditional practices link up across localities and be perceived as a threat, the CCP will move swiftly to crack down. This was the case with a *qigong* (a type of exercise and breathing regime) related sect called the *Falungong* (Skills of the Wheel of Law) that came to prominence after 10,000 of its followers surrounded the party headquarters in Beijing in April 1999 following criticism of its organization. This woke up China's senior leaders to the potential of such faith-based movements to inspire loyalty. This concern and the humiliation that senior leaders felt at being caught by surprise led to a draconian crackdown on the organization and a subsequent campaign to discredit it as a superstitious cult. One public security official commented that what he found really scary was that when they left they cleaned up all their rubbish and left the area clean. No police group would have done that! Thousands of its members have been arrested and it has also led to the investigation of a number of similar organizations.

The Impact of CCP Policy

The CCP's vision of a modern state and its policies has had a marked impact on the physical structure of towns and countryside as well as on people's lives. The CCP came to power in 1949 with a vision of the future that was inspired by that of the Soviet Union. To be modern was to be urban, industrial and with production socialized. The CCP despised the private sphere and policy through the early 1950s was to eradicate what remained of private industry in the urban areas. Yet, at the same time, there was a suspicion of the cities as carriers of indolence, corruption and other traits that ran against the perceived revolutionary heritage.

The effects of post-1949 CCP policy produced a uniform, drab urban environment. With the exception of a few cities such as Beijing, Xi'an and Pingyao that have an imperial heritage, or Shanghai with its confluence of colonial styles, virtually all other cities have adopted the dour, gray architecture of the Soviet era. City walls in many cities, even including much of Beijing, were ripped down to make way for the new, wider roads and work-unit apartment blocks. Those who favoured urban planning that would have afforded greater protection to China's historical heritage were often drowned out by those who favoured the Soviet-style plan. In the anti-rightist campaign of the 1950s and the Cultural Revolution (1966–76), defenders were denounced for their bourgeois and/or feudal thinking.

The desire rapidly to build up the industrial base also had a major impact on the urban landscape as the CCP sought to build up the heavy industrial sector. Smokestack factories became a familiar part of many cities with little notion of zoning and protection of green areas. In part the industrialization of the First Five-Year Plan (1953–57) built on the inheritance of the past. The northeast became the industrial powerhouse with its legacy from Japanese control of Manchuria with chemicals, steel and coal prominent. This made the urban northeast one of the privileged areas of the Maoist period, privileges that have steadily eroded since reforms were introduced from 1978.

The second main area for heavy industrial development was Sichuan, especially Chongqing. This had two origins. First, the Guomindang (the Nationalist Party with which the CCP fought two civil wars to gain power) with its retreat to Chongqing after the Japanese invasion of 1937 moved significant industry to the southwest. This inheritance was built upon by the CCP with the post-1949 policy to industrialize the hinterland as well as security concerns. Following the Sino-Soviet split (1960), Mao became increasingly concerned about war with the Soviets and even the possibility of nuclear conflict. This led to the policy to develop the industrial 'third front' that was based in Sichuan and the further southwest and built on earlier investment in the northwest (Naughton, 1988, pp. 351–86). There was a massive redeployment of investment, almost 50 per cent, from the mid-1960s to the mid-1970s, to build an industrial base and nuclear facility that could resist Soviet attack. It has provided Sichuan and Chongqing with insurmountable problems of outdated industry in the 1990s.

In the countryside the CCP first abolished the old landlord system and, as a result of peasant expectations and pre-1949 policy, land reform was carried out with land redistributed to the household. However, by the mid-1950s steps were taken towards collectivization in order for the state to extract the funds necessary to feed its industrialization programme. The division of China into 50,000 rural communes brought a uniformity to political administration in the countryside that lasted until the early 1980s when they were dismantled and a return of household farming was promoted. The promotion of the communes brought a far greater uniformity to the visual impression of rural life than the varied topography would suggest. It also allowed the CCP to push nationwide policies while ignoring the law of comparative economic advantage. The most damaging of such policies was the promotion of 'taking grain as the key link' to accompany the industrial policy of 'taking steel as the key link'. The former led many communes to turn ill-suited land to grain production. Slopes were cleared of tree cover and grazing land was ploughed under to meet mandatory grain production targets. Not only did this depress local incomes, it also caused significant environmental damage (Shapiro, 2001).

The other major policy that transformed the physical image of the countryside was the promotion of small-scale industry during the Great Leap Forward (1958–60) as a concerted programme for rural industrialization. The most notorious result was the 'backyard steel furnace' that produced a huge volume of steel, much of it useless and consuming scarce resources. Forests and any available resources were torn up to fuel the production of steel. Other experiments such as the creation of small electric power generators and chemical fertilizer plants provided the legacy for an equally dramatic transformation of the countryside in the 1980s and 1990s with the massive growth of township and village enterprises (TVEs).

The Maoist lack of concern and the privileging of production over all other factors enhanced the degradation of the environment. This perspective was enthusiastically adopted by Mao Zedong who saw nature as something to be conquered and tamed and did not appreciate that there are natural limits that resource endowment places on growth. Not only did the development strategy favour rapid exploitation of natural resources to build up the heavy industrial base but also the associated policy of below-cost pricing for water, coal and other inputs contributed further. Walking by office buildings with lights burning in the weekends and past bathrooms with constantly running taps that could not be turned off even if one tried showed the irrelevance of water or electricity prices to workplace and domestic budgets.

The rapid economic growth and urbanization of the years after 1975 have come at the cost of enormous environmental damage and natural resource constraints are a potential brake on China's future development. The political economy of the reforms has in many ways been inimical to the development of an effective policy to control environmental pollution. According to the World Bank (1997g, p. 2), the damage caused from air and water pollution has been estimated at $54 billion a year, amounting to a staggering 8 per cent of GDP in 1995. Of this, the largest amount comes from urban air pollution at $33 billion and water pollution comprising at least $4 billion. The natural resource constraints are significant and the development of alternatives such as hydropower and nuclear energy are expensive and have their own environmental problems (Smil, 1998, pp. 935–51). This exaggerates the use of coal over cleaner alternatives.

With the rise in population and urban expansion there has been a decrease in high-quality arable land, leading to concerns about China's ability to feed itself (the most alarmist account is Brown, 1995). Smil (1995, pp. 801–13) provides a balanced assessment indicating that farmland areas are actually substantially larger than official statistics show, meaning that average yields are lower than reported, and significant opportunities remain for higher efficiencies in production. In particular, Smil points out that if China could cut the annual grain loss of between 60 and 100 million tons, an extra 90 million people could be fed. Despite this, China will become a major importer of grains and a major producer of genetically-modified crops to raise productivity levels.

The cost to the population's health of this environmental degradation is significant. The reliance on coal is responsible for some of China's worst industrial accidents in the mines, especially in the small private mines; China has the highest death rate in the world from mining disasters. The extensive use of coal causes particulate and sulphur air pollution in China's cities. According to the World Bank (1997g, pp. 1–2), particulate and sulphur levels in major Chinese cities exceed WHO and Chinese standards by two–five times. In 1998, according to the World Resources Institute in Washington, eight of the top ten cities with the worst air were in China, with Lanzhou in the northwest topping the list (interview with researchers concerned). In addition, 178,000 people in major cities suffer premature deaths each year from pollution, while indoor pollution, from burning coal and biomass for cooking and heating, causes 111,000 premature deaths each year, primarily in rural China. Some 7.4 million work-years are lost to health damage related to air pollution. In urban areas, the rapid increase in the use of cars and leaded petrol has been a major cause of pollution. The number of cars on the road in Beijing is estimated to reach 2 million by 2003, up from just half a million at the beginning of the 1990s. While Beijing became the first city in January 1998 to ban the sale of leaded petrol, the effect was limited as Chinese cars did not have catalytic converters and the ban did not extend to the purchase of leaded petrol outside of the city. It is estimated that 60 per cent of summer air pollution is caused by car exhausts and that nearly 70 per cent of Beijing children suffer from some form of lead poisoning (*SCMP*, 29 March 1998).

The economic reforms introduced since 1978 have also had a significant impact on the physical look of both urban and rural China while binding the two closer together than in the Mao years. The reforms have released the tight grip of the party and state over local society and have allowed space for the return of local enterprise and even limited private entrepreneurship. Cities in contemporary China are certainly livelier and less homogeneous than in Mao's China. The drab Stalinesque town centres have been transformed in many city centres with the rise of gleaming, glass-fronted skyscrapers housing luxury offices, shopping malls and the ubiquitous McDonald's. These are the new symbols of modernization and much of the old architecture and housing that survived the Maoist blitz has been bulldozed to make way. While it is true that much of the housing was sub-standard, the redevelopment and loss of family homes to move to sterile new apartments far from the city centre have met with resistance and sit-ins.

Historical heritage has often been bulldozed away in the name of a new concept of progress. Kunming was chosen to host the International Flower Exhibition in the late 1990s and this led to a frenzy of development and demolition. As a result, many of the charming old lanes around the Cuihu lake area were demolished to make way for new buildings. When I asked a local official why they preferred demolition to restoration he replied that the old lanes represented the past and backwardness and the foreigners who would come to the Exhibition would think of China as a poor country if they saw them. As a result, communities were broken up and dispersed in the name of modernity. The new buildings represented the future and the modern. Unfortunately, to Western eyes, the building material of choice in southwest China is white tile, making most buildings look like inverted public lavatories covered with opaque deep sea-blue glass.

The new architecture also reinforces the reified view of state power with many new gleaming, marble-decked buildings constructed to house the local party, government and judicial authorities. In Wuxi, an affluent reform-minded city in Jiangsu a couple of hours from Shanghai, I asked local officials about this phenomenon. I wondered aloud whether they thought that such ostentatious signs of state power and public spending were appropriate in the modern world and whether local citizens felt disturbed to see so much expenditure on civic buildings. The local officials were dumbfounded and amused by my question. It had never occurred to them to think about this and when they did they replied that it was indeed appropriate as it was the party that had provided the correct guidance and policies for China's economy to take off. They may be correct and such graphic demonstrations of state power are a universal phenomenon. Certainly there seemed to be no popular angst about such public extravagance. Interestingly, sitting on the hills overlooking the famous lake of Wuxi is not only the Gold Buddha, representing the return of belief, but also the enormous villa that belongs to one of China's top capitalists, Rong Yiren, who also served as Vice-President of China, representing the return to credibility of private capital in China. Showing the continued hostility to private entrepreneurship sponsored by the CCP since 1949, one did hear criticisms of the large ostentatious villa built by Rong. So there in one city, the architecture represents three facets of modern China that have to find a new *modus vivendi*: state power, popular religion and private capital.

The new icons of urban modernity tower above a more varied urban environment that is a product of the reforms. I remember in 1976 the delight with which we greeted a street-seller in central Beijing who was selling home-made toys for a few cents. Now the streets teem with so many vendors that one is more likely to run away and seek refuge from the hawkers and traders. The gradual release first on rural markets and later for rural produce to be sold in the cities has led to a much more diverse urban streetlife. The markets, restaurants and discos are signs of the new entrepreneurship or official organizations moonlighting to make a bit of extra money. The restaurants and nightclubs are filled with the beneficiaries of reform: the private entre-preneurs, those involved in the new economy, the managerial elites and the politically well connected.

The reforms have also changed what is for sale in the stores. In the Cultural Revolution by and large one bought what one could get if you had the money and the correct ration coupons. Entering the department store was not a particularly energizing experience as choice was limited, quality was poor and service distinctly surly. Now film and rock stars are used to promote new products and open stores. Competition has caused even the state-run stores to become more entrepreneurial and to offer service with a grudging smile rather than a scowl. Most of the luxury goods that were kept back in special stores for senior officials and foreigners are generally available for anyone who has money.

Reform has even changed the content of official bookstores such as the Foreign Languages Bookstore on Beijing's main shopping street. Its transformation has been a bell weather of reforms. In the 1970s and 1980s its main stock was the collected works in foreign languages of China's leaders, posters of revolutionary icons such as Stalin and Enver Hoxha and English-language textbooks that carried revolutionary parables or stories of friendship between Chinese and foreign citizens. When I visited in November 2000, there was barely a collected work in sight and no revolutionary icon to be found. In their place were Harvard Business School textbooks and manuals on how to make money or manage financial transactions. The posters had been replaced by a wide choice of Western novels, cassettes and CDs intro-ducing the latest sounds and fashions. Learning English by revolutionary parable has been replaced by learning English through business management.

The one-child-per-couple policy has affected shopping. Toy shops and department stores are now the icons of happy family life with parents lavishing relatively large sums to pamper the 'new emperors' of modern China. As one old party wag commented, they were the hope for greater party accountability in the future. In his view they had been so spoilt and dominated household spending and priorities that there was no way that they would listen passively and unquestioningly to party directives when they grew older! They were more likely to demand results to improve the quality of their life and provide greater accountability.

Not all have money to spend in this new urban China. There have been beneficiaries but there have also been losers – workers in inefficient SOEs, the aged with no family dependents and some migrants. The increasing pressure of marketization and the need to cut costs and increase profits, pressures that will intensify with WTO entry, have caused a rapid increase in lay-offs from the old SOEs. While the worst effects for many have been cushioned either through supplemental income from the state or the retention of low-cost housing and medical provision, there is no doubt that it has been a hard transition for some. The favoured northeast and Sichuan of the Maoist period have become the rust-belts of the early twenty-first century. The word 'yellowing' (*huangle*) of enterprises is commonly heard in the northeastern cities that were the former industrial powerhouses of the Maoist era. It is noticeable that provinces such as Liaoning and Jilin that used to be among the wealthiest in the Mao years have become relatively poorer in the reform period. By contrast Guangdong, one of the poorest provinces under Mao, has become the wealthiest under reform. In fact, three of the richest ten people in China in 1996 were from Guangdong (Benewick and Donald, 1999, p. 25).

Many older workers are bewildered by the changes and are unlikely to find work in the new economy where quite different skills are required than those learned by the traditional working class. Official unemployment figures (around 4 per cent) significantly under-represent the true levels and the regional variation. In northeastern cities such as Mudanjiang, unemployment may even have run as high as 40–60 per cent. Certainly anecdotal evidence would suggest much higher rates. Peddlers in the streets in such towns and the hostesses and prostitutes working in the hotels and clubs tend to be local rather than outsiders as is the case in larger cities such as Beijing.

The impact has fallen unduly heavily on women. In most SOEs, they are the first to be laid off and the last to be taken back. In many state organizations, women are being persuaded to take early retirement – usually around 45 and, on occasion, even earlier. The chance of finding new, legal employment is slim. The elderly and the single have also been vulnerable. With workplaces shedding their social welfare responsibilities and a new system only slowly coming into place, old age or divorce can appear more threatening than in the days of cradle-to-grave socialist care for the elite of the urban industrial working class.

A rise in the divorce rate has been a by-product of reforms and there has been much hand-wringing in the Chinese press. While some see it as a breakdown of social mores, others have heralded it as a positive sign of modernization, pointing to the higher divorce rates in the 'developed West'. The number of divorces had risen to around 1.25 million in 2001, up from fewer than 0.5 million in 1986. Of these divorces, 65 per cent were caused by extra-marital affairs. The northeast provinces have particularly high divorce numbers, perhaps reflecting the economic distress of that area. This might seem low, but for a society coming out of the Mao years of enforced social conformity and repression of sexual desire (unless you happened to be Mao himself) it was seen as a disturbing increase. The rise in divorce rates also relates to people shaking off political marriages that they undertook during the Cultural Revolution. In those years correct class background and political stance rather than feelings of love, were more important for finding urban marriage partners. It led to many loveless marriages in urban China for the now 50-somethings, leading not only to rising divorce rates but also to increases in extra-marital affairs as well as the enormous popularity of books like *The Bridges of Madison County*.

I have sat through many discussions by older urban residents of nostalgia for the old days. Forgetting the famine of the Great Leap Forward and the chaos and violence of the Cultural Revolution, they reminisce of the 'golden days' when life was secure, there was basic healthcare and the streets were safe. For many, reforms have meant bewildering choices, loss of security, rising crime and declining personal safety, and a younger generation who treat their elders with less respect. Some have been attracted by the 'leftist' manifestos published by former Maoist party veterans. These criticize the 'capitalism' and 'materialism' and new inequalities of current policy and call for a return to stricter discipline, party control and central state planning. Others have been attracted to a variety of religious and popular movements such as *Falungong*. This is just the tip of an iceberg as many seek to find something that brings meaning to their life in such a turbulent world.

It is the migrants who have received popular and official blame for the increase in crime, dirt and disease in urban China. While such hyperbole is usually unjustified, migrants are a feature of the post-Mao reforms. There have been previous waves of migration post-1949 but now there are anywhere between 80 and 120 million migrants linking the urban to the rural areas and transforming both landscapes. The decline in farming incomes and the pull of better-paid work in the cities (an average of $600 a year) have led many young men, and increasingly women, to abandon the harsh conditions of rural labour for higher wages in the cities. The construction boom of the 1990s was a major source of employment as was the expansion of TVEs and the foreign-invested manufacturing enterprises that have mushroomed in the Special Economic Zones (SEZs). One further link between the urban and the rural was the rapid expansion through the 1980s and early 1990s of rural industry in the form of TVEs. By 2001, there were some 130 million employees in 20 million enterprises, and in provinces such as Jiangsu and Shandong they employed some 30 per cent of the rural workforce.

However, life in the cities while perhaps not as harsh as in the countryside has not been easy either. Migrants tend to live in sub-standard or shanty-housing or in dormitories provided by their employers. In the former, they often group together in native-place villages. A major problem for the migrants is that their place of registration is still considered to be in the countryside and thus they are denied access to state-sponsored education and medical facilities.

As noted, the migrants have been important to the growth of not only the non-state sector but also the development of the new growth areas of China along the coast. The CCP has promoted this strategy of coastal growth while allowing a progressive running down of the old industrial areas. This began with the promotion of trade as a key component of the new policy and the licensing of the four SEZs in 1979 that provided a series of incentives for foreign enterprises and joint ventures. They were set up primarily to absorb overseas Chinese investment. The programme expanded from the four zones (Shenzhen, Zhuhai, Shantou and Xiamen) under Zhao Ziyang by the late 1980s to a coastal zone development strategy. Shenzhen, the first major zone over the border from Hong Kong, was just a small sleepy village when I first passed through in 1976. On the train ride from the border with Hong Kong to Guangzhou one passed through endless rice paddies, small clustered village hamlets and the occasional water buffalo pulling a plough or swishing its tail while bathing lazily in the river. A decade later, Shenzhen was Asia's newest metropolis with an urban centre full of towering skyscrapers rising from the former paddies. It is now home to over 4 million people (of whom only 1.2 million have permanent residence permits), has foreign investment of $2.7 billion (2000) and an urban *per capita* income of $2700 per annum and a rural *per capita* net income of $1100, making it one of the richest places in China.

Very few rural areas have undergone such a dramatic transformation, but official figures state that the incidence of absolute poverty has dropped from 250 million at the start of the reforms to only 28 million by 2002. As these figures suggest, the reforms have been equally dramatic in their effect on rural China. The communes have been abandoned and farming returned to a household basis. As a result, the wide fields and expanses of land have been divided up into small parcels that are often guarded as crops ripen. The breakdown of communal farming has led to an increase in theft of crops in the countryside.

Migration has also affected the demographics of many rural villages and many who have remained behind have quit farming where there is a viable alternative. While still some 75 per cent of China's population are registered as living in the countryside, farming families are increasingly reliant on non-farm sources of income. This may come from remittances from migrants or from wage labour in township and village enterprises or from household business. In 1996 over three-quarters of the basic incomes of agricultural workers came from this last source (Benewick and Donald, 1999, p. 28). Even for those who remain in agricultural production there has been a shift away from the Maoist obsession with grain production to other products that fetch a higher price in the urban markets. Generally with the low returns for grain production, most keep fields only to fulfil their quotas. For a country that has such a heavy pressure on the available land, it is disconcerting to see so much good agricultural land being abandoned either because families do not want to farm it or cannot because of migration or redeployment to more profitable non-agricultural work.

The composition of those farming has also changed. In many villages, males have moved in search of off-farm employment as have many women of pre-marriage age. This has left farming in many areas to the elderly and married women. Because of the low status and income from these activities, there has been discussion as to whether we are witnessing the 'feminization' not just of agriculture but also of poverty. Many villages seem to comprise only the elderly, children, the sick and married women dealing with all the household and production affairs.

Increased mobility and other social changes have also led to the increase of sexually transmitted diseases and HIV/AIDS. Migrant male workers who have contracted sexually transmitted diseases have brought them back to the village where there may be no adequate healthcare. The spread of HIV/AIDS has also been linked to poverty. Minorities represent 9 per cent of the population but 40 per cent of the absolute poor and 36 per cent of reported HIV/AIDS cases (information from Joan Kaufman). While HIV/AIDS is now spreading among the heterosexual community and from sexual activity with prostitutes, much of the spread has come from needle-sharing by drug addicts and the sale of blood to 'blood snakes' by the poor. China's coercive and social systems are ill-equipped to deal with this situation and an epidemic of major proportions is looming.

Yunnan is typical. In rural and small towns in the province, HIV/AIDS first began to spread among intravenous drug users and subsequently to sex workers. In border towns such as Ruili the explosive mix of drugs and prostitution has caused a major epidemic to develop. I have visited villages in the surrounding area that have been devastated by the death of many of the males and increasingly females. UNAIDS projects 0.3 million AIDS orphans by 2010. One major problem with tracking the spread of a new disease such as this is that local health workers often fail to recognize it. In addition, there are bureaucratic and systemic imperatives that can lead to the spread of the disease being hushed up (see Box 1.3). Local authorities are worried that any adverse publicity would not only bring opprobrium from higher authorities but also would discourage foreign investment. The same fears have prevented local authorities from investigating and exposing the extent of the spread of

---

BOX 1.3

Dealing with HIV/AIDS in Yunnan

In the 1990s, health workers in Yunnan had become so concerned about the level of HIV/AIDS infection among intravenous drug users that they asked a foreign donor organization to support a workshop to promote a range of policies and precautionary measures (such as bleaching and needle exchange) that could help slow down the rapid spread. However, just before the workshop was to be held, the Public Security Bureau intervened to stop the workshop on the grounds that drug use was illegal and therefore could not be talked about publicly. Subsequently, the situation became so bad that the Public Security Bureau was willing to allow the workshop to go ahead. By this time, the health workers felt that the infection rate was now so high among intravenous drug users that such a workshop would be ineffective. They proposed that energy be focused on the next at-risk group, sex workers. Again the Public Security Bureau stepped in to halt the workshop as prostitution was illegal! For drug users, they preferred to rely on lock-up, cold turkey and traditional CCP mechanisms of education and campaigns rather than the kinds of measures that have been successful elsewhere.

HIV/AIDS through the spread of the sale of contaminated blood. While official estimates remain low, many independent organizations project some 10–15 million infections by 2010.

With reforms, rural China has become more varied than in the past, with greater freedom for households to decide on what to produce, where to sell it and how to deploy their labour force. However, reforms have not favoured all in the rural areas, and the extension of household-based farming and markets to areas where they are inappropriate has had adverse effects. For the absolute poor, many of whom live in remote mountainous areas, liberalization and the increased use of market forces have been of little benefit as they have little if anything to sell. In fact, with increased prices for agricultural inputs and the collapse of medical access, their living standards have almost certainly declined. In addition with financial pressures increasing on local authorities many have resorted to raising illegal fees and levies that fall on the poor disproportionately.

The CCP's vision of modernity has also intruded into rural life. Clearly, the CCP still sees the future as urban and industrial. Policy has always privileged these areas but other policies have also impacted on rural life. In particular, the CCP sees nomadic or other traditional farming practices as 'backward'. As a result, CCP policy has tried to organize nomadic and shifting cultivators into more permanent habitats. More permanent settlements, of course, make it easier to control activities and to pursue unpopular policies such as family planning.

In Yunnan, officials have blamed local communities who engage in swidden agriculture as contributing to the soil erosion that has contributed to downstream flooding. In fact, there is little evidence beyond prejudice to support this official viewpoint. Local Chinese researchers have reviewed this practice and have discovered that it is environmentally sound. By contrast, the main periods of environmental destruction came during the Great Leap Forward and the Cultural Revolution (Interviews, November 1998).

The CCP has to rule over this increasingly diverse society while trying to guide China into further integration with the world economy. This is a daunting challenge. The CCP has also to provide an explanation to its people of where the country is heading and offer some kind of a moral compass. This is hard not only because of the diversity but also because ideological orthodoxy appears to run counter to the direction in which the economy and society are heading. It is hard for General Secretary Hu Jintao, or any other senior leader, to provide a genuine vision of China's future as at best it would suggest a radically transformed role for the CCP – and at worst, perhaps, no role at all. If the future is an economy increasingly dominated by market forces and integrated with the world economy, is a CCP that still professes commitment to socialism and the state-owned sector while harbouring suspicion of foreign motives the most effective organization to manage it? However much practice may move away from Marxism, the ideology remains a crucial component of the CCP's self-legitimation (Kelly, 1991, p. 23). To abandon adherence would be impossible.

The gap between official rhetoric and social practice has widened significantly under the reforms and is perhaps even greater than in the Soviet Union and Eastern Europe in the late 1980s. While China's leaders claim 'only socialism can save China' the students laugh that 'only China can save socialism'. The leadership has adopted a number of linguistic phrases that seek to explain current reality while retaining allegiance to socialism. The latest is that China is a 'socialist market economy' while the phrase of 'Chinese-style socialism' has been used to cover a multitude of policies that are difficult to describe as conventionally socialist.

While Chinese society has become less ideological and even more pluralistic, CCP ideology sets limits on how far reform can go. Party leadership has retained its commitment throughout the reform period to socialism however much the definition of its content may have changed. The reforms have not been intended to introduce either democracy or a capitalist economic system but rather to find a way for socialism to survive (on this point, see Huang, 2003, Chapter 2). This explains the residual commitment to the SOE sector, the slow grudging approval given to the private sector and the attempts to make foreign investment support the CCP's socialist objectives. Whether such an approach to development is still tenable is one of the major challenges the CCP faces in the twenty-first century. With the commitment to WTO, there must be serious concern as to whether the socialist core can be retained and even whether certain senior leaders wish to retain it. In a prescient observation Kelly has remarked that one outcome of transition may be the 'installation of a New Authoritarian regime that dispenses with Marxist state ownership and its attendant social welfare functions but retains the self-legitimating apparatus of Marxist ideology' (Kelly, 1991, p. 34).

Certainly within society and even among party members there is little faith that socialism can provide a guiding light for China. Socialism is very rarely raised these days in discussions with foreigners and when mentioned is usually met with an embarrassed giggle by those sitting around the table. When bored listening to the development plans of local officials, I would often ask them about the relevance of socialism to their plans. They usually pulled up short and muttered something about social stability, party guidance and that the kind of socialism being pursued was one with Chinese characteristics. The appeal to the primacy of social stability and the appellation of Chinese characteristics seemed to justify most things one wanted to do. I was chatting with a party secretary from an industrial town near Xi'an (Shaanxi province) in the northwest of China; during our discussions he mentioned that he had privatized virtually all of his local industry and I noted that he appeared to be in breach of central party policy that ruled out the use of the word 'privatization'. He upbraided me, stating that despite having studied CCP history for so long I still did not understand basic principles. He explained to me that the basic principle of party work was to rally around Comrade Jiang Zemin as the core of the leadership to ensure social stability. If he did not privatize the SOEs under his jurisdiction he would be faced with a financial crisis that would lead to social unrest. Thus, far from contradicting party policy, his privatization policy was perfectly attuned to it.

Whether such linguistic conundrums can suffice in the future is hard to say. It is clear that many party members and citizens have a highly instrumental view of the party. As long as it has sufficient patronage to deploy and continues to deliver the economic goods there is little incentive to seek alternatives or to rock the boat. This makes legitimacy highly conditional and the party has struggled to provide deeper reasons for attachment, best seen in its promotion of nationalism. One significant legacy of Deng's reforms is that the overwhelming majority of people do not have to worry about the CCP any more and it does not interfere directly in their lives. This is an important advance from the Mao years and even those of the 1980s, when political campaigns in which all were supposed to participate were commonplace. Withdrawal could be interpreted as lack of support and punishment could be harsh. Now campaigns generally affect only the 66.4 million party members and even then many party members do not have to take them seriously.

Some citizens have not been willing to withdraw into a private realm of activity but have joined a variety of religious and spiritual organizations. A very small number have even joined underground political and labour organizations. Such individuals have clearly transgressed the limits of the permissible and such organizations are broken up and key individuals arrested when discovered. Many more inhabit a grey zone of local religious organizations, clans, lineages, gangs or social organizations that operate at the margins of the politically acceptable.

Providing governance over this diverse people and territory is an increasingly complex challenge. The chapters that follow provide an introduction to how the CCP has governed to date and the challenges it faces in the immediate future. It looks at the organization of the party and the state at the central and local levels, the shifting nature of participation and protest and how the relationship between state and society has changed over time. The final chapters review the key areas of economic, social and foreign policy before looking at important future challenges.

2

China's Changing Road to Development: Political History, 1949–78

After 22 years of conflict with its nationalist rivals domestically and Japanese invaders, the Chinese Communist Party (CCP) took control of Beijing in January 1949 and Shanghai in May the same year. By 1950 the Guomindang (Nationalist) forces retained control only of the island of Taiwan. Though CCP leader Mao Zedong told the Chinese people that they had stood up, the country the CCP now controlled in their name was economically backward, predominantly agrarian and contained considerable opposition to communist rule. Victory returned the CCP to the cities they had been forced to abandon following repression by the nationalists. CCP leaders now had to return the revolution to the cities, build an industrial base and a working class whom they were supposed to represent, create new political institutions and train officials to staff them. Pockets of opposition remained from troops loyal to the nationalists with whom the CCP had fought two civil wars (1927–37 and 1945–49; see Box 2.1) and there was armed fighting with Tibetans who resisted incorporation into the People's Republic of China (PRC). In addition many, especially in the cities and the south, were suspicious of the CCP's motives and intentions. The economy had suffered badly from the dislocation and destruction not only of the civil wars but also the Japanese invasion (1937–45), and the country was suffering from rampant inflation.

Given this inheritance, the achievements by the mid-1950s were impressive. The country, with the exception of Taiwan, was unified, the rural revolution completed, inflation tamed, and solid economic growth achieved. For many older CCP members the early 1950s is remembered as the 'golden age' of steady progress and social stability. One might have thought that China's search for a suitable state form to help the nation modernize and take its rightful place in the world would have ended and institutionalization would have been completed. Yet, only a few years later the CCP led its people

---

BOX 2.1

Key Dates of the Communist Revolution 1911–49

1911 Uprisings bring down the Qing dynasty and Sun Yat-sen is proclaimed President of the Republic of China

1912 14 February, Sun steps down and Yuan Shikai, a former Qing official, takes over

1919 4 May, students protest against their government and the Japanese in response to provisions of the Versailles Treaty at the end of the First World War

1920 November, 'Manifesto of the CP' drafted and the party journal *The Communist* launched

1921 23 July, the CCP opens its founding Congress

1923 June, Third CCP Congress agrees to collaboration with the Guomindang (GMD)

1925 30 May Movement breaks out in Shanghai when International Settlement police open fire on demonstrators

1926 July, Chiang Kai-shek with CCP and Soviet support launches the Northern Expedition to unify China

1927 12 April, Chiang Kai-shek's soldiers massacre communists in Shanghai and a purge of communists begins in many eastern and southern cities

1928 April, Mao and Zhu De unite to form the Jinggangshan base

1933 January, Party Centre flees to the Jiangxi Soviet

1935 15–18 January, enlarged Politburo meeting at Zunyi criticizes past military policy and elects Mao to the Standing Committee of the Politburo

1936 December, kidnap of Chiang Kai-shek by his own troops facilitates formation of second united front

1937 January, CCP moves its headquarters to Yan'an
      7 July, clash between Japanese and Chinese troops at Marco Polo bridge near Beijing provides pretext for full-scale Japanese invasion of China

1941 September, the Rectification Campaign is launched

1945 April–June, CCP Seventh Congress convenes marking culmination of Mao's rise to power
      14 August, Japan surrenders unconditionally

1946 10 October, with the fall of Kalgan to GMD troops the CCP announces that civil war is inevitable

1949 January, Beijing falls to CCP troops and Shanghai falls in May
      1 October, Mao Zedong announces the establishment of the People's Republic of China (PRC)

---

through a series of disastrous movements that ripped apart the ruling elite, caused social dislocation and famine on a massive scale, and culminated in the Cultural Revolution (see Box 2.2). In fact, even in the early 1950s tensions lay just below the surface that derived from the pre-1949 CCP legacy and the application of the Soviet economic model. This chapter first reviews the framework of the debates and tensions within the revolutionary inheritance, and then how Mao and the CCP moved from triumph to disaster, from state-building to state destruction.

BOX 2.2

Key Political Dates, 1949–65

1950   February, China signs the Treaty of Friendship, Alliance and Mutual Assistance with the Soviet Union
May, Marriage Law promulgated
June, Land Law is promulgated
October, China joins the Korean War
1951   February to 1953, 'Campaign to Suppress Counterrevolutionaries'
August to June 1952, 'Three-Anti Campaign' against official corruption
1952   January to June, 'Five-Anti Campaign' to curb the violation of official regulations by private businesses
1953   October, First Five-Year Plan launched, although formally ratified only in 1955
1954   February, Gao Gang charged with trying to seize state power
September, First National People's Congress meets, replacing the Chinese People's Consultative Conference as the highest organ of state power
1955   July, Mao rejects that collectivization could be subordinated to mechanization
1956   February, Krushchev's secret speech denounces Stalin
April, Mao's talk 'On the Ten Great Relationships'
May, 'Hundred Flowers' Campaign' launched
September, Eighth Party Congress acknowledges success of First Five-Year Plan and approves the second to start in 1958
1957   February, Mao widens 'Hundred Flowers' Campaign'
8 June, *People's Daily* article signals start of 'Anti-Rightist Campaign'
September–October, Third Plenum of Eighth Central Committee (CC) adopts radical measures that pave the way for the GLF
1958   May, Second Session of Eighth Party Congress ratifies plans for GLF
1959   10 March onward, Crushing of the revolt in Tibet
July–August, Lushan Plenum, Peng Dehuai criticizes the GLF
1960   July, Soviet Union withdraws all its technical personnel from China
1961   January, Ninth Plenum of Eighth CC adopts economic adjustment policies worked out the previous summer
1962   September, Tenth Plenum of the Eighth CC, Mao stresses the continued existence of class struggle
October, Border war with India breaks out
1963   May, Socialist Education Movement intensifies with publication of the 'Early Ten Points'
1965   November, article by Yao Wenyuan criticizes a play written by Beijing deputy mayor Wu Han claiming it a defence of Peng Dehuai

Parameters of Policy Debate

Two sets of issues framed the policy debates through the 1950s into the 1990s. The first is a set of debates that have been common to all socialist systems operating under a one-party political structure managing a centrally planned economy. The second is a number of tensions that derived from the Chinese revolutionary experience.

The nature of the socialist system (see Kornai, 1992) means that the possibilities for change are limited and the areas of policy debate tend to oscillate along a continuum of a key set of policy alternatives. The main determining features are a centrally planned economy with predominant, if not total, social ownership of the means of production overseen by a hierarchical highly centralized political power structure concentrated within a one-party state and with an atomized society within which the agents of civil society are weak or ineffective. It was only when reformers in the Soviet Union and China began to undermine these pillars that fundamental change has become feasible.

This structure results in recurrent debates on a number of specific questions. In the economic sphere, there is the question of the relationship between the government and the state-owned sector of the economy and the extent of the supplemental role to be played by the collective and private sectors. What is the relationship between consumption and accumulation? How extensive a role should foreign trade play in the development of the national economy? Debates in this field focus particularly on the level of trade with 'advanced capitalist countries'. In addition there have been sharp debates over how best to motivate managers and labourers to work effectively. Should material incentives in the form of bonuses or piece-rates be expanded or should moral exhortation and social recognition be used as a primary form of stimulus?

The cyclical debates have also included the management and administration of the economy. First, in terms of broad economic management there has been oscillation between the role of directive planning and the use of economic incentives to direct the behaviour of economic actors. This is related to specific questions of how much autonomy should be granted and in what functional areas autonomy should be granted to the production enterprises. A further area of debate is between the division of economic decision-making powers between the central administration and its various local agencies.

In the political sphere, there have been oscillations between the level of authority to be enjoyed by party officials *vis-à-vis* other state administrative cadres and enterprise managers. Just how much specific decision-making power should reside with party secretaries? What is the role of the intelligentsia and technicians in the process of policy formulation and how much academic freedom should they be accorded and in which areas? Last but not least there are debates about the extent to which any institution or organization outside of the party-state should be permitted to exist.

In addition to these generic debates, the specifics of the CCP's rise to power contributed legacies that framed the post-1949 debates. The Chinese revolution had been fought in the countryside and this raised a fundamental question about whose interests the new regime would serve: those of the social force that brought it to power (primarily the peasantry), or in whose name it was brought to power (the proletariat); or, as some have suggested, its own bureaucratic structures and personnel.

The preference for the proletariat, if not urban China, was clearly understandable from CCP ideology. Even though the CCP had had no effective contact with the proletariat during the years before seizure of power, its leaders never dropped their commitment to an ideology based on its supremacy and leadership over the peasantry, as represented in the Soviet-inspired vision of the future. As soon as conditions permitted, the party reasserted the primacy of urban work over that in the countryside. However, the socialization drive of the new party-state ran against the material interests of both the farmers and the proletariat. This disregard for the interests of the two primary classes the CCP was supposed to represent derives from the party's 'privileged' position in relation to them before 1949. In the absence of an actual proletariat in the revolutionary base areas, proletarian rule in practice meant rule by its vanguard, the CCP. The party adopted the habit of speaking in the name of the proletariat without the nuisance of having to listen to an actual, existing class. This affected CCP rule after 1949 and its autonomy to act. The party often spoke on behalf of all social forces cognizant that it knew best what was in the real class interest. As a result, after the CCP came to power it enjoyed significant autonomy from the specific interests of all social forces.

This autonomy of the CCP was heightened externally by its relationship to the Soviet Union, the head of the communist movement worldwide. The Chinese revolution was distinct from the 'baggage train' governments that followed the extension of Soviet power into Eastern Europe following the Second World War. The revolution was indigenous and Mao made it quite clear that the CCP was not fighting a war to become the 'slaves of Moscow'. Obviously the influence of Marxism–Leninism as an ideology and the practical help of Soviet Russia cannot be denied, but the end product of Mao Zedong Thought was a distinctive approach geared to and influenced by Chinese realities. The CCP was willing to ignore Soviet advice when it ran counter to national interests and to abandon the Soviet approach to development once its internal inadequacies and its inapplicability to the Chinese situation became apparent. This desire for strong independence was enhanced by China's humiliation at the hands of foreigners in the century before the CCP took power.

Last but not least there was a legacy of institutional overlap and tensions between individual and institution. In the revolutionary war, institutions were very fluid and often the military was a more visible expression of communist power than the CCP itself. Individuals held positions in multiple institutions without any apparent contradiction. It was impossible to identify a senior CCP official, for example, as having a military background or representing a military interest as all senior CCP leaders had been military leaders before 1949. This bred a somewhat cavalier attitude to institutions and their use to achieve other policy objectives.

However, in the CCP revolutionary base area of the Shaan-Gan-Ning in the 1940s more attention was paid to organizational development and the drafting of codes and procedures. CCP stress on organizational stability and ideological orthodoxy went, somewhat paradoxically, hand in hand with the accretion of power in Mao's hands. Indeed, it went even further than this, as loyalty to the organization was reinforced through a campaign to promote the individual of Mao Zedong as the font of supreme wisdom in China's revolution, a campaign that built up momentum from July 1943 onwards. At the time, it does not seem to have occurred to other senior leaders that the build-up of a Mao cult negated the stress on collective leadership and loyalty to the CCP as an organization. While his preeminence did not necessarily have to lead to the abolition of inner-party democracy and serious policy discussion, it was the major factor preventing the institutionalization of more enduring political structures after 1949.

Economic Recovery and the Adoption of the Soviet Model, 1949–55

The CCP's main aims in 1949 were to revive the war-ravaged economy and to eliminate the remaining domestic opposition. If differences remained within the leadership they were hidden beneath a façade of unity. Before 1949 the CCP held a number of base areas in addition to Shaan-Gan-Ning, and their precarious nature and vulnerability to Japanese or GMD attack meant that the party had to rely continually on the support of the poor peasantry and the local elites (see Box 2.3). This made policy more conciliatory even in Shaan-Gan-Ning than it might otherwise have been with economic moderation and political attempts to placate a wide range of social forces. Post-1949 initial policy followed this approach, with populist measures to remove the most obvious inequities of the old system, a moderate economic policy and harsh treatment of those considered enemies of the state. Over time, policy radicalized and increasing sections of the population, including intellectuals, became the focus of CCP criticism. Gradually, the authoritarian strands of the pre-1949 legacy came to dominate over any proto-democratic proclivities. In addition, personal dominance by Mao Zedong over decision-making frustrated the developmental need to build sustainable institutions. As these tensions mounted and the CCP confronted economic failure on a vast scale during the Great Leap Forward, the façade of unity began to crack.

The principles of 'New Democracy', developed by Mao (February 1940) in Shaan-Gan-Ning, with their emphasis on reconciliation and class collaboration were to guide the new state. Naming the new state the People's Republic rather than a people's democratic dictatorship symbolized this. Important practical considerations favoured the adoption of a relatively 'moderate' policy. On assuming power the communists suffered from a shortage of properly trained, administrative, managerial and technical personnel, and they lacked experience in managing a modern, urban, industrial sector. With

---

BOX 2.3

Revolutionary Base Areas

Before 1949, CCP forces were organized in a number of base areas that provided sanctuary, allowed policy experimentation and cadres to develop administrative experience. The main base where Mao and the party headquarters were situated was Shaan-Gan-Ning with its capital in Yan'an. The experiences here provided a blueprint for post-1949 society. Policy combined a moderate economic policy and external relations with tough internal party discipline and the 'mass-line' campaigning style of politics. Apart from Shaan-Gan-Ning there were major base areas in Jin-Ji-Yu-Lu (Shanxi–Hebei–Shandong–Henan) and Jin-Cha-Ji (Shanxi–Chahar–Hebei) regions. The CCP was successful at putting down local roots only where it showed flexibility in adapting policy to local circumstances, where initially it was good at micro-politics. By contrast, attempts to transform local environments to conform to predetermined ideology were unsuccessful. These different base area experiences were often ignored after 1949 and especially during the years of the Cultural Revolution (1966–76) when the focus was exclusively on a CCP history based around the persona of Mao Zedong. When the reforms began in the late 1970s, these varied experiences became important points for alternative policy experimentation. For example, the programme of village elections launched in the late 1980s under the patronage of then National People's Congress leader, Peng Zhen, owed much to his own experiences in Jin-Cha-Ji. Peng hoped that 'controlled democracy' would keep local elites on board and give them a stake in the new politics to prevent them from going over to the enemy. The experiences of Jin-Ji-Lu-Yu are important because key leaders of the reform period such as Deng Xiaoping, Bo Yibo, Wan Li and Zhao Ziyang spent time there. The precarious and fragmented nature of this particular base area meant that policy had to be even more conciliatory than that in Shaan-Gan-Ning. This paramount emphasis on survival meant that a very flexible economic structure was maintained that built on the pre-existing banking expertise of the area and an agricultural policy that very closely resembled that of the 'responsibility system' introduced in China during the 1980s (see Goodman, 1994; Saich, 1994a, 1996).

---

priority given to economic recovery it was necessary to ensure that all available scarce resources were not wasted. This foreclosed the immediate introduction of a full-scale socialist transition strategy. The 'moderate' mood was summed up in the slogan 'three years of recovery and ten years of development'. Policy was to benefit not only the workers and peasants, but also the petty bourgeoisie and those capitalists who had supported the CCP. By contrast, landlords, unsympathetic industrialists, those with foreign interests and those connected with the GMD were to be dealt with harshly.

Policy toward capitalists deemed sympathetic to the revolution provides a good example of the gradualism through which the CCP bound key groups into new forms of state patronage before eliminating them. They were allowed to develop their industries as a prime requisite for the development of a modern economic structure that would then be ripe for socialist trans-formation. Although this meant the initial maintenance of a mixed economy, only the CCP-controlled state apparatus was capable of providing any real coordination. This allowed the CCP to transform the mixed economy to its own advantage without a major disruption in production and distribution. The state took control over both ends of the production process, providing the industrial enterprises with their raw materials through the national ministries and placing orders with the private entrepreneurs for processed and manufactured goods. The state was therefore able to control what went in and what came out. Once privately owned enterprises were tied up in this way, the CCP began to promote the creation of joint state–private enter-prises. This made sense for many of the privately owned enterprises that found it difficult to compete with the state enterprises and that lacked the necessary capital to replace outdated machinery. This movement reached a peak in 1954 and was gradually extended into a programme to 'buy out' the private owners who were paid interest on their shares at a rate determined by the state. This gradualist policy proved to be very successful for the CCP and as early as 1952 industrial production had been restored to its highest pre-1949 levels.

Social and rural policy attacked gross inequalities of the old system and sought to build or consolidate new bases of support. The two most important pieces of legislation were the Marriage Law and the Land Law, both adopted in 1950. The Marriage Law was intended to improve the position of women in Chinese society by according them equality and freedom in their choice of marriage partner. Practices such as infanticide and the sale of children were outlawed.

The countryside was dramatically transformed but radical socialization was postponed. Policy was based on Sun Yat-sen's view that all had equal rights to land and that land should be given to the tillers. This is not to say that the process was peaceful, and up to 800,000 landlords were killed in the land reform campaign (1950–52), while many more were beaten and humiliated by the villagers they had previously ruled over (Teiwes, 1993). Land reform was modelled on policies adopted in the base areas and was seen as crucial for breaking up the traditional social order and power relationships in the countryside. Further, land reform had the advantage of forcing an identity of interest between the peasantry and the CCP by redistributing land to the rural households. This had been a hard bond for the GMD to break before 1949. The fact that most in the party saw land reform as an integral part of the victory strategy before 1949 meant that it was a stage that could not be skipped over on the march towards socialism. The CCP did not wish to fol-low the Soviet mistake of a premature rush to rural collectivization before peasant support and trust had been gained. Finally, the CCP did not have sufficient trained administrative and technical cadres to preside over a collective farming structure. As a result, policy emphasized caution and persuasion and, as before 1949, excesses tended to come from spontaneous outbursts by villagers rather than from directives from above.

The Land Law sought to bring land reform under close party control in an attempt to restrain peasant 'enthusiasm'. A fivefold categorization based on property relations was drawn up to enable cadres to unravel the complexities of rural Chinese life. The law sought to ensure land redistribution to the labourers and the poor peasants while not alienating the middle and rich peasants. This was done to minimize the disruption of production. The category of 'middle peasant' was the vaguest but essentially a middle peasant was one who worked the land without engaging in exploitation. The land worked did not necessarily belong to the peasant. Landlords' land was to be confiscated or requisitioned for redistribution. The blow of being designated a landlord could be softened if the person had supported the revolution. However, the land of the rich and middle peasants, including those designated as prosperous middle peasants, was to be protected. The bulk of land reform was completed in the 18 months after the 1950 autumn harvest. Several hundred million *mu* of land was redistributed among approximately 300 million peasants, giving them between 2 and 3 *mu* each on average. However, there was considerable variation from region to region, and some areas such as Tibet, with which Beijing had signed a short-lived agreement promising 'national regional autonomy', did not undergo land reform at all. With party organizations weak or non-existent, central leaders did not wish to upset the traditional, religious elite.

It was never likely that the CCP would tolerate a household-based farming system for long. As CCP leaders began to think about pushing ahead with socialism, a rural sector based on private farming and markets was anachronistic. CCP leaders also felt that the small units of land would make rational use impossible, the popularization of new farming techniques difficult and large-scale capital construction projects problematic. In addition, the CCP leadership took on the Soviet notion that bigger was better, that fast growth regardless of quality was paramount and that to be modern meant to be urban and industrialized.

These factors meant that gradualism was abandoned and the reorganization of the rural sector into larger collective units began and the role of rural markets was curtailed. The Soviet-style emphasis on heavy industry meant that little capital was available for investment in agriculture, yet more efficient agricultural production was necessary to feed the industrialization programme. The solution was to cooperativize agriculture. This process began slowly at first in 1952 with the formation of mutual-aid teams that shared seasonal work and other chores, but gradually gathered pace until the crash programme of communization was embarked on in the late-1950s.

Mao's view that the 'peasant masses' were raw material for mobilization in time of need meant that post-1949 policy soon treated them as the primary

---

BOX 2.4

Stages of Collectivization in the Chinese Countryside, 1952–59

1952–54 *Formation of mutual-aid teams*. Five–eight households combining for work in particular seasons with up to 20 households cooperating on a year-round basis. Animals, tools and redistributed land were in private hands but labour was pooled.

1954–55 *Formation of lower-stage agricultural producers' cooperatives* (APCs). Voluntary associations of roughly 30 households pooling not only labour but also property, land, farm implements and draught animals. Farmers received income in relation to the proportion of the size of the shares of property originally invested.

1956–57 *Formation of higher-stage agricultural producers' cooperatives*. Containing between 100–300 households, depending on the terrain. Income distribution was now decided on the basis of work-points earned; 750,000 were set up.

1958–59 *Formation of people's communes*. 24,000 communes were set up to carry out not only agricultural work but also such things as industrial work, trade, education, military affairs, health, village administration and social welfare. In 1962 the number of communes was increased to 74,000. Three levels of ownership were introduced: commune, brigade (equivalent to the higher-stage APC) and the production team (equivalent to the lower-stage APC) as the basic accounting unit.

---

source from which to extract resources to feed urban development and the rapidly expanding party-state structure. While the peasants were the immediate beneficiaries of the revolution through the extension of land reform, the need to build up capital quickly led the CCP to take them through the process of collectivization (see Box 2.4). This was resisted by many and communization at best benefited few.

Friedman, Pickowicz and Selden (1991, p. 273) show how by 1952 in the North China Plains extra-village relations once mediated by the market and travel were attenuated by statist restrictions, and how the farmers gradually lost out to a party-state that sought to penetrate society in order to attack tradition and any potential oppositional organizations. Increased party penetration through collectivization into rural social structures brought the activities of clans and lineages under greater scrutiny and control than ever before.

Apart from the landlords, the 'dictatorship of the proletariat' was unleashed on those deemed by the CCP to be 'counterrevolutionaries'. These included GMD supporters, industrialists who were not willing to toe the new party line and who were too critical of CCP practice. The tense post-civil war situation may have caused the campaigns to turn into witch-hunts but many party members seemed to accept harsh measures as justified. One senior party official who was detained briefly in 1943 by the CCP and again in the early 1950s defended party actions. In his view there were indeed many spies, traitors and saboteurs around and this justified harsh, extra-legal measures. For him, the system worked as he was released after investigation with his innocence proven. He was less sanguine about his arrest in the Cultural Revolution. However, the system worked less well for the half a million who may have died in these suppression campaigns. The harshness of CCP action was given further impetus by China's involvement in the Korean War. Before this, the CCP had little to worry about in terms of organized resistance but war increased the communists' fears while, at the same time, enabling them to mobilize the patriotic support that had initially helped them to power. This fear that external threat might lead to internal revolt led to the 'Campaign for the Suppression of Counterrevolutionaries' that was ruthlessly pursued throughout 1951 until the war reached a stalemate. Two other major campaigns were launched during the early 1950s: the Three-Anti Campaign (August 1951–June 1952) that aimed at the abuse of official position to engage in corruption, waste and bureaucratism, and the Five-Anti Campaign (January–June 1952) that sought to curb the violation of official regulations by private businessmen.

Although the emphasis on the need for reconstruction meant that attention was focused on the solution of immediate problems, one decision was taken that had implications for the longer-term development strategy. In June 1949, Mao outlined the policy of 'leaning to one side' that entailed learning from the Soviet Union. This preference was of major significance when, towards the end of 1952, the Chinese economy began to move from rehabilitation to development. This generated the need for greater centralization and the conscious application of Soviet development techniques, certain of which ran counter to the Chinese revolutionary experience. In October 1953, the First Five-Year Plan was effectively launched, although it was not formally ratified until 1955.

With the benefit of hindsight it is easy to criticize adoption of a Soviet-style plan, but at the time the inherent problems in the model and the specific problems of applying it to China were not so apparent. It was the only socialist model for modernizing an economically backward country and, as far as the CCP leaders were concerned, it had already demonstrated its success. Given the challenges China faced and the economic dislocation, central planning appeared to offer a way to distribute scarce resources rationally and effectively. National planning seemed to imply that the diverse war-torn land was indeed one unified nation. Economic centralization matched the political concentration of power that was taking place and would aid the 'consolidation of the dictatorship of the proletariat'. Further, to carry out the industrialization programme, China needed a considerable quantity of financial and technical aid. Given the contemporary climate of world opinion it was obvious that the Soviet Union was the only source of supply.

Initially in China application of the model also appeared successful and an infrastructure for industrial development was rapidly established. The concentration on industrial development meant that 88 per cent of the state's capital investment went to heavy industry: 649 major industrial enterprises were to be built, of which 472 were to be set up in the interior regions – 156 of the total constructed using Soviet advice and equipment. Growth rates were high: industrial production grew at 18 per cent per annum, compared to a target of 14.7 per cent; heavy industry grew at 12.9 per cent. However, agricultural production lagged behind with a growth rate of only 4.5 per cent per annum (Xue, [1980] 1982). Agricultural growth was high by international standards and in relation to population growth (2 per cent), but there were worries about how sustainable this might be and whether agriculture could support the further ambitious industrial expansion and urban growth. Application of the plan also facilitated political objectives with the socialization of the means of production through the nationalization of industry and the collectivization of agriculture.

It was not long before the kinds of problems that have plagued other Soviet systems also began to emerge in China. The concentration on heavy industry soon led to the creation of bottlenecks in the system as well as imbalance in the economy. The obsession with heavy industry and the fixation on growth rates and gross output figures led to neglect of the quality of production and ignored considerations of whether anyone would actually want to buy what was produced. The incentive structures within the system were weak and this meant that worker and management enthusiasm was low. Over time, rates of return on capital declined as did labour productivity. Last but not least, consumption was repressed as funds were accumulated for capital construction.

The Chinese economy was considerably weaker than that of Soviet Russia when each chose to launch its respective First Five-Year Plan: Soviet output *per capita* in 1927 was about four times that of China in 1952; in agriculture, Chinese output was about one-fifth that of Soviet Russia. Some wondered how long the unbalanced growth and privileging of heavy industry could be continued in the Chinese context. Indeed by 1956 Chinese repayments of Soviet loans began to exceed the value of new monetary aid, meaning that China would have to find an effective way to generate investment capital (Lieberthal, 1995, p. 99).

The adoption of the Soviet model of development also meant, to a large extent, the adoption of Soviet management techniques and the creation of a Soviet-style society. While the Soviet model may have had some superficial resonance with notions of order in traditional China, it was at variance with other traditions, as well as running counter to the CCP's own experiences in the revolutionary base areas before 1949. Finally, the Soviet approach to development would lead to the formation of two new elites that proved to be anathema to the populist strain in Mao's thinking. First, there was the new technocratic elite of managers and economic professionals, from whom China's current rulers are drawn, who were needed to design and implement Soviet-style plans and, second, a new political elite of party professionals.

The striking growth rates were not sufficient to allay these concerns and increasingly China's leaders felt that new methods were needed if China was to break out from its economic backwardness. In particular, unless agricultural production could be boosted the accumulation necessary for industrial development could not be met and the rapidly growing population could not be fed. Instead of shifting development priorities to a major programme of agricultural modernization, Mao chose to expand agricultural output by exploiting traditional farming methods at breakneck speed together with a dash for industrial growth. The resultant strategy was the 'Great Leap Forward' (GLF) and its disastrous implementation led not only to massive famine in China but also severe splits about the way forward within the senior ranks of the Chinese leadership.

The Origins of a Chinese Path to Socialism, 1955–62

Although it was not until 1958 that the CCP made a radical break with previous economic practice, there had been earlier signs of disillusionment, and the years 1955–57 were crucial for the rupture. The socialization of industry had moved apace and in 1955 the pace of collectivization of agriculture picked up dramatically. In the economic sphere the main debates concerned the speed of development, the relationship of socialization to technical transformation, and the question of whether the economic process should be decentralized and, if so, how. Mao's view concerning agricultural transformation was signalled in a July 1955 speech in which he rejected the approach that collectivization should be subordinated to mechanization. Mao felt that China's conditions meant that technical transformation would take longer than social transformation and in 1956 he put forward his 12-Year Plan for Agriculture that proposed socialization as the necessary prerequisite for a rapid increase in production. It was a while, however, before Mao's economic thinking gained the support of a majority within the leadership. His plan was shelved with the relatively moderate political climate of 1956, only to be revived again in 1957.

The Eighth Party Congress (September 1956) acknowledged the success of the First Five-Year Plan and approved proposals for a second plan to start in 1958. The new plan again accorded agriculture the lowest priority for allocation of funds but more emphasis was placed on light industry to meet consumer demands. Some decentralization was also introduced to curb the powers of the central ministries but the plan still lay within the Soviet orbit and assumed that socialist transformation required a developed industrial base. Mao, as shown in his views on agricultural development, was moving away from this approach, and it is clear that a serious divergence of opinion was emerging. Given the Mao-centric nature of the Chinese political system, it was clear that once Mao decided openly to throw his weight behind his views, policy would have to shift.

The ground for a major shift in strategy was prepared with decisions taken at the Third Plenum of the Eighth Central Committee (September–October 1957) that adopted the radical measures that paved the way for the GLF. The decision was taken to decentralize power to the regions rather than to enlarge the power of initiative for individual enterprises as proposed by Chen Yun, a revolutionary veteran like Mao and a key economic planner, although limited decentralization of power was allowed to be carried out within individual units. Chen's strategy would have facilitated the use of material incentives to promote production and might have led to a decrease in the influence of the party in the production process. In fact, this approach formed the starting point for reforms introduced in the late 1970s. Mao feared that such a policy approach would encourage an incentive structure that would encourage the growth of 'spontaneous capitalist tendencies'. Decentralization to the regions only would allow greater flexibility but ensure continued party control and conformity with central planning. It would permit mobilization techniques to promote production enthusiasm rather than the use of material incentives. These decisions paved the way for the adoption of the radical approach to development embodied in the GLF.

Two other factors contributed to the radicalization of policy. The first was that Mao had already begun to push social transformation in the countryside, sweeping aside the objections of those who felt that steady mechanization must come first. In July 1955, Mao called for one-half of all households to be in cooperatives by the end of 1957. In practice, the speed of transition was even quicker, with all households so organized by the end of 1956 and communization completed even more swiftly.

Second, significant criticism of the practice of CCP-rule surfaced. The external origins derived from the death of Stalin and Krushchev's February 1956 'secret speech' denouncing Stalin's crimes and attributing them to the cult of the individual. The internal causes derived from resistance by workers and peasants to the rapid pace of socialization. Mao was not willing to go as far as Krushchev in his denunciation of Stalin – to do so might have reflected badly on himself – but accepted that he had made mistakes. It did cause him to think about leadership and he outlined his own methods on correct leadership in the Ten Great Relationships (Mao 1956, in Schram, 1974, pp. 61–83). He reaffirmed that a balance must be struck between democracy and centralism and argued that there would be 'long-term coexistence and mutual supervision' between party and non-party people. This theoretical position, together with Mao's reaction to the 1956 uprising in Hungary and his desire to shake up a party apparatus that he felt was becoming increasingly conservative and institutionalized, led to the launching of the Hundred Flowers' Campaign. Mao felt secure that the intelligentsia basically supported his revolution and that, while he decried the nature of the criticism unleashed in Hungary, what was needed in China was not repression of complaint but the encouragement of open criticism of the party apparatus.

The Campaign was launched in May 1956 and widened in February 1957 when Mao invited intellectuals to raise criticisms and suggested that the party, some of whose leaders were frustrating his plans for social transformation, was not above criticism from those outside. The depth of criticism was, however, unexpected and ranged widely, even calling into question the legitimacy of the party and the revolution itself. Mao was bitterly disillusioned with the intellectual elites and on 8 June 1957 the Campaign was brought to a swift close when the *People's Daily* published an editorial denouncing the 'rightists' who had abused their freedom to attack the party and socialism. This marked the start of the 'Anti-Rightist Campaign' under which hundreds of thousands of intellectuals were investigated, demoted, fired or imprisoned.

Perhaps more alarmingly, the socialization drive of the new party-state had begun to run against the material interests of both the workers and the peasants. Evidence suggests that peasant withdrawal from the cooperatives in the winter of 1956–57 was extensive and was dubbed a 'small typhoon' (Teiwes, 1987, p. 140). Research by Perry shows how the socialization of industry was not universally approved of by the new working class (Perry, 1997). By early 1957 reforms had led to a decline in real income for workers and loss of input into decision-making, leading to an increase in strike activity in Shanghai and other industrial centres. Those protesting, on the whole, were rejecting the process of socialization. Thus, while the immediate causes were economic, the ultimate consequences could have quickly become political. This must have alarmed Mao and the Party Centre and perhaps provides an additional explanation as to why the leadership not only launched a crackdown on 'rightists' but also rallied behind a policy to press ahead quickly to complete socialist transformation.

Radicalization in the political sphere was soon followed in 1958 by the 'Great Leap Forward' in the economy marking a radical break with the Soviet model of development. The GLF represented a return to the mobilization techniques for development used in the Yan'an period. The GLF was based on the premise that the enthusiasm of the masses could be harnessed and used to promote economic growth and industrialization. Mao wanted to fast-forward the development process and an express aim of the movement was to overtake Britain's output of major industrial products within 15 years. Better agricultural production would increase the amount of capital that could be accumulated for investment. The strategy rejected the notion that high-level development of the productive forces was a necessary prerequisite for socialist transformation; its theoretical foundations lay rather in Mao's notion of 'permanent revolution'. Permanent revolution would prevent the institutionalization and bureaucratization of the revolution, with continuing or new contradictions resolved by a series of qualitative changes as a part of the process of realizing Mao's developmental goals. Mao questioned the value of administrative planning copied from the Soviet Union and came down heavily against a detailed planning of economic activities by the central government. The advantages of local initiative, such as the innovation and improvement of basic agricultural implements, were to be brought into play. Local initiative was not to be stifled and the gains from mass mobilization were not to be underestimated. This would leave ample possibilities for the people to be mobilized for capital works and for engaging in the transformation of the social relations of production.

An integral part of the strategy was the policy known as 'walking on two legs'. This promoted the dual use of modern, large-scale, capital-intensive methods of production and traditional small-scale methods. Mao hoped that this combination would tap the huge reservoir of hitherto unexploited resources in the rural areas so that they would be capable of providing their own industrial goods, manure and agricultural tools. The most notorious result of this approach was the 'backyard steel furnaces' that produced a huge volume of steel, much of it useless. Other more successful small-scale projects were the creation of small electric power generators and chemical fertilizer plants. This use of intermediate technology remains the greatest legacy of the movement and many of the small-scale production plants formed the basis of the rural industrial take-off of the 1980s.

Hand in hand with the GLF strategy went the programme of communization that created much larger collective units. By the end of 1959, the 750,000 cooperatives (higher-stage APCs) had been amalgamated into just 24,000 people's communes. The communes carried out not only agricultural work but were also responsible for such things as industrial work, trade, education, military affairs, health, village administration and social welfare. Communal living was introduced in some areas to release more labour for production.

While the GLF was not quite the wild act of voluntarism that it is often portrayed as in the West (Lippit, 1975), the campaign style with which it was pursued and the dominating radical political atmosphere very quickly pushed it to excesses. Most communes and industrial units falsified production figures to show that they were more 'red' than their neighbours. This contributed to setting even higher targets in subsequent plans. It is clear that although many people doubted the exaggerated figures, they were afraid to speak up for fear of being criticized. Planning was rendered totally ineffective. The imbalance within the structure of the national economy, combined with inevitable bottlenecks, meant that stoppages in production occurred and many enterprises overextended their productive capacity.

The communization programme also encountered major problems and resistance. Many peasants resented communal living and the confiscation of private plots. Other problems arose from the unwieldy size of the communes and the lack of competent personnel to administer them. Two external factors further contributed to the failure of the strategy. First, during the summer of 1960 the Soviets withdrew their aid following the Sino-Soviet split. Second, floods and droughts were extremely severe. This latter factor enabled Mao and his supporters to shift the blame for failure onto natural disasters claiming that they were 70 per cent responsible. Foreign observers have always blamed the strategy itself and the post-Mao leadership has been less charitable about the catastrophe, blaming the strategy for 70 per cent of the damage.

From 1959 production in all sectors began to fall. Between 1958 and 1962, China's gross national product (GNP) fell by about 35 per cent. Paradoxically, national consumption at the aggregate level fell only marginally, as the share of national income devoted to investment dropped off sharply. Nonetheless, in many rural parts of the country acute shortages of food caused famine on a massive scale and at least 30 million people died as a result (From Pieter Bottelier; on the famines see Becker, 1996). It was obvious that a different strategy had to be found to restore production and, in particular, assure food supply for the population. Serious opposition first became apparent at the Lushan plenum (July–August 1959) and the main critic was the Defence Minister, Peng Dehuai. Peng attacked across a wide range of issues and particularly criticized the speed with which the programme had been implemented and the exaggeration of figures that made planning impossible, and condemned the commune programme. In addition, Peng criticized party practice, claiming that democracy in the party and the party's relations with the masses were being severely hampered by the 'petty-bourgeois fanaticism' characteristic of the GLF. While the strategy was abandoned in 1960 and Mao accepted some blame, such a direct challenge to his rule was intolerable. Peng was denounced as the leader of an 'anti-party clique' and replaced as Defence Minister by Lin Biao. The plenum, in accordance with a prior agreement, replaced Mao as President of the Republic by Liu Shaoqi to whom powers of policy implementation increasingly passed. This situation was uncomfortable for Mao but ultimately deadly for Liu.

Liu had been the most enthusiastic supporter of the Mao cult in the 1940s but had presided over the removal of Mao Zedong Thought from the Party Statutes in 1956. In the 1950s Liu had favoured a policy that promoted agricultural mechanization before the social transformation proposed by Mao. In the early 1960s, together with Deng Xiaoping, he presided over policies of economic liberalization designed to restore economic health after the ravages of the GLF. Economic policy focused on how to provide correctives to and reversals of the disastrous GLF policy. The period also contained some policy experimentation that formed the initial point of departure for the post-Mao reforms. At the time, the policies promoted provided the basis for the conflicts that broke out in the Cultural Revolution.

The most pressing problem was how to revive agricultural production, and a series of adjustment policies were adopted throughout 1961. The order of priority for economic development was changed with agriculture taking priority over light industry and with the formerly favoured sector of heavy industry placed last. This meant that in rejecting the GLF strategy the Chinese did not resurrect the Soviet development strategy, and a lower growth rate for industry was anticipated than was put forward in either the First Five-Year Plan or the GLF. Further, the communes were reformed and more flexibility over production was granted. Private plots abolished under the radical atmosphere were returned to the farmers who were once again allowed to sell their goods in rural markets. The number of small enterprises assuming responsibility for their own profits and losses was also increased. These changes were encapsulated in the slogan of 'three freedoms and one guarantee'. The communes were not abolished but were greatly reduced in size and the socio-economic functions they had acquired during the GLF were reduced. The basic organization was codified in September 1962 in the 'Regulations of the Work in the People's Communes' (the 60 Articles) and it remained essentially unchanged until the reforms of 1978–83. The number of communes was increased from 24,000 to 74,000, making them more manageable units, and the three-tier structure of commune, brigade and team was reaffirmed, with the team functioning as the basic accounting unit. The size of the teams was decreased so that it comprised only 30 or 40 households. The team became the most important unit in the countryside as it could make the final decisions concerning both the production of goods and the distribution of income.

When provided with an alternative, the farmers tended to reject advanced collective structures. Dali Yang (1997) has shown that after the famine when local leaders and farmers sought any strategy for survival, they chose non-sanctioned ones, especially household contracting for agricultural production. This system took the household as the key economic unit, with it undertaking certain production guarantees with local administrative authorities. While Mao was willing to decentralize certain powers to the production team, re-empowering the household was unacceptable. By contrast, many farmers opted for the household when they had the choice. Rejection of the collective continued even after the crackdown on household contracting began in November 1961; the practice was criticized as representing the 'spontaneous capitalist tendencies of the peasantry'. As late as May 1962, 20 per cent of all rural households adopted a household-based system of responsibility; by the summer this figure rose to 30 per cent. Mao and his supporters at the policy-making centre consistently rejected this preference for household farming and associated market factors as a retrograde step that could lead China astray ideologically. To accept this would have marked a major defeat for Mao and his view of the transition to socialism. This battle over households, markets and socialism was rejoined in the reform debates and policies of the 1980s, and has led Selden (1995, p. 250) to conclude provocatively that:

We must now read the entire history of the PRC at one important level as the persistent – ultimately successful – effort from below to restore the role of markets that socialist party leaders had accepted during resistance but sought to suppress once they were in power.

In the industrial sector a policy of financial retrenchment was introduced to help rationalize production. Thousands of construction projects were stopped or scrapped and investment for capital construction was lowered by 80 per cent. Material incentives were revived as the main stimulant for increasing production and managers were given greater freedom to determine policy in their own enterprises. The workforce was greatly reduced as the 20 million or so farmers who had joined the industrial workforce were returned to the countryside. To prevent future urban drift the residence system was tightened to keep the rural dwellers in the countryside and to make it difficult for workers to change jobs and virtually impossible to change cities. In return, enterprises and work-units would provide cradle-to-grave care for their employees.

The recovery programme was an impressive success with growth, from a low base, averaging 15 per cent per annum from 1962 to 1966 (information from Pieter Bottelier). However the economic recovery and the manner in which it was achieved led to policy divisions resurfacing. By 1964, Mao and his supporters felt that economic readjustment was complete. While there had been undeniable economic gains, they had been attained by increasing the urban–rural difference and by increasing the differentials between various groups in society. The programme had proved especially advantageous to skilled workers and technocrats and the social and political tensions that resulted led some to question whether the programme should be continued. The new priority given to agriculture was not disputed but there were differences over the substance of specific policies. The main source for disagreement stemmed from continued debate over the GLF. Nobody proposed a complete return to the strategy and Mao acknowledged that a more cautious approach to planning was necessary. Even so, Mao was not willing to see all the GLF policies abandoned in favour of ones less concerned about the means through which economic development was to be achieved.

The Radicalization of Politics and the Resurrection of Class Struggle, 1962–78

In the early 1960s, Mao found himself unable to direct the policy-making process and referred to himself as a 'dead ancestor'. His attempts to preserve something of the GLF experiment appeared thwarted, but a speech in January 1962 signalled that he would not remain in the political wilderness. Like his policy nemesis Liu Shaoqi, he stressed the importance of democratic central-ism, but unlike Liu he spoke at great length of the importance of democracy and the continued use of the mass line (see Box 2.5). Mao felt that this approach

---

BOX 2.5

Mao and the 'Mass Line'

Articulated by Mao in the 1940s, the 'mass line' was to be the fundamental organizing principle of the party to ensure that leaders and masses remained united. In his most celebrated statement on the subject, Mao ([1943] 1965) defined the 'mass line' when he instructed that:

In all practical work of our party, all correct leadership is necessarily 'from the masses to the masses'. This means: take the ideas of the masses (scattered and unsystematic ideas) and concentrate them (through study turn them into concentrated and systematic ideas), then go to the masses and propagate and explain these ideas until the masses embrace them as their own, hold fast to them and translate them into action, and test the correctness of these ideas in such action ... Such is the Marxist theory of knowledge.

This approach to mobilizing the masses to reach an objective, with its rejection of bureaucratic practices, gave the party a distinctive style that did much to bring it to power in 1949. Thereafter it helped to consolidate that power by mobilizing the population in a host of campaigns. These were directed at human targets such as 'counterrevolutionaries' and landlords, but also natural ones: pests and diseases and the Chinese earth itself. The intention was that through involvement many Chinese would undergo attitudinal change and learn to 'take the attitude of being the masters', whether by attacking former 'exploiters' or by learning through participation in water conservancy campaigns that the forces of nature could be tamed

In theory, the 'mass line' is about consultation, education, persuasion and eliciting an enthusiastic response. It is not, however, concerned with democracy. Through the 'mass line' it was hoped to combine the benefits derived from consultation with those at lower levels and those of a tight centralized control over policy formulation. Mao and his colleagues were Leninists and the party was the 'revolutionary vanguard', not simply an agency for implementing the wishes of the people. The weakness of the 'mass line' was, ironically, that it reflected in part a traditional view that the masses would accept the leadership's interpretation of their true interests if only these were explained properly.

---

had been abandoned during the years of economic retrenchment. Crucial for later developments, he put forward the idea that class struggle did not gradually die out in socialist society but continued to exist, a point reiterated at the Tenth Plenum of the Eighth Central Committee (September 1962). Using Yugoslavia as an example, Mao claimed that it was possible for a socialist country to change its nature and become revisionist. Mao's insistence on the continuation of class struggle did not predict the massive upheavals of just a few years later and he made it clear that class struggle should not interfere with economic work but proceed simultaneously. Mistakes made by rural cadres were to be treated as 'contradictions among the people'. Out of the plenum grew the Socialist Education Movement (1962–65).

While the leadership supported the new campaign, it is clear that Liu Shaoqi and Deng Xiaoping were more inclined to control the movement, keeping the party in charge and not letting it run out of control and damage the economic revival. Mao and his supporters felt frustrated by what they saw as deliberate attempts to stop mobilization of the masses to weed out corruption and to keep rural cadres on the revolutionary path. By January 1965 Mao had decided that Liu had to be removed (Snow, 1972, p. 17) and the movement radicalized, paving the way for the Cultural Revolution and the death and humiliation of most of Mao's former 'comrades-in-arms'.

In January 1965 a Central Work Conference issued a document that signalled an important shift in the targets of the movement. The document proceeded from the premise that the struggle between socialism and capitalism was present in the party itself. Consequently the principal target became 'people in positions of authority in the party who take the capitalist road'. The document undermined the capacity of the party to control the movement by adjudging that the masses represented the most effective supervision of cadres, and 'peasant associations' were permitted to seize control temporarily if they decided a local administration had been 'usurped' by capitalist elements. As Mao became convinced that the source of the troubles lay at the heart of the party itself, the lines were drawn for the battles of the Cultural Revolution (see Box 2.6).

The Great Proletarian Cultural Revolution is the most complicated and one of the most misinterpreted events in the history of the PRC. Attempts to understand it have not been helped by simplistic explanations that it was a two-line struggle between socialism and revisionism. It is not even clear what Mao really wanted from the movement, and he changed his mind on crucial issues during its course (see Box 2.7). Lieberthal (1995, p. 112) has neatly summarized a number of factors that underlay Mao's thinking. He certainly wanted to get rid of Liu Shaoqi, who died in desperate circumstances in 1969, but seemed to have no other successor in mind. He also seems to have wanted to shake up the bureaucracy, which he did by shattering the central party and state administration leaving the army and radical forces to fill the vacuum. He seems to have seen the movement as one last attempt to keep the revolutionary fires burning, giving the younger generation a feeling for the revolutionary enthusiasm that Mao's own generation had enjoyed. On the policy front there was stalemate in all major areas, although with the exception of education, arts and literature, the early years of the Cultural Revolution did not seem to resolve anything.

What the Cultural Revolution did result in was a shattered social fabric with students required to turn on their teachers, children encouraged to denounce their parents and authority in all its forms held up to ridicule. It unleashed many of the social tensions that had built up under CCP rule and revealed the frustrations of many with the bureaucracy. For a brief period

---

BOX 2.6

Key Political Dates, 1966–78

1966   16 May, Circular marks start of Cultural Revolution
August, Eleventh Plenum of the Eighth CC adopts the 'Sixteen Point Decision', further radicalizing the political atmosphere
1967   February, 'Revolutionary rebels' announce the establishment of the Shanghai commune; Mao rejects it
1969   March, Soviet and Chinese forces clash along the Ussuri River
April, Ninth Party Congress marks the return to top-down rebuilding of party and state
1970   August, Second Plenum of the Ninth CC reveals leadership divisions and subsequently Chen Boda is purged as a 'sham Marxist'
1971   September, Lin Biao's plane crashes in Mongolia
October, China is admitted to the UN; Taiwan's status revoked
1972   February, President Nixon arrives in Beijing
1973   August–September, Tenth Party Congress attempts to forge a new leadership
1974   April, Deng Xiaoping reappears to speak at the UN and by January 1975 is effectively in charge of the government
1975   January, Fourth National People's Congress, Zhou Enlai outlines the 'Four Modernizations'
1976   January, Zhou Enlai dies and Hua Guofeng is appointed acting premier
April, Tiananmen demonstrations used to purge Deng Xiaoping
September, Mao dies
October, 'Gang of Four' arrested
1977   July, Third Plenum of the Tenth CC restores Deng to all his posts
August, Eleventh Party Congress calls an end to the Cultural Revolution
1978   February–March, Fourth National People's Congress announces a new ambitious economic policy
December, Third Plenum of the Eleventh CC announces shift to economic modernization as core of party work

---

of time even the leading role of the party was called into question, as revolutionary committees were formed to fill the political vacuum left by the collapse of the existing administrative structures. A set of temporary organizations emerged at the centre to keep the country running, such as the Central Cultural Revolution Small Group, led by Jiang Qing, and the Working Group of the Central Military Commission. Citizens were exhorted to adulate Chairman Mao and his disjointed sayings became the justification for all policy initiatives and actions. More radical elements in the Cultural Revolution even seemed to eschew any intermediary organizations and envisioned a system that comprised 'Mao in Holy Communion with the masses'. For many the Cultural Revolution resulted in a loss of respect and legitimacy for the CCP as an institution. Once the PLA put the students back in their place, many became cynical towards the party and authority and alienated from the political process, a legacy that has persisted to this day. Certainly at

BOX 2.7

Changing Views of the Cultural Revolution

'All revolutionary intellectuals, now is the time to fight! Let us be united, hold high the great red banner of Mao Zedong thought, rally ourselves around the party CC and Chairman Mao, break the controls of revisionism and all its plots and tricks, so as to wipe out resolutely, lock, stock and barrel, all the monsters and freaks and all the Krushchev-style counterrevolutionary revisionists and to carry out to the end the socialist revolution' (Nie Yuanzi *et al.*, Philosophy Department, Peking University, 25 May 1966).
'I say to you all; youth is the great army of the Great Cultural Revolution! It must be mobilized to the full.
We believe in the masses. To become teachers of the masses we must first be the students of the masses. The present great Cultural Revolution is a heaven-and-earth shaking event' (Mao Zedong, 21 July 1966, in Schram, 1974, p. 254).
'The Great Cultural Revolution wreaked havoc after I approved Nie Yuanzi's big character poster at Peking University, and wrote a letter to Qinghua University Middle School, as well as writing a big-character poster of my own ... It all happened within a very short period, less than five months ... No wonder the comrades did not understand too much. The time was short and the Peking University poster was broadcast, the whole country would be thrown into turmoil. Since it was I who caused the havoc, it is understandable if you have some bitter words for me' (Mao Zedong, 25 October 1966, in Schram, 1974, p. 271).
'The Great Cultural Revolution is not a mass movement, but one man moving the masses with the barrel of a gun' (Wang Rongfen, student, Beijing Foreign Languages Institute, 24 September 1966, in Schoenhals, 1996, pp. 149–50).
'Smashing the "Gang of Four" is yet another signal victory in the Great Proletarian Cultural Revolution...The victorious conclusion of the first Great Proletarian Cultural Revolution certainly does not mean the end of class struggle or of the continued revolution under the dictatorship of the proletariat... Political revolutions in the nature of the Cultural Revolution will take place many times in the future. We must follow Chairman Mao's teachings and continue the revolution under the dictatorship of the proletariat to the end' (Hua Guofeng at the Eleventh Party Congress, 1977, pp. 49, 52).
'The "Cultural Revolution", which lasted from May 1966 to October 1976 was responsible for the most severe setback and the heaviest losses suffered by the party, the state, and the people since the founding of the PRC. It was initiated and led by Comrade Mao Zedong.
[Mao's erroneous "left"] theses must be thoroughly distinguished from Mao Zedong Thought. As for Lin Biao, Jiang Qing, and others who were placed in important positions by Comrade Mao Zedong, the matter is of an entirely different nature. They rigged up two counterrevolutionary cliques in an attempt to seize supreme power and, taking advantage of Comrade Mao Zedong's errors, committed many crimes behind his back, bringing disaster to the country and the people.
Irrefutable facts have proved that labelling Comrade Liu Shaoqi a "renegade, hidden traitor, and scab" was nothing but a frame-up by Lin Biao, Jiang Qing, and their followers.
Chief responsibility for the grave "left" error of the "Cultural Revolution", an error comprehensive in magnitude and protracted in duration, does indeed lie with comrade Mao Zedong. But after all it was the error of a great proletarian revolutionary' ('On questions of Party History', 27 June 1981).

the lower levels much of the struggle in the 1960s and 1970s comprised personal revenge rather than principled struggle, though on occasion the two could coincide. Chinese politics since 1969 has been dominated by the fallout from this momentous movement and even the reforms under Deng Xiaoping's tutelage would not have taken off so quickly without the excesses that had made most tired of the politics of mobilization and class struggle.

Feeling frustrated by the party bureaucracy, Mao turned to an explosive cocktail of the mobilization of students as Red Guards, younger more radical party members who gathered around his wife, Jiang Qing and, crucially, PLA officers loyal to Defence Minister Lin Biao. The movement began in the realms of culture with criticism of veiled attacks on Mao by those who were opposed to Peng Dehuai's dismissal and who were critical of the GLF. Very quickly calls for more proletarian literature led to a major attack on the party establishment.

The '16 May Circular' of 1966 drawn up by Mao and issued in the name of the CC radicalized the movement. The target was identified as 'the representatives of the bourgeoisie who have infiltrated the party, government and the army' and they were described as 'counterrevolutionary revisionists' who wanted to 'overthrow the dictatorship of the proletariat and replace it with that of the bourgeoisie'. While the PLA waited in the wings, Mao unleashed the students who had begun agitation following promulgation of the Circular. In August Mao gave them and their Red Guard groups his blessing.

In August at a CC plenum from which opponents were excluded, the '16-Point Decision' was adopted and this reflected further radicalization. The aim of the movement was now the 'overthrow of those persons within the party in authority taking the capitalist road'. An important part of this struggle was the elimination of the 'four olds', the old values and customs that the 'capitalist roaders' manipulated to enable them to dominate the masses. Clearly if the highest levels of the party were affected they could no longer be relied on to supervise the purification of the lower levels. This meant that it was up to the masses to liberate themselves; under no circumstances was action to be taken on their behalf and the party 'work teams', sent by higher levels for investigation, were criticized for trying to control the movement. Those who held 'incorrect' views were to be persuaded of their errors by reason rather than by force, but in the following months the battling Red Guard groups honoured this more in the breach than the observance. Finally, the decision referred to the electoral system set up by the Paris Commune that appeared to challenge the whole idea of the ruling vanguard party. The new political organizations that evolved in the struggle were to become 'permanent' mass organizations for the exercise of political power.

Following the publication of this decision, debate and fighting between Red Guard groups and their opponents increased and the movement quickly fragmented and became increasingly unruly. Even Mao very quickly became aware of the need to bring the situation under control and to rebuild some kind of party and state structure. Yet, the Red Guards could not be wished away as easily as they had been created. Many opposed the resurrection of a system that they felt was in essence similar to that which they had been trying to destroy. Even among those groups that supported the return of a modified party and state system, there was considerable disagreement about precisely what form it should take.

With the 'masses' divided and the party–state structure in disarray, the process of restoring order fell to the PLA. Mao had already ensured army support through the appointment of his loyal supporter, Lin Biao, as Defence Minister. The result was military Maoism. Mao, with his infallible capability to map out the correct road to socialism, provided the system with its legitimacy, while the PLA provided the institutional continuity and necessary force to deal with 'class enemies'. For a while, it appeared as if Mao wished to extend the PLA's supposed tradition of plain-living and unquestioning loyalty to society as a whole.

Not all in the PLA were happy about this new role. Local PLA commanders were often faced with the difficult task of deciding who were the revolutionary forces. Often they chose to side with the old, local bureaucrats whom they had known for years rather than with the more unruly 'revolutionary rebels'. This put local commanders in conflict with their own central military command. Not surprisingly, the student and other groups who had been promised a new system were disillusioned by these events. Mao had destroyed their faith in the party-state system and now his use of the military destroyed their faith in Mao as the invincible leader.

To run the country, Mao soon rejected the radical ideas of the Paris Commune as the new organizational form and instead the revolutionary committee was proposed. Not all authority was to be considered bourgeois and these committees were to comprise a 'three-in-one alliance' of revolutionary mass organizations, leading members of the local PLA units and revolutionary leading party-state cadres. The first such committee had been set up in Heilongjiang province. By September 1968 the last of the provincial revolutionary committees had been set up and in April 1969 the Ninth Party Congress was convened, marking the abandonment of the attempt to rebuild the system from the bottom up. The need to rebuild was also spurred by the March clashes with Soviet troops along the Ussuri River, clashes that we now know were initiated by China (Goldstein, 2001, pp. 985–97). The clashes following the Soviet invasion of Czechoslovakia justified by the Brezhnev doctrine that asserted the Soviet right to intercede in the affairs of other socialist countries gave impetus to Mao's recognition that rebuilding was necessary. This must have convinced Mao of the need to restore order. It also prompted him to improve relations with the United States that culminated in President Nixon's February 1972 visit to Beijing.

While proclaimed as a Congress of 'unity and victory', the unity was fragile at best and it was difficult to see what the 'victors' had won. The turmoil had done nothing to solve the policy differences and actually created new problems. The Ninth Congress set in motion party rebuilding but differences existed within the leadership about the kind of party it should be, where the new cadres would come from and about the correct role for the PLA. The PLA was the one group really to benefit from the Cultural Revolution and it had acquired a new and vital governing role. Active soldiers headed all but four of the revolutionary committees and almost half of the CC members were from the PLA. The preeminence of the PLA was reflected by the anointment in the new constitution of Lin Biao as Mao's chosen successor.

However, rebuilding the party apparatus would mean that Lin would have to supervise the removal from power of his own support base. While the PLA had been important during the phase of destruction, Zhou Enlai and the revolutionary veterans were to play a greater role in reconstruction. Before the military could agree to withdraw they required assurances that the 'left' and the mass organizations would not carry out reprisals for the brutal way in which some had been treated. This was achieved with the removal from power of Chen Boda and his 'leftist' supporters in 1970. Chen had represented the most radical voice at the centre but he was unceremoniously dumped and criticized as a 'sham Marxist'.

The leadership group around Mao and Zhou could now turn their attention to reducing the influence of Lin Biao and the military. Between December 1970 and August 1971 the provincial party apparatus was rebuilt but the military actually consolidated its position during this process. In addition to the fear of reprisals, PLA reluctance to return to the barracks stemmed from the new-found power of centrally directed units such as the air force and navy that had not exercised political power previously and seemed unwilling to part with it. The death of Lin Biao while attempting to flee to the Soviet Union after an alleged *coup d'état* and the purge of his military supporters at the centre decreased military influence. Recent research reveals that Lin and his generals never had any intention of challenging Mao and certainly did not plan a *coup*, while Mao decided relatively late that Lin should go. The Lin Biao that emerges from recent accounts is sickly and passive and did not rouse himself even when he knew that Mao would purge him (Teiwes with Sun, 1996; Jin, 1999). A series of campaigns was launched against Lin, calling on the military commanders to accept party leadership, with the party rather than the army being once again portrayed as the symbol of national unity.

The question of what kind of party should rule China was resolved less easily, and indeed today still remains the core political issue. As the influence of the radicals was curbed and military influence decreased, increasing numbers of officials who had been purged during the Cultural Revolution returned to senior positions. The best example was Deng Xiaoping, who had been criticized as the 'number two person in authority taking the capitalist road'. In fact, it appears that Mao had always intended to bring Deng back once he had been taught a lesson.

This process of rehabilitation gained momentum at the Tenth Party Congress (August–September 1973). The Congress reflected an attempt to put together a leadership that could command sufficient support to allow economic development not to be disrupted, but at the same time could maintain some of the revolutionary momentum of the Cultural Revolution. In this context the Congress abandoned the attempt to resolve the question of succession by appointing a specific individual in favour of appointing a collective leadership by electing five vice-chairs. However, it was clear that the system was excessively dominated by a 'supreme leader', the institutions attacked in the Cultural Revolution possessed no legitimate authority in the eyes of many, the people who staffed the institutions were severely divided about the way forward, thus paralysing decision-making, and many urban residents had become cynical about the whole political process.

By 1974 Mao and his supporters felt the pendulum had swung too far and they appeared ready to launch a new campaign to consolidate the gains of the Cultural Revolution. On 2 February 1974 the *People's Daily* called on people to 'dare to go against the tide and to advance into the teeth of storms' and a campaign of mass criticism unfolded. Premier Zhou Enlai, who was critically ill, was one of the main targets, together with those such as Deng Xiaoping who had returned to power under his and even Mao's protection. Initially, the conflict was contained and another attempt at ensuring collective succession was made at the Fourth National People's Congress (January 1975). At the Congress, Zhou Enlai outlined the policy of the four modernizations (agriculture, industry, science and technology, and national defence), a policy that he had first presented in 1964. The policy envisaged a two-stage programme, with the first objective being to build an 'independent and relatively comprehensive industrial and economic system' by 1980, and the second being to bring the national economy to the front rank of the world by the year 2000. The Congress appointed a coalition that seemed to represent the opposing groups within the leadership. However, it was very fragile, and fell apart shortly afterwards.

The new economic policy ran counter to the sketchy ideas that Mao and his more radical supporters had begun to develop during the 1960s and 1970s. It is difficult to say that their ideas amounted to a coherent theory of economic transition but it is possible to piece together a nascent strategy that had a number of specific policy consequences (see Christensen and Delman, 1981; van Ness and Raichur, 1983). In the 1950s Mao had already made clear his dislike of Soviet-style administrative planning and preference for decentralization to local-level governments. This he felt would provide greater flexibility but would ensure policy coordination and offer the opportunity for mass mobilization for capital construction works and to transform the social relations of production. Mao also rejected decentralizing economic powers to the production units themselves as well as an incentive strategy based on material incentives.

In his major critique of Soviet economic thinking, Mao proposed a break with the idea that socialism was an independent mode of production (Mao, in Roberts and Levy, 1977). In his view, socialism was a transitional mode between capitalism and communism. As we have seen, Mao did not see socialism as a phase of harmonious and peaceful development, but rather racked by contradictions between the economic base and the superstructure, and that class struggle still persisted. In contrast to his more orthodox Marxist colleagues, Mao felt less constrained by 'objective laws of economic development' and adopted a more voluntaristic approach, as witnessed in the GLF and the Cultural Revolution. Such an approach would permit people to overcome physical and other constraints on development and could also prevent the revolution from stagnating and even a capitalist restoration taking place.

These ideas were developed by the group later denounced as the 'Gang of Four', in particular Yao Wen-yuan (1975) and Zhang Chunqiao (1975). They sought to explain how a socialist economy might regress back to a capitalist one. They identified 'bourgeois rights' and the persistence of capitalist factors, such as commodities and differential wages, as providing a material base for the reproduction of capitalism. Such factors also provided the source of power for a new bourgeoisie to emerge and prosper. Further, the division of labour created an 'intellectual aristocracy' who ruled over the production units, denying the workers access to real power. In their view, it was necessary to enforce the 'dictatorship of the proletariat' to prevent capitalism from being restored and a new bourgeoisie from taking power. Their wrath turned on the policy of the 'four modernizations' and in one of their memorable phrases they claimed they would rather have 'a late socialist train' than 'a capitalist one that ran on time'. To prevent capitalist restoration there would have to be many 'cultural revolutions' to eradicate the remaining capitalist factors.

Their solution had direct policy consequences that affected the lives of hundreds of millions. Intellectuals and those engaged in management were viewed with particular suspicion and were required to undertake regular manual labour and even to spend many years in the countryside to 'learn from the peasants'. This policy even extended to the foreign students in China. Each week the institute leaders would devise manual labour tasks for us students to engage in. We pulled down trees and moved rocks from one end of the campus before moving them back again the next week. We also did a stint on a people's commune just outside of Yangzhou, where the Grand Canal meets the Yangzi. We were a drag on the production of the commune and the local farmers had to be bribed to take us on with a few little household items. Perhaps the most important impact of this policy, as with the 'revolutionary travels' of the Red Guards, was to expose to the urban elite just how poor and backward China really was. It convinced many of the need for drastic reforms.

To prevent the power of a new management class from developing, workers' control of the enterprise was to be secured through worker participation in management. This did not mean, however, that the workers ran the factories, but it did provide various institutional mechanisms through which their voices could be heard. In particular, the 'Gang of Four' sought to reduce and even eliminate the material privileges that could succour the 'new bourgeoisie'. Grades on salary scales were to be limited to reduce income differentials and piece-rates and bonuses were to be curtailed or even eliminated. In the countryside private plots were criticized as was production outside of the plan as the 'tails of capitalism'. On the communes, while more moderate voices wanted to keep accounting at the team level, the 'Gang of Four' wanted to raise it to the level of the brigade as this would make the countryside appear more socialist. These and other measures would eradicate a material base for the 'new bourgeoisie' from emerging. This policy put the collective above the individual and was accompanied by an egalitarian distribution policy and austerity in consumption. Austerity was promoted by campaigns to be frugal and adopt plain living (something Mao's wife, Jiang Qing, never took to apply to herself) and was reinforced through an intricate system of rationing. Combined with the emphasis on 'self-reliance' in production under which most areas produced for their own needs, it meant that consumption was limited to a small number of basic goods.

Finally, the 'Gang of Four' acknowledged a negative view of the role of international trade in development. The principles of 'self-reliance' extended to foreign trade, with it playing at best a residual role, and all efforts were made to restrict the import of bourgeois ideas. In particular, they attacked Deng Xiaoping's plans to import technology on a large scale and to pay for it through the export of China's minerals. They accused Deng of being a traitor and of turning China into an 'appendage of imperialism'.

Given such divergent views it is not surprising that the political coalition soon fell apart. Two main factors accelerated the collapse of this attempt at conciliation. First, the ill-health of the older generation of China's leaders brought the question of succession to the forefront. Secondly, concrete economic plans had to be drawn up for the new Five-Year Plan to be implemented beginning in 1976. This brought the differing approaches to development strategy into sharp focus. While Zhou, Deng and their supporters started convening meetings and conferences to draw up programmes for their growth-oriented policies, their opponents launched a series of theoretical campaigns directed against those whom they saw as 'whittling away' the gains of the Cultural Revolution. The latter group enjoyed little influence in the crucial apparats such as the military and the economic planning system, but instead dominated the education and propaganda systems. Policy practice and party rhetoric began to diverge dramatically. While Zhou and Deng sought to rally production and begin the import of new technologies, their opponents began campaigns using historical allegory to attack what they saw as 'class capitulation at home and national capitulation in foreign affairs'.

Not for the first time in a communist system, it was the death of the 'supreme leader' (Mao in September 1976) that offered a window of opportunity for a radical break with the past. Developments unfolded swiftly and on 6 October 1976 the PLA elite guard, under instructions from the veteran military leader Ye Jianying, arrested the 'Gang of Four' (Jiang Qing and her closest supporters). The 'Gang of Four' had sought to devise new organizational forms that would be able to combine more traditional Leninist concepts with those thrown up by the Cultural Revolution. In practice they used hierarchical means to bring about democracy, and invoked obedience to encourage initiative (White, 1982, p. 6). The organizational forms experimented with failed to gain legitimacy. This fact, combined with the 'Gang of Four's' suspicion of the party and lack of support within its top leadership, meant that they fell back all too readily on the invocation of Mao's name as a source of legitimacy. While they were able to manipulate Mao's vague directives and pro-Zhou and Deng demonstrations in April 1976 to cause Deng's second purge, their grip on power was tenuous. In January 1976, after Zhou had died, it was neither Deng nor one of the 'Gang of Four' who was named acting premier but the little known Hua Guofeng. This indicated that while Mao may have had reservations about Deng, he was not willing to give free rein to his wife and her supporters.

With the arrest of the 'Gang of Four', the challenge of coming to terms with this economic and political legacy first fell to Hua Guofeng, who pursued a policy of 'Maoism without Mao'. For the economy, Hua favoured the 'quick-fix' approach, setting ambitious planning targets and using the selective import of high-level technology to transform the ailing situation. The basis for this transformation was to be the 1976–85 Ten-Year Plan presented to the Fifth NPC (February–March 1978), a plan that owed much to Deng's alternative policy prognosis from 1975–76. The plan set forward a number of optimistic targets and bore resemblance to Mao's 12-year plan of the mid-1950s that had preceded the GLF. However, Hua reversed the previous sectoral priority, placing the emphasis on heavy industrial development rather than agriculture. Some 120 large-scale projects were to be completed by 1985 and an almost 150 per cent increase in steel production was called for. The Maoist obsession with grain production was retained with the call for an increase in production of over 40 per cent.

This initial post-Mao strategy served only to compound the problems. The import of modern technology, the 'Great Leap Westward', far outstripped both China's export capacity and its ability to absorb the imports. The trade deficit with 'capitalist' countries grew from US$1.2 billion in 1977 to $4.5 billion in 1979. There was the notorious case of the modern Wuhan steel plant that would have required more electricity to run it than could be generated to supply the needs of the entire city. Many of the large-scale projects could not be completed because of planning errors and a shortage of the necessary skilled personnel

In the political realm, Hua also failed to address the problems of the Maoist legacy. Little attention was paid to political–administrative reform. For the most part, such problems as were recognized were put down to the excesses of the 'Gang of Four', the 'bad workstyle' to which officials had grown accustomed as a result of the Cultural Revolution, and the remaining influences of a 'feudal' way of thinking. No moves had been made to rede-fine party–society relations or to reduce the excessively leader-dominated system.

Hua and his supporters retained certain ideas from the Cultural Revolution period along with the ambiguities. Further, their attitude towards the party's role in society was designed to complement their optimistic proposals for economic development. Essentially, Hua and his supporters proposed the continuance of the party as a vehicle of mobilization to conduct mass campaigns, both economic and political, to achieve the ambitious economic targets. They persisted with the Maoist ambiguity that while the party was to be in command, the masses were to monitor abuses by its officials. This view caused suspicion of the party to remain while failing to create organizations with legitimacy. It was too dependent on the more 'radical' aspects of Mao's legacy and the creation of a new personality cult around Hua to resist policy shifts to the new economic programme.

Hua Guofeng was never able to come to terms with the problem of leader-ship. He continued the Mao cult and set about creating one of his own. Polit-ically, it would have been extremely difficult for Hua to have dismantled the excessively Mao-centred system as his own right to rule was based on the claim that he was Mao's hand-picked successor. The increasing emphasis from December 1978 onwards on the need to regularize procedures and the mounting criticism of the 'feudal workstyle' did not augur well for Hua's continued occupation of top party and state posts. The restoration of Deng Xiaoping to his posts at the Tenth Plenum of the Tenth CC (July 1977) had not helped Hua. It was clear to all that Deng enjoyed higher military status and prestige than Hua. No matter how much they may have sought to cooper-ate, there was no room in the Chinese political system for two dominant leaders. Indeed, Hua gave up the premiership in September 1980 and his position as party chair in June 1981. The quaint poster that was widely distributed of the aged Mao handing the youthful Hua a piece of paper with Mao's inscription 'With you in charge, I am at ease' smacked far too much of the Emperor passing on the Mandate of Heaven to his chosen successor.

By the late 1970s, it was becoming clear to the group of veteran leaders around Deng Xiaoping that solution of the economic, political and social problems required a major overhaul of the system. While the aggregate figures for the economy do not justify the official CCP verdict that the Cultural Revolution represented 'ten lost years', they mask increasing problems and imbalances in the Chinese economy. After a mild economic recovery in the early 1970s, the growth rate declined, and by 1976 the decline began to assume crisis proportions. In 1976, the average growth rate of the national income dropped 2.3 per cent and the growth of total production was, at 1.7 per cent, below the rate of population growth. In part, the serious Tangshan earthquake of 1976 can explain these poor results. However, it is more plausible to explain the seriousness of the results in terms of the paralysis that gripped China's economic decision-making in the years prior to 1976. This economic downturn was combined with a longer-term dissatisfaction about stagnating living standards on the part of much of the population. The government's consistent overconcentration on accumulation at the expense of consumption meant that rationing, queuing and hours spent on laborious household chores were the daily fare for most urban residents. In the countryside, the attacks on private plots of land and free markets as 'capitalist tails' had caused farmer resentment by undermining alternative sources of income. Although the collective functioned effectively in some regions, many farmers saw it as an alien entity that made unfair demands on their time without supplying just returns. It seems no exaggeration to conclude that China's population had probably had enough of tightening their belts in return for the promise of a bright future.

Behind all this was a ticking population time bomb. Mao's 1950s view that a larger population would increase China's strength had meant that the population had boomed from 540 to 930 million by the time of his death. Unemployment and underemployment were serious problems, and it was clear that a major overhaul was required to resolve the problems; the Third Plenum of the Eleventh CC (December 1978) began to articulate a new policy course.

3

China Under Reform, 1978–2003

The reform programme launched under Deng Xiaoping's tutelage in 1978 affected every aspect of life in China and left no institution untouched. The reforms led to a significant liberalization of previous regime practice in terms of party control over the economy and society. However, it was not the intention that this liberalization would lead to democracy and Deng and his followers preferred to combine the introduction of market forces in the economy with tight political control. While the reforms left the pillar of one-party rule untouched, they undermined the other main pillar of a centrally planned economy with predominant social ownership of the means of production. While Deng and his successors all stressed the need to continue strong one-party rule, even here there was adaptation in the party's role and some began to question whether it was viable for the long-term future. Certainly by the early twenty-first century, this strategy appeared to be a success in economic terms, with the economy averaging 9 per cent per annum output growth, leading to significant rises in incomes. However, the reforms have been deeply contested by those opposed on ideological grounds, or groups that felt disadvantaged by the reforms, or by those who felt that the reforms had not progressed swiftly enough. This chapter reviews the progress of the reforms (see Box 3.1 and Box 3.5: pp. 58 and 80) and the opposition they have generated.

The Third Plenum and the Initial Reform Agenda, 1978–84

The criticism of Mao Zedong and the attempts by Deng and his supporters to dismantle the personality cult meant that Mao's name could no longer be invoked effectively to underpin legitimacy. As a result, they chose to promise a bright economic future for all within a relatively short space of time, meaning that CCP legitimacy would be linked closely to the ability to deliver the economic goods. The political breakthrough for Deng came at the Third Plenum of the Eleventh CC held in December 1978 (see Box 3.1). Deng had formed an alliance with pragmatic planners, in particular Chen Yun, accepting

---

BOX 3.1

Key Political Dates, 1978–96

1978   November, Posters start to go up at Democracy Wall
        December, Third Plenum of the eleventh CC shifts policy to economic
        reform
1979   March, October, Deng puts forward the 'Four Basic Principles'
        October, Democracy Wall writer Wei Jingsheng sentenced to 15 years
        in prison
1980   February, Fifth Plenum of the Eleventh CC rehabilitates Liu Shaoqi
        May, China joins the World Bank and International Monetary Fund (IMF)
        September, Zhao Ziyang replaces Hua Guofeng as Premier
1981   January, Trial of 'Gang of Four' completed
        June, Resolution on party history criticizes both the Cultural Revolution
        and Mao
        June, Hu Yaobang replaces Hua Guofeng as party head
1982   September, Twelfth Party Congress adopts new statutes
1984   October, CC document proposes major urban industrial reform
1985   September, Party National Conference announces major restructuring
        of party leadership
1986   April, Zhao Ziyang presents the Seventh Five-Year Plan that is cautious
        in tone
        September, Sixth Plenum of the Twelfth Party Congress calls for
        improvement in ideological and cultural work
        December, student demonstrations lead to the purge of Hu Yaobang
        (January), and Zhao Ziyang becomes acting General Secretary
1987   October, the Thirteenth Party Congress favours continued economic
        and political reform
1988   Summer, Beidaihe meeting removes Zhao's right to speak on economic
        affairs
1989   15 April, Hu Yaobang dies, sparking student demonstrations
        3–4 June, PLA troops brutally clear students from Tiananmen Square
        June, Fourth Plenum of the Thirteenth CC formally removes Zhao
        Ziyang and Jiang Zemin becomes General Secretary
        November, Deng Xiaoping steps down as head of Military Affairs
        Commission
1992   January–February, Deng tours South China to kick-start economic reform
        September, Fourteenth Party Congress approves renewed economic reform
1993   November, Third Plenum of the Fourteenth Party Congress adopts the
        document 'Establishment of a Socialist Market Economic System'
1995   October, Jiang Zemin delivers 'More Talk About Politics'
1996   March, Taiwan Straits crisis escalates as Li Teng-hui is elected president
        of Taiwan

---

their views of an alternative approach to economic development. In this sense, the initial victory at the plenum was Chen's rather than Deng's. Later developments and the official history that ascribes the new line and its development almost exclusively to Deng has tended to obscure this fact. Deng's usurpation of full credit for the original reform programme and its subsequent radicalization angered Chen, and he became Deng's strongest opponent on the question of pace and extent of economic reform. On a number of occasions, Chen upbraided Deng for ignoring the opinions of others, thus defying the principles of collective leadership that Chen claims had been restored at the plenum.

The plenum implemented three decisions that had a lasting impact. First, economic modernization was made central to all party work. Ideology and class struggle were downplayed and policy-making became more pragmatic, summed up in the slogan 'practice is the sole criterion for testing truth' (the slogan was launched in May 1978) and the corresponding policy line of 'correcting mistakes wherever they are discovered'. Second, despite the plenum's decision to forget about the past and concentrate on the future, the new 'practice' slogan was used both at the plenum and subsequently to reverse a whole series of previous political judgements. These were used both to undermine the basis of legitimacy of Hua Guofeng, the party chairman, and his supporters, and to establish the credibility of Deng's and Chen's policy positions. Essentially, Mao's increasing radicalism in his later years was denounced while previous attempts to moderate 'economic excesses' through a policy of economic liberalization were praised. To award themselves the mantle of popular legitimacy the demonstrations of April 1976 were reassessed and proclaimed a revolutionary movement that had demonstrated support both for Zhou Enlai and Deng Xiaoping. Third, the plenum formed the source for a new policy direction that gradually increased the influence of market forces in the Chinese economy. This was felt first in the rural sector. The plenum ducked two pressing political issues: no assessment was made of the Cultural Revolution nor of the role of Mao. Given that Hua Guofeng and others had risen to power because of these two factors, this was not surprising.

After the plenum, Deng and the more pragmatic economic planners such as Chen Yun and Bo Yibo began to criticize the ambitious economic plans identified with Hua Guofeng and warned of 'economic rashness'. They repeatedly stressed the need to comply with 'objective economic laws', thus rejecting the voluntarism that had plagued policy since the late 1950s. These warnings were reflected in the new economic policies presented to the Second Session of the Fifth NPC (June–July 1979), policies that Chen Yun had a greater role in drafting than Deng Xiaoping. The Ten-Year Plan (adopted in March 1978) was postponed and abandoned at the Third Session (1980). In its place a three-year period of 're-adjusting, restructuring, consolidation and improvement of the national economy' was introduced. Economic priorities were reordered with heavy industry relegated to last place behind agriculture and light industry. The primary focus was to fix targets for the agricultural sector. Rather than leading the economy, heavy industry would receive only such funds as were necessary for its adaptation to meet the needs of the other sectors (Pairault, 1982, pp. 119–48).

Economic policy revolved around the promotion of market mechanisms to deal with the inefficiencies of allocation and distribution that occurred with the central planning system. Awareness of the 'new technological revolution' increased the Chinese leaders' desire to make their system more flexible and thus more amenable to change. To take advantage of the market opportunities, more power of decision-making was to be given to the localities, and in particular to the units of production themselves. Production units were given greater autonomy to decide what and how much to produce, and where to sell. At the core of this system was the ubiquitous contract that was expected to govern economic activity. Correspondingly, material incentives were seen as the major mechanism for causing people to work harder, and the socialist principle of 'to each according to their work' was to be firmly applied. Egalitarianism was attacked as a dangerous notion that retarded economic growth. These reforms of the domestic economy were accompanied by an unprecedented opening to the outside world in the search for export markets and the necessary foreign investments, technology and higher-quality consumer goods.

Change was rapid and dramatic in the rural sector and moderate in the urban sector, while political reform was ineffective and ultimately divisive. The Third Plenum ratified a policy intended to encourage growth in agricultural production by substantial increases in procurement prices and by modernizing agriculture through investments by the brigades and teams (Watson, 1984, pp. 83–108). Through 1979, specific measures were introduced to implement the policy of raising procurement prices. At the same time, policy was relaxed to let different regions make use of the 'law of comparative advantage'. Reversing the policy of the Cultural Revolution, farmers were given the green light to work private plots and engage in sideline production. To allow the farmers to sell their products, for example their above-quota grain, private markets were again tolerated. Rural towns began to emerge again as bustling centres of exchange. The drab, sparsely stocked state-run store was soon supplemented with a street market selling a range of foodstuffs that was far more varied and of better quality. The policy was firmly based on the collective and represented nothing radically new, and was modelled on the policies for economic revival that followed the Great Leap Forward (GLF). The net effect of this policy was, however, to increase dramatically state expenditure on agriculture with well over 1 billion *yuan* of state subsidies provided for grain supplies to the urban areas. This kind of massive state investment was not feasible over the long term and neither was rapid technological transformation and mechanization. China's leaders were confronted by the same dilemma as that in the mid-1950s of how to boost productivity without increasing state spending. This time, the answer was radically different and led to abandonment of the collective through a major restructuring of farmer incentives and away from the use of production quotas and to a focus on the household as the basis of production. This process was encapsulated in the term 'production responsibility system'. It was the farmers themselves who launched the reforms, usually without official sanction. Their abandonment of the collective, while opposed by many local cadres, received tacit support from pro-reform cadres (Zhou, 1996; Zweig, 1997, pp. 12–15 and Chapter 2).

In 1979, farmers in poor areas were beginning to abandon the collective structures and grass roots experimentation took place in contracting output to the household. Gradually this practice spread throughout other areas of rural China. It is worth noting that as late as 1981 Deng remained agnostic as to whether this was a good or a bad thing (personal communication from Fred Teiwes). As practice at the grass roots radicalized, the centre could do nothing but stand by and make policy pronouncements to try to catch up with reality. In this initial stage of reform it is clear that the central authorities were being led by developments at the grass roots level. However, it is important to point out that not all areas opted for decollectivization when given the choice. For example, while poor areas were going back to the household, one commune in Heilongjiang announced a shift to a wage labour system.

For a while, it looked as if the centre might abandon or be forced to abandon its monolithic approach to policy and allow different organizational models to flourish in different parts of China. By 1982–83, however, decisions were taken to standardize the new system and decollectivization was enforced throughout the country with a speed reminiscent of the collectivization of the 1950s. The new State Constitution (1982) returned the political and administrative powers of the commune to the resurrected townships, leaving the communes as an economic shell. The scale of administration was reduced, with 96,000 township governments replacing 55,000 people's communes. In 1983 the 'responsibility system for agriculture' was officially endorsed with the household as the basis for contracting. This was reconfirmed in 1984 when cropping contracts were extended to 15 years and measures were introduced to concentrate land in the hands of the most productive households. Abandonment of the collective as the key economic unit in the countryside was complete. In 1985, it was made clear that the market was to dominate with the announcement that the state procurement system was to be abolished. Instead of the state assigning fixed quotas of farm products to be purchased from farmers, a system of contract purchasing was introduced with all other products being sold on the market. The aim was to improve the distribution of commodities and reward further efficient producers with the expectation that wealthier farmers would reinvest capital and labour in the land. As discussed below, this did not prove to be the case.

Change in industry and the urban areas was much less dramatic. The embedded institutional interests in the industrial sector made a radical overhaul more difficult to achieve than in the rural sector and, as a result, policy was a stop–go affair with radical proposals bogging down once the effects began to bite. Following the adjustment of the years 1980–81, the leadership began to turn its attention to reform of the industrial sector culminating in adoption of the important CC document 'Decision on Reform of the Economic Structure' (October 1984). Policy sought to bring the kinds of incentives and use of market forces that had proved successful in the rural areas to bear in the industrial sphere. The 'Decision' outlined the need for reform and pulled together the piecemeal experiments into a more thoroughgoing reform blueprint. The key was seen as making enterprises more economically responsible and profit retention was introduced and the system of tax-for-profit, introduced in 1983, was confirmed. This replaced the early experimentation with profit contracting and the old system with profits returned to state coffers and losses covered by the state. To enable enterprises to take advantage of the limited market opportunities, managers were to be given greater power of decision-making with respect to production plans and marketing, sources of supply, distribution of profits within the enterprise and the hiring and firing of workers. It was clear, however, that enterprise reform was to form part of a comprehensive reform strategy. Not surprisingly, these reforms created differences of opinion and were resisted by some powerful figures such as Chen Yun. The acuteness of the debate about the way forward was sharpened by the overheating of the economy in late 1984 and early 1985.

It is not true to say that the period witnessed no political reform, but it was limited in scope to administrative reform while more radical proposals for change were criticized. The period 1978–80 was a high tide for suggestions for political reform, with not just the Democracy Wall activists but also highly placed party members floating ideas on far-reaching reforms. Deng Xiaoping indicated his approval for political reform in August 1980 when he called for people's democracy to be developed to the fullest extent possible. According to Deng, it was necessary to ensure that the people as a whole really enjoyed the power of supervision over the state in a variety of effective ways. In particular, they were to 'supervise political power at the basic level, as well as in all enterprises and undertakings' (in Deng, 1984, p. 282). Although Deng's speech was not published officially until 1983, it did set the tone for subsequent discussions about reform, some of which recommended quite far-reaching structural change. This early promise of extensive reform was not combined with sufficient substantive change, thus causing many intellectuals and students to become frustrated. Substantive change was ruled out by the refusal of senior party leaders to accept structural reform that would lead to a redistribution of power to other groups and organizations in society. Orthodox party members were offended by the attacks on the party-state system that were aired during the Democracy Wall Movement of 1978–79 (see Box 3.2), attacks that were sometimes repeated in the official media. The rise of Solidarity in Poland in 1980 convinced them that too

---

BOX 3.2

Wei Jingsheng on the Need for Democracy

'After the arrest of the Gang of Four, the people eagerly hoped that Vice Chairman Deng Xiaoping, who might possibly "restore capitalism", would rise up again like a magnificent banner. Finally he did regain his position in the central leadership. How excited the people felt! How inspired they were! But alas, the old political system so despised by the people remains unchanged.

Is the struggle for democracy what the Chinese people want? The Cultural Revolution was the first time they flexed their muscles, and all the reactionary forces trembled before them. But at that time the people had no clear direction and the force of democracy was not the main thrust of the struggle. As a result, the dictators silenced most of them through bribes, deception, division, slander, or violent suppression. At the time, people also had a blind faith in all kinds of ambitious dictators, so once again they unwittingly became the tools and sacrificial lambs of tyrants and potential tyrants.

Now, twelve years later, the people have finally recognized their goal. They see clearly the real direction of their fight and have found their true leader: the banner of democracy' (Wei, 1979 in Wei, 1997).

Wei was a key figure in the Democracy Wall Movement and was imprisoned from 1979 until 1993, arrested again in 1994 and in 1997 released into exile in the United States.

---

great a relaxation of party power would lead to loss of control. While some were presenting blueprints for a new political structure, party leaders, including Deng Xiaoping, were setting stringent limits to the extent of possible reform. The essential question was how far control could be relaxed to ensure that ideas useful for economic modernization would surface without party dominance being weakened. The experiences of the Hundred Flowers, the GLF and the Cultural Revolution caused leaders such as Deng Xiaoping to be suspicious of participation that took place outside of direct party control. They thus tried to restore the effective leadership of the party while, at the same time, not negating the contributions that 'articulate social audiences' could make to the modernization process.

In effect, this meant that change was to be brought about by a 'revolution from above'. The party was to define the limits of what was acceptable and it was anticipated that continued party control over the process would ensure stability and stop the possibility of degeneration into chaos. This was best seen in the promotion of the slogan of adherence to the 'Four Basic Principles' that Deng put forward in March 1979. These principles enshrined the leadership of the party and adherence to socialism. Many critical intellectuals and students saw the promotion of the principles as an excuse to hold back on genuine political reform. Indeed the principles were used by ideological conservatives such as Deng Liqun to launch campaigns against heterodox ideas in 1980–81 and 1983–84.

Until 1986, Deng was fairly successful in stopping these divisions from becoming destabilizing and the limited political reforms taken had been to his advantage or had supported his attempts to get the Chinese system moving again. The outstanding political issues from the Cultural Revolution were resolved in 1980–81. In February 1980, at the Fifth Plenum of the Eleventh CC, Hua Guofeng's closest supporters were removed from office and the former president, Liu Shaoqi, was posthumously rehabilitated. Hua relinquished the premiership to Zhao Ziyang in September 1980 and resigned as chair of the party in June 1981, turning affairs over to Deng's protégé Hu Yaobang. In 1981, the year of verdicts, the 'Gang of Four' together with 'supporters' of Lin Biao were sentenced and an official resolution on party history was adopted that was critical of both Mao and the Cultural Revolution.

Further, according to Deng, in 1982 China was in the midst of an 'administrative revolution' and measures were introduced to reduce the size of the bureaucracy, eliminate functional overlap, prevent the overconcentration of power in too few hands and recruit new, better technically trained members into the party. In 1982, the Twelfth Party Congress (September) and the Fifth Session of the Fifth NPC (December) codified the new policy directions and organizational changes by adopting new Party Statutes and State Constitution. Deng called the party congress the most important since that held in 1945 that had paved the way for CCP victory after the war.

Economic Troubles and Political Instability, 1985–91

By 1985, there were problems in both the economy and the political realm, with opposition to the reforms becoming more apparent and bursting out for all to see in 1986 and 1989. By the end of 1984, the rapid pace of rural growth had slowed down and, ironically, the next phase of reform adversely hit the farmers' pockets. In 1985 when the state abolished its mandatory grain purchase, prices on the market dropped significantly. This led to several years of cat-and-mouse games between farmers and state agencies, with farmers cutting back on production or buying on the market when prices were low and selling to the state when it was obliged to pay the higher price. In addition, declining returns were setting in as the one-time boost farmers received from the organizational changes and other incentives worked its way through. With the decline in grain yield, and the spiralling state food subsidies paid out to keep the costs down for urban workers, Chen Yun proposed stopping the second phase of reforms. Many farmers were forced back into grain production, which they had abandoned because of its lack of profitability. Not surprisingly, farmers resented the curtailment of their new-won freedoms. Stringent production quotas for grain were reimposed and the attempts to dismantle the state monopoly over distribution were effectively abandoned. Farmers were forced to sell to the state at below-market prices. Further, many farmers left the land either to work in more lucrative jobs in the rural industrial sector, which was by 1984 producing nearly 25 per cent of industrial production, or to migrate to find work in the cities.

In the industrial sector, problems had emerged with the transition to a market-influenced economy. The lifting of price controls and the new incentive system in enterprises led to a major overheating of the economy by late 1984 and early 1985, with a surge in inflation in 1985.

As a result, the Seventh Five-Year Plan presented by Premier Zhao Ziyang (April 1986) struck a note of caution, with balanced growth as its theme. According to Naughton (1995, pp. 175–6), it rates as 'one of the most realistic and sound plans ever promulgated in China'. Growth, while lower, was still projected at a healthy 7.5 per cent per annum, with moderate improvements in social welfare and living standards to keep pace with economic growth. According to Zhao, the slowdown in growth rates would 'avert strain on the economy and ensure the smooth implementation of the reforms'. His worries centred on the twin problems of the tardiness with which industrial reforms had been implemented and the fall in grain output that occurred in 1985. In fact, Zhao came under pressure from deputies from leading grain-producing provinces to increase government investment in agriculture and to pay more attention to grain production. In a significant break with the past, the plan suggested guidance for production figures rather than setting mandatory targets. Zhao saw the plan as providing a solid basis for further advance of reforms. He confirmed that enterprise reform should continue, with enterprises being genuinely responsible for profits and losses. Under the phrase of a 'socialist commodity market' he proposed further extension to the market and also that a new form of macro-management be established with the state gradually moving from mainly direct to indirect control of enterprise management.

Nonetheless, opposition was coalescing and the issue of political reform and the student demonstrations of 1986 enabled opponents to manoeuvre to remove reformist party secretary Hu Yaobang. By summer 1986, it was clear that political reform had become a severely divisive issue within the political leadership. During the spring and early summer, critical intellectuals began to raise ideas for radicalizing the reforms, yet by the end of the year their views had been rejected and Hu Yaobang, who was thought to be sympathetic, had been dismissed from his post as general secretary. A summer 1986 Hong Kong newspaper report referred to a meeting at Beidaihe at which some leaders had expressed the view that, on the whole, the current political system was basically suited to the needs of economic development and that reform could lead to the negation of the party's leadership and the 'Four Basic Principles'. To counter the perceived 'liberal' tendencies of the time, they suggested a strict set of obligations for those engaged in discussions about reform.

Disagreements led to the postponement of an expected decision on political reform until the Thirteenth Party Congress (October 1987). In fact, the Sixth Plenum of the Twelfth Party Congress (September 1986) instead of discussing political reform passed a resolution on the need to improve work in the ideological and cultural spheres. These are issues more closely identified with those seeking to limit the extent of political reform. The opponents of more radical reform continued to link wide-ranging changes with bourgeois contamination. In November 1986, Politburo member Peng Zhen warned against those who yearned for bourgeois democracy 'as if the moonlight of capitalist society was brighter than our socialist sun'. The student demonstrations in late 1986 provided these opponents with their chance to launch a counterattack and remove Hu Yaobang.

The student demonstrations began in the city of Hefei, Anhui province, in December 1986 because of official interference to prevent students from standing in local elections. The demonstrations spread rapidly and combined a mix of student grievance over living and study conditions and concerns over lack of progress on political reform. On the whole, the students threw their support behind Deng and Hu and very few voices raised criticisms of one-party rule. Unlike in 1989, the demonstrations found little support within the broader society, partly because students were regarded as being relatively well off and in part because their demands found little rapport with the public at large. This was different from 1989 when the criticism of corruption found a sympathetic response. The turning point of official toleration was when students in Beijing defied a government ban and held a New Year's Day demonstration in Tiananmen Square (see Munro, 1988).

At the political centre, opposition came from three major groups that were able to ally on occasion to frustrate far-reaching reforms. However, while these groups could frustrate the progress of reforms, they could not roll them back for a consistent period of time. First, there were those who attacked the reforms on primarily economic grounds and who represented the traditional central-planning and economic apparatus. They were concerned about the destabilizing effect of pushing the marketization of the economy too far, too fast. They criticized the overreliance on the market and worried about the 'overheating' of the economy caused in part by the rapid growth of the collective sector, particularly the rural industries. While Chen Yun was one of the main proponents of an increased role for the market, he did view a too rapid introduction of market forces as causing the recurrent economic problems during the 1980s. Chen consistently argued for the importance, and primacy, of planning within the economic system. The defence of the state sector is still reflected in the periodic criticisms of private enterprise and the refusal to redefine property rights in order to protect the state's privileged position in the economy. Chen was particularly concerned about the fall in grain production that occurred in 1985 and the subsequent stagnation after four years of record harvests. He used this to put Zhao Ziyang and the more pragmatic reformers under pressure. Further, this group feared that policy trends would deepen regional inequalities between China's poor hinterland and its more advanced coastal regions. Finally, they were concerned about the mushrooming of corruption that sprung up as a result of the more liberalized policies and increased contacts with the West.

The concern about corruption was echoed by a second group that included Peng Zhen, Hu Qiaomu and Deng Liqun. They were worried about the consequences of liberalization for the social fabric of China. These orthodox party leaders consistently insisted that the party must reaffirm its leading role also in the realm of ideology. They argued that socialism had moral and spiritual goals as well as a material goal, and that only the party could define them. These leaders felt that it was the party's role to dictate the nation's ethical and moral values. In this respect, the party had taken over the traditional role of the state in China. At the Twelfth Party Congress (1982), Hu Yaobang, then general secretary, announced a reversal in the listing of the party's tasks, placing the building of spiritual civilization before democratization, thus making it a prerequisite for democratization. This paved the way for subsequent campaigns for 'spiritual civilization' and against 'bourgeois liberalization' in 1983, 1987 and 1989–90. Further, they saw the 'open-door policy' as a source of problems within the party; a point they were able to get officially accepted in October 1983. An official decision on party consolidation, while stating that the 'open-door policy' had been entirely correct, noted that there had been an increase in the 'corrosive influence of decadent bourgeois ideology and remnant feudal ideas'. It is important to note that one year earlier when Hu Yaobang announced formally that a programme for the rectification of party style and 'consolidation' of party organizations would be launched, he did not cite this as a reason for problems in the party.

Third, there were some senior military leaders who had been closely associated with Mao during the war years and who subsequently provided a rallying point for those disaffected with the reform programme. Such military figures retained a 'leftist' ideology and were concerned by the erosion of Mao's legacy and the tarnishing of his image. Some were disgruntled about the low priority that the military had been accorded within the modernization programme, while others opposed the shift to a less political and more professionalized army. Discontent surfaced among the rank-and-file rural recruits when they saw the new possibilities for making money opening up in the rural areas that they had left behind. The impact of the responsibility system, in the form of providing outlets for making a decent living, caused China to introduce a conscription law in 1984.

Faced with this opposition, Deng Xiaoping was remarkably successful until the end of 1986 in limiting its impact. In 1982, the Central Advisory Commission to the CC was set up. The intention was that the Committee would function as a 'retirement home' for elderly officials, opening up positions in the formal political system for a younger generation more in tune with the demands of the modern world. However, many of those moved to the Commission were not willing to accept a decorative position and 'retire'. Although billed as 'transitional' (it was in fact scrapped in 1992), throughout the 1980s it provided more traditional party leaders with an institutional base from which to launch attacks on the reform programme. The role of the Commission as a focal point for the expression of conservative, orthodox views became more pronounced in late 1987 when Chen Yun became its head following his 'retirement' from the Standing Committee of the Politburo. This undermined somewhat the 1984–85 shake-up of the party and military leadership that had resulted in a major weakening of these groups' influence in formal leadership bodies.

The military's direct political influence was reduced and many elderly officers were replaced by a younger generation more committed to the idea of a less political, more professional military. In December 1984, 40 senior officers of the PLA general staff retired, the largest retirement ever; in January 1985 budget cutbacks were announced; and in April, Hu Yaobang announced that troop levels would be cut back by 25 per cent, some 1 million personnel. To weaken the PLA's political influence, two other important measures were taken. First, in June 1985, a meeting of the Central Military Affairs Commission (CMAC), chaired by Deng Xiaoping, announced a restructuring of the military regional command structure. Apart from reasons of efficiency, this had the effect of breaking up potential powerful regional ties of key military leaders.

The second important step was the shake-up of the party leadership at the CCP national conference held in September 1985. This saw a sharp reduction in military representation on the Politburo. Of the 10 resignations, 6 were military figures and no military appointees were among the 6 full new members of the Politburo. The military establishment resisted, however, one important change to personnel. Deng Xiaoping had tried to pass on his post as chair of the Military Affairs Commission to General Secretary Hu Yaobang. While senior military officers were willing to concede ultimately to Deng's authority, they were not prepared to accept his then protégé. This clearly reduced Hu's prestige and prevented him from forging an alliance with reformers in the military. It presaged later events when Deng was similarly unable to install his second chosen successor, Zhao Ziyang, as head of the Commission. Given the fact that control of the military remains the key to power in China this was a serious blow to the pragmatic reformers and was a worrying sign that later developments confirmed.

The campaign against 'bourgeois liberalization' launched after Hu's dismissal was short-lived and his replacement by Zhao Ziyang seemed to indicate that the attack by the orthodox party members had caused little more than a hiccup in the reform process. This was borne out at the

Thirteenth Party Congress held in October 1987 at which Zhao delivered a speech that on balance favoured commitment to continued reform. Despite containing some elements of compromise, on crucial issues Zhao came down on the side of the reformers. Thus he reiterated the necessity to 'uphold the four basic principles' while pursuing reform but the first five items of his work report dwelt on reform and the conservatives' demand for 'the building of a spiritual civilization' came last on the list. Most importantly, Zhao confirmed that China was in the 'initial stage of socialism', a phase that would last for around 100 years. The major task of this period was to improve material standards and not to wage class struggle. Such a definition was intended to remove the use of ideology to oppose reform. As far as possible, ideology was to be taken out of decision-making. As China was entering uncharted waters, theory was to be defined as policy developed, thus freeing China's decision-makers from the restraints of Maoist dogma.

In the economic sphere Zhao attacked the two traditional shibboleths of state socialism: central planning and state ownership. A dramatic reduction in the role of the plan in controlling the economy was proposed, giving the green light to the non-public sectors. He also advocated not only the use of commodity markets for consumer goods and means of production but also 'markets for... funds, labour services, technology, information and real estate'. Moreover, Zhao broke with the principle that the only source of income was 'distribution according to work'. In the future,

> buyers of bonds will earn interest, [and] shareholders dividends, enterprise managers will receive additional income to compensate for bearing risks, and owners of private enterprises who employ workers will receive some income that does not come from their own labour.

Zhao brushed aside possible accusations that this was making use of capitalist economic mechanisms, with the simple statement that these 'are not peculiar to capitalism' (Zhao, 1987).

However, Zhao's report showed elements of compromise on crucial economic questions. First, the Maoist obsession with grain production was not totally eradicated; Zhao committed China to major increases in grain production in the coming decade. More importantly, Zhao was cautious on the crucial topic of price reform. It had become increasingly obvious that the industrial reform programme would not succeed without a thorough reform of the pricing and subsidy system. Yet each time the reformers put this on the agenda they retreated rapidly in the face of the inflation unleashed. This would become a major issue after the Congress.

Zhao was also clear that political reform should continue, the issue that had led to Hu's dismissal. He reaffirmed that it was indispensable if economic reform was to continue but he was vague on what should be done. He did, however, call for a redistribution of power both horizontally to state organs at the same level and vertically to party and state organs lower down the administrative ladder. The most important measure proposed was the abolition of leading party member groups in units of state administration and work was begun to eliminate them as well as to eradicate those groups that had functional overlap. He also acknowledged that there was now a limited political pluralism under the leadership of the CCP.

Zhao also indicated that policy would push ahead with trying to reduce party influence in the day-to-day management of enterprises. The Party Statutes were amended to reflect this reduced role and in April 1989 at the Seventh NPC a new Enterprise Law was adopted that tried to limit as far as was politically feasible the scope of party work in the enterprise. Indeed, with respect to the role of the party in enterprise management no clear indication was given to resolve confusion over the division of responsibilities between party secretaries and managers. The fact that Zhao neglected the 'Four Modernizations' in his speech was significant. This reinforced the link between economic and political reform. The 'Four Modernizations' demonstrate concern with economic reform and ignore the need for an accompanying 'modernization' of other aspects of society.

However, after the Congress the economy faltered and inflation took off as China experimented with price reform. Initially, it looked as if with Deng's support China might stay the course but by the summer of 1988 Deng started to back away and shifted the blame for the attempts to make a radical breakthrough on to Zhao. The economic situation increased general disgruntlement among the populace while many critical intellectuals were frustrated at what they saw as the lack of political reform. The leadership might have navigated the troubled period without crisis if it had remained united, but the façade of leadership unity began to crack under the strains of management and was blown apart by the massive student-led demonstrations that erupted throughout urban China in the spring of 1989. Zhao tried to use his position as general secretary to limit the ability of the more conservative premier, Li Peng, to divert more radical economic reforms. From the summer retreat at Beidaihe in 1988 came rumours that Zhao was to be prevented from speaking out on economic issues.

The catalyst for widespread disruption was the worst inflation in PRC history in 1988 that began to discredit calls for more radical reform and led by 1989 to a programme of economic retrenchment. Key groups were severely disaffected by spring 1989. Farmers were feeling insecure with the fluctuating grain prices and policies, workers were undergoing lay-offs, all urban dwellers were hit by inflation and critical intellectuals felt betrayed by the dismissal of Hu Yaobang and insufficient political reform. The refusal to engage in serious political reform was compounded by the failure of the urban economic reforms and the declining position of the working-class and state employees. Essentially, urban workers were offered a deal that involved giving up their secure, subsidy-supported low-wage lifestyle for a risky contract-based system that might result in higher wages at the possible price of rising costs and unemployment. Many urban workers decided to reserve their judgment. Their reservation was exacerbated by the leadership's indecisiveness about urban reform, which resulted in a stop–go cycle throughout the 1980s. The insecurity mounted when after 1986 the reforms resulted in spiralling inflation without consequent improvements in material standards. Not surprisingly, talk of price reform and reduction of subsidies created a sense of panic. Zhao's attempts to produce rapid economic results created the inflation of 1988 and 1989, which threatened those on fixed incomes. The resultant decline in living standards added many to the urban reservoir of discontent.

Urban anger was increased by the higher visibility of official corruption. Abuse of public position and private accumulation from public function by the late 1980s was the worst since 1949. By 1989, for many urban dwellers the party's incompetence and moral laxness had eroded any vestigial notions that the party was a moral force in Chinese society. Once the students breached the dams, a flood of supporters was waiting to defend the students and attack the authorities. Student agitation had festered on the campuses since 1986 and critical intellectuals had given regular lectures there. The specific cause of the demonstrations was the unexpected death of Hu Yaobang (15 April) during a Politburo meeting at which it was rumoured he had wanted to discuss education and was engaged in a major argument with party conservative Bo Yibo.

The student demonstrations quickly found resonance with large numbers of the urban citizenry. The initial government response was slow and incoherent in part because of the size of the demonstrations and the pending visit of Soviet President Gorbachev, but also because of severe leadership division about how to handle the demonstrations and future policy direction. Repression was unacceptable until all possible avenues had been tried. This was not just because the party was deeply split but because it was difficult to take violent action against a group that was demonstrating peacefully, singing the 'Internationale' and calling for support of the CCP and further reforms and opening up. Yet entering into dialogue would mean recognition of autonomous organization in society, something that was anathema to orthodox party members. The potential for a tough regime response had been signalled in a *People's Daily* editorial of 26 April issued when Zhao Ziyang was out of the country (see Box 3.3). The editorial condemned the movement as a 'planned conspiracy' directed against the party and constituted a 'political conspiracy' aimed at negating 'the leadership of the CCP and the socialist system'. Despite the early decision to take a hard line, it took another six weeks before the protests could be crushed. Apart from the problem of using force against unarmed students, Zhao Ziyang came to oppose a tough response, favouring instead a limited dialogue.

BOX 3.3

Perspectives on Tiananmen, 1989

'The situation for the people throughout the country has now become intolerable. After a long period of bureaucratic dictatorial government, inflation is out of control, and the people's living standards have slipped. To cover up their extravagance, the small group of ruling officials have issued a large number of various types of government and treasury bonds. They are thereby squeezing every penny out of the people. We appeal to people from all walks of life to come together to fight for truth and the future of China.

Police brothers, soldier brothers: Please come and stand on the people's side. Come and stand for the truth. Do not serve as tools of the people's enemies' (Beijing Workers' Autonomous Union, 20 April 1989, in Ogden *et al.*, 1992, pp. 86–7).

'Facts prove that what this extremely small number of people did was not to join in the activities to mourn Comrade Hu Yaobang or to advance the cause of socialist democracy in China. Neither were they out to give vent to their grievances. Flaunting the banner of democracy, they undermined democracy and the legal system. Their purpose was to sow dissension among the people, plunge the whole country into chaos and sabotage the political situation of stability and unity. This is a planned conspiracy and a disturbance. Its essence is to, once and for all, negate the leadership of the CCP and the socialist system. This is a serious political struggle confronting the whole party and the people of all nationalities throughout the country' (*People's Daily*, 26 April 1989).

'Don't believe us. We tell lies' (Banner of protesting journalists, 4 May 1989).

Q 'What did you expect to get when you first joined the movement?'
A 'I expected improvement in the following two aspects. First, as far as democratic consciousness was concerned, I hoped we could get the same effects of enlightenment as those of the May Fourth Movement. Actually, although the Chinese people strongly desire democracy, they lack consciousness of democracy, and do not understand democracy. I hope that through the student movement, we will make progress in our work toward enlightening the people. Second, I hoped that we could set a good example with regard to the skills for promoting democracy. At the beginning, I hoped that our Students' Self-Government Federation's legal status would be recognized, and could play its role in government administration as an opposition group' (Wu-er Kaixi, one of the key student leaders, 3 June 1989, in Oksenberg, Sullivan and Lambert, 1990, pp. 354–5).

'This storm was bound to come sooner or later. This is determined by the major international climate and China's own minor climate. It was bound to happen and is independent of man's will. It was just a matter of time and scale. It is more to our advantage that this happened today. What is most advantageous to us is that we have a large group of veteran comrades who are still alive. They have experienced many storms and they know what is at stake. They support the use of resolute action to counter the rebellion. Although some comrades may not understand this for a while, they will eventually understand this and support the CC's decision' (Deng Xiaoping to Martial Law Troops, 9 June 1989, in Deng, 1994).

With the start of the hunger strike (13 May) and the involvement of organizations that had close ties to Zhao and the reformers, the demands of the movement began to change. From mid-May onwards they became more directly political and sharply focused. The dismissal of Zhao (19 May) was followed by the implementation of martial law (20 May) and one last attempt at dialogue was made. With Zhao removed and the motions gone through, the way was open for a tough response. Importantly, the demonstration had spread to include huge numbers of the urban population and now not only the students were forming autonomous organizations but also the workers and critical intellectuals. The orthodox leaders were able to use these developments to push for a brutal resolve. During the night of 3–4 June, troops from the PLA were sent in to clear out all protesters from the Tiananmen Square focal point.

Subsequent events showed both the capacity for the orthodox party faction to frustrate those reforms it opposed, and its lack of strength to roll back the momentum of economic reform for long. The scale of the demonstrations also meant that the leadership had to appear to respond to the criticisms. The veteran orthodox party members such as Chen Yun, Bo Yibo and Yang Shangkun together with Deng had effectively taken over decision-making in late April. Their programme had two main elements. First, the policy of economic austerity was strengthened with the intention of restoring the centrally planned economy to pride of place. Second, tight political supervision over society combined with a major political campaign was introduced to eradicate the influences of 'bourgeois liberalization'. While Deng Xiaoping supported the second, the programme of economic austerity entailed attacks on his own reform programme. Deng always maintained a traditional view of political activity that occurred outside of party control and resisted Mao's attempts to open up the party to criticism from outside forces. In August 1989, the *People's Daily* carried a 32-year-old speech by Deng in which he argued that too much democracy was undesirable for China and made clear that the party would remain paramount. The reforms to reduce the role of the party throughout state institutions were swiftly abandoned.

In late June 1989, the Fourth Plenum of the Thirteenth CC announced the removal of Zhao Ziyang and supporter Hu Qili from the Politburo Standing Committee, with Zhao criticized for 'grave errors and mistakes', including 'splitting the party'. He was not allowed to defend himself at the plenum. Shanghai Party Secretary, Jiang Zemin, was appointed to replace Zhao as general secretary primarily on the basis of the effective way he had dealt with the demonstrations in Shanghai. In terms of institutionalization of politics, the manner of Zhao's removal and Jiang's appointment show how little progress had been made. The crucial decisions were made, contrary to the Party Statutes, by a cabal of veteran revolutionaries at Deng's residence and then sent to party functionaries for official transmittal. Veterans Chen

Yun and Li Xiannian had first raised the possibility of Jiang's appointment at a meeting on 21 May and the decision was made on 27 May, after Deng personally moved a motion on the composition of the Standing Committee of the Politburo. They also decided not to announce the decision immediately but to wait for the Fourth Plenum (Nathan and Link, 2001, pp. 260–1, 308–14).

The dismissal of Zhao also opened the way to a critique of the economic reforms, but already by May 1990 there were clear signs that the orthodox attack was being blunted. Critics pointed to their success in bringing down inflation and calming excessive growth as grounds for trusting their economic competence. GNP growth in 1989 was only 4 per cent, the lowest since the death of Mao Zedong, while inflation for the year was calculated at 17.8 per cent but by the end of the year had dropped to around 3 to 4 per cent. Even the collective and private sectors of the economy and the coastal policy for export-led growth came in for criticism. However, the programme of economic austerity imposed in late 1988 and tightened after 4 June 1989 very quickly revealed its limits (Naughton, 1992, pp. 77–95). The austerity programme did not deal with the fundamental structural problems of the economy and, in fact, exacerbated many of them by denying their existence. The economic squeeze dampened demand but did not improve productivity nor remodel the irrational structure as had been promised. Already by early 1990, there were clear signs that the austerity measures were pushing the economy towards a major recession. In October 1989, for the first time in a decade, industrial output fell on a month-to-month basis by 2.1 per cent. In the period January–March 1990, industrial output recorded no growth while that of light industry fell to 0.2 per cent. The previously thriving collective sector was hit hard and by September 1989 the growth in monthly industrial output had dropped from 16.6 to 0.6 per cent. A number of large factories sat idle because of the slowdown in output. In the first two months of 1990 alone, this resulted in 1.5 million urban residents losing their jobs.

Shaken by the economic downturn, and fearing social dislocation, measures were quietly introduced to ease the austerity programme despite resistance by fiscal conservatives at the centre. Many initiatives associated with the disgraced General Secretary, Zhao Ziyang, again became key elements of policy. The role played by the collective and private sectors was recognized and articles began to appear praising their contributions to economic growth. The strategy of coastal development that was closely associated with Zhao was reaffirmed and the reputation of the SEZs was rehabilitated. Government policy also began to deal with the problem of pricing and subsidies. In April 1991, the sharpest price increases for some 25 years were introduced for staple foods, with high-quality rice rising by 75 per cent and wheat prices by 55 per cent. In April 1992, the price of rice was increased again by 40 per cent. These were necessary measures but still not sufficient to allow market forces to work properly in the Chinese economy.

In addition to continuing the programme of economic austerity, the leadership responded, or tried to give the impression of responding, to the movement's political demands. A widely publicized campaign against official speculation and corruption was launched. On 28 June 1989, the Politburo adopted a seven-point programme to deal with corruption. This addressed issues such as closing down firms that had engaged in potentially corrupt activities, preventing the children of senior officials from engaging in commercial activities, limiting perks derived from official position such as entertaining, travel abroad, special supply of scarce goods and driving around in imported cars. Further, one of the students' main demands was met when, on 9 November 1989, Deng Xiaoping stepped down from his last official position as chair of the party's Military Affairs Commission. However, it was clear that such a process of internal regeneration could not be successful over the long term.

Return to Economic Reform, Boom and Moderation, 1992–97

By stealth, the programme of economic retrenchment was gradually being rolled back. However, Deng Xiaoping obviously felt that policy-making by increment or by default was insufficient and that a clear statement of intent was necessary. When the CCP celebrated its 70th anniversary on 1 July 1991, the chances for a dramatic change of course looked slim. The party remained defensive in the aftermath of Tiananmen and felt threatened by enemies from both within and from without. Yet, the party prided itself on the fact that it had ridden out the storm of protest in 1989 and had been spared the consequences of the dramatic collapse of the communist regimes in Eastern Europe and the profound changes then taking place in Gorbachev's Soviet Union. Open dissent had been quashed and inner-party battles kept within acceptable limits. General Secretary Jiang Zemin, in his speech commemorating the party's founding, reaffirmed the hard line by claiming that 'class struggle' would continue for a considerable period of time within 'certain parts' of China. This contrasted markedly with the party line that had dominated since the late 1970s when Deng Xiaoping and his supporters had claimed that class struggle was dying down and that the main focus of work would be placed on economic development. Social harmony was to replace class warfare. In response to the situation in Eastern Europe, Jiang claimed that 'We Chinese communists are convinced the temporary difficulties and setbacks recently experienced by socialism in its march forward cannot and will not ever prevent us from continuing to develop'. As far as the West was concerned, CCP policy was still to focus on resisting the capitalists' presumed attempts to transform China through 'peaceful evolution' (Jiang, 1991, pp. 1–14).

In addition to the need to deal with the structural problems in the economy, two other factors combined to convince Deng Xiaoping and his allies that it was necessary to reassess the hard-line policy and to push China once more along the road to reform. The first was the fall-out from the failed coup in the Soviet Union (August 1991), and the second was the need to lay down a clear agenda for the Fourteenth Party Congress that would define his legacy. While Deng was bitterly critical of Gorbachev for undermining socialism, he realized that unless the CCP could satisfy the material aspirations of the population, it might be destined for the same fate. Debates about the future direction were brought into sharper focus by the fact that the Fourteenth Party Congress was scheduled to be convened before the end of 1992. Party congresses and the fixing of Five-Year Plans are always times of tense debate in China. Policy differences that could be previously contained often spill over into factional fighting and resultant purges. Once a document that will dictate policy for the coming five years has to be written down, it becomes more difficult to paper over the cracks in the leadership. Political differences become increasingly public as the various policy tendencies strive to set the agenda through newspaper articles and controlled leaks.

The year 1992 proved to be a watershed and led to the dramatic economic boom and building craze that characterized much of the 1990s. However, it also led to another round of overheating, forcing the new leadership under Jiang Zemin to articulate a more coherent plan for economic development than had hitherto been the case. Rather than 'bourgeois liberalism', the main theme of criticism in 1992 was 'leftism', namely those opposed to Deng's reforms.

The most dramatic breakthrough came with Deng Xiaoping's inspection tour to South China in January–February 1992 (see Box 3.4). Deng concluded that continued economic reform was vital for the party's legitimacy. He claimed that if China's economic reforms were reversed, the party would lose the people's support and 'could be overthrown at any time' and he ventured the view that it would certainly not have survived the trauma of Tiananmen. Interestingly, Deng absolved both Hu Yaobang and Zhao Ziyang, his first two choices as general secretary, of faults in the economic arena by stating that they had been removed from power because of not opposing 'bourgeois liberalization' properly. Deng went beyond stating the general need for economic reform by implicitly criticizing those who sought to slow down the pace of change. He claimed that economic reform should not 'proceed slowly like a woman with bound feet' but should 'blaze new trails boldly'. Most importantly, Deng announced a major change in the CCP's political line. Ever since the events of 1989, the Chinese public had been told that the greatest threat to socialism in China came from 'bourgeois liberals', termed 'rightists'. As far as the party veterans were concerned, these people were responsible for the unrest that had broken out in 1989. This unrest legitimized the attacks on Zhao Ziyang and his supporters as well as on outspoken pro-reform intellectuals throughout the system. Now Deng told his party members that it was the 'leftists', who opposed further

---

BOX 3.4

Shanghai: A Tale of Two Visits

Even before Deng Xiaoping made his Southern tour (see p. 76), localities had been pushing ahead with reform without waiting for central approval. When Deng visited Shanghai on his inspection tour, the city had begun construction of a new bridge, without central approval, to link the city to the planned massive development area of Pudong across the river. Local officials were nervous about whether to let Deng see the bridge, but after hearing his plea for rapid development they arranged a tour. Greeting Deng, they claimed that on hearing his words the workers of Shanghai had laboured all night in a fit of enthusiasm. Deng smiled and commented that it was not always wise to follow central policy directives.

This visit contrasted with the tense trips of Chen Yun in the mid-1980s, which had been marked by blazing arguments over Shanghai's development. Local officials wished to see Shanghai benefit from the same incentive policies that operated in the SEZs. Chen, by contrast, had insisted that there should be one city in China that remained a model of socialist development and that that city would be Shanghai! In addition, Shanghai was too important to the central exchequer to be allowed significant tax breaks. Shanghai was virtually the only provincial equivalent administration that experienced a lower annual growth rate from 1979 to 1989 than in the period from 1953 to 1978 (Interviews with local Shanghai officials, 1987 and 1994).

---

reform, who presented the greatest problem for China at the present time, something already signalled by Yang Shangkun in a major speech of October 1991. Deng turned his fire on those who argued that economic reform must inevitably lead to capitalism. According to Deng, a market economy did not necessarily imply capitalism any more than a planned economy implied socialism. He refused to accept their arguments that the danger of 'peaceful evolution' mainly originated in the economic sphere. Deng warned against sinking into another ideological impasse. For Deng, the basic line of rapid reform was clear and it was to be upheld for 100 years.

This relaunch of reform caused Jiang Zemin to submit a self-criticism (March 1992) and paved the way for drafting the party congress documents. The rush for rapid growth did not go unopposed, and at the NPC in March 1992 Li Peng ignored Deng's exhortation that 'leftism' was not the major problem and tried to set growth at no more than 6 per cent rather than Deng's 10 per cent. Reality outpaced Li. The Fourteenth Party Congress adopted Deng's calls for rapid economic reform and mediated a figure of 8–9 per cent for the growth rate, reflecting an emerging consensus that China's economy could not withstand too rapid growth without the old problems of bottlenecks and inflation reemerging. The three key aspects of the Congress all reflected a victory for Deng, as did key institutional and personnel changes. First, the Congress praised Deng as 'the chief architect of our socialist reform, of the open-door policy and of the modernization programme' and credited him with developing the 'theory of building socialism with Chinese characteristics'. It thus provided a way out of the sterile ideological battles that were waged over what constitutes socialist mechanisms of development.

Second, the document sanctioned sweeping economic reforms under the formulation of a 'socialist market economy'. This gave a greater role to market forces than that offered by any other ruling communist party to date. While the state was to retain the capacity to make 'macro-level adjustments and control', market forces were to be unleashed to eradicate poverty, while the laws of supply and demand were to ensure the rational allocation of commodities throughout the economy. Indeed, Jiang Zemin even proposed that price levers and competition be used to improve efficiency and 'realize the survival of the fittest'. However, the report steered away from precise objectives, leaving the door ajar for debilitating arguments over the specific implementation of the guidelines. However, it is clear that Jiang saw an increased role for the market and envisaged that the tertiary economy would expand from 27 to 40 per cent of GNP by 2000. The 'open-door' policy also received a clean bill of health and Jiang proposed that foreign capital could be used not only for enterprise technological transformation but also in areas of finance, commerce, tourism and real estate.

Third, the liberal view of economic affairs was paralleled by a strong commitment to political control. There is no mention of the kinds of reforms that Zhao Ziyang had suggested at the Thirteenth Party Congress. The only proposals were to trim the size of the bureaucracy and clear up party and government overlap. Whereas the previous congress had proposed eliminating 'party cells' in government organizations, the proposal now was to strengthen them at all levels. The newly elected leadership produced a clear majority in favour of Deng's economic reform programme and only 6 of the old Politburo were reelected to the new 20-person body. Importantly, the Congress confirmed the abolition of the Central Advisory Commission, which had become an institutional base of support for Chen Yun's sniping at Deng over economic policy.

After the Congress, the economy continued to boom on a diet of foreign investment and real estate speculation and it seemed as if most of urban China had turned into a massive building site. As the saying went, the national bird of China had become the crane. At the same time, inflation also shot up to around 30 per cent by the end of 1994. Through 1993 and 1994, attempts were undertaken to rein in growth and prevent economic distress from turning into social instability. This time, economic retrenchment did not work, GDP grew at 13.4 per cent as opposed to the projected 9 per cent and accelerated further in 1994. Yet another vicious stop–go cycle was in the making and forced a group of reformers gathered around vice-premier and new Politburo Standing Committee member Zhu Rongji to articulate the most far-reaching plan for economic transformation to date. Almost for the first time the leadership seemed to be setting out a programme that would place it at the forefront of the reform process rather than appearing to react to short-term contingencies. Not surprisingly given the ramifications of the plan, it has been deeply contested and most subsequent political debate has revolved around its implementation. Vested interests have deflected policy in a number of key areas and fears of social unrest have been used to slow down the pace of structural transformation.

In November 1993, the Third Plenum of the Fourteenth CC adopted a key economic reform document that argued a renewed role for the centre in managing key macroeconomic levers (for details see Chapter 9), especially in reversing *de facto* economic decentralization. It proposed an extensive role for the market, modernization of the enterprise system and importantly, for the first time, highlighted the need for restructuring the financial system. To back up the reforms, substantial policy innovation would be necessary to deal with the provision of social welfare, especially in the urban areas.

The policies of retrenchment continued, with the regions resisting and often registering growth exceeding the official projections. However, Vice-Premier Zhu Rongji was slowly able to manipulate the remaining macroeconomic levers to calm growth to 8.8 per cent in 1997 and bring inflation to 0.8 per cent by the end of 1997. While Zhu may not have achieved a soft landing for the economy, he had bought time that if used wisely could bring about the kind of transition that would put an end to the stop–go cycles.

From October 1995 onwards there were attempts not only to rein in a wayward economy but also a society that seemed to be evading political control by the party. The economic spurt unleashed by Deng from 1992 was accompanied by an attitude in society that anything went. Public security organs, PLA units and party members began to neglect other duties in order to join the rush to make money. In October 1995, Jiang Zemin delivered a speech 'More Talk About Politics' that supported attempts to exert more control over society. The speech was followed by the registering of religious organizations and the crackdown on underground churches; the reregistering of publications and more concerted attempts to ban unwanted publications and control content; a new law that set tougher limits on the activities of social organizations and tightened controls over their operations (Saich, 2000a); and new restrictions on research collaboration with foreigners in the social sciences. The attempt to revitalize the party and exert greater control over society became a hallmark of Jiang's rule that became even clearer after the Fifteenth Congress. However, many of the controls have proved impossible to implement for any length of time, testifying to the decline in state capacity and threatening to result in continuing friction between the state and elements of society.

Managing Reform without Deng, 1997–2002

It was in this context that the Fifteenth Party Congress and Ninth National People's Congress (September 1997 and March 1998, respectively) were held (see Box 3.5). One additional factor influenced the Party Congress; it

---

BOX 3.5

Key Political Dates, 1997–2003

1997   February, Deng Xiaoping dies
       July, Hong Kong reverts to Chinese rule
       September, Fifteenth Party Congress proposes significant advances for economic reform
1998   March, Ninth NPC new Premier Zhu Rongji unveils a dramatic package of reforms
       November, China Democracy Party leaders arrested
1999   April, supporters of *Falungong* protest criticism by surrounding party headquarters in Beijing, a major crackdown follows
       May, NATO bombing of Chinese Embassy in Belgrade
       September, Fourth Plenum of Fifteenth CC announces a cautious approach to reform
       November, China agrees to terms of WTO entry with the United States
       December, Macao returns to Chinese sovereignty
2000   March, Chen Shui-bian elected President of Taiwan
       September, US Congress passes Permanent Normal Trading Rights for China
       October, Fifth Plenum of the Fifteenth CC agrees to the new five-year economic and social plan that calls for 'relatively rapid economic development' while improving 'qualitative' aspects of growth
2001   March, Fourth session of the Tenth NPC ratifies the Tenth Five-Year Plan
       April, EP-3 US plane makes emergency landing in Hainan setting off a crisis in US–China relations
       July, Jiang Zemin and Putin sign a new 'Treaty of Friendship and Cooperation' – forever friends, never foes
       September, Sixth Plenum of the Fifteenth CC adopts a decision to improve party work-style
       October, Jiang and Bush meet in Shanghai
       December, China enters WTO
2002   February, Bush visits Beijing
       October, Jiang visits Bush at his Texas ranch
       November, Sixteenth Party Congress instals Hu Jintao as general secretary
2003   March, Tenth NPC appoints new government with Wen Jiabao as Premier
       May–June Hu Jintao visits Russia on way to parallel meeting of the G-8 in France

---

was the first time where Jiang Zemin did not have Deng Xiaoping, who had died in February, behind him. In fact, in the couple of years before the Congress, Jiang had been moving cautiously to establish a more independent position while wrapping himself in the mantle of Deng's legacy. Given what happened to all of Mao's chosen successors and the first two of Deng's, a cautious strategy was a wise one.

While the announcements at the two congresses were dramatic, subsequent events blunted some of the more radical thrusts. Jiang's strategy, ably supported by Premier Zhu, had five main strands. First, there was continued commitment to high economic growth that was seen as essential to maintaining social stability. This meant that more attention would be paid to the worries of sparking inflation and getting to grips with the deep-seated financial sector problems. Second, the leadership made the clearest commitment to date of a mixed economy with theoretical continued dominance of the state sector (Jiang, 1997, pp. 10–37). Third, while the party would continue to refrain from an overbearing role in the economy and society, the CCP would be strengthened and its guidance enhanced. Jiang and his supporters clearly saw the party as the key institutional actor at all levels and in all crucial areas. At the same time, the appeal of the party was to be broadened beyond its traditional constituency, as was seen later with the acceptance of private entrepreneurs and Jiang's promotion of the 'Three Represents'. Fourth, the pace of integration with the world economy was to be quickened, best exemplified by WTO entry. Fifth, Jiang carried on Deng's preference for a good relationship with the United States wherever possible.

Contrary to the perceptions of many before the Congress, there were no new ideas for political reform. During 1997, political reform seemed to come back on the policy agenda with a number of suggestions for significant change. For a while, it appeared that Jiang was sanctioning these discussions. While he may have been testing the waters, the main intent was to divert the opponents' attention away from enterprise reform, clearly the most important issue for Jiang. The political proposals put forward amounted to little more than improving the functioning of the Congress system, closer involvement of mass organizations and affirming the value of village elections. In addition, Jiang's main contender as a champion of political reform Qiao Shi, head of the NPC, 'retired' from the leadership. Qiao's removal enabled Li Peng to take over at the NPC.

With the onset of the Asian financial crisis and the realization that China's banking system was as perilously placed as many of those that collapsed in the surrounding countries, reformers were able to push ahead with a comprehensive package of new policies that culminated in Zhu Rongji's presentation at the NPC in March 1998. The first measure to be unveiled was an overhaul of the banking system, the centrepiece of which was the reorganization of the local branches of the People's Bank along regional lines to reduce political interference by powerful provincial party chiefs in lending decisions.

As Zhu Rongji noted, the 'power of provincial governors and mayors to command local bank presidents is abolished as of 1998' (Lardy, 1998a, p. 86).

At the 1998 NPC meeting, Zhu Rongji announced an integrated set of five major reform measures. First, approving plans proposed a decade before, Zhu announced that China would set up a nationwide grain market to ease the country's reserves. Most importantly, China would reduce the massive amount of government subsidies pumped into the system because of the remaining influences of the Maoist obsession with self-sufficiency in grain. Second, the investment and financing system was to be overhauled to prevent wasteful duplication of capital investment, with the Central Bank stepping up its regulatory functions and commercial banks being allowed to operate independently. Third, housing was to be marketized and 'welfare housing' abolished. For those who did not purchase housing, rents were projected to rise to around 15 per cent of the family income. Fourth, Zhu revealed that a new nationwide medical care reform programme would be introduced in the second half of 1998. Finally, the tax collection system was to be rationalized to prevent the levying of excessive fees and levies by local authorities who had been the source of much resentment and social unrest. In addition, Zhu announced a massive restructuring of the government bureaucracy, with half the officials to be laid off and reassigned to new jobs.

In the ensuing five years progress was made in all the areas targeted for reform but the more radical intentions were blunted by interest groups at the centre and the localities. The difficulty of moving ahead on any significant reform shows that the central state is now far from autonomous. Senior leaders lobby on behalf of their ministries to avoid the worst administrative cutbacks, line agencies interpret policy to the benefit of their own sectoral interests and localities seek to pursue their own economic agendas. For example, SOE restructuring has been pursued but there are strong political reasons for central leaders not to be too precipitate – the first and foremost remains the capacity of other sectors of the economy to absorb the absolute numbers of redundant workers and to develop a sufficient social welfare programme. Over the years, the overblown staffs of many of these enterprises have proved to be a political and social solution to the problem of inefficient industrial production but now this is no longer financially viable.

Official figures for registered unemployment at the end of 1996 were 3 per cent (6 million) and had only risen to 3.9 per cent by September 2002. However, this massively underestimates the true figure as it excludes those who have not registered as unemployed, including the large number of workers laid off (*xiagang*) by still-functioning SOEs. Athar Hussein and his colleagues (2002) have calculated real urban unemployment at 12.3 per cent. Not surprisingly the unemployment is worse in the Northeast and Chongqing, homes to much heavy industry and manufacturing industry. Given the situation, local authorities have been very successful at restraining unrest and the inability of workers to ensure independent representation has also moderated strikes (see Blecher, 2002). Wary of potential unrest, subsidies and 'policy loans' are often reinstated to try to reverse the losses in key industries, such as textiles.

Second, the fear of rising unemployment was exacerbated by worries about economic slowdown and the potential impact on employment of WTO entry. In fact by 1998–99 the economy was sliding into deflation, with prices dropping by 2.6 per cent and growth officially estimated at 7.8 per cent, and worries were surfacing not only about this but also about its impact on social stability. Such a growth level would mean serious economic distress for certain sectors of the population and regions. As a result, from the end of 1998, the Chinese government launched a massive public building and infrastructure programme to try to maintain economic growth in the 7–8 per cent range. These policies, while not providing a long-term solution, have settled the growth rate.

China finally entered the WTO in December 2001, building on its extra-ordinary integration into the world economy. Essentially, President Jiang and Premier Zhu realized that guiding the necessary concessions through China's complex bureaucracy would only result in delay and potentially strong opposition. As a result they took the whole process out of the political system and kept information within a tight leading group. As the details were slowly disseminated in China, its people and bureaucracies became wary of what they had signed on to and how it would affect their lives. The views on the impact were mixed and there were a number of alarmist scenarios of rising unemployment, greater inequality, Chinese firms going under because of lack of competitiveness and millions being driven off the land because of lower priced and better-quality agricultural imports. Much of this alarmist literature overestimates the problems and attributes to the WTO effects that are the result of the shortcomings of the old system. However, it is true that the costs of entry – such as unemployment, strikes and rural unrest – are concentrated and visible while the benefits – such as a more efficient economy, cheaper consumer goods and better governance – are diffuse and not visible (Fewsmith, 2001b).

Third, while workers' and rural unrest were kept in check and did not appear regime-threatening, the leadership did become worried about political activism in China. Apparently after a debate about whether open political activism could be allowed, the leadership decided to move quickly to crush any potential opposition. First, in a direct challenge to its rule, activists across China formed the China Democracy Party that after a delay in 1998 was harshly crushed. By the end of the year (November 1998) its key members had been arrested, others were periodically picked up and harassed. Second, in April 1999, members of a *qigong* sect, the *Falungong*, encircled the party headquarters in Beijing in a quiet show of strength to protest against criticism. After a few months of hesitation, in the build-up to the fiftieth anniversary of the PRC, leaders of the group were arrested, thousands of followers picked up and all publications concerning the movement banned.

Fourth, external factors played a role. Not only did the Asian financial crisis that began in 1997 limit China's growth alternatives and help it focus on developing the domestic market but also Jiang and others seem to have been unnerved by the sudden fall of the Suharto regime in Indonesia and the rapid systemic collapse. Here was a man who had presided over a long period of economic growth and who seemed securely in power supported by the military and an authoritarian political system and yet was swiftly swept away by street demonstrations. The potential parallels must have seemed alarming.

Further, the relationship with the United States that had looked so promising in 1998 following Clinton–Jiang reciprocal visits began to sour in 1999 with revival of frictions over Taiwan, human rights and WTO entry as well as unexpected events. Bad relations with the United States always hamper domestic reform attempts. The accidental NATO bombing of the Chinese Embassy in Belgrade in May 1999 caused large anti-US demonstrations in Beijing and a few other cities. The inauguration of President George W. Bush in January 2001 with an administration determined to take a tougher stance on China did not help and the 'relationship' almost fell apart when a US EP-3 reconnaissance plane collided with a Chinese jet fighter over international waters in the South China Sea (April 2001). This caused a tense stand-off before the US crew were returned and the plane was sent back in packing cases. This marked a turning point for the new Bush administration, that realized that some kind of constructive engagement with China was necessary. Exchanges of visits were set in motion, culminating in President Jiang's visit to Bush's Texas ranch in October 2002. In the intervening period, the 11 September 2001 attacks on the World Trade Centre had dramatically changed US foreign policy, with the result that the 'China Threat' notion became less important and China was viewed as an ally in the US 'War on Terrorism'.

Such domestic and international uncertainties combined to cause Jiang to ignore calls for more rapid economic transition and even political reform. He preferred to adopt a cautious approach, with tight political control legitimated by a strident nationalism. It was rumoured that Jiang, under pressure from Li Peng and others, announced that political reform should not be discussed for two to three years. When celebrating 20 years of reform in December 1998, Jiang made it clear that radical or 'Western'-inspired models of economic and political reform were not for China. He chose instead to stress the need to maintain stability and crack down on any potential unrest immediately and reemphasized Deng's use of the 'Four Basic Principles'. In this context, he suggested that the bold reforms of earlier in the year would be moderated for people to adjust to their consequences.

However, Jiang did launch one major initiative with far-reaching consequences. In a speech in February 2000 that was intended both to portray Jiang as a great theoretician and to indicate that the CCP was still relevant to China's future, he raised the idea of the 'Three Represents' (the CCP will represent the advanced social productive forces, the most advanced culture and the fundamental interests of all the people). This became a major campaign and the idea was adopted in the Party Statutes in 2002.

The campaign seeks to portray the CCP as not only leading the new and dynamic areas of the economy but also the newly emerged technical and economic elites. It furthers the process of distancing the CCP from sole reliance on the proletariat the party created 50 years ago. The proletariat is consigned to the past and the CCP now claims a broader constituency of representation. It may not amount to Khrushchev's declaration of the Soviet party as that of the whole people but it appears to move significantly in that direction. The campaign suggests that the CCP not only wants to welcome new constituencies but also to exert leadership over the new burgeoning sectors of the economy. This was accompanied by Jiang's declaration on 1 July 2001 (the CCP's anniversary) that under certain circumstances, private entrepreneurs could become party members, a shift that generated howls of disapproval from the 'old' and some of the 'new left'.

One last unexpected event that caused concern was the public announcement of a massive corruption scandal at the *Yuanhua* Group based in the open city of Xiamen (see Chapter 12). Corruption has been a consistent problem but this case implicated many local officials, implicated PLA intelligence and by association at least one of Jiang's close allies, Jia Qinglin. So shocked was Premier Zhu, whose persistence kept the investigation going, that he stated on national television that the ringleader, who had fled to Canada, 'should be killed three times over' (*Wall Street Journal*, 23 November 2001).

The various party plenums and NPC meetings from 1999 to 2001 confirmed the more cautious approach. Jiang tried to walk a middle line by recognizing the need for a radical shake-up of the state sector without accepting that privatization was necessary. The Fifth Plenum (October 2000) also concentrated on the economy adopting the blueprint for the new Five-Year Economic Plan (2001–05), which was formally approved at the March 2001 NPC meeting. The plan called for achieving average growth of about 7 per cent per annum with the goal of doubling the size of the economy by 2010. Growth under the previous Five-Year Plan had averaged 8.3 per cent. Most importantly, the plan acknowledged the need to improve competitiveness because of pending WTO entry. In fact, WTO entry is one of the major factors pushing the leadership to consider a faster pace of reform in the SOE and financial sectors and brought Premier Zhu back to the forefront of economic decision-making. A number of policy pronouncements indicated that the state banks would clean up their bad policy loans and adopt more commercial criteria for future lending, while even large SOEs were warned to expect to feel the impact of reform in preparation for WTO entry.

The new plan also stressed that economic gains would lead to improvements in welfare and would mean that most Chinese would be able to enjoy a comfortable (*xiaokang*) standard of living, a theme that would mark the Sixteenth Party Congress and the policies of the new leadership. The need to show concern about those disfavoured by reforms led the leadership to claim that the working class would be looked after in the process – an unlikely proposition, given that many localities do not have the funds to provide the necessary support.

Political reform had disappeared from the agenda but the need to fight corruption was prominent although no structural reform was suggested. This concern with corruption must have been the driving factor behind discussions at the Sixth Plenum of the Fifteenth CC that examined a decision to improve and strengthen party work-style. The decision mentioned the problems of 'material temptations' while the communiqué claimed that winning the struggle against corruption within the party was an essential condition for maintaining its power and authority. However, beyond exhortation to work better and honestly nothing was recommended that would get to grips with the deep-seated structural causes.

The Sixteenth Party Congress and Beyond

With these discussions as a backdrop, the question of succession heated up through 2002 and a new leadership was selected at a delayed party congress (November) and at the Tenth NPC in March 2003. On the policy front, the meetings did not offer much new but rather gave the opportunity to Jiang and Zhu to reflect favourably on their years in power. The meetings reaffirmed SOEs as the pillar of the national economy but talked of a new road to industrialization that would continue to explore diversified ownership forms that could still be counted as state ownership. Second, they also affirmed that the leadership needed to pay greater attention to the rural economy while pushing ahead with the policy of urbanization. This would also help meet the policy objective of expanding the service sector of the economy. Third, greater attention was to be paid to the non-economic aspects of reform and getting to grips with the problems of inequality. Jiang Zemin outlined the important objective of keeping up with the times and building a comfortable society (*xiaokang shehui*) that included quadrupling the 2000 GDP (around $900 *per capita*) by the year 2020 (Jiang, 2002).

However, the big issue at the Sixteenth Party Congress was election of the new leadership and what continued role Jiang would seek to play. While pre-Congress some talked of the institutionalization of elite politics with Jiang retiring from all posts, things were not so clear-cut. First, Jiang himself has muddied the waters by retaining his post as Chair of the CMAC. This was portrayed as contributing to stability and ensuring continuity in foreign policy, especially in terms of dealing with the important but often difficult relationship with the United States. Second, it appears that at the first Polit-buro meeting after the Party Congress, new General Secretary, Hu Jintao, proposed that important party issues be referred to Jiang and that he would be the only departing leader to continue to receive minutes of the Politburo Standing Committee meetings. This was to continue even after he relinquished the post of President to Hu (March 2003).

Third, the structure of the Standing Committee of the Politburo suggests that Jiang has retained a strong influence over appointments that could enable him to influence policy over the next few years. The fact that the Standing Committee was expanded from 7 to 9 positions suggests that contention reigned up until the last minute. The expansion looks like a compromise solution that avoided hard decisions being made that might have disfavoured Jiang's supporters and the extra slots appear to be rewards for those Jiang loyalists who would not have been promoted otherwise. Fourth, the unex-pected retirement of Li Ruihuan removed a possible strong opponent to Jiang and a person who might have been able to establish different policy priorities. Aged only 68 (below the unofficial retirement age of 70), Li could have expected to remain on the Standing Committee, possibly even overseeing the NPC. However, like Qiao Shi at the Fifteenth Party Congress, he was manoeuvred into retirement. Importantly, like Qiao Shi, Li went quietly, suggesting that they adhered to the norms of internal party unity in public.

None of this, however, guarantees Jiang's long-term dominance. First, those who are seen as close to Jiang do not necessarily share the same views and represent a variety of institutions that may have differing interests. Second, the title of General Secretary does bestow institutional power on its holder and over time Hu may be able to take advantage of this. It should be remembered that when Jiang become General Secretary, he did not have a natural power base but his shrewd politics and use of the prestige that came with the title enabled him to consolidate power. Jiang does not have the personal prestige of Mao or Deng and without a formal position such as the head of the CMAC, he will find it more difficult than his predecessors to rule from behind the scenes. This may cause some of his 'loyal' supporters to find an incentive to move closer to the new General Secretary. Similarly, when Deng Xiaoping exerted ultimate power behind the scenes he was seen to represent the consensus view of the revolutionary elders such as Wang Zhen, Peng Zhen, Bo Yibo and Li Xiannian. Jiang's generation is far less illustrious and calling together 'his (divided) elders' – Li Peng, Li Ruihuan, Zhu Rongji, Qiao Shi and Li Lanqing – would not necessarily enhance his prestige and he may find that it hampers consensus-building.

The Party Statutes were amended to include Jiang's 'Three Represents' and also to make it easier for private entrepreneurs to become party members. However, the Congress offered virtually no indication about the new directions in political reform and rehashed dominant themes of the Jiang years: administrative fine-tuning, improvement in the quality of public officialdom, mention of the rule of law, firm party control over the reform programme and a tightening of the party's grip over the state sector. Despite this lack of encouragement, as in previous post-Congress periods there was a flurry of articles and suggestions about reform (see Chapter 12) and the old mantra that 'economic reform needs political reform' from the Zhao Ziyang years was revived.

In March 2003, the leadership transition was completed when Hu Jintao was appointed as the new President and Wen Jiabao as Premier with a new essentially technocratic cabinet. It also confirmed the course of economic policy and undertook a further but much milder round of government restructuring. With so much on its plate, the NPC delayed amending the Constitution until its 2004 meeting. Most important in the government restructuring was the establishment of two new commissions to oversee the banking sector and asset administration and a new food and drug administration that seemed to indicate that the new leadership was serious about moving more toward a regulatory model for the state. Of equal significance was the change in name of the State Development Planning Commission to the State Development and Reform Commission that would guide the overall reform efforts.

The new leadership under Hu and Wen has been at pains to portray themselves as more open, efficient and concerned about the plight of the poor. In the eyes of many, Jiang represents the interests of China's new economic and coastal elites, yet even in the latter years of Jiang's rule there was increasing concern about inequality and the potential threat this might pose to stability.

Around the Party Congress, there were signs that the leadership has understood the seriousness of these problems but beyond recognition and certain symbolic gestures, concrete polices were lacking. Following the Congress, some measures such as those for migrants have been introduced. Jiang Zemin in his report to the Congress stated that efforts would be made to improve pension, medical and unemployment insurance and basic subsistence payments for urban workers. Further, he said that the government should play a more active role in narrowing the income gap while continuing the programme to develop the West.

In the run-up to the conference, a number of Chinese reports played up the fact that both Hu Jintao and Wen Jiabao had spent significant phases of their career in poorer Western provinces. This is in marked contrast to Jiang, Zhu Rongji and Li Peng who worked in the developed metropolis of Shanghai or in the central ministries and bureaucracy in Beijing. The implicit message that the new leadership would show greater concern for those who have not benefited as well from the reform programme was deliberate.

It was of symbolic importance that the first two public visits by Hu Jintao as General Secretary were not to the glitzy cities of Shanghai or Shenzhen but rather to Xibaipo, a town Southwest of Beijing where Mao Zedong plotted his final push on Beijing in 1949, and Inner Mongolia. Hu's numerous references to 'plain living and hard struggle' in the speech he delivered at Xibaipo were clearly intended not only to draw a line of legitimacy from Mao but also to indicate that the agenda for building a comfortable society would include a broader constituency.

Following the Congress, the new leadership has adopted a number of policies such as trying to integrate migrants better into urban facilities that are relatively easy to promulgate. Importantly at the January Central Rural Work Conference, the party called for the countryside to be accorded the highest policy preference and acknowledged that rural problems were even more intractable than those of the urban areas. The CC decided that most of any additional funding for education, healthcare and culture will be allocated to the rural areas. Perhaps most importantly the Conference stated that it was necessary 'to make further adjustments to the structure of national income distribution and fiscal expenditure'. If this goes beyond allocating more funds as the economy grows to actually redistributing resources to the countryside it would be an extremely significant policy shift. However, given the current power structure and the benefits the coastal areas enjoy any substantive redistribution of resources will be strongly resisted.

Before the new leadership could effectively develop a strong profile they were knocked off course by a crisis from an unlikely source. It probably never occurred to Hu and Wen as they surveyed the policy minefields ahead of them that the first test would come from the health sector with an outbreak of Severe Acute Respiratory Syndrome (SARS) that would have a global impact. In November 2002, this new disease broke out in Guangdong province but was initially covered up and eventually infected people not only elsewhere in China, primarily in Beijing, but also in a number of other countries throughout the world. However, once they decided to act in April 2003, Hu and Wen presented themselves as modern managers with a problem-solving orientation who were concerned for the welfare of the people. By contrast, Jiang Zemin and his supporters looked irrelevant and initially were invisible, although they tried to regain some ground by bringing in the 'Three Represents' and stressing that economic development must not be ignored in the attempt to eradicate SARS. In the traditional 1 July speech (2003) to commemorate the founding of the party, Hu did not display any new ideas for reform but rather praised Jiang's theory of the 'Three Represents', rather than discussing internal party reform as some had hoped, thus indicating the limits on his capacity to carve out a new political agenda should he so wish.

By June 2003, with SARS appearing resolved, the new leadership could try to return to establishing its policy priorities but tensions are apparent and contradictory signals abound. While both Hu and Wen had called for honest reporting about SARS and its impact, other directives were sent out to make sure that the media was not able to exploit this to gain greater press freedom.

Various outspoken magazines and newspapers were censured for bold reporting and a clamp was put on reporting a different disease – encephalitis B – that had broken out.

In part this, may just be put down to a conservative establishment trying to reassert itself but also events are linked to Jiang Zemin and his supporters attempting to reassert their continued relevance. Jiang and his group did not come out well from SARS and two other events weakened Jiang's position. The first was the delayed announcement that 70 Chinese sailors had died in a submarine accident: Jiang, as head of the CMAC, must have been affected by this. It may even be the case that some party elders signed a letter suggesting that he resign from the CMAC at the end of 2003; a number of writers have complained about the problem of the military having two heads (Jiang and Hu) to respond to.

Second in June another corruption scandal broke out, this time in Shanghai involving Zhou Zhengyi, who must have used local connections to obtain illegal or improper loans and land-use rights from Shanghai banks and departments. No one has suggested that Jiang is involved but the fact that it has taken place in Shanghai, his bailiwick, and must have been known to some of his protégés does not reflect well. However, this does not mean that his force is spent, far from it. His supporters have stopped media reporting of the corruption and have tried to ensure that they are involved in the investigation. Further, party and media outlets have again begun to trumpet the relevance of Jiang's 'Three Represents'.

The inner-party jostling is a distraction that the new Hu–Wen leadership can do without, yet it will be difficult for them to launch new policy initiatives until they have consolidated power. This is unfortunate as there is a wide range of institutional, financial, and social challenges that require urgent attention, as discussed in the chapters below.

4

The Chinese Communist Party

While the CCP has resisted all attempts to challenge its political power, the reforms have led intentionally and unintentionally to significant changes in its role in the political system, its relationship to state and society, its capacity to command obedience and its membership. It is clear that the CCP today, while still committed to a Leninist model of political control, is far from the party that set the reforms in motion in the late 1970s. Policy within the party and its relationship with other institutions is more contested than in the past. With 66.4 million members it is an extremely diverse organization with a wide range of political beliefs represented. This chapter first reviews the party's organizational structure and membership and then looks at the changing role of the party in the political system.

Party Organization and Membership

Although there are 8 other political parties in the PRC that accept the established system, the only one that matters is the CCP. The Party Statutes adopted in September 1982, with minor revisions, outline the current thinking about organizational affairs. They describe a traditional Leninist party structure, more akin to the old Communist Party of the Soviet Union (CPSU) than that outlined in the more 'radical' statutes adopted in 1969, 1973 and 1977. However, reforms have also brought a number of changes to party organization and to membership composition.

The basic organizing principle of the party is democratic centralism that demands that the 'individual is subordinate to the organization, the minority is subordinate to the central committee'. This creates a hierarchical pattern of organization in the shape of a pyramid. At the bottom is the network of some 3.51 million 'primary party organizations' based in work-units, neighbourhoods or in villages and where there are 3 or more full party members. Above this is a hierarchy of organization running upwards through the county and provincial levels to the central bodies in Beijing (see Figure 4.1). The second important principle is that of collective leadership – this is designed to avoid the tendency toward one-person rule inherent in such a hierarchically organized structure. In fact, the statutes expressly forbid 'all forms of personality cult'. Party

FIGURE 4.1

Organization of the Chinese Communist Party (CCP), 2003

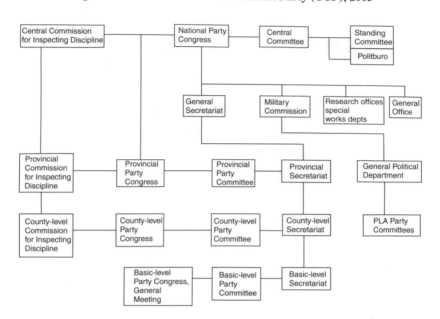

committees at all levels are called on to 'combine collective leadership with individual responsibility under a division of labour'. The third principle concerns the protection of minority rights in the party and seeks to enable individual members to hold different views from those of the organization and bring them up for discussion at party meetings. If there is serious disagreement, the individuals can present their views up to and including the CC. They must continue to carry out policy while awaiting a decision. However, neither party norms nor internal discipline function according to such rules and regulations and personal networks and factions riddle the party and there is a continual tendency towards personal rule over institutionalized rule.

While non-institutional factors were most obvious in the Mao period, they have persisted down to the present. The most recent manifestation was the campaign to build up the image of Jiang Zemin as the unchallenged leader of his generation and that was also intended to allow him to dominate politics after his retirement. While this may well prove impossible given both his more limited charisma and the changed nature of the political environment, it is interesting to note that the organizational structure pushes any leader along the same course. Those around Zhao Ziyang (general secretary 1987–89) and now those around Jiang Zemin have all stressed the importance of concentrating power in the hands of their preferred leader to ensure policy continuation and that power would be redistributed at a later unspecified moment in time. We shall have to see whether the same logic works with current

BOX 4.1

Neo-Authoritarianism and Neo-Conservatism

These theories show the fascination of the post-Mao leaderships with the need for an authoritarian power structure during the economic transition, and in particular for a strong paramount leader.

Ideas about neo-authoritarianism began to appear in 1986 but the theory became more important as a justification for holding power in late 1988 as the reforms began to falter. It was the first clear non-Marxist theory to emerge from within the party (Kelly, 1991, p. 30), although it retained the notion that the political superstructure is determined by the economic base. Its proponents suggested that the gradual extension of market mechanisms could create the necessary basis for democracy that China currently lacked. A strong central authority (and even a strong man) was necessary to push through the policies to create the basis for change. On his removal, Zhao was criticized for this theory.

Shortly after the collapse of the Soviet Union, theories started circulating promoting neo-conservatism, elements of which provided the basis for the rise of nationalism. Supporters of this view essentially want statism to replace communism with carefully guided economic reform and an authoritarian political structure to prevent possible social dislocation leading to chaos and upheaval. They rejected the programme of wholesale privatization, the issuing of shares and the opening of a stock market. They consider these measures unsuitable for the state sector and would restrict them to smaller enterprises with severe losses. The role of the party was to change, abandoning its revolutionary rhetoric and adopting *Realpolitik* for its guiding principles. In addition, the CCP should strive to take control of the economy, building up an asset base as formidable as that of the GMD on Taiwan. Finally, they saw the demise of the Soviet Union as offering new opportunities for revitalization. It would no longer be necessary to rely on Marxism to justify rule but the CCP could now operate on the basis of the 'national interest' and to stress the indigenous nature of the Chinese revolution. While some of its economic thinking has been pushed aside by the speed-up of reform, it formed the basis for the rise of nationalism in the 1990s (see Sautman, 1992; Liu and Lin, 1989; Kelly, 1996; Saich, 1993).

general secretary, Hu Jintao. This explains the fascination with theories of neo-authoritarianism under Zhao and neo-conservatism after 1989 in China (see Box 4.1).

The most striking feature of leadership in the PRC has been the dominance of the system by a paramount individual. From 1949 until his death in 1976, Mao dominated the party and leadership through a combination of political cunning and ruthlessness when necessary (for an unreliable account by his doctor that gives a sense of Mao's power and personality see Li, 1994). After a brief interregnum, Deng Xiaoping dominated the leadership from 1978 until his death in 1997. While Jiang Zemin strove to become the paramount leader upon Deng's death, China has clearly changed. Jiang has great power but it derives more from his institutional positions as head of the party, army and state than his own personal prowess. While he is trying to remain the power broker after his formal retirement, he will never invoke the authority of Deng, let alone Mao.

Policies in all spheres up until the mid-1990s bore the hallmark of Mao or Deng. Despite the CCP's formal emphasis on the norms of democratic centralism and Deng's stress on the need for institutionalization, it is clear that the party has not devised an enduring mechanism for regulating leadership debate or for dealing with leadership succession. This will be one of the great tests of the transition from Jiang Zemin to Hu Jintao. Whether this can be handled without the eruption of factional fighting within the party will be closely observed. Successful long-term transition, while not amounting to institutionalization, will mark considerable progress.

Anointment by the paramount leader has been the norm of succession. However, such attempts to bestow legitimacy have rarely been successful. Mao designated two successors (Liu Shaoqi and Lin Biao), both of whom were subsequently jettisoned before in his dotage he picked Hua Guofeng who could never escape the legacy. Similarly, Deng Xiaoping lost two successors (Hu Yaobang and Zhao Ziyang) before acquiescing in Jiang Zemin. Depending on the patronage of one individual is clearly problematic and places constraints on the capacity to develop an independent power base. The 'successor' cannot stray too far away from the policies and networks of the patron for fear of being denounced as a traitor who has betrayed the patron's trust. While Hu Yaobang appealed privately to Deng on a number of occasions to retire, thus opening up the way for Hu to consolidate power, Zhao pursued his claims by taking Deng's retirement for granted. Yet the attempts to develop their own policy positions and networks of support that would survive Deng's death brought them into conflict with their patron.

Jiang Zemin was fortunate that Deng remained alive long enough for him to consolidate his power sufficiently to survive the death of his patron. He also learned from the removal of his two predecessors, Hu Yaobang and Zhao Ziyang, that it was not wise to push one's own policies independent of the paramount leader. Jiang played an extremely shrewd game, revealing that he was an enormously skilful insider politician, in not offending Deng or other factions in the party and appearing to be all things to all people. It was only as Deng's health deteriorated dramatically that he began to stake out his own terrain more generally.

Jiang has not picked a successor and his favourite, Zeng Qinghong, has suffered from association. Zeng was not promoted to full Politburo membership at the Fifth Plenum of the Fifteenth CC (September 2000) as expected and this disqualified him from having a shot at becoming general secretary when Jiang stepped down. As a result, Jiang has been compelled to go along with the generally accepted choice, Hu Jintao, who has effectively been groomed to be leader for a decade since Deng Xiaoping singled him out. This gives Hu an independence but it also sets him the problem of not appearing too obviously to undercut Jiang's authority.

Personal power and relations with powerful individuals are decisive throughout the Chinese political system and society. While this may decline as the reforms become more institutionalized (Guthrie, 1999), most Chinese recognize very early on that the best way to survive and flourish is to develop personal relationships (*guanxi*) with a powerful political patron. Thus, the Chinese political leadership is riddled with networks of personal relationships and is dominated by patron–client ties (see Nathan 1973; Pye, 1981, 1995; Nathan and Tsai, 1995). This system of patron–client ties lends itself easily to the formation of factions within the leadership. The basis of such factions is shared trusts and loyalties dating back decades. This process of faction formation also relates to institutional and regional interests but the nature of the personal ties makes it difficult to identify such interests clearly. The venom with which an individual is denounced is often difficult to understand unless one knows that person's history and relationships. Similarly, on occasion an individual is attacked as a surrogate for a top leader who is the head of one of the patronage systems. This means that we must understand the informal nature of the Chinese body politic to comprehend the nature of policy-making. Dittmer, like a number of other writers, gives primacy to the role of culture in defining the importance of informal relationships in the political process. Informal politics, in his view, prevails at the highest levels (Dittmer, 1995, pp. 1–34; Dittmer, Fukui and Lee, 2000).

The overdependence on personal relationships makes the Chinese political leadership extremely unstable. Despite the impressive appearance of the CCP as an enduring organization, it is in fact vulnerable to very rapid breakdown. When disputes break out among the leaders of the factions and patron–client networks, this has ramifications throughout the system, often leading to large-scale purges of personnel who are deemed to have supported the 'wrong line'. These purges are accompanied by campaigns against particular individuals or groups of individuals who have deceived party members and the masses and led the party away from its correct line. Rather than reasoned debate of policy faults, the most common form of attack is to dole out personal abuse (see Box 4.2).

The response of the leadership to the student demonstrations of mid-1989 showed how this system of individual power relationships built up over decades remained far more important than the rule of law and the formal functions people held. The events also highlighted how in the absence of institutional mechanisms for accommodating serious divisions, the system still desperately needed a Mao-like figure to perform the role of final arbiter in policy disputes. Increasingly, Deng Xiaoping slipped into the same pattern of personalized rule as Mao. This tendency was noticed not only by the Democracy Wall activists of the late 1970s and the student demonstrators of

---

BOX 4.2

Criticism CCP-Style: Chen Boda's Denunciation of Wang Shiwei

The denunciation of the critical intellectual, Wang Shiwei, occurred in the Shaan-Gan-Ning base area during a major campaign to enhance party unity. The style of criticism is the prototype for subsequent CCP attacks on critical intellectuals and party members who have run foul of the 'correct party line'. Wang attacked the inequalities that were being perpetuated in the Shaan-Gan-Ning and chided the authorities for saying that life there was better than outside and that the problems were nothing to worry about. The persecution of Wang and his colleagues put an end to a more cosmopolitan strain of thinking in the CCP as Mao drove to exert a new orthodoxy. His accuser below, Chen Boda, was a secretary to Mao and was a main source of the Mao cult. He rose to national power in the Cultural Revolution before being purged himself as a 'sham Marxist' in 1971.

> Wang Shiwei's thinking contains a strain of Trotskyism that is antimasses, antination, counterrevolutionary, and anti-Marxist, and which serves the ruling class, the Japanese imperialists, and the international fascists...
>
> In my view, it is too bad that while his [Wang's] clothes are quite clean, his soul is very dirty, base, and ugly. We can find in him various manifestations of all the dirtiest elements that can be found in humanity. His filthy soul rides in tandem with his real life...
>
> I think that he could be as great as a 'leech'. This kind of leech hides in water; when people walk in water, it crawls on to people's feet or legs, using its suction to get into their skin and suck their blood. It can only be removed when people beat it. We think that Wang's 'greatness' is like [the greatness of] this kind of worm; it is truly 'great' (Chen Boda, 1942, in Saich, 1996, p. 1108).

---

the late 1980s, but also by Deng's opponents at the top of the party. The more orthodox economist, Chen Yun, rebuked Deng for abandoning the notion of collective leadership that had been agreed on in the late 1970s; Chen warned Deng not to set himself up as an Emperor by avoiding listening to the views of others. Such criticism notwithstanding, a secret party decision was taken in 1987 that all important matters had to be referred to Deng for his approval.

The same process has occurred with Jiang Zemin. First, in May and June 1989, comments of Deng's were circulated within the party stating that Jiang was to be considered 'the core' of the party's 'third generation of leadership' – Mao having led the first and Deng the second. This became the mantra for all party leaders to recite. However, it has been followed by Jiang's attempts to ensure his influence beyond 2002 when he stepped down as party general secretary. Many expected the Sixteenth Party Congress to mark an institutionalization of leadership transition with the first peaceful transition from one general secretary to another. Jiang was to be hailed as a bold leader who would willingly step away from power and be remembered for his contribution to political institutionalization. This characterization carries an element of truth but events around the Congress moderated such a positive spin (see Chapter 3).

Association with Jiang also had adverse affects in terms of popularity. Jiang's protégé, Zeng Qinghong, fared well, rising from an alternate member of the Politburo to fifth rank on the Standing Committee of the Politburo and being appointed vice President at the NPC meeting. However resentment of those thought to be close to Jiang meant that they generally received low votes at the NPC: Zeng received only 87.5 per cent of the vote to be vice President, the lowest vote on record. Jia Qinglin, Jiang's choice to head the CPPCC, received 92.7 per cent, the second lowest vote of all. Other supporters of Jiang, such as Huang Ju and Chen Zhili, received the lowest votes of the new vice-Premiers (242 abstentions or negatives out of 2,935) and State Councillors (358), respectively.

The Party Congress and the Central Committee

In theory, the top of the party pyramid is the NPC, or its CC, which takes over the Congress' functions when it is not in session. In reality, power lies within the Political Bureau (Politburo), its Standing Committee, and to a lesser extent within the secretariat. The Congress should convene once every five years and as a part of the post-Mao institutionalization this has indeed been the case (see Figure 4.2). The number of delegates attending the Sixteenth Party Congress (8–14 November 2002) totalled 2,114. Such a large number of delegates meeting over such a short space of time means that it is rarely, if at all, that anything of consequence is seriously debated. However, the symbolic function of the Congress is extremely important in terms of providing a display of power and unity, and more important 'milestones' in the party's history. Importantly, the Congress formally elects, although in reality it approves, candidates to the CC that are proposed by the outgoing Politburo and senior leadership.

When the Party Congress is not in session the CC is, in theory, the leading body of the party. Although it meets more frequently, usually once a year in plenary session, its size (198 full members and 158 alternates at the Sixteenth Congress) again indicates that it cannot be the main focus of decision-making in the party. Debates seem to have become more lively but again plenums are convened primarily to approve a party draft document. These plenary sessions are not necessarily restricted to members and alternates, and may include other important personnel who are involved in the decision to be ratified. The draft decisions are usually worked out by the senior leadership during their summer retreat to the Beidaihe seaside, interestingly abandoned by Hu Jintao in 2003. Plenums normally last a couple of days and decisions taken are usually published in the form of a communiqué.

FIGURE 4.2

Central Organization of the CCP (simplified), 2003

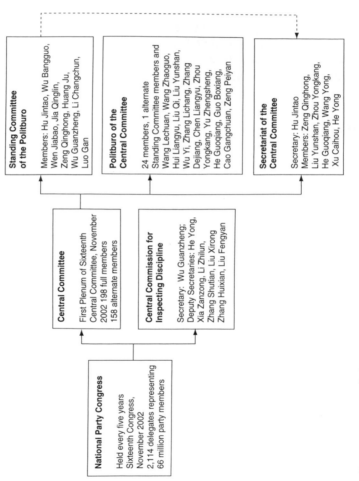

Note: ──────► = elects ────────► = nominates. The Secretariat is *nominated* by standing the committee of the Politburo, 'subject to endorsement' by the CC.

The fact that it is effectively a rubber stamp to decisions made elsewhere does not mean that the CC is entirely uninteresting for study. First, it is vested with a number of formal powers, such as electing the Politburo and its Standing Committee and the general secretary. When there is division on lists among the senior leaders, CC members can have a marginal impact on the elections. In addition, the CC is important as a transmission belt passing down policy proposals and receiving ideas concerning their feasibility and implementation. Finally, membership on the CC is a good indicator of trends in the political system, and a study of the composition indicates what the leadership considers important at any one time and how this changes over time. In turn, the study of any such change over time will reveal the changing requirements of the leadership.

The number of full members oscillates in the range of 170–200, while that for alternates varies from just over 100 to 150 or more. The position of alternate provides a training opportunity for future promotion to the full CC. The first on the alternate list will be promoted to the full CC should a member die or be removed from office. There have been a number of trends discernible during the reform period concerning the level of education, regional and gender representation and the level of military involvement. The education level of delegates has risen and the average age has dropped since the Eleventh CC was elected in 1977. At the Twelfth Congress (1982) only 55 per cent had a college education of any form but this had risen to 98.6 per cent at the Sixteenth (2002). By contrast, average age has dropped. By the time of the Eleventh CC in 1977, age had steadily increased, indicating that power had not yet passed into the hands of a successor generation but merely from one section of the same generation to another. It stood at 65.9 in 1977 (Goodman, 1979, p. 47). The major turnover during the early 1980s when Deng forced most of the veterans into retirement, meant that the age at the Thirteenth CC dropped to a low of 55.2 and remained in the mid-50s thereafter (55.2 at the Sixteenth). Also, the CC has become more technocratic over time, with 56 per cent of the members at the Fifteenth having a professional background in science, engineering, management and finance compared with 40 per cent in 1992 (Baum, 1998, pp. 153–4).

Regional and functional representation has also changed over time. At the Ninth CC (1969) the dominance of central officials was radically reversed, with 59 per cent of members drawn from the provinces as opposed to only 31 per cent at the time of the Eighth CC in 1956. This trend reached a high point during the 1970s when the percentage of those from the provinces in the CC was over 60 per cent. Throughout the 1980s and 1990s, the situation of the 1950s was restored, with 26 per cent provincial representation in 1992 and 32 per cent in 1997 and 32.8 per cent in 2002 (65 members). With Jiang's emphasis on fusing party and state power, state councillors and ministers booked the largest increase in CC seats at the Fifteenth CC, raising representation from 18 per cent in 1992 to 26 per cent (Baum, 2000, p. 26); this was maintained at the Sixteenth with 30 per cent (Fewsmith, 2003, p. 7). The military has retained a significant voice on the CC even though its representation has been weakened at the highest levels of the party. Not surprisingly, given the destruction of the party after the Cultural Revolution was launched, military representatives on the Ninth CC accounted for 50 per cent, a figure that declined to 31 per cent by 1977 as the civilian apparatus was restored. This bottomed out at 17 per cent in 1987 but the increased military influence after 1989 saw representation rise again to almost 25 per cent where it has roughly stayed (22 per cent in 2002). The one group consistently underrepresented is women. Under Mao, there had at least been rhetoric to support the inclusion of women within the leadership and this was reflected in a 1973 CC that had 10 per cent women. This declined to 7 per cent in 1977, 5.3 per cent in 1992 and only 2.5 per cent in 2002! So much for holding up half the sky.

The Politburo, Secretariat and General Secretary

The attempts to institutionalize life at the party centre led to changes in the relationship between the party's leading organs. During the 1980s and 1990s, institutional power in the party has shifted among the Politburo, its Standing Committee and the Secretariat under the general secretary, a post restored in 1982 when the position of party chairman was abolished.

At the Thirteenth Party Congress, Zhao Ziyang announced an important adjustment in the relationship between the Politburo and the Secretariat. The Party Statutes adopted at the Twelfth Party Congress (1982) legislated that the Politburo, its Standing Committee and the general secretary and the Secretariat were all to be elected by the CC. This resulted in the Secretariat and the Politburo acting as competing sources of power. This is not surprising given that one of the reasons for the resurrection of the Secretariat was because at the time Deng Xiaoping and his supporters could not gain a natural majority in the Politburo. In fact, there was even talk of the Politburo being abolished. In theory, the Secretariat was to handle the day-to-day work of the party, becoming its administrative nerve centre. The Politburo and its Standing Committee would be freed to concentrate on taking important decisions on national and international issues. In practice, it placed the Secretariat in an extremely powerful position, as it supervised the regional party organs and the functional departments of the party that should, in theory, have been responsible directly to the CC and the Politburo. This access to information and its control functions meant that it could function as an alternative power base to the Politburo.

Zhao Ziyang announced a clear change in this relationship, downgrading the Secretariat with respect to the Politburo. The Secretariat was reduced in size from 10 to only 4 full members (excluding the general secretary) and one alternate and was made the working office of the Politburo and its Standing Committee. Instead of being directly elected by the CC, its membership is now nominated by the Standing Committee of the Politburo and approved by the CC. A practical indication of the decline of the power of the Secretariat was the announcement that in the future agendas raised by the State Council for policy-making by the Politburo or its Standing Committee would no longer be 'filtered' by the Central Secretariat. However, in practice, it functioned as Zhao Ziyang's support base in the party centre. Zhao and three of his supporters in the Secretariat were removed at the Fourth Plenum of the Thirteenth CC on 24 June 1989. Similarly, under Jiang Zemin it was useful to use the Secretariat to work around the Politburo and its size started to rise again (7 members at the Fifteenth Party Congress). Under Jiang all members were on the Politburo or its Standing Committee, whereas under Zhao only 2 members were on the Standing Committee of the Politburo. Under Hu Jintao, it seems to be becoming more functional with 2 (including Hu) from the Standing Committee, 3 from the Politburo and 1 alternate member each from the CMAC and the Central Discipline Inspection Committee (CDIC).

The Politburo and its Standing Committee are the most important organs of the party and lie at the centre of the decision-making process. The Statutes give no idea about the extent of the powers of the Politburo and its Standing Committee, and simply state that they are elected by the CC, that the Politburo convenes the plenary sessions of the CC and that when the CC is not in session the Politburo and its Standing Committee exercise its functions and powers. We know little about the actual workings of the Politburo, except for the fact that its meetings are frequent and that discussion is said to be unrestrained. The increasing size of the Politburo over time (11 members in 1949 and 25 including alternates in 2002) meant that in 1956 the Standing Committee was set up as a kind of 'inner cabinet'. This committee has functioned continuously since 1956, and it is the highest collective authority in the party.

Under the reforms there have been attempts to formalize membership of these two bodies on the basis of functional representation, and upper age limits have been introduced. However, membership is subject to fierce lobbying and the stress on institutionalization can give way to more pragmatic concerns. Standing Committee membership should comprise not only the general secretary but also the premier, the heads of the NPC and the Chinese People's Political Consultative Committee (CPPCC) and the CDIC. This usually leaves 1 or 2 places over which senior leaders wrangle and try to manoeuvre their protégés into place, although the membership was expanded to 9 at the Sixteenth Congress. Interestingly, at the Fifteenth Party Congress no military leader was appointed to the Standing Committee, a factor that suggests that the civilian leadership wants to assert its control more clearly. This continues a gradual decline in military representation at the highest party levels. When Deng and Mao were alive this was not such a great problem but for Jiang and Hu it is more difficult given their lack of military experience.

The other members of the Politburo are drawn from a combination of functional and factional backgrounds. The Sixteenth Congress saw a dramatic turnover of personnel with 6 out of 7 old Politburo members retiring and 15 new members among the additional 16 Politburo members. The regional party apparatus provides the most substantial block in the Politburo but essentially represents the richer coastal areas of China. On appointment the new Politburo has the party secretaries of Jiangsu, Beijing, Tianjin, Shanghai, Guangdong and Shandong, as well as the former party secretaries of Beijing and Shanghai. It appeared as though the party secretaries of Sichuan, Chongqing, Hubei, Xinjiang and Zhejiang were to be added. With the exception of Zhejiang, this would have been a marked recognition of the need to give some voice to the inland provinces and those that have not fared so well from reforms. However, all except the secretaries of Hubei and Xinjiang have been moved to other posts. This means that Sichuan, the most important province in the West of China, and Chongqing, the most important Municipality, still enjoy no representation at the highest levels, despite the campaign to develop trade with the West. The appointment of the Xinjiang secretary has more to do with the centre's intent to maintain its territorial integrity and to resist any moves for autonomy rather than those of poverty and inequality. Some have suggested that the Xinjiang secretary may serve a role as a new leader in the fight against 'terrorism'.

This means that to all intents and purposes the new Politburo resembles the old with traditional major municipalities (Beijing, Shanghai and Tianjin but not Chongqing) and the wealthy coastal province of Guangdong enjoying representation while the inland and poorer areas of China are excluded. Given this, one may presume that the policy will continue to be biased in favour of the 'haves' while rhetoric will continue to be paid to the needs of the 'have nots'. It is clear that regional leadership is now an important stepping-stone to the top. Of the 22 civilian members of the Politburo, 20 have served as top provincial leaders, and 5 of the 9 Standing Committee members have served for over 10 years (Li, 2003, Table 1). For the new Politburo at the time of the elections more were drawn from the central party organizations (8) than from government organs (5); this had been 6 and 11 respectively, at the 1997 Congress.

A few other features are worth noting about the Politburo. This is one of China's youngest Politburos with an average age of 60.6 years as opposed to 63 at the Fifteenth Congress and 72 back at the Twelfth Congress in 1982 (Zheng and Lye, 2002, p.2). The trend of a younger leadership is matched by that of a better educated one. However, reflecting the pre-Cultural Revolution emphasis on technical training, imported from the Soviet Union (although none of the current leadership trained there) all the Standing Committee members are engineers, as are the majority of Politburo members. This helps explain both the increasing policy pragmatism and the general belief that there is a technical solution to society's problems if only the correct formula can be found. In fact, 4 of the 9 Standing Committee members graduated from Beijing's prestigious Tsinghua University; 5 of the civilian members of the Politburo have considerable work experience in Shanghai, giving some credence to Jiang's critics. Last but not least there is only 1 woman among the full and alternate members.

Institutionalization is dispensable, as are age requirements. Two examples, one from the Thirteenth Congress and one from the Fifteenth Congress, demonstrate this point. Attempts to institutionalize membership on the basis of functional occupation as stated in the 1982 Party Statutes was abandoned at the Thirteenth Congress. According to the Statutes, the heads of the Military Affairs Commission (Deng Xiaoping), the CDIC (Qiao Shi) and the Central Advisory Commission (Chen Yun) had to be members of the Standing Committee. Deng presumably felt it was better to face ridicule for yet again ripping up the Statutes than to have his strongest opponent, Chen Yun, still in the Standing Committee. As a result, neither Deng nor Chen served. Also, given Deng's and Chen's ages it would have made the policy of introducing 'new blood' look utterly ridiculous. However, rejuvenation can also be broken if other reasons are paramount. This was shown at the Fifteenth Party Congress. While no mandatory age for retirement had been agreed for senior cadres, age limits were used as a mechanism for Jiang to remove his chief rival Qiao Shi by declaring that all over 70 should retire and that he himself was willing to do so. However, party elder Bo Yibo is said to have stressed that the key was unity and rejuvenation and that Jiang as the designated 'core' of the 'third generation' should remain. The others had no choice and reluctantly stepped down (Baum, 1998, p. 151). By contrast, Li Ruihuan, a vocal opponent of Jiang, was manoeuvred out of the Politburo, despite being under 70.

Discipline Inspection Commissions and Party Schools

While institutionalization is still not enshrined, the need to restore party discipline after the Cultural Revolution has led to the revival of the commissions for inspecting discipline and the party schools. Both systems have been resurrected to overcome the problems of bureaucratism, bad work-style, opposition to agreed party policy and the rampant corruption that pervades the party. The schools such as the Central Party School are expected to educate party members in the way that they should behave and in the running of the party. The Central Party School runs short-term (3-month) and 1-year training programmes for officials, both to create an *esprit de corps*, but also to prepare them for promotion. The party has clearly decided that it, rather than the state, is the most important organization for pursuing reforms and has exerted much effort to train the targeted personnel. Contrary to perception, the atmosphere at the school can be very open and critical. It was, for example, at the Central Party School that reformer and Politburo member, Tian Jiyun, made his famous speech in April 1992 ridiculing 'leftism' and signalling that

China was going to break free from the policies of tight economic control that had followed 1989. After reiterating his support for the thrust of Deng's 1992 southern tour, Tian suggested that perhaps the 'leftists' in the party leadership might want to set up their own SEZ in which salaries and prices of goods would be low, and queuing and rationing would be commonplace. There would be no foreign investment, all foreigners would be kept out, and no-one would be able to go abroad. Bootleg tapes of the speech were one of the hottest selling items in China through the spring of 1992. Similarly, but in less eloquent fashion, Jiang Zemin spoke to the Party School in May 1997 and outlined the report that he would deliver to the forthcoming Sixteenth Party Congress.

For participants, attending the Party School has a number of advantages. First, it is a mark of honour within the party to be singled out. Second, it gives local officials a privileged inside view of current senior party thinking that will enable them better to second-guess the situation once they return to their locality. Third, it provides an ideal source for networking among up-and-coming leaders. Last, but not least, most participants find it very peaceful, providing them with a few months of tranquillity to read and catch up on the various chores that work had prevented them from completing.

Discipline inspection commissions are important agencies in the attempt to reestablish a system for dealing with discipline and monitoring abuses within the party. This system replaces what the party saw as the arbitrariness and unpredictability of the Cultural Revolution. It was also a clear expression that although the party recognized the breakdown of the Cultural Revolution, it was not willing to entrust monitoring of its membership and its behaviour to non-members and to submit them to any external democratic supervision. In explaining the tragedies and incompetence of the past, the party has always prided itself on the fact that it alone had righted the wrongs. During the reform period the party always resisted any attempts or suggestions to be held accountable to society and the citizenry. This frustrated its attempts to eradicate the corruption that senior leaders, including Jiang Zemin, have identified as a threat to continued CCP rule. Indeed it is now common for senior leaders and the head of the CDIC to comment that work-style and relations between the party and the people are issues that have a close bearing on the party's survival. It has also meant that cases of party corruption that are exposed are done so either because the leadership wants to make an example to discourage others, or because of factional in-fighting.

The Commission has concentrated on promoting the restoration of internal 'party life', and has drafted guidelines that would prevent the personalization of politics and restore Leninist norms of collective leadership. In addition, it has tackled such problems as the evaluation of accusations made against Liu Shaoqi in the Cultural Revolution (declaring him to have a clean bill of political health), preparing the materials against the 'Gang of Four', and the investigation of Beijing Party Secretary, Chen Xitong, and his associates on charges of corruption. Chen, a political enemy of Jiang Zemin, was eventually sentenced to 16 years imprisonment.

Central Military Affairs Commission

The Central Military Affairs Commission (CMAC) is the main vehicle through which the party ensures control over the military system. There is also a state commission but its composition is identical and is clearly irrelevant. The state commission was formed in 1982 to give the impression that the military came under control of the state rather than the party. This was done in particular with respect to possible reunification with Taiwan; the military was thus portrayed as one arm of the Chinese state rather than the CCP. The CMAC is clearly more important than the Ministry of National Defence and is the highest policy-making body for military affairs and the highest command organ for military operations. In reality, the Ministry of National Defence is subordinate to the CMAC rather than to the State Council. The CMAC has existed under one name or another since 1931, when it was established on the instructions of the First All-China Soviet Congress. Personnel appointments to the CMAC give an indication both about the strength of the military in the system and about the paramount leader. Until his death, the CMAC was headed by Mao, then briefly by Hua Guofeng, then by Deng Xiaoping, and finally by Jiang Zemin. While the military may have deferred to Mao and Deng, they resisted Deng's attempts to place his first two chosen successors, Hu Yaobang and Zhao Ziyang, at its head. Jiang Zemin moved carefully to consolidate his control over the military and was judicious in his promotion of generals and key senior military personnel loyal to himself. His growing power was reflected in the fact that at the party plenum in September 1999, Jiang was able to install his successor Hu Jintao as the vice-chair of the CMAC, after two years of attempts. Hu now shares the position of vice-chair with two others known to be close to Jiang, Generals Guo Boxiang and Cao Gangchuan (both of whom were added to the Politburo at the Sixteenth Party Congress). Cao serves concurrently as Minister of National Defence. The fact that Jiang refused to cede his position as chair is what gives him his residual consider-able political power. It will be interesting to see when and under what circumstances he hands this position over to Hu. It will also be interesting to see whether his protégé, Zeng Qinghong is then appointed as a vice-chair.

Membership

While the total party membership is huge (66.4 million in 2002), the CCP has always prided itself on its exclusivity, with membership representing less than 5 per cent of the total population. Its Statutes give no evidence of this exclusivity, and contain detailed rules governing the admission of members and the duties and behaviour required of them. The actual criteria for membership have changed over the years, reflecting shifts in ideology and recruitment policies. In contrast to a number of its forerunners, the 1982 Statutes acknowledge that class background is no longer a significant factor in China and they provide an extremely broad definition of eligibility. This was amended further in 2002 when the category 'any other revolutionary' was amended to 'advanced element of other social strata' to reflect the more inclusive nature of the 'Three Represents'. Thus, membership may be sought by: 'Any Chinese worker, farmer, member of the armed forces, intellectual or advanced element of other social strata who has reached the age of 18 and who accepts the party's programme and statutes and is willing to join and work actively in one of the party's organizations, carry out the party's decisions and pay membership dues regularly.'

To become a probationary member an applicant must be supported by existing members, accepted by a party branch after 'rigorous examination', and approved by the next highest level of party organization. Probation normally lasts for one year during which time the candidate's progress is assessed and education is provided. If all goes well, full membership will then be granted by the general membership meeting of the party branch and approved by the next higher level. Members who violate party discipline are subject to various sanctions, including warnings of varying degrees of severity, removal from party posts, probation and expulsion from the party. The party can also propose to the 'organization concerned' that an offender should be removed from non-party posts. A member subjected to discipline has the right to be heard in his or her own defence and has a right to appeal to higher levels.

Although exclusive, party membership has risen steadily since 1949 when there were only 4.5 million members to reach 66.4 million in 2002 (see Figure 4.3). Despite this steady growth, there has been considerable variation in the nature of recruitment. During the reform period the party has had to undergo a massive process of renewal to bring in the kind of recruits who had the requisite technical skills for development. During the Cultural Revolution, and even before, insufficient attention was paid to the recruitment of the educated and the young. The 'Gang of Four' took the blame for their emphasis on worker, peasant and soldier recruitment that left the party ill-equipped to manage the modernization drive. To build up their own support, they were accused of pursuing a reckless speed of recruitment and promoting new cadres at the 'double quick' ('helicopter cadres'). The new recruits joined at a time when rational rules and regulations were under attack, meaning that these members were unfamiliar with traditional Leninist norms. By the time of the 'Gang of Four's' arrest, 43 per cent of all party members in Shanghai had been admitted during the years 1966–76 and it was claimed that a 'handful of them' did not even know what 'the Communist Party, communism or party spirit' were (*SWB: FE*/6341). The flurry of books published during the 1980s as a part of party education campaigns contained the most basic questions that party members were expected to answer in tests to assess their capability.

FIGURE 4.3

Party membership, 1921–2002

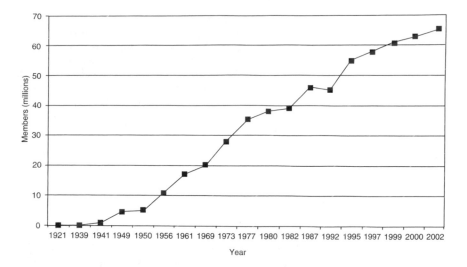

When starting the reforms, poor education levels were a general problem. In 1984 only 4 per cent of members had received a higher education and over 50 per cent were either illiterate or had been only to primary school. Moreover, in 1978 only 27 per cent of members had a senior middle-school education. By 1995, this figure had risen to 39.9 per cent and to 43 per cent in 1997, while by mid-2002 52.5 per cent had completed high school and 23.2 per cent were university graduates. At senior party levels, the party is now highly educated and technically competent, but at county level and below the problem of elite renewal remains serious. Whereas in 1950 nearly 27 per cent of members were under 25, by 1983 this had fallen to less than 3.3 per cent. Recruitment has had an effect and by 1995 those under 35 had risen to 21.1 per cent and to 22.3 per cent by mid-2002. Not surprisingly, not only are women underrepresented in the leadership but throughout the party as a whole. In mid-2002 only 17.5 per cent of members were female; however, there is evidence that recruitment of women is increasing; since 1995, just over 20 per cent of the new recruits have been female. By contrast, recruitment among the non-Han peoples roughly reflects their percentage of the population as a whole (6.2 per cent in 2002 and 8.01 in 1990).

Although the high standards demanded by the Statutes are not always met in practice, membership can require a high degree of commitment and considerable sacrifice of personal time. On occasion, party members have had the unpleasant task of implementing policies that were widely disliked, for example the enforcement of family-planning policy. Many local party officials have confided to me that their most hated task is overseeing the implementation of this policy (see Box 4.3).

BOX 4.3

Party Duty and Personal Choice

When I was a student in China at the end of the Cultural Revolution, the Campaign to Criticize Lin Biao and Confucius had just wound down. Politically, the campaign comprised a major attack on Zhou Enlai and his more moderate economic policies; socially it attacked many traditional practices. While chatting, one of the Chinese students told us of her distress at having to go periodically from Nanjing University to the surrounding communes to lecture the farmers on the evils of Lin Biao and Confucius. They were not welcoming, said they had no interest in or idea of what she was talking about, and told her in no uncertain terms to stop wasting their time and get back to the university. She often returned in tears. When we asked her if she could avoid this humiliation, she replied that it was her duty as a party member and while she could claim sickness once or twice, further absence would be noted and a demerit placed in her personal file.

During the Cultural Revolution many members were particularly vulnerable to the violent oscillations of the Maoist political process and were subject to savage criticism. Many members suffered simply by backing the losing side in a particular dispute. Over time such oscillations have led to dramatically different reasons for joining the party. For many, the attractiveness of party membership diminished as a result of the record of past failures and excesses that tarnished its image. Recent policies for agriculture, the emphasis on encouraging and rewarding the professionally competent and party withdrawal from interference with much of daily life have also made it increasingly possible for some to pursue relatively well-paid and responsible jobs without membership.

However, membership keeps rising, indicating that there must be incentives for joining. Membership still confers great benefits for career advancement and also now the acquisition of economic resources. Politically, the party is still the only game in town and thus remains the locus of political power and few can achieve real political influence without membership and a record of political activism. I have met party members who are Maoists, Stalinists, more Friedmanite than Milton Friedman, Shamans (traditional religious leaders), underground Christians, Anarchists, and Social and Liberal Democrats. With no other political home to go to, virtually all with political ambition will try to enter the CCP to pursue their political agenda.

In the Maoist era, the vast majority of responsible jobs in the state and mass organizations went to party members who often had few other qualifications. Deng Xiaoping's insistence on the need for an elite of competent moderniz-ers in all walks of life has meant that political reliability alone is no longer regarded as a sufficient qualification for a senior appointment. However, party credentials remain necessary for a wide range of sensitive positions and are a major advantage for many other jobs. Moreover, wage scales in China are highly differentiated and those in senior positions enjoy relatively high incomes, commensurate pensions, superior accommodations and access to innumerable perks. There is also a range of 'informal' advantages. Although the precise nature has differed over time, these have always included access to information denied to the general public; an increased ability to obtain 'good' education and to use 'connections' to advance the careers of one's children; opportunities to travel at state expense; the right to use cars in a country where private car ownership is still limited; and the opportunity to enjoy a certain amount of wining and dining at public expense. The privileged position of party membership and the access it brings has been a major cause of corruption in China.

The party is now faced with the dual challenge of making membership relevant to today's youth while not attracting only those who see it as a vehicle for personal gain. Jiang and his supporters with the 'Three Represents' campaign have tried to make a case for continued relevance, claiming that the party represents the most advanced scientific and productive forces and a broader constituency than the traditional working class. In the rural areas, the party has used the village elections to attract new members who have a degree of popular legitimacy. However, senior CCP members have argued about just how accommodating they should be towards new social forces that are products of reform. In particular, debate has centred on the new private entrepreneurs whom orthodox party members see as having no place in the CCP. In the July 2000 issue of the party's theoretical magazine, *Zhongliu*, the fact that too many business people were joining the party was denounced. *Zhongliu* opined that in some coastal areas, 50 per cent of all new recruits were private business people; in Qinghui county near Shanghai, there were said to be 158 capitalists in the local party and 36 of the county's party cells were run by them. As long as the CCP allows no other opposition to exist, it will have to find a way to be more inclusive of such groups or risk their alienation. In July 2001, celebrating the 80th anniversary of the CCP, Jiang broke the deadlock, announcing that under certain circumstances private entrepreneurs would be welcomed to join the party. It is reported that 100,000 private entrepreneurs applied to join the party immediately after Jiang's speech and 10 provinces were set up as experimental sites (Dickson, 2003, p. 104). However, as noted, this was confirming existing practice. Apart from the value of such inclusion, recruiting private entrepreneurs would have financial benefits for the party: if they only joined the other political parties, this could weaken the CCP's financial viability.

A 2002 national survey of private entrepreneurs showed that 29.9 per cent had joined the CCP, an enormous jump from the 16.6 per cent in 1997 (*Beijing Review*, 20 March 2003, p. 17). However, this jump is attributable in major part to the fact that many SOEs and collective enterprises had been converted to private enterprises and their heads were party members. Dickson, who has conducted a fascinating survey of private entrepreneurs and their values, reaches an even higher figure of 40.4 per cent, but again this is biased by the large size of the enterprises (Dickson, 2003, p. 108). No matter what the exact figure, the political consequences are liable to be significant especially at the local level.

The Role of the CCP in the Political System

The most important question for reform of the political system is that of the correct role for the party and its relationship to other organizations. CCP dominance has been felt in all walks of life as the party sought not only to control the legislature and executive but also to dictate the nation's moral and ethical values. Not surprisingly, suggestions for reform have focused on the need to decrease the party's influence over the day-to-day affairs of other organizations. Since fundamental reform in this respect would lead to a decrease in the party's power, it has been strongly resisted. This resistance led to the dismissal of two general secretaries, Hu Yaobang (1987) and Zhao Ziyang (1989). However, by both design and by unintentional effect the reforms have curtailed the party's power in certain respects.

The Legacy of the Cultural Revolution

A major challenge in the reform era has been to deal with the legacy left by Mao Zedong from the Cultural Revolution. The Cultural Revolution witnessed an unprecedented attack on a ruling Communist Party. This attack was all the more astonishing since it was initiated and led by the leader of the party – Mao Zedong. At a superficial level, there are obvious parallels with the CPSU under Stalin. Indeed, the conscious attempts to revive party life since Mao's death seem comparable with Khrushchev's attempts following Stalin's death. Certainly, under Stalin the party was emasculated. This is demonstrated by the virtual atrophy of the regular party organs. The Party Congress did not meet between 1939 and 1952 and the CC did not fare much better. The CCP did not hold a congress between 1958 and 1969. In the Soviet Union under Stalin there was a relative eclipse of the party as the supreme institution of power at the centre. As Stalin's personal power moved into the ascendant, that of the party declined. Again one can find a parallel with the party under Mao.

However, there are important differences. Despite Stalin's destruction of his opponents in the party (politically and, invariably, physically), the downgrading of the party's importance and the growth of the personality cult, he always claimed to be acting in the name of the party and invoked its name to sanction its actions. Mao in destroying his opponents and, for a while, the party, was willing to invoke his own authority against that of the party. While Stalin turned to the state administration and the public security forces to attain his objectives, Mao appealed to the masses and later the army to break down the old system. While Stalin destroyed the old Bolsheviks and began to replace them with a managerial elite, Mao tried to extinguish the 'new class' and inject revolutionary zeal into the emerging managerial ethos.

Although differences existed between Mao and his supporters on questions of the nature of the ideal form of the party, his thinking on organizational issues influenced the whole programme of party rebuilding until the late 1970s. Mao's attitude to organization of any form was ambivalent. While he saw leadership as necessary to guide the revolution forward, he was suspicious of those who occupied leadership positions. He was constantly aware of the possibility of leaders becoming alienated from the masses and adopting bureaucratic postures. In the 1960s, this trend of thought led Mao to believe that the party itself provided part of the basis for the emergence of a new class dedicated to serving themselves rather than the masses and socialism. If the party as an organization had a tendency towards bureaucratism and if its top leaders could be seduced along the 'capitalist road', purely internal party mechanisms of control could not be relied upon.

Leaders were exhorted to maintain close contacts with the masses, formalized through programmes such as those for cadre participation in manual labour. The masses, for their part, were expected to exercise supervision over the leadership and offer criticism. The internal party control mechanisms that had operated before the Cultural Revolution were abolished. They were replaced by a faith in a leadership committed to revolutionary values and in the power of the masses to point out problems as they arose. The chapter on organizational principles in the party statutes adopted by the Ninth and Tenth Party Congresses (1969 and 1973) referred to the need for 'leading bodies to listen constantly to the opinions of the masses both inside and outside the party and accept their supervision'. The post-Mao stress on the need to reestablish an institutionalized system for maintaining party discipline and the virtual elimination of a role for the masses in determining the party line meant that such references were dropped in the 1982 Statutes. The organizational principles referred only to the need for higher party organizations to pay constant attention to the views of the lower party organizations and rank-and-file members.

Mao's ambivalence meant that he could not provide his supporters with a clear idea of the precise organizational forms that he preferred. Despite the attempts to separate the party as an organization from the individuals in the party who were under attack, the effect was to undermine the party's prestige. This brought to the fore the question of legitimacy. With the discrediting of the party as a source of authority and legitimacy in the Chinese polity, the tendency was to resort to the invocation of Mao's name. The fact that the Cultural Revolution did not, or was not allowed to, develop alternative forms of organization only compounded the problem.

The post-Mao leadership not only had to devise a proper relationship between the party and society but also to deal with the issue of excessive dominance by one person. While Hua Guofeng was unable to come to terms with this, Deng Xiaoping recognized the need to address this legacy and return, as he phrased it, to a 'conventional way of doing things'. By this he meant having the CCP return to a more traditional Leninist role with collective leadership, predictable rules governing the power of the higher over the lower levels and a tight grip on state and society.

The reforms have changed the role of the CCP in significant ways even as it retains its all-powerful role in the system and is willing to crush any potential opposition. This was shown most clearly in the crushing of the student-led demonstrations of 1989 and again in December 1998, when leaders of the China Democracy Party were given heavy sentences. The need for change also came from the recognition that a revolutionary mobilizing party would not suit the needs of the new plans for economic modernization and that the CCP was now a ruling party. However, a variety of factors set constraints on the extent of change. For example, the traditional Leninist rejection of organizational pluralism, the fear of internal unrest, the collapse of the CPSU and the fall of Suharto all caused Deng and Jiang Zemin to favour limited change, a development model under which increased market influences in the economy are accompanied by authoritarian political rule. One hallmark of Jiang's rule, emphasized at the Fifteenth and Sixteenth Party Congresses, has been the attempt to reassert party control over state and society.

Talk about political reform was legitimized by Deng Xiaoping in August 1980 when he proposed that a mere tinkering with the system and a removal of what were seen as irregularities in party work caused by the Cultural Revolution were not enough (Deng, 1984, pp. 280–303). This had followed Deng's 1978 observation that party leadership was to be limited to 'political leadership' and was not to substitute for the government and other organizations in the system. He eschewed using the phrase of 'overall leadership' (Deng, 1983, p. 113, from Zhao, 1997, p. 13). The new development strategy adopted at the Third Plenum of the Eleventh CC (December 1978) accentuated the need for change. The policies introduced to stimulate the use of market mechanisms combined with attempts to decentralize economic decision-making were not readily served by a rigid, overcentralized political system dominated by the party and staffed by personnel who felt most at home hiding behind administrative rules and regulations. Leaders such as Deng Xiaoping and his supporters began to realize that the demands of a modern economy required a greater differentiation and clarification of roles for China's institutions.

During the early 1980s, a number of initiatives were undertaken to reform the political system, including the adoption of new Party Statutes and State Constitution, measures to trim the bureaucracy, attempts to improve the quality of the cadre force and steps to promote more effective citizen participation. The party even changed its self-definition. The 1982 Party Statutes refer to the party as the 'vanguard of the Chinese working class' rather than as the 'political party of the proletariat and its vanguard'. The term 'working class' is more neutral than that of 'proletariat', the latter term conjuring up visions of class struggle. This suits the emphasis that was placed on the tasks of economic modernization and the downgrading of the role of class struggle. Also, importantly, the CCP now defines intellectuals as an integral part of the working class. This attempt to reach out to broader groups in society is shown by the fact that the 1982 Statutes claim that the party is the 'faithful representative of the interests of all the Chinese people'. This claim did not appear in any of the previous Party Statutes, not even in those of 1956, Statutes that were also adopted at a time when the main emphasis was placed upon economic development. However, a major overhaul of the party's role has been resisted and cadres baulked at the idea of curtailment of their power. Even the most reform-minded members of the establishment realized that there would be limits to the permissible. As in other periods of liberalization in the PRC, as indeed in all state-socialist societies, there were differences of opinion about just how much the grip of the party could or should be relaxed. Recognition that the party cannot control everything and trying to define what its leading role means in practice leaves plenty of room for disagreement.

The notion of continued party leadership is enshrined in promotion of the slogan of adherence to the 'Four Basic Principles'. These principles were first put forward by Deng Xiaoping in March 1979 at a Central Theoretical Work Conference, in response to the Democracy Wall Movement of the late 1970s and the heterodox views put forward at the Conference by the party's own senior intellectuals. After initially using the movement in his political struggle against his opponents in the party leadership, Deng had no further use for the movement and wished to set limits to non-party-sanctioned activity. Adherence to the 'Four Basic Principles' indicates that there are limits to the reforms and suggests a range of obligations for those engaged in discussions about political reform.

A further limit to wide-ranging reform was the general consensus shared by senior party leaders that political reform should be dictated by the needs of economic reform. Only such reforms would be initiated as were necessary to keep the motor of economic reform running smoothly. Jiang Zemin and his supporters were swayed by those using arguments about economic development rather than Marxism to justify authoritarian rule, drawing the conclusion from the swiftly developing economies of East and Southeast Asia that the modernization process required a strong centralized political structure, especially in the early phases, to prevent social divisions from undermining it. They hoped that this would help them push through unpopular measures without mass protest. Quite simply, they equated democratization with chaos, and chaos with underdevelopment (Saich, 1992, p. 1159).

Differing Views of the Party's Role

Within the top leadership, opinions on the role of the party in the political system have moved between two main polar points: the pragmatic reforming and the traditional orthodox. These two viewpoints served as points on a continuum around which different opinions clustered at crucial moments. Certainly they were not the only views expressed and the paramount leaders Deng Xiaoping and Jiang Zemin shifted between the two viewpoints as circumstances dictated. For example, in the spring and summer of 1997, Jiang Zemin appeared to be giving licence to wide-ranging discussion of political reform only to endorse a fairly orthodox statement of the party's role at the Fifteenth Party Congress held later that year. Again at the Sixteenth Party Congress in November 2002, he confirmed that China would never copy Western political models, a statement that came after the sentencing of the leaders of the China Democracy Party.

Zhao Ziyang provided the fullest articulation of the pragmatic view at the Thirteenth Party Congress (1987). The term 'pragmatic' is used as the reforms proposed are designed primarily to improve economic efficiency. Zhao indicated that future reforms would have to deal with some of the core issues of the party's role and structure as inherited from the Leninist model, developed during the pre-1949 struggle for power and intensified under the centrally planned economy. This role and structure did not suit the demands of a more decentralized, market-influenced economy where flexibility, efficiency and the encouragement of initiative were key values. Zhao made it clear that political reform was indispensable if economic reform was to continue, and with an unusual rhetorical flourish stated that the CC had decided that 'it was high time to put political reform on the agenda for the whole party' (Zhao, 1987, p. iii).

The proposals called for a redistribution of power, both horizontally to state organs at the same level, and vertically to party and state organs lower down the administrative ladder. The party had so dominated, and continues to dominate, the legislature, the executive and the judiciary as to make their independence a fiction. The intention was for the party to exercise political leadership but not to become directly involved in the routine work of government. In particular, Zhao proposed that the dual holding of both government and party posts would be stopped, party administrative departments that carried out the same functions as those in the state sector were to be abolished along with the system of party committees ruling over academic and economic organizations. Most importantly, the system of party core groups in government and other non-party organizations was to be abolished. After the Party Congress, these reforms began to be implemented throughout the system, but the harsh atmosphere that followed the crackdown in the summer of 1989 led to a reversal.

Zhao even acknowledged that there existed a limited political pluralism under the leadership of the CCP. Breaking with the monistic view common to CCP thinking and the idea of uniform policy implementation, Zhao acknowledged both that 'specific views and the interests of the masses may differ from each other' and that '[a]s conditions vary in different localities, we should not require unanimity in everything' (Zhao, 1987, pp. iii–iv). Similarly, the group recognized that experts and intellectuals should be given a greater degree of freedom as a prerequisite for their contribution to policy-making. In turn, they had to be given guarantees that they would not be punished tomorrow for what they said today. This leads not only to a greater tolerance of 'dissent' but also to the protection of people's rights by the legal system. Genuine elections are seen as important not just for allowing mass participation in the decision-making process but also to ensure that those in leadership positions have the support of their constituencies. Yet this acknowledgement of a limited pluralism was not intended to lead to the accommodation of factions within the party, something that had been suggested by some reform-minded intellectuals. Such reforms were seen as the only way to maintain party leadership in a time of change.

Similarly, the group recognized that experts and intellectuals should be given a greater degree of freedom as a prerequisite for their contribution to policy-making. In turn, market-oriented reforms required that new groups in society be given the chance to participate in the process of both formulating and implementing the reforms. In this changing environment, the pragmatists realized that the party had to find a new role for itself and devise new institutions to mediate between the party and the officially sanctioned sections of society. Pragmatic reformers did not see this as weakening party control, far from it. Such reforms were seen as the way to strengthen party leadership. The clear definition of roles with the removal of the party from administrative work would strengthen its political leadership. This thinking underlay the more pragmatic response to the student-led demonstrations that sought to negotiate rather than to eliminate the voice of the protesters.

While neither Hu Yaobang in late 1986 nor Zhao Ziyang in mid-1989 saw the student protests as a major threat, the traditionalists in the party saw them as a challenge to the very fundamental principles of party rule. Crucially, Deng Xiaoping decided to side with them. Whereas Zhao appeared willing to make concessions to the students' demands, his opponents felt that no retreat was possible as it would lead to a collapse of socialism. Their reaction to the events and their brutal repression of the students served only to highlight their fear of spontaneous political activity that occurred outside of their direct control. It is this view of the threat from autonomous organizations that dominates the thinking of the majority of the senior leadership at the present time and that has caused them to move hard against any independent organization, whether it be an openly political organization such as the China Democracy Party or a faith-based movement such as the *Falungong* or the underground religious movements.

Deng always maintained a traditional view of political activity that occurred outside of party control and resisted Mao's attempts to open up the party to criticism from outside forces. The general caution derived from his Leninist heritage had been reinforced by experience of the Hundred Flowers Campaign, the Cultural Revolution and the democracy movements of the late 1970s and late 1980s. In all these movements, the party as an institution came under attack and the associated political instability led Deng to conclude that too much democracy was undesirable in China. To ignore the masses was dangerous as this might lead to greater unrest, a view reinforced by the events of the Cultural Revolution. However, the party itself would decide whether to take any notice of the views expressed, and whether it was qualified to continue in its leadership role was a matter for the party alone. This was an explicit rejection of 'Big Democracy' as proposed by Mao Zedong, under which non-party masses would be allowed to have a say in party affairs. The earlier political campaigns also greatly influenced those such as Jiang Zemin who went through the movements of the 1950s and 1960s as new party recruits trying to work their way up the system. The one notable exception is Premier Zhu Rongji, who was one of the victims of the anti-rightist campaign. Crucially for Jiang's view is the fact that he owes his position as general secretary to the events of 1989 when he was recruited from Shanghai to run the party. The elders seemed impressed by his firm but non-violent handling of the demonstrations in Shanghai, including shutting down the city's liberal newspaper, and Deng recognized that the Beijing party leadership had been discredited by the crackdown and none could be promoted to general secretary.

The traditional orthodox view opposes wide-ranging political reform and too much loosening of party control because of the consequences of liberalization for the social fabric of China. Proponents seek to run the party and its relationship to society on orthodox Leninist lines. Efforts to relax the party's grip over state and society are resisted and they seek continually to institutionalize party dominance. In particular, they are concerned about attempts to loosen the control of the party in the workplace. With the decentralization of limited decision-making powers to the work-units, it is felt important that the party retains a strong role in the enterprises to stop the work-units from deviating too much from central party policy. Thus, there is a stress upon the need for party strengthening at the grass roots level and the concern that political and ideological work continues to be taken seriously.

From the 1990s this view dominated, with the result that a number of reforms instigated at the Thirteenth Party Congress were reversed or slowed. Jiang Zemin and his associates made it clear that the party remained central to the reform process and that they trusted the party only to lead reform from within all organizations. This was reflected in a number of measures. First, at the Fifteenth and Sixteenth Party Congresses, Jiang referred to the need for political reform but offered much thinner fare than Zhao had in 1987. Not only did he predictably reject a Western-style political system but also Zhao's earlier stumblings towards acceptance of pluralism. Instead he proposed 'multi-party cooperation and consultation under party leadership' and increased control over the press and media. Such reforms as were proposed were in terms of strengthening the legal system, consolidating the programme of village elections and continuation of the civil service reforms (a cornerstone of the Fourteenth Party Congress proposals).

At the Sixteenth Party Congress, Jiang stated quite clearly that 'party leadership' was fundamental to ensuring that the people were the 'masters' and that China was 'ruled by law'. He stated that to 'run the state well we must run the party well first'. In terms of the party's relationship to the state he said:

> We will support people's congresses in performing their functions as organs of state power according to the law, in ensuring that the party's views become the will of the state and that candidates recommended by party organs become leading cadres of the organs of state power through legal procedures and in exercising supervision over them.

Generally, throughout the 1990s party control was tightened whenever possible. It became common practice again for senior party figures to take on important state functions – best symbolized by Jiang himself (who was president of the state, general secretary of the party and chair of the CMAC) and Hu, who succeeded him in the first two; presumably the third will follow. In addition, through the early 1990s, the party core group system in non-party organizations was strengthened and generally the authority of party committees and secretaries was boosted. This was particularly seen in the new law on higher education and with attempts to control the rapidly expanding NGO sector. The draft education law presented in late 1998 surprised reformers by reconfirming the preeminence of the party secretary at higher education institutions *vis-à-vis* the president or administrative head, seen throughout the university system as a major setback for academic freedom and the vitality of the universities. A number of senior university officials felt that while it might not affect premier universities too badly, as the party secretary would have to be well educated and relatively open-minded to survive, it could be stifling for the less prestigious colleges (interviews, September 1999), where party secretaries might be able to pull rank more easily. For the NGO sector not only did the CCP promote new regulations (1998) to try to bind social organizations into a Leninist hierarchy, but it also reactivated the use of party cells within non-party organizations to try to ensure control and monitoring. In early 1998, an internal circular called for the establishment of party cells in all social organizations and the strengthening of party work in those where a cell already existed.

The party's leaders also realized that its power had atrophied or had been undermined at the grass roots level and a movement was launched in late

1994 to rebuild party capacity. The urgency of this endeavour stemmed from the fear of unrest that was growing in both urban areas as workers were laid off, and in rural areas as farmers rioted against the increased corruption and the imposition of excessive illegal fees and levies. A spate of reports in late 1994 and early 1995 referred to the poor state of party organizations, especially those in the countryside that suffered from weak and lax discipline. Official figures referred to some 8 per cent of the country's 800,000 rural organizations being paralysed. One researcher, based on conversations with officials, assessed that up to one-third of party organizations in urban enterprises and villages had stopped functioning (Zhao, 1997, p. 18). Such problems led the Fourth Plenum of the Fourteenth CC (September 1994) to adopt a decision to strengthen party-building. Over the next two years, just over 900,000 party functionaries were sent to the countryside to try to breathe life back into party organizations. By June 1995, the party was claiming success, with 800,000 branches having been rectified. The reality was different, and even official press reports continued to refer to the lax discipline in many rural areas: of 50,000 villages that had formed the initial focus of the campaign, only 80 per cent had been certified as effective (Lam, 1999, p. 139).

Finally, Jiang Zemin has used old-style ideological campaigns to try to instil discipline among the rank-and-file party members. The most notable were the 'Three Stresses' and the 'Three Represents' launched in 1999–2000 to build unity and to consolidate the power of Jiang as the paramount leader of the post-Mao period.

However, these attempts did not significantly restore party prestige and the party-strengthening campaigns did not have an enduring effect. The primary reasons were threefold. First, the increased social space that the party allowed was filled by a range of heterodox ideas and beliefs. The reforms of the 1980s and 1990s were not only accompanied by sharp debates among the party leadership but also by the public expression of quite unorthodox ideas. The party found it difficult to maintain its system of patronage for certain intellectual groups and social organizations while slowly losing control over the discourse that was filling the public spaces. Increasingly, public discourse was breaking free of the codes and linguistic phrases established by the party. These discourses revealed a weaker party and one whose authority was being slowly undermined. In the villages, for example, party control was challenged by the revival of traditional religious practices, and temples became places for not only worship but also the kind of reciprocity that was previously solely controlled by the party. The party has had to struggle against the revival of local religious leaders, clans, and triads as well as being challenged in some areas by private wealth. For some it has meant taking on multiple roles of being the party secretary and the local religious leader. One thing that is certain is that the party has become more contested and embroiled in daily life.

Second, the party itself lost much legitimacy in the eyes of many because of the extremely high levels of corruption that accompanied the reforms and the close identity of interest between business and official party position. As the historian Meisner (1996) has pointed out, with no commercial middle class when markets were introduced, it was local party officials who acted as the entrepreneurs and who became rich as a result. The pursuit of economic riches without genuine marketization and democratization and where power remains hierarchically structured with information dependent on position resulted in corruption being institutionalized. A system of state, society, party and bureaucratic reciprocities based on networks of favour, kinship, friendship and association has become the operational norm. Public enterprises controlled by the state became in practice fiefdoms plundered by those who ran them, with a market system in which goods and services were less important than power and prestige. The combination of party appointment to controlling positions and a dual economy created a hybrid economic formation that one might refer to as '*nomenklatura capitalism*'. The real good of value in this form of market is information that can be traded for money – or, more often, for further power (Apter and Saich, 1994). Party membership is crucial in this process.

Third, with the emphasis on economic development and the shift in the party's fundamental legitimacy to its capacity to deliver the economic goods, the objectives of party and state were not always synonymous. Neither is the obedience of party members at lower levels guaranteed. The party needed to affect its policy intent through mobilization of both party members and organizations at all levels and the implementation and enforcement by state organs. Local governments in pursuit of local developmental goals may take policy options that at best conflict with party policy and at worst run counter to it. The party cannot count on state organs for automatic policy support. A good example was the privatization of SOEs that was rife at the local level but deeply contested at the centre. This caused a fundamental tension between the party's traditional Leninist vanguard role and its other roles as an integrating mechanism and development agency.

These trends led one analyst to suggest that the party had abandoned its desire for ideological correctness and disciplined grass roots organizations to ensure maximum penetration into society. Instead it became a network of bureaucratic elites whose primary purpose was to retain power to protect their own interests (Zhao, 1997, p. 20). In all probability, the decline in attention to the grass roots comes more from default and lack of capacity than design.

The drive to maintain institutionalized party dominance provides stability and assurances as well as status for party cadres. However, at the same time this drive does much to explain the stifling of initiative that was increasingly apparent during the reform period. Previously, in combination with the dual-pricing system, it provided the structural basis for corruption that was heavily criticized not only by student demonstrators but also in the official Chinese press. The concentrated nature of power and the lack of a genuine system of accountability meant that party officials at all levels were in a unique position to turn professional relationships into personal connections for financial gain. Given this structure, the idea that the problem could be resolved by the punishment of a few middle-ranking officials and an ideological campaign to instil correct behaviour in cadres was a non-starter. It is a fundamental problem that affects CCP rule over the long term and will be returned to in Chapter 12.

5

The Central Governing Apparatus

Post-Mao policy has led to a revitalization of the state sector, with a renewed stress not only on the state's economic functions but also its legislative and representative functions. Policy also required the state to withdraw from its previous overbearing role and reduce administrative interference, and led to a major redistribution of power both horizontally and vertically with significant *de facto* powers decentralized to lower-level administrative units (see Chapter 6). This chapter first discusses some of the aspects of governance that do not appear on the organizational charts, then describes the structure of the central state apparatus, the legal and coercive system and the military in the political system.

Institutional integrity and jurisdictional authority have been less important than in many countries. Indeed it is the role of the state, including its judicial organs, to implement party policy. Yet state organs and individuals have a great capacity to distort party policy during the process of implementation. Not just Mao Zedong but also local leaders have intervened in the governing process to amend outcomes to suit their own preferences.

It is no surprise given China's immense size, the large population and attempts to retain a unitary state structure that the organization of government is very complex. While it is an authoritarian system, authority is, as Lieberthal (1992) has suggested, 'fragmented' both horizontally and vertically through the system. As a result, it is also a 'negotiated state' (Saich, 2000a), where local governments and even individual institutions vary in nature depending on the relationship they have negotiated with other parts of the *apparat* (see Chapter 8 for further discussion). The problem is compounded by the fact that formal organization charts often hide as much as they reveal about where real power lies in the system. The question of party dominance was dealt with in Chapter 4 and the relationship between the centre and the localities is covered in Chapter 6. Here a number of other important issues are briefly considered.

First, as noted in Chapter 4, despite the stress in the post-Mao period on the need to move to a rule of law and away from personal dictate, it is still a system where individuals hold immense capacity to circumvent formal regulations. This is true not just at the centre but also at the local levels, and it is difficult to tell the real extent of a person's power from their position on an organizational chart. One example of this is the system of personal secretaries that senior leaders maintain (Li and Pye, 1992). The party elite can choose their own secretaries and thus that person's loyalty will be primarily to the senior leader rather than to any organization as a whole. They often come to form a trusted inner cabinet acting as the 'eyes and the ears' of the senior leaders. Many of them may later go on to develop important political careers of their own.

Second, there are a number of organizations and relationships that do not appear on any chart but that are important for understanding power and control. These are the leadership groups at the centre, the organization of various systems that coordinate work and policy in broad functional fields and the relationship between line command and horizontal command (for a fuller description of these see Lieberthal, 1995, pp. 192–207, 169–70). To coordinate work across a particular field, the central leadership organizes a small group that is usually headed by a member of the Standing Committee of the Politburo. The group may be set up to oversee a particular problem at a particular time or they may be more permanent, such as those that oversee party affairs, agriculture, propaganda, economics, foreign affairs or state security (Hamrin, 1992). These more permanent groups are often referred to in China as being 'gateways' (*kou*) that link the elite to a functional area within the party and state system. In the past, control of crucial 'gateways' was a source of conflict. In the late 1980s when Zhao Ziyang was moved to be CCP general secretary for example, he fought with Li Peng, the new premier, for control over the economics 'gateway'. Through his control, Li was able to keep him out of the loop on a number of key policy issues (interview with official concerned). By the end of the 1990s, interviews with relevant officials suggested that these 'gateways', with the exception of party affairs and propaganda, had declined in importance. Control over finance and economics had shifted effectively to the groups working under the State Council system, reflecting greater professionalization of the system, and others such as agriculture met only once a year before the main party-work conference.

Below these senior leadership groupings functional bureaucracies are grouped together in what the Chinese call a 'system' (*xitong*), and Chinese commonly refer to themselves as working in a particular *xitong*. The *xitong* should coordinate policy and attempt to monitor its implementation: no easy task in such a dispersed bureaucratic system. *Xitong* has a narrow and a broader meaning; some use it to refer to all the units within the jurisdiction of a particular ministry or commission, while others might refer to the broader group of functionally related bureaucracies that cross individual ministry or industry lines (Barnett, 1967). While there are many *xitong* in this second sense, Lieberthal (1995) identifies 6 major ones: party affairs, organization and personnel, propaganda and education, political and legal affairs, finance and economics and the military. These *xitong* link to the leadership groups at the centre and while they may provide some coordination, they are not entirely effective for either implementation or feedback.

The problems of bureaucratic coordination have resulted in tensions between what Schurmann (1968, pp. 188–94) refers to as a 'vertical' and 'dual' rule that proximates to what the Chinese call *'tiao'* (branches) and *'kuai'* (areas). The dominance of one over the other will affect how central policy is implemented and how authority is exerted. *Tiao* indicates that a ministry at the central level has control over all the units at the lower levels that come under the scope of its jurisdiction. As a result, the flow of information and command runs vertically up and down the system. *Kuai* indicates that the party committee at each level would be the primary point of authority coordinating the activities of the organizations within its geographical jurisdiction. It amounts to a form of dual rule as the unit at the lower level is responsible to the corresponding departments of the line ministry and the higher levels as well as to the party committee at the same level. In the first pattern, it is the line ministry or equivalent that exerts a 'leadership relationship' (*lingdao guanxi*) over those below, whereas in the second it is the party at the same level that enjoys this authority.

Which of these relationships dominates varies over time and one Western author has interpreted post-1949 history as a struggle over the dominance of *tiao* or *kuai* (Unger, 1987). The system of vertical control was adopted under the First Five-Year Plan, but it caused the growth of specialized bureaus at the lower levels that were responsible to the corresponding departments at the higher level but that were resistant to party supervision at the same level. This did not lend itself to the kind of political mobilization preferred by Mao, that was to be led through the party system at the various levels. As a result, in 1956 the Eighth Party Congress adopted the system of branches. In practice this enabled the party to keep control over the state system as the party committee at each level was the only body capable of coordinating the activities of all other units. During the Great Leap Forward, following the 1957 decentralization measures, the party took almost complete control over the state administration at lower levels and ministries of the State Council were effectively cut off from their functional departments at the lower levels. On the whole the dominance of *tiao* leads to the development of large industrial systems, while the dominance of *kuai* supports a policy of local self-sufficiency with the development of autarkic economic systems. The reforms have tried to move China away from this tug of administrative war but the main result has been greater *de facto* independence for the localities to pursue their own development strategies within broadly defined guidelines.

Given this background, one might wonder whether it is worth spending much time on the formal organization structure at the centre. However, as Blecher (1997, p. 117) has pointed out, at the very least the formal institutions shape the overall nature of the state and politics and it is thus important to understand them, how they function and how they interrelate. Second, slowly but surely China has been moving towards a greater institutionalization of the policy process and the central institutions have became a focal point for lobbying by diverse groups and interests as they formulate rules and regulations. Third, the central state has presided over a massive body of legislation to support the economic and social reforms since the 1980s. If China is to complete its transition to a market economy, it will require a competent national government to adjudicate disputes, to interpret the rules, to give concrete form to the emerging norms and to devise new institutional forms.

Central Government

The Constitution

The question of whether it is worth studying the formal aspects of China's political system is even more apparent when one talks about the relevance of the Constitution to actual political practice. While much of the important politics in China is informal and thus parts of the Constitution cannot be taken at face value – for example, rights extended in one part may be contradicted in another – as a whole it does provide a useful guide to the leadership's thinking about the present situation and gives an indication of the way in which they would like to see it evolve. In this sense, like the three previous State Constitutions, the 1982 version and its amendments provide the reader with a good barometer for China's political, economic and social climate (Saich, 1983a, p. 113). This is clearly demonstrated with the leadership's evolving acceptance of the non-state sector of the economy. At the NPC meeting in March 1999, the role of the non-state sector was elevated from being 'a complement to the socialist public economy' to 'an important component of the socialist market economy'. Similarly, the change of the phrase 'counterrevolutionary activities' to 'crimes jeopardizing state security' reflected China's attempts to move towards international norms on legal issues.

The PRC has been governed by four Constitutions. The years immediately following the establishment of the regime were a time of radical political, social and economic restructuring and it was not until September 1954 that the first Constitution was adopted detailing the new state structure. Inevitably, it owed much to the Soviet system of government and paralleled that of the party with three levels of government below the centre – the province, the county or municipality and the town or commune. With minor changes, this structure has remained the same since. The first Constitution effectively ceased to operate in 1966–67, when the Cultural Revolution (1966–76) resulted in the disruption of established institutional arrangements and produced new structures and processes that had little, if any, constitutional validity. The second Constitution was adopted in January 1975 and reflected the more radical atmosphere of the Cultural Revolution. This was replaced by the third constitution, adopted in March 1978, that marked the initial attempts to restore the pre-Cultural Revolution system. The current Constitution was adopted in December 1982.

In general the 1982 Constitution reflects the leadership's concern to create a more predictable system based on a clearer separation of roles and functions and a system of clearly defined rules and regulations applicable to everyone. The Constitution defines the nature of the state as 'a socialist state under the people's democratic dictatorship', a concept similar to the 1954 definition of China as a 'people's democratic state'. These two Constitutions were adopted during periods when the emphasis in policy-making was on economic development. Clearly, the intention was to use a definition that incorporated as many people as possible, thus limiting the number of people to be considered as enemies of the state. This accords with the utilization of united front tactics by the pro-reform leadership in the 1980s. Vital to this approach was the downgrading of the importance of class struggle in Chinese society – a decision announced at the Third Plenum of the Eleventh CC (December 1978). Thus, the fiercer definition used in the 1975 and 1978 Constitutions of China as 'a socialist state of the dictatorship of the proletariat' was no longer deemed applicable.

All communist regimes suffer from the problem of party penetration into state affairs. In China this problem has been particularly acute, and during the Cultural Revolution any pretence at distinction between the two was effectively abolished. Thus, at the start of the Cultural Revolution, the organs of party and state at the non-central levels were identical. The revolutionary committee, which replaced the pre-1966 party and state organs, initially combined the functions of both in one committee. Even after 1969 when the party structure was gradually rebuilt, confusion persisted concerning the correct division of responsibilities between the party and the revolutionary committee. To resolve this problem the post-Mao leadership abolished the revolutionary committee and restored the pre-Cultural Revolution system of local government.

The 1982 State Constitution reflected the attempt to free the state sector from the grip of the party. Unlike the more 'radical' constitutions of 1975 and 1978, the power of the party was played down in the Constitution. Reference to the party as the 'core of leadership' was dropped, as was the claim that it was the citizens' duty to support the party. Mention of party control now appears only in the preamble, where its leading role is acknowledged in the 'Four Basic Principles'. Yet, in practice, it is clear that the state's freedom for political manoeuvre remains circumscribed and limited.

The National People's Congress and the Chinese People's Political Consultative Conference

Since its creation in 1954, the NPC has been the highest organ of state power, but prior to this, during the period of the Common Programme (1949–54), the highest body was the Chinese People's Political Consultative Conference (CPPCC). In September 1949 the CPPCC met in Beijing to proclaim the establishment of the People's Republic of China (PRC). The CPPCC was a manifestation of the united front policy, which meant that many of its members were non-communists, but its ultimate purpose was to bring about its own replacement as the most important administrative body. The meeting elected the Central People's Government Council and the Government Administration Council, the forerunner of the State Council, and approved the Common Programme and the Organic Law that provided the principles of organization for the new state structure.

The CPPCC still functions, headed by a member of the Standing Committee of the Politburo, and has become a lively forum for discussion and policy suggestions on prominent social, economic and foreign policy affairs. It now meets annually, around the same time as the NPC. With the stress on harmony rather than class conflict it provides liaison with other political parties and promotes united front work, providing a discussion forum for some non-party intellectuals and figures prominent in other walks of life who have no party affiliation. At the session held in March 2000, there were calls for more private entrepreneurs to be recruited in light of their growing economic and political weight. In fact at the March 2001 session lack of effective representation was a complaint causing CPPCC head, Li Ruihuan, to call a review of how various sectors of society were represented (*SCMP*, 13 March 2001, Internet edition). This was reflected at the Tenth CPPCC (March 2003) where among the 2,238 delegates, 65 represented the 'non-state' sector; also included were some accountants and lawyers. There were 33 heads of major SOEs. The CPPCC provides the party and the NPC with expertise that is helpful for policy-making. The Ninth CPPCC (1998–2003) put forward 17,722 proposals of which 44 per cent were related to economic issues, 28 per cent to science and education and 27 per cent to legal reforms.

For CPPCC members, it provides a voice to influence policy-making over a range of economic and social questions. Evidence suggests that proposals from the CPPCC do have some impact, although it should be pointed out that they do not deal with fundamental questions of policy but rather with technical matters, environmental questions, or social issues. In discussions with CPPCC members over the years, they have identified two other values of membership. First, members are allowed to see an array of internal party and state documents that the general public is not allowed to see. Second, membership allows them to pick up subtle and not so subtle changes in the political winds before they are more generally apparent. This can afford them the time to adjust their public views and practices accordingly to head off any potential criticism.

At all levels, state power is vested in people's congresses. The highest organ of state is the NPC, which is composed of deputies elected by the provinces, autonomous regions and municipalities directly under the central government, and by the armed forces. The NPC is elected for a term of five years and holds one session in each year. To date, there have been nine national congresses held.

The Constitution vests in the NPC a wide range of powers and functions. It has the power to amend the Constitution, to make laws and to supervise the enforcement of constitutional and legal enactments. Formally it has a significant role in appointment of senior state officials. It elects the president and vice-president and shall 'decide on the choice of the Premier of the State Council upon the nomination of the President'. The 1978 Constitution stated that this be done 'upon the recommendation of the CC'. Similarly the NPC shall 'decide on the choice of vice-premiers, state councillors and ministers upon nomination by the Premier'. Some offices, however, are at the NPC's disposal without such constraints. Thus, it is empowered 'to elect' the chair of the Central Military Commission, the president of the Supreme People's Court and the Procurator General (see Figure 5.1). It also has the power to remove from office all those listed above, from the president downwards. The NPC is also entitled to examine and approve the national economic plan, the state budget and report on its implementation, to 'decide on questions of war and peace', and 'to exercise such other functions and powers as the highest organ of state power should exercise'.

At first glance these powers seem extensive, as indeed they are, but in practice it is not the NPC that controls them. Major decisions and appointments are made by the party, usually ratified by the CC before the NPC and passed on to the NPC for its 'consideration'. Within the party, normally the legal and political group of the CC or a special drafting committee will assess the proposed legislation and present its views to the CC. As O'Brien has noted, from its inception the NPC has lacked the organizational muscle to tell the State Council, ministries or courts what to do (O'Brien, 1990, p. 79). Further, the NPC has too many delegates (2,984 at the 2003 Tenth Congress) and meets too infrequently to really exercise its powers. Thus, the NPC elects a Standing Committee to act on its behalf when not in session. Because of its smaller size (approximately 150 members), it can hold regular meetings with comparative ease. Since 1987, the Standing Committee has met every two months. This body conducts the election of deputies to the NPC and convenes it. The 1982 Constitution adopted important increases in the powers of the Standing Committee; it has been given legislative power and the power to supervise the enforcement of the Constitution. When the NPC is not in session, the Standing Committee can examine and approve partial adjustments to the state plan and budget, and it is hoped that this will provide the state with flexibility and speed when reacting to problems in the economy. The Standing Committee's power of supervision over state organs has also been increased.

That said, it is clear that the NPC has strengthened as an organization; it has institutionalized and strengthened its input into decision-making in ways that are not an overall threat to party dominance, and its outcomes have become

FIGURE 5.1

Central Organization of the Chinese Government, March 1998

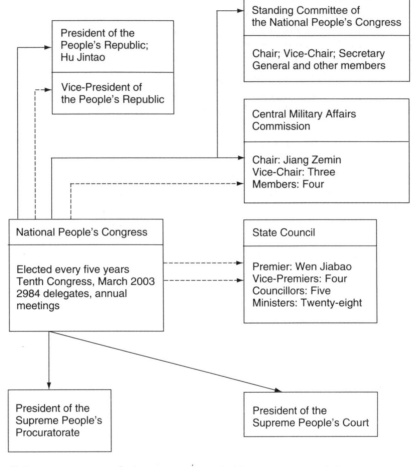

Note: ─────► = elects; ------► = decides on recommendation.

less easy to predict, as seen in its higher number of dissenting votes on legislation and personnel appointments. As with other parts of the political system, the party cannot guarantee absolute support and has accepted a looser form of control than in the Maoist days when the NPC was simply stocked with model workers and peasants, pliant intellectuals and senior party leaders. However, 68.4 per cent of delegates to the Eighth NPC were CCP members (Cabestan, 2000, p. 7) and this rose to 71.3 per cent at the Ninth (*FEER*, 6 March 2003).

It seems that this form of looser control was accepted by Jiang Zemin after a brief attempt to exert party control after 1989 (for details see Tanner, 1999, p. 111; 1994, pp. 397–402). In February 1991, a CC document outlined that party leadership was, henceforth, to be limited to establishing overall policy direction, with the Politburo reviewing and confirming draft laws before they were sent to the NPC for final discussion and approval. It was also acknowledged that most articles would not need detailed review and that certain 'less important' laws might not even need to be reviewed by the Politburo. The document also made subtle changes in the relationship between the NPC and the ministries and agencies under the State Council. Through much of the 1980s the NPC had been reactive, responding to legislation as it was submitted from the State Council system. Now it was required that ministries should report significant political laws they were drafting to the NPC leadership in advance. In addition, NPC leaders were placed in charge of working out any problems with such legislation with the Politburo or the Secretariat.

In a further sign of regularization, the March 2000 session of the NPC passed the 'Legislation Law' that sought to bring some clarity to the question of who could make laws on what and when. Most importantly, the new law made it clear that only the NPC could draft law in areas regarding basic human rights, litigation and taxation. In other areas the State Council, local governments and congresses could still legislate. Second, it endorsed the rights of local legislatures to pass laws when national legislation did not exist. However, once national law is passed, then the legislation must be brought into line. (The centre had been embarrassed in 1993 when Shenzhen passed its own Company Law after launching China's first stock exchange.)

The reforms have also breathed life into the debates at the NPC meetings, but while challenging its image of being a 'rubber stamp' it is far from functioning as a Western legislature. As O'Brien (1990, p. 178) has concluded, reform of the NPC system has led to limited inclusion as a substitute for liberalization, not a sign of it. There have been reports in the Chinese press about policy debates conducted during the sessions and voting has become far from unanimous. The particular individual who chairs the NPC still makes a difference but there is an increasing sense in which the chair also comes to represent the institutional and policy interests of the NPC. Thus under the leadership of the orthodox Peng Zhen in the mid-1980s, the NPC acted to hold up reform legislation on the question of bankruptcy and a new enterprise law that was designed to increase the power of managers at the expense of party committees. It was only when Peng was replaced by the reformer Wan Li that the delaying tactics ceased. By contrast, given his previous experiences in the pre-1949 base area of Jin-Cha-Ji, Peng pushed and promoted experimentation with village elections and presided over a draft law regularizing them nationwide.

It is interesting to note that when Li Peng became chair in 1998, while not known for his democratic credentials, he became a champion of both the programme of village elections and the role of the congress system. In this, Li has followed in the footsteps of his three predecessors as chair, Peng Zhen (1979–88), Wan Li (1988–93) and Qiao Shi (1993–98). All three made speeches about the need for the NPC to shed its passive role and to provide serious monitoring and evaluation of party policy. Peng had been secretary general of the NPC in the 1950s and he voiced support for the assertiveness of the NPC and an increased institutionalized role in policy-making. Following the events of 1989, Wan held the view that 'further policy mistakes and catastrophes could be avoided if the party used the NPC as an institutionalized device for listening to the complaints of the people' (Tanner, 1999, p. 107). The NPC system became a strong platform for Qiao Shi's promotion of the rule of law and the right to engage in elite party politics, significantly a battle in which he ultimately lost to the party general secretary, Jiang Zemin. Jiang himself inevitably stressed the need for NPC delegates to hold to the party line. Under the leadership of Li Peng this received more attention and at the NPC session held in March 2000, he called for deputies to 'support the party's leadership over the work of the people's congress' (*SCMP*, 10 March 2000, Internet edition). This 'party-first' concept seemed to roll back some of the increased powers that Li's predecessor Qiao Shi had carved out for the NPC. While Qiao strove to increase NPC capacity to supervise the party as well as the government, Li seemed more content to boost its powers over government and judicial units. In line with Jiang's and Li's wishes, the power of the party cell over CCP NPC legislators was strengthened. This tightening of control was even more apparent at the non-central levels where 23 party secretaries from the 31 provinces or equivalents also headed the legislature, something that Zhao Ziyang's reforms had tried to stop.

The clash of views between the orthodox leaders who still see the NPC as having only a 'rubber stamp' function and those who favour genuine debate was highlighted at a number of NPC sessions. At the March–April 1989 session the orthodox premier, Li Peng, clearly saw the session as simply necessary to provide the seal of approval for his proposals for economic retrenchment. To ensure his objectives were met, he tried to muzzle both China's domestic press and the delegates to the congress. Indeed, China's most strongly pro-reform newspaper was barred from sending reporters to cover the proceedings. The rest of the Chinese press corps was told not to cover the delegates' complaints, only their positive remarks. Delegates were asked not to raise troublesome issues but to confine themselves to patriotic displays of support for central policy. Such attempts to ensure that only the bright things of socialist life were covered is more reminiscent of the Cultural Revolution years than the 'open-door policy' pursued under Deng Xiaoping.

However, these strictures could not prevent some of the discontent coming to public view and the NPC Rules of Procedure passed by the meeting contained a clause that delegates should enjoy immunity during debates. Questions raised at the meeting by delegates reflected a more independent spirit and showed how increasingly difficult it had become to stage-manage such events. The biggest success of the dissenting voices was the temporary halting of the project to build a huge dam across the Yangzi River that would have major social, economic and environmental consequences. Some 270 delegates criticized this project during the meeting and consideration of construction was to be delayed until 1995 at the earliest. Given that this was a pet project of Premier Li Peng, perhaps many felt that this was also a way of making a personal snub. However, shortly after the events of 1989, Li Peng brought the issue back to the NPC, muzzled all criticism and bulldozed the measure through at the March 1992 NPC session. Resentment was even displayed at the special treatment that the coastal areas received. In his work report, Li Peng supported the policy of rapidly developing the coastal regions and a special motion was passed that gave Shenzhen, the city and SEZ over the border from Hong Kong, special privileges in terms of drafting its own legislation. Opposition was shown by the fact that 274 delegates voted against the motion while a further 805 abstained – a record at that time in NPC voting.

While this may have been an initial high tide of NPC assertiveness, events a couple of months later showed that on any vital issue the NPC was a mere sideshow to the decisions made by the senior party leadership. In May 1989, after the State Council had promulgated the imposition of martial law, around one-third of the NPC's senior leaders signed a petition calling for its standing committee to be convened to consider this step (Hu, 1993, pp. 3–34). There was also the hope among many demonstrators that then NPC Chair Wan Li might return from his overseas trip and call the NPC to order and provide a constitutional resolution to the friction that was dividing the party, state and society. On both counts people were disappointed and the NPC was shut out of any meaningful role.

In the 1990s, the NPC picked up its role of occasional assertiveness and was especially robust in monitoring the annual work report of Premier Li Peng, demanding numerous revisions. In general, the NPC tried to exert greater scrutiny over the different *apparats* within its jurisdiction. For example, the NPC Finance and Economic Subcommittee heard reports from relevant ministers on economic development. With such senior economists as Li Yining and Dong Furen among its ranks, it is not surprising that ministers and their teams were challenged and heavily criticized. Negative votes have been increasing. Tanner (1999, p. 123) has compiled the statistics for the known votes in the 1990s and has concluded that large numbers of dissenting votes became common. Of the 23 known votes on personnel appointments and other motions in the 1990s, 6 received dissenting vote totals of over 20 per cent. Of 12 known votes on draft laws since 1989, dissenting votes exceeded 10 per cent on seven occasions, 20 per cent on five and reached 32–41 per cent on three occasions.

The NPC has also been willing to express its disapproval of candidates for vice-premier positions whom it feels lack competence and are clearly being appointed for factional reasons. Even Jiang Zemin's election as president in March 1998 was not unanimous, with 2,882 votes in favour, 36 against and

29 abstentions: not a large number but interesting all the same given the enormous build-up of Jiang's pre-eminent status that had followed the Party Congress (1997). In fact, as most positions only have one candidate, negative votes can tell much about a candidate's popularity. Thus, while Li Peng received 2,290 (85 per cent) of the votes at the Ninth NPC, Zhu Rongji received 2,890, with only 60 abstaining or voting against (Cabestan, 2000, p. 10). Wen Jiabao in 2003 only had 19 abstentions or votes against. Yet even the reformist Premier Zhu Rongji has had problems getting through legislation. For example, in April 1999 the Standing Committee of the NPC voted down a new Highway Law because of the fuel tax that it intended to bring in. Zhu's intention was to use the fuel tax to raise revenue to substitute for the myriad of local tolls and levies on road users from local officials. Some delegates resisted because they claimed this was a return to central planning and others pointed out that the tax would increase the costs to farmers, because the farmers would be taxed if they purchased fuel even though the vehicles were to be used on their land and not on the roads. The Standing Committee voted 76–6 for the legislation with 42 abstentions: 78 votes were needed to pass it. In November 1999, the legislation was presented again and was passed. On this occasion, the Finance Minister assured the legislators that the impact of the fuel tax would be offset by paying compensation to the farmers in accordance with their farm size (Interview with legislators concerned).

In addition, the NPC has found a popular cause with respect to law, order and corruption. It has been highly critical of various reports of the heads of the judiciary and the procuracy, reflecting popular disenchantment with the legal system. At the Ninth NPC, the candidate for chief prosecutor received only 65 per cent of the votes. Many voted against him both because of his age (66) and because they felt that a career as minister of railways was perhaps not the best legal training. In addition, nearly half of the delegates voted against the annual work report of the procurator-general, the largest negative vote in NPC history. This resulted in greater consideration being given to the report and delegates' views the following year. At the Tenth NPC the court report received a 79.4 per cent approval rating while that for the procurator received 74.6 per cent approval.

How the NPC will develop in the future is, like all things, difficult to predict, but it is the hope of many reformers in China. They feel that the institutional strengthening that has taken place and the professionalization of NPC staff will lead to an even more assertive role on policy-making and implementation and that it will even begin to hold the party to greater accountability. Periodically since the early 1990s suggestions from party reformers have been submitted, suggesting that direct elections be introduced for provincial level congresses, leading eventually to national elections.

Certainly a rolling back of the NPC's role is unlikely in the immediate future. It has carved out an institutional space for itself that is supported by significant individuals and interests within the system. In addition, as legislation becomes more complex and specialized more power will move to those with the necessary skills to research and draft more elaborate regulations. The NPC is well placed in this process, with a number of specialized committees including legal affairs, finance and economics, education, foreign affairs, environment and agriculture. Its staff expanded significantly during the 1980s and 1990s and many of those newly recruited were well qualified and committed to building the rule of law and helping the NPC assert its role more strongly in the political system. During the mid- and late 1990s, I met a number of NPC staffers and was struck both by their professional capacity and their belief in what they were doing. Many see the NPC as an important part of China's future and are convinced that its influence will grow. The Research Department of the General Office has begun an active programme of study, seminars and exchanges with its counterparts in other countries of the world, including France, Germany, Italy, Japan, the United Kingdom and the United States. In one seminar of these professionals in the mid-1990s, I was surprised that despite the systemic differences there was a common language spoken. NPC staffers were interested to hear the French and Germans discussing the advantages and disadvantages of a presidential system, what happened when the prime minister and president were in conflict, how staff dealt with getting absentee and overworked legislators to understand complex pieces of legislation; they were amused to hear from the British how Byzantine books of precedent can be used to keep legislators safely under the thumb of professional staffers.

The State Council

The highest organ of state administration remains the State Council, which is the executive organ of the NPC. In theory, it is responsible and accountable to the NPC and its Standing Committee and is, in effect, the government of China. It is able to submit proposals on laws to the NPC or its Standing Committee as well as to formulate administrative measures in accordance with the laws; to exert leadership over the non-central levels of administration as well as the ministries and commissions; to draw up and put into effect the national economic plan and state budget; and to oversee public order and safeguard the rights of citizens. The work of the State Council is presided over by an executive board composed of the premier, vice-premiers, state councillors and the secretary general.

Under the State Council are the various ministries, commissions, committees, bureaus and ad hoc organizations, the total number of which has varied over time. There has been a general tendency for the number of such organizations to expand followed by attempts at retrenchment. Prior to the attacks on the administration in the Cultural Revolution there were 45 ministries and commissions, whereas by the time of the Fourth NPC (1975) this had been reduced to 29. With the reforms, the number had ballooned to 52 by the end of 1981. In 1982, this was cut again to 41 with the number of ministers and vice-ministers reduced from 505 to 167 (Saich, 1983b, pp. 634–6). In part, the ebb and flow of personnel numbers derived from the lack of an effective retirement system in the 1970s and 1980s. True to form, the number of ministries, commissions and other offices under the State Council crept up again to total 86 by 1992.

The rise in the number of cadres and of the administrative organs under the State Council became too expensive for the state to cover. The need to streamline was intensified by the state's deteriorating budgetary situation. In 1991, 36 per cent of total financial expenditure went to administrative and operating expenses. This led under Jiang and Zhu to a continuous attempt from 1992 both to reduce the size of the bureaucracy and to change its functions from direct governance to more indirect regulation. The first step was to reduce the offices under the State Council from 86 to 59 while reducing government employees at all levels by 25 per cent and State Council employees by approximately one-third. There were some 4 million cadres working for the central government with 35 million working in the localities in 1996, up from some 18 million when the reforms began. The first objective was to slow the growth by introducing a retirement system, finding alternate work for cadres and then cutting the absolute number. By the mid-1990s the growth rate had been slowed. In the early 1950s the ratio of cadres to population was around 1: 90 but by the 1980s it had fallen to 1: 25, by 1996 it had eased somewhat to 1: 34.

However, the cuts were still insufficient, and the Ninth NPC (March 1998) announced an institutional 'revolution' to produce a more efficient, well-integrated and standardized administrative system that would meet China's needs. The then Secretary General of the State Council, Luo Gan, in announcing the programme, stated that many functions appropriated by government organs be given back to society and handled by commercial enterprises or new social intermediary organizations. Luo noted that the government had 'taken up the management of many affairs that it should not have managed, is not in a position to manage, or cannot manage well' (see *FBIS-CHI-98-068*). This overload not only led to a massive wage and administrative bill but also detracted from the government's capacity to carry out its work effectively. Luo traced a primary cause of this problem to the fact that the administrative system had evolved with a planned economy. There was insufficient separation of government and enterprise and the government was directly involved in enterprise production and management with the result that it had set up a large number of special economic management departments. The overall objective was to strengthen macroeconomic regulation and control departments while reducing the specialized economic departments, social services departments were to be reduced with individuals and social organizations taking on greater responsibility, and legal and supervisory departments were also to be strengthened.

In practice, this meant cutting the existing 44 departments under the State Council to 29 ministries, commissions, administrations and banks with a further reduction to 28 at the Tenth NPC (March 2003). Twelve actual ministries were dissolved together with three commissions, and four new major ministries were created to absorb some of the defunct departments. In addition, the old State Planning Commission was renamed the State Development Planning Commission and then the State Development and Reform Commission that was put in charge of guiding the overall reform programme. In the domestic trade area, changes were dramatic. First, the State Economic and Trade Commission (SETC) that was set up in 1993 absorbed the ministries of coal, the metallurgical industry, machine-building industry and internal trade, which were all turned into bureaus under its jurisdiction. Having completed this task, in 2003 the Commission itself was abolished with its duties farmed out to various other ministries. In 2003 the formerly powerful Ministry of Foreign Trade and Economic Cooperation was dissolved into a new Ministry of Commerce that will oversee both international and domestic trade.

Control over SOEs that had been with the SETC was placed under a new State Asset Management Commission that would function as a holding company for government stakes in the SOEs. The expectation is that the Commission will reduce its holdings over time. The creation of this Commission marked part of an attempt to move to a regulatory state and was accompanied by the creation of a China Banking Regulatory Commission and a State Food and Drug Administration. The former took over certain powers from the central bank to oversee the restructuring of the banking sector and reducing the non-performing loans. The latter is modelled on the US administration that oversees the food and pharmaceutical industries

This restructuring allowed Premier Zhu to announce in March 2003 that in addition to the reduction from 49 to 28 state agencies, one-quarter of the State Council's departments and a further 9 state industrial administrations had been abolished resulting in a 50 per cent reduction in the workforce. However the cuts have been resisted. A number of ministries tried to use arguments about social stability to resist too deep cuts in their staff: they argued that with too many lay-offs there might be a greater chance of social unrest. At the same time, ministries such as foreign affairs and state security argued for an increase in their staff quotas. The former argued that with China's integration into the world proceeding apace it required more qualified personnel. The latter argued that with social stability paramount it needed more staff to guarantee this. The Bureau of Internal Trade, which was downgraded from a ministry and was scheduled to be abolished and submerged fully under the SETC, looked to the United States and foreign examples for salvation. It argued that even the United States, the most market-oriented country, retained the equivalent of a Ministry of Commerce (Interviews with officials concerned). Although the Ministry of Commerce was created, the old Bureau had taken a major hit, having reduced its staff from 842 to 160.

Clearly not all the employees from the various ministries became unemployed. Some former government departments were shifted to become economic entities, some staff were allocated to the industrial sector while one report stated that the government had instituted a scheme whereby 13,000 places in universities were to be provided for the laid-off cadres. This was simply a bureaucratic reshuffling, with responsibility shifted to the universities that were themselves under pressure to cut back on staff.

It remains to be seen whether this latest round of bureaucratic retrenchment will be more successful than other attempts. Previously, after an impressive start the numbers have quickly climbed again. However, there are grounds for optimism that while the numbers may creep up again, they will not rise to the levels of the 1980s. The reform attempts of the 1980s were hampered by a number of factors in addition to the lack of an effective retirement system. Most important was that attempts to streamline the bureaucracy were launched at the same time that other demands such as revamping the legal system, regularizing economic activities and dealing with international trade, were causing a bureaucratic expansion. In the 1980s a government job was still thought of as the best and there was very little in the way of a private sector to absorb those laid off. By the turn of the century the situation was quite different. Government was not the job that people aspired to and there were many good alternative opportunities for those sufficiently qualified who wanted to leave government. Second, a functioning retirement system had been put in place that reduced the incentive for many to stay on the active payroll. Third, after 25 years of reform the role of government in the economy and society has changed and many are cognizant of this fact and feel that a less extensive government apparatus is needed. Last but not least, China can no longer afford to pay for such a large government infrastructure neither at the central levels nor in the localities.

The Legal System, Coercive Control and Rights

When the reforms began in the late 1970s, the legal system was effectively at ground zero. What had not been undermined by the campaigns of the late 1950s was destroyed in the Cultural Revolution. The first task in rebuilding the legal system was to devise a system of rules and known procedures to govern people's daily lives to provide reassurance and comfort after what was described as the anarchy and lawlessness of the previous decade. In major part this entailed a resurrection of the Soviet-inspired system that was set up after 1949. However, as economic reform took off this was equalled in importance and even surpassed by the need to legislate for the new economy. As China opened up more to the outside world there was the pressing need to introduce legislation that would reassure foreign investors and slowly move this area of law towards international practices. This will take on greater importance as China enters the WTO. As Premier Zhu announced (Zhu, 2003) in March 2003, the State Council reviewed 2,300 foreign-related regulations and policies, abolished 830 of them and revised a further 325.

This combination of factors means that the Chinese legal system operates under a complex set of influences that often contradict one another. The more recent influences come from European law, especially with regard to the state, from US law, mainly felt through international investment and trading practices, and sit aside the longer-term inheritance from Soviet practice and Marxist theory that subjugates the law to the needs of the state. All these influences lay over Chinese traditional practice that has not emphasized a regular legal process in a Western sense, and that has not been overconcerned about formal institutions. Not surprisingly, the end result is that 'China does have a set of institutions for the preservation of social order and governmental authority, but these institutions operate on very different principles from institutions usually called "legal"' (Clarke, 1995, p. 92).

The legal system is simply one specific cog in a bureaucratic machine that is built to achieve state objectives. It enjoys parity with other bureaucratic entities and thus there is no immediate notion that the decision of a court is binding on another administrative agency or across different geographical locations. This means that once a court decision is made, the judiciary may have to negotiate with other agencies to realize the desired outcome, or the court decision may simply be ignored or be unenforceable (see Box 5.1). This kind of system means that enforcement is variable, depending on the power of the administrative agencies concerned. Thus, while enforcement of environmental regulation has remained weak, public security agencies have a greater capacity.

In addition to the bureaucratic fragmentation that often prevents the enforcement of a court decision, there is the fact that all law is seen to be in the service of 'socialism', meaning that the party can override any legal decision and intervene where it thinks appropriate. The binary nature of politics and law, like propaganda and education, in the CCP's view is shown by the coupling of the two characters *zheng* and *fa* in Chinese. Thus, the relevant party committees are political–legal affairs committees and the major specialized legal training university in Beijing is called the University of Political Science and Law.

From 1954 to 1966 a legal system of sorts developed and over 1,100 statutes and decrees were promulgated to add to the handful of very wide-ranging, vague and highly politicized directives of the early years. Attempts to enjoy 'socialist legality' were overridden by party interference in the form of political campaigns, and the legal system as such was dominated by the public security organs. The police agencies were responsible for the maintenance of public order; the investigation, arrest and detention of suspects; and the administration of the prisons and 'Reform Through Labour' camps.

BOX 5.1

The Problem of Implementing Court Decisions

The Centre for Women's Law Studies and Legal Services of Peking University takes on the litigation of selected cases that centre staff believe to be of significant importance for women or that are in some ways representative. One woman came to them who had been abused by her husband and wished to file for divorce. This sounds simple; the Centre took on the case and won the case for the woman. The settlement included the decision that she and the child should have the housing, with the husband moving out. However, the housing was allocated through the husband's place of work and despite the court order the workplace did not act. Their reason was that housing was tight, they could not move the husband, and the woman did not have an entitlement in her own right to housing at the work-unit. The woman therefore had to remain living with her abusive husband. The court had no mechanism to enforce its ruling. The Centre did not leave things there. During President Clinton's visit (1998), Hillary Rodham Clinton and Secretary of State Madeleine Albright visited the Centre to highlight China's progress in establishing the rule of law. The case was presented by Centre staff at the meeting and the problem was very quickly solved in the woman's favour after it was widely reported by the foreign correspondents accompanying the presidential visit. In another case, the Centre won against a Beijing employer for failure to pay wages to 80 women over a period of two years. He acknowledged that this was the case but simply declared that he had no money to pay them with. The court had no capacity to enforce payment.

Although prosecution was supposedly the function of separate prosecutorial organs, these tended to be subordinate to the police. They also enjoyed legal powers in some instances to imprison offenders without the formality of a trial.

It may not have been law in the Western sense but there were some understood norms that people could grasp. For example, those with a 'bad' class background (landlords) would receive harsher punishment for the same transgression as would a worker or peasant. Similarly, a party cadre could get off punishment more lightly if they confessed their guilt, turned in others and displayed repentance for their 'crime'. There is evidence that many police took their job seriously, went to considerable pains to collect and sift evidence, and usually arrested someone only after they had built up a solid case. The exception was in political campaigns that soon undermined any attempt to establish norms.

The Cultural Revolution finally destroyed even these small semblances of predictability. The legal organs themselves were early points of attack and were labelled as 'bourgeois' by those who sought to abolish them. One of the important bodies abolished was the People's Procuratorate that had operated between the public security forces and the people's courts, rather like the District Attorney's office in the United States. Its powers were given to the police at the various levels, meaning that to a large extent the arbitrary power of the police became enshrined in the Constitution. However, especially in the first years of the Cultural Revolution the police themselves also came under attack. In one province alone it was claimed that 281 police stations were sacked, over 100,000 dossiers were stolen, and large quantities of guns and ammunition seized. For many police power was replaced by the summary justice of the Red Guards who set up their own 'people's courts' and prisons.

Given this inheritance, it is impressive the extent to which the legal system has been rebuilt and the feeling of security guaranteed for most citizens. However, problems remain, especially with respect to the dominance of the police in the legal system and the interference of the party at all levels of the political system. Not surprisingly, the new leadership displayed a massive display of revulsion against the anarchism and brutality of the Cultural Revolution period. The first step was to try to heal the political wounds. From 1977 the leadership began a lengthy process of investigation that resulted in the reversal of verdicts on hundreds of thousands of people who had suffered unjust punishments ranging from demotion to death. However, the leadership was careful not to allow criticism of the system as a whole and blame was placed squarely on the shoulders of the 'Gang of Four' for leading many astray. In addition, the leadership was very cautious about allowing investigation of the pre-Cultural Revolution system as a source of troubles. This is the theme of an interesting film, *Legend of Tianyun Mountain* (1980). The film's main theme is that the difficulties that plagued China as it entered the 1980s stemmed not just from the Cultural Revolution, as the 1981 official resolution on party history decrees, but derived from the 1950s and especially the anti-rightist campaign in which Deng Xiaoping played a prominent role (Pickowicz, 1989, p. 46). What emerges from the film is not identification with the 'good' cadres who had been harshly treated during the Cultural Revolution, but their exposure and replacement as heroes by those persecuted a generation before.

The process of regularization is covered by the phrase 'socialist legality' and Jiang Zemin's stress on the need to build a 'rule of law'. Thus a system of rules and regulations was to be created to replace the more arbitrary and uncertain situation of the Cultural Revolution. The fact that it was *socialist* legality set certain constraints and retained for the party the major role in deciding what was, and what was not, a crime. Further, it is clear that when Jiang and his advisers use the phrase 'rule of law' they do not mean a system that gives primacy to law above political considerations and party policy. Instead it is a way to manage power, regulate the economy and discipline society in light of the rapidly changing circumstances. In this sense, while it might provide greater predictability it is just another weapon in the arsenal of party control.

The process comprises two main elements. The first has been to resurrect the legal system, enact significant numbers of regulations and slowly to allow professionalization and differentiation of function within the legal system (for an excellent account of this rebuilding see Lubman, 1999). The second has been to protect citizens' rights and use law to show that it is indeed of significance. This second aspect has witnessed far slower progress.

In terms of legal rebuilding, the State Constitution adopted by the Fifth NPC (1978) resurrected the procuratorate system and after the NPC session there were concrete manifestations of the drive to restore law and order. This included the establishment of a Commission for Legal Affairs, the resurrection of the Ministry of Justice, the regularization of the people's courts system, the introduction of a series of laws and the reestablishment of law programmes at various key universities. Drafts of seven laws were presented to the Second Session of the Fifth NPC (June 1979), including the organic laws for the people's courts and people's procuratorate and, most importantly, the first criminal code and law of criminal procedure. These laws came into effect on 1 January 1980 to serve as the basis for the new socialist legality. A revised Criminal Procedure Law was passed in March 1996 to take effect on 1 January 1997 and an amended Criminal Law was adopted in March 1997 and went into effect on 1 October 1997. These provide a good window on how far the legal system has changed, and how far there is still to go in building a more impartial legal system.

The code of criminal law and the criminal procedure law were designed to promote the idea of equality of all before the law. The criminal law brought together in one relatively short document the major categories of criminal offence and the range of penalties they were likely to attract. Punishment could be given to anyone 16 or over, and of sound mind. The law paid attention to the need for stability, rejecting various legacies of the Cultural Revolution. Thus penalties were laid down for extracting confessions by torture; gathering a crowd for 'beating, smashing and looting'; bringing false charges; unlawfully incarcerating a person; and 'seriously insulting' a person by any means, including the use of wall-posters to spread libel. As Lubman has noted, the law, however, 'remained faithful to a politicized view of the criminal law' (Lubman, 1999, p. 160). The law paid great attention to what it termed 'counterrevolutionary' crimes; 24 articles dealt with this problem – included were not only predictable activities such as plotting to overthrow the government or leading armed rebellions, but also using 'counterrevolutionary slogans... to spread propaganda inciting the overthrow of the political power of the dictatorship of the proletariat and the socialist system'. These were the first official definitions of 'counterrevolutionary' behaviour, thus making it formally a crime to work against communism. In September 1989, the mere fact that six Tibetan Buddhist nuns shouted the slogan 'Independence for Tibet' was enough to have them arrested and five of them sentenced to three years of 'reform through labour'. According to Lubman (1999, p. 161), despite the various new provisions, the fundamental nature of the original law has not been altered. Most importantly, the need to move towards internationally accepted norms has meant that the crime of counterrevolution has been scrapped and replaced by the phrase 'crimes of endangering national security'. This definition can, in practice, still subsume all that was previously determined to be counterrevolutionary. The second major change reflects the increasing importance of the economy in law-making, with a large number of economic crimes added, such as smuggling or the making of false statements.

The Law on Criminal Procedure made meticulous arrangements for the handling of criminal cases, and carefully defined the rights and responsibilities of the legal organs and those accused. The role of the procuratorate is to exercise authority to ensure the observance of the Constitution and the laws of the state and to protect the rights of citizens. It decides whether to approve a request for arrest by a public security department, and also whether the person, if arrested, should be held criminally responsible. This was a marked change from Cultural Revolution practice. The public security organs are responsible for investigation of crimes, detention and arrest of suspects; the courts are to convene the public trials. In the 1980s, a number of amendments expanded police powers of detention and this, combined with the annual 'strike hard' campaigns launched in 1983, sanctioned a much more quota-driven, politicized form of policing once again. The continued role of the party is shown by the fact that all key appointments in both the procuratorate and court system fall under the *nomenclatura* system.

The Law also outlined an array of punishments, ranging from surveillance to the death penalty, including the particular Chinese decision of a two-year suspension of death sentence during which time the accused has the opportunity to show if she or he had 'reformed'. It also emphasized such basic procedures as that the accused was entitled to defence and that the court could appoint someone to defend the accused if they did not do so themselves, that the accused or the advocate could see the material pertaining to the case and that no one could be convicted on the basis of a statement unsupported by other evidence. In theory, police were, with certain exceptions, expected to arrest people only upon the production of a warrant from the procuratorate. After arrest, a detainee's family was normally to be informed within 24 hours and the procuratorate was to examine and approve the arrest within 3 days. Trials were to be public unless state secrets were involved and there were to be proper appeals procedures.

The revisions to the law were long in gestation and much fought over, with the public security organs unwilling to give up their powers to greater scrutiny and control by the procuracy and the courts (for a fascinating account of the amendments and the political background see Lawyers' Committee, 1996). Of the 164 articles in the original law, 70 have been amended and 2 eliminated, with 63 new articles added. The principal revisions were with respect to arrest and detention, defence counsel, initiation of prosecution and trial proceedings, while the regulation of investigation, evidence, appeal and review of death sentences were largely left alone (Lawyers' Committee, 1996, p. 19). The revisions eliminated a major method of police detention, called 'shelter and investigation', that allowed them to hold people indefinitely. Some estimate that after the promulgation of the original law, 80–90 per cent of arrests were first subjected to this method (Lawyers' Committee, 1996, p. 22). However, the concerns of the police were addressed by relaxing the standards for arrest and increasing the scope and length of pre-arrest detention. The Lawyers' Committee report (pp. 30, 32) argues that on the whole there has been some movement towards greater protection of the rights of suspected criminals in pre-trial detention, but certain aspects actually weaken restrictions on the use and length of pre-trial detention, and it still leaves China far from international norms in this area.

With respect to the trial process and the right to counsel there are some significant improvements. With respect to the trial, the revisions seek to differentiate more clearly the judge's function from that of prosecutor and defence lawyer and to give a greater role to the trial itself, with the evidence being reviewed during the trial rather than beforehand by the court. In addition, lawyers will now be able to see their clients from the moment that the case materials are transferred to the procuratorate for a decision to prosecute. However, both these advances can be removed by the decision that the case in question involves state secrets. This might seem a normal condition but the definition of what constitutes a 'state secret' is very open-ended, and in the past even maps, weather and disease information have been classified as such.

Last but not least, the revised law suggests movement towards the norm that there is a presumption of innocence. The amendment was made to state: 'In the absence of a lawful verdict of the people's court, no person should be determined guilty.' This would suggest that, unlike previously, the procuratorate cannot make a decision on guilt. However, the Lawyers' Committee report (1996, p. 63) concludes that the revisions result in 'little movement toward genuine acceptance of the presumption of innocence'. As the report states, many other aspects of the legislation that would facilitate this are severely restricted or simply absent. For example, suspected criminals may still be subject to lengthy pre-trial detention, there is no recognition of the right to remain silent, no exclusion of illegally gathered evidence and no right not to testify against oneself. The right to remain silent has been a major point of contention between the public security forces and reformers, who see its absence as a practice open to abuse and forced confessions.

As the above suggests, there has been progress towards greater regularization in law and the protection of individual rights, and it is true to say that most Chinese enjoy more individual freedom of choice than at any time since 1949. The party has taken itself out of much of daily life, and as long as one is law-abiding things are more predictable than they used to be. Party influence in the legal system remains considerable and is not restricted only to political offences. With the setting of quotas in the annual 'strike hard' anti-crime campaigns, there is strong pressure on the police and perhaps even encouragement to flout regulations on due process in order to meet targets. However, as student demonstrators in 1989, members of the China Democracy Party and of the spiritual movement *Falungong* have seen, once targeted as a political enemy the full force of the coercive state apparatus comes into play. In fact, although 'shelter and investigation' was removed from the revised Criminal Procedure Law, other forms of administrative detainment remain available to the police to pick up political suspects and to keep them under lock and key for significant periods of time. The most used is 'reeducation through labour' that allows detention from one to four years, and while used for misdemeanours it is also used to hold political dissidents. Recently, coming under increasing international scrutiny, China has begun to charge political dissidents under its criminal law, accusing them of tax evasion or consorting with prostitutes, as was the case with Peng Ming, the founder of the China Development Union, an opposition group set up in the mid-1990s.

The rise in political activity outside of the party's direct control has eroded somewhat the initial post-Mao concern with individual rights that had been so mercilessly flaunted in the Cultural Revolution. Like other communist states and a number of authoritarian Asian leaders, China has conceived of human rights in collective rather than individual terms. In so far as the four state constitutions promulgated since 1949 have enshrined the rights enjoyed in 'bourgeois' democracies, these have regularly been negated by other constitutional provisions, by actual practice or, in some instances, by subsequent constitutional amendments. The PRC has, in fact, gone to great lengths to restrict personal choice and it was only after Mao's death that attempts were made to bring about liberalization and to establish a predictable system.

The post-Mao leadership stress on the equality of all before the law was reflected in the 1982 Constitution with the restoration of the 1954 stipulation to this effect. Indeed the renewed emphasis on citizens' rights (and duties) and on the need to treat people in accordance with known rules and regulations is reinforced by the fact that the chapter on Fundamental Rights and Duties of Citizens is now placed second in the Constitution whereas in all previous Constitutions it stood third after the chapter on the State Structure (Saich, 1983a, p. 119). Interestingly, the 1982 Constitution did drop two citizens' rights from the 1978 Constitution. These are the freedom to strike and the freedom of the 'Four Bigs' – the right to speak out freely, air views fully, hold great debates and write big-character posters. The latter freedoms were considered too closely associated with the style of expression associated with the radicalism of the Cultural Revolution. The deletion of the right to strike was clearly influenced by events in Poland and the rise of Solidarity. One senior leader put up the rather weak defence that the reforms of the democratic management of enterprises meant that workers did not have to resort to the strike weapon as a means for redress of grievance. In this person's view, 'striking is not only disadvantageous to the state, but also harmful to the interests of the workers' (Hu, 1982, p. 17).

The question of rights has become a key point of contention not only domestically but also internationally, all the more so since the events of 1989. China has clearly resented external pressure on its rights record but has still felt compelled to defend it and to imply that it does indeed conform to internationally accepted norms. However, China has a poor understanding of these norms, as witnessed by its decision to sign the two UN covenants on rights (October 1997 and October 1998). China does not seem to have appreciated that by signing the covenants it is accepting that there are international norms concerning the freedom of organization, right to work, procession and formation of political groups that transcend national boundaries. China's leaders appear to have thought that they could sign on and then hold off implementation by retreating behind sovereign borders and talking about different histories and national conditions. The international human rights regime has been one forum in which China has been active in trying to shape guidelines. It has fought to resist scrutiny of domestic abuses while trying to focus attention on the actions of 'hegemonists and imperialists'. China has been a strong advocate of the right to development and has stressed that providing food and livelihood for its people takes precedence over rights of political expression and demonstration.

China has been particularly adamant in preventing monitoring of human rights by international agencies from leading to criticism of its domestic practices. It was particularly stung by the critical resolution in August 1989 adopted by the UN Subcommission on the Prevention of Discrimination and Protection of Minorities, the first time that a permanent member of the Security Council had been censured on human rights grounds in a UN forum. Subsequently, it fought a hard battle to escape criticism in the annual Geneva meetings of the UN Commission on Human Rights over the objections of the United States and the European Union. To escape this possible avenue of censure, China has moved to situate discussion of its human rights record in less intimidating bilateral forums. China declared its willingness to conduct discussions with countries on a one-to-one basis so long as pressure at Geneva was dropped. This was an effective strategy to marginalize concerted international censure of China's human rights abuses. In an interesting move in 2003, the United States decided not to propose a motion to criticize China at the annual Geneva meeting. After years of getting nowhere, the Bush administration decided a new approach, taking the Chinese leadership at its word that without Geneva there could be fruitful bilateral discussions and progress on specific issues concerning religious tolerance, political detainees and the excessive use of the death penalty.

However, like the former Soviet Union, China has tried to manipulate the 'international human rights game' and gain international concessions by timing the release of a few political prisoners (see Nathan, 1994, pp. 622–43; 1999, pp. 136–60). As the Soviet Union found, this is a difficult game to play. China's leaders have now acknowledged to the international community and their own people that they accept that certain UN-defined rights are universal, and that like it or not these can be held up to international scrutiny. Not only does this open up China to evaluation in terms of international norms, something it finds difficult to accept, but it also legitimizes debates on human rights domestically, something it finds problematic. Indeed, legal reformers in China have seized on the signing of the two covenants to provide an impetus for reform of some of the most problematic areas of domestic law, including eliminating the excessive use of the death penalty and avoiding the courts by sentencing people to reeducation through labour, and amending the criminal law to include things such as the right to remain silent. In fact, as one prominent legal specialist stated while China joined the economic mainstream 20 years ago, it now needed to join the human rights mainstream (Interview, September 1999).

The Military and the Political System

The PLA has formed an important element of state power in China, has stepped in to save the CCP at crucial moments and its support is crucial for any aspiring leader. That the role of the PLA has changed under the reforms is clear, but how it will continue to evolve and what the consequences are for the political system are less clear (for an excellent overview see Shambaugh, 2002). Neither Jiang Zemin nor Hu Jintao enjoy the prestige and authority within the military of either Mao Zedong or Deng Xiaoping. Mao and Deng were both significant military leaders and as such enjoyed an authoritative standing with their colleagues. This enabled them to convince the PLA to act in ways that were not necessarily in the military's best interests. This included Mao ordering the PLA to enter the fray of the Cultural Revolution and Deng ordering the military to clear Tiananmen Square of student demonstrators on the night of 3–4 June 1989. Both actions tarnished the reputation of the PLA in different ways. It is improbable that Jiang or Hu could enjoy such automatic support from the PLA, and will have to lobby its leaders, listen to its concerns and find ways to address them, while trying to promote a corps of officers that could be considered loyal. Within the new confines, Jiang has shown himself to be a capable political operator; however, support is more conditional than ever before. Continued support will depend on results not just in terms of providing the PLA with sufficient hardware and policy input in those areas that it considers vital to its interests, but also more broadly by guaranteeing economic growth and social stability.

Traditionally the PLA, unlike armies in the West, has been more than a professional standing army and has enjoyed a much wider field of operation than that of a bureaucratic pressure group competing for scarce resources. The role of the PLA – which includes the navy, the airforce and those divisions concerned with nuclear weaponry – in the Chinese political system owes its origins to the pre-liberation struggle. No consideration of the post-1949 communist regime can afford to ignore the importance of the military. Shambaugh (1997, p. 127) has even described the nature of the regime at its outset as one of military conquest. As he writes 'it is essential to view the CCP's victory as an armed seizure of power following protracted military campaigns'. Not only did many of China's citizens first witness the military conquest of the PLA before they met their new CCP leaders, but it was also the PLA that seized control of many of the factories, enforced land reform and played a leading role in reconstituting regional and local governments.

Certainly, the influence of the military was important before and after 1949, but this should not be taken to mean that the CCP was or is a military regime. However, the militaristic heritage has influenced CCP politics in significant ways, and it has also deeply affected the CCP's language. While Marxism, especially in its Leninist form, is punctuated by the language of struggle, particularly that of class, the terminology of the CCP is one of war: war on class enemies or the struggle to achieve production targets or the battle to overcome nature. This language combined with the mobilization campaigns that accompanied policy initiatives or denunciations of enemies explains, in part, the severe nature of post-1949 Chinese politics.

The positive view of the military in the PRC has been widely held. Individual soldiers or units have frequently been promoted as models for emulation because of their embodiment of the communist spirit. The best-known example of this is Lei Feng, the soldier who was put forward in the early 1960s during the PLA campaigns to study the thought of Mao, again after the fall of the 'Gang of Four' in 1976–77 and finally for young people to learn from after the party had called in the PLA to crush the student-led demonstrations in 1989. Essentially, the messages to be drawn from the study of Lei Feng are to be loyal, obedient, serve the party faithfully and unquestioningly and know and accept your place in the hierarchy. In the summer of 1998, the PLA was portrayed heroically fighting the summer floods. This helped restore prestige, which had fallen not only by its firing on unarmed students in 1989 but also by its various shady business dealings in the 1990s.

Before 1949, party and military leaders were often interchangeable and since 1949 many leaders have held concurrent party and military positions. Apart from causing institutional overlap, the liberation struggle has affected the functions of the military since 1949. The conditions during the Long March and in Yan'an and the need to rely on the population to wage guerrilla warfare meant that the PLA became a multifunctional body carrying out education and production tasks. The legacy of the past and the military success led Mao Zedong not only to have a highly favourable view of the military *per se*, but also as a participant in the political system. When Mao sought to purify the ranks of the party and state during the Cultural Revolution he turned to the army for help because he felt that under Lin Biao's leadership it embodied the 'true spirit' of the revolution. The military was seen to embody the plain-living, selfless values that Mao felt the party elite had abandoned.

Since 1949 there have been various attempts by some leaders to downgrade this 'traditional' role of the PLA and to 'professionalize' it by concentrating on its purely military functions. The most concerted and successful of these attempts has been since 1978. The fundamental question remains whether the military in politics acts as a homogeneous group pursuing military interests against those of other *apparats*, or whether the most important leadership differences cut across the different *apparats*. Related to this question are the often-quoted dichotomies of 'red' versus 'expert', and of 'politicization' and 'professionalization'. In fact, the military, especially at the non-central level, has always been involved in politics – but it is important to understand the nature of that involvement and how it has varied over time. Also the use of the singular term 'military' can be misleading because different factions have existed within the military itself.

Under Mao, the two main issues that involved the military – the purge of Peng Dehuai and the rise of Lin Biao and the PLA's intervention in the Cultural Revolution – were the result of broader political issues rather than those of a military interest. It is true that the removal of Peng Dehuai as Defence Minister followed the mid-1950s attempts to modernize the PLA along the lines of the Soviet army, but his fall was linked to a much deeper criticism of Mao's voluntaristic approach to development. On the military side Peng, as the commander of the People's Volunteers during the Korean War, had been affected by the large-scale losses and the inadequacy of the Chinese equipment. This and the Soviet example had led him and others to think about the need for military modernization. However, after the Korean War and with the Great Leap Forward, Mao made it clear that the PLA was to place a greater emphasis on its non-military work. This conflict over the PLA's roles provided the background to the military aspects of Peng's criticisms at the 1959 Lushan Plenum (Gittings, 1967, pp. 225–34). However, Peng did not limit himself to an attack solely from a military standpoint. He attacked the whole range of the policies pursued, even to the extent of telling Mao how the revolution in the countryside should be carried out. One can argue that a change of overall strategy might have benefited the military by allocating more money for investment in heavy industry, but this is not the same as saying that Peng acted as a military man airing his professional grievances. He acted as a senior Politburo member rather than a disgruntled Minister of Defence (Charles, 1961, pp. 63–76).

Peng's replacement as Minister by Lin Biao led to a revival of the Yan'an traditions but not all modernization work stopped. For example, the nuclear programme was continued but a greater emphasis was placed on the PLA's non-military roles. Political education was intensified, the system of political commissars was strengthened and party branch committees were revived in all PLA companies and party cells in platoons. In 1964, a campaign to 'Learn from the PLA' was launched and as Mao became increasingly convinced that the solution to China's future lay in its past he turned to the PLA for help.

Groups in society were asked to compare themselves to those in the military, the training of militias was increased and a large number of military personnel were transferred to civilian units. Under Lin's leadership the main strategy for the PLA was enshrined in the notion of the 'People's War'. The revolutionary credentials of the PLA were boosted further in 1965 when it abolished ranks and insignia and introduced the 'Down to the Ranks Movement' for officers. Mao was using the PLA to bypass an administration that was reluctant to implement the radical policies of the Socialist Education Movement, and it was not surprising that he turned to them to impose his will in the Cultural Revolution.

While it may not have been the original intention for the PLA to intervene in the Cultural Revolution, once launched the military's involvement became inevitable. The PLA was the only remaining organization with national authority and the only one capable of carrying out the necessary public security role. The engagement also created frictions within the PLA and an eventual wariness of a direct role in politics on the part of many. While Lin Biao encouraged the left and tried to prevent it from attacking the Red Guards, his regional commanders often chose to side with the 'old' regional leadership.

The Cultural Revolution, although not a military takeover, did result in a massive increase in military involvement in the Chinese political system. With the national party network destroyed, the PLA replaced it as the backbone of organization throughout the country. Of the chairs and vice-chairs of the provincial revolutionary committees, the PLA had the largest representation (42 per cent) of the three-way alliance of revolutionary cadres, PLA and mass representatives. At the time of the Ninth Party Congress (1969) the military was in a powerful position, with 20 of the 29 provincial revolutionary committee chairs having a basic affiliation with the military. While the Congress was to signal the rebuilding of the party apparatus and the return of the military to the barracks, this did not happen immediately. Lin Biao was designated Mao's successor and leaders from centrally directed units enjoyed power that they had not experienced before. These leaders favoured continuing the status quo of 1969 with PLA members staying in their civilian positions without resigning from the army. Regional commanders were also reluctant to return to the barracks and hand over power to the radicals for fear of reprisal.

This stand-off was resolved only with the purge of Lin Biao and five other members of the Politburo in 1971 (see Teiwes and Sun, 1996; Jin, 1999). The purge brought to the fore divisions in the PLA between the regional commanders and the leaders of the centrally directed units, and between those who favoured a professional, military role for the PLA and those who favoured a more political role. Powerful regional commanders in the Politburo did not rally to Lin's side, not only because it was Mao's wish but also because he had become increasingly identified with the left with whom many regional commanders had clashed. Those who favoured a more professional military sought a withdrawal from political work and might have harboured grudges against the central military leaders for not protecting them from Red Guard criticisms. These two divisions, combined with the fact that Lin Biao could not assure Mao that the military would withdraw from politics, meant that Lin found himself in a position where he could satisfy no possible supporters.

Lin's fall provided the starting point for a long process of modernization in the military and a change in its political role, first back to resembling that of the pre-Cultural Revolution years but subsequently to one of substantive change. While withdrawal from direct involvement in politics and modernization and professionalization were to become key themes under Deng, it is important to remember that the new era was launched by what in effect was an illegal *coup* in which the PLA played the key role. On 6 October 1976 Politburo member, Wang Dongxing, with the support of Ye Jianying and other veteran revolutionaries, led the elite 8341 Unit of the PLA to arrest the 'Gang of Four'.

Deng shared Mao's favourable views of the PLA but also recognized the need for its modernization, without adding extra financial resources, and for the PLA's withdrawal from the broader political arena to be confirmed. Under Deng during the 1980s, three main areas were highlighted for modernization – military equipment, military cadres and military thinking (Xu, 1979). In 1975, when Deng was Chief of Staff he had already pushed the need for a revamp of the military and in case people had missed this he had the following to say in 1980 (*People's Daily*, 5 March 1980):

In the past we spent rather a long time mechanically copying the experiences of the army during the years of war... Things are different now... Even the army is different today. In the past the army was a matter of millet plus rifles and you could go into battle if you knew how to fire your gun, use the bayonet and throw a grenade ... The area of knowledge [now] is much broader. Today's army cannot get by using its past experiences, which is precisely the problem we must strive to solve.

However, Deng also made it clear that military modernization would figure last in the 'Four Modernizations' and that it would have to happen without an increased allocation of financial resources. In 1985, Deng outlined that PLA units would have to diversify their revenue sources as a result of the declining budgets (Shambaugh, 1996b, pp. 276–7). This coincided with the moves to reduce the PLA by around 1 million troops, other organizational reforms and a significant change in military strategy. The notion of 'People's War' was dumped and in 1985 Deng put forward the view that China no longer faced imminent attack from the Soviet Union and that the need was to focus on peacetime production and economic construction.

Initially, PLA economic diversification started with a CMAC directive to engage in self-reliant agriculture and sideline production to try to cover some of the decline in the central government's food subsidy (Yeung, 1995, pp. 159–60). However, it soon led to massive involvement by the PLA in production for civilian consumption, import and export (legal and illegal), the construction of hotels and entertainment centres and even retailing. This involvement expanded yet further after Deng Xiaoping's 1992 trip to the south. PLA enterprises were able to take advantage of military benefits, including a tax rate of only 9.9 per cent compared to 33 per cent for other firms. This engagement in business led to serious problems of corruption and decline in morale with which Jiang Zemin has had to deal. By the early 1990s, this entrepreneurial engagement had become extremely significant. The PLA admitted to having 10,000 enterprises, with much higher independent estimates, and commercial earnings in the range of $5 billion by 1992 (Shambaugh, 1996b, p. 277). These included 9 major conglomerates and as many as 70 automobile plants, 400 pharmaceutical factories and 1,500 hotels (*SCMP*, 31 January 2001, Internet edition). In the Shenzhen SEZ in 1992 there were 500 PLA-run enterprises that accounted for 10 per cent of the total industrial output value of the zone (Yeung, 1995, p. 164).

The policy to modernize and professionalize the PLA has been successful. The new strategy for the PLA is to be prepared to fight a 'limited war under high technology conditions'. In addition, as Mulvenon (1997) has noted, the education level of PLA officials has increased, combined with an increasing functional specialization. In his view, the PLA has undergone the shift from the revolutionary generation to a new post-1949 cohort that is more experienced in modern warfare and consequently more inclined to modernization and doctrinal evolution.

This does not mean that the PLA has had no political role under either Deng or Jiang. The nature of this role has changed, however. It is still the case that it would be impossible to become the paramount leader in China without PLA backing. Deng's first two choices as successor, Hu Yaobang and Zhao Ziyang, were not accepted by the military leadership and were never able to consolidate their position on the CMAC. Conservative members of the military played an important role in bringing about their downfall. In addition, it was the PLA that came to the aid of the CCP on the night of 3–4 June 1989 when troops cleared Tiananmen Square of the remaining student and other protesters. While there were rumours of divisions within the military over how to handle the situation, once there was a clear line of command and it was clear that Deng was using his prestige to call them in, discipline held up well.

The events of 1989 caused a temporary reverse in attempts to keep the PLA further away from politics, but there is no evidence that as an institution the PLA had a desire to become embroiled again in elite politics. However, it appears that the Yang brothers had a different idea. Yang Shangkun, at the time president of the PRC and first vice-chair of the CMAC, had been a strong supporter of Deng's in rallying PLA support and in moving for the dismissal of General Secretary Zhao Ziyang. Yang Baibing, his half-brother, was secretary-general of the CMAC and chief political commissar. Many had seen Yang Shangkun as a potential patriarch of China's system after Deng's death, and Deng may have moved to remove him to limit this possibility and to strengthen the chances of his latest choice as general secretary, Jiang Zemin. It also seems that both were unpopular among key figures in the PLA who lobbied Deng to curtail their power (Saich, 1994b, p. 1149), while others were disturbed by the politicization of the PLA and the investigations launched by the younger Yang to review actions in Tiananmen.

The king-making capacity of the PLA is something that Jiang Zemin has appreciated and he has made great efforts to court the military while promoting a new generation of military leaders that will be loyal to him. However, he cannot count on the PLA for automatic support in the way that either Mao or Deng could, and continued PLA support will be much more performance-based. That said, Jiang has been very skilful in his handling of the PLA, but his refusal to step down from heading the CMAC may have created problems for Hu and has made the process of institutionalization less clear.

In the view of Joffe (1997), one of the main specialists on PLA affairs, three factors have influenced the PLA in the post-Deng period to provide it with unprecedented potential to wield political power. This potential is moderated by professionalization and countervailing political factors. First, the authority of the 'paramount leader' has changed dramatically with the passing of Deng and the ascendance of Jiang. While Jiang and his successors will be able to derive authority from their institutional positions, they cannot count on automatic support on all issues all of the time. This seems to have pushed Jiang to personalize his leadership over the military. Second, the military now has more say over discrete policy-making areas that it deems to be of immediate concern. These cover not just matters concerning their own internal affairs but also issues relating to sovereignty and foreign policy. Third, Joffe sees a growing separation between the party and army and this has highlighted the potential for increased policy conflict.

Jiang Zemin inherited a situation where PLA representation on the Fourteenth CC (1992) was at the highest level since the Eleventh CC (1977). However, there were only two Politburo members, the elderly Liu Huaqing, who was also elected to its Standing Committee, and the politically emasculated Yang Baibing. The fact that Liu (then 76 years old) and Zhang Zhen (78), old Deng allies, were elected first vice-chairs of the CMAC reveals the problems that Deng had in finding a younger generation of leaders whom both he and the military could trust. Both Liu and Zhang had stepped down from the CC in 1985!

Jiang's first objective was to promote into key PLA positions people who would owe their position to his patronage. Second, he moved to strengthen party and political mechanisms within the PLA, while publicly lavishing praise on the PLA as an institution and increasing its budget every year. In 1994–95, with an eye to Deng's pending demise, the CMAC was overhauled, Jiang promoted 27 lieutenant generals to the rank of full general, while the leadership down to group army commands was reshuffled (Shambaugh, 1996b, pp. 270–1). Importantly, Defence Minister, Chi Haotian, and former PLA Chief of Staff, Zhang Wannian, were appointed vice-chairs of the CMAC and in a major breakthrough for Jiang, at the Fifteenth Party Congress they replaced the retiring Liu Huaqing and Zhang Zhen in the Politburo. For the first time, Jiang had a senior CMAC leadership that he had appointed. Significantly, no PLA representative was elected to the Standing Committee of the Politburo. This may signify the triumph of party control over the military but more likely it confirms Baum's assessment (1998, p. 155) that with Jiang as General Secretary the PLA does not need one of its own members present to safeguard its corporate interests. However, this has become a problem at the Sixteenth party Congress where the practice has been continued but where Jiang Zemin is not even a member of the CC and where General Secretary Hu Jintao's name is mentioned far less frequently in the PLA media. Finally, in June 2000 Jiang promoted a further 16 officers to the rank of full general, including four vice-chiefs of the General Staff and three vice-chiefs of the General Political Department. This further strengthened Jiang's control over the senior positions within the military and also provided rewards for loyalty to a number of them (*SCMP*, 22 June 2000, Internet edition).

Backing up these personnel changes, Jiang has both praised the military and strengthened the institutional mechanisms for party control while promoting a number of campaigns to express loyalty, increasingly loyalty to Jiang rather than to the party. Extensive efforts have been made to breathe life back into the commissar system, party committees in the PLA and the discipline inspection system (Shambaugh, 1991, 1996b). The PLA became a major promoter of Jiang's notion of the 'Three Represents' and its media has glorified the theory and lionized Jiang as its leader and inspiration.

While Jiang did manage to gain public loyalty from the PLA, this did not mean that he would not go against their interests when these were considered detrimental to the nation as a whole. One development that caused concern over conflict of interest was the PLA's enormous business empire, the seeds of which were sown in the 1980s but the fruits of which blossomed in the 1990s. Many of those who profited were the children of senior cadres and they have been involved in a number of scandals. Not only the civilian leadership has been worried about this and the associated corruption, but senior military figures have also expressed concern about the corrosive effect on military discipline, preparedness and morale. Jiang was apparently also disturbed about the corruption that was involved with some of the PLA 'business' ventures. As a result, Jiang, with the support of key figures such as then Defence Minister, Chi Haotian, decided to remove the PLA from business or at least to reduce its role significantly. In November 1994, a CMAC directive banned units beneath the group army level from conducting business activities, and in July 1998 Jiang made the bold announcement that the PLA would withdraw from its business activities within the year.

The programme of divestiture has been more successful than one might have imagined given the immense financial empire, and showed clearly how senior leaders saw the PLA's dealings as counterproductive. The disengagement was one of the most contentious decisions made by Jiang, and his fortitude surprised many. The revelation of questionable activities of PLA-run enterprises that came to light in the process (smuggling, gun-running, prostitution) has sullied the PLA's reputation. A dramatic fall in smuggling has resulted from this policy and it is no surprise that the customs department announced a 41 per cent increase in revenue in the year 2000 ($27 billion in total). The divested companies were placed under a newly created office, the National Transfer Office, under the SETC. Over the first two years, 6,000 companies with assets of around $24.1 billion were transferred but only 900 remain, the others having been closed down or merged. Included were 9 major conglomerates that accounted for around 75 per cent of the PLA's business empire (*SCMP*, 31 January 2001, Internet edition).

To sweeten the pill of this programme, Jiang had to promise an increased budgetary allocation to offset the decline in external revenues and it is clear that different branches of the PLA used this as a means to extract inflated budgets from the state in compensation for supposed business losses. It is thought that senior PLA figures negotiated with Premier Zhu Rongji compensation of around $6 billion, having asked for around $8.6 billion (*SCMP*, 9 September 1998), but initial payouts disappointed the PLA. However, perhaps only as little as $1.2 billion was paid in March 1999 (*FEER*, 13 July 2000) and the PLA was granted a 13 per cent budget increase that was to include compensation for military enterprises and double-digit increases followed annually until the Tenth NPC (March 2003) that allocated an increase of only 9.6 per cent. At first sight this is puzzling, but it probably results from the general fiscal stringency and the international attention that the high budget increases attracted. If the latter is a major cause, it may be that further funding is being concealed rather than reduced. If it is the former, the PLA will have to compete with many other priorities for future funding. Ironically, one problem in trying to assess the value of PLA enterprises stems from the fact that the PLA has tried to conceal the true extent of its business operations. In addition, progress was hampered not just by difficulties in deciding what exactly was a PLA business but also by problems of finding jobs for laid-off workers, clearing up the bad debts left behind and assessing accurately the financial liabilities. It seems that some units had tried to palm off loss-making enterprises while finding creative registrations to keep those that were profitable.

In recent years, the PLA has played a more assertive role in policy areas that it considers important and has been one of the main proponents of nationalism and promotion of the national interest. With the collapse of the Soviet Union and the change in the geopolitical situation, it became clear that China would be freer to assert its own national interest without regard to ideology or existing power blocks. Combined with the decline of Marxism–Leninism as providing policy guidance, a more assertive expression of national interest emerged and this was particularly strong in the military. With economic performance now providing the main source of legitimacy, Jiang has used nationalism as a way to build up a broader base of support. However, he has had to be careful that this does not turn into a more dangerous xenophobia. Senior military figures have taken a hard line on issues such as the reunification with Taiwan and the relationship with the United States. In 1995–96, after the United States had given a visa to then President Lee Teng-hui of Taiwan, the PLA was the most powerful voice pushing for a more aggressive response. Again during the 2000 presidential elections on Taiwan, the PLA was the harshest group advocating pressure on the United States and Taiwan to make sure that independence would not be considered. Similarly, the PLA as an institution remains the most suspicious of the United States and since the accidental NATO bombing of the Chinese Embassy in May 1999 and the EP-3 incident (April 2001) has been the most difficult organization to persuade of the need to resume normal relations.

Whether Hu Jintao is able to take control of the PLA as effectively as Jiang Zemin remains to be seen but Jiang's refusal to give up his post and the campaign of adulation within the PLA have created potential problems; they set back the process of institutionalization and reflect the worst aspects of personal idolatory in the Chinese political system. This will not help coordination between the civilian and military apparatuses. Jiang is not even a CC member, and yet the military must answer to him. As Mulvenon (2002) has noted, while Deng kept control of the military to pursue radical reforms, Jiang has remained because of personal ambition. The outbreak of SARS in 2002–03 provided the latest example of poor coordination, with the military hospitals and system clearly not feeling the compulsion to report the number of infections to the civilian authorities. It seems that the dysfunctional nature of being the servant of two masters has been noted within the PLA and covert criticism of loyalty to Jiang has been voiced. The reporting of the submarine accident in which 70 sailors died in late April 2003 was China's worst publicly acknowledged military accident and could be used to reflect badly on Jiang, and it was rumoured that a group of party elders had signed a letter urging him to step down by the end of 2003.

6

Governance Beyond the Centre

The relationship between the centre and the localities has undergone significant changes with the reforms. This chapter outlines the organization of government away from the centre and then examines the role of the province in the political system. The reforms have also led to significant regional inequality that is providing a major challenge to governance. Finally, the chapter reviews the changing centre–locality relationship especially as it has been affected by fiscal reforms. While the centre tries to exert political control over the localities through the system of party-sanctioned appointments of leading personnel – the *nomenclatura* system – its fiscal capacity and its moral authority have declined. State revenues only amounted to 16 per cent of GDP in 2001, down from 36 per cent in 1978, and most localities increasingly have had to deal themselves with the serious problems that confront them. The revenues had dropped as low as 11 per cent. The decline in state revenues created pressures at all levels and in all Chinese government agencies to meet recurrent costs from locally generated sources. Increasingly, political outcomes are determined by local power structures and resource allocation. Within the same province and even in adjacent counties one can see radically different socio-political outcomes deriving from the reforms. What are the consequences of this for the nature of the local state and what are the consequences for governance and policy?

The Organization of Local Government

Since the abolition of the 6 administrative regions in the mid-1950s, the most important administrative level has been the province and the municipalities. Unlike the former Soviet Union, the PRC has always been a unitary multinational state. Constitutionally, all nationalities are equal and 'big-nation chauvinism' and 'local-nation chauvinism' are equally opposed. All nationalities are theoretically free to use their own languages and there are constitutional arrangements for regional autonomy in areas inhabited by non-Han minorities. But there is no right to secede: 'All the national autonomous areas are inalienable parts of the PRC.' The real level of autonomy is, in any case, extremely limited and since the late 1980s, Beijing's fears of resistance to its rule in Tibet and Xinjiang have meant that the limited autonomy that was enjoyed in the early years of reform is now highly constricted.

The non-central government is administered through 22 provinces (although official PRC sources count Taiwan to total 23), 5 autonomous regions, 4 municipalities directly under the central government, and 2 Special Administrative Regions (SARs). The notion of a SAR was included in the 1982 Constitution with an eye to the return of Taiwan and also Hong Kong and Macao to Beijing's sovereignty. In July 1997, Hong Kong was handed over by the departing British colonial administration and in December 1999 Macao was handed back by Portugal. Administration of these two SARs is covered by Beijing's concept of 'one country, two systems' that guarantees that for a period of 50 years they will be able to keep their previous economic and political systems. Thus, Hong Kong will be able to retain its capitalist economic system under a chief representative (effectively nominated by Beijing) and a partially elected legislature.

Under the provinces and equivalents, there is a three-level administrative network of prefectures, counties and cities, and townships and districts (see Figure 6.1). The prefecture does not constitute a level of political power, and therefore does not set up people's congresses and people's governments but instead has administrative agencies set up by the province. The leading members of these agencies (administrative commissioners and their deputies) are not elected but are appointed by the higher levels. The three levels of government below the centre – province, county and township – are organized in basically the same way as the centre, with government and party organizations paralleling one another. The people's congresses are the local organs of state power and are able to elect and recall members of the people's governments. In June 1979, the people's governments replaced the revolutionary committees that had been set up during the Cultural Revolution. The people's governments at the provincial level are elected for 5-year periods while those at the county level and township level are elected for 3 years. The people's government is the administrative (executive) organ of the People's Congress and is responsible to both the People's Congress and its Standing Committee at the same level, and to the organs of state administration at the next higher level, and is ultimately subordinate to the State Council.

The powers of the local people's congresses have been increased to allow them to adopt local regulations, and at and above the county level standing committees were created to carry out the work of the congresses on a more permanent basis. Shenzhen, for example, became the first SEZ to be granted legislative power by the NPC, quickly followed by Xiamen. In 1996, this power was also granted to Zhuhai and Shantou. Guangdong seems to be taking the lead and appeared to grant to its three SEZs (Shenzhen, Zhuhai and Shantou) powers to make local laws that would be adopted after a 4-month period of review by the legislature. This built on the NPC legislation and the

FIGURE 6.1

Levels of Government Under the State Council, 2003

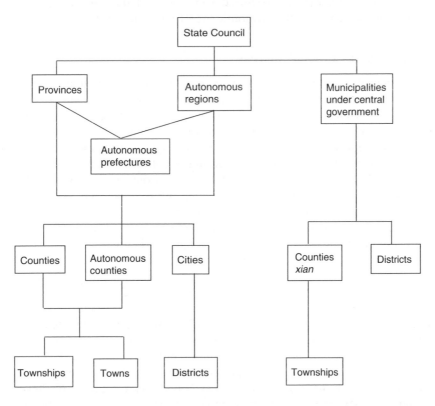

Note: In addition there are the two Special Administrative Regions (SARs) of Hong Kong and Macao that will retain their existing political and economic systems for up to 50 years.

powers were also extended to the provincial capital, Guangzhou (*SCMP*, 19 September 2000, Internet edition).

Before 1978 the legislative and administrative organs (standing committees of people's congresses and people's governments) were not separated. Previously, when the people's congress was not in session these powers were exercised by one body, the revolutionary committee. Furthermore, neigh-bourhood and villagers' committees were written into the 1982 State Con-stitution as 'the mass organizations of self-management at the basic level'. The election of the committees is covered in Chapter 7.

The most important change in local government under the reforms is that the people's communes, set up during the Great Leap Forward (1958–60), no longer function as both a unit of economic and government administration. Now the township operates as a level of government and with the decollect-ivization of economic life throughout the countryside the commune has disappeared altogether as an organ of substance. The changes were designed not only to strengthen the state at the lowest level, but also to improve economic performance. Under the old system it was claimed that the party committees interfered too heavily in the economic life of the countryside.

The Province as a Unit of Analysis

The provinces and four major municipalities form the most important level of sub-national administration in the Chinese system. This has been the situation since the establishment of provinces (*sheng*) during the Yuan Dynasty in the Thirteenth century. In today's China, administratively the province carries the equivalent rank to a ministry in Beijing and its party secretaries and governors are important politicians in the political system, brokering the desires of the centre with the needs and wishes of the localities. It gives these leaders great power and potential but also offers great risks and requires careful management skills to play this role well.

While formally all provinces carry the same rank, it is clear that some are more important and carry more political weight. Variation across the provinces and even within provinces is enormous. Many would be substantial countries in their own right in terms of population, geographic size and endowment of natural resources. Five provinces have populations in the range of 70 to around 90 million people – Henan, Shandong, Sichuan, Jiangsu and Guangdong. The population of Sichuan was almost 120 million before Chongqing was established as an independent municipality in March 1997. By contrast, the population of Tibet numbers only 2.4 million but it is geographically big – 1.2 million km^2. While not as big as the largest province (Xinjiang – 1.6 million km^2), it dwarfs a province such as Ningxia that is a mere 66,000 km^2, let alone the Municipality of Shanghai that is a mere 6,431 km^2. Yet, Shanghai has economic muscle with a GDP *per capita* of 17,403 *yuan* compared to Tibet's 2,332 *yuan* or poor Guizhou's 1,796 *yuan*. The GDP of China's largest provincial economy, Guangdong, was over 80 times that of Tibet in 2001.

The economic might of Shanghai and Guangdong make them important to the centre. Shanghai has traditionally been a major cash-cow, while Beijing has spent much of the reform period trying to figure out how to get hold of more of Guangdong's recent wealth. They clearly pull more weight in discussions in Beijing than does a poor northwestern province such as Ningxia or Gansu. However, poor Tibet and other sparsely populated border provinces are important to the centre for strategic reasons. They cover 60 per cent of the land mass and house only 6 per cent of the population and are home to many of China's national minorities. Beijing has had cause to wonder about their loyalty in the past and garrisons them heavily for fear of external threat, and in the cases of Tibet and Xinjiang for internal opposition.

Given the sheer size of China and this diversity, despite the formal administrative conformity, it is difficult to make too many coherent generalizations about policy implementation across provinces. Virtually all writers on the subject agree that not only has the relationship between centre and province become more complex since the reforms began but also that with increased control of financial resources there is more capacity for creative local leadership than in the past. The increasing provincial control over vast resources, the decline in the moral authority of the centre, and China's previous history of fragmentation and warlordism have led some writers to surmise about a possible break-up of China (see Jenner, 1992; Segal, 1994). Despite the economic growth of provinces such as Guangdong and the reorientation of a province such as Yunnan towards Thailand and Southeast Asia for foreign direct investment (FDI) and trade, this has been no more than wishful thinking (see Huang, 1995a, pp. 54–68). To date, when the centre has really wanted to impose its will on a significant issue it can, and the provinces have been willing to go along with this.

The only provinces where a breakaway might be a reality are Tibet and Xinjiang. Here, the relationship with the centre is qualitatively different and it has had to resort to violence on a number of occasions to exert control. Despite the process of moving in Han Chinese to dominate the political and economic apparatus of these two provinces, considerable opposition has remained to Beijing's dominance. In both cases this is aided by a history, language and culture that provides an alternative point of reference to Beijing's official story of unity. It is also helped by Tibetan loyalty to the exiled Dalai Lama and in Xinjiang by the various Muslim groups in the newly formed independent states that emerged from the break-up of the former Soviet Union.

The relationship between the centre and the localities is not necessarily one of a zero-sum game, and most may feel that they have more to gain by remaining within a collaborative framework with Beijing than suffering the cost of trying to wriggle free, something that would be impossible in any case unless CCP rule were to collapse. Further, as Goodman (1997, p. 2) has pointed out, it was Beijing's intent that each province should develop its comparative advantage as a fundamental component of the economic reform programme. Indeed, as new research is now indicating, the natural endowments and political skills of provincial leaderships have become key determinants of the development of particular provinces (see especially Goodman, 1997; Cheung, Chung and Lin, 1998 and Hendrischke and Feng, 1999).

With the provinces playing such a critical role in the political system and with their leaders forming an important group, it is not surprising that there should be attempts to integrate those with possible conflicting ideas into the national decision-making framework. This has taken a number of forms. The NPC's annual meetings have become a major venue for meshing central priorities with the needs of individual provinces. Until the new revenue-sharing system was passed in 1994, NPC sessions had become focal points for sharp arguments between provincial delegations and central financial leaders over the division of revenues. Representation at the NPC is organized along the lines of provincial jurisdiction and all sub-provincial delegates operate as a part of a provincial delegation, especially during small group discussions (Cheung, Chung and Lin, 1998, p. 10). Even many senior central leaders are appended to provincial delegations, preferably where they may have worked or been born, or sometimes even where they have no connection and may not even have been.

The rising influence of the provinces in the political system has also led to increased representation on central party organs. The CC has consequently been enlarged to include provincial personnel and this percentage has increased over time. The Fourteenth Party Congress (1992) witnessed a significant increase in representation of the provinces (Saich, 1992, pp. 1148–9), a trend that was maintained at the Fifteenth and Sixteenth Congresses (1997 and 2002). Provincial representatives formed the largest block of delegates, topping 70 per cent in 1992. While representation declines at higher party levels, the provincial bloc remains important. On the CC, provincial representation rose from 49 seats (26 per cent) in 1992 to 65 (32.8 per cent) in 2002, with all but one province (Jiangsu) having the first secretary elected. This is an anomaly, with the secretary of one of the most influential provinces securing only alternate member status that will presumably be rectified. While central state ministers and councillors increased their representation from 34 (18 per cent) to 60 (30 per cent), the provincial bloc remained dominant. As was seen in Chapter 4, there are 6 members of the 24-person Politburo who are provincial leaders, with another 14 who have served as top provincial leaders. The regions of course have differing interests, but provincial leaders provide the largest bloc in the current Politburo. It is clear that provincial leadership, especially Shanghai under Jiang Zemin, provides a reservoir of talent for the centre and it is now expected that before taking on a significant central ministerial post one should have at least a couple of years' experience at the provincial level. Thus, for many of those who serve at the provincial level their career is still with the centre.

Despite this trend, it is interesting to note that the number of 'natives' serving in the provincial administration has risen under the reforms. Throughout China in 1965, this group comprised only 35 per cent of provincial leadership but this had risen to 41 per cent for provincial party secretaries in 1985 and 44 per cent for governors and vice-governors in 1988 (Chung, 1998, p. 435). Goodman suggests that this trend increased in the 1990s and notes that most of those who have become party and government leaders at the provincial level have significant work experience in the province, heralding a break with past practice (Goodman, 1997, pp. 8–9).

Ultimately, Beijing has the power of control over appointments and this makes it difficult for any provincial leader to defy the Centre for too long. In fact, Yasheng Huang (1996a, pp. 655–72) has argued that economic decentralization has been accompanied by a strengthening of China's unitary political system. In particular, he highlights the continued role of the

Organization Department in the appointment, management and promotion of officials. Thus, the party retains a very powerful institutional mechanism for rewarding and punishing non-central officials. The system is now one of 'one-level downward' management that replaced the two-level downward system in 1983. This means that the Centre directly appoints and removes only 7,000 cadres, a reduction of some 6,000 from previously. Certainly this is a good mechanism for controlling provincial level officials given that many see their career prospects in terms of transfer to a national ministry or equivalent. One only needs to see the fawning over Jiang Zemin's local trips or latest pronouncements by provincial party secretaries and even governors to see how powerful this can be in keeping local officials in line publicly.

In the 1990s, Jiang Zemin made it a top priority to reorganize the Beijing municipal leadership and the Guangdong provincial leadership, both of which were seen as too independent. Jiang was able to use a spectacular corruption scandal to get rid of Beijing Party Secretary, Chen Xitong, and his supporters in April 1995, and eventually was able to install one of his entrusted followers in Guangdong to try to break up the local politics. Especially with Guangdong it will be interesting to see how long the 'outsiders' can dominate over the 'native sons'. In Guangdong the presence of the CCP is historically weak and was first felt as an invading force from the north after 1949. As Goodman has noted, the party apparatus in the province is seen as being less important than the government administration (Goodman, 1997, p. 6). In fact, some of the senior officials sent down from Beijing to bring Guangdong back under central control claimed they felt uncomfortable working there, were shut out from the informal politics and longed to return to Beijing (Interview with officials concerned, 1999).

The centre has also set up more indirect means to control the provinces, including developing rules and regulations for local administrations and improving administrative monitoring through better auditing, collection of information and disciplinary inspection (Huang, 1995b, pp. 828–43). These new mechanisms complement traditional control mechanisms such as ideological campaigns or party-school system training programmes. In 1987 to try to control corrupt and other unwarranted behaviour, the Ministry of Supervision (abolished in 1959) was revived and the General Auditing Administration was set up to monitor the fiscal affairs of both firms and government agencies (Huang, 1996b, p. 662). They have met with only limited success, however. Huang also notes that central administrative control over the provinces has increased through the regularity of personnel changes and is demonstrated by the administrative uniformity across provinces and the tenure characteristics. In a prescient study of inflation and investment controls Huang shows how political and bureaucratic centralization shapes the incentive structure of local officials and affects their economic behaviour. When the centre really wishes to implement a policy and moves coherently, local officials will comply even at significant cost to their own economic interests (Huang, 1996a).

That said, the situation has changed significantly from the Mao years. In Chung's view (1998, p. 430) the pre-reform role of the provinces was relatively simple, 'disseminating Beijing's policy directives and monitoring subprovincial compliance with state plans'. They were left largely to rely on their own efforts under the policy of 'self-reliance' that produced a cellular structure. The power of the centre led most to see provincial leadership more as a vital cog in the transmission of the centre's ideas to the provinces – ensuring that political power rested exclusively with the centre (Falkenheim, 1972, pp. 75–83). In an early comprehensive study of the first provincial party secretary, Goodman (1980, p. 72) concluded that 'there is little to suggest that the first secretary has been a local leader rather than an agent of central control'. While there may still be an element of truth in this for the first party secretary, the picture is more nuanced for the provincial leadership as a whole. Some have seen them as policy entrepreneurs or as agents with multiple principals in the capital and in the province (Cheung, 1998, pp. 14–15). Lieberthal and Oksenberg (1988, p. 344) have defined the provincial level as 'a gatekeeper guarding and providing access to the local levels'. It is these latter roles and how the leadership mediates between the Centre and its local constituencies that has received most attention in recent literature.

The provinces have been important to the Centre and also to particular leaders in terms of providing incubators for reforms. In fact, Susan Shirk (1990, pp. 227–58) shows that Deng Xiaoping's reform strategy as a whole was dependent on the support of provincial governments that were willing to push ahead with reform in the face of recalcitrance from more cautious bureaucrats in Beijing. The most recent example was in January–February 1992 when Deng went to south China to kick-start economic reform once again after the pace of reform had been slowed in response to the demonstrations of 1989 and the ousting of Zhao Ziyang.

Consistently, reforms at the local level have provided the basis for national implementation. Thus, Goodman (1986, p. 181) has observed that 'national decision-making was frequently an incremental process involving provincial experimentation before a final decision was reached'. It is well known that what became the household responsibility system was first experimented with by Wan Li, when he was in charge of agricultural policy in Anhui and by Zhao Ziyang in Sichuan. Zhao was so successful in turning around grain production that the Sichuanese thought up the little ditty '*yao chifan, zhao ziyang*' (if you want to eat food, then look for Ziyang – the sound *Zhao* meaning both 'to look for' and being his family name). Both were promoted to the central levels because of their success.

The attitude of the local leadership can influence how swiftly a new policy or reform measure is taken up. Shortly after the attempts to introduce the household responsibility system nationwide, collectives in Heilongjiang announced a switch to a rural wage system, the complete antithesis of the new policy. In fact, a wage system was probably in the interests of the farmers in the northeast who worked on highly mechanized communes; the return to small family farming did not appear to be in their immediate economic interests. Similarly, leaders in Shaanxi opposed the policy until 1982, a couple of years later than other provinces, and also rejected the idea of promoting rural collective enterprises as a major growth engine. Lane (1998, pp. 212–50) puts this reluctance to be inventive in reform down to the legacy of the revolutionary struggle in the province, the lack of central incentive and a general conservatism that meant that local leaders were more attached to the centrally planned economy than their southern counterparts.

The experiment with SEZs provides another good example of both the desire of reformers at the centre to have a local base for experimentation and the importance of local leadership to pursue an opportunity. The zones were set up in the 1980s to receive foreign technology and to be reform laboratories. While Guangdong grasped the opportunity once offered and became a pioneer of reform, recording consistently high growth rates, Fujian's leaders were more cautious though offered the same package. Fujian did not develop a coherent local package to take advantage of central policy. Similarly, they were slow off the mark with Deng's 1992 speech that launched another massive expansion of provincial-led growth (Lin, 1998, p. 420). Apparently, officials in Hunan were kicking themselves for missing the implications of Deng's 1992 speech. He had first made the comments while on an inspection tour there and they were too slow to pick up on the policy shift and to promote it. This lost them favour with Deng, and made them slow off the mark subsequently (Interview with officials concerned, May 2000).

The provinces also provide the centre with a reliable organization to fine-tune policy and allow more flexibility with implementation than would otherwise be the case. The provincial people's congresses can promulgate local legislation so long as no national legislation exists or as long as it does not conflict with the objectives of national legislation. The centre also provides the power of discretion to the province to flesh out the details of national legislation and to arrange the schedule for its implementation (Cheung, 1998, p. 10). Thus, for example, while Beijing has decided that there should be a minimum wage, the provinces decide the appropriate level within their jurisdiction, not Beijing.

With more at stake, rivalry between provinces has also intensified and it is still the case that many provinces trade more internationally than they do with other provinces in the country. Provinces have often acted to prevent raw materials leaving to other provinces while erecting high tariffs to prevent goods from other provinces entering that might undermine local industry. A classic case was when Guangdong sent trucks to Sichuan to buy silkworm cocoons directly from the producers, while the Sichuan authorities responded by setting up armed blockades to prevent them from leaving the province (Breslin, 1995, p. 68). Similar 'wars' occurred over wool and other vital raw products (see Watson, Findlay and Du, 1989, pp. 213–41; Zheng, 1994, pp. 313–14).

Regional Inequality

One major problem for the centre to deal with in this new relationship has been the rapid increase in regional inequalities. The provinces do not have an incentive to redistribute wealth and the centre's disposable funds for redistribution have declined. The new economic development strategy has led to new geographic losers and winners. While coastal areas have been able to develop their economies very rapidly, the western inland provinces have not fared so well by comparison. The reforms have reversed the fortunes of a number of provinces that enjoyed relative wealth under the centrally planned economy. Guangdong was one of the poorest provinces in the Mao years but has benefited enormously from the policies of international trade and economic liberalization. By contrast, the most prosperous provinces of the Mao years that benefited from the emphasis on heavy industry (Liaoning, Jilin, Heilongjiang) have suffered significant relative decline under the reforms. Such provinces have struggled with very high levels of unemployment, ageing industry and infrastructure and social welfare bills that are increasingly difficult to meet.

The inland provinces have lobbied the NPC to increase their resources and to accord them the same kind of privileges that have been given to the coastal areas. This the centre consistently refused to allow until the mid-1990s when the leadership became more worried about regional inequality as a source of instability. Even with the 1994 reforms that were designed to guarantee Beijing's revenues, it is clearly the case that richer provinces turn over far less of their surplus to the centre than previously.

The concentration of FDI has exacerbated the regional inequalities, contributing further to the greater wealth concentration in the coastal areas. In 2000, Guangdong alone received 25.7 per cent of FDI, the three major municipalities of Shanghai, Beijing and Tianjin received 17.6 per cent and Jiangsu province 13.5 per cent. By contrast, the 9 provinces and 1 municipality in the northwest and southwest of China received only 3 per cent of all FDI (calculated from figures in *China Statistical Yearbook*, 2002, p. 633). While annual growth in *per capita* rural income from 1988 to 1995 averaged 4.71 per cent for China as a whole, it was 11.66 per cent for Jiangsu, 9.33 per cent for Beijing and 7.11 per cent for Guangdong. In the southwest it was only 0.72 per cent for Guizhou, 0.62 per cent for Sichuan and 1.26 per cent for Yunnan (Khan, n.d., p. 36). As a result, the average 1998 rural income for the coastal areas was about twice that of the southwest, and Shanghai was 3 times higher. In urban areas real income was also consistently higher, with Shanghai enjoying real income approximately twice that of the northwest and 60 per cent higher than that in the southwest.

These trends have caused major migration flows, with anywhere between 80 and 120 million people moving to find work on a temporary or more per-manent basis. Significant numbers have been attracted to the employment opportunities offered in the SEZs, along the coast and in major municipalities in the manufacturing sectors that have developed with foreign investment. This has led to a breakdown of the old residence control system that kept the farmers out of the cities and protected an intricate system of benefits and allowances that favoured the urban over the rural. Currently, the government does not provide welfare or education for these migrant families and they are not integrated into local government service provision. As China opens itself to greater foreign investment, labour mobility will increase and this will require a major rethinking of traditional government service provision that can no longer be based on place of birth. It is interesting to note that Guangdong, the destination of many migrants, took the lead in reform in this area. It began to allow farmers who had stable jobs and accommodation to obtain residence permits in small townships, allowing them access to the same social welfare benefits that are enjoyed by other urban dwellers (*SCMP*, 2 June 2000, Internet edition). These measures have become national policy (see Chapter 10).

While the central government has continually stressed that more attention has to be paid to the poorer interior, this has not translated into a coherent policy approach, and the powers that the coastal provinces have won will not be given up easily. China is pursuing an extremely inegalitarian development strategy, especially in comparison with its East Asian neighbours that it seeks to emulate. China's central leaders have been concerned by the growing disparities and have launched classic central-planning policies to try to stimulate growth in the western parts of the country. For example, from 1980 more developed provinces or municipalities were 'teamed' with poorer provinces; the objective was to get the richer provinces to invest in the poorer ones or to undertake major infrastructure projects. Provincial leaders have had little choice to go along with this, but it is clearly not a main priority for them and many of the investments are of dubious value. For example, in Xishuangbanna in Yunnan province, Shanghai Municipality built a hotel for tourists, many of whom come to see transsexual shows. Most of the profits are repatriated to Shanghai (Discussions in Xishuangbanna, November 1998). There are also formal 'twinning' arrangements between coastal provinces and the interior. Thus, for example, Shanghai is teamed with Yunnan, Beijing with Inner Mongolia, Shandong with Xinjiang and Guangdong with Guangxi. Interestingly, the poor province of Guizhou is teamed with the four cities of Dalian, Qingdao, Shenzhen and Ningbo.

The main response to deal with regional inequality has been the 'Develop the West' policy that was launched in late 1999 and confirmed at the Tenth NPC (March 2003). It comprises 12 provinces but excludes very poor provinces such as Jiangxi. The policy was to rely on state-led funding for infrastructure combined with political persuasion and arm-twisting of the more developed provinces to shift investment to the interior provinces. A Leading Group on Developing the West was set up, headed by the Premier and with an office under the State Council. Initially $6 billion was set aside for use in 2000. In fact, despite the fanfare state commitment has been quite limited. Most of the projects announced were already scheduled and many provinces sought to shift the costs of current projects to the central exchequer. Increased funding is to be provided through state bank loans and those from international financial organizations and preferential loans. If the funding is not diverted from more productive investment it should help. Many analysts feel that the initiative to 'Develop the West' serves rather more political purposes than genuine development needs and there is resentment from those provinces excluded. An OECD report states that better integration of China's regions is important not only for equity reasons but also as it is becoming an impediment to meeting other development goals. It points out that key features of the initiative such as using 'growth poles' and launching major infrastructure projects without taking into account regional demand and supporting declining sectors of the local economy have not worked elsewhere, and there is no reason to suspect that they will work in China (OECD, 2002, p. 41).

There is little imagination in central policy and health and education barely merit a mention. Many of the current problems in the region stem from previous bad central policy, in major part from Mao's policy of the 1960s to build a 'Third Front' to help China survive a potential Soviet invasion. About 20 million people and many factories were moved from the coast to the hinterland and a large number of industrial and military projects were carried out. They nearly bankrupted the economy in the 1960s and now they sit as millstones round the necks of local leaders who have to deal with falling revenues and large numbers of laid-off state workers.

Not surprisingly, given the economic structure many local leaders have remained more wedded to the old central-planning techniques than their colleagues in the east. For example, in Yunnan and Sichuan the state-owned sector of the economy remains dominant. It is interesting to note that the country's first national agricultural census published in 1998 reported that there were 5 times as many farmers engaged in private ventures in the east than in the west, and 4 times as many individual household enterprises; 33 per cent were engaged in non-agricultural production in coastal areas, compared with 15 per cent in the East (*SCMP*, 9 March 2000, Internet edition). This suggests that a radical overhaul of economic structure might be more beneficial, together with major investments in education, rather than pumping money into state-run infrastructure projects. Given the poor construction of many of the major state investment projects to date, and the corruption that has siphoned off money earmarked for development or poverty relief in the past, there is little cause for optimism that this policy will be successful in helping to bridge the gap. In fact, it is reported that Beijing is awash with requests from the interior provinces for large infrastructure development projects that specialists see as lacking credibility (Interview with officials concerned, May 2000). A far more judicious use of investment would be in basic education and health-care facilities.

Relations Between the Centre and the Localities: The Fiscal Picture

While the central state apparatus has the capacity to react to problems when acute or perceived to be regime-threatening, its relationship with its local branches has changed significantly and it does not command automatic allegiance. Just how much it has changed has been the topic of considerable debate; however the topic is not as new as some of the recent literature suggests and ever since 1949 the CCP has fretted over the appropriate relationship between the centre and the localities. Debates have focused not only on how much power could be ceded downwards, but also to which administrative level it should be devolved. In the debates of the mid-1950s, once it was decided that the overcentralized Soviet model was not suitable for China's needs, Mao and Chen Yun differed over whether decentralization should be to geographic regions that would keep the party in control and allow for mobilizational politics or whether more authority should be devolved to production enterprises allowing a more incentive-based economic strategy.

The most important element in the reform period has been the decentralization of powers away from central government agencies to those at lower levels, especially the effective decentralization of the fiscal system. This more than any other factor accounts for local variation. Getting the financial picture right is vital to any discussion of the relationship between the centre and the localities. Before the most recent fiscal reforms, only about one-quarter of all state expenditures occured at the central level and the major responsibility for financing infrastructure and providing social welfare occured at the local level. However, government revenue as a percentage of GDP declined to only around 11 per cent in 1995 before rising to 16 per cent in 2001.

The structure of the fiscal contracting system that was institutionalized in 1988 gave local governments a powerful incentive to encourage economic expansion but limited the centre's capacity to benefit sufficiently from this expansion (Yang, 1994, p. 74). Before the major overhaul of 1993–94 (see below), the reforms had transformed a province-collecting, centre-spending fiscal regime to an essentially self-financing regime for both the centre and the provinces (Zhang, 1999, p. 121). Provinces collected and spent up to 70 per cent of budgetary revenues and while the provincial role for collection had declined in comparison with the Mao years, it had increased for expenditures.

Dali Yang (1994, pp. 61, 63) has argued that the extractive capacity of the state has not been in significant decline during reforms, but rather that there was a realignment between the centre and the localities. By 1992, the central government's share of revenue was almost 39 per cent, having declined from 51 per cent in 1980, while collection had risen to 28 per cent from 20 per cent, and expenditure had dropped from 51 per cent to 31 per cent (Zhang, 1999, p. 120). In Yang's view the key fiscal problem is that the set of economic institutions that were set up to manage a planned economy do not work well in an economy that is increasingly directed towards the market. Le-Yin Zhang (1999, p. 130) claims that any decline in budgetary revenues stems from the poor performance of the SOEs and the incapacity to tax effectively the growing non-state sectors of the economy. It is not caused either by the introduction of the revenue-sharing system or evasion by local authorities.

Government revenue as presented in Chinese statistics comprises two major components: the unitary budget and the extra-budgetary funds (EBF) for both the central and the local governments. The unitary budget comprises the taxes, fees and revenues collected by state financial offices and is subject to formal budgeting by the centre. The Ministry of Finance provides the central supervisory role together with the local authorities (Wedeman, 2000, p. 498). The EBF cover officially sanctioned charges such as surcharges from taxes and public utilities, road maintenance fees and incomes from enterprises run by various administrative agencies. Originally, the largest part of these funds came from the retained profits, depreciation and major repair funds from the SOEs. The EBF became increasingly important during the reforms; in 1992, they amounted to 110 per cent of the budgetary revenue. However, in 1993, the definition of this fund was changed to exclude the portion from SOEs that had comprised 79.9 per cent of the 1990 total (Zhang, 1999, p. 123). The EBF, while reported to higher administrative levels are, to all intents and purposes, subject to control and oversight only by the local authorities (county or township). The local financial bureau manages to fund the plans of the local administration accordingly. Not surprisingly, it is difficult to calculate what the real value of the EBF is, and one official review reported that the real amount for 1995 was probably 1.6 times that recorded in official statistics. These officially sanctioned EBF do not include the various revenues collected locally without central authorization. If one adds these extra-establishment funds that by their very nature do not turn up in the statistics, the total sum of revenues available was the same in the early 1990s as at the start of the reforms; 39.5 per cent as compared with 40 per cent (Zhang, 1999, p. 123). Those observers who have suggested a major decline in the state's extractive capacity have relied on the official budgetary revenue and this has indeed declined by almost 60 per cent. The alarmism that some have sounded about the decline of state capacity is in this sense unwarranted. What is important is the changing nature of the centre–local fiscal relationship and the changing role and importance of the different funds as controlled by the centre and the localities.

In 1994, a major reform of the financial system was implemented to stabilize the fiscal relationship between the centre and the localities. The old system that had operated, with minor modifications, from 1979 had the following features (based on Wong, 2000a, p. 54). First, all revenues accrued to the central government with expenditure budgeted by the centre. This meant that the EBF were crucial to local authorities. Second, the revenue system was industry-centred with agriculture irrelevant for the generation of budgetary revenues. Third, the tax system was simple, with few types of taxes. Fourth, not surprisingly, tax administration was straightforward. This system was very redistributive, Shanghai gave up 80–90 per cent of collected revenues while Guizhou financed fully two-thirds of its expenditures from central subsidies.

For the centre the intention was to raise the ratio of its budget to GDP and the ratio of centrally collected revenue to total budget revenue (Zhang, 1999, p. 131). In addition, the intention was to eliminate distorting elements of the tax structure and to increase transparency (Wong, 2000a, p. 55). The objective was to raise the centre's share of state revenue to at least 60 per cent, with 40 per cent as central expenditure and 20 per cent as transfer grants to local governments. The reforms introduced the tax-sharing system, and formalized it in the Budgetary Law that came into effect on 1 January 1995. This had been on the policy agenda since 1985 but experimentation in 9 provinces began only in 1992 (the following account draws from Zhang, 1999, pp. 131–8, and interviews with officials concerned). The intention was to delineate clearly the division of responsibilities between the centre and the localities with respect to spending responsibilities, while allowing the centre a significant role in the redistribution of revenues. This required clarifying the division of spending responsibility, how taxes would be divided between the centre and the localities and how to divide the administration for the collection of central and local taxes.

There are now three sets of taxes. Central taxes include items such as customs duties, income (personal and institutional) and consumption taxes, and profit remittances from central enterprises. Second are the central–local shared taxes, the most important revenue stream including VAT (75 per cent for the centre and 25 per cent for the localities), resource tax (100 per cent of offshore oil to the centre, other resource taxes to the localities) and securities' trading stamp tax (evenly divided for those provinces participating). Third are the local taxes that include business taxes and income taxes from local enterprises that do not fall into the first category, individual income tax, urban land-use tax, property and vehicle tax, stamp duty and agriculture and husbandry taxes. The centre hoped that this would regularize a system to replace the unseemly squabbling that took place with the localities and usually reached a peak of threats and counter threats just before the annual NPC session. To achieve its objective the centre had to concede that the provinces would be guaranteed revenues in line with a base year of 1993 with a special transfer payment mechanism for the provinces. Not surprisingly, provincial leaders boosted revenues to gain maximum benefit. The provinces were compensated for any shortfall against the 1993 baseline as well as receiving a payment of 30 per cent of any increases in the central government's revenue from value-added tax (VAT) and consumption tax in that province over the previous year.

This new system has raised central revenues as a percentage of the total but also has had adverse effects on local governments that are dealt with below. The ratio of the budget to GDP has been raised as well as the ratio of centrally collected revenue to total budget revenue. For 2001 centrally collected revenue exceeded that of locally collected revenue – 52.4 per cent as opposed to 47.6 per cent (calculated from *China Statistical Yearbook 2002*, p. 61) – thus overcoming the initial tendency of the localities to collect only for themselves. The centre's share of budgetary revenues grew from 2.8 per cent of GDP in 1993 to 6.2 per cent in 1998 (Chung, 2000, p. 46), still one of the lowest levels in the world. The funds are insufficient for the state to play a major role in redistributive policy given their other financial obligations.

The Consequences for Local Governance

There are a number of consequences for local governance. First, some have raised the spectre of unruly provinces and the possibility of disintegration. While unlikely, as noted above, trends do suggest a more nuanced relationship and more local variation in development in accord with revenue generation. Combined with the decline in the party's moral authority and legitimacy, some have argued that there has been a potentially unhealthy rise in the power of the regions (see for example Wang, 1995, pp. 87–113; Yang, 1996, p. 364). There is some truth in this, and Wang's (1999) work together with Hu Angang raises legitimate concerns about the consequences of the significant regional inequality that has been an integral part of the reform strategy.

Montinola, Qian and Weingast (1995, pp. 50–81) have interpreted the trend in a positive light, arguing that what is developing is 'federalism, Chinese Style'. Local governments have primary control over behaviour, policy and economic outcomes with each autonomous in its own sphere of authority. They credit this with placing limits on central control and providing richer localities with substantial independent sources of revenue, authority and political support. At the same time it induces competition among local governments, serving not only to constrain their behaviour but also to provide them with a range of positive incentives to foster local economic prosperity. However, the problems or advantages do not arise from the decline in the fiscal capacity of the state as a whole, but rather from how revenues are collected and controlled. Given the mess that the centre has often made in directing the national economy, perhaps it is just as well that its capacity is curtailed. However, as discussed above, it is not so clear that the centre has lost its capacity to control the provinces and there is considerable evidence that the localities can also devise irrational development plans.

The fiscal inequalities have also led to enormous variation in the provision of public goods and services. The main systemic incentive at the present time is for local governments to stress revenue mobilization at the expense of other distributional and growth objectives (Park *et al.*, 1996, p. 752). As Park and his colleagues (p. 751) have noted:

> heightened pressures on revenue starved local governments may lead to over-investment in revenue generating industrial enterprises, [encourage] bureaucratic predation of enterprise resources and regional protectionism, and [divert] attention away from long-term development strategies.

Their conclusions were based on research conducted in a county without a financial surplus situated in Shaanxi (northwest China). The province itself has consistently run fiscal deficits exceeding 20 per cent of expenditures, making local governments increasingly self-reliant in terms of meeting expenditure responsibilities. Deficit provinces and counties had also suffered from the decline in the fiscal transfers from the central state, something that the 1994 reforms were designed to reverse.

At the same time, popular expectation of the kinds of services that local authorities should provide has not declined. A successful resolution of this dilemma lies with a couple of initiatives – first, by increasing the tax base of the government, a solution explored by the World Bank and favoured by the Chinese central government. Second, and more importantly, through a re-think of the kinds of work in which the government should be engaged, its relationship to the local community and the acceptance that many functions previously managed by the state in the field of social welfare and asset development will have to be taken on by the local communities themselves. This is preferable to the policy of squeezing the rural poor through levies and fees as often favoured by local authorities. In a system increasingly influenced by market mechanisms, it is not possible to rely on administrative fiat to direct local implementation of policy.

The changes are causing local governments to meet recurrent costs from locally generated revenues. Especially in resource-deficient areas this has driven them to short-term planning in place of long-term development design. The 1994 tax reform requires local counties to hand over 75 per cent of VAT, but they have increased obligations. This is pushing local administrations to derive more funds from management fees, fines and other sources of extra budget (or off-budget) revenues. This has led, for example, to the local Chaoyang branch (Beijing) of the fire brigade using its privileged access to high-pressure water to operate a car wash out of the fire station, and the Qianmen police station (Beijing) to purchase a Sichuan restaurant to be able to generate funds to pay off informers. It has also had more perverse effects, with local governments running prostitution rackets through their hotels and Karaoke bars, doctors relying on kick-backs from pharmaceutical concerns and nature reserves struggling to restrain poaching by villagers only to turn around and contract out extraction to logging, fishing or mining concerns.

VAT is the key tax in the 1994 reform and accounts for over 60 per cent of total taxes collected causing a significant and sometimes unexpected impact on the government's fiscal revenue (Lin, 2001). Reassigning taxes on liquor and tobacco to the central authorities has taken a heavy toll on a province such as Guizhou, which in 1993 derived 45 per cent of its revenues from this. Richer provinces will have a greater opportunity to offset such VAT losses and consumption tax revenues from other local taxes and asset sales.

The financial base of counties and townships has also suffered, with the centre taking over the most lucrative taxes and leaving the localities with low-revenue-bearing taxes that are the most cumbersome to collect. A study by the Development Research Centre of the State Council found that in Xiangyang County (Hubei) from 1994 to 2000 the amount handed over to the central authorities increased 150 per cent but central government transfer payments to the county rose by only 34.2 per cent. One can see the impact on the provision of public goods. For the primary education budget, the township and villages contributed 34.33 per cent, the county 6.25 per cent and the provincial government (including the central transfers) only 0.1 per cent.

Thus it is not surprising that the use of EBF and the self-raised funds (*zichou zijin*) has been increasing. A 1995 nationwide audit suggested that EBF amounted to 6 per cent of GDP (the formal budget was only 12 per cent) and some experts think that the real figure is much higher. Official statistics for 1996 show that total tax revenues levied by governments at various levels amounted to 10.2 per cent of national GDP but fee charges collected amounted to around 13 per cent of GDP, and the margin is thought to have grown since then. Christine Wong estimates the EBFs to amount to 12 per cent of GDP as compared to an official budget of 14 per cent in 2000 (Wong, 2000b). This financial reality is not only perpetuating but also exacerbating existing inequalities between and within regions. In poor and remote communities where marketization has barely begun and where the scope of economic activities will always remain limited, local treasuries have little recourse other than the elimination of services. In many poorer parts of China, rural medical health schemes have been wiped out and access to schooling has been drastically reduced.

Increasingly, many poor regions rely on EBF for even the reduced services they can provide and evidence suggests that this is increasing. According to Yasheng Huang (2001), in 1991 extra budgetary expenditures for education were around 15 per cent of budget expenditures as compared with 8 per cent in 1979. Guizhou Province derives fully 80 per cent of its educational funding from such sources (Discussion with provincial vice-governor, May 1997). Park *et al.* (1996, p. 767) calculated that in Shaanxi 86 and 89 per cent, respectively, of provincial consolidated revenues and expenditures were from EBF. It is precisely this kind of funding that is most vulnerable in an economic downturn.

In poorer counties, even these funds are scarce and local administrations are dependent on the self-raised funds to cover costs. These are fees derived from the township and village levels and usually fall outside of auditing scrutiny by higher levels. They are often referred to as the three arbitraries (*sanluan*): arbitrary taxation (*luan shoufei*), arbitrary fines (*luan fakuan*) and arbitrary expropriation (*luan tanpai*) (Wedeman, 2000, p. 490). Just before the reforms of 1994 were introduced, the division of revenues at the township level was 74 per cent from budgetary revenues, 6.5 per cent from EBF and 20 per cent from self-raised funds (Wong, Heady and Woo, 1995). These extra fees and levies have been the source of considerable unrest in the countryside, and the centre has tried continually to clamp down on their use. The latest State Council circular prohibiting them was issued in June 2000, but so long as local administrations have bloated staffs and are cash-strapped the problem will not be resolved.

At the same time, local governments are still under pressure from higher-level agencies to fulfil certain tasks of economic production and social development without receiving funding. Researchers in the Translation Bureau of the Central Committee (Rong *et al.*, 1998) have named the current structure of local government a 'pressurized system' that needs to be reformed to accommodate a more open democratic system of cooperation. In their view, the *de facto* decentralization has meant that higher-level agencies put administrative pressure on lower levels of government, as manifested in the political contract system. This system divides up and sets tasks for organizations and individuals at the lower levels and they are expected to fulfil them within a prescribed period of time. This political contracting and the responsibility system for fulfilling the tasks by local leaders provides an important incentive framework guiding their behaviour. While certain objectives can be missed, some performance targets must be met or promotion will be denied. For example, all local officials are charged with meeting family-planning targets and maintaining social stability while many counties require townships to meet fixed revenue-generation requirements (Interviews with local officials).

The financial pressures lead to the preference for a development plan that maximizes short-term revenue over longer-term needs and that is balanced with social and welfare priorities. In particular they result in a desire to expand TVEs as a first priority, as these are seen as the most stable sources for local income. This is the case irrespective of whether the locality concerned is relatively wealthy or poor (see Box 6.1). In addition to the change in fiscal stimulus, decollectivization and the return to a household-based farming system removed agriculture as a viable source of financing for local governments (Oi, 1992, p. 115). It has led many inland counties to try to ape the coastal areas in setting up similar kinds of industries, irrespective of whether there is the necessary skilled labour force, a sufficient infrastructure and a market for the product itself. Local leaders have also developed strategies for hiding revenues from the higher-level authorities. In Liaoning, for example, some $4 million annually in electricity fees was kept away from provincial

---

BOX 6.1

Misguided Development in Rural China

In Pingchang County, Sichuan province, the financial pressures led one well-meaning local leader to devise a strategy that not only brought him into conflict with much of the rural population, but also did not bring the desired economic results. He had heard that other counties had become rich through silk production so he set out to build a silk-spinning plant on the outskirts of the county town. Next he needed the raw silk to start the process and ordered all the rural households to plant a quota of bushes and to hand in a quota of silkworms at the end of the season. This did not go well and was resisted by many of the farmers who either did not wish to turn over land for this purpose or knew that the land was not suitable. If they did not plant the requisite number of bushes and deliver the quota of silkworms, however, they would be fined. Eventually, the opposition caused the county head to give up requiring all households to plant the bushes and restricted the policy to some 15 townships that he felt were most suitable. He stated, however, that he would not give up the quotas, meaning that while the other households would not have to plant the bushes they would have to pay the fine – twice in fact, once for not meeting the quota for bushes planted and again for not meeting the quota of silkworms. In fact, we calculated that of the revenue he claimed came from the silk production, almost 80–90 per cent came from the fines. This made it very difficult for him to abandon this mistaken policy as the local administration was dependent on the revenue. Eventually, he was persuaded to abandon the project. There are many local leaders who would not be so persuaded and would be driven solely by the desire to rack up revenue from various illegal sources (Field visit, November 1995 and 1996).

---

coffers by county governments. The province sold the electricity to the counties at 0.3 cents but the county sold it to consumers for 1.25 cents. Without transparency the local population was unable to discover the mark-up in price that benefited their local leaders (Interview with provincial-level official, November 1999).

The various demands of the different line agencies come together at the individual household level. Villagers in a poor rural village in Pingchang County, Sichuan, told of how the household had to weigh up the competing demands to plant enough trees to satisfy the forestry bureau, enough grain for the grain bureau, to raise enough pigs to sell to the local state, while being mindful of staying within the family-planning quota and having to provide a certain number of days of *corvée* (forced) labour to the local government. It is clear that for most villagers, especially those in poor areas, despite the development of market exchanges the role of the local state is still the defining factor in their lives.

Dealing with exorbitant fees also leads to invention on the part of farmers. Chatting with a farmer in one poor county in Sichuan we totted up 120 such illegal levies that were levied on his household (Interview, November 1995).

As a result, farmers adopt a number of strategies for evasion or feign compliance. For example, in this county the farmer had to deliver 8 pigs to the local authorities at a fixed price. Obviously he had to deliver some, but could pay a fine for those not delivered. He calculated that he could deliver 4 and pay a fine for the others, which he sold for a higher price on the free market. This price exceeded the price of the fine and so he figured that both he and the local government were happy.

This raising of arbitrary fees and levies has been the root cause of the increasing number of riots in the countryside, especially when the funds have been misused. For example, in Daoling township, Hunan province, officials collected $200,000 from local farmers to build an electricity station but the money was diverted to other purposes. As a result, several thousand farmers demonstrated, which resulted in the call up of 1,000 armed police to put down the riot (Yu, Sun and Jiang, 2000, p. 17). To try to curb the problem of illegal fees and levies the government has decided that they should be replaced with a fixed tax that should not exceed 5 per cent of the farmers' annual net income. This national programme is based on a successful pilot in Anhui province that had been associated with a 25 per cent rise in farmers' disposable income. Premier Zhu hoped to raise the agricultural tax collected from $3.6 billion to $6.0 billion, with the central government providing $2.4–3.6 billion in subsidies to offset shortfalls in revenues (*Xinhuanet*, 15 March 2001). This would be a major success if it could be realized, but a number of observers are not convinced of its viability. It might lead to a drop in the revenue of already cash-strapped local governments, leading to the cutting of services and the funding of public infrastructure. Some have even defended the current system of fee collecting for ad hoc projects as suitable for China's current situation. However, it is clearly open to abuse and without staff reductions much of the revenue goes to salary support.

The overstaffing of local governments is seen as a root cause of many problems and financial pressure is increased by the need to meet the wage bill and cover entertainment allowances and vehicle costs for local officials. Together, these items comprise the overwhelming majority of expenditures for local administrations. Indeed, a number of reformers have suggested that local unrest could be best tackled by drastically cutting the number of local officials who rely on illegal fees and levies to cover their salaries and benefits. One village I visited had money only for administrative expenses; even then, many local governments have difficulty meeting the wage bills. In central and west China and even Shandong, some townships had not paid their officials for 9 months in 2000 (Interview, September 2000). One national survey from the late 1990s showed that in a medium-sized county with a population of around half a million and with 5,000 administrative staff, 60 per cent had their salaries covered by financial revenues; 30 per cent had to raise their salaries themselves and 10 per cent found their salary by fining farmers directly. The situation is even worse at the township level (40,000 population with 100 staff). Here 35 per cent collect their salary directly from farmers (Guo, 1998, pp. 34–5).

This overstaffing has underpinned Zhu Rongji's attempt drastically to trim local government employees. However, it is much more difficult to implement the policy at the lower levels. While provincial-level cuts were pursued in 1999, cuts at county and township levels were delayed until 2000 because of fears of social instability with lay-offs from SOEs already beginning to take a toll. Provinces such as Liaoning lobbied hard given the broader unemployment challenges they face. Premier Zhu announced a partial success in March 2003 when he announced that administrative personnel had been cut by 1.15 million, far short of his announced goal of 2.5 million in 1999.

As at the centre, the number of government agencies is to be reduced. At the municipal level, the number of different committees and departments is to be reduced from 61 to around 45, from 53 to around 40 at the provincial levels, while in poorer or less populated provinces the cut is to be deeper, to around 30. Some have begun to suggest an even more radical approach by abolishing the township as a formal level of government. They see the township as redundant and a level of government that is difficult to control and extremely lacking in transparency. They propose that there could be just county administrative offices at the township level and thus many departments could be abolished or merged and the whole paraphernalia of the people's congress and people's political consultative conference done away with (Interviews, Beijing, May 2002). The county would be a sufficiently large entity that if all fiscal matters were located there could deal with redistribution issues. However, local government is such an important employer in the countryside, especially in poor areas, that many see township abolition as destabilizing. In poor areas, economic reality is enforcing change as townships have to merge because of financial pressures, causing a retrenchment of public services. This has been the case in Tibet, for example, and elsewhere. The intention is that any savings made from downsizing government will go to increase the salaries for those who remain. Given the parlous financial situation, there might not be much extra cash to distribute. Some have complained that if the staff cuts are not sufficiently deep, the levies on farmers at the local level will increase yet further to cover salary hikes. Reflecting these financial pressures, it was announced in December 2002 that the expected official pay increase would be put on hold.

While in many poor areas the state's presence is still overbearing, there are examples from wealthier areas of the local state trying to reduce its bureaucracy and interference in society while increasing accountability. For example, in Qindu District, in Xianyang next to the major northwest city of Xi'an, local officials have decided that the government system is too large for the local economy. District party and government offices are being fused and they expect to reduce the number of officials by 50 per cent. The restructuring of the local government reflects the changing economic structure of the district. The district has undertaken a major programme of industrial overhaul, shedding its SOE sector and encouraging the private sector to expand. By 1998, of the 57 SOEs and collective enterprises (of which 29 are SOEs) under the District's control, 56 had undergone ownership 'transformation': 26 had been converted into some form of shareholding arrangement, 12 had been declared bankrupt or merged, 2 had become joint-capital cooperative ventures, 8 had been sold off through a public auction including to owners from outside of the District, 2 placed into trusteeship and 6 were joint-managed joint ventures. This put the District ahead of its plan for the year 2000 for privatizing (*siyouhua*) 90 per cent of its enterprises. In 1998, the number of private enterprises increased to 412 (from 202), while the number of new households engaged in commercial activities topped 4,000. According to the Party Secretary, this transformed the government's relationship with the enterprises from that of a 'parent' to a market-based one, and was accompanied by a major restructuring of local government organs (see Box 6.2).

The administrative restructuring reduced pressure on the budget, and to reduce this further the system of official cars was abolished, with officials receiving monthly subsidies for travel. Bureau heads would receive 400 *yuan* per month, with deputies receiving 200 and ordinary cadres receiving a range from 50–30, according to the bureau they worked in. The disposal of official cars without further purchases was estimated to save 2 million *yuan*. However, not all were convinced of the value of the savings. One of the laid-off drivers claimed that all that had happened was that he had been made redundant and his salary given to a local official. With these financial savings, the local government was able to decree the abolition of 114 administrative fees charged by the different bureaus. These included the fee for a labour permit, labour contract, leaving the province for work purposes, child health inspection, marriage book, permit for family planning, fee for management of a TVE, fee for bicycle maintenance and the fee for taking agricultural machinery on the road (Interviews in Qindu and Qindu CCP Committee, 1999).

With most problems having to be resolved *in situ*, local resources and their distribution concern the majority of people's lives. Many local officials may well be party members but they are also members of the local community, and where there is a moderate increase in local accountability through village elections and transparency regulations they have to take this seriously (see Chapter 7). While most observers agree that the economic powers of local governments have been enhanced through control over local industry and EBF, there has been considerable disagreement about the emerging nature of the relationship between the local state and society. This chapter concludes with some comments on the effect on local officialdom, while the broader question of changing state–society relations is reviewed in Chapter 8. The tendency in the literature has been to dwell on the fusion of political and economic power at local government levels and to suggest that the state is

---

BOX 6.2

Restructuring Local Government: Qindu District

Qindu district, near Xi'an, launched a major programme to shed its SOEs and other collective industries. This was followed by a significant restructuring of the local government agencies. The extensive economic reforms meant that the Economics and Trade Bureau (*jingmao ju*) was dissolved as the 22 enterprises under its control had dwindled to just 1. Its residual functions had been taken over by a Comprehensive Economic Management Bureau (*zonghe jingji guanliju*) that covers all economic work, except agriculture, with a total staff of only 7 or 8 people. Given the importance of the non-state sector of the economy, a Private Economy Development Bureau (*siying jingji fazhanju*) was set up together with a Township and Village Enterprise Bureau (*xiangzhen qiyeju*). Other departments were merged and thus the former Plan Bureau and Statistics Bureau were merged into one new entity. Importantly, the office of the District Party Committee and that of the government were merged into one new office. This reduced work overlap and improved the implementation of government decrees. Bureaus such as those for agricultural machinery and transportation were to be transformed into commercial entities, while keeping the old appellation and public seal for internal use. The party secretary calculated that they had reduced the number of agencies by 25 per cent and the staff on payroll by 20.8 per cent, putting it on the way to meeting the 50 per cent cut demanded by Premier Zhu.

These cutbacks still left a fairly complex administration to manage 400,000 people spread over 251 km^2. Under the party system there is: the joint office with the government, the party committee, organization and propaganda bureaus, the political and legal affairs committee, the commission for discipline inspection, the party school and the party research department. Under the government there is the office of the people's congress and that of the consultative congress. There are the bureaus of: industry and commerce, finance, agriculture, water management, flood control, development of the private economy, construction and environment, land, comprehensive economic management, plan and statistics, education, letters and visitors, family planning, personnel, labour and social security, public security, civil affairs, audit, justice, prices, culture and sports, TV and radio, technology supervision, health, science and technology, environmental protection, supervision and archives. There are departments of: agricultural industry and united front, and offices of: asset management, reform of economic systems, spiritual civilization, the elderly, protection of secrets, publications and military draft. In addition there are centres for emergency services and general services for administrative agencies. There is a research office and one for supervision and guidance for education. Last, but not least, there are the mass organizations whose staff are funded by the government: the youth league, women's federation, the labour federation, industrial and commercial bureau, the disabled federation, and the handicrafts association (Interviews and Qindu CCP Committee, 1999).

---

either predatory or displays some variant of local state corporatism or clientelist structure (Oi, 1992, pp. 99–126; 1999). What this has meant to local cadres has also been open to different interpretations. Not surprisingly, those who see local corporatism or clientelism as the dominant paradigm feel that the power of local officials has been enhanced by increased control over resources for distribution to those within their jurisdiction. Chinese researchers under Xu Yong have argued that, despite the village elections, the head of the villagers' committee acts as much as an agent of the state as a representative of the villagers (Zhang and Xu, 1995; Xu 1997). Victor Nee (1989, pp. 663–81) proposed that, on the contrary, the new opportunities in the local economy provided individuals with control over financial and other resources independent of local cadre power. However, the increasingly widespread practice of buying and selling official posts suggests that much can be earned from them. Sayings such as the following have become commonplace in the countryside:

> If you bribe your superior 10,000–20,000 *yuan*, you have just checked in. If you offer him 30,000–40,000 *yuan*, you have registered for promotion. If you give him 80,000–100,000, you will get promoted.

The predatory nature of local leadership is reflected in the popular use of phrases such as *wuzi dengke*, and the complaint by locals that they are required to provide cadres the best housing, the prettiest women in the village to marry and the fattest pigs to slaughter for the celebration. *Wuzi dengke* traditionally had a positive meaning in Imperial times, with a father whose five sons all passed the examinations to become officials. In Republican China it became a term to criticize the abuses of Nationalist officials, and it has been revived to describe the predatory habits of local rural officials. The *wuzi* stand for gold, silver, houses, cars and women.

The reforms have clearly led to an extremely varied pattern of local development, with local officials enjoying greater financial freedom from higher levels and being less dependent on higher-level approval for career advancement and economic reward. However, as Nevitt (1996, pp. 39–40) notes, the vertical chain of career advancement is more a concern for those at the municipal and provincial leadership level than for those at lower levels of township and village.

What these developments mean is that it is at the local level that one should look for substantive change and that questions of rights, accountability and transparency mean something for the vast majority of people. It is also at this level that the general impression of a system in stasis is challenged by the vibrancy and inventiveness of solutions to problems. Society has become very dynamic, and not only institutional needs but also the institutional fabric of state–society interactions have become more complex. Much experimentation is taking place with basic level organizations and institutions, which all makes for a very messy kind of China and one that defies simple categorization. The one thing that is certain is that the rapidity of change has been staggering and there is every reason to expect that it will continue.

Political Participation and Protest

Until the reforms began in the late 1970s, China was distinctive for political participation mobilized by the party leadership to show public support for their policies. This chapter looks first at the distinctive features of sanctioned participation under Mao Zedong, such as mass campaigns and the use of role models, and how this participation changed during the reform period. The remainder of the chapter looks at the existing mechanisms for citizen participation, such as sanctioned mass organizations, electoral participation and membership in non-governmental organizations (NGOs). The chapter concludes with an analysis of dissent and protest both within the party and outside.

In a formal sense, there has been a very high level of participation in China, especially in the Mao years. Indeed ever since the founding of the PRC, mass participation has been a distinctive feature of the Chinese political scene. As Oksenberg (1968, p. 63) suggested, it has not been a matter of 'whether' one participated but of 'to what extent'. The key question, of course, is how meaningful such participation is. Does such participation impact on the political agenda or is it limited to public expression of support for centrally agreed policy preferences? Here, opinions in the literature differ widely and there are distinct differences between the Mao years and after 25 years of reform. While the CCP sees maintaining high economic growth rates as its major challenge, an equally decisive issue is how to accommodate the expanding citizen demands and participation. While greater and more meaningful participation is recognized as necessary for economic development, severe differences of opinion have arisen concerning how autonomous that participation should be and what the correct role of the party is in guiding such participation.

Mao Zedong and Participation in Theory and Practice

The need for participation received strong emphasis in the thought of Mao Zedong. For Mao, it was not sufficient to accept passively a policy – one must be seen to support it actively. In theory, this participation was not to be restricted solely to expression of policy support but was also intended to apply to the process of policy formulation. This notion was embodied in the principle of the 'mass line'. Through the mass line it was hoped to combine the benefits derived from consultation with those at the lower levels and those of a tight centralized control over policy formulation. This has its roots in Lenin's notion of 'democratic centralism', but Mao added the important feature that the process should apply not only to the party but to society as a whole. However, this does not mean that Mao was willing to accept the existence of different, competing groups in Chinese society. Mao's speeches at the Yan'an Forum on Art and Literature in 1942 made it perfectly clear that he rejected a plurality of views in favour of conformity to the revolutionary tasks prescribed by the party at a given time. Although he was later to attack the party, he was still unwilling to accept a plurality of views among the masses who were expected to display loyalty towards him.

Despite this, throughout the 1950s and 1960s Mao appeared more ready to open up the system to more meaningful participation, albeit unstructured, than his colleagues in the top party leadership. In the 'Hundred Flowers Campaign', Mao wished to subject party policy to the criticism of intellectuals and scientists thus drawing them more closely into the political process. The strength of their criticisms, however, shocked Mao and caused him to become disillusioned in the scientific elite and to turn to the participation of the 'masses' as the main driving force in his development strategy. The idea of the power of the masses to transform objective reality through a series of mass campaigns became an important element of the Great Leap Forward (GLF) strategy. As Gordon White (1983, pp. 157–8) observed, development was to be:

> generated through popular mobilization and intense politicization, a strategy reflecting Mao's confidence in the tremendous potential of the *masses* working within *collective institutions* under the leadership of a *revolutionary party*. (Emphasis in the original)

Again in the mid-1960s, Mao was willing to encourage the direct participation of groups outside of the party to prevent the institution itself from becoming a vehicle for 'capitalist restoration' (see Chapters 2 and 4).

With the benefit of hindsight, it can be seen that the realities of the GLF and the Cultural Revolution radically diverged over time from the stated intent. Initially both movements seemed to open up new mechanisms for participation, and the Cultural Revolution, in particular, let the genie of a relatively spontaneous mass participation out of the bottle. China's people had an unprecedented opportunity to attack their 'bureaucratic leaders', read classified materials and express their opinions openly. Yet this participation was unstructured and random and contributed to the disintegration and factionalism that caused Mao to move to 'restore order'. In particular, such a system of mass participation could not be regularized; indeed such participation would have been anathema to Mao at his most radical. Mass participation in the GLF did not lead to the breakthrough in economic development that was expected, but planning and coordination were rendered a virtual impossibility and widespread famine was experienced. Mass participation in the Cultural Revolution certainly led to the destruction of the old party elite, but proved incapable of providing a suitable organizational form that could oversee the process of modernization. This has remained a key challenge right down to the present time.

The 'Gang of Four' was unable to deal with this legacy and, according to Gordon White (1983, p. 163):

> they failed to break with the structural and normative logic of Leninist [i.e. Stalinist] political economy by offering an alternative 'associationist' model of socialism which would have transferred real, not symbolic, power to the population.

Their top-down attempts to enforce democracy and insistence on unity while calling for initiative were unlikely to stimulate any genuine participation. The result was that the breakdown of the party's authority and the inability to revive it or to produce a substitute created an excessively leader-oriented source of legitimacy (Saich, 1983c, p. 750).

An area heralded by some as a major triumph of the Cultural Revolution was workers' participation in management; yet as Walder (1982, p. 221) demonstrated, reality was at considerable variance with rhetoric. The experiments in this area did not, he claims, lead to greater worker participation but conversely 'power became concentrated in the hands of a single administrator at each level of the factory, especially after 1967'. Similarly, the operation of the mass line and the use of mass campaigns produced unintended results. Significantly, the mass line was intended by Mao to check bureaucratic excesses and prevent a routinization of institutional work that would lead to corruption and the divorce of the leaders from the led. What Mao himself did not appear to realize was that the mass line and the organizational technique of the mass campaign might themselves become routinized and counterproductive.

Not surprisingly, the political twists and turns and the manipulation and mobilization of the population to support the goals of the various factions gave rise to a deep and bitter cynicism and apathy on the part of many. The Cultural Revolution had opened up information and horizons to hundreds of thousands, especially youths, before the army and later the 'Gang of Four' closed the lid back down on the system. The cynicism and apathy led to the alienation of many from the political system.

Modernization and Participation Since Mao

The renewed stress on the primacy of economic modernization since December 1978 has produced parallels with other periods when the demands of economic development have required the party to relax its grip over society and to devise mechanisms to incorporate the views of various groups. However, in many respects, and various setbacks notwithstanding, the party has gone further than at any time since 1949 in its attempts to take account of the increasing heterogeneity that its modernization programme has produced. The experience of the excesses of the Cultural Revolution showed China's leaders the kind of problems that could arise if the flow of ideas and information from society was cut off or unduly distorted. Thus, the post-Mao leadership realized that a higher degree of participation by sanctioned groups was both desirable to promote modernization and was inevitable given the proposed rapid changes that they hoped to bring about. However, the experience of the Hundred Flowers, the Cultural Revolution, the Democracy Wall Movement and the student movements of the 1980s caused the leadership to be suspicious of participation that took place outside of its own direct control. Thus, Jiang Zemin launched a number of movements to restore the effective leadership of the party and to control social space while not negating the contributions that 'articulate social audiences' could make to the economic programmes.

There is no intention to make the party or the state apparatus genuinely accountable to the citizens of China. It is a tricky policy to follow and it has been impossible for party members to remain immune from the influence of different social groups and for the party organs to channel fully the activities of the new organizations that have sprung up in recent years. The tacit recognition by the party of the existence of other groups in society should not be interpreted as the emergence of a 'pluralist' political system. It is an attempt to finesse self-regulated and autonomously defined political organizations by incorporating those groups the party leadership sees as important into the existing modified power structures and spaces. In this attempt at 'revolution from above', groups are 'created' by the party and state rather then being 'recognized'. Thus, as Jowitt (1975) has noted in the context of Eastern Europe, the move of the party from insulation from society to integration within it can be interpreted as an attempt to prevent an arising plurality of definitions by revising the structure of the regime and the party's relationship to state and society. The party moves to accommodate the increasingly wide range of articulate audiences to thwart or limit the possibility of alternate political–ideological definitions. This is best seen recently with the decision to allow private entrepreneurs to join the party.

There are clear limits to the permissible: the party had to remain in control and activities had to take place within a framework laid down in the relevant state decrees. This was first signified by the promotion of adherence to the 'Four Basic Principles' that were put forward by Deng Xiaoping.

Further, democracy in so far as it was promoted was prefaced by 'socialist' and was not interpreted as an end itself but as a means of achieving the party's central task of economic modernization (see, for example, *People's Daily*, 11 January 1980, p. 1). As the party recovered from the trauma of the Cultural Revolution and began to book some economic success, its confidence rose and it began to reassert its role as the guardian of ideology once again.

Jiang Zemin shares this basic approach and in the late 1990s tried to channel participation along more structured lines through those institutions that are officially sanctioned. From October 1995, following his speech 'More Talk About Politics' the leadership has tried to reassert party and state control over business, society and the localities. These attempts intensified after the 1996 Sixth Plenum of the Fourteenth CC adopted the resolution on the need to build a 'socialist spiritual civilization'. The challenge raised by the formation of the China Democracy Party, the existence of *Falungong* and the strikes and protests over the lay-offs caused the party to try to reassert its relevance. The China Democracy Party questioned the CCP's right to political monopoly, the support for *Falungong* challenged its right to moral authority and the strikes questioned whether the party could protect the working class it had created during the process of industrialization. To meet this challenge, in 2000 the party launched a major campaign under the name of the 'Three Represents' in a further attempt to display its relevance in a changed world (see Chapter 3). Without considerable structural reform, it will not be enough.

Impact on the Sanctioned Organizational Structure of Representation

As Chapter 5 has shown, there has been a revitalization of the state sector with the people's congress system and the consultative congresses playing a more lively role than in the Mao years. In addition, official policy tried to integrate experts into the decision-making process, to influence key groups in society more indirectly by binding them into organizations that are dependent on regime patronage, improve democracy at the grass roots and sanction a limited number of social organizations.

The attention paid to economic growth in place of class struggle has led to a more empirically based approach to the solution of problems in place of an overreliance on ideological criteria. This approach was first reflected in the use of the slogan 'practice is the sole criterion for testing truth' (or more simply 'seek truth from facts'), and the corresponding policy of 'correcting mistakes whenever they are discovered'. This emphasis on practice and a more empirical approach to decision-making have led to greater value being placed on consultation and discussion. It also resulted in the upgrading of the position of intellectuals in ideological and material terms. Gone are the Cultural Revolution references to intellectuals as the 'stinking ninth category', and instead intellectuals are defined as an integral part of the working class. This 'ideological upgrading' has been accompanied by attempts to improve their work, housing and salary conditions, and intellectuals have been given greater freedom within their fields of professional competence. There has been an explosion of professional journals and convening of meetings to facilitate the exchange of views. Professional societies have mushroomed as further forums for the exchange of ideas and as organizations on which the party and state leading bodies can draw for expertise. Many of these organizations have been drawn into inner-party debates through their provision of advice to different policy tendencies within the top leadership. Other organizations have used the newly granted public space to challenge the boundaries of acceptable discourse.

As in earlier periods when economic modernization has been pushed to the fore, various groups of experts have been drawn into the process of policy initiation and implementation. This has been particularly noticeable in the case of scientists and technicians. Thus, they were closely involved in the drafting of the 1956 Twelve-Year Plan for Science and Technology, the 1975 plans to support Zhou Enlai and Deng Xiaoping's modernization programme, the ambitious 1978 Ten-Year Plan for Science and Technology, and the 1985 Party Decision on the Reform of the Science and Technology Management System (see Saich, 1989a, Chapter 1).

Participation and the Eight 'Patriotic' Political Parties

The revival of the 'united front' approach and the increased reliance on experts has led to a revitalization of the eight other political parties in the PRC. Contrary to the view that these parties would pass away with the generation that spawned them, they have survived and have begun to recruit growing numbers of members. The CCP sees these other parties as providing a useful link to the intellectuals who it cannot draw directly under its own influence and as playing a pivotal role in mediating with influential Chinese abroad. For example, the *Jiusan Society* is composed mainly of intellectuals from scientific and technical circles and the CCP has sought to take advantage of those connections.

It appears that, with Deng Xiaoping's approval, Zhao Ziyang and his advisers set up an ad hoc group in January 1989 to draft a plan to expand the role of these parties. Although this was in the more liberal atmosphere before the 1989 crackdown, it may be interesting as a possible future reform measure. According to Seymour (1991, p. 3), by May the proposals were ready and they included: a greater role for these parties in the organs of state power; the suggestion that they be consulted on the choice of state leaders; and their participation in the formulation of state principles, policies, laws and decrees. Non-communists were to be included in government and judicial work.

Many in China perhaps rightly see these parties as merely subservient lackeys of the CCP meekly doing its bidding. As one wall-poster in 1989 noted: 'it is better to get divorced than to be a concubine of the other party.

Democratic parties, become independent while it is still not too late to speak for the people' (in Ogden *et al.*, 1992, p. 135). While they may not have spoken for the people, they have used the new opportunities to press the interests of their own members. The Democratic National Construction Association, composed mainly of people from financial and business circles, even contemplated the possibility of setting up a genuine opposition political party rather than one that operated under the tutelage of the CCP. They have all, however, conspicuously kept their distance from any attempts by others to set up an opposition party such as the China Democracy Party.

Since the repression of the demonstrations in June 1989 and the emergence of multi-party systems in Eastern Europe, the CCP has been at pains to stress the unique nature of its own multi-party system to forestall any moves to genuine independence by the preexisting parties. Articles have stressed the acceptance by the other 8 parties of the CCP's leadership. In an interview, the then Chair of the Democratic National Construction Association stated that CCP leadership was the prerequisite and guarantee for multi-party cooperation. Contrary to views expressed by his association a year or so before, he noted that his party was not a 'party out of office or an opposition party' (Lu, 1990). However, the idea of enhanced access for the democratic parties has persisted. At the time of the Tenth CPPCC (March 2003), delegates expressed the hope that not only would multi-party cooperation be strengthened but that one of their number might be appointed state vice-president. There was precedent for this with the industrialist, Rong Yiren, having served from 1993 to 1998, but in the end Jiang Zemin's protégé, Zeng Qinghong, was appointed. Hope springs eternal.

The Mass Organizations

To head off potential mass opposition, the party seeks to extend its organization, coordination and supervision of as much of the population as possible. Traditionally, the party has relied on what it terms 'mass organizations' such as the trade unions and the Women's Federation, a two-edged sword as it provides a mechanism of participation to officially sanctioned groups but makes the formation of autonomous union organizations or women's organizations impossible. By subjugating sectoral interests to general party policy, the party allows such organizations the autonomy to organize their own activities within a broadly defined framework, and to support the pursuance of legitimate rights of their members in so far as they do not override the common good, as defined by the party. In return, the party expects unconditional support for its broader political, economic and social programmes.

The unions for the most part have been engaged in conflict avoidance, or conflict management, and with mobilizing support for party policy. Even before the events of 1989, however, there was frustration with these officially sponsored trade unions and pressure built up to take a more active promotion of their members' interests. In a July 1988 symposium sponsored by the official union, it was proposed that the unions should play down their political role as a conduit of party policy and concentrate on protecting the workers' economic and welfare interests (Interview with union official, 1991). In the 1990s, the unions tried to pursue this role while remaining loyal to the party. Many working within the official union movement recognized the problems inherent in this construct and that many workers see them as stooges for the party rather than as their representatives. The party moved hard to crush any attempts to provide independent representation for labour; those who were involved in the 1989 attempts to set up an autonomous labour union received much more brutal treatment and punishment than did the students.

In 1989, two things in particular shook the orthodox party members and made them fear that they might be confronted by a Solidarity-type situation in China. The first was the donation given by the official trade union to the students and its calls for senior leaders to enter into dialogue with them. The fact that the official trade union appeared to be going over to the opposition within the party was outdone by the establishment of an independent workers' organization that rejected party rule entirely. The foundation of the Capital (or Beijing) Workers' Autonomous Federation, independent of the official workplace-based unions, was a direct affront to the party's claim to be the sole representative of the working class, and it was interpreted by orthodox party members as a 'counterrevolutionary' organization.

Thus, activists within the union are reduced to exploiting whatever space the party cedes or trying to ensure that policy is implemented at the local level. For example, in the early 1990s the All-China Federation of Trade Unions (ACFTU) successfully took up workers' demands for a 5-day week to replace the 6-day system, and tabled motions to this effect at the annual NPC sessions. They also tried to work on the protection of workers' rights in the Korean, Hong Kong or Taiwan-run sweatshops but have usually been thwarted by local political leaders who are afraid of scaring off investors. The adoption of the 1992 Union Law represented a high point for the official union when it was able to convince the party leadership that it needed to present a semblance of autonomy to retain credibility among its members.

However, such actions have done little to convince the rank and file of its viability. Over 64 per cent of workers in SOEs do not turn to the ACFTU but to informal networks for support when their rights are infringed (Lee, 2000, p. 55). The strength of the Union is further eroded by its declining fiscal base, with many enterprises and members unwilling or unable to pay, trends exacerbated by the large number of SOE lay-offs. Despite the continued attempts to deny autonomous space to labour, Lee (2000, p. 57) has estimated that since 1989 several underground unions and initiatives have surfaced including the Free Trade Unions of China, the League for the Protection of the Rights of the Working People, the Hired-Hands Workers' Federation and the China

Development Union, among others. However, it appears that the key organizers have been dissident intellectuals.

Similar tensions are evident with the All-China Women's Federation. Croll (1984, p. 3) has noted that the common trend is for the Women's Federation to be marginalized politically and for it to be placed on the defensive in representing women's demands, especially where these demands are seen to be conflicting with the overall priorities of political and economic development. These tensions were particularly evident during the preparation for and convocation of the UN World Conference on Women and the NGO Forum held in Beijing in 1995. The Women's Federation had to tread a careful line between opening up more political space to improve the situation of women in China and gain credibility with the international women's movement while not alienating the CCP. The CCP was more interested in the prestige of holding a major UN Conference and reversing the international criticism that had followed the crushing of the 1989 demonstrations than highlighting the plight of women *per se*. The tension led to deep divisions within the Women's Federation between those who wished to forge better links with the international movement and its agenda and those who wanted to toe the party line. This came to a head when the party leadership decided to move the NGO forum to Huairou, a small town some 15 km outside of Beijing. The CCP forced the Women's Federation leadership to defend the decision, a decision much derided by the international women's movement and many national governments. However, the mere fact of preparing for the Conference integrated the official Chinese Women's Federation and the hastily created NGOs into an international network and focused on key issues that have had an impact in China far beyond the Conference itself. Many of the groups set up or tolerated for the NGO Forum are still in existence, providing invaluable support for women. But official ambivalence remains. In the 'Beijing plus five' follow-up meeting held in New York in early 2000, the Women's Federation invited a number of NGO representatives to join the official delegation but informed them that they should not speak up at the meetings (Interview with members of the delegation).

However, under the reforms the Federation has undertaken a more strident role in defence of women's interests at the national level while at the local level its branches have sometimes been at the forefront of key policy experimentations. By the Federation's Fifth Congress (1983), it had already taken up a more active role in speaking out for women's interests. Thus, while the main task of the Fourth Congress (1978) was to publicize and gain support for China's modernization programme, the Fifth Congress identified itself closely with women's interests. Yet, interestingly, it was the government that prompted this reorientation in response to the adverse effects on women of the 'one-child family campaign'. According to Croll (1984, p. 3), the government warned the Federation that it would be a 'gross dereliction of duty' should they let the problem of infanticide and violence against mothers of daughters run its course and not become involved. Having received the green light, the Federation seized on the opportunity and published a series of other abuses and began to campaign against male domination. This has led, in concrete terms, to the promulgation of local new laws against discrimination and to the opening of legal counselling offices for women. In March 1985, the Number Eight Legal Counselling Office opened in Beijing, the first in China devoted to women's rights.

In addition, activists have set up NGOs to work under the umbrella of the Women's Federation. For example, the group of women activists gathered around the magazine *Rural Women Knowing All* has undertaken work ranging from sexual health of rural women, to hotlines for migrant women, to raising concerns about the high levels of suicide among young rural women. The effectiveness of this group comes not only from the social commitment of its members, but also because a number of the key figures are senior members of the All China Women's Federation. The key figure in the group is one of the chief editors of the *China Women's Daily*, the official organ of the Federation. This has meant that the group can use the infrastructure and staff of the Federation to publish their own journal specifically targeted at rural women and to ensure that important policy issues are taken up in the official newspaper. As a result, such issues are immediately in the domain of key policy-makers with respect to issues concerning women. A number of the local federation branches have been inventive in policy implementation; for example, some have set up rural microcredit schemes targeted at poor women and legal counselling centres (see Box 7.1).

BOX 7.1

Providing Legal Aid to Rural Women

In late 1995, the Qianxi Rural Women's Legal Centre was set up to deal with the implementation of laws and regulations affecting women's rights. The county is a rural area about 200 km outside of Beijing. The Centre is headed by Ms Wang Shuzhen who is also the head of the county's branch of the Women's Federation. The Centre uses the network of the Women's Federation, having set up a branch in each of the county's townships, some 17 in total. The costs are covered for a number of paralegals and a smaller number of trained lawyers who provide education and legal services, usually at the weekly rural markets. Its quasi-official position has also brought it the trust of the local administration and it has trained a number of legal workers at the township level specialized in women's rights issues and they are especially active in informal dispute resolution. In addition, the Centre has helped train police officers and established a special women and children's division in the local county court. The county now participates in a Ministry of Civil Affairs project to look at how the representation of women in the elected village committees can be boosted (Interviews with those involved).

New Social Organizations

Not only has there been a revival of activity in these more traditional organizations, but new social organizations have also developed. These range from clubs such as philately associations, to the China Family-Planning Association set up by the government Family-Planning Commission to receive foreign donor funding, to groups such as Friends of Nature that operates as freely as one can in the field of environmental education. Naturally the further the group is along the spectrum of party-state sponsorship towards autonomy, the more vulnerable it is in terms of administrative interference (Saich, 2000a, pp. 125–41). As regulations have tightened control, the number of social organizations registered nationwide has fallen from 186,666 in 1996 to 134,000 at the end of 2001 (Ding, 2003, p. 235). In addition, there were 700,000 civilian not-for-profit institutions, which were set up by enterprises, social groups or individuals to provide social services (Deng, 2002, p. 26). This category includes private schools, hospitals, community service centres, vocational training centres, etc. (Meng, 2002, p. 10). With greater social space created by the reforms and with the state unable or unwilling to carry the same range of services and functions as before, organizations with varying degrees of autonomy from the party and state structures have been set up. They have been allowed or have created an increased organizational sphere and social space in which to operate and to represent social interests, and to convey those interests into the policy-making process. They not only liaise between state and society but also fulfil vital welfare functions that would otherwise go unserved.

The party and the state have devised structures and regulations to bind these organizations to state patronage and to try to control their activities. For example, in 1998 regulations were adopted that sought to incorporate them more closely with existing party and state structures. These included the need to register with a sponsoring state agency that would oversee and be responsible for the organization's activities, while banning 'similar organizations' coexisting at the various administrative levels. There cannot be two national trade unions, for example. This helps to control representation to a smaller number of manageable units and has been used to deny registration for some groups. It ensures that the 'mass organizations' continue to enjoy monopoly representation and cannot be challenged by independent groups seeking to represent the interests of women or workers.

The state's intent is clear: it is to mimic the compartmentalization of government departments and limit the horizontal linkage. This favours those groups with close government ties and discourages bottom-up initiatives. It keeps people with different opinions on the same subject from setting up 'opposing' interest groups. However, many organizations have found ways to evade such controls or to turn the relationship of state sponsorship more to their own advantage. Many social organizations have also been effective in negotiating with the state to influence the policy-making process, or at least to bring key issues into the public domain. Two examples are noted here, one the China Family-Planning Association set up by the official Commission to operate as its NGO, what people refer to as a GONGO (Government-Organized NGO), and the other the environmental NGO, Friends of Nature.

The first provides an interesting example of the extent to which GONGOs function in the traditional Leninist 'transmission-belt' framework, and to what extent by operating at one level removed from government they can open up social space and provide policy innovation. The Association was set up by the State Family-Planning Commission (SFPC) to operate as its NGO, to bring in international funding from which the Commission was blocked, in part by the hostility of the US Congress, and to be a member of organizations such as the International Planned Parenthood Federation. While it is charged with promoting official family-planning policy, the Association has become sensitized through its international contacts and grass roots policy experimentation to the needs of women and the inadequacies of the current methods of policy implementation. The Association, particularly its local branches, has run a number of innovative projects on problems to do with sex education for young people, income generation for women, public health education and raising women's awareness about their rights. Through its pilot programmes, the Association has affected the government's approach to family planning and conducted experiments to shift from a target-driven, quota-based system of family planning to one that is more client-driven, offering choice of contraception combined with education. This is reflected in the launch by the SFPC in 1995 of experimentation in 5 rural counties with an approach to family planning called 'Improving Quality of Care'. This project and its subsequent expansion have emphasized reorientation towards a reproductive health and more client-centred family-planning programme. Currently, over 300 counties and districts have been selected as pilots (Interviews with officials concerned). In addition, the commission has not always been able to control the association entirely and the latter has begun to develop its own organizational identity and ethos.

Broadly speaking, those groups working in the fields of education and environment have been permitted or have negotiated a relatively free space. Friends of Nature provides a good example of how effective an organization can be when it is run by an energetic, charismatic individual who has a powerful vision of what they wish to achieve. The fact that this individual is Liang Congjie, grandson of Liang Qichao, and has been a member of the Chinese People's Political Consultative Conference obviously helps. Liang has been able to use his talents, connections and political skill to steer Friends of Nature through a number of successes. In particular, his group was involved with the attempts to protect the habitat of the golden monkey that was being hacked away by illegal loggers in Yunnan. This was an issue that caught the attention of young people in Beijing and provided the possibility for Friends of Nature to engage in policy advocacy. Students at the Forestry Academy in Beijing and at other campuses began to hold peaceful candlelight vigils for the monkeys; this greatly worried not only the Beijing Municipal authorities but also some central leaders. They were worried that the students' vigils might turn to something more sinister but, at the same time, knew they could hardly break up the actions. Friends of Nature began to mobilize public support for the monkeys' cause and its members wrote letters and petitions to central leaders while mobilizing friends in the media to publicize the monkeys' plight. The combination of social mobilization, media spotlight and central leaders' fear of student action caused them to adopt decisions to reinforce the ban on illegal logging. Friends of Nature managed to extract a decision from the local authorities to ban the activities to preserve the golden monkeys' habitat (Knup, n.d., p. 12; Dunn, 1997, pp. 12–14).

Despite the various concerns there is also growing official recognition that NGOs have a role to play in welfare provision, broadly defined. CCP general secretary, Jiang Zemin and Premier Zhu Rongji recognized the necessity of further development of NGOs at the party and state congresses of 1997 and 1998. In his speech to the Fifteenth Party Congress, Jiang stressed the need to 'cultivate and develop' what he termed 'social intermediary organizations' as the reform programme proceeded (Jiang, 1997). With the state downsizing and many local governments strapped for cash, there may be little choice.

Following the two congresses, more ground has been marked out for such organizations to develop. In a major departure from past practice, the current 10-year plan for poverty alleviation explicitly states the need to bring NGOs on board to help implement government development projects in poor areas (State Council, October 2001). The NGO meeting sponsored by the China Foundation for Aiding Poor Areas called for the government to set up systems for bidding and tendering to ensure fair competition and to break-up government monopoly over the implementation of such projects. Indeed there is ample evidence to show that NGO-run projects have been more successful in meeting their goals in alleviating poverty than similar government-run programmes. In fact former head of the China Charity Federation, Yan Mingfu has stated that he believes government should delegate most social services to NGOs and volunteer organizations in order to deliver better help to people (*Toronto Star*, 5 September 2001).

Participation at the Grass Roots and the Role of Elections

Perhaps the most meaningful form of participation for the vast majority of individuals is that which affects their immediate work or living environment.

In China the workplace, which for many is also a social unit, has been a focus of political attention for the leadership. The working class, with their allies the farmers, are supposed to be the 'masters of society', but the truth of this assertion is debatable. In the urban sector, indications suggest that while more meaningful participation has been taking place at the workplace, this is still far from adequate. In the countryside, there has been the extensive programme to introduce direct elections in the villages, the effectiveness of which are contested.

Urban China

The main forum for workers' participation is the workers' representative congress that operates mainly in SOEs although also present in other urban work units. According to regulations promulgated in July 1981, the congresses were not to be viewed as advisory or supervisory, but as 'organs of power' through which the workers and staff were to 'run the factories and supervise the cadres'. In reality, control is relative, not absolute, and the functions and powers of the congresses are limited to factors such as the objectives of the state's overall plan, the level of direct interference by the party committee, and the accountability of the factory director. An official union poll in 1988, for example, showed that only 51.5 per cent of workers asked believed in their status as 'masters', a figure presumably inflated given the official nature of the poll (*Workers' Daily*, 16 August 1988, p. 3).

While enterprises might not be under workers' control as such, evidence does suggest that workers' congresses do fill important functions relating to production and welfare (Saich, 1984, p. 167). In addition, with the massive lay-offs in recent years, the congresses have become actively involved in negotiations about the level of lay-offs and the compensation package provided. In fact, for most SOEs the lay-offs have to be approved by the workers' congress. To deal with arbitration in 1987, the State Council resurrected the labour dispute arbitration system, which had been abolished in 1955 (Lee, 2000, p. 47). According to Lee, by 1997 around 270,000 labour dispute mediation committees had been set up in enterprises and 3,159 at county, city and provincial level. The issues covered have expanded through the 1990s and now cover wages, fringe benefits, occupational safety and health, contract disputes and termination of contracts of permanent workers in SOEs. The number of enterprise mediation cases totalled 820,000 with 450,000 cases of labour arbitration handled. The establishment of this system reflected leadership awareness that there was a lack of formally sanctioned channels through which workers' grievances could be expressed and that workers were increasingly tending towards unsanctioned actions such as strikes and go-slows.

Lee's research (2000, pp. 47–8) shows that the provinces or municipalities with the highest number of arbitrated disputes are Guangdong, Chongqing,

Shanghai, Fujian and Jiangsu, where economic growth has been most rapid. Most of the cases are from the SOE sector, with private enterprises making up the smallest percentage. Not surprisingly, most disputes are economic, with wages, welfare and social insurance payments being the most common cause. This confirms work done on other periods of time when it has been possible to monitor labour grievances (Saich, 1984, pp. 157–9). The key question is, of course, the degree of success that workers enjoy in these arbitrated disputes. Here, the picture is mixed. Grievance was redressed in 50–80 per cent of cases, depending on the locality. However, as we have seen in Chapter 5, success in court does not mean the decision is acted upon. In one county in Beijing, of the 441 employees involved in disputes in 1993–94, 66 per cent were later dismissed by employers (Lee, 2000, p. 48).

In terms of residence, the urban residents' committees (*jumin weiyuanhui*) have played an important role, although more in terms of monitoring behaviour and ensuring compliance with policies such as family planning than in providing a mechanism for participation. In the past, the role of these committees was less important than work-based committees in terms of the everyday life and needs of most urban residents. This may change in the future with the expansion of the non-state sector of the economy, and with the work-unit providing less in terms of housing and social welfare benefits. With individuals taking increasing responsibility for these, urban committees may take on greater importance. Across China, there are 119,042 residents' committees with over half a million members, with each committee having between 3 and 7 members headed by a director. They cover an area encompassing between 100 and 700 households, but some cover 1,000 (Read, 2000, pp. 807–8).

The image of many residents' committees as of old men and women who snoop on the affairs of the locals has been changing. In Beijing, by the end of 1997 the average age of members fell from 60 in the 1980s to 54. In Shanghai, 95 per cent of the members had a minimum of middle-school education (Read, 2000, p. 812). In the 1990s, a number of committees presided over local businesses and commercial rentals and younger personnel who had entrepreneurial skills were hired. These entrepreneurial activities boosted the finances of the committees, and in prosperous areas membership became valued.

Reformers have seen these committees as playing the same kind of role as the villagers' committees. Like their rural counterparts, they do not form part of the formal state structure but are considered as a grass roots, autonomous mass organization. There have been suggestions that urban electoral reform should begin with these committees and through the 1990s trial elections took place. In some cities the residents' committees were renamed as 'community service committees' whose leaders were subject to recall by the population. In May 2000, Beijing announced that it would sanction 'open and fair' elections for members of the 5,000 residents' committees in the city. They would be elected for a period of 3–4 years. From the beginning of 2000 experimentation had taken place in 200 of the committees in Beijing, while another 20 cities outside of Beijing were also engaged in experimentation (*AFP* and *UPI*, 24 May 2000). Of increasing importance in urban China are the owners' committees. Many SOEs and other government organizations have been engaged in selling off their housing stock, meaning that a large number of apartment blocks are now in private hands. As a result, new owners' committees are springing up to manage affairs. To date, little research has been conducted on their role and functions.

Village Elections and Villagers' Committees

The use of direct elections conducted in a fair and free manner would represent a major change in the relationship between the state and society by forcing the former to be more responsive and providing a degree of accountability to the latter. The most noteworthy step in this direction has been the attempt to introduce elections for villagers' committees (*cunmin weiyuanhui*) since 1987. However, the process of the election has been complex and contested and the impulse to set up villagers' committees was guided primarily by the need to restore some kind of governing structure to China's 930,000 villages. This formed part of a set of measures to restore governance to the countryside and it included the use of Village Representative Assemblies and Financial Transparency Committees and the open publishing of the village accounts.

With the dismantling of the commune system, an administrative power vacuum was left at the village level. While the township took over the government functions of the commune, a new organization called the villagers' committee was to take over those of the brigade. The first experiments with elections took place in Yishan County, Guangxi, where villagers began to organize committees to oversee village administration, to address the needs of infrastructure and to deal with public services and order. These experiments were approved by the provincial and central leadership (Epstein, 1997, p. 406). This new organ, which was to manage public affairs, was mentioned in the revised State Constitution of 1982 but was fleshed out only by the Draft Organic Law on Village Self-Governance passed by the NPC in 1987, a definitive version of which was promulgated in late 1998.

In the meantime, village management had collapsed in many parts of rural China or operated policies that were at variance with state demands on villagers. As Kelliher (1997, pp. 31–62) has pointed out, the starting point for gaining acceptance for village committees was to appreciate that there was a political crisis in the countryside that probably could be solved only by letting the villages govern themselves. As with arguments for political reform more generally, the reason given for promoting elections for villagers' committees was instrumental: they would provide better leadership and self-governing villages would enforce unpopular state policies more effectively than was the situation currently. These observations, based on a survey of the literature by Kelliher, are borne out by visits to various villages I undertook through the 1990s.

The source for the elections were both the system that had been implemented in Taiwan in the 1950s but, more particularly, the CCP's own experiences during the 1930s and 1940s with village elections in the Jin-Cha-Ji Revolutionary Base Area. Peng Zhen, who had championed this earlier programme, was head of the NPC in the 1980s and was the main driving-force behind the Draft Organic Law. Peng's reflections on this earlier experience are interesting for understanding the 1980s. His main concern was how to build political power in the base area in such a way that party committees would be able to retain control of the policy process in the decentralized and fragmented environment. He wished to ensure that the party could guide the political process while giving local elites a stake in running the villages. To do this, he established a system of directly elected village councils, which would then provide local administrative officials. This indirect system would prevent the traditional village leaders from automatically ensuring their election to official positions of power, as the party was guaranteed one-third of the seats in the council. Higher-level administrative positions were not to be elected directly ensuring CCP control over the system as a whole (Saich, 1996, pp. 975, 1017–38).

Naturally the specific environment of the 1980s is different but the logic is the same for the establishment of villagers' committees, with state power needing to be reconstructed in many villages after the introduction of the household responsibility system. This process was heavily contested and it took almost four years for the Draft Law to be passed and, despite numerous proposals, it was only in 1998 that a final version of the law was ready. While some villagers' committees had been established spontaneously between 1982 and 1987, official experimentation began in the subsequent two years in 1,093 pilot counties in 14 provinces. Thereafter, the experiments moved to full scale and by mid-1995, elections had been held twice in 30 provincial-level jurisdictions, with 20 already conducting the third round of elections.

However, Civil Affairs' figures show the slow progress of the work. In 1990 only 15 per cent of village committees were deemed to 'operate reasonably well', while 65 per cent suffered because of poor cadre performance and 20 per cent existed in name only (Datta, 1996, p. 95). Commenting in July 1998, Zhang Mingliang, the official in charge of this work, noted that 40 per cent of villages still needed to improve their election practices, decision-making, administration and supervision (*China Daily*, 13 July 1998), a number he was still using in April 1999 (*China Daily*, 9 April 1999). Independent research suggests even slower progress. One Chinese analyst estimated that by early 1997 no more than 10 per cent of Chinese villages had held good competitive elections. Research conducted in late 1997 by

O'Brien and Li (2000, pp. 485–6) suggests that from their sample of 478 villages, only 45 per cent of individuals asked thought that their village committee was elected.

A total of 3–7 people are elected to serve for a term of 3 years. China has established some 920,000 committees with nearly 4 million committee members. The committees are entrusted to deal with all administrative matters of the village, including tax collection, budgets, public goods and services, public order, social welfare and dispute resolution. The committees are overseen by a village representative assembly that is comprised of all village residents over 18 years of age (Lawrence, 1994, pp. 61–8). The assemblies were promoted by a 1990 Ministry of Civil Affairs circular and over half of China's villages had established them by the mid-1990s. Their role and the requirement that all villages set them up was written into the revised 1998 law. To some extent, this move represents a step away from direct accountability in the village. In some villages these assemblies comprise only the heads of households. These assemblies not only monitor the work of the committee but also in some cases oversee the work of the party committee, monitor all accounts and expenditures and can make policy proposals.

State dominance is apparent in the process of the establishment and development of the villagers' committees. The presentation ritual on visiting a village committee is almost always the same and is delivered by the villagers' committee head, if that person is the party secretary or deputy secretary. On occasions where the head is not a party member, the briefing is usually chaired by the village party secretary, before handing over to the village head to fill in the details. This reveals the complex relationship between the villagers' committees and party committees, a point returned to below. After the geographical and statistical details, the briefing turns to the terrible problems that used to exist in the village: corruption, conflict over resource allocation, marital disputes and last but not least the failure to carry out family-planning policy effectively. The establishment of the villagers' committees are then credited with clearing up these problems and with enforcing effectively state policy in the villages. In fact, it has clearly been a tactic of reformers to show that villages with functioning committees actually result in the people doing what the state wants better. Rarely does one hear arguments based on the fact that they enhance the power of the people rather than those of the state (Kelliher, 1997, pp. 70, 75). In villages I visited that were not part of a project on village elections, especially in poorer areas of southwest China, villagers when asked were much vaguer about the committees, how and when they were established and what they did.

Despite statistics that show that not all those elected are party members, far from it, interference by the party and higher administrative levels are commonplace (see Box 7.2). In Diaotai Township, near Xianyang City, Shaanxi, in 1998 10 of the 12 villagers' committee heads were not party members (Interview with party secretary, May 1998), an unusually high figure. From the

---

BOX 7.2

Township Interference with Village Committees

Local party leaders of Diaotai Township, Shaanxi Province, who came to investigate the villages in June 1996 discovered many problems, including spending that was out of control. They knew they could not simply dismiss the old guard and put in place those whom they favoured. In their view, the existing elections had not produced a leadership committed to a pro-reform agenda. They complained that one village with 11 party members had proposed an unsuitable candidate who was over 65 years old, while another had had the same leader for 20 years. To gain control they decided to establish a village-level people's congress (*cunji renmin daibiao dahui*), not to be confused with the village representative assembly (*cunmin daibiao huiyi*) to which the committee is answerable. They thought this would expand democracy in the villages even though it eschewed direct elections. Each 10 households were to elect by secret ballot 1 representative to this congress. Despite discussions, the Township officials did not believe that the same results could be attained through direct elections for the villagers' committee. In their view, the household method selected representatives who were of 'higher quality'. In particular, they felt that the cultural and educational levels of the women were too low for them to be able to vote properly by themselves. When asked about women's involvement in the meetings of the congress, it was pointed out that this was not very convenient because busy schedules meant that the meetings were usually held after 10 o'clock at night! (Interview with local officials).

1995 elections, statistics show that in Shandong some 24 per cent of village heads were not party members, in Fujian 48.8 per cent and in Jiangsu 42 per cent of the total of elected members were not from the party (Wang, 1996, p. 300). The percentage of those village heads who are party members rather than also party secretaries appears to be higher nationwide. Pastor and Tan (2000, pp. 504, 510) suggest that 80 per cent of village heads are party members. In Shanghai, the figure was 92 per cent while in Zhejiang it was only 62 per cent. The distinction of whether one was a party member before the election or only joined afterwards is important. The elections have provided a source of trusted new leadership for the party and a popular elected member might be asked to take on the job of party secretary. In all villages where there is a functioning party branch or cell it convenes a meeting to consider the implication of the election.

These figures do not imply total party dominance of the process but it should be remembered that while the village committees only fall under the guidance (*zhidao*) of the township level of government, they operate under the leadership (*lingdao*) of the party. Not surprisingly, there are many cases of the party stepping in to affect villagers' committee affairs. For example, four democratically elected village leaders from Yuezhuang, Shandong Province, were arrested when they called for a land redistribution that was opposed by party officials. In fact, they had beaten the candidates favoured by the local party officials and had led a demonstration of some 500 villagers over the land redistribution (*AFP*, 13 November 1999).

It is clear that some township cadres have not been satisfied with the expansion of elections as it has undermined their capacity to intervene directly in village affairs to obtain the outcome they desire. This tendency is reflected in attempts to limit the direct, secret ballot as the main electoral form and propose indirect elections or the use of public meetings to approve the elected by acclamation. These latter forms give the party and higher level administrative agencies a greater capacity to control the electoral outcome. Even among reform-minded leaders, there is a tendency to influence outcome and not trust villagers to make their own choices. The widespread view among local officials is that the 'quality' of the farmers is too low and that they are a breeding ground for feudal and superstitious ideas and backward practices.

There is great variance in the system and one must remember that it is basically only some 15 years since the elections began and that for many there may be greater control and accountability than in the past. Many reformers who support the elections have publicly stressed the 'statist' component of the elections while privately expressing the hope that the process itself will develop accountability and build a more democratic culture that will gradually be transferred upwards in the administrative system. They may be correct in this assumption. The rise in corruption has caused the central party leadership concern as they fear that it may undermine their legitimacy to rule. In this context, it is interesting to note an increased interest in the role that competitive and open elections might play in monitoring, restraining and disciplining local officials (*China Daily*, 11 June 1998, pp. 1–2).

In June 1998, the CC and the State Council issued a joint Circular that stated 'open and democratic management of village affairs is conducive to developing grass roots democracy in rural areas, and will guarantee the direct exercise of democratic rights by farmers'. Particular stress was placed on promoting villagers' capacity not only to participate in management, but also to closely monitor the 'performance of the leadership they have elected'. Further, the Circular notes that all major matters must not be decided or resolved secretly but made public to villagers and suggests that each village have a public board to publicize details of all village affairs. On the party, the Circular calls on village branches and committees to hold regular democratic elections and never to try to delay the holding of elections. This follows the spirit of Jiang Zemin's comments to the Fifteenth Party Congress (1997) that democratic activities should be expanded and transparency increased at the grass roots level, while at the Sixteenth Congress (2002) he stated that extending democracy at the grassroots level was the groundwork for developing socialist democracy.

In the villages, as the Circular suggests, there has been an increase in emphasis on the role of democracy itself rather than the purely 'statist' instrumental value of the elections. For example, in Liuyin village, Shaanxi Province, the local party secretary claimed that what the villagers hated most was the lack of democracy. In this village, finances are published openly every year with full accounting for receipts and expenditures. In addition, all party cadres must undergo an open evaluation meeting each year. However, even here the village committee is felt to be lacking as an organization that can function properly on behalf of the village. As a result, leaders have established a village affairs' forum (*cunmin yishihui*) that acts, according to the party secretary, as a kind of village political consultative conference. To expand representation, each 15 households elect one delegate. This organ serves in addition to the village representative assembly (*cunmin daibiao dahui*) that is seen as too cumbersome (Interview, May 1998). The practice has been spreading and has been promoted in the journals of the Ministry of Civil Affairs. The forum may not take decisions but discusses ideas raised by the villagers to be presented to the party and villagers' committees. The final decision on implementation is with the villagers' committee.

While a strong logic for the establishment of the villagers' committees might have been to enforce state policy, those in richer areas actually preside over rapidly rising revenues. While villagers' committees in poorer areas might be more concerned with how to raise revenues to cover salary and basic welfare requirements, richer villages preside over extensive income from local enterprises and make decisions that concern village investment in areas such as road-building and hospital development. According to Dearlove (1995, pp. 126–7), in the early 1990s in Fujian, committees had revenues for public expenditure that amounted to 44 per cent of total *per capita* village income. By contrast, a poorer rural committee in the same province could only raise 3 per cent of total *per capita* income. In Guankou village, Henan, the committee presides over 13 companies ranging from building materials to processing agricultural products to a 1,000-head pig farm. This has enabled the committee to avoid illegal levies and fines and have one agricultural tax for all. In addition, funds cover all road-building costs and it was able to build a two-storey 100-bed hospital. Even in the poorer nearby Fangshan village, 350,000 *yuan* had been invested for road repair, relieving farmers from forced unpaid labour (Interviews with village officials, June 1996).

The richer the village, the more there is to disperse. Lamasi village near Chengde, Hebei, in 1997 invested 500,000 *yuan* in upgrading power infra-structure and put 340,000 *yuan* to improving the village primary school. In 1998–99 it planned to invest 6 million *yuan* to build a cable car up a nearby scenic mountain, but shelved the project because of concerns that the Asian financial crisis might reduce the number of visitors. For some, at least, the politics is real and deliberations are meaningful. A Civil Affairs' official in charge of election work told a foreign press conference convened by the Foreign Ministry in February 1995 that vote buying had occurred. He used this to counter the claims that the elections were meaningless by stating 'why buy votes if there was nothing to gain out of being elected?'. In some areas, it is reasonable to conclude that greater public control over local decision-making has increased and that the need to place a record of results in front of the electorate has led to greater accountability of the local officials.

Township Elections

Reformers have tried to push the idea that the success of village elections should lead to raising direct elections to the level of the township. However, dealing with township government is more complex and deeply contested. Most importantly, the township forms the lowest level of state administration and thus its officials are state cadres. Their appointment, evaluation and approval procedures are decided within the set of relations between the township people's congress and the county congress, the party committee for the township and that at the county level. Township leaders come under the party's *nomenclatura* list meaning that the party must oversee and sanction even those leaders who are to be elected through one means or another. The township is thus nested within the party and state networks and is the key interface between state and society.

A number of localities took Jiang Zemin's comments to the Fifteenth Party Congress to extend the 'scope of democracy' at the grass roots level and to establish a 'sound system of democratic elections' for grass roots organs of power as a green light to experiment with township elections. Support has come from within the people's consultative conference system and the Ministry of Civil Affairs (MOCA) that oversees the village elections. In March 1998, the MOCA official in charge of elections drafted a document suggesting that township elections might be carried out if conditions were ripe. This was rejected by the Politburo, although Wen Jiabao (the current premier) among others was said to have supported the idea during discussions at Beidaihe (He, 2002, pp. 11–12). This did not kill the issue, however, and at the March 1999 Chinese People's Political Consultative Conference session, 35 members of an agricultural sub-committee proposed that the Legal Work Committee of the National People's Congress should study and introduce a law to promote direct election of township leaders (*SCMP*, 9 March 1999). The request went unanswered and in April 1999, Zhang Mingliang, then the official in charge of village elections at the Ministry of Civil Affairs, stated that once uniform conditions were in place in the villages, direct elections could be initiated for the townships. However, as he acknowledged elections were not functioning properly in 40 per cent of villages, it could be a long wait. Even Premier Zhu Rongji suggested support at a news conference in March 2000 (*Renmin ribao*, 16 March 2000).

In the midst of these discussions, reports of the first direct election of a township head in Buyun, Sichuan Province, stirred great interest within China and abroad that this might mark the extension of direct elections from the village to the township level (see Li, 2000; Li, 2002; Saich and Yang, 2003). On 31 December 1998, 6,200 voters from 11 villages voted for 3 candidates after gaining approval from the municipal leadership in Shizhong. The winner received 50.19 per cent of the vote and was sworn in on 4 January. Previously the township head had been appointed as everywhere else: proposed by the local party branch and approved by the township and county people's congresses. The event caught senior leaders in Beijing by surprise, and a news blackout was ordered. On 19 January the authoritative *Legal Daily* criticized the election as unconstitutional and, to date, higher-level party and state leaders have not sanctioned the direct election of township leaders; in July 2001 a Central Committee document tried to call a halt to experimentation by declaring that the direct election of township heads was unconstitutional and contrary to the organic law on local people's congresses and people's governments.

However, this has not stopped local experimentation with forms of selection that provide greater feedback on potential candidates but that do not fall foul of the Constitution. For example, in Shizhong they have been using a method called 'open recommendation and selection' to find suitable township heads and party secretaries. Unlike the banned direct election, it is a process that uses some electoral procedures to enable a representative group broader than the township people's congress but not the entire electorate to have a strong role in candidate selection. It is different from the traditional way of party selection of officials through the *nomenklatura* as it entails a higher degree of openness and competition. However, it is more open than it is competitive. The final candidate from the process is recommended to the township congress for the person to be 'elected'. This does not mean that the party's Leninist predilection has been abandoned. Practices such as this are important for the party in terms of gauging support for candidates they want to promote and for throwing up new talent. It helps to deal with the institutional decay in the countryside that some have remarked on.

Non-Sanctioned Participation

Despite the development of such formally sanctioned channels of participation, as well as other mechanisms such as petitioning and letter writing, it is clear that the reforms have given rise to unprecedented political activity outside of these channels, some of which has been anti-systemic. Such actions have included use of the 'weapons of the weak' (Scott, 1985), cynical jokes and songs, dissent within the party and major demonstrations and riots to signal economic and political plight.

Especially in urban China, the younger generation is much more committed than their parents to individualism and self-pursuit and pays scant attention, if any, to official party-state definitions of what is correct, socially defined behaviour, or orthopraxy to use Watson's (1992) term. The party has begun to lose control over the discourse that is filling public spaces. Increasingly, public discourse is breaking free of the linguistic phrases established by the party. As one wall-poster at the Chinese People's University in mid-May 1989 stated, loyalty to the party equalled 'subservience and blind faith as a result of [intellectual] castration and loss of the ability to have any independent thought' (Ogden *et al.*, 1992, p. 227).

Urban China is awash with the kinds of jokes, mockery and cynicism that continue to erode the legitimacy of the party. When students at Beijing University talk of two factions, the *ma pai* and the *tuo pai*, they are not referring to the Marxist and Trotskyite factions of party hagiography but to those who play mah-jongg and those who want to pass the TOEFL test in order to go abroad. Even the singing of official, patriotic songs is used to mock the authorities. Immediately after the suppression of the demonstrations in 1989, academics at the Chinese Academy of Social Sciences were encouraged to sing patriotic songs. The choice by a group of elderly women of the children's song 'I love Beijing Tiananmen' was not only a poignant reminder of what had happened in the nation's capital but the sight of grown women marching singing a children's song critiqued the infantalization of the adult population that the party has sought to bring about.

While these anecdotes may not be overwhelming as evidence of party weakness, they do point the way to a partially submerged discourse that is clearly at odds with the official one. As in many other authoritarian regimes in the throes of transition, it is the writers and other creative intellectuals who have been at the forefront of bringing this discourse into the public eye and have opened up another world for us to see in China. Official histories and accounts of key events are a key element of CCP rule; they provide the meta-narrative to legitimize the hegemony of the ruling party. Underground literature during the Cultural Revolution, the 'roots literature' of the mid-1980s and the various styles of the 1990s have all eroded belief in the official narratives. These literatures reveal 'heroes' who are not necessarily party members, colourful local histories and vibrant sexuality that proves to be just as much a driving force as the ideological fervour displayed in official party writings. With faith in the orthodox eroded and alternatives presented, protest becomes more acceptable.

Protest in Society

There is no doubt that open protest has increased since the 1980s and persisted even after the massive student-led protests of 1989. Hardly a day goes by in China without some workers' demonstration over lay-offs or unpaid wages, farmers' unrest over land issues or excessive taxes, or go-slows or stoppages being reported. The vast majority of these protests are not overtly political and derive from economic grievances that are a product of the reforms. Major causes are the industrial restructuring, the pressures on local governments to raise their own revenues that leads to illegal levies, the manifest increase in inequality and the high-handed behaviour of local officials. While the causes may be contemporary, the alliances formed in protest and the symbols used may often resemble the traditional. As Perry and Selden (2000, p. 8) have remarked, 'traditional forms of contention are being revitalized in a new sociopolitical context, sometimes creating new public spaces with new economic bases'. They and others have also remarked on how some protesters have invoked the Maoist notions of egalitarianism and fairness, combined with traditional mores, to critique the inegalitarianism currently promoted. One of my favourite instances concerns a rural leader who rose up in the mid-1990s in Hunan to challenge the state and to demand the restoration of a Taiping Heavenly Kingdom system of equal fields. Through a vision, the leader also revealed himself to be the younger brother of the Taiping leader Hong Xiuquan and thus also a younger brother of Jesus Christ. Whether out of fear or respect many farmers from a score of villages were said to have followed him until the army was sent in to break up the movement. In good classical fashion, the leader was said to have melted away into the mountains and was never caught (Interview with Hunan official, January 1999).

The rise and persecution of *Falungong* (The Wheel of Life) presents a clear case of a movement that became political because of the acts of repression by the CCP. Its popularity also underlined the decline in the CCP's capacity to provide a spiritual vision for its people. *Falungong* was originally registered with the official China *Qi Gong* Science Research Society. The Society decided that it was a Buddhist sect and as a result deregistered it in February 1997. It counted among its many members senior retired cadres, especially from the military, and many women who believe that its exercise regime will enhance their health. The sudden appearance of some 10,000 supporters in April 1999 who surrounded the party headquarters in central Beijing woke up senior leaders to the potential of such faith-based movements to inspire loyalty. This concern and the humiliation that senior leaders felt at being caught by surprise led to a draconian crackdown on the organization as well as similar ones and the subsequent campaign to discredit them. For a leadership generation trained in the high Stalinist belief in the role of science and technology to transform society, that people could believe in such a movement must have been the source of immense bewilderment. *Falungong* was banned in July 1999 and a major campaign was launched to discredit it and to weed out party members. Thousands of followers have been rounded up and party members who refused to break ties have been expelled. Party members were instructed to criticize the movement and denunciation and depiction of the movement's 'evil deeds' and 'ulterior motives' dominated evening television. In October 1999 the Standing Committee of the NPC issued an anti-cult law designed to legalize the repression of *Falungong* and similar organizations. Most of my Chinese friends complained bitterly not about *Falungong* but about the fact that their favourite television programmes were taken off the air over the summer while the campaign was waged.

As noted, most protest has been confined to narrow material interests. In the urban areas, most collective protests have come from the forced acquisition of homes for redevelopment, the failure to meet payments either for salary or pensions, or from lay-offs. A smaller number of actions have come from citizens who have been duped in some kind of investment or pyramid selling scam. Not surprisingly, figures for such unrest are hard to come by but anecdotal evidence and the level of reporting in the papers suggests that they increased through the 1990s. Internal reports compiled by the Ministry of Public Security recorded a national total of 480 strikes in 1992, 1,870 in 1995 and 1,740 in the first nine months of 1996 (Lee, 2000, p. 49). In terms of taking to the streets, in 1995 official statistics indicate protest marches involving over 20 people rose to a record high of 1,620, including over 1.1 million people in over 30 cities (Lee, 2000, p. 51). In 1992, official statistics from the Ministry of Public Security reported over 540 cases of illegal demonstrations and assemblies and over 480 strikes involving hundreds of thousands of workers (Perry, 1995, p. 321).

In the countryside, the main bones of contention have been the imposition of illegal levies and fees, land disputes and resistance to unpopular policies such as those for family planning. While Deng Xiaoping was complacent in 1989 that there was no threat to CCP rule as long as the farmers remained faithful, by 1991 he had changed this assessment to state that the continued existence of the CCP depended on looking after the farmers better. Since then outbreaks of farmer unrest have continued unabated. It seems that by 2000 Jiang Zemin had come to the same conclusion as Deng and the Hu–Wen leadership have stressed the primacy of dealing with rural issues such as stagnating incomes and illegal fees. Perhaps they may not threaten the overthrow of the CCP, but continued protests erode legitimacy and undermine the party's capacity to enforce its will across the countryside.

The rural riots have been episodic, usually targeted against local officials rather than the system as a whole. Many seem to hold the traditional view that if higher-level officials know of the problems, they will step in to resolve them. One major wave of protest was in 1992–93 with cash-strapped local governments not only putting extra burdens on the farmers but also paying them in IOUs for grain and other produce delivered to the state procurement agencies. An official report noted that there were 1.7 million cases of resistance in 1993, of which 6,230 were 'disturbances' that resulted in severe damage to persons or property. Of these, 830 involved more than one township and more than 500 participants and 78 involved more than one county and over 1,000 participants. The actions injured or killed 8,200 township and county officials and 385 public security personnel were killed. In the first four months of 1994, the protests even increased, with 720,000 protests of which 2,300 were deemed serious with the death or injury of nearly 5,000 township and county government personnel (quoted in Perry, 1999, pp. 314–15). As a result, CCP leaders issued a stream of directives asking local authorities to cut illegal fees and levies and to resist from the practice of issuing IOUs. In addition, the legal village and township tax was not to exceed 5 per cent of the previous year's average net *per capita* income. In 1991 this tax nationally averaged out at 7.94 per cent. In the 1990s, central pressure does seem to have brought the tax down to the 5 per cent range but this has presumably led to the raising of funds from illegal levies (Bernstein and Lü, 2000, p. 743).

One problem for the regime has been its declining capacity to police the countryside, which is related to the problem of limited fiscal revenues (see Chapter 6). A survey revealed that only one-third of the nation's townships had police stations and judiciary assistants, with one-quarter of the police stations having only 1 or 2 agents. The researchers also noted that in much of rural China, religious powers or clans had replaced grass roots regimes (Zhang and Xu, 1995, p. 426).

The political threat of such urban and rural unrest stems from the party's historic claim to represent these two classes. The party has also been subject to complaints from others whom it would normally count on for automatic support – the elderly and veteran party members. A number of elderly who are members of groups such as *Falungong* have been alienated, as have those who have not been receiving their pensions on a regular basis. In addition, there have been a number of cases of sit-ins organized by the elderly when they have been faced with forced eviction as city centres are redeveloped, often without adequate compensation and consultation with lifelong residents. One such confrontation took place in Beijing near the Workers' Stadium where a group of elderly residents used to take up positions each day to defend their old houses against destruction by the municipal authorities. The stand-off took almost a year to resolve before a deal was made that was acceptable. Of greater concern may be the disregard with which a number of the older party members, who are concerned about the rampant corruption, are held by the younger local leaders (see Box 7.3).

Protest Within the Party

Most protest in contemporary China is not regime-threatening as long as the party itself stays united, continues to eliminate any focal points of opposition and retains a monopoly over representation and coercion. The main systemic threats have arisen when the senior party leaders have fallen out among themselves. Most of the time, party discipline and codes of conduct make it very difficult for an individual or group to oppose the general policy line at a particular time. While local leaders can ignore or deflect central directives, strategies for central leaders are more complex. They must work incrementally to change policy, either by building a new coalition and consensus or

---

BOX 7.3

Comrade Zhou Fights Corruption

Since the mid-1990s Mr Zhou Wei, a party member of over 40 years standing, had been organizing protest in the northeast city of Shenyang against corruption and the local party's disregard for the elderly, the workers and the farmers. Apparently he found enthusiastic support in this endeavour from many of his older comrades. They enjoyed a number of notable victories, raising the monthly benefits of retired cadres and exposing various instances of individual corruption and high-handedness. His actions led to his arrest and sentence for 2 years to re-education through labour. The party was able to use its internal disciplining mechanisms to deal with him. In 1998 he was stripped of his party membership for organizing 119 trips to petition the government, involving 17,000 people. The expulsion order stated that he 'should have set an example of observing the party's political discipline, conscientiously protecting the party's image and protecting a stable and unified political situation'. Subsequently 15 top government officials in Shenyang, including the mayor and 500 others, were removed, but the party officials in charge of legal affairs, discipline and personnel were left in post. The mayor, given a suspended death sentence, had been fêted domestically and internationally as a model leader but he presided over a city riddled with corruption and gangsters. The executive vice-mayor, who was executed, was said to have squandered $4 million in public funds gambling in Macao and Las Vegas. A journalist who has exposed the corruption in a Hong Kong magazine was jailed for 9 years (*New York Times*, 2 July 2000 *Washington Post*, 8 March 2002).

---

through licensing experiments together with local leaders to provide proof of the viability of an alternative policy approach. Opposition to the party line as a whole is much harder, as is public opposition. If one is opposed to the party line there is little recourse other than to seize power and denounce the previous power-holders for deviating from the 'true line'. This is what happened when the 'Gang of Four' was arrested in a coup in October 1976 by troops under the command of veteran Marshal Ye Jianying.

To oppose party policy publicly is difficult, but is more likely to be tolerated if the critique comes from the 'left' rather than from the 'right'. Historically, those individual party members and groups that have criticized the party for not being liberal enough or for not pursuing market-oriented reforms more seriously have either received internal party sanctions that have made further promotion difficult or have been expelled from the party. Party culture has always made criticism from the 'left' safer. This tendency was identified as early as 1937 by Liu Shaoqi when he suggested in a letter to the CC that methods in ideological struggle had always been excessive and had created a situation that blocked 'calm discussion' of problems within the party. Further, he noted that the hallmark of the party was 'leftism', which in turn had exacerbated the factionalism within the party (see Saich, 1996, p. lix). In the 1990s, the senior ideologue, Deng Liqun, sponsored a series of criticisms of the reforms that highlighted the abandonment of socialist principles in favour of free-market economics and greater bourgeois influences. These circulated widely within and outside of the party but Deng received no known sanction. One suspects that if the intensity and severity of the attacks had been from a party member espousing a 'rightist' point of view, that person would have been expelled from the party.

On a number of occasions the CCP has been rocked by dissent where inner-party strife or disagreement has allowed China's broader population to become involved. The first occasion was in the 'Hundred Flowers' (1956–57), launched by Mao as a response to de-Stalinization in the Soviet Union and the Hungarian uprising of 1956. Mao suggested that what was needed was not the repression of complaints but the encouragement of open criticism of the party apparatus. The campaign was opposed by those in the leadership who favoured a more guided and limited form of criticism. Given what they thought was a green light by Mao, citizens unleashed a torrent of criticism about the bureaucratic nature of the system and demanded greater freedoms such as competitive elections, a free press, effective trade unions, academic freedom and an independent judiciary. Mao was not amused and shut the movement down with the 'Anti-rightist campaign'. As we have seen, the outpouring of dissent and political activity in the Cultural Revolution was also at the instigation of Mao in order to unseat his opponents in senior party positions. This time, public criticism came from both the left and the right but both were ultimately suppressed.

Divisions in the Party and Dissent in Society

In the post-Mao period, there have been two significant bouts of dissent, the first with the Democracy Wall Movement of 1978–80 and the second with the student-led demonstrations of the late 1980s culminating in the events of 1989. Unlike in the Mao years, neither was prompted by a senior leader and both began spontaneously. However, they came at times when the leadership was divided about the way forward and then split about how to deal with the protests. In November 1978, many of the ideas expressed during the 'Hundred Flowers' campaign received a second airing and initially it was tactically useful to Deng Xiaoping in his inner-party struggles. The movement took its name from the 'Democracy Wall' in western Beijing where people congregated to put up wall-posters and to express their grievances. The main stimulus to action was the redesignation of the 5 April 1976 Tiananmen Incident as a positive act that represented the people's attempt to remove the 'Gang of Four'. The demonstrations had been used as an excuse to remove Deng Xiaoping from all his posts for instigating a 'counterrevolutionary' incident. This reversal of verdict seemed to imply that 'the masses' had the right to make their views known and to criticize their leaders.

The dissent differed significantly from dissident movements in the other communist states in that it did not have the support of leading intellectuals. China's leading scientists and writers had already been recompensed for their suffering in the Cultural Revolution and were being given exceptional freedom and responsibility in the service of the state. One person shocked a group of British sinologists with his denunciations of the participants, suggesting that they would rock the boat for China's 'genuine' intellectuals. The movement was made up of those disadvantaged by the Cultural Revolution who did not have the necessary power and/or connections to seek proper redress in the new politics. Thus, many of the complaints focused on individual injustices that had been suffered (see Seymour, 1980; Goodman, 1981).

The most detailed and serious criticisms were to be found in the unofficial journals that were generally produced by young people of 'middle-class' families whose education had been stopped by the Cultural Revolution and who were too old to resume it after Mao's death. Many had participated in the Red Guard movement and had eventually come to realize that their naïve idealism had been simply manipulated by the elite. Their cynicism and sense of betrayal was heightened by the fact that they had tended to end up in relatively menial urban jobs with no great prospects for improvement. Most of the activists who edited or wrote for the unofficial journals wanted democratization within a framework of socialism; they were not opposed to the party as such.

However, the most famous figure, Wei Jingsheng, was critical of both the communist system as a whole and Deng Xiaoping in particular. He was a 30-year-old electrician at the Beijing Zoo who was the son of a party cadre but had made the mistake of joining a Red Guard faction opposed to Mao's wife, Jiang Qing, and had suffered as a result. His essay *Democracy – The Fifth Modernization* went beyond criticism of the Cultural Revolution system and Mao to suggest that the current leaders were no better. He attacked Deng for having thanked Mao for restoring him to office in 1973, but for failing to thank the Chinese people whose efforts had restored him in 1977. He urged greater democracy for China as a part of its modernization strategy, suggested that the respect for human rights under socialism was not as effective as the leadership maintained and called for sacrifice to bring about democracy (Wei, 1997, pp. 199–212).

In March 1979, Wei was arrested and sentenced to a lengthy prison term in October and a general crackdown on dissent was launched. At its height the 'Democracy Wall' movement probably embraced only 200–300 activists. In the early 1980s, dissent was sporadic and often directed against specific policies rather than the political system itself. However, in 1986 and more particularly 1989, major demonstrations broke out in Beijing and a number of other cities that provided a more fundamental challenge to the leadership. Yet neither of these movements produced the kind of well-thought-out critiques as presented by Wei Jingsheng, for example.

Both rounds of demonstrations have to be seen in light of the unfulfilled promises for political reform that had been presented by Deng Xiaoping as an important part of the reform programme; a part he was prepared to sacrifice to more orthodox party leaders to keep his economic reforms on track. Here we shall just focus on the 1989 demonstrations (for the 1986 demonstrations, see Munro, 1988). These demonstrators were different from those of the earlier Democracy Movement; the participants were not the victims of the Cultural Revolution but those who stood to gain most from the newly emerging system. As a consequence they wanted to place their concerns for a better future on the agenda.

The student-led democracy movement of 1989 was one of unprecedented scale that rocked the party to its foundations and came within a few days of bringing the leadership down (see, for example, Saich, 1990; Calhoun, 1994). Unlike the previous movements, shortly before it was crushed it began to bring together students, intellectuals and workers into one movement. Ever since 1981 orthodox elements in the Chinese leadership had been frightened of a Solidarity-type phenomenon in China. The coming together of workers with students and the creation of an autonomous workers' federation was more than the leadership was willing to tolerate. The fact that the federation and the students had taken over Tiananmen Square, the political heart of China and the symbol of communist power caused them to retaliate with massive force to try to crush once and for all the growing demands for greater democracy (Apter and Saich, 1994, Chapter 9).

As in 1986, the demonstrations took place against the background of a perceived defeat for the reformers in the party. The March–April 1989 meeting of the NPC made it clear that the then general secretary, Zhao Ziyang, and his pro-reform allies had lost the policy debate. Premier Li Peng put forward a programme of tight economic austerity combined with attempts to curtail political liberalization. The immediate catalyst for the student demonstrations was the death of the previous general secretary Hu Yaobang on 15 April 1989. As with the demonstrations of 1986, the demands were simple and were not articulated in an elaborate, systematic way. Essentially, the students called for a significant relaxation of regime practice, with greater freedom of speech and the press and the curtailing of the corrupt practices of the leadership and their children. The simplicity of the demands perhaps partly explains why they found such a massive following, a following that included many party members themselves. The students portrayed themselves as patriots who simply wanted to enter into a dialogue with their own leadership. For the most part, the movement began with the idea of reform from within. It was only later that more radical demands were made. Some of the students began to call for the formation of a nationwide citizens' organization like Solidarity that could deal openly and directly with the government. In this respect, it is clear that much of the inspiration for the students derived from reforms in Poland

and Hungary and from the reform programme launched by Gorbachev in the Soviet Union.

This does not explain why the students received such massive support by mid-May from the citizens of Beijing. This is explained by the fact that both the political atmosphere and the economic situation had declined noticeably since 1986 and the reservoir of discontent in the urban areas had risen greatly. Indeed, the manner of Hu Yaobang's dismissal caused many intellectuals who had previously been willing to set aside their doubts and accept their newfound prestige to become disillusioned with the top party leadership. Further, it was clear to many that the party had no clear idea over the future direction of the reforms. The economic problems in the urban areas, particularly inflation, caused further erosion of acquiescence to party rule, particularly among those government employees on fixed incomes and the industrial working class.

Despite such factors, it is important to note that the students had been demonstrating a full month before the intellectuals and workers actively supported them. In particular, the hunger strike of mid-May brought the students enormous support. This combined with the feeling that the movement had reached a crucial phase encouraged many ordinary citizens to take to the streets. Also, by now the student movement had unwittingly become part of the power struggle within the top party leadership between Zhao Ziyang and his opponents. The massive increase in the size of the demonstrations, and particularly the appearance of workers and government employees on the streets between 15 and 18 May, prompted the orthodox party members to take harsh action, culminating in the massacre on the night of 3–4 June 1989. The suppression of the movement revealed in brutal fashion just how far the orthodox party leaders were from allowing any significant political activity to take place outside of their control.

Spontaneous movements are seen as undermining the ruling party's hegemonic position. Indeed, the ruling party has no mechanism to explain such a direct challenge to its 'leading position' within state and society. The existence of an autonomous workers' organization, for example, directly challenges the ruling party's claim to represent the highest form of working-class consciousness. Such a clear challenge cannot be accepted and the party will seek to crush the autonomous organization and denounce it as a 'counterrevolutionary' organization.

Similarly, once the movement gains momentum it is difficult to pursue any course other than one that will result in conflict. Strong emotions, once released, are notoriously difficult to bring back under control. The movement tends to develop a life of its own and often tends towards a fundamental critique of the state itself. If the state cannot see the necessity to redress the 'just grievances', then there must be something wrong with the state itself. The critique tends towards the moral and often assumes an iconoclastic form. The strength of the opinions held often closes off the solution of compromise through negotiation.

This highlights the key problem of non-sanctioned political and social movements in a state-socialist context. The political space in which they must act is extremely limited and any noticeable increase in activity is liable to lead to confrontation. The capacity to develop is restrained by the fact that to expand they must confront highly centralized political institutions whose incumbents will repress or otherwise try to control collective action when it arises. Whether original intent or not, the outcome is to seek the overthrow of the system itself.

8

The Chinese State and Society

Chapters 4–7 have revealed the extent to which state and society have changed since the death of Mao. This chapter takes a broader view of these changes by analysing the changing nature of state–society relations. First, it reviews the Mao years and the legacies it inherited from traditional China. Second, it looks at how the reforms have impacted on state–society relations and how researchers have tried to categorize the changes.

The Maoist Period: An Autonomous State and a State-Dominated Society

The CCP took over from the traditional political culture the notion of an omnipresent, penetrative view of the state. Unchallenged by other organizations (there was no organized church as in the West), the state assumed an all-embracing role that included defining correct ethical values on the basis of the prevailing interpretation of Confucianism. The local official was to embody and proselytize these values and the 'masses' were expected simply to follow the examples provided for them. The recurrent campaigns launched by the CCP in the 1980s and 1990s to combat 'spiritual pollution' and to 'build a spiritual socialist civilization' were just the latest manifestations of this phenomenon.

The state thus assumed the role of educator. In the same way that couplets hung in public places in Imperial times exhorting Confucian values, so huge billboards in the PRC beam out messages for the people to love the party, the army and the nation. This approach is strengthened by the traditional view that people possess innate goodness, and that the proper education will enable them to achieve their full potential. In practice, however, 'goodness' was equated with those attributes that the imperial authorities deemed desirable for the maintenance of the existing social order, and the use of education to inculcate 'correct' ideas was fully accepted as part of government policy. Communist China has promoted role models in the same way that the village lecturers of the Qing dynasty were required to use examples of virtuous behaviour for purposes of emulation. Equally, those deemed guilty of anti-social behaviour were criticized; their names were posted in public places and remained there until they showed contrition for their acts. Thus the communist glorification of moral exemplars and vilification of 'negative

213

examples' has an Imperial past. A stroll through a village during a major vilification campaign will reveal not just posters denouncing the villains, but also sets of creative cartoons lampooning them.

As discussed in Chapter 4, this tradition lent itself to the use of mass mobilization and campaign movements combined with a distrust of independent intellectual criticism, which was thereafter associated with a lack of loyalty. The concept of 'loyal opposition' was unknown. Historically, the state did not acknowledge the legitimacy of an opposition as a necessary part of the political system. This sharply defined the role of intellectuals within traditional society with political control of literature and other such pursuits being widely perceived as legitimate. The scholar-officials who were the product of this system often possessed great political power and social stature. In turn, because most scholars were officials, it worked against the striving for intellectual autonomy. Intellectual autonomy was dangerous and would most probably end up in loss of position or even moral and social exile. In the same way as the dynasties built up their armies of scholars to write up their official histories and to provide arguments for their legitimacy, so too has the CCP built up its coterie of 'establishment intellectuals' (Hamrin and Cheek, 1986).

Most writers agree that the leaders of the post-1949 state not only inherited China's traditional statist disposition but also that they sought far greater control over and penetration of society than their Imperial and Nationalist predecessors (Wittfogel, 1957; Tsou, 1986). This desire for control derived in part from pre-1949 experiences but also from the process of power consolidation in the 1950s. The result was what Tang Tsou (1983) has termed 'feudal totalitarian'. While for Tsou the CCP was the 'monistic' centre of power, it was not a monolith. Importantly, Tsou highlights the distinction between personal leadership combined with mass mobilization and the totalitarian tendency of the party. The former is a more extreme form, as the system has even less restraint in terms of formal rules or norms.

Not surprisingly, Western scholarship in the 1950s and 1960s focused on the structures of the new state and how they were used to penetrate society, an approach heavily influenced by studies of the Soviet Union (see Schurmann, 1968). However, it is worth cautioning that state penetration was never as consistent or extensive as may have appeared from the outside. The swift revival of social networks and traditional practices once reforms began and the public expression of heterodox ideas suggest that popular culture and local networks of resistance were more pervasive than initially thought. Further, as the sociologist Wank (1998) has noted, the local consequences of structures and policies promulgated by the Central state could create incentives at the 'grass roots for behaviour and actions that deviated significantly' from their intent.

The first and foremost feature of the new state was its relative autonomy from the forces and classes in Chinese society (see Chapter 2). Second, the new state assumed the traditional role as the provider of society's moral framework and compass. This was completed in the Shaan-Gan-Ning Border Region where Mao Zedong consolidated his leadership over the party and cajoled acceptance of his brand of pragmatic Marxism through the Rectification and Rescue Campaigns of 1941 to 1944. Third, the central organizing principle of the state was hierarchical, with parallel vertical structures that made horizontal relationships almost impossible to maintain. In addition, the system of household registration (*hukou*) ensured that a sharp distinction was maintained between the relatively privileged urban dwellers and their disadvantaged rural cousins.

Fourth, authoritarian tendencies in the CCP were brought to the fore by the autonomy of the post-1949 state and the lack of influence by society over its apparat. Selden (1971) in his path-breaking study of the communists in the Shaan-Gan-Ning, argued that there was a democratizing potential in the CCP and that there was an effort at community-building with a genuinely participatory ethos. However, in his later work he acknowledges that a fine line separated popular mobilization in the Shaan-Gan-Ning from repressive commandism (Selden, 1995), and Keating has argued convincingly that the populism that Selden observed was always combined with the authoritarian and state-strengthening ambitions of the CCP cadres (Keating, 1994).

Authoritarianism was always present in the CCP's drive to establish power. Not surprisingly, this became more apparent once the party assumed national power and lost its privileged role as agent of the progressive forces of history. As Friedman, Pickowicz and Selden (1991) discovered in their study of Raoyang in the North China plain, features of socialist dynamics and structures could produce brutal outcomes as the system became stronger. Seeds planted well before 1949 in such systemic factors as a security force set up to crush arbitrarily and mercilessly those dubbed 'counterrevolutionary', and a notion of socialism that treated all accumulated wealth as resulting from exploitation, could be used against society in extreme and arbitrary fashion after 1949.

While official CCP history and some Western accounts portray peasant support as crucial to CCP success, the peasantry was only a short-term beneficiary, through land reform, of the revolution. The need to build up capital quickly led the CCP to collectivize the peasantry's recently awarded lands as the CCP leadership viewed the peasantry as the main source for extraction to fuel urbanization and the rapidly expanding state apparatus. Their economic gains of the early years of the revolution were soon lost and collectivization culminated in the disasters of the GLF (see Chapter 2).

By the mid-1950s, CCP policy clearly saw no significant role for the market in allocating goods and services. This not only had a detrimental effect on the quality of rural life but also led to the eradication of intermediary organizations that operated within the market economy and in the spaces between the local state and family. The CCP vigorously sought to suppress lineages, clans and other organizations that might have presented a moral alternative or different organizing principle to the state in the countryside.

While industry was favoured over agriculture and industrial workers over farmers, the CCP retained a contradictory attitude towards the urban. Cities represented the home of the proletariat and the advanced production forces, but they were also the home of sin and temptation that could lead to the sapping of the moral vigour of the revolutionary forces. In part, this ambivalent attitude derived from the fact that CCP rank-and-file, if not party leadership, was overwhelmingly rural and not only had qualms about entering the urban arena but also brought along a strong anti-intellectual bias. This anti-intellectual bias enjoyed senior party leadership support, as witnessed through the extreme personal attacks in the Shaan-Gan-Ning on critical intellectuals such as Wang Shiwei and the attempts to manufacture ideological conformity through the various campaigns. This, in part, accounts for the ferocity of many of the post-1949 urban campaigns, especially those directed against intellectuals.

Research by Elizabeth Perry (1997) reveals that even if the working class was relatively privileged, it did not universally approve of the socialization of industry. By early 1957 reforms had led to a decline in real income for workers and loss of input into decision-making. Thus, the socialization drive of the new state had begun to run against the material interests of both the peasantry and the proletariat. The CCP's rise to power afforded it considerable autonomy from all classes and social forces, an important factor influencing its policy choices after 1949.

In a number of studies of the developmental state in East Asia and Latin America, it has been argued that especially during the initial phase of industrialization a strong and autonomous state is an advantage as it can push ahead with contentious but necessary policies. It will not be captive to vested forces domestically or external pressures that would work against the national interest. The Chinese state was certainly strong and autonomous but its practice in the late 1950s and 1960s reveals the economic and social carnage that can ensue if the bureaucracy pursues injudicious policies without any countervailing social forces or controls.

The creation of a dual rural–urban society was solidified by the household registration system (*hukou*) that ensured state resources were channelled primarily to the cities at the same time as substantial portions of the rural surplus were transferred to urban industry, the military and other state priority projects. The post-1949 origins of the system derived from the desire to get many of the refugees in the urban areas back to the countryside. The programme proved successful both because it was voluntary, but also because the state was able to offer to many land and/or money to leave the cities. In addition, the state did not announce that it would effectively close the cities to its rural population (Cheng and Selden, 1997, pp. 28–9).

As the country moved from restoration to reconstruction of the economy, the CCP began to adopt more specific regulations about the need to control migration flows. Urban residents, following the 1953 census, were issued with registration books and directives began to appear to control rural–urban movement. Finally, in June 1955 regulations were promulgated for a permanent system for household registration that covered both the urban and the rural areas. Importantly, the new regulations made movement from rural to urban areas extremely difficult and even strengthened monitoring of movement within the countryside and from city to city. While the GLF saw one last major exodus to the urban areas, in 1960 the household registration system was invoked to return people to the countryside. As Cheng and Selden (1997, p. 45) remark, the system as it evolved from 1960 onwards was quite distinct for both China and socialist systems more generally. People were now registered permanently to a particular place on the basis of their birth, or for women the place of the person they married. It 'established and reified a permanent spatial hierarchy of positions that were transmitted across generations'.

Migration up the spatial ladder from rural to urban or from a small city to a major metropolis was hardly ever granted. This locked the population into vastly different socio-economic structures in terms of remuneration and the provision of public goods and services. With the exception of the Cultural Revolution when many urban dwellers were 'sent down', a significant phrase that reveals much about how the state viewed the countryside, most Chinese rarely travelled and knew little about the world outside of their own neighbourhood. The system was reinforced not just by the registration controls but also by the elaborate system of ration coupons for grain and other basic goods that were place-specific. Unless one had national grain coupons, which were reserved for only very special Chinese and foreigners, one could buy food only in one's own administrative jurisdiction. The lack of an open urban food market meant that it was difficult to migrate spontaneously.

As the 1950s progressed, the Chinese state concentrated ever more welfare resources on urban inhabitants while enforcing the countryside to practise self-reliance. The associated structures formed a system that exerted control over China's population and locked them into a dependency relationship based on the workplace. In the countryside this was the lowest level of the collective, normally the production team within the commune. This structure had the advantage of fragmenting the society and dividing it into a honeycomb of local communities that would make organization to oppose the CCP all but impossible. The CCP with its network of local members and vertically integrated command system could sit astride and control the local communities.

In urban China, the workplace (*danwei*) became a system to ensure social control (Walder, 1986; Lü and Perry, 1997). Housing was allocated through the workplace as would be welfare benefits, holidays and even, later, the permission for when and how many children to have. Lü and Perry (1997) define five basic features of the *danwei*: it controls personnel, provides communal facilities, operates independent accounts and budgets, has an urban or industrial role and is in the public sector. The system eschewed horizontal contact between workers, students and farmers thus contributing to a system of vertically defined control and the cellularization of society for many functions (Shue, 1988). While the cellular structure of Chinese rural society was long apparent (Skinner, 1964–65), CCP organizational structure and pre-1949 operations dramatically influenced the notion of using this as the organizing principle for society as a whole post-1949. The cellularization of life as reflected in the *danwei* system was inherent in the cell system of the CCP developed before 1949 when horizontal contact was eradicated for fears of discovery and betrayal leading to the destruction of the organization as a whole.

The workplace system became the defining system for urban organization and has, in many ways, remained so until today. The system also entailed a hierarchy of benefits and quality of life. First, the elite were those workers who had a job in the state-owned sector or the government bureaucracy. Secondly, within the state sector itself there was a very uneven provision of goods and services dependent on the wealth and status of the enterprise. Employment in a large Shanghai state enterprise would provide one with better housing, schools for children and retirement prospects than work in even a large factory in a small city in the hinterland. Labour mobility was not encouraged and one was likely to work one's whole life in the work-unit to which one was assigned upon graduation from school or college. In fact, an employee had to get permission from the workplace to change jobs, giving great power to the personnel department of the work-unit. This power of control was strengthened by the fact that each employee had a dossier (*dang'an*) kept by the department of personnel that contained not just biographical detail but also information about political attitude and performance in campaigns. For women, biological information on their menstrual cycle was also kept so that family-planning quotas could be implemented better. The notion of *danwei* and one's own identity was so pervasive that on answering the phone or on meeting someone for the first time, almost always the first question would be 'Which *danwei* do you belong to?'. The reply would help one gauge whether the interlocutor was superior, equal, or of inferior status. In fact, when the reforms began, a number of young urban Chinese who desired to shock put the affiliation on the ubiquitous name card as 'No *danwei*'. This was seen as a sign of rebelliousness and non-conformity to existing norms and structures. As discussed in Chapters 9 and 10, reform of this workplace system is crucial to the CCP leadership's attempts to restructure the urban economy successfully.

The lack of a need to be responsive to social forces and the eradication of all potential opposition outside of the party meant that policy-making became increasingly monolithic and less grounded in socio-economic reality. Once ideology began to dominate policy-making, disastrous policy choices were made, which brought the authoritarian trend within the CCP to the fore. The coincidence of state and village interests during the war years hid the tension between state-strengthening and popular sovereignty, and the overall statist thrust of the CCP left some room for local independence. Not surprisingly, this became more apparent once the party assumed national power.

The tendency towards coercion was heightened by traditional statist culture, the dominance of the party over all other institutions and the tendency towards individual domination by Mao Zedong over the decision-making process. China's traditional culture viewed state and society as constituting a moral and ethical unity inseparable from one another. Cadres were expected to define those official values that would 'regulate all social relationships, with rule conceived of as much in terms of preaching and setting moral examples as of administration' (Whyte, 1991, p. 255). This fitted well with the form of Marxism–Leninism developed by Stalin and Mao that claims the unique capacity to interpret the linear progress of historical development and to be able to develop correct policy prescription on that basis (Saich, 1995). By the time the Cultural Revolution broke out, this 'unique capacity' effectively belonged to Mao Zedong alone.

These factors further strengthened the paternalistic nature of the authoritarian party and its state *apparat*. While Mao Zedong was referred to as the 'great teacher' and the party took on the role of political socialization, a policy of 'infantalization' of society was pursued. That is to say, individuals were treated as children who did not know what was in their own best interests. Senior and local officials felt it their role not only to represent the population, but also to think on their behalf and take all important decisions in their interests. Since the party and its leaders were 'infallible' because of their capacity to analyse the unilinear flow of history, policy failure was traced either to deliberate sabotage by class enemies or the inability of the 'masses' to respond properly or because of their low educational quality (*suzhi taidi*). Ultimately, this system also removed individual responsibility from the officials, as they were merely acting on behalf of the masses.

The arrogance of officials under this system was staggering. Jiang Qing, when asked by US historian Roxanne Witke why she could watch old Hollywood movies but the masses could not, replied that while she knew how to understand the films in context, the Chinese masses did not; their political level was too low (Witke, 1977). In 1977 I had personal experience of this system. In Anyang, I witnessed a parade of followers of the 'Gang of Four' who were being taken to be executed. While the atmosphere was that of a carnival and local people were happy to talk with foreigners and have their photos taken, when word reached higher-level officials, they were not so happy. During subsequent interrogations we were told that the 'masses' were very upset and demanded that all photos be confiscated. When questioned further the well-dressed official, with his foreign-made wrist watch, commented that the masses did not actually know what was in their best interests and that he spoke on their, 'better', behalf. Such a response also removed any individual responsibility from the official concerned as he was acting on behalf of the masses rather than taking a personal decision for which he could be blamed later. The intrusiveness has persisted into the reform period and many officials, even reformers, have no clear notion that citizens may have a private realm away from the prying eyes of the state. I accompanied a popular, local official who ran a microfinance scheme in villages a couple of hours south of Beijing to visit participating families. On entering the household, the official immediately walked over to a chest of drawers, opened them, took out some personal papers, including the repayment book, and began to read them. Such an action was natural for the official and it did not raise a concern from the family either. It says much about the intrusiveness of the state and its agents in daily life and its acceptance by the local population.

The system of intense bureaucratic control over distribution, the increasing arbitrary control over personal life and the concentration of power in individual hands undermined social cohesion and trust in officials and laid the basis for the corrupt behaviour by officials that dogs the system to this day. So much control over so many resources made it inevitable that officials would use their positions to extract benefits from their local communities. Walder (1994; see also Oi, 1989a, 1989b) and others have noted that party authority was founded upon a citizen dependence upon officials for satisfaction of material needs and for access to career opportunities. One of the most abusive forms was for the commune or brigade party secretary to demand sexual favours from 'sent-down' educated young women who wished to return to the urban areas for study. Often the communes had a shortage of qualified people or there was lack of interest among the local farmers, meaning that it was difficult for local officials to meet quotas. Not surprisingly, such activities increased cynicism towards officialdom and a disrespect for those in authority who were seen as self-serving rather than 'servants of the people'. Paradoxically, perhaps, the structure led to an expansion in the use of connections to obtain goods, often those to which one was entitled, and an increased reliance on the immediate and extended family. These tendencies that became more pronounced during the Cultural Revolution persisted into the reform era and provide the underlying basis for the more spectacular corruption witnessed in recent years.

Through the 1950s and 1960s the party developed a highly centralized state apparatus that was far more capable of penetration into society than was the traditional Imperial system. The level of penetration was facilitated by the takeover of power in 1949 and the liberation of the party from reliance on any social forces. It was a party-led bureaucracy that primarily served its own interests, with all independent social forces having been neutered during the socialist transformation. In addition, in as far as was possible, the various post-1949 political movements had eradicated intermediary organizations beyond the family. Land reform and collectivization eliminated lineages, religious sects and gentry-dominated voluntary organizations from rule over rural social life (Whyte, 1991, p. 262).

Yet the institutions of the state were not institutionalized and operated primarily to implement party policy. Indeed, one can even speculate to what extent, especially from the mid-1950s, they functioned as institutions to implement the political will of one person, Mao Zedong. A completely Mao-centred approach to Chinese politics leaves many gaps in our knowledge of the workings of the political process, but Mao's role cannot be ignored. It is ironic that although Mao played a crucial role in devising the 'rules of the game' and associated institutions, it was he who was instrumental in causing their breakdown when he resorted to alternate channels of communication and a more personalized form of politics. One of the most crucial tensions in post-1949 politics was the position of Mao Zedong among the 'collective leadership'. His dominance prevented the institutionalization of political structures that could have regularized policy-making. The most extensive analysis that policy-making and institutions were dominated by Mao has been provided by Teiwes and Sun (Teiwes, 1990; Teiwes and Sun, 1997, pp. 151–90, 1999). This work demonstrates that even at the best of times there was a tension between Mao's supreme position and the demands of party documents that a collective leadership style be practiced. Their analysis reveals that for the most part when Mao was committed to a particular policy, no one dared to resist, or at least not for long. Politics at Mao's court seemed to go no further than second-guessing Mao.

Teiwes and Sun (1997) reject Bachman's attempt (1991) to understand the politics of the period by viewing them through an institutional lens. Bachman portrays Mao during the period leading up to the GLF as critically constrained by key institutions. Teiwes and Sun show that senior leaders and the central bureaucracies could play significant roles only when Mao was willing to tolerate this, as during the *fanmaojin* episode. This was in 1956–7, when Mao allowed policy debate to oppose moving ahead too quickly on economic transformation, caution that was abandoned in the GLF. Bachman's account sees the key dynamic for the GLF as lying with the victory of the 'planning and heavy industry coalition' led by Li Fuchun and Bo Yibo over their bureaucratic rivals in the 'financial coalition' led by Chen Yun and Li Xiannian. He portrays Mao as ignorant of the details of economic affairs and thus unable to undertake initiatives by himself. What Mao could do was choose between plans that were drafted by the bureaucracies concerned.

This attempt to explain the politics of the period as shaped decisively by institutional interests is rejected by Teiwes and Sun. They point to Mao's unchallenged authority and claim that the leadership followed him into the new venture with an extraordinary degree of enthusiasm. However, this does not entirely resolve the issue of how much was Mao's own view, and how much was impressed on him by various bureaucratic interests. On this point, Teiwes and Sun claim that Bachman's conclusions that policies had begun to shape the GLF a good half-year before the Third Plenum are dubious. They see the crucial Third Plenum (1957) as a product of Mao's thought and claim that there is no evidence of planners pushing Mao in a more radical direction than he would have chosen himself.

While the emergent system appeared as a strong state, it undermined the capacity of the CCP to rule effectively and to inspire strong bonds of loyalty from its citizens. Not only did the attacks of the Cultural Revolution lead to economic stagnation, it actually weakened the capacity of the state to maintain effective control for any extended period of time. In the most radical phase of the Cultural Revolution (1966–69), the party effectively substituted for the state and with the party taking over many state functions, there was only the party to blame if, and when, things went wrong. The system, while high on coercion, was low on information flows. This meant that feedback on policy was inefficient and inaccurate, with those lower in the hierarchy passing up only information that those in higher positions wanted to hear. Yet, paradoxically, even though this was not Mao's intention, the Cultural Revolution enabled the young people of China to read and learn more about the inner workings of the system than had been the case before. In addition, the travels that many had undertaken as Red Guards and the periods spent forcibly in the countryside by many had revealed to them the harshness of rural life, a harshness that clashed dramatically with the Maoist images of the rural idyll with which they had grown up. Further, Mao's inspiration to attack the party-state authorities, and indeed all authority, bred a disrespect for authority among the people. Subsequently, the savagery with which the radical movement was squashed, the manner in which Mao seemed to turn his back on the 'revolutionary youth' once they had destroyed his party colleagues, and his attempts to rebuild the party-state apparatus, caused many a young rebel to become disillusioned with the 'Great Helmsman'. These factors combined with the stagnating economy meant that there was a population receptive to a radical shake-up of the system once Mao died, the 'Gang of Four' were arrested and Deng Xiaoping returned to power. It also explains the energy of reform ideas that poured out in the late 1970s and early 1980s, both from the official press and in the unofficial journals. While Deng's decisions to squash the Democracy Wall Movement of 1978–79 and the recurrent campaigns against 'bourgeois liberalism' showed that there would be limits to the extent of significant political change, the economic reforms have radically reduced the capacity of the state to intervene in society.

State–Society Relations under Reforms: A Negotiated State

The economic reforms launched by the CCP in December 1978 led to a relaxation of party control over the economy, society and ultimately over public discourse, in part by design and in part by default. Reforms have led to a major transformation of urban and rural society (see Chapter 1). Once social spaces were opened up by the party and state's tactical withdrawal, this led to both the pressure for a further opening up of space and the filling of it with unorthodox ideas.

The reforms in China share certain features with those in other former state-socialist systems. There has been a progressive decline in the state control of the economy, with powers devolved from state agencies to enterprises, and a decrease in the use of mandatory planning mechanisms and a concomitant increase in the use of market forces to guide distribution and, increasingly, production choices. The role of the market has been gradually extended beyond goods and services to labour, now increasingly seen as a commodity (Tomba, 2001), and capital. By contrast, there has been concerted resistance to allowing the development of a market in political ideas. The process has been accompanied by debates over diversification of the ownership structure of the economy, with a marked increase in the collective and private sectors. In addition, there has been an increasing appreciation that law can play a role in moderating official excesses and governing relations between state and society, and that there should be increased accountability of officials not only to the party but also to society.

The economic changes have redefined the social structure and are changing the distribution of power between state and society, have altered the principles on which society is organized and the ways in which it interacts with the state apparatus. Chinese society has become more complex as a result in terms of both structure and attitudes and at the same time has become more fluid and dynamic than at any time since the early 1950s. There is greater social and geographical mobility and horizontal interaction and integration has developed as the vertical and cellular boundaries of the traditional Leninist system have become more porous. Finally, there has been a significant redistribution of economic power away from the state and its ancillary agencies and towards groups, new or reformed institutions, households and perhaps even individuals.

These trends were seen clearly in the reforms accepted by the Fifteenth Party Congress and the Ninth NPC (1997–98) that mark a significant retreat of the role of the state in regulating society (see Chapter 3). Over time, the political consequences of this are liable to be considerable. The partial withdrawal of the state and party from people's lives has led to a revival of many traditional practices, the emergence of new organizations to fill the institutional void and the appearance of new trends in thought to fill the spiritual void. However, this does not necessarily mean that the party's power will be eaten away, as a mixed picture emerges if we look at the 'moral resources' possessed by those who either oppose or do not fully support the party-state. While it is true that public discourse is breaking free of the codes and linguistic phrases established by the party-state, it is also clear that no coherent alternative vision has emerged that would fashion either a civil society or a rapid construction of a democratic political order. From the party's point of view, what is lurking in the shadows waiting to pounce on any opening that would allow freedom of expression is revivalism, religion, linguistic division, regional and non-Han ethnic loyalties.

What we have seen is a progressive undermining of the party's own heroic narrative of its central role in the revolution (see Box 8.1) and reemergence of popular religion, class and even secret societies providing not only alternative sources for belief but also as sites for reciprocity and welfare distribution. In the urban areas, there is also the emergence of a focus on individual desires and wants, something that will be enhanced further by the single-child policy. This is reflected in material culture, music and much more hedonistic literature, all of which conflict with the party's traditional collectivist ethos. Thus, while party propaganda tells us that 'women hold up half the sky', Shanghai writer, Wen Hui, tells us women 'have much more freedom than women fifty years ago, better looks than those of thirty years ago, and a greater variety of orgasms than women ten years ago' (Wen Hui, 2002, p. 90). Individuals are rejecting the collectivist ethos and believe that they have more to gain through the pursuit of their own self-interest rather than supporting the collective. This is problematic for the CCP as it still professes belief in socialism and all socialist systems are based on some variant of collective individualism (Apter and Saich, 1994).

To some extent, the party is right to be afraid. At present, the most clearly emerging alternative foci of identity are ones that tend to weaken centripetal forces. The most obvious are the re-statement of Tibetan and Uighur cultural identities that have led to a number of clashes between local demonstrators and the internal security apparatus and the PLA. Similarly, coastal China is not only moving away from Beijing in terms of its economic policy but also in terms of cultural identity. In Guangdong, this is reinforced by the use of the Cantonese language and the interactions with Hong Kong. In Fujian, this is strengthened by the ties across the Taiwan straits.

With the 'belief vacuum' at the centre, traditional belief systems and organizations are beginning to reemerge, such as popular religion, clans and even secret societies. Not only in the countryside but even in the suburban areas, temples are once again becoming sites for worship and hubs in an intricate system of reciprocity and welfare distribution. In southern China particularly, clans and lineages have reappropriated the role of local self-organization that was partly taken away from them after the communist conquest swept down from the north in the late 1940s. Secret societies are once again flourishing in China and contacts have been established with their counterparts based in Hong Kong and farther afield. Groups such as the *Falungong* have provided not only exercise outlets for Chinese citizens, but also spiritual outlets that the party has been swift to crack down on.

In urban China, while the party's official discourse has ceased to be hegemonic and the voice of alternative discourses is readily heard, no new dominant discourse has emerged. What is emerging is the individual as focus.

BOX 8.1

The Party, the Revolution and Modern Film

Chen Kaige is a film-maker whose film *Yellow Earth* angered many party veterans for its portrayal of conditions in a village on the shores of the Yellow River in Northwest China before the communist victory. The film cut to the core a number of the basic myths of the party's narrative about its rise to power. The village is shown as having a continuing history broken only by when the rains come and whatever ills nature may inflict upon it. The struggle is against nature not a class struggle against landlords as portrayed in official party history. If this were not enough, portrayal of the party is remote. Yan'an, the centre of the revolution, is most notable by its absence. This at a time when official histories claim that the party was active in raising peasant political awareness and thereby arousing them to help the party defeat the Japanese invader. The only trace of the party is a soldier who is collecting folk songs. When he does intervene it proves disastrous even though his intention is benevolent if paternalistic. The film casts doubt on the whole Yan'an enterprise and undermines it as the legitimizing myth of communist rule. In one poignant moment the soldier asks a goat-herder boy to sing a local song, a song that he expects will celebrate peasant survival amidst the harshness. He is shocked by what he hears:

When the pomegranate flowers, the leaves start showing,
My mother sold me off to him, without me knowing.
All I ever asked for, was a good man to wed,
But what I ended up with was a little piss-in-bed.
When you piss, I'll piss along,
Curse you, you can piss with me.
In spring next year, when the flowers blossom red,
Frogs will start croaking, under the bed.
Right to the East Ocean, flows a river of piss,
To the Dragon King's palace under the sea.
The Dragon King laughs, as he hears the piss:
This little piss-in-bed is in the same line as me.

The perplexed soldier replies with a song typical of the sterile eulogies of the CCP.

(Translation adapted from Barmé and Minford, 1988, pp. 256–7)

This is impossible for party veterans to contemplate with their stress on a discourse of the 'collective'. The new emphasis might all too easily lead to the realization of oneself as an individual citizen of China rather than as a subjugated element of the masses of the PRC. At present, the only binding factor is the desire to make as much money as quickly as possible and to live a relatively untroubled life.

These trends are best seen away from the political centre where concerns with political conformity are less stringent. In some ways, China at the non-central level begins to resemble descriptions of the traditional. Official vertical reporting is in Marxist terminology (rather than Confucian) and economic statistics will be cooked to conform to centrally set targets. Traditionally, officials passed up Confucian accounts of their locality while many were themselves practising Buddhists, Daoists or whatever. In many areas of China, party organs have atrophied or have become economic service organs. Central officials often mention that half or more of party organizations at the local level do not function well. With the party's withdrawal, as we have seen, traditional belief systems and organizations – popular religion, clans and even secret societies – are beginning to make a comeback. In Sichuan and Yunnan, I have met local party officials who are shamans or Daoists, combining party rule with local spiritual leadership. One survey of a Catholic area in Northern China concluded that the reputation of village cadres was markedly lower than that of local religious leaders (Wu, 1997, pp. 54–62).

Of Civil Society, Corporatism, Predation and Negotiation

It is not surprising that these tumultuous changes have prompted both Chinese and Western scholars to reconceptualize the relationship between state and society. The problem of definition is compounded by the fact that we are trying to deal with a moving target, a state and society in transition. We are dealing with not only the dynamics of the interaction and how this has changed over time, but also with the changes within the state sector and society. What appeared as a predatory local state may evolve later into one of social partnership. We are also dealing with a country where multiple models of state–society relations may be operating at the same time. It is clear that the local state apparatus in Wenzhou, Zhejiang Province, with its privatized economy operates in quite a different way from a neo-Maoist showcase on the north China plain. As Baum and Shevchenko (1999, pp. 333–4) have pointed out, there is considerable ideological confusion concerning the analysis of the state in China.

While social space has opened up, the state has continued to retain a great deal of its organizational power and has moved to dominate the space and reorganize the newly emergent organizations. This is resulting in new hybrid forms of public/private that are difficult to define precisely. That the public clearly dominates in most cases is reflected in the growing interest in the ideological sphere in China by younger intellectuals with statist ideologies of neo-authoritarianism and neo-conservatism.

Given this phenomenon, China's traditional culture and the previous practice of CCP rule, it is surprising that the concept of civil society received so much scholarly attention during the 1990s. The rise or reemergence of civil society was seen as an important component or even precursor of democratization in China. This search for the signs of civil society was sharpened by the large-scale, student-led demonstrations of 1989 in China and the collapse of the former Communist regimes of Eastern Europe. The number of people who participated and the rapidity with which they formed autonomous organizations caused some to argue that the movement heralded the emergence of a civil society in China (Sullivan, 1990). Observers of the Soviet Union have argued that the collapse of the empire power and of Communist parties in the East European satellites was aided by the development of a civil society that operated independently of the party-penetrated state and society. Gradually, the logic runs, this undermined the official structures and organizations, leaving nothing but a hollow edifice easily toppled. This prompted scholars of contemporary China to see if a similar phenomenon was at work there.

Initial literature on civil society and contemporary China focused on the areas of conflict between society and the state. Almost all types of nonconformity or anti-regime behaviour were cited as evidence of an emerging civil society. This, however, is too simplistic. One of the major reasons that the 1989 protests failed was the absence of a framework of a civil society on to which they could graft. In addition, it is clear that to thrive a lively civil society needs a competent state structure and impartial legal system. Without this the free-for-all is more likely to produce an uncivil society, as in Russia.

Recent writing has taken a more nuanced view but still emphasizes the need for organizations of civil society to enjoy autonomy *vis-à-vis* the state. This includes social groups that want to operate independently of the party and state structures such as private business enterprises, trade or professional bodies and religious organizations (Gold, 1990; Whyte, 1992; Dean, 1993). While such accounts provide useful descriptions of what might constitute elements of a civil society, and where one might look for them, they run the risk of viewing civil society as inevitably pitted against the state and developing *against* the state. Deng and Jing (1992), in one of the main Chinese analyses of civil society, also take as a given that it refers to a 'private sphere of autonomous economic and social activities based on principles of a voluntary contract'.

Such approaches underestimate the role the party and the state are playing in sponsoring significant changes that lead to organizational innovation that could be a precursor to civil society. State entities have given birth to many of the new social organizations in China, known as GONGOs. Many of the original briefcase companies (*pibao gongsi*), small mobile businesses where all the paperwork could fit in a briefcase, were set up by state employees who were moonlighting from their state jobs. For example, researchers from the Chinese Academy of Social Sciences, the nation's premier think-tank for the social sciences, have to report for work only two mornings a week and publication requirements are minimal. Their housing is subsidized by the work-unit, as are their medical expenses, basic salary and other costs. Thus, costs are minimal should they wish to go into business and they can use state-subsidized offices and facilities to pursue entrepreneurial goals. Should the company fail, they can simply walk away and start again. This phenomenon has also occurred at an institutional level. One of Beijing's largest SOEs runs about 30–40 enterprises under its umbrella, ranging from collectives, through private companies, to joint-ventures. At its peak, 25–30 per cent of FDI in China is estimated to have been 'round-trip capital' exported to Hong Kong and then reinvested in China.

To try to address this complexity, Frolic (1997, pp. 48, 56) uses the notion of a 'state-led civil society'. This seeming contradiction in terms accounts for Chinese authoritarianism that is creating change from the top-down as an adjunct to state power. This civil society is created by the state to help it govern, co-opt and socialize potentially politically active elements in the population. This helps Frolic to avoid the pitfalls of portraying civil society as against the state and it permits a dynamic interaction between society and the party and state structures. It also suggests a potential in the relationship that proponents of corporatism as an explanatory model run the risk of missing.

As we have seen in Chapters 6 and 7, there has been a significant redistribution of power, a revitalization of 'mass organizations' and the creation of new entities. Some suggest the structures arising under this reordering may not amount to a civil society but instead resemble 'state corporatism'. Their continued existence, not to mention degree of influence and well-being, depend on the whim of the party and the state. In one way or another, all these authors are trying to get to grips with state-dependent interpenetration. As Baum and Shevchenko (1999) point out, the principal attraction of corporatist models is their ability simultaneously to acknowledge the pluralizing socio-economic changes induced by market reforms and the continued dominance of the Leninist party-state. This allows writers to explore the opening up of social space while explaining continued control through more indirect mechanisms of coordination and co-optation.

Applications of corporatism to China have come in various forms. The work of Chan (1993), Saich (1994c, 1994d) and Unger and Chan (1995) have used it to refer to the co-optation of the mass organizations as their roles have changed during the reform period. By contrast, Oi (1999) has used the notion of local state corporatism to explain the process of explosive rural economic growth that took off in the 1980s and continued into the 1990s. This model seems appropriate for those areas such as in southern Jiangsu that have a legacy of collective-run industries that formed the basis for TVE development. Oi shows how the change in incentives allowed local communist officials to play the key role in fostering this growth through local government entrepreneurship. The loss of agricultural revenue from decollectivization, combined with hardened budget constraints, while granting local governments greater rights over any surplus, were crucial. This meant that for those leaders willing to take up the challenge there was a major opportunity to develop the rural industrial economy. In Oi's view (1999, p. 11) 'collectively-owned industrial enterprises served better both the political and the economic interests of local cadres during the initial stages of reform'. In this process, local officials acted like a board of directors in their management of village affairs. Walder has explored this idea in his analysis of local governments as industrial firms (Walder, 1995a, pp. 263–301; 1998a, pp. 62–85). In Walder's view, the key question for a transitional economy is not whether the government should play a role, but what that role should be. A number of other writers have taken up similar themes in looking at the local state as developmental (Blecher and Shue, 1996) or entrepreneurial (Duckett, 1998).

However, as we saw in Chapter 6, the resources available to the local state vary enormously and this affects the nature of entrepreneurialism. Local leaders with no industrial base have either had to build one, often with disastrous results, or have been predatory. Sargeson and Zhang (1999, pp. 77–99) challenge Oi's and Walder's findings even for more developed areas on the basis of their study of a sub-district of Hangzhou, capital of Zhejiang Province. They question the general applicability of the assertion that local governments with strong property rights have acted as entrepreneurs fostering economic development and meeting social demands through the development of collective industries. Their study shows that local government officials put their own objectives above not only the aims of the central government but also above those of the local community. They assert that the notion of 'local state corporatism' mistakenly 'conflates the interests of local governments, individual officials and the members of local communities, and also fails to consider broader implication of concentrating property and power in the hands of lower-level governments and officials' (1999, p. 79). With the lack of accountability the local community is excluded from the decision-making process and has no choice other than to go along with the decisions of the 'board of directors', whether they benefit the local community or not.

With the promotion of shareholding in the latter part of the 1990s, it has become clear that local officials in a number of areas have used their official positions to acquire major benefits for themselves, families and associates. As one local official in southern Jiangsu commented to me on hearing Premier Zhu's bold reform plan of March 1998, 'one last chance to get rich'. In one village I visited in May 1999 near Wuxi, Jiangsu Province, the three key members of the party committee ran the village's major businesses. They complained that the pittance they received for party work (300 *yuan* a month) was no incentive. What was an incentive, however, was that they had used their positions of power to gain majority shareholdings in the enterprises. One survey by Chinese researchers concluded that most village cadres did the job only for economic benefit, while 90 per cent of villagers refused to be village team heads as the salaries were too low and often could not be paid anyway (Li, Wang and Tang, 1994, p. 32).

The situation is worse in resource-deficient localities or those that are dependent on one product. The work of Guo (1999, pp. 71–99) in Jinguan township in northwest Yunnan reveals this. It is a poor township where the local administration forced the farmers to plant tobacco. This generated revenue for the township government because of a good revenue-sharing agreement with the county-level government. For the province as a whole the tobacco industry provides 70 per cent of the revenues. Since 1991, the local county has obliged 11 of the 18 townships to grow tobacco and excluded only those in the mountainous areas where the conditions were clearly not conducive. Not surprisingly the farmers were unhappy as the tobacco took land away from their capacity to grow rice and they earned less from tobacco. The county government derives enormous revenues, however, as it operates a sales monopoly and has the highest agricultural tax at 38 per cent. To buy compliance of the township authorities, the county signed a revenue-sharing agreement that allowed the township to keep two-thirds of the tobacco revenue. This cosy agreement ran into problems at the end of 1993 when a bad harvest combined with the government's harsh extraction policy to cause public protests. Compulsory tobacco production was abandoned in 1994 but Guo surmises that this was because of the general 1994 fiscal reform that adjusted the sharing of tobacco revenues between higher and lower levels of government. When the county reintroduced the tobacco quota in 1996, there was no coercion, with the result that only 10 per cent of the quota was met (Guo, 1999, p. 77, n. 16).

The picture is different again in areas with a high degree of privatization. Unger and Chan (1999, pp. 45–74), in their work on Xiqiao township in Guangdong, show how the criteria for success in private enterprise and public office are beginning to converge. The local township government does not need to levy any general taxes on village households and has been strongly in favour of local private business. As they conclude (1999, p. 73), this experience counters the general writing on local government in two significant ways. First, local officials do not give priority to publicly owned industry over the private sector and, secondly, they do not insist on relationships in which private enterprises are subordinate to and dependent on them. Zhang (1995) confirms these findings with his research on Wenzhou in Zhejiang Province, where private business is highly developed. He found that the enterprises were guided by the market and the local administrations did not interfere with their production of business activities.

Thus, empirical research questions the general applicability of the notion of corporatism. Corporatism as a theory captures well the top-down nature of control in the system and how citizens are integrated into vertical structures where elites will represent their perceived interests. However, such explanations risk obscuring both important elements of change and oversimplifying the complexities of the dynamics of the interaction. It can mean that researchers pay less attention to the benefits that members of the 'subordinate' organizations derive. What are the attractions and benefits of participation, or at least acquiescence, with this process? New social organizations, for example, can have considerable impact on the policy-making process by retaining strong linkages to the party and state, far more than if they were to try to create an organization with complete operational autonomy. The inter-relationships are symbiotic rather than unidirectional. Those social organizations with close government links often play a more direct role in policy formulation than in other developing counties as they do not have to compete in social space with other NGOs for dominance and access to the government's ear on relevant policy issues (Saich, 2000a).

In the same way that the local state in China shows enormous variation in its nature, each social organization in China has negotiated with the state its own niche that derives from a complex interaction of institutional, economic and individual factors. In some cases the outcome may be a close 'embedded' relationship with the state (Evans, 1995), in others it may entail formal compliance while operating strategies of evasion and circumnavigation of the state. The work of O'Brien (1994) and Ding (1994) has explored the consequences of such strategies. O'Brien has suggested that co-opted groups become embedded over time in the system and, through this process, acquire viability and legitimacy.

Ding uses the notion of 'institutional parasitism' in his study of critical intellectuals during the 1980s. These and related groups do not seek institutional separateness, but rather seek to manipulate official and semi-official institutions for their own advantage. In Ding's analysis a single institution can be used for contradictory or even conflicting purposes and functions while the boundaries between institutional structures are vague and indeterminate, with subsidiary organizations sheltering under umbrella-type organizations.

These kinds of explanations come close to allowing for the complexity of the current system, and the institutional fluidity and ambiguity that operates at all levels is even more pronounced at the local level. A focus on vertical integration and lines of administrative control, while ignoring the way in which the relationship is negotiated, ignores important horizontal relationships in society. As government downsizes further, citizens have greater responsibility for their own welfare and more functions are devoted to national and especially local social organizations, people will look more to the local provider of public goods than the central party and state directives and regulations. This will become more important as the wealthy business class is given more freedom over how it chooses to dispose of its money.

As the historian Timothy Brook (1997, p. 23) has noted, emphasis on the vertical 'minimizes the capabilities and opportunities that people exercise regularly to communicate horizontally and form cooperative bodies'. He suggests that we should be more aware of 'auto-organization' as a more cooperative principle of social integration at the local level.

Social scientists tend to dislike open-ended theories and to seek to close down the range of options available for interpretation through a process of imposing order and logic. The idea of each organization and the nature of each local state being the result of a process of negotiation tries to do justice to the complexities of social reality in China. In the field of state–society relations, we need to develop explanations that allow for the shifting complexities of the current system and the institutional fluidity, ambiguity and messiness that operate at all levels in China, and that are most pronounced at the local level.

9

Economic Policy

Chapters 9–12 look at the policy areas of the economy, the social sector, foreign affairs and at future policy challenges. First, we shall introduce a few key issues related to the institutional environment for policy-making and implementation.

Policy-Making and Implementation

Most literature on policy-making in communist systems has highlighted the monolithic and top-down nature of the process. The prime concern has been with the monolith and its totality and the actions of a cabal of key leaders who transmit policy direction through the party to be implemented by a sub-servient bureaucracy. As White *et al.* (1990, p. 216) commented, until the late 1980s it 'was not generally believed that the communist states possessed anything that could properly be called a "policy process"'. The overriding policy demand was to build up heavy industry and to achieve the highest possible rate of economic growth. That different parts of the bureaucracy might pursue different interests or that there might be significant variation in input or even that groups might have an input was not taken very seriously. Despite this dominant view of a monolithic and closed decision-making process, even before the reforms there has been significant policy variation and experimentation throughout China. While this was less visible under Mao's rule, it has become more apparent as China has tried to introduce market influences into a centrally planned economy.

The start of the reforms had the added advantage that sources became more readily available, data improved and fieldwork and interviews with those working in China became possible. This made it easier to locate the effect of the bureaucratic setting on Chinese politics and to investigate how these structures affected the policy process.

The most important analysis of the institutional setting is that of Lieberthal and Oksenberg (1988) with their study of policy-making in the initial development of large-scale energy projects. They conclude that the policy-making process is not entirely rational, they do not see a direct relationship between the problem and the solution and the policy outcome may not be an actual response to the problem that triggered the decisional process. Rather, the connections are more likely to be 'complex, loose and nearly random' (1988, p. 14). They argue persuasively that it is necessary to understand the bureaucratic structure as it creates or compounds the problems and is a necessary ingredient for understanding typical policy outcomes (1988, p. 17). Their study leads them to conclude that the bureaucratic structure in China is highly fragmented, making consensus-building central and the policy process protracted, disjointed, and incremental. This leads to three operational consequences (1988, pp. 22–3). First, problems tend to get pushed up the system to where supra-bureaucratic bodies can coordinate response and have sufficient leverage to bring together the different parties. Second, the fragmentation of authority means that at each stage of the decision-making process strenuous efforts have to be made to maintain a basic consensus to move forward. Third, for a policy to be successful, it needs the concerted support of one or more top leaders. This fragmentation is accentuated because the party is no longer able to perform the vital role of integrating the bureaucracy to improve both the formulation and implementation of policy.

This structure and the energy needed to keep a policy on track reveal why it is unwise to pursue too many strong policy objectives at the same time. On his appointment as Premier, Zhu Rongji announced a dazzling array of policy priorities for reform, ranging from cutting the bureaucracy to revamping the grain system to restructuring social welfare. With energy dissipated across so many policy areas, it was impossible for him to keep on top of all of them and with a recalcitrant bureaucracy and considerable vested interests digging in, his most ambitious schemes have been diverted. Consequently, Zhu had to pull back and set his sights on one or two main priorities and to try to keep the momentum moving forward while making grand statements about the remaining objectives. New Premier Wen, by contrast, has not announced such a grand strategy but has made it clear that he will continue attempts to restructure SOEs and bad policy loans, while paying more attention to the rural sector.

Lieberthal (1992) has developed the idea of bureaucratic fragmentation further with his concept of 'fragmented authoritarianism'. This highlights that while the system may be pluralist in terms of interests and highly fragmented with each level having to negotiate horizontally and vertically, it is certainly not a democratic process. For Lieberthal (1992, p. 8), authority just below the apex of the political system is fragmented, disjointed and structural and has increased as a result of the reforms pursued since 1978. This means that bargaining is a crucial element of the political process (see Lieberthal and Oksenberg, 1988; Lampton, 1992). We have seen in Chapter 6 the complex relationship between the centre and the localities, especially related to financial questions, and how adept lower levels have become at protecting their own interests against higher-level institutions and those at the same administrative levels. This process of bargaining and negotiation makes it difficult to accept one particular approach to policy-making or to be able to predict accurately policy outcome, as each organization will attempt to bend policy to its own advantage. The resultant system is extremely complex with enormous institutional fluidity, ambiguity and messiness as Chapter 8 demonstrated.

The complexity is increased by the challenges of policy implementation. There is no doubt that the implementation phase of the policy process is critical yet it is often ignored by researchers, bureaucrats and national and local policy-makers. However, it is precisely this phase that determines the nature and success of a policy reform initiative and implementation may often lead to an outcome quite different from that intended and anticipated by analysts and policy-makers (Grindle and Thomas, 1991, esp. pp. 121–50). Grindle and Thomas note that many assume a linear model of implementation where a proposed reform gets on the agenda for government action, a decision is made and a new policy or institutional arrangement is implemented either successfully or unsuccessfully. Failure usually results in a call for greater effort to be made to strengthen the institutional capacity or to blame it on the lack of political will. However, a 'policy reform initiative may be altered or reversed at any stage in its life cycle by the pressures and reactions of those who oppose it' (1991, p. 126). These responses can happen either through the reactions of society in a more public arena or in the more closed bureaucratic arena where opposition from vested interests may be mounted. Further, the government simply may not apply enough resources to ensure a successful policy outcome.

Despite the strength of the Chinese state and its ability to bring enormous resources to bear for limited periods of time in a narrow range of policies, China has suffered from all these problems with implementation and has been especially poor in monitoring and follow-up. As noted above, bargaining and negotiation are key features of the Chinese policy process. Lampton (1992, pp. 57–8) sees bargaining as a fundamental form of authority relationship, and outlines five consequences. First, decisions are generally arrived at slowly because the process of consensus-building and negotiation is protracted. Second, it is difficult to say precisely when a decision has been finalized: most decisions are made 'in principle' and then are still open to amendment. Third, even once a policy is adopted, negotiations among and between various levels of the hierarchy can result in significant adaptation. This is what Naughton (1987) refers to as the 'implementation bias', whereby all central policies will be bent in favour of the organization or locality responsible for implementation. Fourth, it is a mistake to set too many high-priority goals simultaneously. Fifth, because bargaining is so extensive, the legal framework is poorly developed.

Most of the problems that China faces with implementation are not unique to China and plague all systems, but some are more acute. In particular, China's size and diversity makes it especially important that policy remains flexible to account and that policy-makers receive accurate information for policy design and on feedback once policy begins to be implemented. A number of problems have hampered this process in China, ranging from the logistical to the political.

Politically, the party still does not welcome dissenting views. While the principle of democratic centralism may not be applied as rigorously as in the past, the party still has very weak mechanisms for providing feedback on policy implementation. There has been a growth in Internet chatrooms associated with party and state organizations for citizens to express views to complement the traditional system of letter writing, but these remain constrained. The use of informal surveys of the performance of local officials is also increasing. The absence of a free academia and media seriously restricts the quality of feedback that the party can gather on how their policies are being received by the population. The party has loosened up somewhat, especially in the realms of reporting on environmental affairs and consumer rights, but it is still virtually impossible to address the systemic nature of the problems to encourage a genuine public debate. The leadership may have put a premium on improving the population's education, but it still does not trust them to use it creatively.

While there is a more pluralistic input to decision-making, with different think-tanks or agencies preparing reports, the limit on the range of views they can put forward is still restricted. Even the reform-minded Premier Zhu Rongji does not like to be challenged by evidence that contradicts his own perception of reality. One senior academic decided to confront him over the inappropriate policy towards restricting the grain market. The Premier asked him whether other economists had the same view, to which the academic replied almost all. At this the Premier exploded in replying that he found this very strange as all the economists with whom he had spoken agreed that the Premier was correct (Personal communication from the academic concerned). There are other examples of this behaviour by Zhu. They reveal that it is still judicious to present what leaders want to hear rather than what they need to hear. Policy was, however, amended a couple of years later. In fact, raising a problem too soon, even if the analysis is correct, can have adverse consequences. It is more judicious to wait until a consensus emerges that a policy is not working before offering alternatives.

Economic Policy

There can be no doubt that in economic terms the reforms launched by Deng Xiaoping and his allies have achieved considerable success. Since 1978, high growth rates, rising *per capita* incomes and massive increases in foreign investment all appear to tell the same positive story. But if the story is so positive, then why is there so much concern about the state of Chinese economic health? While it is true that progress has been enormous, the headline figures hide a number of potentially worrying trends and new problems. First, growth in the late 1990s declined before stabilizing at 7–8 per cent with the impact of massive state investment in major infrastructure projects. Growth for 2001–05 is projected at 7 per cent. Second, the state-owned sector of the economy has deteriorated badly and most of the growth has been in new sectors of the economy, such as the collective, foreign invested and the private sector. These latter sectors have kept China afloat while the SOEs have become an increasing burden on state coffers. Third, this has put an enormous strain on the financial sector and many wonder whether it can cope with the accumulated losses. Such worries were heightened by the Asian Financial Crisis and what it revealed about fiscal vulnerability in the 'Asian Miracle'. Fourth, in the rural sector there have been concerns about stagnating incomes, the decline in the dramatic growth of the TVEs and whether China can continue to feed its growing population. Last, but not least, China's entry into the WTO will have a massive impact on all aspects of the Chinese economy, and many analysts are uncertain how well it will manage the transition. In particular, WTO entry will cause further redundancies in the state sector, reduce fiscal revenues and dramatically shift the CCP's traditional preference for self-sufficiency in basic food supply. At the same time, WTO entry offers the potential for growth in new sectors of the economy, particularly in the high-tech and service industries, and over the long term should be generally beneficial. Morgan Stanley economist, Andy Xie, has calculated that the necessary economic restructuring could lead to a growth rate of 9 per cent during 2006–15 (*The Economist*, 10 March 2001, p. 24). The question remains as to whether China can weather the initial storm. The remainder of this chapter begins with a discussion of gradualism and 'shock therapy' as a transition strategy, followed by an outline of the general contours of reform. Then rural, industrial and financial policy are reviewed in greater detail.

Gradualism or 'Shock Therapy' as a Transitional Strategy

The academic debate between those who favour 'shock therapy' as the best way to restructure the former socialist economies and those who have sought a more incrementalist approach has concretized for many into a debate about the relative merits of Russian and Chinese economic policy. At first glance, China's reform experience would seem to argue persuasively for a gradual approach to economic reform. As Rawski (1999, p. 153) has announced 'we are all gradualists now'. He and others such as Naughton (1999) have demonstrated how transitional systems in which the market is not yet fully established can generate very high growth levels. In fact, a gradual transition will provide an opportunity for the development of new or reformed institutions that can help guide the process to a market economy. Qian, Roland and Lau (1999) have suggested that the form of decentralization in China has actually allowed the development of effective institutions that can better coordinate the economy and allow for more effective local experimentation. As the case of Russia shows, the premature introduction of markets where there was neither a culture nor the institutions for dealing with them can have catastrophic effects. Much of the argument hinges on the view of the role ownership and property rights have in the transition. As Stiglitz (1999, p. 45) has argued, China has demonstrated that a country does not have to have a perfect legal structure with property rights clearly clarified to attract foreign capital or to encourage domestic investment.

Not surprisingly, senior Chinese leaders have heralded their approach as a better model for emulation. They have been horrified by what they have witnessed in Russia and have used this as a strong warning to persuade their own population to rally behind their leadership. In the period after the collapse of the Soviet Union, Chinese newspapers were full of scare stories about the harshness of life in post-communist Russia. Articles were run about former university professors who were now reduced to selling second-hand clothing in the streets. Demonstration of the superiority of the Chinese approach is vital to the leadership's interests as their legitimacy to rule depends almost exclusively on their capacity to deliver the economic goods, or at least to persuade people that any other alternative would only be worse.

Whether WTO entry can be considered beneficial or not to the Chinese economy depends on whether success has come from the development of new institutional forms (such as the dual-track pricing mentioned above or SOE contracting) or because its economic institutions have converged with those typical of a developed WTO economy. If the 'gradualists' are correct then WTO membership could create problems as it will constrain the leadership's capacity for exceptionalism and experimentation (Woo, 2001). The economist Jeffrey Sachs and his main collaborator, Wing Thye Woo (Sachs and Woo, 1994; Woo, 1999, pp. 115–37) have suggested that China's success has come in those areas where reform has been most radical and where institutions have begun to resemble those in a regular market economy. Thus, China's approach may not necessarily be better than that of Russia and, no matter what else, they argue that it is not and cannot be a model for other transitional economies given its particularity. In their view, performance to date merely reflects the different starting points of the two countries, with Eastern Europe and the former Soviet Union being overindustrialized while China is an economy based on peasant agriculture. In this sense, they see China as resembling more its neighbours in East Asia where there were huge initial gains to be made from the transfer of workers from low-productivity agricultural pursuits to those in the higher-productivity areas of industry. In fact, they see the major areas of growth coming from precisely those areas of the economy that did undergo the most radical transformation, such as the dismantling of the communes. In terms of institutional innovation, Woo (1999, p. 119) concludes that they are 'simply imperfect substitutes for normal market institutions that would have provided China with at least as rapid growth, and at less cost in terms of long-run distortions'. Thus, while in their view, growth in China has occurred in spite of 'gradualism', 'shock therapy' in Russia and the former Eastern Europe was inevitable as other attempts at gradual reform and dual-track reforms had already failed repeatedly. Sachs and Woo are correct that initial conditions matter, but they have downplayed some key issues that arise from China's experience that are now being raised by other mainstream economists such as Stiglitz (1999) and Rodrik (1999).

Three factors were important among China's initial conditions (see among others Boone, Gomulka and Layard, 1998). First, even under Mao the Chinese economy was highly decentralized and this allowed for the varied experimentation to take place, for the take-off of the TVEs, and for certain areas to encourage foreign investment. Second, this did not mean that the state itself was weak and China did not suffer from the kind of implosion of the state witnessed in Russia. Whatever its foibles, as we have seen in earlier chapters, the Chinese state has continued to govern and in recent years has even begun to claw back its control over some revenues. Third, there is the point highlighted by Sachs and Woo that China was over-whelmingly agrarian and thus there was much capacity for growth just through 'normal development'. Eastern Europe and Russia could not simply redeploy people from the rural to the industrial sector; they had to redeploy within an already overloaded and inefficient industrial sector. In Russia, privatization was rapid and contributed to market collapse rather than its development. As Stiglitz has observed, the failure of privatization to provide the basis of a market economy was not an accident but a predictable conse-quence of the manner in which it occurred. Last, but not least, the changes and the end of the Cold War led to a massive collapse in production for the military sector. This altered the pattern of government spending and delivered a further blow to the heavy industrial sector.

Despite such differences in initial conditions and the possible relevance of China's transition to the countries of Eastern Europe and Russia, it still does raise a number of interesting points. First, an effective state structure is a precondition for any hope of effective reform. Certainly, the role of the state in the economy will change with a narrower set of interventions and less direct administrative interference. Polanyi (1944), in his study of the creation of the market in Britain, pointed out long ago that a competent state is a prerequisite for any successful extension of the market. The state must adjudicate the increasingly contentious nature of economic market transactions. In addition, the state must manage the key macroeconomic vari-ables, deal with revenue collection and distribution and provide minimum social services and welfare guarantees.

Second, the starting point for reform does matter, and it is preferable to start with the existing social and political institutions and try to stimulate incremental transformation through the judicious use of incentives. An unregulated and ungoverned market will produce chaotic results. The alternative approach is what Stiglitz denounces as an 'institutional blitz-krieg'. Third, the precise role that property rights plays in this process is more ambiguous than orthodoxy might suggest. As Rawski (1999) notes, they may play a less important role than economists usually ascribe to them. Market structures and the institutional arrangements surrounding business enterprises often exercise greater influence over performance, efficiency and profitability than the nature of ownership (for China, see Steinfeld, 1998). Private monopolies will not necessarily function any better than state-run ones, what matters is how the competition is regulated. The state as a large business is more likely to be interested in gaining a monopoly position than in securing fair competition for all.

However, this does not mean that China's economy is not without problems and a number of the most acute stem from delayed reform, giving some weight to the views of Sachs and Woo. This debate has been given new impetus with China's entry into the WTO. In later work they have argued explicitly that the dual-track approach to transition may cause such a high long-term cost for constitutional reform that it may outweigh the short-term benefits of buying-off vested interests (Sachs, Woo and Yang, 2000). Deng Xiaoping was very successful at ensuring that there were no significant losers in the first phase of reform and that those who did lose out were small in number and politically marginalized. While it might have been easier economically to push through the reform of the state sector in the 1980s, the political will was lacking. CCP leaders did not wish to affect adversely the privileged working class that they had created after 1949. Now that the reform has become of paramount economic importance, it has become politically more difficult because the costs have become much higher. Gradualism allows opposition to further reform to develop. A hybrid system that is neither fish nor fowl provides ample opportunities for the officials who run it to engage in corrupt practices, exploiting the disjunctures between the plan and the market. The SOE lobby in China still has considerable residual strength, not just from the workers affected and the ministries created to run it but from the fact that the vast majority of state revenue (perhaps 80 per cent) comes from the SOE sector and consumes 60 per cent of household savings through bank loans. This puts a limit on the speed of future reform as a pre-cipitate collapse of the sector would be disastrous for many vested interests, not least those of the CCP. Real and potential resistance to further reform lies behind the reformers' desire to get China into the WTO to provide the kind of external disciplining mechanism for SOEs that is no longer possible to encourage internally. It also has the political advantage that foreigners can be blamed for the pain that will be experienced by many, rather than blame being put on the CCP.

To some extent, the argument is not about whether these are alternate modes of transition but rather whether there is a third way between capitalist markets and state planning. In fact, it might be more correct to rec___ debate in terms of questions of the speed of the transition and the sequencing of reforms. Kornai, the Hungarian economist, has highlighted the fact that different reforms might need to be conducted at different speeds (Kornai, 2000). In his view, macroeconomic stabilization needs to be carried through quickly, whereas privatization might take a much longer time.

In addition, as Rawski (1999) has now come to argue, the problems in the Chinese economy are structural rather than cyclical, as the current leadership tries to suggest. In particular, he highlights the largely unreformed investment mechanisms that still tilt the Chinese economy toward a 'distinctly non-market behaviour', seen most clearly in the continuing huge seasonal fluctuations driven by investment plans.

General Policy for Economic Reform

In December 1978, the CCP CC decided that the focus of future work would be economic modernization and that all other work must be subordinated to meeting this objective. The CCP's legitimacy was shifting effectively to the capacity of the leadership to deliver the economic goods. This approach resulted in significant changes in the relationship between the plan and the market, and the party and the economic decision-making apparatus, with previous regime practice significantly liberalized. This focus on the economy and the attempts at systemic transformation have not gone unchallenged, and until the mid-1990s remained the focus of considerable dissension. Serious debate now revolves around not whether there should be a transition, but the speed of it, and how to moderate its anticipated effects on China's social and political fabric.

The stress placed on economic modernization by Deng Xiaoping and his supporters had specific causes. First, living standards for much of the population in the late 1970s had barely risen from those in the late 1950s. The government's overconcentration on accumulation at the expense of consumption meant that rationing, queuing and hours spent on laborious household chores were the daily fare for most. The lack of consumer goods was offset by the fact that few had sufficient disposable income to buy them. In fact, in 1977 the average wage of state employees was 5.5 per cent lower than it had been in 1957; that of industrial workers was 8.4 per cent lower (partly explained by the addition of many younger workers to the labour force). Given the 'anti-bureaucratic' rhetoric of the Maoist era, it is interesting to note that the average wage for government employees was almost the same in 1977 as it had been in 1957. In the countryside, the attacks on private plots of land and free markets as 'tails of capitalism' had caused peasant resentment by undermining alternative sources of income. The Chinese population had had enough of tightening their belts today in return for promises of a bright future tomorrow.

Second, the failure of the initial ambitious post-Mao strategy to improve economic performance significantly caused the leadership to focus more sharply on the need for fundamental economic reform. The ascription of blame to the policies of the 'Gang of Four', with the associated policy of returning to a 'golden age' before they ruled, was seen to lead to a dead end. It was increasingly recognized that the main problems were deep-seated structural ones. Also, the ambitious pursuit of 'Maoism without Mao' under Hua Guofeng's leadership had led to serious short-term problems, such as a towering budget deficit and increasing inflationary pressures. The politically inspired measure of offering the urban labour force increased wages and bonuses to win their confidence and allegiance was exhausted.

Third, the party was faced with a serious problem of legitimacy. The continual twists and turns of policy since the mid-1950s left the party's claim to be the sole body in society capable of mapping out the correct path to socialism looking a little thin, to say the least. Nor could Mao's name any longer be invoked to legitimize policy. Thus, the party began to promise a bright economic future for all within a relatively short space of time. More than any other post-1949 leadership, Deng Xiaoping and his supporters tied their legitimacy to their ability to deliver the economic goods.

The new policies revolved around the promotion of market mechanisms to deal with the inefficiencies of allocation and distribution that occurred within the central state planning system. Awareness of the 'new technological revolution' increased the Chinese leaders' desire to make their system more flexible and thus more amenable to change. To take advantage of market opportunities, more power of decision-making was to be given to the localities, and in particular to the units of production themselves. Production units now have more autonomy to decide what to produce, how much and where to market the products. At the core of this system lie the ubiquitous contracts that are expected to govern economic activity. Corresponding material incentives are seen as the major mechanism to stimulate people to work harder, and the socialist principle of 'to each according to his work' is to be firmly applied. Egalitarianism is attacked as a dangerous notion that retards economic growth. This is best reflected in Deng's much-quoted dictum 'to get rich is glorious'. These reforms of the domestic economy have been accompanied by an unprecedented opening to the outside world in a search for export markets and the necessary foreign investments, technology and higher-quality consumer goods (see Hartford, 1990, pp. 61–9).

Importantly, in terms of initial success, the reforms did not have a blueprint, and the centre often appeared to be responding to policy innovation at the local level. The Chinese themselves referred to this as a process of 'Crossing the River by Feeling the Stones'. However, as Rawski points out, this dignifies the approach somewhat as it implies that there is a bank on the other side that it is the objective to reach. Even in the initial stage, however, the state played a key role. Once the central leadership had decided that a local experiment was suitable, it would try to enforce it throughout the country. As explained below, this was the case with the introduction of the rural household responsibility system.

By 1993–94, the central leadership had decided that a more coherent set of central policies was necessary to prevent the economy from overheating, and to prevent runaway inflation and local initiative and growth from escaping from central macroeconomic control. For the first time, the centre drew up a comprehensive statement of its reform plans and articulated them again in 1997–98. As Naughton (2000, pp. 56–7) has perceptively pointed out, by 1994 the reform agenda of the 1980s was basically completed and now the leadership had to deal with the tough parts of reform, such as the SOE system, the institutional impediments to rural–urban labour flows, the banking system and the integration of domestic markets with foreign competition.

In November 1993, the Third Plenum of the Fourteenth Party Congress adopted a crucial decision on the 'Establishment of a Socialist Market Economic System', the details of which were thrashed out at a meeting held in Dalian in June 1993. The back-drop was the feeling that excessive decentralization had caused the centre to lose control over key macroeconomic levers of the economy and that prudent recentralization was necessary. Much of the devolution had been by default rather than by design, with some real decisions on fiscal, monetary, financial and foreign exchange issues residing with the localities. For the state to meet its reform objectives, it became clear that both prudent recentralization and institution-building was necessary. The starting point for the decision was the increasing problems the central government was having in securing its financial base and maintaining macro-control over the economy.

The decision had a number of components. First, a 'modern enterprise system' was to be established that would include reform of the organizational and managerial systems. Clearly defined property rights would be central, with each enterprise becoming genuinely responsible for its profits and losses and bankruptcy as a real option. Government interference would be reduced to enable the enterprises to function properly in the marketplace. Second, it fleshed out the extension of the market in the Chinese economy that had been raised at the Fourteenth Party Congress. Crucially, for the first time, a CC document saw that economic reform required reform of the financial system – including taxation, banking and monetary systems – and laid out objectives. A rational division of taxes between the centre and local authorities was to be devised to replace the annual tug-of-war that currently existed. In monetary policy, the major reform was to allow the People's Bank of China to function as central banks do in other countries. It was to implement monetary policies in an independent manner and to distance itself from provincial political interference by letting the head office take responsibility for the regulation of the scale of the loans. Further, the document recognized that more flexibility needed to be introduced into the social security system and that serious problems existed in the agricultural system.

Subsequent policy has marked a clear commitment to a mixed economy, with theoretical continued dominance of the state sector and with attempts to shift to a more regulatory state. However, the impact of the Asian Financial Crisis and the slowing growth rate led to a programme of massive state investment to keep up growth. Growth rates in 2002 were sustained by a 23 per cent increase in fixed asset investment. It is important to remember that despite all the headline figures of China's FDI and its exports, its growth is driven predominantly by domestic demand. According to calculations by Wong and Chan (2002), each 1 per cent increase in domestic consumption generates 0.66 per cent more GDP, each 1 per cent increase in domestic investment generates 0.30 per cent, while each 1 per cent increase in net exports generates only 0.33 per cent. This enables China to maintain its growth rate with greater independence from the global economy and with China's high savings rates, the government can mobilize a huge pool of savings for infrastructure investment.

Some have been critical of this approach, suggesting that it cannot perform as a long-term substitute for serious structural reform and a greater role for the non-state sector. This is true, but in institutional terms China's consolidated public debt is not high and the government has concluded that with private aggregate demand falling and monetary policy not providing stimulation, government spending is the key to maintaining macroeconomic stability. However, caution is still necessary not only because of bail-outs for bad loans and pension obligations that could balloon but also because China has a low capacity to service its public debt. As we have seen, its revenue-raising capacity remains low, at about 16 per cent, as compared to 21 per cent in the United States.

Agricultural Policy

Economic reforms began in the agricultural system and have been the most radical. Yet the two most dramatic policy developments, the household responsibility system and TVE development, were unexpected, deriving more from spontaneous local initiatives than government planning. However, many problems have remained, with stagnating incomes and problems concerning land tenure and access to credit. The rural sector will receive a major impact from WTO entry that will cause a significant shift from China's traditional autarky to policies that will seek to profit from China's international comparative advantage.

While the industrial reforms of the 1980s and early 1990s presented very little that had not been tried in the Soviet Union and Eastern Europe, the agricultural reforms represented a 'big bang' and radical new departure, throwing up the question of whether there was still a socialist agricultural system in China (on this period, see Watson, 1984; Hartford, 1985). However, the success of the early 1980s had soured by the end of the decade and has remained a policy headache since.

At the time of Mao's death, the Chinese countryside was organized on the basis of communes (set up during the GLF, 1958–60). These communes functioned as the highest level of economic organization in the countryside and as the basic level of government there. Below the communes were production brigades and teams. For most farmers, the teams were the most important unit, as they made the final decisions concerning both the production of goods and the distribution of income in accordance with the work-points accumulated. While the radicals of the Cultural Revolution tried to force this level of accounting upwards (see Zweig, 1989), the reforms of the 1980s placed many of the functions in the hands of the individual household. The old commune system lent itself to central planning, large-scale production and unified distribution, precisely those aspects of rural policy that the reforms set out to undermine.

Initial post-Mao policy sought to encourage growth in agricultural production by substantially raising procurement prices and by modernizing agriculture through brigade and team financing. At the same time, policy was relaxed to let different regions make use of the 'law of comparative advantage'. Also, private plots of land and sideline production were stressed as playing an important role in agricultural growth. To allow the peasants to sell their products – for example, their above-quota grain – private markets were again tolerated. This policy was firmly based on the collective and represented nothing radically new.

In December 1978, it was decided that the procurement price of quota grain would be increased by an average of 20 per cent, above-quota grain by 50 per cent and cotton by 30 per cent. The impact was immediate; this single act did more than anything else to lift large numbers of peasants out of poverty. However, the result of this policy was to increase massively state expenditures on agriculture. The Ministry of Finance and the provinces began to spend well over 1 billion *yuan* per year subsidizing grain supplies in urban areas, helping to account for the state budget deficits of 1980 and 1981. In addition, the policy of agricultural modernization did not bear fruit. A new strategy had to be found that would raise agricultural incomes, permitting modernization but without significantly increasing state investment.

The most important subsequent reform was the introduction of the house-hold responsibility system. Although this was introduced in December 1978, initially it did not entail any significant undermining of the collective. However, by 1980 the more radical form, contracting various activities to the household, was becoming commonplace despite official denials. The household was clearly becoming the key economic unit in the countryside. This house-hold contracting system makes the rural household the nucleus of agricul-tural production, working on a clearly stipulated piece of land for a specific period of time. The contract includes all raw materials and means of production except land-use rights and access rights to irrigation facilities, the latter rights being made available by the collective. Later legislation confirmed this situation and extended the cropping contracts to over 15 years, encouraged the concentration of land with the most productive households, encouraged capital flow across regions for investment and reduced the funds that the collective could demand from the peasantry.

The lack of security around land tenure led to further increases in the length of the contract and in 1993 it was announced that new contracts would be for 30 years, something confirmed in both the Land Management Law (August 1998) and the Rural Land Contract Law (effective in March 2003). The two laws also sought to protect against the illegal seizure of land by local officials who then sell it for commercial development, while providing derisory compensation. The Ministry of Land and Resources stated that, according to official figures, from 1999 to 2002, 0.3 million acres had been seized from 1.5 million farmers. Farmers are empowered to transfer land-use and to derive income from its use while local authorities are banned from revising the contract or confiscating the land during the contract period. This law marks a massive step forward in recognizing farmers' rights but it is still weak in terms of how to deal with local authorities that refuse to issue contracts. Also it does not appear to rule out land readjustments that may involve partial reallocation because of changing demographics, something that has occurred in the majority of villages.

The policy amounts to *de facto* privatization of land, and now that contracts can be bought and sold, it resembles more closely a private land market. However, contrary to the general belief that all farmers would be in favour of such guarantees, interesting research by Kung and Liu (1997, pp. 33–63) reveals a more nuanced picture. Their study of 8 counties reveals that 62 per cent preferred the situation under which land was periodically reassigned among families in response to changing demographics. In fact, only 14 per cent of those surveyed said that they supported *de jure* land ownership. It was true that a majority (65 per cent) favoured longer contracts, but those from more affluent villages consistently preferred shorter-term contracts.

This seems to challenge the conventional view of the security of property rights and the relationship to family investment in agriculture. A number of factors are important. First, it may just be that the interviewees felt uncomfortable about appearing to be pushing at the limits of what was tolerated policy. Second, Kung and Liu stress the desires of the farmers for a more fluid system. This they trace to the persistence of the strong egalitarian spirit that has remained in many villages despite the inegalitarian reforms launched from 1978. With no social security system for the overwhelming majority of farmers, land is an important guarantee and periodic redistribution can help deal with demographic fluctuations. Third, it clearly reflects general practice in many rural villages. In many villages that I visited in the early 1990s, land was periodically reassigned irrespective of the existence of contracts. In fact, Kung and Liu (1997, p. 54) note that at the end of 1996 barely over half of China's villages had renewed land contracts in line with 1993 policy, and only 20 per cent were contracts for 30 years. Most of the contracts were signed for 10, 5 or even fewer years. They attribute this also to farmers' desires based on their survey. However, it is clear that village authorities are reluctant to relinquish such a major mechanism for exerting power and patronage. As we have seen earlier, state power in the countryside remained strong throughout the reforms.

In fact, even the introduction of the household responsibility system was more complex than some authors have suggested, who see it as a case of farmers exerting their power over hesitant and obstructive bureaucrats (Zhou, 1996). In 1979, a mere 0.02 per cent of production teams had adopted the household responsibility system, but by the end of 1983 this figure had risen to 97.8 per cent (Yiping Huang, 1998, p. 158). In many areas the new system was not the result of spontaneous farmer dismantling of the collective agricultural structures but enforcement of a new policy line from above. This was especially the case in Heilongjiang where the mechanized grain-farming appeared to favour collective structures. Unger (1985–6, pp. 585–606) conducted a survey of emigrants to Hong Kong from 28 villages in China. Of the 28 villages, 26 had decollectivized to family-based agriculture by the end of 1982; 24 claimed that the type of system adopted was decided above the village level and only in 2 villages had village cadres and farmers taken the initiative themselves. With the massive extension of the policy through 1983, direction from above can only have increased.

In January 1985, in a further radical move, the state announced its intention to abolish its monopoly over purchasing and marketing of major farm products. Instead of the state assigning fixed quotas for farm products to be purchased from farmers, a system of contract purchasing was to be introduced. All products not purchased in this way could be disposed of on the market. Clearly, the aim of this reform was to improve the distribution of commodities and further reward efficient producers. It was hoped that this would encourage wealthier peasants to reinvest capital and labour in the land. Essentially, the contract procurement system was intended to establish a market relationship between the state and the peasantry and between the urban and rural areas.

This new measure was a massive shock to the agricultural system and challenged the old economic assumptions on which it was built. It led to the breakdown of the unequal terms of trade between the rural and urban areas under which an estimated 600–800 billion *yuan* had been extracted from the peasantry over a 30-year period. New channels opened for the circulation and marketing of surplus grain and other agricultural products. However, the state could not increase the price of grain to the urban dwellers and thus returns on grain production began to decline and in some instances money could even be lost on grain production. For example, between 1983 and 1985, average prices paid for chemical fertilizers rose by 43 per cent and those for pesticides by 83 per cent, reducing net income gained from 1 hectare of grain by about 30–40 per cent. In comparison with cash crops, grain production was no longer a lucrative activity.

The initial agricultural reforms had thus provided a major boost to the rural sector, but by 1985 were beginning to falter. Grain production increased from 305 million tons in 1978 to 407 million tons in 1984, only to fall back to 379 million tons the following year, the second largest fall in grain production in PRC history. Further growth in rural incomes began to slow, from 17.6 per cent per annum from 1978–84 to only 5.5 per cent by 1987. Finally, the income gap between rural and urban areas that had been coming down began to widen again, and by 1986 it was 2.33: 1, worse than it had been at the beginning of the reforms.

From 1985 onwards policy vacillated primarily over what to do about grain production and procurement. Until the late 1990s rural policy was left in a never-never land that was governed neither by the market nor the central plan. Also affecting rural production was the state's decision to cut its investment in the agricultural sector from 10 per cent of the capital construction budget in the period 1976–80 to 3.9 per cent for 1986–90. In part, this cut was to make up for the massive subsidies that were necessary to cover the increased price of grain. CCP fear of urban unrest made it impossible to pass on the price rises to residents. The expectation was that the collectives and/or individuals would take up the investment, thus offsetting the reduction in state funds. The effective collapse of the collectives as powerful economic entities sealed off one of the alternative sources of funds. The newly emerged townships used their funds to invest in the TVEs, a point returned to below. Initially, individual households were wary of reinvesting profits because of their uncertainty about how long it would be before policy would change yet again. When they did begin to invest, it was not in grain production but in more lucrative cash crop or sideline production. These problems led the state to abandon the contract procurement system before the reform had been properly carried out. Under the system there was dual pricing, with the state buying the grain needed for urban consumption and state industry at artificially low prices, while allowing surplus grain to be sold at free-market prices. Eventually, the difference between the two price systems was to be eliminated. Unfortunately, this system had been introduced following the bumper harvest of 1984 when the market price of grain was below the state purchase price; by 1985, it was already back above this price and continued rising. The level of exploitation that had been disguised thus became clear to the farmers. Further, this system meant that when grain was scarce, market prices would go up further, thus making the 'exploitation' even greater.

Policy since 1985 comprised a cat-and-mouse game between the farmers and the state, with no clear resolution and, as Aubert has noted, all
attempts to liberalize grain trade have failed (Aubert, 1997–8, p. 72). This
may well change with WTO entry and the appointment of Wen Jiabao as
Premier. The following is based on Aubert (1997–8) and Yiping Huang
(1998). Following the fall in production, the use of contracts to purchase
grain and cotton were once again made mandatory in 1985 and 1986.
Grain production stagnated and actually dropped in 1985, 1988 and again
in 1991. Agricultural growth in general slowed from 7.4 per cent from
1979 to 1984 to 3.8 per cent in the period 1984–94, and grain production
showed a steeper decline. Between 1982 and 1984, it had grown at 8 per cent
but this dropped to 0.9 per cent in the period 1984–94). The response
was to raise grain prices significantly in 1989 to try to boost production
and in 1991 grain market reform was once again accelerated, with state
prices for grain again significantly increased. The next attempt was to
abolish the grain ration system in the urban areas. Urban ration levels
were set too high and actual consumption was far lower. In 1992, urban
market prices were raised to reflect the price of rural production in an
attempt to reduce the heavy burden of grain subsidies in the state budget.
This resulted in a 140 per cent price increase for urban rations but direct
subsidies were provided to avoid unrest and help urban families absorb
the initial impact.

In 1994 the State Price Bureau was abolished, signalling the intention of
the state to end its wholesale intervention in pricing policy. In addition, the
mandatory procurement quotas were abolished, with the State Grain Bureau
expected to buy 'fixed quantities at market prices'. Contracts were set with
the market price to be paid at the time of sale and production was intended
to match urban need. The trade market was opened to competition from
other traders. As a result, the State Grain Bureau was unable to match the
competition and many farmers preferred to sell to private traders. This
led to a fall in state procurement and a 17 per cent rise in the price paid
for grain.

The new policy unravelled as a result of the severe macroeconomic problems
that China faced from 1993–95. At the end of 1993, huge price rises occurred,
deriving initially from a rice shortage in South China – the inefficiency of
China's storage system meant that it was unable to use up the ample stored
grain reserves. In 1994, food prices rose 32 per cent, adding 12.1 per cent
(about 55.8 per cent) to the overall inflation rate. The reversal was swift.
Grain coupons were back in many cities in 1994 and in March 1995 a new
grain policy was announced that required all provincial governors to be
responsible for the supply in their own provinces. In May 1995, the State
Price Bureau was reestablished. The 'dual-track' pricing system of quota and
negotiated prices was reinstated but there was a growing gap between the
two, with the result that in 1996 quota prices had to be increased by 40 per cent.

This meant that since the grain trade reforms of the 1990s began, the quota had risen threefold. This did have the effect of significantly improving farmers' income, with a net income of 1,926 *yuan* in 1996, up 45 per cent from 1990. However, stagnating incomes remained a problem, with Zhu Rongji announcing in 2003 that they had risen from 2,090 *yuan* in 1997 to 2,476 *yuan* in 2002; urban incomes had risen from 5,160 to 7,703 *yuan* in the same period (Zhu, 2003).

The cost to the state in terms of the subsidies was enormous and policy was back to square one. In 1996, the official amount of subsidies for grain, oil and cotton amounted to over 31 billion *yuan*, 35 per cent up on 1995. The boom for the farmers also burst in 1996 when a record harvest (505 million tons) triggered a dramatic fall in grain prices. While many recognized that China needed to break out of this vicious cycle, the mentality of grain self-sufficiency and the fears of social instability have not helped. While Zhu Rongji defended this system of indirect subsidy at the Tenth NPC (March 2003), reforms had been set in motion earlier and his successor, Wen Jiabao (who has significant experience with rural policy) set about dismantling the old system. The old policy was associated with corruption at the State Grain Bureaus and a huge financial burden for the state that was hard to carry. A final blow to the notion of grain self-sufficiency was dealt by WTO entry.

Before the recent reforms, state prices and procurement plans covered about 80 per cent of marketed grains (about 20–25 per cent of the total crop) and all of the cotton crop. Grain procurement bureaus bought from the farmers at subsidized prices. For the farmers, while it did provide a guarantee that crops would be bought, it had negative effects that income often could not match rises in farm input prices and many local governments often diverted funds earmarked for grain purchase to more lucrative pursuits.

The grain procurement bureaus were kept afloat by loans from the Agricultural Development Bank (ADB) that had to be repaid only once the grain was sold. This produced a large empire that profited from the old system. It controlled 80 per cent of the grain wholesale trade and 50 per cent of the retail trade through 52,000 urban retail enterprises. There were over 1 million employees. They were often able to arm-twist the state into lending more money as maintaining grain self-sufficiency was a key priority. WTO entry will halt these kinds of hidden subsidies and while some have tried to claim that the removal of subsidies will adversely affect China's grain farmers, the truth is that it will be these procurement agencies that will be worst hit. Little was passed on to the farmer. In Anhui Province, the central government provided procurement bureaus with around 4 billion *yuan* each year, but only around 400 million *yuan* was passed on to the farmers. The agencies are also a source of corruption, buying grain at low state prices and then selling on once market prices move higher.

Premier Wen signalled an end to this system and in June 2003 the government announced that it would pay subsidies directly to the farmers. The farmers will decide what to plant based on market circumstances and will receive government subsidy if the market slumps. The state grain bureaus will have to compete with private grain merchants without their preferential loans. This policy is based on experiments carried out in 2002 in two counties in Anhui, often a rural reform leader. In one county, the reform resulted in laying off half of the staff and its official thought that with loans cut off it was debatable whether it could compete. Whether Premier Wen will be more successful than his predecessor in attempting to marketize grain production will be a major test of his leadership.

WTO entry will also have a major impact on grain production while benefiting labour intensive farm work such as horticulture, livestock and fisheries (Ke, 2001). Gradually, China will drop its dependence on domestic grain and eventually the domestic costs and inefficiencies of production may lead it to become a net importer because of demand from the rapidly growing livestock sector. WTO will favour the eastern provinces and disfavour those in the west and the central regions while the shifting dynamics of grain production will adversely affect the northeast, an area already suffering from SOE lay-offs.

These problems and the unrest that has come from stagnating incomes and rising local levies have moved rural policy back to the centre of the policy stage and under Premier Wen it has become a key priority. The land concentration, the loss of work in grain farming and the recognition of the link between poverty and exclusive engagement in agricultural, especially grain production, will cause even more people to move off the land in the future. In fact, this has been promoted by the government with its tolerance of increased migration (see Chapter 10), its desire to boost rural enterprise development and push on with urbanization. Zhu Rongji at the March 2001 NPC meeting recognized the link between poverty and agricultural work when he announced that towns and small cities would be allowed to expand to provide more job opportunities for China's farmers. With an urbanization rate of only 30 per cent, China lags well behind other developing countries, suggesting that such expansion might be possible.

These changes will impact further on rural labour and will increase the numbers moving off the land. The Ministry of Agriculture calculated that by 2005 there would be 600 million labourers in the countryside, of whom only 168 million would be required for agriculture. Surplus labour in the countryside has been a major problem during the reforms and 200 million have been absorbed by work in the TVEs or through migration to the urban areas. However, with the slowdown in the urban economy, exacerbated by SARS that sent many migrants home, and the tighter budget constraints for the TVEs, these employment alternatives look less appealing.

TVEs have been hailed as one of the wonders of the reforms by Chinese and foreigners alike. By the mid-1980s with farmer income stagnating, one of the best ways to increase it was to stimulate non-grain and non-agricultural production. A major consequence was the rapid expansion of

TVEs that at one point were employing over 100 million people, up from around 25 million in 1978. In 1990, those working in this sector surpassed the number of employees in SOEs. The development of these enterprises, as we have seen in Chapter 6, also meshed with the political requirements of local governments, who saw them as a regular source of revenue in a resource-constrained environment.

The TVEs built on one of the enduring legacies of the GLF, the commune and brigade-run industries that had been set up to serve the rural areas. However, these were not little budding sprouts of entrepreneurship and were restricted to the production of the 'five products' of iron and steel, cement, chemical fertilizer, hydroelectric power and farm tools. Their role was limited and in 1978 the rural areas accounted for only 9 per cent of industrial output, while 90 per cent of the rural labour force was engaged in agriculture. However, it is true that employment in rural industry was increasing at 20 per cent per annum from 1970 to 1978 (Naughton, 1995, pp. 144, 146). The reforms changed this and while initial policy measures were intended to use rural industry to divert more resources to the country-side and strengthen the collective, policy changes had a dramatic effect on its role. The results were unexpected as Deng Xiaoping noted 'what took us by complete surprise was the development of TVEs.... All sorts of small enter-prises boomed in the countryside, as if a strong army appeared suddenly from nowhere. This is not the achievement of the central government...This was not something I had thought about. Nor had the other comrades. This surprised us' (*Renmin ribao*, 13 June 1987).

Of special importance was the decision to relax the state purchasing monopoly on agricultural goods, making them available to local rural indus-try. It soon became the most vibrant part of the economy, soaking up excess rural labour, processing agricultural products and diversifying production into a range of consumer goods and products for export. The growth rate was explosive, with rural industrial output growing at 21 per cent per annum from 1978 through to the early 1990s. By 1997 they produced almost 28 per cent of China's GDP and nearly 50 per cent of all industrial exports (Johnson, 1999, p. 11).

The presence of a ready labour force was crucial to the expansion of the TVEs and the introduction of the household responsibility system made this available. Moreover, it was a relatively cheap labour force compared to what industry had to pay in the urban areas. At the same time, costs were at or near market prices for water, electricity and raw materials, unlike for the SOEs that received their inputs at heavily subsidized rates. While taxes on TVEs were low (indeed, they were granted an initial 3-year tax break), budget constraints were much harder than in the SOE sector. This meant that there was a greater incentive to produce things that would have a market and that would produce a good rate of return on investment. Finally, these TVEs were extremely flexible in terms not just of what they could produce but also in terms of their organizational structure (Naughton, 1995, pp. 156–7). They ranged from those run by local governments to ones that were more genuinely independent in nature. However, as Wong (1988, pp. 3–30) has shown, through the 1980s most of the supposedly collective TVEs operated in practice as private enterprises. The use of the term 'collective' became a flag of ideological convenience to what was becoming the wholesale privatization of rural enterprise.

The growth of these rural enterprises was particularly strong in areas such as Southern Jiangsu (*Jiangnan*) and around peri-urban Shanghai. In fact, the enterprises in Southern Jiangsu gave the name to the *Jiangnan* model of development based on the profusion of small-scale rural industry. In these areas, their growth was closely linked to the proximity of urban SOEs. With the shift to the taxation system for SOEs from the previous profit transfer system, they had money to invest and many began to outsource their production to the rural enterprises where land and labour were considerably cheaper. For example, in 1988, Jiangsu, Zhejiang and Shandong, while accounting for just 17 per cent of the rural population, had 43 per cent of rural industry, with half of all township and village-level industrial output (Naughton, 1995, p. 154).

However, in the later part of the 1990s dramatic changes took place in the TVE sector. First, the retrenchment of the economy caused many TVEs to go under; some estimates have suggested that 30 per cent went bankrupt. Second, they became more capital-intensive, and as a result little new employment was created. Third, their limited and dispersed distribution networks and poor management became more of a liability. Fourth, the tendency noted by Wong of TVEs to hide effective privatization became more apparent. Research by Park and Shen (2000) on 15 counties in Jiangsu and Zhejiang revealed a massive trend towards privatization. In 1994 only 92 of the 415 enterprises surveyed were private, but by 1994 the total was 231 and it has risen since. The magazine *Caijing* reported that by the end of 2001, 93.2 per cent of the 85, 000 TVEs in Southern Jiangsu had switched to private or stock companies. The consequences of this trend are hard to predict, but with the challenges of WTO entry it is unlikely that this sector will provide the kind of employment opportunities as in the past.

Industrial Policy

Reforming the industrial sector has been the most difficult challenge for the central leadership as it goes to the core of the economic system that was set up under the central plan. Reform undercuts the interests of powerful bureaucracies that were set up to run the system and the working class of whom the CCP was to represent the most advanced elements. As a result, reform has been stop–go. Throughout the 1980s and the early 1990s, leaders generally backed off from reforms whenever representatives of the heavy industrial sector squealed loudly enough or when the fears of social instability arose. This changed, however, by the latter part of the 1990s when it was clear that difficult reforms could be delayed no longer.

One might even ask if China needs an industrial policy as SOEs have become a net destroyer of assets while the rapidly growing and more productive non-state sector is penalized and starved of the necessary capital for development. Industrial and fiscal policy supported declining sectors of the state-owned economy that the CCP created from the mid-1950s onwards. Whether a strategy of 'picking winners' did or did not work in the past, it is hard to implement in a world of WTO. Right or wrong, WTO regulations and practices try to prevent the kind of development strategy that was practised throughout East Asia from the 1960s on. It is clear that international pressure will force the Chinese government to undertake a more market-based strategy. Should China not adjust its policy it will run the risk of substantial friction with the WTO and especially with the United States.

Delay in fundamental reform also initially derived from the lengthy learning process that the leadership underwent in grappling with this sector. It took a long time for central leaders to realize that simply stressing technological up-grading, improved management, limited autonomy and expanded market forces did little to improve the health of SOEs unless the external environment was significantly reformed and a proper sequencing of reforms introduced. Indeed, as the work of Steinfeld (1998) has shown, tinkering with these aspects could actually make the situation worse. As he argues (1998, p. 4), China lacks the key institutional mechanisms needed to make corporate governance, and by extension property rights, function for producers in complex market settings. The problem is compounded by the fact that many SOEs have become net destroyers of assets, with what they consume being of far greater value than what they produce. The dilemma for the government is that they still provide significant revenue for all levels of government: in 1995 amounting to 71 per cent of total revenue.

From the mid-1990s two important reforms were introduced to attempt to reform this sector. The first was the establishment of a social welfare system independent of the individual enterprises and regulated through the government (see Chapter 10). The second was to harden the budget constraints by gaining control over bank loans, trying to introduce better discipline over lending and commercializing loans.

Just as the reforms of the agricultural sector began to run out of steam in 1984, the leadership turned its attentions to reform of the urban industrial sector. By 1984 pressure had increased for further reform of the industrial sector as it was clear that the industrial system was unable to meet properly the needs of the increasingly commercialized, decentralized agricultural system. Indeed, the reformers used the successes of the rural sector to argue for the implementation of similar measures in the industrial sector. However, it was much harder to transfer these experiences to the urban environment where production was more socialized and bureaucratized.

The need for further reform and the reform experiments to date were recognized in the CC 'Decision on Reform of the Economic Structure' of October 1984. This decision chronicles the problems of the industrial economy, noting that 'defects in the urban economic sector...seriously hinder the development of the forces of production'. The measures proposed offered a more thoroughgoing reform than the piecemeal experimentation that had previously taken place. However, in 1985–86, 1988 and again in 1990 when problems became apparent, orthodox leaders tried to bring the reforms to a halt by reasserting the levers of administrative controls at the expense of market forces.

The key to the industrial reform programme was to make enterprises more economically responsible, and most important was the introduction of enterprise profit retention. In 1983, a system of tax for profit was introduced and this was adopted in the 1984 Decision as a policy for all enterprises. This new system replaced the old system of requisition of profits or covering losses and the initial reform experiments of profit contracting. The intention was that the tax system would stabilize state revenues and force enterprises to become more fiscally responsible.

To ensure that enterprises could take proper advantage of the limited market opportunities, managers of factories and other enterprises were given greater power of decision-making with respect to production plans and marketing, sources of supply, distribution of profits within the enterprise and the hiring and firing of workers. While this provided the carrot, it was recognized by some that there should be a stick with which to beat inefficient enterprises. Thus, a draft bankruptcy law was presented, and in August and September 1986 an enterprise in Shenyang won fame by becoming the first enterprise to be declared bankrupt since the founding of the PRC. However, this measure provoked a strong reaction from opponents and reformers alike. A decision on the law was shelved and in December 1986, the Standing Committee of the NPC reached a compromise by adopting a 'trial law' to come into effect 3 months after a general enterprise law had been adopted. The Enterprise Law was eventually adopted in 1988, also after having been delayed from adoption at the March 1987 NPC meeting.

While opposition to the bankruptcy law centred on whether this had a place in a socialist economy, opposition to the enterprise law focused on the relationship of managerial authority to party control. The enterprise manager not only had constraints from the external environment in terms of decisions on key factors such as sourcing of inputs, sales of products, mandated staffing and wage levels, but had authority problems within the enterprise itself *vis-à-vis* the party committee. The phrase used to describe the experiments launched in 1986 was the 'managerial responsibility system' rather than the previous description of the 'managerial responsibility system under the leadership of the party committee'. This was an attempt to make a clear demarcation between the party and the day-to-day administration of enterprises and emphasized the need for the manager to be able to act on certain matters without always first asking for the approval of the party committee. Dissension was so severe that when Zhao Ziyang discussed this at the Thirteenth Party Congress (October–November 1987), he avoided the problem by declaring that party organs must see that managers could undertake leadership but that the party must play a supervisory role and guarantee that industrial policy was carried out properly. This just continued the same messy lines of control.

However, the passage of the Enterprise Law in 1988, by adopting the 'managerial responsibility system', seemed to resolve the debate by moving the party committee out of direct management. The events of 1989 did not lead to repudiation of the Law but opponents used the demonstrations to insist again on the paramount position of the party committee in the enterprise and have reiterated this periodically since. They have also been able to seize on Jiang Zemin's notion of the paramount position of the party in the political system to justify intrusion, despite the adoption of various directives encouraging greater enterprise autonomy. For example, State Council regulations issued in July 1992 stipulated 14 areas where SOEs were legally entitled to autonomy, including hiring and firing and allocating investment capital.

As with the farmers, the main incentive to make workers work harder and raise labour productivity was to be a material one. Wage rises, bonuses and piece-rate systems were all tried to increase worker productivity, although to date the results have not been remarkable. The politics within enterprises often have meant that the same bonuses are handed out to all and are seen as a part of the basic wage, thus undermining their purpose. Along with the carrot there also came a stick – the 'iron rice bowl', the name given to the system under which it was impossible to fire workers, was abolished. Lifelong tenure was replaced by a system of fixed-term labour contracts. In October 1986, a new labour contract law and supplementary regulations were introduced to cover the recruitment and dismissal of undisciplined employees. This new system was intended to reward those who worked well, provide the basis for dismissal of bad workers and, at the same time, cut down the costs of social security and welfare. Resistance to this new contract system was strong. Essentially urban workers were being offered a deal that involved giving up their secure, subsidy-supported, low-wage lifestyle for a risky contract-based system that might entail higher wages at the possible price of rising costs and unemployment. Leadership vacillation on the reforms persuaded workers to reserve judgement.

While the central administrative controls were being weakened, they were not being replaced by adequate market mechanisms. In 1988, this led to major economic problems of overheating and attendant inflationary tendencies. In 1988, industrial production increased 17.7 per cent, well above the proposed

8 per cent. While looking good on paper, this economic growth put an enormous strain on the energy and transport sectors where growth rates hovered around the 5 per cent mark. These problems of imbalance aggravated the inflation rate. Official figures showed an inflation rate of 21 per cent for 1988, but most reliable unofficial estimates for urban areas placed it at around 35 per cent. Beginning in 1992, after Deng's trip to the south there was another boom in economic growth, with inflation again shooting up to around 30 per cent by the end of 1994. The differing leadership responses to these two periods are interesting. In the 1980s, a programme of austerity was introduced to calm growth and a number of the reforms were slowed down, a process that gained momentum after the demonstrations of 1989. However, the 1993 and 1994 attempts at economic retrenchment did not work: GDP growth was 13.4 per cent, well above the projected 9 per cent. This forced then vice-premier Zhu Rongji and his supporters to articulate a more dramatic plan for economic transformation to try to break out of this vicious cycle.

The question arose as to whether reform would be pursued any more vigorously this time. There were strong political reasons for central leaders not to pursue swift enterprise restructuring. The first and foremost remained the capacity of other sectors of the economy to absorb the absolute numbers of redundant workers and to develop an adequate social welfare programme. Over the years, the overblown staffs of many of these enterprises proved to be a viable political and social solution to the problem of inefficient industrial production, but now this was no longer financially feasible. Economic pressures made it impossible for the centre to sit on the fence while the localities were pursuing *de facto* privatization.

Some figures display the seriousness of the problem faced in the mid-1990s. Of the 100,000-plus industrial SOEs, World Bank figures suggest that perhaps less than 10 per cent were fundamentally viable. SOEs absorbed 60 per cent of national investment; received total subsidies amounting to one-third of the national budget, and net credit to SOEs reached over 12 per cent of GDP in 1995. Importantly, 50–75 per cent of household savings, mediated and directed by state banks, went to finance SOE operations. The World Bank (1997b, p. 1) estimated that in 1996, 50 per cent of SOEs lost money (unofficial estimates are higher). For the first quarter of 1996 the SOE sector slid into the red for the first time since the establishment of the PRC, with a net deficit of around $850 million.

It must have become apparent that over the long term government resources would be insufficient to pay depositors and bondholders if SOEs were unable to service bad debts. At the same time the state, with a declining revenue base, was unable to offer the same kind of bail-out, and subsidies declined. This made it virtually impossible for many SOEs to meet their full range of social obligations and even salary payments, thus in turn speeding up the need for pension, medical and housing reform. SOEs employ fully one-third of China's medical staff and some 600,000 teachers and adminis-trators (Hughes, 1998, p. 73). The cost of social insurance and welfare funds as a proportion of the total wage bill rose from 13.7 per cent to 34 per cent in 1995 (UNDP, 1998, p. 65). It is not surprising, then, that bankruptcies in 1996 rose by 260 per cent on the year before and that lay-offs rose despite official concern: the total of 6,232 bankruptcies exceeded the total for the previous seven years combined.

Such statistics led the party leadership to decide, in a risky venture, to cut themselves loose from the working class that they had created in the 1950s and to reduce working-class expectations about what the state could provide. Rhetoric is still paid to the importance of the leadership of the working class, and policy is to give priority to finding work for laid-off workers. The reality, however, is that many are on their own to find new work in an eco-nomy that is increasingly unfamiliar to them and that requires very different skills than those they learned under the Soviet-inspired system.

These serious reforms have produced a dramatially transformed industrial landscape. The main thrust of reform has been to correct the problem of growth at increasing cost by improving investment efficiency, forcing the SOEs to become more market-oriented and replacing policy-driven bank subsidies with real loans at market rates. This led Premier Zhu to announce at the March 1998 NPC meeting that the leadership would strive to resolve the problem of the SOEs within 3 years, an impossible task but one that sets down a target to aim for. In September 1999, the CC adopted a decision on the further reform of SOEs; not surprisingly, it represented a compromise that sought to steer a middle course. Thus, it did not mention radical local practices such as the sale of the large number of state firms, nor did it cite targets for converting large state firms into shareholding companies. However, it did encourage SOEs to pull out of certain sectors of the economy where there were adequate alternatives and once again stressed a mixed ownership system. Yet, the question of managerial autonomy was still ambiguous, as the document stressed the importance of guidance of enterprises by party committees. Party organs were described as the political nucleus within enterprises. At the same time, it called for a modern corporate system to be established with clear ownership and the separation of the enterprise from government administration. Enterprises were to enjoy full management authority and assume full responsibility for profits and losses.

The other important points were that state-owned assets were to be reor-ganized and the formation of large enterprise groups was still to be the focal point, under the policy of 'grasp the large and release the small' (*zhuada fangxiao*). This meant that small- and medium-sized enterprises (SMEs) would be turned into a variety of non-state forms through the expansion of shareholding systems, formation of joint-ventures or sale to interested parties (see Huchet, 2000). For the 500 or so large enterprises (originally 1,000) that the state intends to keep under its control, the proposed models are the conglomerates of the *keiretsu* in Japan and the *chaebols* of South Korea. With an eye to past practice, the document stated that the large enterprise groups should be formed by the needs of the market rather than by administrative means. The market was also to ensure the survival of the fittest through the encouragement of mergers, standardization of bankruptcy procedures, lay-offs and the encouragement of reemployment projects. To soak up the unemployed, greater political coverage was given to the non-state sector of the economy.

Local leaders saw the policy of promoting shareholding as a great opportunity to shed themselves of responsibility for the state sector and to raise some much-needed capital as well. Nationwide figures show that by the end of 1997 one-third of the 500,000 township-run enterprises (not SOEs) had been sold off or turned into shareholding cooperatives (*SCMP*, 21 June 1998). However, the potential for corruption and official speculation was great and clearly a number of local officials saw this as a major windfall or one last chance to get rich at the state's expense. Official estimates calculate that 'spontaneous privatization' with the stripping of state assets cost the state $6 billion a year over the years since 1985 (Hughes, 1998, p. 75). While state assets were diverted into individual pockets, the state was left to cover the debts. An equally severe problem was local authorities forcing workers to buy shares in enterprises so that they qualified as shareholding cooperatives. It is unclear how pervasive this practice has been. For already failing institutions, it is unlikely that these one-time infusions of cash will turn such enterprises around and local officials are liable to be confronted by angry workers who have lost their life's savings. In addition, workers have been frustrated when they have discovered that their buy-in has not bought them a seat at the decision-making table; the majority of shares are held by the old management or local officials, who received them as a reward rather than through purchase.

Amazing as it may seem given the experiences of South Korean and Japanese conglomerates with respect to the Asian Financial Crisis and its aftermath, senior Chinese officials still feel that they are viable. In their view, during the initial developmental phase such industrial conglomerates can play a positive role, and they claim that they will abandon the model before it has out-lived its usefulness. There may indeed be some efficiency benefits to derive from the formation of larger entities. As Huchet (1999, p. 5) points out, China holds some unenviable records for the fragmentation of its industrial structure. For example it has 8,000 independent cement producers against 1,500 throughout the rest of the world. China's leading company has only 0.6 per cent of the national market; it has 123 manufacturers of cars and 1,500 steel works. Thus, in part the drive for mergers comes from the enormous surplus production capacity in Chinese industry as well as the demands of WTO entry. The leadership feels the need to build up a certain number of world-class, major conglomerates to compete in the global economy: the dream of being in the *Fortune 500* list seems irresistible! In 1997, China announced its hope to develop 120 such worldbeaters, companies such as Changhong in Sichuan, already the seventh-largest producer of televisions in the world. These conglomerates will get priority not only with access to loans but also when listing on the stockmarket, including those overseas. They are also allowed to set up finance companies for internal use and trade overseas without going through state training companies (*FEER*, 21 May 1998, p. 12). In a further boost, in November 2002 China allowed foreigners to buy non-tradable shares in listed companies and announced that it would allow foreigners to invest in unlisted SOEs from January 2003 (*Reuters*, 12 November 2002).

The key problem is that ministries and enterprises often see the reform as an invitation to develop monopolies that rely on political connections to ensure privileged access to funding. In addition, many of the larger, genuinely profitable companies are forced to take on smaller companies that would go bankrupt without such protection. This has been a common complaint of the very successful Hai'er group based in Qingdao that produces refrigerators and other household appliances. The problem with the policy, as Huchet (1999, p. 16) astutely notes, is that of trying to meet multiple objectives that may not be compatible. He notes that the policy is designed, apart from getting a few companies on the *Fortune 500* list, to solve the problem of overcapacity and fragmentation of the industrial structures; to reduce the losses made by SOEs while avoiding bankruptcies that would produce unemployment; and finally to simplify the management of public assets by assigning it to groups organized into holding companies. Thus, the policy runs the risk of undermining precisely those groups that are emerging as genuine market leaders.

Is the policy of reviving the SOEs working? On paper, yes, but the picture is mixed and pressures are increasing on the financial system. By the end of 1999 and throughout 2000, officials were beginning to highlight figures that showed the situation for loss-making SOEs starting to turn around. In 2000, official estimates of profits for the sector were $11.75 billion, a 78 per cent increase over 1999 with a further rise in gross profits in the first 8 months of 2001 of $18.7 billion (*AFP*, 28 October 2001). This turnaround is not surprising. First, many of the really hopeless cases have been taken off the state books through mergers and acquisitions with more profitable companies. Second, from 1994 the state has sold off, bankrupted or contracted out many small- and medium-sized SOEs that were owned by non-central authorities. One survey found that in 19 provinces by the end of 1999, 75 per cent of such SOEs had changed their ownership structure. Third, Asset Management Companies have bought up the debt for many of the larger enterprises which have thus been moved off the books of the SOEs, some $160 billion in 1999 and 2000. Most importantly, the SOEs are no longer paying a large amount of interest on their bad loans. In this way many bankrupt SOEs have turned around from basket cases to seemingly profitable enterprises overnight.

Whether the problem of SOE inefficiency is really resolved or not is an entirely different matter, and many of the SOEs have avoided the necessary structural reforms to enable them to compete in the WTO market.

Certainly we are looking at a restructured industrial and employment landscape. However, recent figures suggest that the benefits of these one-shot measures are diminishing. Little has come from the kind of increased efficiency that would signal a lasting turnaround. For 2001, it was estimated that 43 per cent of SOEs lost money, while 5,200 out of 6,000 SOEs that formed the core of reform efforts reported losses. Also in September, for the first time since early 1999, the rate of SOE losses increased (*AFP*, 28 October 2001).

In May 2003, general secretary Hu Jintao decided to launch a new approach to streamlining and improving the performance of the SOE sector. While Jiang's report to the Sixteenth Party Congress reiterated prior policy, including calling SOEs 'the pillar of the national economy' while continuing to diversify the nature of public ownership, Hu's approach differs. It abandons the primary focus of selling off smaller SOEs that had produced much corruption: some estimates put the loss of state assets at $41 billion. The new plan separates ownership and management of SOEs, with ownership transferred from various ministries to a central State Assets Commission. The Commission has taken over 196 of the largest SOEs with combined assets of $834 billion, including the national airline Air China, national oil companies and major telecommunications, steel and auto companies (*Economist Intelligence Unit*, 28 May 2003). The new Commission hopes to enhance management, reduce corruption and try to restructure 30–50 SOEs to become internationally competitive. Success, however, is far from certain and the wisdom of creating another bureaucratic structure to resolve the SOE problem is debatable. Many officials who have gained from the old system may resist while local governments and ministries may rush to sell off their remaining assets before they are taken over.

We have seen above the major role that rural industry has played in China's recent development, but the private and non-state sectors in the urban areas have also been expanding and gaining increasing political acceptability. Diversification of ownership with the collective and private enterprise sectors providing competition is also seen as a way to improve the SOE sector. The entry of foreign firms, first through joint-ventures and subsequently as wholly foreign-owned enterprises, was seen as providing both the necessary capital, technological up-grading and enhanced management. The share of the non-state sector in industrial output rose from 22.4 per cent in 1978 to 73.5 per cent in 2000 while the private sector grew from 2 per cent in 1985 to 16 per cent in 1998 (Yusuf, 2000, pp. 24–5). The People's Bank of China has estimated that by the end of 1998, the private sector contributed 43 per cent of GDP, 48 per cent of employment and 31 per cent of fixed asset investment (Saich, 2003).

It is clear that the state sector will not be able to provide employment for those laid off and for the estimated 11–12 million new entrants each year onto the job market. Hu Angang (quoted in *The China Quarterly*, June 2000, p. 611) noted that with GDP falling in 1998 only 3.57 million new jobs had been created, the smallest percentage increase in employment (0.5 per cent) since 1949. Employment in SOEs and collectively owned enterprises had fallen by 10.273 and 4.704 million, respectively, in 1998, and a further 5 and 3 million in 1999 (*China Statistical Abstract*, 2000, p. 36). There was thus a need to find other avenues of employment.

One route for employment expansion is the service sector, which in China employs a low percentage of employees in comparison with other countries at a similar developmental level. Hu Angang estimated that allowing foreign investment into this sector could generate a boom of 40–50 million jobs. The other main option for employment expansion is further development of the private sector. At the end of 2001 the number of private enterprises was 2.03 million, up 34 per cent over 2 years and the number of employees was 27.14 million (20.21 million in 1999) (*Beijing Review*, 20 March 2003, p. 14). With better protection and access to adequate credit the sector could expand further. Laid-off state workers and even many fresh college graduates look towards the sector for future employment. To many young Chinese it offers the attractions of a wealth that was unimaginable for their parents and a freedom from bureaucratic procedures and state intrusion into one's life that SOE work offers. While this might be true for some of China's new millionaires, reality is far more complex and many labour in sweatshop conditions with minimal labour protection and little chance for financial advancement. As Parris (1999, p. 267) has noted, in 1990, while average SOE workers enjoyed a salary of 2,500 *yuan* annually, 11 per cent of individual entrepreneurs made less than 1,000 *yuan* and only 9 per cent of private business owners made over 80,000 *yuan* annually. Perhaps the largest private sector exists in the city of Wenzhou in Zhejiang province. Wenzhou is physically isolated from the rest of the country and suffered from very little state investment. Drawing on its own resources and traditions it developed a flourishing private sector long before it was politically acceptable. By 1997, state production accounted for only 8 per cent of total industrial production, down from 15 per cent in 1988. Its growth rates were high, exceeding the national rates by a wide margin and it cornered significant markets for buttons, leather, shoes and clothes, and more recently it has begun to develop chemicals and electronics.

The growth of the sector has been accompanied by grudging acceptance and a battle over constitutional reform that sought to give the private sector better recognition, legal protection and to reduce political interference, thereby providing better access to credit and other necessary resources. Policy has moved far from the Seventh NPC (1988) that allowed private enterprises with more than 8 employees to enjoy legal status for the first time since the early 1950s (Parris, 1999, pp. 265–6). During the 1990s after Deng's relaunch of economic reforms the sector grew rapidly. In addition to the need to provide employment, it became clear that those provinces with a higher level or private enterprise were also those that enjoyed a higher growth and standard of living. For example, in Wenzhou and Taizhou, where the private economy is dominant, there is very little unemployment in contrast with towns like Mudanjiang in the Northeast that are dominated by old SOEs. Some 54 per cent of the 2.03 million private firms at the end of 2001 were in the rich coastal areas of Jiangsu, Guangdong, Zhejiang, Shanghai and Beijing while only 14 per cent were located in the West (*SCMP+*, 17 July 2002).

As noted, the sector was provided with political legitimacy in 1997–98 (see Chapter 3) and in 1999 the State Constitution was amended to note that the non-state sector of the economy was an 'integral part of the socialist economy' replacing the previous formulation that it 'supplements' the state sector. Politically, of course, acceptability was granted on 1 July 2001 when Jiang Zemin welcomed private entrepreneurs to join the party. Policy changes have also been introduced to boost the sector. For example, in 1998 the banking sector was instructed to shift from lending quotas to using profitability as the main criterion and this was accompanied by attempts to shift lending away from enterprise financing to consumer financing. More export licences have been granted to private firms, allowing them to acquire foreign exchange; in 2000, 'IPOs' were to be allowed not just for SOEs while in 2002 the State Development and Planning Commission abolished a number of restrictions on investments by private firms.

Despite progress, problems still exist for the sector and the tax evasion and extravagant lifestyles of a few of the very rich have damaged the reputation of the sector and played to traditional prejudice against private entrepreneurs. Zhu Rongji was said to have become apoplectic when he discovered that some of the wealthiest people in China paid less taxes than he. Measures to promote the sector have been accompanied by a crackdown on corruption and tax evasion by individuals and an attempt to improve tax collection. The main complaint, apart from insufficient political recognition, is that of access to good business opportunities and credit to develop. The main state banks still tend not to lend to private enterprises and only one private bank exists in China. At the same time, it is very difficult for private companies to raise capital on the stockmarket. Opportunities for expansion are constrained and while lucrative sectors such as telecommunications are open for foreign investment, they are effectively closed to domestic private enterprise. It seems probable that in 2004, the NPC will make a further constitutional amendment to establish equal treatment for state and private property. This will facilitate revision of other existing laws (*Xinhua*, 3 March 2003).

Financial Sector Reform

A key component for the success of economic reform in general, and SOE reform in particular, is the restructuring of the banking and financial sectors (see Huang, Saich and Steinfeld, forthcoming). In the 1980s, financial reform was not really thought of as a part of economic reform, and if considered it was interpreted in the very narrow sense of banking reform. With a weak fiscal system banks were essentially used to meet the state's development objectives. However, by the mid-1990s reformers recognized the need for the overhaul of the sector and the necessity of cleaning up the banks' bad debts. This was given extra urgency, first by the Asian Financial Crisis and then by WTO entry that threatened a meltdown of Chinese banks unless they could improve their accounts.

With the main role of state banks being to feed the SOE sector, they built up a huge portfolio of non-performing loans, the true extent of which no one really appears to know: some have estimated it to be as large as 25 per cent of GDP (Naughton, 2000, p. 66). Bottelier (2000, p. 2) asserts that the true net equity value of the large state commercial banks (before the transfer of the non-performing loans to asset management committees) is almost certainly negative. He asserts that to revive the state banks it will require not only internal restructuring but also at least $200 billion in fresh capital, and possibly much more (Bottelier, 2000, p. 3). The situation with rural credit cooperatives is even worse.

Since Zhu Rongji took over responsibility for reform of the sector, considerable progress has been made, even though the remaining problems are huge, the largest unresolved reform issue in the eyes of some (see, for example, Lardy, 1998b). Zhu set in motion a series of reforms designed to free state banks from local politics, to allow the Central Bank to play more of a regulatory role and to get the non-performing loans off the books of the banking system. In 1994, the banking system was divided into three types of banks: commercial banks, policy banks and cooperative banks, with a limited but increasing role for private banks. The four major banks remained under the authority of the state but were given greater capacity to make loans on a commercial basis. These four banks (the Industrial and Commercial Bank, the Bank of China, the China Construction Bank and the Agricultural Bank of China) account for up to 70 per cent of the domestic banking business. It is important to remember that in China financial assets are essentially concentrated in the banking system as capital markets are small and bank loans are the most important source of capital for enterprises. The state's capacity for direct lending for its priority objectives was entrusted to three newly-created 'policy banks' (China Development Bank, the Agricultural Development Bank and the Export Import Bank of China) that would look after government-mandated lending. Despite this intent, the division has not been so clean in practice. The four commercial banks are still directed to lend to SOEs and they will also purchase bonds from the policy banks.

The next major steps were taken in 1998. With the onset of the Asian Financial Crisis and the realization that China's banking system was as perilously placed as many of those that collapsed in the surrounding countries, reformers were able to push ahead with financial sector reform. The first measure to be unveiled was an overhaul of the banking system, the centrepiece of which was the reorganization of the local branches of the People's Bank along regional lines to reduce political interference by powerful provincial party chiefs in lending decisions. The former 31 provincial branches of the People's Bank of China were reduced to 9 regional centres. As Zhu Rongji noted, the 'power of provincial governors and mayors to command local bank presidents is abolished as of 1998' (Lardy, 1998a, p. 86). 'Reduced' rather than 'abolished' is probably a more accurate assessment. The People's Bank of China was to strengthen its regulatory functions and operate more as a central bank, an authority it was granted only in 1995. However, central leaders remain ambivalent about commercializing the banking system and see state banks as a mechanism to fund the state's severe fiscal shortfalls (J. D. Langlois, in *Asian Wall Street Journal*, 12 October 2000).

The People's Bank of China showed its new teeth briefly in 1998 and 1999 when it moved to close the insolvent Guangdong International Trust and Investment Corporation. Such corporations, of which there are around 200 in China, were set up primarily to raise foreign capital for domestic use. The fact that the primary creditors were foreigners led most to believe that the central authorities would step in to help for fear of repercussions. Zhu's decision to allow the closure to go ahead was a clear signal both to domestic institutions and foreign lenders that, in the future, rules would be applied more consistently.

Massive problems remain, and at the July 2000 session of the Standing Committee of the NPC the chief auditor criticized the state-owned banks for their sloppiness in financial management. According to his report, two of the banks held 10.1 billion *yuan* in off-book assets and 790 million *yuan* in petty cash that was said to have cost the state 10 billion *yuan*. The audit found 170 cases of malpractice that had involved 221 people and 14.6 billion *yuan*. Not surprisingly, the State Council decided to send inspection teams to monitor the performance of state financial institutions. This parallels Zhu Rongji's decision in 1999 to appoint 100 special inspectors to investigate the books of the 500 largest SOEs.

In 2003 at the NPC it was decided to set up a new oversight organization for the state banks, the China Banking Regulatory Commission, to help them improve corporate governance, shift lending to commercial criteria and intensify the effort to recover non-performing loans (NPLs). Official figures claim that the NPLs had been reduced to 24.1 per cent in March 2003, down from 26.1 per cent at the end of 2002. The objective is to reduce the

NPLs as a percentage of total lending by 2005 to 15 per cent (*Financial Times*, 29 May 2003).

The main measure to get NPLs off the books was the creation of an Asset Management Committee (AMC) for each of the 4 commercial banks. The capital is provided by the Ministry of Finance and they are owned by the central government, not the banks themselves. To help clear up the problem of SOE debts, the AMCs acquired at face value, loans from banks to SOEs. Initially 600 SOEs were selected to receive these benefits, later expanded to 1,000. These SOEs were selected on the principle that they could become solvent once their debt was cleared, that there was a future market niche for them and that they were well managed. However, it is inevitable that some must have got onto the list because of local politics and connections rather than because of objective criteria.

The programme has not worked and creates a dilemma as to whether further bail-outs should be used. In 1999 and 2000 some $169 billion worth of bad loans were transferred to AMCs, about 18 per cent of China's GDP in 1998 (Ma and Fung, 2002). Of this amount only 6 per cent has been disposed of and recovery rates have not surpassed 10 per cent (Lardy, in *Financial Times*, 22 June 2001), well below the officially anticipated 30–40 per cent. Perhaps most amazingly the NPLs in the sector have gone up or at least not declined substantially. The bank recapitalization and the AMC transfers have not resolved the NPL problem. The transferred NPLs amounted to under 50 per cent of the NPLs at the 4 banks, perhaps because the banks never fully disclosed their real problems. The AMCs have also run into problems with the cash recoveries that are below their interest obligations, thus creating cash flow pressures. As a result, the government has tried to speed up asset recovery and this led to China's first international NPL auction.

The banks have clearly not resolved their own NPL problem. The main reason for this is that their customer base has not changed, it is still the major SOEs (Woo, n.d.). As we have seen above the sector is still deep in debt. The AMCs, through the debt-for-equity swaps, were expected to gain a role in restructuring SOEs. However, Steinfeld (2000, pp. 22–7) in late 1999 found that the AMCs had little capacity or power genuinely to reorganize the SOEs. In fact, he notes that enterprise managers felt that the purpose of reform was to preserve assets as they were currently deployed in the existing firm. Many enterprise leaders felt that the fact that they had been put on the Commission's list was proof enough that they were a good company and required no further interference in their management affairs. As we have seen above, with no change in business practice, many are sliding back into debt.

The urgency of resolving the SOE and banking problem is heightened by the agreement signed on WTO entry between China, the United States and the European Union. The consequences of what China has signed are enormous. By 2005, there will be no restrictions on foreign banking activity in China and prudential not national criteria should apply. Already in 2002 foreign banks were able to conduct local currency work with corporate customers. Unless the AMCs and China's banks are able to clear up the debts within 5 years, the challenges could be enormous and create a banking crisis in China. Even with the AMCs taking over much of the current bad loans, but only the pre-1996 non-performing policy loans, the banks will have dramatically to improve their future lending habits. The consequences for the macroeconomic situation will be far-reaching. Bottelier (2000, p. 2) has predicted that to prepare its banks for international competition, China will have to accelerate the liberalization of domestic interest rates, seek fuller integration between domestic and international capital markets and accelerate towards full convertibility of the currency. The dilemma is whether China can afford another recapitalization of the banks. In international terms, China's consolidated public debt is not too bad. Thus financially it is possible, but the question remains as to whether it is another case of throwing good money after bad.

Thus, despite extraordinary progress in economic reform, China's leaders face enormous future challenges. These stem from the problems of delayed reform and will provide a major test for the skills of the next generation of leaders. While there are grounds for pessimism, China has survived remarkably well to date and has avoided the various doom-laden scenarios that have been offered abroad. On the positive side, there is broad recognition that there is no alternative but to move ahead, and in the latter half of the 1990s China's leadership moved to a more comprehensive vision of the nature of reform and begun to adopt a better sequencing for the reform programme.

10

Social Policy

The effect of reform on social policy has been no less dramatic than on economic policy. Reforms have produced new inequalities, a dramatic rise in the disparity between welfare provision in rural and urban China and an abandonment of the compact for cradle-to-grave social welfare for the privileged industrial working class. While the reforms may have raised the standard of living for the vast majority and shifted China along the road to a market economy, China's policy-makers have met considerable problems devising policies to bridge the social transition. In this respect, China has confronted similar problems to other transitional economies in designing a new welfare system that is affordable and equitable (for other transitional economies, see Bird and Wallich, 1993; Kornai, 1997). This is not surprising as reforms entailing major institutional change are inherently slower and more complex than macroeconomic stabilization and liberalization measures (Nelson, 1997, p. 256).

In the boom years of the early 1990s little attention was paid to the social consequences of the reforms and there was a general assumption that high levels of economic growth would resolve all problems. However, by the end of the 1990s it was clear that not all had benefited equally from reforms and that inequality and differential access to services had become a major problem. The grandest response was the programme to Develop the West launched by Jiang Zemin, but there have also been other significant changes that have redefined the role of the state in welfare provision. The new leadership of Hu and Wen has made addressing the problems of social inequality a key feature of their administration. Recognition that the state and its agencies can no longer handle its welfare obligations has led to the emergence of new service providers, some of which are operating on strict market principles, while others are taking a more philanthropic approach (see, for example, Wong and Flynn, 2001). Reforms have also changed notions of entitlement, with access to services much more tightly tied to financial capacity than in the past. The linkage of service provision to ability to pay has produced new inequalities and exacerbated old ones. In particular, there has been a dramatic rise in the disparity between welfare provision in rural and urban China and an abandonment of the old cradle-to-crave social compact for the privileged urban working class. Not only has this led to policy challenges to devise new institutions and mechanisms for service provision but also raises more fundamental questions about citizenship and entitlement. To whom does the state have an obligation to provide welfare, and at what level?

The challenge is different for the urban and rural areas. In urban China the challenge is to shift from a system of severely frayed safety nets for the urban working class officials majority to a clearer articulation of what China's citizens can expect in terms of welfare guarantees. In rural China, it is more a question of putting basic systems in place that can cover healthcare and education. The resultant policies should address the dualistic development strategy that privileges the urban over the rural. The literal fencing off of the rural from the urban during the Mao years made it easier for the city dwellers to enjoy their privileged position. The reforms have begun to tear down this fence and, as a result, it is increasingly difficult to justify this privilege in political terms. With increased market reliance and with the huge influx of rural migrants to the cities the two worlds are now inextricably linked and they often share the same neighbourhood. The inequity of providing education and medical services to one while denying it to the other has become a source of tension, especially at a time of economic slowdown (UNDP, 1998, p.9).

President Hu and Premier Wen will have to deal with such inequities if they wish to project the image of serving the interests of the whole nation rather than of a small urban elite. Migrants and those who remain in the countryside need a clear indication from the central leadership as to whether citizenship, in terms of access to social welfare, will be extended to them through a gradual increase of access to social security and insurance schemes or whether they will be left to their own devices, private sector provision and family-based support. There have been encouraging signs of recognizing these problems.

This chapter looks first in general terms at the question of social policy and the transition in China, and then discusses a number of specific policy areas. As it is impossible to cover everything, it highlights a number of questions that are exemplary: the difficult policy area of family planning, the attempts to cut the Gordian knot of urban workplace-based welfare, healthcare provision in the rural areas, the situation of migrants and poverty alleviation programmes.

Social Policy and the Transition in China

China shares two basic points of departure with all other countries in terms of how the welfare system is structured. First, the ideology and value system provide the basis for decisions about who gets what level of welfare support, and for how long. Second, the structure of the economy and the level of economic development affects the kind of welfare choices that can be made. Welfare is a crucial part of the institutional framework of the economy and attempts are being made to coordinate the two to meet the regime's objectives.

Under Mao, the welfare system was seen as subservient to the demands of the economy and to the pursuit of socialism. In practice, this meant that social policy was closely tied to a development strategy that kept the rural and the urban separate and privileged provision of the urban and industrial sectors over the rural and the agricultural. At the same time, the organization of the collective in the countryside and the inconsequentiality of cost meant that, for its developmental level, rural Chinese enjoyed a good preventive healthcare and basic education system. While they were subsequently derided, the paramedics of the Cultural Revolution known as 'barefoot doctors' do seem to have provided decent vaccination programmes and preventive care for many who would not have received them in other developing countries. This redressed somewhat the urban bias of the system.

George and Manning (1980), in their study of social welfare in the Soviet Union, suggest a definition for a socialist social policy that rests on the fundamental premise that the private market has been largely or completely abolished and that the means of production are in the hands of the government. This gives the government, in reality the CCP, enormous discretionary power over decisions related to social policy in comparison with capitalist systems where individual insurance schemes may be predominant. In theory, social policy can be used to promote ambitious goals of social engineering, even more so than in the North European welfare states, as there should be no fundamental conflict of interests between the various sections of the community. Social policy can be thus another tool in the government's kit to build the communist society. This certainly enabled the CCP to institutionalize its development priorities and reflect the vested interests of the communist *apparat*. Even under Mao these have not been redistributional in nature and post-Mao there has been no attempt to eliminate social inequalities and to build a classless society. Policy has provided selected targeting of state assistance and has shunned an elaborate system of universal entitlements. In fact, China's current development strategy is highly inegalitarian and deviates considerably from those of its East Asian neighbours whose economic development China is so keen to follow. *The People's Daily* (31 August 2002) reported a Gini coefficient of 0.457 as against 0.33 back in 1980. While China is not as unequal as countries such as Brazil (0.61) or Mexico (0.52), normally thought of as highly unequal, it has surpassed other large developing countries such as India (0.38) and Indonesia (0.32). Welfare policy has been used as a safety net in the urban areas to catch those thrown aside by the economic juggernaut that is under constant pressure to increase more with increased efficiency.

The development of social policy went hand-in-hand with the nationalization of urban industry and rural collectivization. The system developed has broken down under the reforms with the financial collapse of many SOEs, the rise of the non-state sector, and decollectivization in the countryside. However, the underlying premise that the best way to alleviate poverty and improve welfare is to boost production has been accepted by the post-Mao leaderships. They have eschewed policies of significant income redistribution to the poor and welfare will be expanded only as production increases. The obsession to boost production figures has never been seriously challenged by a need to divert resources away from immediate investment in production. Mao rejected any notions of 'welfarism' for the new workers' state and this has been faithfully adhered to by his successors. As Deng Xiaoping pointed out in 1980, while China had to increase education spending as it was among the 20 countries in the world that spent the least relative to GDP, this did not mean that China should become a welfare state. He noted that 'developing production without improving the people's livelihood is not right' but 'calling for an improved livelihood without developing production is not right either and cannot be attained'. However, before the reforms began, ideology did act as a constraint on too great an increase in inegalitarian distributional policies. This made the policy shift to a more inegalitarian wage policy and to an openly inegalitarian development strategy more difficult to introduce.

The reforms have also eroded the full, or near-full, employment policy operated by the CCP. Until the late 1990s, social policy was designed to encourage as great a participation as possible in the labour force through providing support that would allow women with children to work. Now the tendency is to lay off women, first in SOEs, or persuade them to take early retirement, often at age 50 or earlier. Second, unemployment relief was hard to come by, thus forcing those who could work into the labour force. With the current downturn in the economy, this is more difficult to achieve. Third, as many people as possible were encouraged to work. Before the reforms, urban China had a string of factories in which those who were physically handicapped worked. This increased production but also provided them with a wage, making them useful to the family and integrated them into a social network. With the financial bottom line now paramount, many of these factories have closed down, with negative consequences for many of the handicapped. With no effective welfare system to support them, they are now seen as a burden on the family and make up one group of the new urban poor.

The Chinese system for social welfare administration enjoys two distinctive features. First, as with other areas there has always been a high degree of decentralization and even during the high tide of the collective period what one got varied largely in accordance with where one lived. Second, there was a strong emphasis on collective self-reliance and mutual aid. The first port of call was the family and then the collective in the countryside, or the neighbourhood committee in the urban areas. Welfare needs and social policy more broadly have been met at the level of the urban workplace, the urban neighbourhood committee and the rural people's collectives and now villages. These three networks dependent on party policy and under direction from higher administrative levels were responsible for deciding not only the appropriate level of welfare support but also, more importantly, for the financing and delivery of the services. This provided the population with a reasonable measure of security and education in what was a surplus-labour, low-income economy. However, even in the 1980s the state was often unable to provide the support it guaranteed. For example, any one with a disability should be eligible for welfare benefits and support from their workplace of the Ministry of Civil Affairs. Yet 67 per cent of those with disabilities received basic subsistence from their families and only 3 per cent from the state (Zhong, 2001). For much of the time the stringency of the household registration system prevented large-scale rural–urban drift, and in the Mao years China's cities were remarkable for the lack of shanty-town development and migrant labourers.

Self-reliance has been and remains an important principle for social policy in China. Administratively, this requires the basic-level administrative organizations to develop capacity in line with their own resources rather than to rely on hand-outs or redistribution payments from higher levels. In practice, it means that individuals might be provided with minimum levels of subsistence, but for the rest they would rely first and foremost on the family and then borrow from village funds in the countryside before receiving actual welfare. The CCP sets down general guidelines, such as for a minimum wage or the need for unemployment relief, but it does not apply a standardized rate or system across the country.

As a result, inequality of provision is inevitable, not only across geographic divisions but also from work-unit to work-unit within the same urban district, or from village to village within the same township. This was true also when the communes were in operation. In one commune near Guangzhou, only 3,000–6,000 out of 15,000 households were participating in the collective medical schemes. In part, these low participation rates stemmed from the voluntary nature of the scheme and it was often the wealthier who pulled out. Many did not wish to subsidize the medical expenses of their poorer neighbours (Discussion with farmers, Yangzhou Commune, 1977). In fact, Du Ying from the Ministry of Agriculture has claimed that by the mid-1970s the majority of commune and brigade-run health cooperatives had already collapsed or existed in name only because of lack of trust by farmers in local officials (Du Ying, 2000, pp. 36–7).

A number of problems have stemmed from this system that require urgent attention during the transition. The cost of even the limited welfare provided has become too high for the state to cover. Welfare costs rose from 3.1 per cent of Gross National Product (GNP) in 1978 to 6.2 per cent in 1990. Of this amount, 85 per cent went to cover costs for employees in urban enterprises. The costs of medical and pension provision rose the most rapidly and amounted to 50 and 21 per cent of these expenditures, respectively (Leung, 1995, p. 221). The financial crisis in the SOEs means that they can no longer carry the economic burden of providing the previous levels of social welfare for their workers. The abandonment of the commune has meant that the collective health structures have all but collapsed and especially in the poorest regions have yet to be replaced by a new system. The introduction of market incentives and a regard for profitability that did not exist previously has led basic-level institutions to shed their social costs or to turn them over to a fee-for-service system. The impact of this is seen particularly with respect to healthcare. In the mid-1970s China was frequently praised by international organizations for the level of healthcare provided given its low income level, yet in the *World Health Report 2000* the World Health Organization (WHO) ranked China 188 out of 191 countries in terms of the fairness with which its healthcare operates, 144th for overall performance and 139th in terms of healthcare *per capita*. While ranked above most African countries, it is ranked below other large developing countries such as India, Bangladesh and Indonesia. In terms of health quality achieved, it ranks somewhat better (61), but this may be because of the residual impact of the old collective medical system.

The bifurcation of development strategy into rural and urban components has set different starting points for reform and presents different challenges for policy resolution. Up until 1979, most had some kind of minimum guarantee, either through a job in the urban areas or the use of communal land in the countryside. In the urban areas, for those in SOEs there was social insurance provision and the workplace supplied housing and medical benefits. For the rural population, the government offered relatively little but there were provisions through the collective agreements. The support provided by the state was through the local offices of the Ministry of Civil Affairs. This was to provide the 'five guarantees' (to food, fuel, clothes, healthcare and burial) to the destitute with no family to care for them. This was subsequently extended to the urban areas. Those in the urban areas who worked in the non-state sector did not qualify for social insurance but did have access to social relief and welfare services, dependent on a means test. These are dispersed in two ways, either through the firm to laid-off workers or through the Ministry of Civil Affairs to those families whose income falls below a set minimum. Receipt of the first is especially unpredictable as it depends on the willingness and ability of the firm to pay. The second is more predictable but the numbers in receipt have been rising rapidly. In April 2000, there were 2.81 million urban Chinese receiving it, but this had risen to 19.3 million by July 2002 (*Xinhua*, 19 July 2002 and *China News Service*, reported in *China Online*). According to the Ministry of Civil Affairs, in April 2000 there were 2.81 million urban Chinese receiving minimum living subsidies, with the amount ranging from a monthly high of 319 *yuan* in Shenzhen to a low of 143 *yuan* in Nanchang, Hohhot and Yinchuan (*China News Service*, reported in *China Online*).

While social welfare has been subordinate to economic policy, failure to introduce effective policies has undermined state policy. For example, the lack of a social security system for those working outside of the SOEs and the household responsibility system in the countryside are the two major obstacles to lowering the birth-rate. Many desire children as an insurance for old age. Interestingly, just before their abolition a number of more prosperous communes began to introduce pension schemes. They acknowledged that this would help with both family planning and with reducing the differences between the city and the countryside.

Redressing these problems will be a major challenge for Hu and Wen, coming at a time when the urban proletariat already sees its status and benefits being eroded by reform. Further, any significant shift of resources would adversely affect the urban professional health and education networks that can be relied on to resist. Like most regimes, the Chinese leadership reflects the political bias of the most powerful, vociferous and visible groups and ignores the needy (Graham, 1997). As a result, it has focused policy on the needs of state officials, has been receptive to the policy prescription of its professional classes and has sought to soften the blows of the market transition for the urban proletariat. By contrast, it has left the rural poor, the migrants and the non-state-sector employees to their own collective devices and has ensured that they have remained politically marginalized.

Family Planning: Problems of Policy Coordination and Policy Evasion

The lack of policy coordination across different line ministries and the adoption of conflicting policies are familiar problems. For example, the quotas that each local bureau of a ministry sets for local farmers are decided independently of one another, with the result that the individual household becomes the point for reconciliation of conflicting demands to produce grain, plant trees and raise livestock. Here we look at the conflicting policies of the promotion of the 'one-child policy' and the household responsibility system (White, 1987, pp. 307–9).

The introduction of the household responsibility system set up incentives for households to increase family size rather than comply with the tightening of family-planning policy. Two primary reasons accounted for this. First, when land was initially parcelled out, it was allocated on the basis of household size and thus there was a benefit in having a larger family. Demographics played a major part in who got rich first in a village, with those families having a larger labour force of working age benefiting more than those families with both very young children and old grandparents. Second, the desire to increase family size derived from the dismantling of the collective welfare system in the countryside. The policy message appeared to be that if you wanted to get rich and be looked after in your old age you needed more children. This was clearly true, but it was not what policy-makers had intended and they were concerned about the baby boom that Mao had set in motion in the

late 1950s. They feared that the rapidly increasing population would undermine the economic gains that they hoped would come from the reforms.

The one-child family policy, introduced in 1979, has been one of the most
unpopular policies in China, especially in the countryside. In the urban areas
not only is political control easier but also there are stronger economic
incentives for families to consider a smaller family size. While many in China
recognize the need to control population and may even feel that the policy is
a correct one, many also have specific reasons about why it should not apply
to them. The state set up an elaborate administrative framework throughout
the system to monitor programme implementation. There are around
400,000 officials at the township level and 1 million in the villages. The State
Family-Planning Commission (SFPC) sets the national birth-rate and the
provincial quotas, it is then the responsibility of local family-planning
officials to set out the birth quotas for their administrative jurisdiction. The
burden for family planning falls on women and little attempt is made to
involve men in the process. In each work-unit or administrative jurisdiction,
there is a list kept of whose turn it is to conceive and often lists are kept of
the menstrual cycle of women to facilitate control.

The fact that family planning was given the highest priority as a task for
local officials meant the implementation often became coercive, even if this
was not the intent of central policy-makers. For local officials one can meet
all other quota targets but if that for family planning is missed then promotion
is not possible. This and the general pressures generated by a quota-driven
system have led to the frequently reported abuses of forced abortions and
the forced sterilization of women.

However, even with such attention there has been policy evasion and ultimately policy amendment. In fact, the policy was not applied to minority
households and in most of the countryside *de facto* policy was for 2 children
or even 3. With increasing financial opportunities, those families no longer
dependent on the state for grain and other basic products could afford to
raise more children. In addition, they could afford to pay the fines that
would be imposed on them. There have also been many cases cited of local
officials who also preferred to pay the fine rather than reject the child. Other
strategies have been used to evade this, such as not registering births of
female children, or parking children with friends and relatives when officials
may come round, or the repugnant use of female infanticide.

As a result, it is hard to say just how reliable Chinese population statistics
are. The objective is to hold population to 1.6 billion by 2050 from the
current 1.28 billion. There are clearly many more people than official statistics
reveal, while in some counties the reported discrepancy between female
and male children is alarmingly large. One study shows that underreporting
of births accounts for between 50 and 70 per cent of the differential sex ratio
at birth (Zeng *et al.*, 1993). The same study also claims that female infanticide accounts for 5 per cent of this differential (see also Li, 1992). Part of the

discrepancy may be accounted for by underreporting, but clearly not all. The current census shows the sex ratio of males to females as 106.74: 100, resulting in 41.27 million more men than women. However, at birth the ratio is 119.92: 100 and by age four it is 120.17: 100. Jiangxi and Guangdong have ratios of 138.01: 100 and 137.76: 100, respectively, with rural Guangdong at a rate of 143.7: 100 (Zhang Yi, 2003, pp. 66, 73). Walking through many villages it is clear that the policy has not been applied as stringently as officials suggest. In summer 1997 I was in a village just a couple of hours south of Beijing visiting women who were participating in a microfinance scheme supported by the Ford Foundation. In the first house, there were 5 or 6 children playing around. I asked the women how come there were so many children in the house given the family-planning policy, to which she replied that most belonged to neighbouring families. In the neighbour's house I was met by the same situation and the same answer! In February 2000, the Chinese press reported that in Tanba township in Wuzhou city, Guangdong province, about 5,500 families had 3 or more children, with 2 having 10. Even party members were not following the policy. In one village with 25 party members, 21 had 3 or more children (*SCMP*, 28 February 2000, Internet edition).

The negative aspects of policy implementation have led some academics, members of the women's federation and the Family-Planning Commission itself to push for policy change and to bring China's family-planning programme into line with international norms. The Chinese government signalled acceptance of these norms when it signed on at the International Conference on Population and Development (Cairo, 1994) to a declaration that rejected coercive population policies and recommended that family-planning services be augmented by other measures that ensure women's reproductive health. It reconfirmed its commitment at the UN Conference on Women (Beijing, 1995). A pathbreaking study by Zhu Chuzhu *et al.* (1997) set out both the positive effects of the programme but also the negative effects. They pointed out how it is the woman who bears the responsibility for contraception and the pressures that she comes under from home and from officials. Men will often pressure the woman to have another child if the previous children are female but it is the woman who will be the object of the wrath of the family-planning official for breaching the policy. Interestingly, the study mentions the stress that implementation also places on family-planning officials who have to enforce a policy that they know is not popular and that makes them the target of abuse within their own community. They also highlight the fact that the preference for sons generates the high sex ratio at birth and excess female infanticide. The sex ratio at birth in China stabilized around 106–107 in the 1960s and 1970s but increased rapidly from 107.7 in 1980 to 113.0 in 1992, well above the normal rate of between 105 to 107 (Zhu *et al.*, 1997, pp. 169–70). As a consequence of these ratios, around 1 million men per year will probably not find a marriage partner. This will certainly drive up the bride price in the rural areas and will result in increased illegal trade in women and in prostitution. The demographics resulting from this policy will also present major problems for the construction of urban and rural welfare programmes.

Such findings and the greater engagement of family-planning officials in international organizations have led to experimentation to improve the policy. Apart from the gradual policy relaxation in the rural areas, in the year 2000 provincial administrations began to moderate the policy for those now entering childbearing ages. The original intention was that the 'one-child policy' would apply to only one generation and now most provinces have decided that if both parents are single children they may have a second child.

Further integration with other policy areas is also necessary for the problems to be overcome. First, China needs to develop a pension scheme not only for the urban areas but also for rural China that will alleviate reliance on the family as the primary source of support. Second, the family-planning programme needs to be integrated with rural development policy more broadly so that the kinds of policy conflicts noted above are smoothed over. Third, and most importantly, the work method of the family-planning agencies needs to be changed from a quota-driven, top-down operating agency to a service-oriented organization that relies more on participatory and educational approaches than in the past. There is evidence that this is beginning to happen through experimentation at the local level.

Reform in the SOEs: Cutting the Gordian Knot

In urban China, the main concern of China's leaders has been how to move from a system of enterprise-based welfare to one where the government is the main provider and upholds minimum support levels. This has involved dismantling the hierarchy and privileges that existed within the planned economy and smoothing out the inequalities that existed between the units under the plan and those outside of the system. This involves challenges to develop mechanisms to include the private sector and a question as to whether to integrate the large migrant populations into the urban systems. If the answer is 'yes', which services, and how? This is causing a diversification of service providers in urban China, with increasing acceptance of the role of the market in providing service, a demand for cost recovery rather than highly subsidized provision and an increasing space for non-governmental organizations to operate.

The move to a more market-influenced economy has revealed the high costs that welfare provision has placed on the SOEs and the increasing incapacity of this sector to bear those costs. In addition, the existing institutional structure inhibited the further development of a labour market. Labour mobility was highly restricted by the fact that pensions, medical care, but most importantly housing belonged to the work-unit. One of the most important days of the year was when enterprises announced the division of new housing units or reallocations for the next year. Many people would time their weddings to coincide with this division, while others might rush back from a trip overseas so as not to be left out. Many families have adopted the approach of '1 family, 2 systems'; one would work in the state sector to ensure maximum state benefits while the other would work in the private sector where financial rewards could be higher but where there would be no housing provided. Not surprisingly, the system also became prey to ever-increasing demands. While the workers made no direct contribution to benefits and paid little in rent, the improvement of benefits was a continual bargaining point at the workplace. Before stricter financial discipline was instituted, it was relatively easy for enterprise leaders to cede on this in return for industrial peace.

The fiscal crisis changed all this. Reforms have been experimented with since the mid-1980s, but it was in 1998 that Premier Zhu announced an end to the enterprise-based, cradle-to-grave care that the Chinese industrial working class and government employees had come to expect. The policy thrust has been to ensure greater individual responsibility through contributions to pension and medical insurance and the privatization of workplace housing stock. At the same time, the old 'iron rice bowl' of permanent employment has been smashed.

China does not have a current pensions problem, but unless it acts soon, demographics will turn unfavourable by around 2010 and then it will have a major policy headache on its hands. In terms of policy priorities, the leadership recognizes it has a problem but not necessarily one of the most urgent to be solved. However, as discussed below, procrastination on this reform carries very high costs a few years down the road. The enterprises inherited the responsibility for the management and payment of pensions during the Cultural Revolution when the trade unions, which previously managed them, were dismantled. We are seeing the development of a more integrated system out of the fragmented parts and the introduction of market elements, albeit rather tentatively.

Once reforms began to bite and SOEs sank deeply into the red in the 1990s, enterprises began to run into problems with meeting pension obligations and reform was necessary. Evasion became more common; compliance in many cities dropped from 90 per cent at the beginning of the 1990s to 70–80 per cent by 1995 (World Bank, 1997d, p. 2). The World Bank (1997d, p. 3) also calculated that total pension reserves in 1995 were less than 1 per cent of GDP and the accumulated surplus by the end of 1996 was insufficient to cover pension obligations for even 6 months. Further, the demographics are not good. In 1995, there were 10 workers for every pensioner, but there would only be 3 by 2050. Whereas contribution rates were only 3 per cent of payroll when China began its system in 1951, they had risen to 20 per cent by the mid-1990s. Unless something is done, by 2033 Chinese estimates suggest they will require payroll rates of around 40 per cent. Major industrial cities such as Shanghai, where the family-planning programme has been particularly successful in reducing the birth rate, are ageing fast. In Shanghai some have somewhat facetiously raised the suggestion that there should be a financial incentive to increase family size! The number of people over 60 was 18 per cent in 1999, up from 3.6 per cent in the early 1950s, and is set to peak at around 30 per cent in 2030 (*SCMP*, 21 September 1999, Internet edition). The impact is clear to see, with many inner-city schools closing down or becoming boarding schools for non-Shanghai residents, and with many worried about who will look after them in old age.

The attempts to reform the enterprise pension system were drawn together in a State Council document of 1997 that was influenced not just by domestic experimentation but also by input from World Bank staff. This called for the unification of public-pillar benefits, the standardization of the size of individual contributions, and unified management of the funds (Zhao and Xu, 1999, p. 1; see also Box 10.1). The first two pillars would provide a

---

BOX 10.1

Designing a New Pension System

The new pension system proposed for China intends to construct individual pensions from three pillars. The first pillar is a defined-benefit public pillar for redistribution. This is to be funded by a payroll tax of 13 per cent drawn from pre-tax enterprise revenues and would guarantee a replacement rate of 20 per cent of the average wages at the time of retirement, if a minimum of 15 years was contributed. The second pillar is a mandatory-funded, defined-contribution pillar for each worker. This is to be funded through a payroll tax of 11 per cent and would comprise both enterprise and individual contributions (later, solely individual contributions). On retirement, the worker would receive a monthly payout that equals the account balance divided by 120. This assumes a life expectancy of 70 and a wage growth rate that equals the interest rate. If 35 years of contribution are made, then this pillar is expected to provide a replacement rate of 38.5 per cent. The third pillar is a voluntary supplemental pillar managed by each enterprise separately or through an insurance company.

Importantly, the first two pillars would provide a replacement rate of almost 60 per cent, the figure that the World Bank suggested as being a realistic target. It would also bring China in line with practice elsewhere in the world. Previously, Chinese pensions had been very generous in relative terms by providing a replacement rate of 80–90 per cent. This was already untenable for many enterprises on the pay-as-you go system that predated reform. The only source for paying the pensions of retired workers was from current operating funds. To protect cash-strapped SOEs, enterprise contributions to the new plan were not to exceed 20 per cent of the total enterprise wage bill, but because of local practice this was raised to 30 per cent.

replacement rate of around 60 per cent, redressing the generosity of the existing system that was becoming increasingly difficult for SOEs to pay. The lack of a unified system and the regional variance on contribution rates caused some enterprises to withhold payment. For example, the Sichuan iron and steel producer, Panzhihua, joined the local pooling system in 1986 but in 1992 the iron and steel sector began its own pooling system (11 industrial sectors were allowed to form a pooling system) with lower rates. As a result, Panzhihua refused to pay the higher rates in the geographic pool and accumulated a debt to the local pension fund of 300 million *yuan* (Zhao and Xu, 1999). This practice was quite common.

Three further steps were taken to provide the policy framework for this new system. First, in the March 1998 restructuring of the State Council, a new Ministry of Labour and Social Security was established to provide more effective coordination and to oversee implementation. Second, in August 1999 a new State Council document was issued building on the previous reforms. The 1997 document had called for pooling of pension accounts at the provincial level but now it was specified that the provinces should have a unified contribution rate and a unified management of funds by the year 2000. It also sought to clarify the responsibilities for who did what at the local level. Most importantly, the responsibility for the collection and distribution of pensions was removed from the enterprises themselves to municipal social insurance bureaus. To ease the way toward provincial management, each province was to set up a 'readjustment fund' that was to be used to backstop pension obligations and to iron out inequalities between the different municipalities within the province. In a major disincentive for local officials, the document announced that any surplus would be disposed of at the provincial level and most of the money would be invested in central government bonds.

Last but not least, in January 1999 the State Council issued regulations to expand the contribution base to take account of the diversified urban economy. By the end of 1997, while 93.9 per cent of SOEs were in social pension programmes, only 53.8 per cent of urban collectives and 32 per cent of joint-ventures, private enterprises and the self-employed were in such a scheme. Migrant workers were also to be brought into the programme and the 11 industrial sectors that had their own social pooling systems were to be folded into the provincial system. This expansion of the system was to be completed by the end of June 1999 and the number of workers participating in the pool would be increased by 26 million (31 per cent) to reach a total of 110 million (Zhao and Xu, 1999). The rationale for this is obvious. First, if the non-state sectors could escape the payroll tax, then workers would have even less incentive to stay in the SOEs and would move to other sectors where their monthly costs would be lower. Second, the state needs increased participation to be able to cover the bills of the current retirees and the large numbers that will retire from the SOE sector in the coming years.

In making this transition, the government needed to deal with the thorny question of how and when to fund the individual accounts as part of the new pension plan. This meant that they needed to strike a balance between three policy goals of meeting the obligations of current pensioners, not placing too heavy a tax on the workforce and minimizing the payment requirements to future generations.

The policy has been clarified dramatically in the last few years but implementation still lags and a number of serious problems exist. First, encouraging a unified rate is one thing but getting compliance is another. Most provinces have acquiesced in allowing the municipalities to set their own rates based on current obligations rather than risking raising the rate. In many instances, rates were already above the stipulated 20 per cent, especially in the old industrial areas of the northeast and Sichuan. For example, in Jiamusi (Heilongjiang province), the contribution rate was often above 33 per cent of the total wage bill (Kennedy School of Government, 1999). As a result in 2000, the State Council raised the contribution rate for enterprise payments to the social security fund to 30 per cent but no longer required enterprises to pay into personal accounts, thus raising employee contribution to 11 per cent.

The decentralized functioning of the fiscal system has not helped. Pension funds can be major sources for investment funds for the localities and thus the incentive has been to find ways to make it difficult to integrate pooling at a higher administrative level. A 1998 survey revealed that local governments had diverted over 10 billion *yuan* from social security funds to projects that had nothing to do with pensions. The Ministry of Labour and Social Security said that $2.1 billion had been embezzled from the system from 1996 to March 1998 (Wang Xin, forthcoming).

Further, many of those in a financially healthy pool have not seen the incentive of being merged at a higher administrative level that would include a town such as Jiamusi. There has been resistance to joining provincial pools and some towns have refused to contribute to the adjustment funds. If there is no alternative the incentive is to spend out any surplus before joining and even to run up a deficit before joining. This occurred when the 11 industrial sector pools were merged with the provincial-level pools and industries moved to spend the surplus, raise benefits and encourage earlier retirement. The same problems arose when the county-level pools were merged into the provincial pools. In 1993 Guangdong had the largest reserve in provincial redistributive funds of all provinces, but by the end of the decade it had been spent out.

Enterprises have also been reluctant to contribute, even those that have the funds to pay. By the end of 1999, non-payment by enterprises amounted to 38.3 billion *yuan*, with over 200 enterprises owing in excess of 10 million *yuan* (*SCMP*, 16 December 1999, Internet edition). Lack of payment has been the source of a number of demonstrations and unrest and the government has usually moved quickly to make up payments. At the end of 1999, a joint statement of the Ministry of Labour and Social Security, the State Economic and Trade Commission (SETC), the Finance Ministry, the China Securities Regulatory Commission and the State Industrial and Commercial Bureau announced new penalties for defaulters. This included a ban from listing on stockmarkets, setting up joint-ventures and subsidiaries, setting up new branches and expanding scope of business. However, as with other admonitions, its impact has been limited as in June 2000 the Minister of Labour and Social Security once again stated that non-payment would not be tolerated. He acknowledged that another 1.45 billion *yuan* had been added to the unpaid total in the first 5 months of the year and that payment delay had occurred in 19 provinces (*Xinhua*, 22 June 2000).

The move to integrate the non-state sector into the programme has also met with mixed results, as there has been ambivalence not only by companies themselves but also by local authorities at imposing what amounts to an extra 30 per cent cost through the payroll tax to these businesses. A number of provinces have thus allowed cities to set lower rates for the private sector. Officials in Qingdao (Shandong province) lowered the contribution rate in 1999 for private companies from 25 per cent to 11 per cent of the payroll, with an additional 7 per cent to be paid by the workers (Kennedy School of Government, 1999).

There are problems with shifting the pooling to the provincial level. Essentially, the provinces can manage the revenues but staff from the towns and counties remain responsible for the collection of the pension funds. The lower levels would lose the incentive to collect revenues efficiently as they would not preside over any surplus. At the same time, they could seek to buy off potential local unrest by raising benefits as any deficit would be charged back to the provincial level.

To date one of the most successful administrations has been Shanghai, which enjoys a relatively competent administration and has been able to generate sufficient revenues. It is in the process of issuing a social insurance card for all residents that will consolidate unemployment insurance, health insurance and pension payments in a computerized system. The scheme is administered by the Bureau of Labour and Social Insurance and operates independently of all enterprises in the Municipality. This scheme is more likely to be successful than the pilot scheme running in Liaoning Province, which will rely heavily on central government handouts. Liaoning has been selected to establish provincial pooling for its social security fund in a 3-year experiment. Again benefits such as pensions will be managed independently of the workplace (*Xinhua*, 8 July 2001). According to the provincial governor, 5 million people have to pay the pension for 6.88 million as well as supporting 2.68 million retired workers (*SCMP*, 11 March 2002). Neither of these is likely to provide a viable model for the rest of the country. Few would be able to emulate Shanghai's advantages and the central state will not have sufficient funds to bail out many more provinces.

As can be seen, progress to date is mixed. The major question for the future is the pension system's long-term financial viability. In part, this depends on how high a priority the central leadership places on funding pension reform. The answer appears to be high but not high enough, given other pressing issues. By 1999, the number of retirees totalled around 27 million, with the system as a whole having only 4 in work for each retiree. In 1998, the pension system ran a deficit for the first time and by 2000 the deficit was $4.3 billion; 21 provinces had deficits and only 10 were in surplus. Reserves were down from 100 billion *yuan* in 1996 to 58.7 billion *yuan* in mid-1999. This situation could not continue indefinitely. A number of scandals also occurred, with local authorities losing significant amounts of pension funds in bad investments, thus raising the question of the people's trust in the government to manage their money effectively. As one senior official muttered to me at an international meeting on pension reform 'Well, would you trust the Chinese government with your money?'.

Perhaps the biggest problem of all is that the system remains one of pay-as-you-go, despite the new pillars that are to be constructed to provide greater long-term viability. The individual accounts are notional, that is 'real money' is not being accumulated as there is nothing in them. This means that current pension obligations are still being financed out of current revenues, while the financing for the future is not being accumulated. By about 2025 the system will be overwhelmed and contributions from the contemporary workforce will not meet pension obligations. There is also the tendency to set contribution rates at a low level in order to reduce the future pension obligations and if rates of return are lower than the opportunity cost of the capital, evasion and non-compliance will follow (Zhao and Xu, 1999).

There are various estimates of the implicit pension debt. The World Bank (1997a) has calculated a range between 46 and 69 per cent of GDP while Wang *et al.* (2001) have estimated it to be 71 per cent in 2000 and Dorfman and Sin (2000) have suggested a figure of 94 per cent. This is actually low in comparative terms since the pension coverage is limited to a relatively small percentage of China's total labour force. For example, in the United States it is 113 per cent. In fact, if the central government acts soon and adopts adequate measures, the fiscal costs should be manageable (Ma and Zhai, 2001). A number of suggestions have been made but a greater use of the market is the most promising. As a short-term measure, budget expenditures have been increased. At the March 2003 NPC meeting, the Finance Minister announced a 38.6 per cent increase in the social security budget to help those in difficult circumstances and to head off unrest. However, the strong competing budgetary demands make this difficult to maintain over the long term. Second, there was an aborted attempt to consider the implicit debt part of the national debt and to raise funds through the sale of state assets, a programme formally endorsed by the State Council in June 2001. It was swiftly abandoned in October 2001, by which time share values had dropped by 1,000 billion *yuan*.

Current thinking is to introduce a specific social security tax (now operating in 16 provinces) but a better long-term strategy is to open up the pension funds to a market-driven approach and to move away from centralizing pension pool administrations and trying to reduce evasion and non-compliance by administrative means (see Zhao and Xu, 1999). Of course, for the private sector to take over management of pension funds would not only require a psychological leap for China's leaders but also would demand a proper regulatory infrastructure to be put in place. The transition costs would be reduced considerably by creating a fully funded system, with the public pillar over time drawing on general fiscal reserves and the individual accounts managed by a private and decentralized system.

However, there are some positive signs and economic necessity will probably force a faster pace of market-driven change. In 2000, it was reported that the pension system was running a $4.3 billion deficit. Partly in response, the Ministry of Labour and Social Security together with the Boshi Management Company announced that perhaps as much as 15 per cent of pension funds could be invested in stocks with another 10 per cent in treasury and corporate bonds (*China Daily*, 25 May 2001). This marks a significant shift away from current practice that allows investment only in bank deposits and government bonds. This would aid further the attempts to separate social welfare payments from enterprises.

Most important was the establishment in September 2000 of the National Council for Social Security that oversees the Social Security Fund with investment management delegated to qualified asset managers with the exception of investment in bank deposits and the purchase of government bonds in the primary markets. In early 2003, important changes were indicated in the way the $15 billion that it oversees could be deployed. The Fund is expected to cover the shortfalls in provincially managed pension funds estimated at around $800 billion. Clearly its rate of return in 2001 of 2.25 per cent is not enough to meet demand and it was announced that some $3.6 billion would be invested in stocks with more local funds to follow. Some 10 domestic fund managers have been invited to apply to invest the funds. This is a major step forward but the skills of fund managers will have to be enhanced and better oversight will be needed.

Providing Adequate Healthcare in Urban China

The reforms have led to very varied access to healthcare, with the urban areas still relatively privileged in terms of spending, access and quality. In general, government health spending is inadequate – 3.8 per cent of GDP, as opposed to WHO-recommended levels of 5 per cent for developing countries. Spending is also heavily biased toward the urban areas and the state's financial commitment to rural health services has been declining as a percentage of the total medical and health expenditures, from 21.5 per cent in 1978 to 10.5 per cent in 1991. However even within the urban areas problems beset healthcare provisions. The 2 formal insurance schemes, for government employees and SOE workers, cover just 15 per cent of the population but accounted for 36 per cent of health spending in the mid-1990s (World Bank, 1997c, p. 55). While there has been a continuation of healthcare provision for those able to pay, there has been a decline in quality of service for many and a disastrous collapse in the provision for the rural and urban poor. Under the pre-reform system, considering the low income levels, the supply of public goods was quite impressive, especially in the areas of irrigation, education and public health (for a contrary view, see Eberstadt, 1988). However, the shift to a market system has disrupted the capacity of the local state to provide public goods efficiently, especially in the case of healthcare. Even irrigation systems have suffered under the reforms. One survey suggested that 60 per cent were in need of repair (Ministry of Agriculture, 1999, pp. 38–42). According to Lu Mai (1999, p. 1), a major reason for this decline is that the Chinese leadership has not seen healthcare as directly related to economic growth and it has, therefore, received a lower priority for investment.

In urban areas, initial reform experimentation began in 1988 with the system of free medical provision at the workplace. Progress was slow because of strong resistance, greater than with pension reform as the use of medical insurance schemes would affect virtually all in urban China. Again fiscal crisis has pushed reform forward. In 1988, the annual growth in the expense of medical care grew at 40 per cent, having increased from 26 per cent the previous year. Growth declined significantly over the next few years to 18 per cent in 1991 but edged up to 22 per cent in 1993–94 when another attempt was made at reform (*China Labour Statistical Yearbook*, 1998, pp. 40, 505). At the same time, enterprises had less money to contribute to medical provision, while the costs of healthcare provision were rising. For example, in 1992 the Shenyang Internal Combustion Factory was able to provide its 4,500 workers and pensioners with almost free medical care. This cost the factory around 70,000 *yuan* a month. By the end of 1997, the factory had not been able to pay wages for 10 months and had a monthly healthcare budget of between 5,000 and 7,000 *yuan* (*FEER*, 16 October 1997, p. 64). Profitable factories, by contrast, have been able to cover costs and pay them in a timely fashion. Even here there can be frustration with the enterprise signing contracts with specific hospitals to which the patient must go first, even if it is not the most suitable for their specific ailment. Such problems were compounded by the rise in medical costs by some 25–30 per cent per annum through the 1990s, as hospitals and clinics sought to become profitable.

Recourse to private medical schemes was not only alien to Chinese socialist culture but also too expensive for those most in need. In 1997, the cheapest private insurance available in Shanghai to those over 50 but under 65 was 600 *yuan a* year and would cover up to 8,100 *yuan* of hospital costs. For the poorest 10 per cent, the most vulnerable, such as the retired, unemployed or workers at effectively bankrupt SOEs, this would take a big cut out of their income of 3,785 *yuan* per year.

In November 1994, reform was piloted in Zhenjiang in Jiangsu and Jiujiang in Jiangxi, both with populations of around 2.5 million, in what was referred to as the 'two-Jiang model' (for details see World Bank, 1997c, pp. 56–9; Yu and Ren, 1997, pp. 448–50). Pilots were also run in Shanghai and Shenzhen and the success encouraged the government to extend the 'two-Jiang' experiments to 2 additional cities or prefectures in each province, making a total of 50 sites. The experiments provided a mixture of individual accounts and social pooling. Workers would contribute 1 per cent of their annual salary, with the enterprise providing a further 10 per cent. These funds went to newly set up insurance centres that committed them to individual and public medical insurance accounts. The split was roughly 50–50. The costs are also shared on the demand side; if the worker falls prey to a serious illness, the individual account is drawn on first. Once exhausted, the worker pays up to 5 per cent of annual salary for treatment and then cost-sharing kicks in, with the government covering 80–95 per cent of other costs. However, for major illness the individual liability is considerable and is enough to drive an average family into poverty.

The results were good in as far as they went. Coverage for those in loss-making SOEs increased, the costs of expensive medical tests were cut, the annual rate of growth in aggregate hospital expenditures declined by 23–28 per cent, and inpatient and outpatient visits declined (World Bank, 1997c, p. 58). However, as Gu has observed (2001), a number of shortcomings were also observed. First, the total coverage rate was low, as it covered only 11.5 per cent of urban employees. Second, with the exception of Zhenjiang, employees from non-profit and administrative units had not participated. Third, there was a considerable degree of fragmentation of the programmes and there was no capacity for portability. This last factor also undermined the capacity for improvements in labour mobility.

As a result, in January 1998 the government proposed, and elaborated further later in the year, a new scheme to be in operation by the end of 1999. This required the establishment of a 'basic health insurance scheme' to be set up in all cities and all enterprises and employees were expected to join. This included non-state enterprises and those of foreign enterprises and joint-ventures. Under the new scheme, employee contribution is raised to 2 per cent of the annual wage and the employer rate is 6 per cent of the total wage bill. The employee's contribution and 30 per cent of the employer's contribution are paid into the individual account and the rest into the pooled account. The individual accounts are to be used for minor medical bills, while those in the pooled accounts will be used for major treatments that would include hospitalization (*SCMP*, 8 and 25 January 1999; and Gu, 2001). The payments from the pooled accounts will pay out a minimum of 10 per cent of the patient's annual wage and a maximum of 400 per cent. Any amount over this is to be covered from commercial insurance. The designation of a maximum was expected to reduce costs and would be used only for designated hospitals.

Importantly, the new system divided off the provision of medicines from hospital provision. One of the main ways for hospitals to generate revenues had been through the sale of medicines. For many, this accounted for more than 50 per cent of income, while some calculated that at least 30 per cent of the state's expenditure on health was on unnecessary medication. Doctors, being lowly paid, generated further income not only from 'donations' from patients who wished to be treated but also from kickbacks from pharmaceutical companies and through purchasing of unnecessary medical equipment. Thus, Beijing has more than 70 CT scanners, more than the total in England, and Nanjing hospitals have three times as many CTs as London (*SCMP*, 25 January 1999). In the future, hospitals must earn their income from treating patients and surgery. Given the financial incentives, one suspects that this will lead to a lot of unnecessary surgery.

The hope is that the new system will unify the existing myriad of different health schemes into a standardized programme. It will be a compulsory universal scheme that should provide those enrolled with the financial means to meet their health costs without causing massive financial distress to the family. However, resistance to the reforms has persisted and the factors preventing full participation in pension systems have also operated in the healthcare sector. In addition, it is clear that many hospitals have not dropped their sales of medicines. In May 2000, Chinese officials were still complaining that many hospitals still derived half their income from this source, claiming that in some of the smaller hospitals this revenue comprised 70–80 per cent (*SCMP*, 29 May 2000, Internet edition). China's leaders want to introduce competition among hospitals, allowing patients to choose rather than being allocated to a specific hospital, to improve efficiency, and former vice-premier Li Lanqing even suggested that public tenders for drug provision could be introduced. However, the vice-governor of Guangdong province suggested that reforms were not moving as well as planned and were resisted by cash-strapped hospitals. She said that many hospitals were more concerned with the financial bottom line than the patients' health and were even renting their space and name to unqualified clinics (*SCMP*, 14 June 2000, Internet edition).

Migration

The rural and the urban are more closely linked than in Maoist days, despite the lingering obstacles to the integration of labour markets, and this is seen most visibly by the huge number of migrants in the cities (for an excellent study, see Solinger, 1999). Migration has been a significant feature of reform, with estimates ranging from 80 to 120 million people on the move. Urban temporary migrant labour was estimated at 94 million in 2002 (*China Daily*, 23 January 2003). Restricted by the household registration and grain-rationing systems, migration began slowly in the early 1980s but with the emergence of a market in grain for migrants (legalized in 1986) and the provision of other goods and services outside of the plan it began to take off in the mid-1980s. This pull factor was complemented by the push factor once the initial rise in agricultural incomes began to decline from 1984. Migrant labour had been crucial to the urban economic boom, whether in supplying the labour to the foreign-invested factories in coastal China, providing the construction crews for the massive building expansion, or feeding the burgeoning service sector, ranging from hotel and restaurant workers to the more unseemly services of prostitution and bar hostesses. It has also been crucial to rural development, in terms of remittances and also because migrants have returned to the villages and brought back with them capital, new skills and social networks that extend beyond the narrow village confines (see Murphy, 2002).

While their economic benefit to the urban areas has been significant, their social status is extremely low, and only in the late 1990s did urban authorities begin to consider integrating the migrants into social service provision. The shift in thinking was primarily stimulated by central leadership concerns that they might be a source of instability and that falling outside of urban administrative jurisdiction they might be evading family-planning regulations. Migrants have been subject to the same abuse and caricature as in other parts of the world and have been blamed not only by the permanent urban residents but also in the official press for the breakdown in law and order, the increased messiness of the urban areas and the difficulty for laid-off SOE employees to find new work. There is evidence that the influx of migrants has increased crime, with figures suggesting that they have been responsible for 30 per cent of crime in Beijing and 70 per cent in Shanghai (World Bank, 1997e, p. 55). However, in terms of the labour market, most evidence suggests that they are not in direct competition with laid-off SOE workers, taking jobs that the latter would not consider.

Debates over their role also has an institutional and political dimension. Basically, the old Ministry of Labour (now Labour and Social Security) favoured keeping tight controls on migration and wanted to keep as many as possible down on the farms, whereas the Ministry of Agriculture has been more positive about the role of migration and the benefits it brings to rural development. Migrant communities have been easy targets for the national and local authorities concerning the problems of urban China and there have been occasional movements to reduce their numbers or eliminate their communities. For example, after the arrest of Beijing party chief Chen Xitong (1995), the new municipal authorities, with the support of then Premier Li Peng, decided to move against the largest migrant community in Beijing (Zhejiang village). As a part of the campaign to clean up Beijing after the fall of the corrupt leader, the new leadership wanted to give the impression of being active and demolishing the unlicensed housing in the village was one act that it thought would be easy and popular. The village survived and thrived. However, residents are now concerned that Beijing's bid to host the Olympics in 2008 will lead to another attempt to reduce the number of migrants living in the city (Interviews, Beijing, January 2001). Xinjiang village in Beijing was a source of concern for security reasons as it was suspected to house terrorists who favoured independence for the province. As a result, it was heavily policed and the authorities have tried on a number of occasions to break it up. In contrast with these negative views, there are cases where the large influx of migrants has turned around stagnant urban district economies such as in Fengtai in Beijing, home to Zhejiang village, or has created new cities, such as Dongguan in Guangdong. The economy of Dongguan has grown 20 per cent per annum since 1990 and, as a result, its 50 enterprises employing 5,000 residents have grown to comprise 20,000 foreign-invested enterprises with a population of 500,000, of whom over 90 per cent are migrants (World Bank, 1997e, p. 56).

Most migration is rural–rural, however, and of short duration. In the late 1990s there were probably around 40 million long-term migrants with the number increasing to 70 million if one includes daily commuters from the countryside and self-employed workers who travel from home to locations outside for their work (Lohmar, Rozelle and Zhao, 2000). In general, central policy has now shifted to an acceptance that migration plays a positive role in development, especially for the rural areas, but seeks to control the flow to manageable levels. For example, migrants have to obtain a permit from their local public security bureau and the destination locality indicating that there is a specific job to go to. Major cities such as Beijing have also tried to protect certain work from the migrants and to protect the possibilities for laid-off SOE workers. For example, the hotel trade was deemed off-limits but the regulations are frequently flouted by the hotels themselves. In one of the most prestigious hotels in Beijing, local residents are interviewed for jobs and their residence papers are copied. The copied papers are then used for cheaper migrant labour and shown to inspectors when they come around to investigate.

The ability of the authorities to control labour flows is restricted by the 'push' factor from the villages where surplus labour is massive. The main resource for finding jobs is through village and local networks rather than through the state agencies. Only 15 per cent of migrants find jobs through the local labour bureaus and employment offices (World Bank, 1997e, p. 55). Most of those working as nannies (*baomu*) in Beijing either found work through personal introductions from someone already employed, or by making their way to the informal labour market that grew up beside Beijing's main railway station. A high percentage came from Anhui province. Zhejiang village is a good example of the process and also of the complexity of many migrant communities. It comprises around 100,000 residents and has set up its own schooling system and clinics and hospital, staffed by those from Zhejiang with medical licences, has its own security forces and essentially pays a large annual fee to the local authorities to leave it alone. Recruitment for workers to come to the village, which has cornered much of the clothing and leather business in Beijing, takes place in Zhejiang and those selected are sent on to Beijing. This includes many from outside of Zhejiang itself (about 50 per cent). For example, many of those engaged in the most menial tasks are recruited in Anhui and sent to Zhejiang for initial training before being sent to Beijing to work. The village originated by outsiders renting space from locals who saw this as an easy way to make some quick money. Subsequently, the migrants began to buy up run-down buildings that they used for the workshops and dormitory sleeping quarters. By 1992, the district leaders allowed groups in the 'village' to construct some 40 new buildings (Interviews in Zhejiang village, 1997 and 1998; and Xiang, 1996).

Although the wages of migrant workers are lower than those for urban residents, their main problem is the lack of access to social services and welfare facilities. Although the SOE system is under attack, migrants are not properly integrated into any system and it reached the policy-makers' attention only in the late 1990s. If accommodation is provided, it tends to be very rudimentary, either in the form of segregated dormitories or tents or temporary shacks. The sanitary conditions are poor, creating significant problems as migrants generally do not have health coverage. Those who do will probably be covered only for direct work-related injuries and not infectious diseases or other sicknesses. This places the burden on the already weak rural social infrastructure as when one gets sick the only way to avoid expensive urban treatment is to return to the village to be looked after by the family. Until the end of the 1990s, migrant children were not allowed to enrol in state schools, thus meaning that they missed out on education, were returned to the village on reaching school age, or their parents had to pay for their education in private schools. While state regulation requires local authorities to provide education for all school-age children, urban local authorities have interpreted this as meaning only those with a residence permit and thus migrant children have been excluded. The negative effect of this policy has been recognized by some local authorities, and in 1998–99 some Beijing districts, for example, began to recognize migrant-run schools and issue them licences.

The new leadership under Hu and Wen pulled together experimental reforms in the first State Council document of 2003 to date that acknowledged the problems of migration but confirmed that it was an inevitable part of China's progress. In March 2001, the central government had decided to promote reforms in small towns based on prior experiments. This permitted residency in small towns and townships for all those from rural areas who could demonstrate legal employment and a place to live. While restrictions have subsequently been eased for some larger cities, major municipalities have sought to control the flow. Importantly, in November 2002 migrants were given the political status of being a part of the working class. In January 2003, the State Council confirmed that unfair restrictions on migrants were to be lifted and they were to be accorded equal treatment with urban residents when applying for work. Wages were to be paid in full and on time, while living and working conditions were to be improved. Perhaps most significantly, urban education departments would have to recognize schools for migrant children and provide them with equal education access. Many of these demands are honoured more in the breach than the observance, but the official recognition is important. Finally, the beating to death by police of a university graduate in Guangzhou (in March 2003) because he did not have his temporary residence permit with him led to criticism of police powers to detain and search migrants. As a result in June, the State Council passed new regulations that mandated local governments to set up shelters that will fall under the Ministry of Civil Affairs. The new regulations expressly forbid extortion, abuse and forced labour.

The effect on life in the village has also been significant. Remittances for those families that have someone working outside the village are important. Typically, migrants send home between 20 and 50 per cent of their income, and in Sichuan and Anhui this accounts for an average of 20 per cent of household income and 50 per cent of cash income (World Bank, 1997e, p. 57). While this narrows the disparities between urban and rural China, it exacerbates inequalities within the village. Given that the majority of migrants are male, although female migration has been increasing, some have written about the feminization of agriculture and even of poverty, given that solely agricultural work delivers little income.

Inequality and Healthcare in Rural China

By contrast to the urban areas, most in the countryside are left to depend on the family and, in times of desperation, on collective funds. However, this does not mean that reforms have not benefited the countryside and one of the most remarkable effects has been to lift more than 200 million people out of dire poverty. Yet, it is also true that inequality has risen, collective rural health services have been paralysed by the reforms and some 28 million still remain below the official poverty line. New policies will be necessary to resolve these problems.

While there is significant variation across regions, within the cities and within the rural areas, the most significant inequality is between the urban and the rural. This has fluctuated under the reforms and in the initial period income inequality actually declined. At the start of the reforms official statistics showed a *per capita* income variation of 2.36: 1 (1978) that declined to under 1.9: 1 by the mid-1980s (Whyte, 1996, p. 17). It rose to 2.42: 1 in 1988 and declined modestly to 2.38: 1 by 1995 (Khan and Riskin, 1998, p. 250) but rose again to 2.8: 1 in 2000. While China as a whole is not among the most unequal countries in the world, this urban–rural ratio is the highest in the world, according to the International Labour Organization (ILO). Most countries do not exceed 1.6: 1. Considerable wealth concentration is taking place; in 2003, one survey of bank deposits revealed that 0.16 per cent of the population controlled 65 per cent of the nation's $1.5 trillion liquid assets, giving China the highest wealth concentration in the fewest hands (*SCMP*, 29 March 2003).

Within the countryside, Khan and Riskin's fascinating study (1998, p. 238) shows that the Gini ratio of rural income distribution in 1995 (0.416) is at the high end for developing countries in Asia. The most important factor accounting for this inequality is income from wages, making up 40 per cent of the overall inequality (on this, see also World Bank, 1997e). Other factors are access to receipts from private and other enterprises, and non-farm household activities. This leads Khan and Riskin (1998, p. 240) to conclude that income composition for the rich and poor in the countryside is very different. The rich enjoy wage employment, non-farm entrepreneurship and transfers from the state and collectives. By contrast, the poor derive most income from farming, the rental value of owned housing and, to a lesser extent, private transfers. However, China is a classic dual economy with massive agricultural surplus labour and a modern urban sector, making it hard to reduce the inequality. The best long-term strategy is to promote urbanization and expand the service sector, but this will create a short-term rise in the Gini coefficient.

Income alone does not account for all the inequality and costs of health-care take a higher percentage of rural disposable income than for urban residents while insurance is less readily available. While some inequality may be inevitable with the transition, policies or policy inaction have heightened the polarization. Healthcare and universal education have vanished for the most vulnerable populations while regressive social policy has made the situation worse, with the poorer paying more in taxes and fees while the richer have received subsidies.

In terms of policy, these findings imply that off-farm employment should be boosted as this is the surest way to raise incomes. Indeed, Chinese researchers often calculate that some 150–200 million in the countryside are surplus to labour requirements. However, not all will necessarily join a flood of migration to the large cities. One of the most remarkable aspects of China's development has been the growth of the rural enterprises, but this sector is going through a major restructuring and it is unclear how much more of the labour it can soak up (see Chapter 9). China also needs to break down the barriers between the rural and the urban, as best represented in the house-hold registration system. This will be difficult to achieve in the present atmosphere of SOE lay-offs and leadership concern about social unrest. In essence, the leadership would rather keep the problems down on the farm where they can be more easily isolated and dealt with. An urban China teeming with laid-off workers and rural migrants is the recipe for an explosive mix that Beijing would rather avoid. In terms of those remaining to work in the countryside, WTO entry will provide new challenges and will make it difficult for the state to boost incomes through subsidies – and, in any case, the prices of most products are now at or near international levels. Nyberg and Rozelle (1999, p. x and *passim*) suggest three further measures to improve the growth of agricultural income. First, factor productivity needs to be increased; second production should be diversified into labour-intensive, higher-value commodities; and third, investment in transport and other marketing infrastructure should be increased to reduce marketing costs and enable farmers to increase their share of consumer expenditures. Foreign investment would help with the process of increased industrialization of Chinese agriculture.

This income inequality and the financial pressures on the local state in China are accounting for the huge variation in the provision of public goods and services during the transition. As the World Bank (1997e, p. 23) has shown, access to health and education services was still widely available in the 1980s but became more dependent on incomes in the 1990s. In 1998, 22.2 per cent of those in high-income areas were covered by cooperative medical facilities, but only 1–3 per cent in poorer areas was covered (Zhu, 2000, pp. 41–3). Spending on rural healthcare has been declining while the cost of care has been increasing. In 1998 the unit cost of an outpatient visit at a county hospital was four times higher than in 1993 while at the township level it was twice as expensive.

The effects of this are becoming readily apparent. Surveys have shown that one-third of those needing to see a doctor cannot because of cost while two-thirds of those requiring hospitalisation cannot afford it. In 1993 in relatively wealthy Zhejiang province, infant mortality per 1,000 live births was around 20 and secondary school enrolment was over 60 per cent, whereas in poor Guizhou the figures were 60 and 20, respectively. A study of health conditions in 30 poor counties found that maternal death during childbirth was 216.8 per 100,000, as compared to a rural average of 114.9 (Meng and Hu, 2000, p. 67). Both the infant and maternal mortality rates are closely correlated with the use of pre-natal care and attended safe delivery, two preventive services that have been adversely affected by the privatization of healthcare in rural China. The focus on cost recovery has hampered poorer areas from providing good facilities, and the capacity for richer areas to invest more in education, health and infrastructure means that the inequalities will increase further over time.

The lack of sufficient state finance means that the extended family will provide the social support for those in the countryside but changing demographics has caused the realization that over the long term it cannot be the sole provider. In 1992, the Chinese government began limited experimentation with rural pension schemes in selected peri-urban areas in the wealthier coastal regions (this description is based on discussions with Stephen McGurk and officials of the Ministry of Labour and Social Security). The programme is overseen by the Department of Rural Social Insurance in the Ministry of Labour and Social Security. This was driven by the realization that the impact of family-planning policies made the nuclear family the norm for many and that out-migration was skewing the demographics of communities. It is not uncommon in villages with high out-migration to see only the old and the very young, with women predominantly engaged in farming activities. Although many peri-urban and wealthier areas are still counted as rural in terms of household registration, they have become heavily industrialized with a pre-dominance of TVEs. The pension programme has expanded gradually, and by the end of 1998 voluntary rural pension schemes organized by local government covered some 82 million farmers in 30 out of 31 provinces, with combined assets in excess of 14 billion *yuan*. Not surprisingly, the average contributions are very low (starting at 4 *yuan* per month) and average payments were only about 75 per cent of the nationally designated poverty line (560 *yuan*). There were 557,900 beneficiaries who received this (Zhang, 1999, p. 187).

The schemes operate through voluntary individual contributions supplemented by collective payments that are accumulated in individual accounts owned directly by the individual. The responsibility for asset accumulation and the right of control is with the rural household and within one jurisdiction there is a single unified scheme that facilitates labour mobility sectorally if not geographically. The problem is that the operational and financial management of these funds is with a single government agency at the county level. This concentration at the county level has meant that transparency and accountability are weak. This has resulted in a number of cases of fund mismanagement, either through embezzlement by local leaders or through unwise investments that have frittered the money away. In 1999, to try to provide better management of these funds, Premier Zhu Rongji proposed that the schemes should be commercialized. However, given the weakness of the insurance and banking sectors, it is not clear that this would ameliorate the situation.

As noted above, the impact of the transition in the rural areas on healthcare provision has been dramatic. The Ministry of Public Health calls for 8 per cent of rural budgets to be spent on healthcare but actual resource allocation falls far short of this. Even the national government allocates only 2.4 per cent of its recurrent health budget to healthcare services and 1.2 per cent of the capital construction fund (Nyberg and Rozelle, 1999, p. 20). At the provincial level, from 1982 to 1993 *per capita* health expenditure in wealthier provinces such as Zhejiang and Guangdong increased only at just over 2 per cent, while in a poorer province such as Guizhou it was only 0.4 per cent. In Ningxia, expenditure actually dropped by about 0.7 per cent and in Liaoning the collapse of the SOEs meant that expenditure dropped by 0.3 per cent (World Bank, 1997e, p. 23). It is the case that the vast majority of this financing was spent in the urban areas. With the loss of the pre-paid collective medical system with the disbanding of the communes in the early 1980s, some 90 per cent of rural households have to pay directly for almost all of the health services used (World Bank, 1997c, p. 47).

Beginning in 1981, healthcare facilities were instructed that they should cover recurrent costs, with the exception of staff, from user charges and by the mid-1980s preventive care facilities were also charging on a fee-for-service basis (Hu and Jiang, 1998, p. 192). Coverage in the collective system dropped dramatically, from almost 80 per cent in 1979 to only 2 per cent in 1987 before improving to around 10 per cent by the mid-1990s. Thus in terms of national health spending, while the collective schemes accounted for 20 per cent in 1978, by 1993 they only accounted for 2 per cent (UNDP, 1998, p. 37). As the World Bank concluded in its 1996 report (1996b, p. 127), 'the downturn in China's health performance relative to its income level coincided with agricultural reform that reduced the ability of the village to tax the peasants'. This has resulted in the return of some diseases thought to have been eradicated, the rapid and underreported spread of HIV/AIDS and the rise since the mid-1980s of prevalence rates for infectious diseases such as hepatitis and tuberculosis. Official figures show infant mortality rising from 34.7 per 1,000 in 1981 to 37 per 1,000 in 1992, whereas UNICEF estimates that by 1997–98 the figure was 52 and that it was 4 times greater in poorer regions (Cailliez, 1998, p. 37). This decline in services led Dr Marcel Roux, the head of Médécins Sans Frontières in China, to comment that

> Healthcare is better in Africa, for sure. There, people are organized and there are good African physicians and health workers but in China, they don't have the knowledge, the structures or people to make it work. (*SCMP*, 19 October 1999, Internet edition)

The basic problem of healthcare derives not primarily from the lack of facilities decried by Dr Roux but from the change of the ownership structure of village networks and the nature of the incentive system that has arisen from these changes (UNDP, 1998, pp. 36, 38). The rural healthcare apparatus has a three-tier structure. At the village level, there are some 1.44 million health workers trained in the basics of care. Essentially, they provide a referral system to the higher levels. Importantly, they charge a fee for their services and are allowed to prescribe medicines for which they can charge. At the township level, there are some 52,000 hospitals that carry out basic medical tasks such as simple surgery and treating infections. At the county level, there are some 4,000 hospitals that carry out major operations and care. Above this, the province funds the referral and specialist hospitals (on funding see Bloom *et al.*, 1995).

In the villages most of the health workers no longer work in a cooperative but for themselves, and the number of private clinics has risen rapidly. This is also true for the urban areas, and the quality is very variable. The number of health professionals in private practice rose from 18,000 in 1981 to 172,185 in 1995 (Hu and Jiang, 1998, p. 194). The buildings they use are often unsanitary, staff are poorly trained and there is little incentive to upgrade facilities. In poor rural areas, it is quite a common sight to pass rows of farmers on saline drips in the street outside run-down clinics. Many local healthcare workers seem to think that such drips are the cure for many ailments. Not surprisingly, diagnostic capabilities are extremely weak, leading to incorrect diagnosis or the lack of recognition of 'new' diseases such as HIV/AIDS. As in the urban system, the sale of medicines is the most lucrative form of income for these local health workers who can retain especially high percentages for Western pharmaceuticals; 3 months training is sufficient to be able to prescribe drugs. Not surprisingly, preventive medicine has been eschewed in favour of expensive curative approaches, which increases the financial burden on the rural household. The choice in the poor areas is stark if major illness strikes. Either wait and die or run up economic burdens that will take decades to pay off.

The chaotic state of rural healthcare attracted the leadership's attention and in December 1996 a National Conference on Health in Beijing was convened to try to fix the broken system. The change of tone was remarkable as the leadership shifted from presenting its healthcare system as a shining example to other developing countries to one of concern about its collapse (discussion with participants; Cailliez, 1998, pp. 42–3; for the joint CC and State Council Decision, see *Health Daily*, 18 February 1997). The political centre was clearly alarmed at the social consequences of financial decentralization and it tried to put forward a coherent policy to restore standards and access to healthcare. First, it was declared that spending in the national budget would be raised from 2 to 5 per cent, something that has not been achieved. Further measures sought to revive preventive healthcare and public hygiene awareness through education. The proportion of the government's budget for spending on preventive care dropped from 23 per cent in 1978 to 18 per cent in 1994 (Hu and Jiang, 1998, p. 192). Village doctors were to receive a pay boost to bring them in line with government officials and to stop the reliance on kickbacks and other non-sanctioned revenues.

The most important measure was the reconfirmation of the 1994 decision to restore the cooperative medical system. In this respect, China has suffered from 'state withdrawal' and the lack of public funding, training and regulation. Evidence clearly shows that where there is a functioning cooperative medical system, utilization rates of the medical services increase, especially the demand for clinic care and hospitalization. This is one clear case where the 'public good' argument would appear to apply and the government needs to tighten the regulatory framework to ensure that guidelines on health are followed and that in poor areas better provision is provided at central government expense (see Box 10.2).

BOX 10.2

New Experimentation with Cooperative Medical Provision

One of the first experiments took place in Sichuan in 1989–90, involving 26 villages in 2 counties (World Bank, 1997c, pp. 49–50). Premiums were 1.5 per cent of average income and those insured could freely visit village and township facilities, but visits to the county level were only in an emergency or on referral from the township. Participation rates were high: 90 per cent with a re-enrolment of 95 per cent after the first year. Administrative costs were kept low at only 8 per cent of total reimbursements. The need for some kind of catastrophic insurance was clearly shown as 11.5 per cent of the covered population used 70 per cent of total health expenditures. In poor areas, for such schemes to work, it is necessary to diversify contributions away from the household and to use the village social welfare funds and government allocations for poverty relief. One study of 30 poor counties in the mid-1990s found that household contributions to funding community health funds made up about 50 per cent, with about 20 per cent from the village funds and 16 per cent from the government (*China Network*, 1996). These experiments were drawn together in an announcement in July 1994 (*People's Daily*, 2 July) that proposed community-based healthcare schemes for the rural areas. It was to be a voluntary system, with each community organizing its own collective financing for basic healthcare. In line with the experiments to date, the funding base was to be diversified with priority given to preventive services.

The fact that the need to build a cooperative medical system was reiterated once again in 1996 suggests that little progress has been made. In fact, there is little evidence of any significant improvement of medical provision in the poor rural areas since then. Variation and non-compliance have been widespread and the frequent requests by the centre to reduce financial burdens on farmers have been interpreted by some as meaning that they should not have to contribute to medical schemes. Ultimately the central state has been unable to fund the medical system and local governments have little incentive to comply with its directives.

Poverty Alleviation

One rural policy area where the government appears to have been successful is in poverty alleviation where official figures show over 200 million have been lifted out of absolute poverty since the reforms began. In 1978, official figures revealed some 250 million rural people living in poverty (30.7 per cent of total rural dwellers), whereas by 1985 those with incomes below 200 *yuan* (1985 prices) had fallen to 125 million. By the end of 2002, official figures stated that just 28 million remained in absolute poverty. However, closer inspection revealed a more complex picture, and less success for direct state intervention than Beijing claimed.

First, the figure that China uses for its poverty line is only $0.66 per day (in 1985 purchasing power parity (PPP) dollars) whereas the usual World Bank standard is $1.00 per day. This figure would reveal a total approaching 200 million (22–24 per cent of rural dwellers and 18.5 per cent of the population as a whole) still in poverty, while the $2.00 per day standard would render a total of 53.7 per cent of total population. This puts it roughly on a par with Indonesia (15.2 and 66.1 per cent, respectively) and considerably better off than India (44.2 and 86.2 per cent, respectively) (World Bank, 2001, p. 280). It should also be remembered that there is a rapidly rising population of urban poor who are a product of the reforms. The Asian Development Bank (ADB) calculates a total of around 14.8 million in 2001 while the number of urban residents who received the minimum subsistence support was 21.4 million in March 2003. Such figures clearly underestimate urban poverty and do not include the migrant population.

What these figures show is that despite tremendous progress there are a significant group in the countryside who have not been helped by state policies, a very large group just above the poverty line who are very vulnerable and a smaller but increasing group of urban poor who are the creation of the reforms. The basic view of the government has been that people are poor because of physical disadvantage (such as living in remote areas) or lack of reform. The Jiang–Zhu leadership seemed to follow the notion of 'trickle-down', giving primacy to rapid economic growth accompanied by limited targeted interventions. As inequality became a political concern in the late 1990s a more pro-active 'Develop the West' policy was promoted. The Hu–Wen leadership recognize this is not enough and would like to enhance mechanisms for redistribution during the urbanization drive. However, policies of redistribution raise questions about targeting of the poor, whether such funds will be used optimally and has to ensure that redistribution does not work against development of the most productive parts of the economy.

Targeting to date has not been effective. Some have pointed out the paradox that the most dramatic decline slowed to a halt in the mid-1980s, just as China was setting up a poverty alleviation programme (UNDP, 1998, p. 86). In fact, in a centrally planned economy the simple act in the late 1970s of increasing state purchase prices of staple goods between 30 and 50 per cent followed by the introduction of market incentives did more than any other single policy to move people out of poverty. Even more dramatically, recent work has suggested that the main determinant of the exodus from poverty has been economic growth more broadly and that there is no statistically significant relationship between poverty incidence and poverty investment. Poverty investment has been ineffective (Rozelle *et al.*, 1998). Problematically for current policy, as poverty levels fall it is becoming more difficult to pull the remaining people out of poverty by relying on economic growth alone.

The slowdown in the reduction of poverty alleviation, in part, was inevitable as those who could be helped quickly by the new reforms had moved out of poverty and the more intractable cases remained. The majority of these extremely poor communities are in inhospitable environments, often in fragmented upland villages with poor infrastructure and with little if any agricultural surplus to market. In fact, for many in this group the introduction of market reforms had a negative effect as the farmers did not benefit from the increase in prices and access while the costs of their inputs and consumer durables rose. This convinced the Chinese state that a massive push would be necessary to raise this group out of poverty. As a result, in 1984 it set up a special agency under the State Council, the Leading Group for Poverty Alleviation, with poverty-alleviation offices at the county and township levels to coordinate policy. It invested a huge amount of funds and devised a number of specific policies targeted at the counties where it thought the poor were situated.

From 1986, the central state and the provinces began to identify 'poor counties' to be the recipients of targeted poverty-alleviation interventions. For even a moderately poor county it was beneficial to be listed as one of the counties to receive benefits and dispensations and intense lobbying took place both at the national and the provincial level. Of the initial 258 officially designated national poor counties in 1986, only one-third actually met the criterion of a rural net income *per capita* below 150 *yuan* in 1985, thus showing the intense politicization of the process. By 1993 there were 331 designated counties and the total was expanded to 592 in 1994, despite the fact that the total number of poor had fallen, according to official statistics, from 120 million in 1985 to 80 million in 1993 (Park, Wang and Wu, 1999, pp. 6–7). In addition, 2 of the 10 poorest counties in China were not among those designated (Nyberg and Rozelle, 1999, p. 97). The new poverty line was set at 320 *yuan* in 1993 prices.

The main problem is that the targeting is not very effective. Many of the absolute poor live outside of these counties and the distribution of funds within the designated counties is not effective in supporting the poorest households. The National Statistics Bureau estimates that one-third of the rural poor live outside of the 592 counties while some studies suggest that it may even be 50 per cent (UNDP, 2002, p. 35). The leakage of funds through misappropriations, bad investments and use by the non-poor households has meant that effectiveness is low. The UNDP has calculated that some 55–75 per cent of poverty-alleviation funds did not reach poor households (UNDP, 1998, p. 102). Within the counties, the money is not properly directed to poor households and is usually divided out evenly between poor and non-poor townships. Spreading the money evenly over the 200 million inhabitants of these counties where only 21 million absolute poor lived in 1998 meant that benefit to the poor was outweighed tenfold by distribution to the non-poor (World Bank, 2000, pp. xvi–xvii).

Some local leaders do not even distribute the funds in this way and they are seen as a useful supplement to local state income; with the lack of transparency the funds are often siphoned off to support pet projects. This was a problem, especially in the early and mid-1990s before central policy swung back to attempt to target the household. The World Bank (2000, p. xxiv) has calculated that in 1992 and 1993, around half of all poverty-alleviation subsidized loans were lent to industrial enterprises. By the mid-1990s, this strategy of copying the successful counties in developing TVEs had run its course and many poor areas were in severe financial difficulty. One local leader I questioned about his decision to continue pumping funds into a bankrupt enterprise was revealing. He stated that these funds were for poverty alleviation and that the wages paid were higher than the money the people could earn on the land. Thus pumping money into an unprofitable enterprise was meeting the state's objective of raising his people out of poverty. His, as it turned out, incorrect assumption was that the poverty alleviation taps would remain open indefinitely. However, in the mid-1990s the focus for subsidized loans was switched back to the household.

There are three main programmes for poverty alleviation: the subsidized loan programme managed by the Leading Group and the Agricultural Bank of China (ABC) (responsibility was returned to it in 1998 from the ADB that was set up in 1994); the food-for-work programme managed by the State Development and Planning Commission; and the budgetary grant programme. As suggested above, the impact of these programmes on helping the poorest has not been significant and there have been serious distortions in implementation. The second and third programmes will be discussed briefly and the loan programme at more length below.

In 1986, the central government increased by 33 per cent the amount of development capital for the Ministry of Finance to direct to counties for investment in poor areas. The budgetary grants totalled 2.7 billion *yuan* in 1997 (Park, Wang and Wu, 1999, pp. 21–2) and were complemented by a number of other special funds for poor areas, and tax breaks. These earmarked funds have been subject to diversion to cover local government operating costs, especially salaries, and the general budgetary pressure has often made it difficult to raise the amounts needed.

The 'food-for-work' programme began in 1984 and was initially conceived of as a programme to use the stocks of surplus grain procured by the government after the 1984 harvest. However, it evolved into a programme to finance much of the rural road construction, agricultural infrastructure and maintenance of water systems. Driving along rural mountain roads one is struck by the frequency that one comes across small teams working on road maintenance with crude tools and doing much of the heavy work by hand. In fact, much of the main road system in the mountainous areas is in remarkably good shape. However, this of itself highlights a problem with the programme as a policy for helping the poorest households in the countryside. The objective is to improve the infrastructure for the community as a whole and not to maximize employment opportunities for the poor. The hope is to improve the capacity for growth within the administrative area with the expectation that the benefits will trickle down to help the poorest. The resources provided by the central authorities are expected to be matched by the local authorities, but this is rarely the case. In fact, in a number of counties I visited they counted the labour of the farmers as their financial input. This labour went unpaid by the local authorities! This has been a major problem for the poor as it effectively amounts to yet another tax burden. Zhu and Jiang (1996, pp. 75–107) carried out research in three poor provinces and discovered that 40 per cent of the households surveyed did their work without receiving any payment. It is probably also the case that local governments have simply used these projects to substitute for construction projects that they should have carried out with their own funds in any case.

The subsidized loans are run through the ABC, now supposedly a commercial bank, at heavily discounted rates of around 3 per cent loaned over a 3 to 5-year period. Over time the effectiveness of these loans in reaching the poor has declined. Such cheap capital is attractive to local governments and wealthier individuals for their own projects and much of the money is captured by those for whom it is not primarily intended. In addition, the banks are now under pressure to cut their losses and this has provided disincentives for the ABC to loan to poor households (World Bank, 2000, p. xiv). The costs of administration in dealing with scattered households often in inhospitable terrains are high, and given the low enforced interest rates they cannot be profitable. On-time repayment has been below 50 per cent. Also, as land is contracted out from the collective to the household, the farmer is not able to offer land as collateral on the loan. These factors incline the ABC to lend to what it thinks will be money-making projects that usually involve enterprise development.

The decision in 1996 by the Leading Group to focus attention for loans on poor households has led to a boom in interest in microcredit schemes. In 1997, a number of provinces began to authorize the use of poverty-alleviation funds for such schemes and in 1998 the Leading Group emphasized that microcredit should be expanded to all provinces. Small-scale lending schemes have been very successful in other Asian countries, not only in targeting the poor but also in building up the lending infrastructure and gaining high rates of return, well above those experienced in China. Local groups in China have been highly innovative and programmes have been run by local offices of the poverty-alleviation bureau and the women's federation targeting poor rural women (see Box 10.3). Programmes modelled on those of Grameen Bank in Bangladesh or Cash Poor in Malaysia have been introduced by international organizations such as the UNDP and private organizations

---

BOX 10.3

Microfinance and Women

The natural beauty of Xiling township (Yixian, Hebei province) belies the poverty that exists in the villages, especially as one moves into the mountains. With the new highway, it is only about a 3-hour drive from Beijing and the villages on the plain are dotted along the river and scattered among the imposing Imperial tombs that are the main tourist attraction of the region. Away from the tombs the roads soon give way to tracks that are difficult to navigate in the winter.

It is also the site of China's first experimentation with a Grameen Bank-style microfinance scheme for poor rural women who have no collateral. The scheme began in October 1993. The women are grouped in 6–8 households with an elected head who has the primary responsibility to convene meetings and ensure that the loans are repaid on time. By the end of 1997, the scheme had expanded to 4 townships with 31 villages and 2,000 households that have received loans totalling 4.8 million *yuan*.

The effect on women's lives has been dramatic. One of the participants had run into financial trouble because her husband was unable to carry out heavy agricultural work because of a heart condition. She used her first loan to purchase seeds and began market gardening. By the second year she had purchased plastic sheeting and had set up two greenhouses. Her transformation was dramatic. From a woman who shuffled around looking at the ground she had developed a confident gait, knew all the local market rates and was instructing other women in the village on her tricks of market gardening.

Another woman used her loan to raise pigs. I asked what she intended to do with her new found 'wealth'. She replied that she wanted to buy a television so that her daughter would be a part of the world culture!

---

such as the Ford Foundation. As of 2002, internationally sponsored programmes were supplying around 70 million *yuan* per year while government schemes were providing around 775 million and rising (Interview, Beijing, January 2003). In 1998 it was also decided that the loans should be distributed through the local branches of the ABC rather than the poverty-alleviation offices to ensure better supervision. The poverty-alleviation offices were to be responsible for organizing the households into groups and to help with ensuring repayment. This structure reduces incentives for the office to ensure a well-functioning system and, as shown above, the branches of the ABC have little incentive to manage the programme.

These institutional factors and the enforced low lending rate mean that microcredit schemes will not provide the 'magic wand' the Leading Group is hoping for and will not be as successful as their counterparts elsewhere in Asia. The interest rates cannot cover operating costs, which in turn will make it impossible to make such programmes sustainable. In fact, one senior official from the Leading Group stunned international participants at a meeting to discuss poverty strategy. The person commented that they did not understand why foreigners kept talking about sustainability and above-market interest rates as there was no need for the lending programmes to become sustainable. The low-interest loans would lift people out of poverty and then the whole scheme would be stopped in any case! Such thinking is hard to shift, as is state policy on low interest rates, and without such changes another financial disaster looms. Research by Park and Ren (2001) has demonstrated that internationally run programmes tend to function better than the government schemes. Average repayment rates in government schemes are declining to between 50 to 70 per cent, well below the threshold to make them viable.

Poverty-alleviation work is an area where the government seems willing to accept a role for NGOs. In a major departure from past practice, the new 10-year plan for poverty alleviation explicitly states the need to bring NGOs on board to help implement government projects in poor areas (State Council, 2001). A meeting convened by the China Foundation for Aiding Poor Areas in October 2001 calculated that incomplete statistics suggested that resources mobilized by the NGO sector amounted to between 18 and 28 per cent of the total funds for poverty alleviation in the second half of the 1990s (Information from participants). Since its establishment in 1989, the Foundation raised over $60.4 million in cash and kind to help the rural poor in central and western China (*China Daily*, 4 August 2001). Similar organizations with close party and state ties have also been important in fund-raising for welfare projects. Perhaps the best known is the Youth Development Foundation set up by the Communist Youth League, which launched Project Hope to build primary schools and provide scholarships for poor children. Project Hope has provided aid to all the officially designated poor counties in China and in 1996 its funding for primary school construction accounted for 8.8 per cent of the county-level budget for capital construction for education (National Research Centre, 1998, pp. 3, 5).

A more comprehensive and participatory approach to rural development would help. Current policies are implemented by different, vertical bureaucratic hierarchies with little attempt to integrate them effectively. Further, there is very little consultation with farmers about what they actually want in terms of help, and little effort to build with them sustainable participatory institutions. The paternalism of CCP rule is evident, with many local officials convinced that the farmers do not know what is in their best interests. The phrase 'their cultural quality is too low' (*suzhi tai di*) is frequently used by local officials to justify why they do not ask farmers for input on the projects they are designing and implementing.

To resolve the problems of poverty and rural social policy more generally, the Chinese government needs to develop an approach that integrates social and economic development policy, is pro-poor and more participatory and inclusive. Obviously urbanization, if well conceived, will resolve much of the problem but in the meantime the structure of public finance hugely disfavours the rural areas. The main thrust of economic policy is to achieve rapid growth, often by shifting resources away from the poor and then returning some funds through limited poverty alleviation interventions. Rural net taxes are highly regressive so that in 1995 the top decile of the rural population appropriated 133 per cent of all net subsidies, while the 2 poorest deciles paid nearly half of all net taxes (UNDP, 2002, pp. 37–8). Investment patterns, as we have seen, favour the coastal and urban areas. However, any major reallocation of resources is liable to be politically unacceptable. Improvement of rural infrastructure and investment in education and health might be feasible.

A complementary approach would be to think about the demand side rather than just the supply side, as governments tend to do. There is a need for better research on poverty in China that is participatory. Well-intentioned government poverty-alleviation and economic development programmes have been hampered by inaccurate assumptions about poverty, and by the fact that poor people themselves have had little to say in the design and implementation of such programmes. In the uplands, some local governments have squandered scarce resources in failed attempts to mimic the development strategies of wealthy coastal areas without regard to local conditions and capacities. Others have overemphasized the need for subsidized credit and relief, undermining local initiative while deepening dependency.

In addition to increasing the effectiveness of design and delivery of government programmes, it is also necessary to create conditions that enable the poor to cast off poverty on their own, which is often a matter of ensuring that they are able to secure access to and control over productive resources and credit. Strengthening the rights of farmers and rural communities to manage and derive benefits from the natural resources on which they depend is one of the keys to securing sustained improvements in the lives of the rural poor.

11

Foreign Policy

The end of the Cold War at the beginning of the 1990s, the US–China agreement on WTO entry at the end of the 1990s and the shift in the US position following the 11 September 2001 terrorist attacks have provided dramatic challenges to China's foreign policy formulation. The disappearance of US–Soviet superpower rivalry meant that China had to reconfigure its international position without the room for manoeuvre that had been offered by the Cold War. It also brought the latent antagonisms in the relationship with the United States to the forefront. Combined with the West's reaction to the military quelling of the student-led demonstrators in 1989, it has brought an uncertainty to the relationship that has continued to this day and will continue to influence relations in the twenty-first century. China's entry into the WTO builds on the extraordinary economic integration into the world economy that has taken place since the reforms began and shows China's leaders' commitment to being an active member of the world economic community. At the same time, it presents new challenges for the leadership in terms of just how much foreign presence China is willing to tolerate and how destabilizing the foreign presence will be to native industry. The US focus on the 'War on Terrorism' after 11 September has brought unexpected benefits for China as it has quietened the 'China as a threat' voices, but has raised fears about potential US unilateralism following the 2003 war with Iraq. This chapter considers first China's perceptions of global integration and how this may hamper success. Second, the chapter looks at the changing nature of the relationship with the United States and Russia. Third, it reviews China's position within the region before concluding by looking at the economic dimension of China's foreign relations.

China and Globalization

The November 1999 agreement between China and the United States on China's terms of accession to the WTO, following its signing of the two UN covenants on human rights in 1997 and 1998, appears to signal the Chinese leadership's intent to be a part of the global community. By signing these agreements, China has implicitly acknowledged that international monitoring is justifiable, not only for domestic economic practice but also for political behaviour. However, in practice, while China clearly wants to be a respected member of the international community, it is deeply conflicted about how active and what kind of a role to play in international governance (Saich, 2000b). Like other countries, China wishes to derive the macroeconomic benefits of globalization but is uncomfortable with the costs of social, political and cultural readjustment. Similarly Western observers have been ambivalent about how to deal with the rise of China's economic power and its integration into global frameworks of governance. Some, taking their cue from historical parallels with the rise of new powers such as Germany and Japan at the turn of the twentieth century, see conflict as inevitable; others argue that the changed international situation makes successful accommodation feasible. The strongest expression of the conflict school is Bernstein and Munro (1997) while a more balanced assessment is presented by Nathan and Ross (1997) and Johnston (2003). Certainly it has been the approach of all US presidents from Nixon on that the more China could be engaged with the international community the better. The latest example was Clinton's fight with Congress during 2000 to have it approve permanent normal trading status with China as a part of the preparations for WTO entry, a measure finally signed into law in October.

As in the rest of the world, in China there has been a boom in publications about globalization. The overwhelming majority concentrate on 'economic globalization', with less attention paid to 'cultural globalization', mainly interpreted as the domination of American cultural products, and virtually no consideration given to the impact on governance. While the impact of globalization is best seen in the economic sphere, there are also consequences for governance.

Xenophobic outbursts and leadership manipulation notwithstanding, withdrawal from deeper integration into the world economy and its evolving structures of governance is impossible. This point was made emphatically when, despite significant domestic opposition, Jiang Zemin and Premier Zhu Rongji pushed ahead with a deal with the United States on the terms of accession for WTO. This reflected the leadership's need to deliver further economic progress to strengthen its legitimacy and this progress can be delivered over the long term only through the increased trade, foreign investment and a more disciplined domestic economy that WTO membership would bring. Entry in 2001 was not only important for national pride and to fulfil Jiang's desire to steer China to great power status, but also for very pragmatic economic reasons. In 1999 with FDI dropping, foreign interest in China waning and domestic reforms stumbling, early entry was seen as the best way to stimulate the economy. This was compounded by fears that barriers to entry might rise subsequently, especially as the next round of talks would cover two issues of vital interest to China – agriculture and trade in services. By joining early, China was hoping to forge alliances to secure policies more beneficial to its own national concerns.

Despite this more accommodating approach to foreign trade and capital, in crucial respects both Deng Xiaoping and Jiang Zemin's approach (and one must presume that that of Hu Jintao will not differ significantly) has mirrored that of their nineteenth-century predecessors in the 'self-strengthening movement' which sought to import Western techniques and equipment while keeping out new cultural and political values. This previous policy of selective adaptation proved shortsighted. The Chinese did not comprehend the inter-related nature of Western societies and failed to see that Western technology could not be easily disentangled from the social and cultural matrix in which it was embedded. It remains to be seen whether the CCP will be more successful in gaining the benefits of globalization without accepting its under-lying premises. For example, WTO membership seems to presume not only a liberal trading order, but also an independent legal system that constrains government as necessary, transparency, accountability and a relatively pluralistic political order.

Since Mao Zedong initiated contacts with the United States and engin-eered the PRC's entry into the United Nations (UN) in the early 1970s, the general consensus has been that China has moved from rejection of the inter-national status quo to acceptance. However, it is more correct to say that China has acquiesced in the international order and while it has been a joiner, it has not been a doer or rule-setter for international governance. In major part this has been because the main priority has been for China to develop its own economic strength and it has seen international organizations as helping it meet this objective. From 1977 to 1996, China's membership in international government organizations rose from 21 to 51 and in international NGOs from 71 to 1,079 (Kim, 1999, pp. 46–7). This has made China reluctant to challenge the existing rules of the game unless they directly confront Chinese claims to sovereignty or economic interests. In addition, coming out of a period of self-imposed exile, China had very few administrative personnel who could work in international organizations to advance China's interests effectively.

Second, as a latecomer to all international governmental organizations, China did not participate in the drafting of the 'rules of the game'. The incap-acity of China to change significantly these 'rules of the game' to suit its national conditions has reinforced its perception that international govern-ance is structured essentially to pursue the agenda and interests of the West, especially the United States. This was apparent in the official response to the Seattle meeting of the WTO (1999) that criticized the 'small number of economic superpowers' that had tried to dominate proceedings over the interests of the developing countries (*People's Daily*, 6 December 1999, p. 7). China's self-told history of 150 years of shame and humiliation at the hands of foreigners, the anti-imperialist thrust of Leninism, the party's own legacy of distrust and betrayal and the leaders' tendency to interpret decision-making in terms of a 'zero-sum' game mitigate against constructive engagement and interaction with the existing international governing structures.

Compounding this is the fact that the CCP has never been successful in transnational governance. Its attempts in the 1960s and 1970s to lead a loose coalition of nations to oppose 'US-hegemonism' and 'Soviet revisionism' failed, as did its attempts to fund pro-Maoist groups to destabilize neighbouring governments in Asia. Not surprisingly, Deng Xiaoping's advice to his colleagues and successors was not to take the lead in international affairs, lean toward the United States, and concentrate on economic development. However, this is difficult for a nation with a psychology that emphasizes the superiority of Chinese culture and that sees an international leadership role as a right to be reclaimed.

Such sentiments can lead to instability when combined with the more strident nationalism promoted, or acquiesced to, by President Jiang Zemin and his advisers. While China is currently open for business, distrust of foreigners and significant periods of closure have been common. We have seen that the 'Gang of Four' criticized Deng Xiaoping for his attempts to promote foreign trade (Chapter 2), but Premier Zhu Rongji suffered similar accusations of treason once the United States published what it claimed were the terms he had agreed to for WTO entry during his US visit in April 1999. The sudden and xenophobic outpouring of anti-foreign sentiment following the accidental NATO bombing of the Chinese Embassy in Belgrade on 7 May 1999 and the downing of the US EP-3 in April 2001 revealed how close to the surface distrust of foreigners still lies.

Since 1989, the Chinese leadership has been fairly successful in manipulating public opinion to instil nationalism as a legitimizing core value. However, the CCP has been careful to set limits to the ramifications of a strident nationalism that might challenge its own position. Thus, while initially supportive of the anti-US demonstration in May 1999, it quickly reined them in once they began to criticize the ineptitude of the government's response. While this appeal to nationalism may aid the regime's short-term stability, it presents two challenges in terms of governance. First, it mitigates against constructive involvement in international organizations as rising nationalism compromises the ability of the nation-state to deal with internationalism. Second, it reinforces the outdated notion of sovereignty that still underpins the current leadership's perceptions of the world. By and large China is an Empire with a Westphalian concept of the nation-state trying to operate in an increasingly multilateral world. In fact, what China wants is an economic order that is international in terms of the benefits it brings but not necessarily global if that means decentring decision-making away from the nation-state.

China has displayed a basic suspicion of multilateral frameworks and has generally preferred to lock discussions into bilateral diplomacy. Thus, in the agreement with the United States on the WTO, China quickly asserted that the organization stipulated that 'regardless of size, all member countries enjoy equal rights' (*People's Daily*, 6 December 1999, p. 7). This suspicion is even more acute on political and social issues. China was quick to condemn

President Clinton's attempts to bring labour standards into WTO consider- ations and commented that the 'so-called labour standards were nothing but a covert form of trade protectionism' and confirmed that labour conditions were nobody else's business and that there should be no interference on this issue 'by other countries in the name of protecting human rights' (*People's Daily*, 6 December 1999, p. 7). That said, in recent years, China's leaders seems to have accepted that multilateral institutions might work to check US power and to promote China's interests, and they seem more comfortable with them.

These trends explain the seeming contradiction in China's international behaviour. China wants to be taken seriously and President Jiang Zemin, in particular, has sought a role in global governance through what he has termed 'Great Power Diplomacy' and the forlorn objective of creating a multipolar world in one that will clearly be unipolar in terms of real power well into the twenty-first century. The dedication to sovereignty and a territorial definition of China that is the most expansive in history, and China's reluctance to move discussions out of bilateral frameworks, causes uncertainty in the region. It also means that China is more willing to join regimes that govern the international economy, but is less enthusiastic about those regional or global frameworks that would place real restrictions on Chinese military capabilities (Economy and Oksenberg, 1999, p. 21; Swaine and Johnston, 1999, pp. 90–135). The CCP and the military have been adamantly opposed to any attempts to establish an Asian collective security system, primarily because they do not wish to give Southeast Asian nations a forum in which to criticize collectively its claims to sovereignty in the South China Sea (Kim, 1999, p. 56; more generally on engaging China, see Johnston and Ross, 1999).

It can also lead to decisions that are described as principled in China but that appear petty to others. Of particular importance in this respect is China's concern to deny international space to Taiwan and to punish those countries that show sympathy towards Taiwan's views. One extreme example was China's veto in the Security Council (February 1999), something almost unpreced- ented, against the continuation of the UN Preventive Deployment Force in Macedonia, because of the latter's switch of diplomatic recognition to Taiwan in January. Sadly, in light of subsequent events, China's Ambassador to the UN, Qin Huasun, did not mention Taiwan as justification but said that peacekeeping forces were no longer necessary as Macedonia has 'apparently stabilized in the last few years' (*New York Times*, 26 February 1999, p. 11). With the outbreak of SARS on Taiwan, China agreed in April 2003 to allow a 2-person WHO group to visit as a 'humanitarian' gesture but the officials were not allowed to speak with the Taiwanese Minister of Health or other senior officials. However, China was at pains to make sure that this would not lead to a political opening and, as usual, China killed in committee Taiwan's attempt to gain observer status at the WHO.

China often has a poor understanding of international norms (see Chapter 5 for human rights) and it needs to be able to feel comfortable with the framework for international governance that it seeks to join. Many important issues beyond the directly political and economic, such as environmental protection, drug smuggling, trafficking in women and HIV/AIDS, need China's active participation to resolve. In turn, other major nations need to incorporate China as a more equal partner and to build China's reasonable concerns into the architecture of international governance. China, for its part, needs to reduce its suspicion of hostile foreign intent and adjust its outdated notion of sovereignty to accept that some issues need transnational solutions and that international monitoring does not have to erode CCP power. Without accommodation on both sides, China will remain a rather grumpy, unpredictable player in international governance.

China and the Great Power(s)

As China entered the 1990s two major events significantly affected its foreign policy. The first was the fall-out from the repression of the 1989 demonstrations that produced a strong backlash from the Western nations. The honeymoon period that China had enjoyed with the West throughout the 1980s abruptly ended and rights abuses that the West had been muted on suddenly became the focus of extensive media and political attention. Second, the tearing down of the Berlin Wall and the subsequent collapse from power of the Soviet Communist Party dramatically affected Chinese foreign policy. China found it hard to adjust to the new world order, even more so as Chinese leaders are used to thinking in terms of an overarching framework based on ideological premises that provides structure to policy and relationships. China had settled into a foreign policy premised on the notion that international politics would be dominated by the existence of a bipolar relationship between the two superpowers. This afforded China the opportunity to play off the one against the other and create more space for itself in international affairs. With the balance upset, China began to feel vulnerable and marginalized in world affairs.

The main advantage to China was that it was now free to pursue more unashamedly its own national interests without reference to ideological considerations. As an internal document published shortly after the failed coup of the hard-liners in Russia (1991) stated, China needed to move away from letting moral judgements and ideological considerations predominate. National interest should be put first and foremost and it was no longer necessary to dress up policies in socialist rhetoric. It concluded:

China is a great power, it should forthrightly establish a general strategy in keeping with its great power status. Moral foreign relations cannot be conducted any longer, the principle of national interest should take the guiding role (Translated in Kelly, 1996, pp. 13–31).

This would certainly keep China from repeating the messy involvement resulting from its radical anti-Soviet stance of the 1970s when it provided support to Pinochet in Chile and UNITA in Angola. With no superpower rivalry, China had less interest in Third World conflicts as it did not matter so much who won. This may change again over the next 20 years as China begins to become more oil-dependent on the Middle East. Iran and Saudi Arabia are China's two main oil suppliers and imports from the Middle East account for 50 per cent of the total imports, a figure expected to rise to 80 per cent by 2008. However, in this case engagement will be a result of pragmatic economic need rather than ideological necessity.

China moved quickly to establish diplomatic relations with both former pro-Soviet regimes in the developing world and with the newly independent states that emerged from the breakup of the former Soviet Union. The reasons were twofold. First, China wished to deny Taiwan the chance to exploit any possibility to establish diplomatic relations. Second, in recognizing the new Central Asian states, China wished to preempt the chance that they might become supporters of Muslim fundamentalists within China.

The first Gulf War (1991) provided China with the chance to improve its standing as a global actor and work to overturn some of the sanctions imposed after 1989. It used its role in the UN Security Council in the offensive buildup to side with the US-led coalition. However, as it became clear that force would be used, it abstained in the crucial Security Council vote that authorized the use of force against Iraq. The overwhelming US military might shocked the Chinese high command and for the leadership more broadly there was the concern that the new multipolar world they were touting would be unipolar and US-dominated.

As a result through the 1990s no new basis for a relationship between the United States and China was forged. The Chinese leadership sought, despite domestic opposition, to maintain Deng Xiaoping's legacy of a neutral or pro-US international orientation that would help facilitate China's ambitious plans for modernization. This meant that despite attempts to improve the relationship on both sides, suspicions remained and unforeseen events could often set the relationship into a tailspin. On the positive side there were the 1994 Clinton decision to de-link trade and human rights (reversing his 1993 executive order conditioning Most-Favoured Nation (MFN) status on human rights, protecting Tibet's culture and allowing broadcasts into China); the June 1998 Clinton statement on the 'three nos' (see below); the November 1999 agreement on terms of WTO entry; and the signing into law in October 2000 of provisions for China's permanent normal trading status. The 'three nos' were apparently communicated to Jiang Zemin by Clinton in the summer of 1995 and relayed orally during Jiang's visit to the United States and then mentioned publicly by Clinton in Shanghai in June 1998. They refer to no recognition of Taiwanese independence, no support for two Chinas or one Taiwan and one China and no endorsement of Taiwan's entry into any international organization for which statehood would be required. This abandoned the two-decade-old policy designed to preserve the right of Taiwan's people to self-determination (Tucker, 2000, p. 251).

On the negative side was the general impression by China that it did not count in US policy-making and the perception that the United States had an active, if undeclared, policy to contain China. There was the casual way in which President Clinton appeared to deal with the 1995 invitation of then Taiwanese President Lee Teng-Hui to visit his *alma mater*, Cornell University: Chinese foreign minister, Qian Qichen, had been assured that no invitation would be issued, only for President Clinton under pressure from Congress to turn around and relent. The 7 May 1999 accidental bombing by a US aircraft of the Chinese Embassy in Belgrade, causing considerable damage and loss of life, only served to compound the frustration and feeling of helplessness.

The new Bush administration that took over in January 2001 seemed to confirm China's worst fears as it adopted a much more confrontational stance and a seemingly more sympathetic view of Taiwan. The collision between a US spyplane and a Chinese jetfighter (April 2001) resulting in Chinese loss of life and a tense standoff, marked a new low in the relationship. However, it also had the effect of awakening some in the new US administration to the fact that some kind of constructive dialogue with China was necessary.

In diplomatic terms China was a major beneficiary of the 11 September 2001 terrorist attacks on the United States. It was hard to establish a political rhetoric of China as a threat or enemy when Al-Qaeda terrorists had just flown two fully-loaded civilian aircraft into the World Trade Centre and the Pentagon. China has been seen as cooperative in the 'War on Terror' and in many ways the relationship is in better shape than at any time since the 1980s. It is debatable, however, whether the relationship would survive another unexpected accident and mutual suspicion is still strong on both sides (for a thoughtful set of essays, see Vogel, 1997).

China was supportive of US actions in Afghanistan but was far more cautious about the US-led invasion of Iraq in 2003. China was willing to let countries such as France and Germany take the lead in criticizing US plans and its avoidance of the UN system once it was deemed unsupportive. However, China has not publicly criticized the United States and the United Kingdom for its dominance of the post-war decision-making and has instead lobbied quietly for a significant stake in Iraq's reconstruction contracts.

In terms of cooperation, there are a number of joint strategic concerns about keeping the peace in the Asia-Pacific region and preventing a new arms race. The need for a good collaborative relationship is seen most clearly with the problem of North Korea (see below) where China is a key player and is generally viewed as having played a constructive role. In addition both countries have a vested interest in preventing an escalation of conflict between India and Pakistan. Economically, there should be an incentive to find the way to a good relationship and there are a number of other issues on which collaboration would be beneficial, such as environmental pollution, with the United States as the largest producer of greenhouse gases and China rapidly catching up.

In February 2003 in his speech at Tsinghua University, President Bush commented that 'China is on a rising path, and America welcomes the emergence of a strong and peaceful and prosperous China'. Strong voices on both sides doubt this, and in China US attempts to remain the one dominant superpower are viewed with alarm. US troops are now stationed in Afghanistan and Central Asia as well as traditional bases in Japan and South Korea and a possible collapse of North Korea, it is feared, would bring US troops right up to the Chinese border.

However, four major problems exist in the relationship between the United States and China, of which Taiwan remains the most contentious, but the US intentions on missile defence are of increasing concern. The first is the question of human rights that has become a major issue in the relationship since 1989. The breakdown in bipartisan support for a constructive engagement with China has led to a more powerful voice for human rights activists and religious groups critical of China's record. This has included groups focusing specifically on China such as Human Rights in China, groups that have a broader mandate with a particular concern about China such as Human Rights Watch, labour unions and Christian groups that are concerned about persecution of believers in China. There is also a strong lobby that is concerned about the situation in Tibet and what is seen as the destruction of Tibetan culture and the swamping of Tibet with ethnic Han Chinese. The United States has tried a number of means to try to force China to shift its stance on human rights and improve its record of governance. These have ranged from private diplomacy to public criticism to the use of international forums and the threat of economic sanctions (Harding, 1997, pp. 165–84). In particular, there is the annual introduction by the United States of a resolution to condemn China for its human rights abuses in Geneva at the meeting of the UN Commission on Human Rights. China has worked successfully each year to undermine this resolution and from 1997 onwards has been successful in breaking European and Oceanian support. Many nations have come to see the resolution as a fruitless exercise that makes no progress and only makes building relations with China even more difficult. In 2003, the Bush administration took a new approach and did not sponsor a motion critical of China's human rights record. The administration decided to take China's comments that not exerting public pressure but engaging in quiet diplomacy would bring greater progress. It was also intended to give the new leadership a chance to ameliorate the situation without appearing to succumb to US pressure. The previous year, the United States and China agreed that the East Turkestan Islamic Movement operating in Xinjiang was a terrorist organization, thus giving Jiang Zemin something concrete to show for his support of the US 'War on Terror'.

Second, there are a number of frictions around trade and investment and not all of these will be smoothed away by the WTO agreement. Despite the omnipresent McDonald's in urban China, US businesses have complained of the hidden barriers to entry in China and hope that WTO rules on transparency will clear them from the path. In particular, US companies have complained about piracy that has resulted in annual losses for the pharmaceutical businesses estimated at around $400 million and a similar amount for software, books, films and music. The periodic high-profile crushing or burning of pirated materials and collaboration with Pinkerton's in China has not stemmed the growth. By contrast, the Chinese have complained about US restrictions on technology transfer from the United States, with the latter often holding back on the most advanced technology not only for commercial reasons but also because of concerns about military adaptation.

Although China is the United States' fourth-largest trading partner, there has been considerable friction about the level of the US trade deficit. This mirrored earlier US concerns with Japan and Taiwan. With these now moving up the development chain much of the anger has focused on China using its cheap labour to promote exports of goods such as toys, clothing and computer components. Nobody denies that the deficit has risen rapidly as China's exports boom, but there are considerable differences about how the deficit is calculated and whether it is structural and will continue to grow. Official US figures claim the deficit to have exceeded $100 billion in 2002 while the Chinese claim that it is at most half of this amount. Independent assessments that discount factors such as re-exports through Hong Kong (half of bilateral trade) also produce a much lower figure than the US official statistics. WTO entry, while providing benefits for China in terms of textile exports, should offer a boost to US exports, possibly up to $5 billion a year. In addition, US investment in China will increase and a significant amount of exports to the United States are from US-invested firms. This is distinct from Japan's exports to the United States, that are made up almost entirely of local products manufactured by their own companies.

Third, there are a number of problems related to arms control and arms proliferation. The United States has been concerned by what it sees as uncontrolled Chinese arms sales in the developing world, especially to what it sees as 'rogue states' such as Iran and North Korea. Of more recent concern has been the sale of dual-use technology that in some cases China has a legal right to transfer but might breach unilateral promises made to the United States, as in the case of the transfer of missile technology to Pakistan. From China's perspective, the most problematic issue was the decision by the United States to move forward with plans that would lead to deployment of a national missile defence system that would shoot down incoming missiles. China was angered that when the United States was thinking about deployment of this new system it was concerned to engage in discussion with Russia but viewed Chinese concerns almost as an afterthought. It is a system that the Bush administration has a strong commitment to building.

China has three specific problems with the development of this system. The first is that it would be destabilizing and would lead to an arms race in Asia as countries move to develop enough missiles to overwhelm the US capacity to shoot them down. Chinese officials have talked about building up their own missile capability from around 20 to 120 or 150 nuclear warheads. Second, they feel that despite US protestations to the contrary, the system is really part of the US strategy to contain China and is effectively directed against China rather than against the 'rogue states', as claimed by Washington. China's posture has been one of opposition to US troops stationed in Asia and they see the missile defence system as an extension of US military encirclement of China. This suspicion had already been raised when the United States and Japan renegotiated their defence agreement in 1996. China also views this agreement as directed against it. Third, and crucially, China sees the development of the missile defence system as designed to protect Taiwan against an attack from the PLA. To try to impress on the United States the seriousness with which it sees this development and the potential for protecting Taiwan, a number of officials have denounced it in official meetings, the army press has warned of missile attacks on US cities and in 1995 General Xiong Guangkai told one US official that in the end the United States would care more about Los Angeles than about Taipei (*Wall Street Journal*, 11 July 2000).

This brings us to the fourth and most important problem, the question of Taiwan, that China views as an internal matter left unresolved from the civil war. For many years, the Taiwanese leadership shared Beijing's view but simply disputed who was the legitimate ruler of the one China. Recent developments in internal politics on both sides of the Straits have made the situation more complex. As far as China is concerned, this is a domestic matter that the United States should not be involved in, and it has continually pushed for the United States to accept its position and to halt weapon sales to Taiwan that it claims makes Taiwan more likely to pursue independence. The latent danger of military conflict was highlighted by the dramatic events of 1995–96. As noted above, China's leaders reacted angrily to President Lee Teng-hui's invitation to Cornell University and felt that President Clinton had deceived them. This was a shock to the Chinese foreign policy establishment and made senior leaders wake up to the role of Congress. They had always been used to the US President making China policy, often without consultation with Congress. This had been the case with the secret negotiations opened by Nixon, with moves by Carter to normalization and when Bush had sent a secret emissary after 1989. Their mode of operation had been that the executive branch of the United States makes China policy, and the legislative goes along with it. It took China's policy-makers a while to realize that in the post-Tiananmen environment this had changed.

Beijing began military exercises in the Straits, suspended talks with Taiwan and showed its diplomatic displeasure. It showed its military teeth in 1996 as President Lee campaigned to become the first democratically elected President of Taiwan. With China launching missiles into the Straits as a warning, the United States dispatched two battleships to the area. In a sense, the brinkmanship was useful in clarifying the limits of the possible. For Taiwan, it made it clear that any moves to independence would be harshly met by Beijing and that there were limits to their capacity for diplomatic manoeuvre. For China, it indicated that under certain conditions the United States would intervene to protect Taiwan, something that China had thought it would not do. For the United States, it clarified that its historical involvement remained very much alive and that it would remain actively involved, like it or not. Subsequently, US policy has been driven by the fear of war over any move by Taiwan to declare independence, hence President Clinton's announcement of the 'three nos' during his 1998 visit to China.

For China, one of their worst nightmares was realized when opposition DPP member, Chen Shui-bian, was elected President of Taiwan in 2000, defeating the officially backed GMD candidate. However, it is clear that lessons were learned from 1995–96 and the hawks on all sides were kept in check. While Beijing's rhetoric was loud and harsh, its actions were more calculated and a 'wait-and-see' attitude prevailed. Since his election President Chen has shown a conciliatory attitude and affirmed that he would not declare independence unless attacked by the Mainland and he has offered to meet Chinese leaders at any location to discuss any topic, including the 'one-China principle'. China has balked at the last point, claiming that it is non-negotiable and implies Taiwan's acceptance that there is only one China and that that China is the PRC. Beijing's response to date has been to let other forms of contacts go ahead outside of official channels. At the same time, Beijing has also accepted the visit of delegations from various Taiwanese political parties. Thus, in July 2000 delegations from the pro-unification New Party, the GMD and the People First Party visited and it was suggested that President Jiang had approved a DPP visit as long as it did not comprise senior government officials (*SCMP*, 17 July 2000, Internet edition).

The Jiang and Hu leaderships both seem to feel that with the significant expansion of business and trading links that the situation is turning in their favour. They hope to use the same tactics as with Hong Kong of detaching the business elites and persuading them to put pressure on the Taiwan authorities to come to a solution that is politically acceptable. In March 2003, President Hu stated that China would look to ordinary Taiwanese residents as a partner for reunification. The increased interaction in trade, tourism and cultural exchanges has also complicated politics on the Mainland. In 1995–96 and in 2000, those provinces that have benefited most from Taiwanese investment such as Fujian lobbied Beijing not to cause them economic hardship by driving away Taiwan investors. Despite this, Taiwan investment in China in 2002 accounted for half of the island's outward investment while the Mainland replaced the United States as Taiwan's largest export market, running a trade surplus of $25 billion.

China has not trusted the motives of Chen's administration and has resisted any substantive dialogue. Beijing's hope is that the GMD candidate will win the Presidential election in March 2004 and that this will facilitate forward momentum on establishing direct flights and investment links. However, there are pressures on Jiang Zemin and Hu Jintao, who has taken over as the head of Taiwan policy, to set some kind of a date for resolution. There has been an increasing impatience among the senior leadership that the United States and Taiwan are trying to draw out discussions to prevent reunification. Some hawkish elements have even viewed China's holding of the Olympics in 2008 as a problem, as this would mean that aggression against Taiwan was impossible for the foreseeable future (Interview January 2001). There have been rumours that in 2003 at CMAC meetings Jiang Zemin set a deadline of 2011, the hundredth anniversary of the founding of the Republic, for reunification. This may increase the pressure and expectation of tangible results that may lead to more precipitate action if not well managed.

The remaining frictions and tensions in the relationship with the United States have led the Chinese leadership to try to raise its international profile and knit together its own set of strategic alliances. The leadership desperately want to believe that the world can be multipolar, even though this view is ridiculed by some of the country's own academia. The attempts were begun by Jiang but will be continued by Hu. This lay behind China's 'rediscovery' of Europe and Africa, both continents having been the target of senior visits since the late 1990s.

It also led to attempts to breathe new life into the relationship with Russia that began with President Yeltsin and has continued with his successor, Putin. Since 1996 the leaders of both countries have talked about a 'strategic partnership' to build a multipolar world. In January 2001, China announced that it would sign a new treaty of friendship with Russia, clearly timed to put pressure on the new Bush administration to warn it to take Chinese concerns seriously. The Bush administration was not moved. In May–June 2003, President Hu travelled to Russia on his way to attend a parallel event to the G-8 meeting in France. Together with Putin they vowed to boost the 'strategic cooperative partnership'.

However, it is difficult to see in what context the relationship would be strategic. Their joint opposition to the NATO actions in Yugoslavia did not stop the United States from meeting its objectives and their joint opposition to the US-led invasion of Iraq was similarly ineffective. Trade is very limited ($6 billion a year, far short of the $20 billion projected in 1996), and while China has seen some potential in new markets in Russia and the new states on its borders, this pales in comparison with the current and potential trade with the United States. The primary benefits for China are to secure its lengthy border against possible military threat and to access Russian military technology and natural resources. In fact, Chinese purchase of Russian weaponry, including submarines, guided-missile destroyers and advanced fighter aircraft, accounts for most of the trade. The most important aspect of Hu's visit was the agreement to build a 2,400 km pipeline to transport Siberian oil to the large Northeast China oilfield of Daqing. Previously, it was expected that Russia was more interested in serving only Japanese energy needs. President Hu also signed a symbolically important agreement with the 'Shanghai Cooperative Organization', a body set up by China and 5 central Asian states to form a regional security and trace block that could also serve as a counter to the US military presence. Showing the importance China attaches to the organization, the permanent secretariat that was agreed upon was to be in Beijing, not Shanghai.

Ultimately, for China and Russia the relationship is a secondary one to that with the United States. The enthusiasm with which either pursues the relationship will wax and wane dependent on the state of China–US relations. Russia might even find weapons sales a useful bargaining chip in its relationship such that it might be willing to limit further sales to gain US favour.

China and the Region

While Taiwan is the major sovereignty issue in the region, China has disputed claims with most of its neighbours including Russia, India and Vietnam, with all of whom it has fought a border war. In addition, it has territorial disputes with Japan and with a number of Southeast Asian neighbours over the demarcation of territorial boundaries in the South China Sea. Despite China's seat on the Security Council and Jiang Zemin's talk of 'big-country' diplomacy, China's interests are overwhelmingly regional (see Hinton, 1994, pp. 348–72). While China claims that it has no hegemonic ambitions in the region, its previous support to liberation movements in Asia, its rapidly growing economy, its relative military capacity and the ongoing territorial disputes make it the major cause of concern for most countries in the region.

Although much of China's foreign policy is rooted in Asia, at the conceptual level in the past it has rarely thought in regional terms at all. This was because its foreign policy was driven by the relationship between the superpowers and by ideological factors. China's leaders are now being forced to develop a regional policy and to think more carefully about engagement with regional institutions such as the Asia Pacific Economic Cooperation Forum (APEC) and the ASEAN Regional Forum (ARF). Increasingly, Beijing has begun to see the development of a 'Greater China' cultural and economic sphere that would include Hong Kong and Taiwan and that would benefit from more open markets in Asia. This was clearly indicated in November 2002 when Premier Zhu Rongji signed a commitment with the Association of Southeast Asian Nations (ASEAN) to form a free trade area by 2010; there is a little irony in China appearing as the leader of economic liberalization throughout the region. A deal was also signed to prevent clashes in disputed areas of the South China Sea. Through the 1980s, China enjoyed considerable success with ASEAN nations, helped by the situation in Kampuchea, and it was noticeably successful in allaying fears about its revolutionary past; this was seen most strongly with the restoration of diplomatic ties with Singapore and Indonesia.

However, difficulties remain in addition to the territorial conflicts, and most countries are worried about China's growing economic might. A number of the regional economies are complementary to China's but a number are also in competition. Countries such as Vietnam, Indonesia and Thailand are more likely to run into competition with China through their own production of textiles, light manufacturing and basic consumer goods. Indeed, one important reason for Vietnam agreeing to a major trade deal with the United States in July 2000 was its concern about the consequences of the recently signed deal between the United States and China. By contrast, Japan should be a natural partner with its capital, advanced technology and high-quality capital goods; however, this relationship is thwarted by political history, mutual suspicions and the concern of other ASEAN countries that Japan should not commit itself to China to the detriment of others.

Travelling around South and Southeast Asia in 2002–03, it was remarkable how often one heard fears expressed about China's development and how the countries would lose foreign investment to the expanding Chinese economy. Yet a Deutsche Bank study in 2003 showed that while China took 53 per cent of the region's FDI in 1995, it took 54 per cent in 2000! In the same period, Taiwan increased its FDI from 2.3 to 6.5 per cent and South Korea from 2 per cent to 13.6 per cent. That said, what we are clearly seeing is a reorganization of the production chain in Asia, with China becoming the most important assembly and manufacturing hub.

Japan is the most important bilateral relationship in the region. Despite the obvious compatibility of the two economies, two-way trade has suffered a number of problems and Japanese economic involvement in China remains far below its potential. The reasons have included the normal frustrations that foreign investors face, combined with the suspicions that both countries harbour about the other as a result of the Japanese invasion in 1937 and China's view that it has not yet made a satisfactory apology for its treatment of the Chinese during the occupation. This was very apparent in Jiang Zemin's 1998 visit to Tokyo, during which his attempts to elicit an apology from Japan's leaders were received negatively. Ill-feeling over the legacy of war was heightened by Prime Minister Koizumi's visit to the Yaukune Shrine to honour Japan's war dead in 2002. More recently, the renewal of the US–Japan security guidelines has caused Beijing concern and heightened its view that Japan plays an important role in the US attempts to constrain China. The presence of US troops in Japan and discussions of the theatre missile defence have increased these worries.

China and the United States have a common strategic interest in ensuring that there is no conflict on the Korean peninsula and that North Korea does not become a full nuclear power. For China, this anxiety is heightened by US arguments that North Korea is one of the countries against whom the missile defence system would be deployed and forms one of the three countries in President Bush's 'axis of evil' (Iraq and Iran being the others). The situation is tricky for Beijing, and both rapprochement between North and South and deterioration of relations present problems. The announcement by North Korea that not only was it developing nuclear weapons but that it already had nuclear capacity provided Hu Jintao with his first major crisis and challenged Beijing's preference to coax North Korea out of its shell, promote mild reform and keep it as a buffer against the US presence.

In mid-2000 the two Korean leaders held a summit that appeared to hold out the chance for rapprochement. The fact that Kim Jong-il, the North Korean leader, made his first trip abroad to Beijing just prior to the summit showed the continued importance of the relationship despite Beijing's establishment of diplomatic relations with the South in 1992. However, China's influence has been waning at a time when it needs it to strengthen. The North has been wary since China established relations with the South and its leaders are not convinced of the viability of China's economic reforms and their transferability to North Korea. Both Chinese and United States officials have expressed the same dismay about the North, and see it as a somewhat bizarre system that has an antiquated economy and an ineffective political system.

North Korea's provocation of the United States while the latter was involved in the conflict with Iraq raised problems for all concerned. The North seems to believe that it is next on the US hit-list and has stated that it will dismantle its nuclear capacity only if the US formally renounces military action and begins a programme of sizeable economic aid. US military action against the North is highly problematic given the close proximity of the South Korean capital and US and South Korean troops to the border. For the newly elected South Korean President, who had stoked up anti-Americanism during his campaign and who favours rapprochement, North Korea's actions are undermining.

These countries, including Japan, are looking to China to play a pivotal role in bringing North Korea to heel and starting an effective dialogue. Initially, China was reluctant to be publicly engaged and accepted North Korea's view that this was a bilateral issue between the United States and North Korea. However, through 2003, China's position began to shift. Many academics and members of the foreign affairs community were critical of China's hands-off approach, stating that it needed to think more clearly about the national interest. The last thing Beijing would want is a nuclear North Korea as this would encourage Japan and South Korea to pursue their own nuclear options and give credence to US claims for the need for a missile defence system with deployment in the region. However, action would mean compromising one important principle of China's foreign policy, non-interference in the affairs of another country. Despite waning influence, China does still control significant oil and food supplies to North Korea and in late February 2003, China shut down oil supplies for three days to protest North Korea's behaviour. In late April, China sponsored the first trilateral talks with North Korea and the United States. Although these talks failed to break the stalemate, they were an encouraging step forward.

For President Hu, unused to foreign affairs, this is a major challenge but China's engagement is crucial to any solution. China has a vested interest in restoring the status quo ante so that limited rapprochement might aid economic reform in North Korea and prevent regime collapse. China's preferred course is for a lengthy period of coexistence during which North Korea could adopt Chinese-style reforms that would leave the governing party in power presiding over a more liberalized economy. This outcome is looking less likely. The worst outcome for China would be system collapse that would bring even more migrants pouring over its borders and US troops even closer.

China's Foreign Economic Relations

One of the most striking aspects of the pragmatic post-Mao foreign policy has been the important role that economic factors have played. As late as 1977, the Chinese press was insisting that China 'would never receive foreign loans' and 'never allow foreigners to meddle in the management of our enterprises'. Despite the occasional hiccups and the frustrations of many foreign business investors, the speed of change has been staggering. Starting in 1979 Chinese development strategy shifted from import substitution, the privileging of accumulation over consumption and viewing foreign trade as irrelevant to economic growth, to an active interaction with the world economy in which foreign trade – and, latterly, investment – were seen as major engines of growth. China entered the global markets at a fortuitous time and with its cheap and abundant labour supply benefited from the rapidly unfolding globalization of the manufacturing process, rapid strides in telecommunications and internationalization of capital markets.

The economic figures speak for themselves. The ratio of foreign trade to GDP rose from 12.6 per cent in 1980 to 39.5 per cent in 1995; from 1990 to 2000 trade quadrupled from $115 billion to $475 billion (of which over 60 per cent is concentrated in Asia, with the United States accounting for 21 per cent of exports and 12 per cent of imports). In 2001 China's trade surplus was over $30 billion, 2.9 per cent of GDP, but it is worth noting that as a percentage it has declined every year since 1997. Using official exchange rate conversion, the trade: GDP ratio is 40 per cent, indicating that China's economy is relatively open (Huang, 2000, p. 3). The rise in the ratio was the

322 *Governance and Politics of China*

seventh most rapid among 120 countries (World Bank, 1997f, p. 2). However, it is worth pointing out that it was only in 1993 that China surpassed its 1928 level of two-way trade comprising 2.6 per cent of the world total; the total had fallen to only 0.6 per cent in 1977 (*The Economist*, 20 November 1999, p. 25). Now it is around 5 per cent of the world's total, but has accounted for around 50 per cent of the net increase in world trade (information from Pieter Bottelier). It is moving quickly, however, and by 2002 China had become the sixth trading nation in the world and is anticipated to be the third largest trader by the end of the decade. FDI, having appeared to peak in 1998, has moved ahead again, but about 60 per cent comes from Hong Kong and Taiwan. It is important to note that the nature of this investment changed from the 1980s to the 1990s. In the 1980s the concentration was on light industry, producing labour-intensive products that used simple production techniques and processes. From 1992, the new investors were Asian multinational corporations that invested in infrastructure, real estate and financial services (Yasheng Huang, 1998, pp. 5–6). This represented 40 per cent of FDI flows. China's own FDI in 1994 of $16 billion was second only to Taiwan among developing countries (however, Hong Kong and Macao were recipients of 61 per cent). Foreign reserves (excluding gold) touched $321 billion in 2003.

The desire for foreign technology combined with the constraints at the end of the 1970s meant that China turned to a variety of methods, both commercial and non-commercial, as well as boosting trade (for the politics of this, see Howell, 1993). The first major step was the adoption in 1979 of the Joint Venture Law, amended in 1990, that not only led eventually to equity joint-ventures but paved the way for the establishment of contractual joint ventures and wholly-owned foreign enterprises. This was China's first foray into the world of FDI. China also began to take medium and long-term loans on generally favourable terms from foreign organizations, governments and international organizations, such as the International Monetary Fund (IMF) and the World Bank. In 1986, the passage of the Law on Wholly Foreign-Owned Enterprises marked a further stage in the acceptance of foreign capital as a key plank in development policy.

Especially important was the decision in 1979 to establish four Special Economic Zones (SEZs) (Shenzhen, Zhuhai, Xiamen and Shantou) to function as export processing zones. They were important as pilots of reform for the rest of the Chinese economy and many new laws and regulations were tried out here. For example, there was the Labour Contract Law and the first piece of legislation issued by any level of the Chinese government that purported comprehensively to regulate business contracts between Chinese and foreign entities. At the same time the zones kept the rest of the Chinese economy isolated from the outside world, something considered good by Chinese conservatives and regrettable by Western economists. The more flexible economic policies were extended to 14 more coastal cities in April 1984 and Hainan island, which in 1988 became an independent province and was given the same powers as the original zones. In August 1987 the whole of Hainan was decreed a SEZ with more liberal policies than those currently in operation elsewhere. The strategy evolved by January 1985 to establish three large development triangles along the coast based around the Pearl River Delta, the Min River and the Yangzi River. The Yangzi development was seen as part of the resurrection of Shanghai as a key financial and trading centre, with the new development of Pudong as the focal point.

These zones were to operate as a 'window' for the introduction of technology, management techniques and information. The belief was also that 'trickle-down' would benefit the hinterland of China, and at the 1989 NPC meeting Premier Zhao Ziyang's 'coastal-strip strategy' was accepted. However, it was not without critics and even at the NPC meeting 300 voted against and 700 abstained. Essentially, the poorer areas were disgruntled with what they saw as the continued preferential treatment of already wealthy areas. Others criticized the economic benefits as negligible; they complained of the diversion of large amounts of funds to develop infrastructure and communications in the zones in exchange for which little advanced technology was brought in with only a small fraction of total output being exported. Some even suggested that the problems stemmed from the fact that there was no central planning in the zones. Last, but not least, there were attacks on the zones as carriers of a variety of 'bourgeois' afflictions that would undermine the communist edifice. However, the zones survived such attacks, even those that followed the 1989 crackdown and the removal of Zhao Ziyang. Rapidly, their 'specialness' became commonplace as many provinces and even towns took their own initiative to open free zones for foreign investors, even when there was no legal basis to do so. At the end of the 1990s, in its efforts to develop the western part of the country, the government formally allowed localities to increase the tax benefits for foreign investors.

Many have been dazzled by the levels of FDI going into China and most multinationals have been keen to gain a foothold in the Chinese market, but China's experience with FDI has been more nuanced than the headline figures reveal. This has been persuasively argued by Yasheng Huang (1998, 2000, 2003) who argues that the large amount of FDI reveals a fundamental weakness in China's economy, rather than strength. While there was gradual growth through the 1980s, Huang shows that the real take-off occurred between 1992 and 1994 and that the institutional imperatives on the Chinese side for FDI did not necessarily match the intentions of China's central policy-makers.

The FDI flows accounted for 73 per cent of the total FDI from 1979 to 1994, and a major stimulus came from the entry of new investors, including Taiwan and South Korea. In addition, there was the shift in investment noted above from simple manufacturing processes to more capital-intensive areas. This coincided with reforms in 1992 that were designed to remove sectoral restrictions on the use of FDI. The overall figures also conceal the regional variation of the importance of FDI: for example, in the 1990s inflows contributed 25 per cent of Guangdong's capital formation, while in Shenzhen it was in excess of 50 per cent.

As noted above, the rationale for opening up to FDI was to bring in advanced technology and capital. However, as Huang shows, certain institutional and policy characteristics increase the demand for FDI to a level in excess of what is justified by the demand for these two items alone. Of particular importance are two factors we have noted earlier in different contexts: the negotiated nature of the Chinese state and the impact of decentralization. Enforcement in China is largely discretionary and the localities have significant powers to renegotiate with Beijing the actual implementation of policy. Some have simply ignored central directives to make their own deals with foreign investors. When combined with investment demand by enterprises and the soft-budget constraints on them, this drives up the demand for FDI. The use of FDI can help avoid taxes and help the enterprise to gain reduced tariffs on certain imported goods. The benefits of FDI for domestic enterprises also led to the extensive phenomenon of 'round-trip' capital: these are funds that Chinese SOEs shift to Hong Kong and then reinvest in China as FDI. In 1991 there were 400 Chinese firms investing in Hong Kong and this number had risen to 2,000 by 1994. By 1993, China's cumulative investment of $20 billion exceeded that of Japan, making it the largest single investor. While this might help the individual enterprise it may cause a loss to the central state in terms of lost tax revenue. Last, but not least, Huang notes that much of the domestically oriented FDI does not contribute to financing new capacity but rather the acquisition of existing assets of SOEs. With the problems faced by SOEs and the government rejecting wholesale privatization, the only viable buyers are foreign companies.

In terms of the effectiveness of meeting central policy goals, Huang concludes that policy has failed for importing technological hardware but that the picture is mixed with respect to factors such as acquisition of new organizational techniques and managerial skills. Most of the enterprises that have foreign investment are labour rather than technology-intensive. Even in Shanghai, 80 per cent of such enterprises are judged to be 'labour-intensive'. Certainly large amounts of foreign capital have come in, but this happened at a time of a general significant rise in capital flows to developing countries. As we have seen, the primary use of FDI is often to evade restrictions on domestic enterprises, thus suggesting that it may not be used optimally. The FDI has also not been allowed to flow to the private sector of the economy where more effective use could be made.

The last vital component of early policy to open China's economy and integrate it into the world economy was the decentralization of the foreign trade apparatus. In the Mao years there was a highly centralized system of foreign trade agencies governing international economic relationships. The disadvantage of this system was that a large bureaucratic organization was situated between Chinese exporters and their foreign customers and Chinese importers and suppliers overseas. In fact, direct contact between buyers and sellers was discouraged. There was no incentive to trade because the foreign trade agencies retained all foreign exchange earnings for remission to the central government.

With the reforms, the number of state trading agencies increased and some companies were given the right to trade directly. Foreign trade companies were encouraged to form joint operations with productive enterprises so that for the first time there was a single entity responsible for production and marketing. In September 1984, the trading companies were transformed through regulations that converted them from government agencies with an official monopoly over certain product lines to competitive economic entities responsible for their own profits and losses. At the same time, the Ministry of Foreign Economic Relations and Trade lost its direct managerial control over state trading companies (in 2003, it was merged into the new Ministry of Commerce). Localities and enterprises were given a greater incentive to produce for the international market by allowing them to retain a portion of foreign exchange that they earned through foreign trade. This set of reforms stimulated an increase in foreign trade from $20 billion in 1978 to over $70 billion in 1986, and the ratio of exports to national output grew from 6 per cent in 1978 to 14 per cent in 1986. By 1994 the number of foreign trade corporations engaged in exporting was estimated to be around 9,400 and those importing at 8,700, while thousands of SOEs had direct trading rights (World Bank, 1997f, p. 12).

However, through most of the 1980s periodic surges were not balanced by export earnings, leading to balance of payment deficits. This was particularly a problem in 1985 immediately after the reforms when the central authorities' decision to boost the purchase of foreign goods to soak up the 1984 excessive wage increases combined with the loss of central control over imports, as localities acquired, legally and illegally, foreign exchange with which to buy consumer goods. The trade deficits led to the devaluation of the *yuan* by 20 per cent in December 1989 and by a further 10 per cent in November 1990 to make its products cheaper on the world market and to improve the trade balance. In fact, in December 1990 China posted its first trade balance since 1984, and with the exception of 1993 it has run a surplus ever since, reaching $43.6 billion in 1998. There was a sharp drop in 1999 to $29.7 billion, strengthening calls for WTO entry. In June 2003, the figure stood at $22.2 billion for the previous 12 months. Currently China, with a *de facto* peg to the dollar, has benefited from the dollar's decline leading to calls throughout the region for a revaluation of the Chinese currency and claims that China was exporting deflation.

By the end of the 1990s it had become apparent that the success of China's overall reform objectives would be determined by international factors outside of China's control. This was already the case before the agreements were reached between China and its major trading partners on WTO entry. The policy of raising foreign capital through the production of export goods depends on the health of the international economy and especially the views of the US Congress, while the need for advanced foreign technology imports depends on the status of Western import controls, a fact that was brought home to Beijing's leaders in the brief period of sanctions after 1989. There is no doubt that China is now integrated with the global economy and the fate of its domestic reforms are now more dependent on trends in the international economy than ever before. Previously, as Pearson (1999, pp. 187–8) has noted, the core of the Chinese economy had remained somewhat insulated from the competitive pressures of the world economy and the impact of trade had been more limited on the domestic economy than the figures might lead one to presume.

When implemented fully, WTO entry will have a significant impact on China's involvement in the world economy. The deals agree that eventually foreign companies will be able to own up to 50 per cent of joint telecommunications ventures, Premier Zhu offered the prospect of 51 per cent in April 1999, and foreigners will also be able to invest in Internet companies (previously, China had prohibited foreign investment in this sector). The deals were also particularly important for reducing tariffs. This was a particular concern for foreigners as in the early 1990s China's average tariffs were among the highest in the world, exceeded only by Egypt, India, Pakistan and Thailand (World Bank, 1997f, pp. 13–14). With tariffs falling through the 1990s in most developing countries, this put China under pressure to follow suit. The WTO agreement followed some earlier reductions announced in 1995 and brought the average down from 24.6 per cent to 9.4 per cent overall, and 7.1 per cent on US priority products. Participation in the Information Technology Agreement will eliminate all tariffs on items such as computers, telecommunications equipment and semiconductors. There are particularly deep cuts in the tariffs on cars, with the rate scheduled to fall from between 80 and 100 per cent to 25 per cent by 2006. In the agricultural sector the cuts in tariffs will come down from 31 per cent to 17.5 per cent and to 14 per cent for US priority products. In a major concession to US manufacturers and agricultural exporters, China agreed to relax its tight control over trading rights and distribution services, opening up repair and maintenance sectors as well as storage and transport.

In the financial and insurance sectors there were also dramatic concessions. Currently, foreign access in these areas is highly restricted; foreign banks are not allowed to conduct foreign currency business with Chinese clients (corporate or individual) and severe restrictions are applied geographically on the establishment of foreign banks. China agreed to full foreign access for US banks within five years; after two years foreign banks were to be allowed to conduct local currency business with Chinese firms and this would be extended to individuals three years later. There would also be national treatment for Chinese and foreign banks. Immediately upon accession, non-bank financial companies would be able to offer car financing. In the insurance business, China agreed to award licences solely on prudential criteria and eliminate geographic limitations within three years and expand the scope of activities. For life insurance, 50 per cent ownership would be allowed and life insurers would be allowed to choose their own joint-venture partners. For non-life insurance, China would allow 51 per cent ownership on accession and wholly-owned subsidiaries two years later.

Finally, there was a series of measures to deal with the problems of dumping, export surges and subsidies to the SOEs. The United States would be able to retain its anti-dumping policy for 15 years after China's accession to the WTO; and for 12 years the United States would be able to operate the Product Specific Safeguard that would protect against Chinese import surges that could cause market disruption there. There was a particular concern with textiles, and China agreed to extend safeguards to respond to increased imports into the United States until the end of 2008 (four years beyond the expiration of the Multi-Fibre Agreement (MFA)). With respect to the SOEs, China agreed that the enterprises would make purchases and sales based solely on commercial criteria and that US companies would be able to compete on non-discriminatory terms and conditions.

It is clear that such an agreement will have an enormous impact, not only on China's economy but also on its overall future development strategy. More than ever before China's success will be entwined with the performance of, and the demands of, the international economy. The questions remain why China should agree to this and what benefits it sees deriving from WTO entry (see Saich, 2002). First and foremost, China had very little choice, as not entering might have afforded protection over the short term for its economy but would have shut it out from the benefits that would accompany membership. For example, if China was outside of the WTO, it would more easily fall prey to unilateral sanctions for not just economic but also political behaviour. China's leaders were shocked by the post-1989 burst of Western sanctions and concerned about the US propensity to threaten sanctions against other regimes in the world that it does not like or that do not follow its policy lead. Also, although the MFA was a separate issue and China was protected until 2008, it feared that if it was not in the WTO it might become the target of textile quotas from a number of Western nations unable to apply them to countries within the WTO.

Second, China's desire to be an important player on the world stage means that it must be a member of key organizations to influence policy-making. Simply being outside is not acceptable and does not fit with Jiang Zemin's desire to project an image of a powerful country that needs to be consulted on major world affairs. Importantly, if China did not gain early entry into the WTO, a number of decisions would be made that would affect its vital interests without it having any input. Trade in services and agriculture are looming issues, as are the questions of workers' rights and environmental protection. On the first two, China has a strong economic interest in being part of the debate, whereas China does not feel that the latter should be a part of the WTO discussions at all. It needs to join before crucial decisions are made in such areas.

Third, a number of senior leaders seem to have concluded that without some strong external disciplining mechanism, economic reforms might grind to a halt as vested interests resisted further forward momentum. In essence, there is nothing in the WTO agreement that does not support the leadership's stated desire to move towards a market economy and, especially on the SOEs and the financial system, there will be pressure for more fundamental reform. It is always useful for a politician to have someone else to blame for tough decisions and, in China's case, who better than foreigners?

Fourth, WTO entry will bring a number of specific economic benefits to China. With Chinese economic growth slowing during the late 1990s and the state investment programmes showing limited signs of success at best, it is clear that new sources of growth must be found. A number of Chinese economists have suggested that WTO entry could add 2–3 per cent growth, enough to add 10–15 million jobs. In particular, WTO entry would improve market access for Chinese goods to major markets in Europe, Japan and the United States, especially for textiles and fashion goods, and telecommunications equipment. Further, as noted, FDI dropped in 1999 and WTO entry was seen as a way to boost FDI and to encourage more US and European FDI to supplement Hong Kong and Asian capital. In particular, China wishes to direct more FDI to develop the service sector which must expand significantly if China is to be able to absorb the surplus rural labour and laid-off industrial workers. One unintended effect may be increased foreign control over the private sector, which has been starved of funds because of official bias. If Beijing continues to prop up and privilege a moribund SOE sector, it may find that foreigners are funding the fastest-growing sector of the economy.

12

Challenges in the Twenty-First Century

As China entered the new century, it was clear that reforms had made enormous progress but the country was still far from being strong and wealthy as its leaders desire. The growth of its economy, its entry into the WTO and its permanent seat on the UN Security Council meant that it was being taken increasingly seriously in world affairs. However, there are considerable challenges ahead with the economic transformation and China has not clearly identified its role in the international community. This final chapter looks at three additional challenges that the CCP must confront if it is to survive the transition successfully. The first is the systemic corruption that has arisen because of economic opportunity combined with the lack of accountability. Second, there are the challenges deriving from new communications technology. Third are the dangers that arise from insufficient political reform.

The Internal Challenge: Corruption

Corruption has been a problem in all transitional systems and China has not been able to escape its effect. A string of Chinese leaders have railed against the effect that the widespread corruption has on undermining the legitimacy of the party, but none have been willing to suggest the kind of structural reforms that would help tackle it. Deng Xiaoping, Jiang Zemin and Hu Jintao all highlighted the rise in corruption as an issue that could affect the party's ability to survive, and reformers and conservatives alike have used the issue of corruption to push their own agendas. Reformers argue that corruption is caused by the incomplete nature of reform and suggest the best solution is to complete the market reforms and push ahead with political reform to make officials more accountable. Conservatives claim that corruption is caused by lack of party discipline and the increased Western influences that have entered with the economic opening. As Deng Xiaoping commented, you cannot open the door without letting in a few flies, although in China's case it is more like a swarm. Conservatives prefer to combine ideological campaigns with severe restrictions on how far the market should be expanded.

Jiang Zemin has tried to toe the difficult line between acknowledging that corruption has become a major problem but not accepting that the system is at fault. He accepts the premise that the party itself can combat corruption through public punishment of a limited number of senior officials, morality campaigns and tightening internal disciplinary mechanisms. This follows traditional CCP logic that while the party has made mistakes, it has always been the party that has corrected them and that people should trust it to do so in the future. As is shown below, it is difficult to see such methods being sufficient to stop the levels of corruption from rising further.

The pursuit of economic riches without genuine marketization and democratization and where power remains hierarchically structured with information dependent on position and party membership lies behind the corruption of party members. This is not a new phenomenon, it is just that now with the increased commercialization and moneterization of the economy there is more to be corrupt about, and the stakes can be higher. It is not easy to gauge the extent of corruption, but it has clearly increased with reforms and has become much more visible. A study of corruption by senior officials conducted by Tsinghua scholars Hu Angang and Guo Yong (available at www.china.org.cn) found that before 1992 the amounts involved had never exceeded 100,000 *yuan*. Of the 37 cases post-1992, 27 exceeded 100,000 *yuan*, with 12 cases in excess of 1 million and 4 cases over 10 million *yuan*.

In the Mao period, most of the corruption was kept hidden behind what appeared outwardly to be relatively plain living. It usually took the form of dining at public expense and travel on the state's ticket. It could take more venal forms of ruthless persecution of villagers under local-party official control. For example, a court proclamation put up in Nanjing in 1977, revealed how vulnerable people sent down from the cities to work in the communes were to the party secretaries. Many wanted to return to the city for education but this could happen only if the party secretary of the commune approved. In this case, the party secretary had used his power to demand sexual favours from some 16 young women in return for processing their applications; showing the hierarchical principles, the deputy secretary had demanded sexual favours from only 12.

The system of intense bureaucratic control over distribution, the increasingly arbitrary control over personal life and the concentration of power in individual hands undermined social cohesion and trust in officials and laid the basis for the corrupt behaviour by officials that dogs the system to this day. Walder (1994, pp. 297–323) and others have noted that party authority was founded upon citizen-dependence upon officials for satisfaction of material needs and for access to career opportunities. This system increased cynicism towards officialdom and a disrespect for those in authority who were seen as self-serving rather than 'servants of the people', as the official ideology claimed. Paradoxically, perhaps, the structure led to an expansion in the use of connections to obtain goods, often those to which one was entitled, and an increased reliance on the immediate and extended family. These trends became more pronounced during the Cultural Revolution and have persisted into the reform era and provide the underlying basis for the more spectacular corruption witnessed in recent years. This has been supplemented by the collusion between individual entrepreneurs and party officials.

The reforms have presented officials with far greater opportunities, political and social controls have relaxed and financial decentralization has provided greater motivation to engage in corrupt activities. At the March 2003 NPC meeting, the procurator-general announced that since the previous full NPC (1998) 207,103 cases of corruption had been investigated of which 5,541 were considered major cases involving over 1 million *yuan*. These major cases had involved 12,830 officers at the county level or above. This represents, in part, the greater seriousness with which the party leadership has taken corruption since 1998. At the 1998 NPC meeting, fully 40 per cent of the delegates voted against the report of the procurator-general, signalling their disgust with the rising tide of corruption and the laxness of the authorities in dealing with it.

For such a big country, such figures do not seem particularly large, but it is just the tip of the iceberg. The big cases have been spectacular. It is estimated that during the 12-year rule of the former corrupt mayor and later party secretary of Beijing, over 18 billion *yuan* disappeared from the municipal coffers. In 2000, it was discovered that a vice-chair of the NPC had pocketed over 40 million *yuan* and was found out only when he was recorded gambling in Macao, losing heavily, and not batting an eye over the losses. In a massive smuggling scandal in Xiamen, it is estimated that at least 80 billion *yuan* had gone missing. By the end of 2000, major cases that reached high in the party had also been unveiled in Shenyang (Liaoning province), Shantou (Guangdong) and in the State Power Company. The diversion of public funds occurs at all levels. For example, a mixture of corruption, negligence and shady investments had caused losses of over 1 billion *yuan* from Shanghai's medical, pension and housing funds (*SCMP*, 10 August 2000, Internet edition). In September 2000, about 1,000 farmers in one county and a further 300 in another township demonstrated to protest the embezzlement of funds by officials. In the township, the farmers' homes had already been knocked down but there were no funds available for their resettlement (*SCMP*, 29 September 2000).

As in other countries, major infrastructure programmes are magnets for considerable corruption. The most recent example is the huge project to dam the Yangtze River at the Three Gorges, a project already billed at $72 billion and designed to boost electricity by 10 per cent and to tame downstream flooding. This on-and-off-again project was a favourite of former Premier Li Peng, making discussion of associated corruption impossible. After he moved to chair the NPC in Spring 1998, more information about the scale of corruption involved has slowly but surely been made public. An audit of the resettlement project revealed that 473 million *yuan* had been misappropriated (8.8 per cent of the total funds audited) and used to build offices, dormitories and to set up companies (*Xinhua*, 28 January 2000). In addition, in July 2000 it was reported that 97 government officials involved in the project had been found to have engaged in corrupt practices. One official was condemned to death for stealing 15 million *yuan* to invest in a hotel, while another stole 650,000 *yuan* from one of the resettlement accounts. Apparently a further 425 million *yuan* is still missing and while staff at the Three Gorges Economic Development Corporation had not been paid for 11 months, their boss had run away with over 1 billion *yuan* (*SCMP*, 3 May 2000, Internet edition). Between 1.5 and 2 million inhabitants are scheduled to be moved, and the diversion of resettlement funds has also been causing unrest.

The partial reforms combined with the weak legal system have been a structural cause of corruption. In the 1980s, one of the main sources of corruption was the dual-pricing system under which officials could acquire goods at low state-regulated prices and then sell them on at a higher market price. This was gradually eradicated, especially after 1992 as the number of goods sold at controlled prices was drastically reduced. However, other causes have arisen, such as those provided by the conversion of enterprise ownership and the associated asset-stripping that has taken place (see Ding, 2000, pp. 1–28).

One particular group to have benefited from the opportunities provided by the incomplete reforms and the state's continued control over information and resources has been the children of senior cadres, especially those in the military, referred to as the 'Princeling's party' (*taizi dang*). They formed a focal point of the 1989 student-led protests that criticized 'official speculation' (*guandao*). By the late 1980s many urban dwellers felt that Chinese society had become one 'on the take' where, without a good set of connections and an entrance through the 'back door', it was virtually impossible to participate in the benefits of economic reform. In this situation, the sight of children of high-level officials joy-riding in imported cars was a moral affront to many ordinary citizens. To try to give the impression of responding to these concerns the leadership launched a widely publicized campaign against corruption. On 28 June 1989 the Politburo adopted a seven-point programme to deal with corruption. This addressed issues such as closing down firms that had engaged in potentially corrupt activities, preventing the children of senior officials from engaging in commercial activities and limiting perks derived from officials' positions such as entertaining, travel abroad, special supply of scarce goods and driving around in imported cars (*Beijing Review*, 1989, 32(32), pp. 7–13). However, especially since 1992 the situation has become even worse. Much of the money is made in the underground economy, estimated at around 1 trillion *yuan* in 2002 (*SCMP*, 2 January 2003) (see Box 12.1).

BOX 12.1

The Rainbow Economy

The underground economy is booming in China with the reforms, and it is estimated that China's gross domestic product (GDP) would have been 10 per cent higher in 2002 if this had been calculated into the official figures. The exposure of corruption in the Northeast city of Shenyang (see Box 7.3) revealed the deep links between officials, entrepreneurs and gangland. Millions of dollars were gambled away. Officialdom seems to have been 'wedded' not only to mistresses but also to mobsters whose networks reached far and wide. Some have even suggested that money from ill-gotten gains is a major factor causing the increase in income inequality. Researchers at Tsinghua University claim that if one included unpaid taxes and other illegal income the Gini coefficient would have risen in 2001 from 0.42 to 0.49.

So common has illicit economic activity become that some describe the economy in terms of five colours:

Black represents money from robbery and theft
Blue represents smuggling, often associated with customs and the navy
Red represents official corruption, being the colour of the party
White represents gains from drug trafficking
Yellow represents money from pornography and the sex trade.

The value of being an official is reflected in the return of the traditional practice of 'buying and selling official posts' (*maiguan maiguan*). In Hepu township in Guangxi province the going rate for the position of deputy party chief was $10,000, $2750 to be a bureau chief and $2500 to run a small neighbouring town (*International Herald Tribune*, 12 March 1999). In one county in Anhui the position of grain station chief cost $3620 (*FEER*, 20 August 1998, p. 13), a good position at that time to exploit the gap between state-mandated prices for grain and the full market prices. As with all things, it is difficult to know how widespread the practice is, but it is an issue openly talked about in many of the localities that I have visited.

Spectacular as these cases may be, ordinary citizens are more concerned about the everyday small corruption that makes their life complicated: the red envelopes filled with money to get to see a doctor or to get the prescription that is one's right, the illegal fees that are paid to the schools to make sure that children get the education they are promised, and so on. Popular displeasure with their officials and the corruption that pervades their lives is shown by the commonplace sayings and jokes. Local people often complained to me that they are required to provide cadres the best housing, the prettiest women in the village to marry and the fattest pigs to slaughter for the celebrations. The 'four basic principles' of the party have been reworked as:

In eating, the basic principle is for other people to invite you.
In things you desire, the basic principle is for people to give you them as gifts.
For one's remuneration, the basic principle is to do no work.
As for one's wife, the basic principle is who needs her? (From David Cowhig)

Generally Chinese are not very confident in the leadership's capacity to deal with corruption effectively. A survey of the Beijing-based private polling company, Horizon, released in December 2000, makes for sober reading. Only 12 per cent of its over 2,000 respondents were very confident about the fight against corruption. By contrast, 40 per cent had little or no confidence in the government's attempts (Information from Horizon staff, January 2001).

Faced by such problems, the leadership has been unwilling to accept that there is a systemic problem and has continued to rely primarily on ideological exhortation and internal mechanisms such as the use of discipline inspection commissions (CDICs). The commissions were abolished in the Cultural Revolution and reestablished as the primary mechanism for dealing with discipline and monitoring abuses within the party. The approach has clearly not worked and the commission has often been blocked from carrying out investigations by powerful local party barons. This has led the central party leadership to consider de-linking local commissions from reporting to the party committee at the same level. It may be that in the future, provincial and municipal commissions may report directly to the central commission. The hope is that the regional commissions will become more independent but this will not answer the fundamental question of *Quis Custodiet Ipsos Custodes* – 'Who Will Guard the Guardians?'

The party has rejected the idea that there is a role for an independent monitoring authority, but it has given more licence to the media to expose examples of corruption at the grass roots level. However, given party control over publishing and especially television, such exposés work under severe constraints and it would be impossible to reveal the wrongdoing of a senior official without Politburo approval. That said, the press has become livelier in this respect and television programmes such as *Law and Society* and *In Focus* do push against the limits, and their reporters are often abused by local powerholders. In fact, it is remarkable how mentioning official corruption moved from being taboo at the beginning of the 1990s to being a major topic of discussion in the media by the end of the decade. It is also clear that some leaders feel that the media can play a more important role in exposure. In late July 2000, a senior figure from the CDIC praised the media for its role in exposing corruption and helping to clean up the party (*Xinhua*, 27 July 2000); however, he stressed that the work of the media should be pursued in collaboration with local discipline inspection commissions. Unauthorized investigation is not tolerated. In 1998, An Jun set up a group called Corruption Watch that grew to have 300 members across 12 provinces and uncovered some 100 cases of corruption. For his efforts, An was charged with subversion of state power and sentenced to prison (*SCMP*, 18 April 2000).

This presents the party leadership with a dilemma, as the more corruption is reported, the more people are liable to see the party as lacking credibility. The reluctance to pursue senior figures unless there is political gain only increases this tendency. For example, the exposure of Beijing Party Secretary, Chen Xitong, and his supporters in 1995 would not have happened without the factional in-fighting with General Secretary Jiang Zemin. The fact that he was not sentenced until 1998 is indicative of the resistance within the party to his sentencing and the delicacy with which the case had to be treated. It gave Chen the dubious honour of being the most senior official behind bars for corruption. Similarly, the huge corruption scandal that unfolded in Xiamen during 2000 also became embroiled in elite party politics (see Box 12.2). The case was brought to trial in September–October 2000 and it appeared that a small number of local officials were executed, including the chief of the Xiamen customs and the deputy head of the provincial police. The protection of key central officials raises questions about the impartiality of the investigations, while some senior leaders resented Jiang Zemin's protection of Jia Qinglin and his promotion to the Standing Committee of the Politburo and as head of the CPPCC. The exposure of the case in the international press in early 2000 probably led to the decision to execute a vice-governor of Jiangxi province, the arrest of one of the vice-chairs of the NPC and a number of other medium-ranking officials around the time of the annual NPC meeting. The vice-governor had siphoned off some 4 million *yuan* and thus earned the title of the most senior official to be executed since 1949. This was to forestall possible criticism from delegates that the party was again being lax in pursuing corruption. The title was held only briefly, as the NPC vice-chair, Cheng Kejie was executed in September 2000 for taking some 41 million *yuan* in bribes while heading the government of Guangxi province (*Xinhua*, 31 July and 15 September 2000). The *People's Daily* (31 July 2000) acknowledged explicitly that Cheng's case was to be used as a 'negative example and cautionary lesson' for others. The case formed the centrepiece of the CCP's latest campaign to eradicate corruption within the administration.

In 2002–03, there was a shift in focus to investigate high-profile individual entrepreneurs who had evaded taxes or who had been implicated in collusion with and the bribery of local officials. Perhaps completing the story of Shenyang's corruption was the arrest of Chinese-born Dutch passport holder, Yang Bin. He was arrested after the North Korean government had appointed him to head an export-processing zone on the border. The lack of consultation with Beijing was clearly a step too far and he was swiftly arrested and his shady land deals and bribes landed him in jail. His most audacious project was a $360 million Holland village theme park that seemed to deplete the resources of his orchid growing business. Certainly before his arrest he was often seen with local leaders as well as some from the national level. The corruption scandals have left their mark on Shenyang and its brief boom in the mid-1990s has been exposed as primarily a scam. It has also affected the remaining officials who, the new mayor claims, do not work as there are no bribes to provide an incentive (*SCMP*, 17 April 2002).

The party is pursuing a number of policies to try to improve the situation, but none of them is likely to have the desired effect without broader political reform that removes the structural incentives for corruption. This has not been lost on Chinese analysts, a number of whom have begun to write about the link between corruption and political structure as an unintended effect of economic reform (see, for example He, 1998). In addition to the sentencing of key malfeasors and ideological exhortation, the party has tried to improve the quality of the judges, to professionalize the civil service, to raise pay for government officials and to make the financial activities of local administrations

---

BOX 12.2

Politics and Corruption: The Case of Xiamen

High-level politics became embroiled in the spectacular smuggling case of the *Yuanhua* (Farewell) Group based in Xiamen. Political connections first led to the investigation being delayed and sidetracked and attempts to protect the image of a Jiang Zemin protégé. Around 80 billion *yuan* is the usual figure said to have been involved in the smuggling and other scams run by *Yuanhua*. However, the real figure may even be as high as 150 billion *yuan*. The smuggling covered firearms, vehicles, crude oil and electrical items. The fact that senior figures from not only the provincial level but also Beijing and the PLA have been involved deadlocked resolution of the case for some time. It is claimed that the PLA, especially the Navy and the General Staff Department, the police, the Ministry of State Security, customs, banks and various personnel, economic and foreign trade departments were involved. The patron was a former vice-Mayor of Xiamen and he was allowed to escape to Australia and several children of senior party officials were allowed to flee. Most importantly, Lin Youfang, the wife of Politburo member Jia Qinglin, was involved. Ms Lin was the head of the Fujian provincial Import and Export Corporation, the trading organization of the provincial government; it seems inconceivable that she was not aware of the corruption. This presented problems for Jiang Zemin as Jia was not only an ally but also Jiang's choice to replace disgraced party secretary Chen Xitong in Beijing. Too active pursuit of the case would reach high into the party and undermine party credibility further. Jiang was at pains to display his confidence in Jia. It took three years for the Politburo to authorize action on the case and then apparently only after Premier Zhu had threatened, in summer 1999, to resign unless something was done. The case was brought to trial in September–October 2000 and 84 people were sentenced, including 11 sentenced to death. In late 2000, a second round of trials was underway. The protection of key central officials raises questions about the impartiality of the investigations while some senior leaders have resented Jiang Zemin's protection of Jia Qinglin and his subsequent elevation.

more transparent. All these measures will help, but as long as there is no systemic reform or independent control over the activities of party officials, the impact will be limited. Political credibility notwithstanding, senior officials at the central and provincial levels should not be that difficult to control; the power elite is not that numerous. If the village elections were made more effective, this would give people greater control over who was elected to local leadership, especially if the party was made more accountable. The big problem is controlling the activities of those at the county and township level who can resist scrutiny from above and below. Moving up the level of direct elections has been suggested by some in China would be a start, but it is resisted by many officials at this level.

The External Challenge: The Information Revolution

The advent of the information revolution and the need for information that is delivered reliably and at high speed provide a major challenge for governance. The embarrassment caused to the CCP by the exposure of its cover-up of SARS during the winter of 2002–03 shows how porous the country's information system is and how vulnerable it can be to cross-border information flows. However, the Chinese government has committed itself strongly to the development of the Internet and has invested some $50 billion in telecoms and data-processing hardware. China's leaders realize that if their aspirations for major power status are to be realized they have to adopt these new technologies, and they see a great potential for the development of e-commerce despite the obvious current obstacles.

The Chinese government has traditionally practised a system of information control and censure, with an intricate grading process for who at what level was allowed to see which kinds of information. For example, in June 2002 the Propaganda Department issued a circular to its local branches calling for tighter control over the media leading up to the Sixteenth Party Congress, it banned or put tight controls on 32 subject areas. Banned were obvious topics such as details on violent news, scandals and pornography but also the advocacy of private ownership and constitutional amendments to this effect, excessive coverage of China's foreign soccer coach and the misuse of funds for Project Hope (a charity associated with the Communist Youth League, a power base of Hu Jintao). *Xinhua* official reports were to be used when covering major accidents or epidemics of animal diseases, while events such as the soccer World Cup, private entrepreneurs being selected as party delegates, blood selling, the impact of the WTO and lawsuits brought by civilians against government officials were all to be 'carefully reported' (*FBIS-CHI*-2002-0621).

There has been a substantial tradition in China of managing information flows to ensure that the state is the primary, if not sole, provider of information. The CCP has tried to channel information flows so that they are vertically linked and it has eschewed the horizontal flow of information. This has meant that access to information in the Chinese system has formed an important basis for power and the ability to provide the correct interpretation of the past has provided the legitimacy to decide on current policy (Saich, 1995, pp. 299–338). Under such a system, the real basis of exchange is secrets and privileged access to information. However, the advent of the Internet makes it much more difficult for the CCP to manage information flows and to ensure that its view of events prevails (see Box 12.3).

BOX 12.3

Governing in the Age of Information Pluralism

The terrible tragedy of the death of over 40 people, mostly children, in an explosion at a school in Fanglin village, Jiangxi Province (March 2001) revealed how difficult it is to control a story in the world of the Internet and information pluralism. In an unusual step, at a press conference at the March 2001 NPC, Premier Zhu Rongji announced that the explosion had been the action of a single madman who had blown up the school. The explosion was an embarrassment to the leadership following a series of accidents that highlighted the poor work safety conditions that existed in China. Coming at the time of the annual NPC meeting in Beijing compounded the problem. It is unusual for a Chinese leader to comment on such an issue and to make such a categorical statement. It is unclear who had advised him on the issue and why he chose to confront it so bluntly. Some have even speculated that he was set up by his political opponents.

The area in Jiangxi is famous for its production of fireworks, and local villagers claimed that not only were fireworks stored at the school but also that the children worked on making them to earn extra income for the school's coffers. The local villagers informed the domestic press, the Hong Kong press and the foreign media of their views and that a major cover-up was underway. Their story was confirmed by county officials reached by phone. A curfew was imposed, the school was bulldozed, preventing any genuine investigation and outsiders were prevented from entering the village. However, Zhu's official version of events was undermined by access to the Internet and the foreign media. Chatrooms very quickly filled with alternate versions of what had happened and called on the government for a better response. Interestingly, the local press in China was also assertive in contradicting the centre's account. This caused Zhu the following week to make an apology for the explosion, he stuck to his original explanation but admitted that up until two years before fireworks had been manufactured at the school. This had stopped in 1999 when an explosion at a fireworks factory in a nearby village had killed 35 people. Importantly, Zhu stated that it was the Hong Kong and foreign press reporting of the villagers' version of events that had caused him to check on what had happened. He had sent a 6-person undercover team to investigate. However, it is debatable what they could discover and how anonymous they could be in a rural village community. This inability to manage the news as effectively as in the past is indicative of challenges that will increasingly confront the CCP in the future (*New York Times* and Associated Press reports).

This system can starve leaders of the reliable information they need to make appropriate policy decisions. The more coercive the regime, the more that which passes up is what leaders want to hear; negative information is suppressed and its agents repressed. What globalization demonstrates better than at any point in the past is that at a certain developmental point – that is, where the need for information becomes very great – it becomes extremely difficult to reduce coercion without inviting vast structural change. In the Soviet Union prolonged coercion and bureaucratization so deprived the state of the capacity to innovate that eventually it broke apart. What appeared at the top as rational public planning was based on a jerrybuilt system of deals and private negotiations (Apter and Saich, 1994, Chapter 9).

In the Soviet Union not only did little accurate information filter to the top, the top rejected and suppressed what little it got. Nor could the directors of such a highly centralized state system trust one another or their party representatives. Once the move was made to transform the Soviet Union into a high-information, low-coercion system, the entire organizational structure unravelled. This is precisely the problem that the current leadership in Beijing is trying to grapple with. It is not surprising that the rapid spread of the Internet and new information technology has caused unease among those managing the system as it threatens their monopoly over the flow of information. This does not mean, however, that the CCP cannot set up new systems of control or that there will be an automatic progression from more Internet users to greater political pluralism.

In a number of respects, the leadership of the CCP has treated the Internet in the same way as it has traditional print forms. It has tried to institute a system of controls that will allow it to participate in the benefits of faster information flows without having to open up the information system and allowing in the disadvantages of views and information that may challenge the CCP's interpretation of events. First, it has only authorized 4 networks for international access in order to control information flows. New regulations issued in October 2000 required Internet content providers to obtain Ministry of Information approval for joint-ventures or any business cooperation with foreign investors, and are to be held responsible for blocking 'illegal content' and 'subversive content' from spreading through their web sites (*Xinhua*, 2 October 2000). In addition to pornographic materials, it has also blocked access to the websites of publications such as the *New York Times*, CNN, those human rights organizations that are critical of China and groups that are pro-Taiwan or pro-Tibet. In addition, the state has forbidden China-based websites from using news derived from websites that are situated outside of the Mainland. This has resulted in a number of service providers in China dropping news services from their menu and concentrating on 'safe' areas of information provision, such as sports and entertainment. In addition, traditional media forms are prohibited from using material derived from any website.

To gain better control over the sector, the CCP has introduced a number of key pieces of legislation and carried through institutional reorganization. In March 1997, the amended Criminal Code included three new articles outlining 'serious crimes' of leaking or misusing information. At the end of 1997, the Ministry of Public Security published its 'Regulations on Security and Management of Computer Information Networks and the Internet' that made it a crime to damage national security and disclose state secrets. In January 2000, the State Secrecy Bureau published its own detailed regulations concerning state secret protection and the use of computer information systems on the Internet. In May 2000, personal websites were banned.

Organizationally, in April 1996 the State Council set up the Steering Committee on National Information Infrastructure to coordinate Internet policy until its functions were absorbed by the newly-created Ministry of Information Industry. The Ministry was created in 1998 and includes the former ministries of posts and telecommunications, radio, film and broadcasting and the 'leading group' on information policy. The Ministry is the primary regulator for this sector, thus reducing the potential for bureaucratic fragmentation, and it reports directly to the State Council. The Ministry of Public Security has set up a Computer Management and Supervision Office to deal with crimes involving computers and had hired some 2,000 people nationwide by 2000. In February 1999 the State Information Security Appraisal and Identification Management Committee was established to coordinate the anti-cyber crime campaign. It is directly under the State Council (Foster, 2000, pp. 33–4).

The Ministry of Information Industry, particularly under its former head, Wu Jichuan, has been hostile to allowing foreigners market access, for both political and commercial reasons. In fact, in early November 1999, Minister Wu was loudly trumpeting that foreigners would not be allowed to become involved in the development of Internet operations in China and he was very hostile to the supposed offer in April 1999 that foreign firms could eventually take a 51 per cent stake in telecommunications. In principle, the agreement on the WTO should significantly alter this situation and China has ceded that the Internet is open to foreign investment. Telecommunications companies will be able to control up to 49 per cent of telecommunications service companies upon accession to the WTO, and 50 per cent after 2 years. However, cases will be dealt with on an individual basis and it is the Ministry itself that will make the decisions on granting licences. This, in combination with political sensitivities and local protectionism, would suggest that there will be a concerted attempt to restrict foreign access in the Internet sector, especially for Internet service providers (ISPs).

The Chinese leadership is clearly aware that it cannot completely control the flow of information or access to forbidden sites by its citizens. Its intention is to lay down warnings about the limits of the permissible and to deter the casual browser from becoming too inquisitive about the world outside. In this limited respect, it may be successful. Even though China has become extremely porous in terms of information flows, there is scant evidence to suggest that this alone has challenged the CCP's monopoly on political interpretation for the majority. It should be remembered that in 2000 90 per cent of its households were still without telephones and 99 per cent of the population did not have access to networked computers (Shao, 1998, p. 12). However, usage is developing rapidly. While in 1990 there were only 10 million telephone lines, by 2000 there were 125 million, with 2 million being added each month. Mobile phones have boomed from 5 million in 1995 to over 57 million in 2000 (*Economist*, 22 July 2000, p. 24). While still low by developed-country standards, this is about three or four times the rate in India. The rise of Internet users is also dramatic, with as one would expect a heavy preponderance in the major eastern cities and the wealthier provinces. By the end of 2002 there were reported to be 59.1 million Internet users in China, up from 22.5 million just two years earlier (for regular updates see China Network Information Centre, http:/ /www.cnnic.cn). However, the rate of increase was slowing somewhat as most of those who were enthusiastic and had affordable access were already online. Of these users, the highest percentage is in Guangdong (9.5), followed by Jiangsu (8.1) and municipalities of Shanghai (7.1) and Beijing (6.6). At the bottom are Tibet (0.1), Qinghai and Ningxia (0.3), Hainan (0.4) and Guizhou (0.8). Of those online, 59.3 per cent are male, 55 per cent are 24 or younger, 62.5 per cent access at home while 53.1 per cent use it for information and 24.6 per cent for entertainment.

It is likely that China's response to the Internet will be differentiated, with much stricter controls on news and political information and practices and controls that more clearly match international practice for e-commerce dealings. Indeed, there are new opportunities that the Internet brings for China. Chinese will be the second language of the Internet and may even become dominant. This provides propagandists in Beijing with untold new opportunities to try to shape a Chinese political culture that stretches well beyond its physical boundaries.

However, even in the commercial area there are security concerns that can be played upon by ministries and other groups in China to restrict foreign access. For example, in January 1996 the State Council announced that the *Xinhua* news agency, run by the government, would in the future be responsible for the distribution of all on-real time economic information that was disseminated by agencies such as Dow Jones and Reuters. This would totally defeat the purpose of such services. The official reason given was to check content to ensure that there were no inaccuracies in the information provided or nothing that was hostile to China. The real reason was the manipulation of leaders' fears of unrestricted information flows to use the argument of state security to obtain an economic monopoly. *Xinhua* was apparently left out of the spoils of the new technology and saw this as a good way to make money (Interviews with representatives of foreign companies involved in these negotiations).

There can be no doubt that a China that is increasingly wired and connected internationally will be more difficult for the CCP to control. The rise of 'virtual communities' that transcend traditional jurisdictions and even sovereign boundaries is difficult for China's current generation of Soviet-trained leaders to contemplate. It is far removed from their notions of modernity where planning, heavy industry and electricity represented progress.

SARS revealed again the fundamental tension between a regime structured to control information and a society that is savvy about communications. Treating citizens as children who need to be spoonfed information and hear only good news is no longer viable when urban elites are part of a global information community tracking down and trading information online. You cannot have a domestic system saying that there is nothing wrong while cyberspace tells China's citizens that there most certainly is a problem. It is not even a question of who is correct, it is dysfunctional. It is also dangerous and threatens to undermine the social stability that the leadership desires to ensure economic development. If there is no trust in domestic reporting, people will turn to foreign sources or listen to rumour, leading to greater levels of discontent and distrust. Denial and cover-up can only work against the leadership's long-term interests.

The Final Challenge: Good Governance and Political Reform

The biggest challenge facing the CCP in the twenty-first century is to provide good governance and grapple with the political consequences of its own programme of economic reforms. Confronted by the potential for social unrest, the Chinese senior leadership has preferred to slow down the pace of reform once it bites and perpetuate a system of authoritarian political control. The question is whether Hu Jintao will break out of this pattern. While dramatic change is highly unlikely, the new leadership seems to be tolerating limited discussion and quietly reviewing local experimentation with transparency and accountability. In addition, many expect Hu to start with a series of reforms to make the party more democratic internally.

There was little by way of systematic thinking on political reform offered by the Sixteenth Party Congress but there have been some positive glimmerings subsequently. As we have seen in the chapters above there has been a dramatic expansion of the market, estimated by Hu Angang (Personal communication) in 1999 at 80 per cent. In 1978, before the reforms began, the state controlled almost all output from the service sector, 94.4 per cent of agricultural production and 97.5 per cent of industrial production was sold at state fixed prices. Despite such changes, the policies of the state and its organizational structure still do not reflect governance of a mixed economy, with the continuation of preferential policies for the state-owned sector, progress but continuing bias against the private sector and an administrative structure that cleaves too closely to that of the pre-reform era.

Many observers expected that with the expansion of the market economy, the role of the state would decline in transitional economies, including China. However, this has not been the case and reform has brought with it state expansion into new areas while old functions have not necessarily been terminated (based on Saich, 2003). Indeed, a withering away of the state may not be the most appropriate approach. One of the primary problems in post-communist Russia has been the lack of an effective state apparatus to guide the process of market transition. A market economy without an effective enabling environment of rules and regulations implemented by a relatively impartial judiciary results in an anarchic free-for-all.

First and foremost an effective, as distinct from strong, state structure is a precondition for any hope of successful reform. Certainly, the role of the state in the economy will change with a narrower set of interventions and less direct administrative interference. However, an increase in state capacity is a prerequisite for an effective market to function. The state must adjudicate the increasingly contentious nature of economic market transactions. This means that it is the obligation of the state to establish a sound legal system. In addition, the state must manage the key macroeconomic variables and ensure that economic and investment policy is not distorted by price-fixing or subsidy supports that have outlived their rational lifetime. It must deal with revenue collection and distribution, and this will help the state to provide minimum social services and welfare guarantees to protect those who are vulnerable in the shift to a market economy.

Far from making governance easier, the shift to less administrative inter-ference and curtailing the direct provision and administration of services makes it more complex. The Chinese state has added to its old monopoly functions new regulatory roles that are broader and more complex than before, and that will become even more complex as China eases its way into the WTO. The Chinese government needs to dismantle old ministries and organizations, adapt the roles of others while creating new ones to serve the needs of a WTO world.

The experience of Russia provides a salutary warning that it is preferable to start with the existing social and political institutions and try to stimulate incremental transformation through the judicious use of incentives. An unregulated and ungoverned market will produce chaotic results. The altern-ative approach is what Stiglitz (1999) denounces as an 'institutional blitz-krieg'. Neither is wholesale privatization of functions an answer. The precise role that property rights plays in the transition process is more ambiguous than orthodoxy might suggest. As Rawski (1999) suggests, they may play a less important role than economists usually ascribe to them. Market struc-tures and the institutional arrangements surrounding business enterprises often exercise greater influence over performance, efficiency and profitability than the nature of ownership. Private monopolies will not necessarily function any better than state-run ones, what matters is how the competition is regulated. The key factor is 'control' rather than 'ownership'. As Rodrik (1999) has noted, formal property rights will not have a significant effect unless they confer control rights and 'sufficiently strong control rights' may be effective in the absence of formal property rights. The development of TVEs in China might be a good case in point.

So how are we to make sense of this with reference to the role of the state in China? Merquior's (1993) general assessment that 'The truth is that we have simultaneously too much state and too little state' applies well to China. Or, put another way, the Chinese state is too directly involved in those areas that can be better left to the market of civil society and has absented itself from certain key areas where the public good argument supports greater involvement. With respect to fiscal capacity there is 'not enough'. Increasing the state's fiscal capacity will go a long way to resolving many of the governance challenges that China is facing, but this alone is insufficient and much remains to be done for government to shift, to use the World Bank's phrase from 'rowing' to 'steering' future development.

While many observers had anticipated enthusiastically that the Sixteenth Congress would provide a renewed impetus for political reform and expected the new leadership to grapple with this area, the Congress offered virtually no indication about new directions and rehashed dominant themes of the Jiang years: administrative fine-tuning, improvement in the quality of public officialdom, mention of the rule of law, firm party control over the reform programme and a tightening of the party's grip over the state sector.

The main potential for promoting reform would appear to lie with the ability of people and organizations to exploit the deliberate vagaries of the 'Three Represents' and 'socialist political civilization' to experiment with cautious reform initiatives. The Congress confirmed the view that the party remains the central actor in the reform process and the leadership trusts only the party to lead reform within all organizations. For the CCP, one starting point for reform would be to recognize and formalize the existence of factions within the party. This would permit citizens to see more clearly the divisions that exist in the party about the way forward. The factions could be formalized with their own publications, and be forced to compete for citizen support. The test of whether factions can coexist comes when policy difference becomes acute or when the system is in crisis, as in 1989. It appeared that in the late 1980s the system was moving to greater tolerance of opposing factions within the party and that the costs of defeat were less severe. Zhao Ziyang, however, missed the opportunity to recognize the open existence of policy-based factions when he pushed ahead with closing down the conservative party theoretical journal (*Red Flag*) and replaced it with a flagship of reform (*Seeking Truth*) (Saich, 1989b). The events of 1989 dispelled that myth but open recognition of party factions remains a suggestion of reformers.

There are in Jiang's report some words that may offer encouragement for the continuation of attempts to enhance transparency and to provide limited accountability over officials. Interestingly although Jiang made the usual comment that 'We should never copy any models of the political system of the West' this was not accompanied by the usual denunciation of the separation of powers that is a key feature of Western democracies. The introduction of the idea of socialist political civility mentioned above may provide a cover for political experimentation. As noted by Li Yuwang in *China Reform Daily*, 'democratic politics' form the core of developing political civilization with Chinese characteristics. In his view, 'An advanced political civilization includes a regularized and perfected democratic political system, as well as the accompanying mechanisms for political activity and oversight of these institutions and mechanisms'. He sees people's democracy lying at the concept's core and adds interestingly that 'its significance lies not merely in values, but also in institutions and organizations'. The Central Party School's publication, *Study Times*, ran a similarly upbeat article by Xu Hongwu, who interpreted the phrase as meaning 'expanding democratic participation, enriching the forms of democracy' and 'actively and steadily advancing reform of the political system'. He acknowledges that in some regions and units, the lack of reform has become a 'bottleneck' damaging social development. However, he warns that the fate of the Soviet Union must not be forgotten and that the party leadership and a socialist orientation were vital for success. It should not include 'unlimited democratization and ideological pluralization'.

It has been noticeable that since the Congress there has been a modest increase in articles calling for more political reform and the old mantra that 'economic reform needs political reform' has been revived. This is surprising as the Congress did not appear to offer much in the realm of political reform. It does, however, seem to be a post-Congress phenomenon that there is an upswing in demands for political reform. One of the most outspoken calls for reform has come from Li Rui, a former secretary to Mao Zedong and deputy head of the organization department, who spent much of the 1960s and 1970s in prison. He follows the prevailing view that it is the party that is crucial for reform, but turns this around by challenging the party to democratize itself, starting with the centre and its senior leader. He even criticizes Deng Xiaoping for not encouraging political reform. It will be interesting to see whether this is a sustainable trend or just another of the periodic upswings in discussion about the need for political reform that is shut off once the demands become too strident.

What may be more enduring is the idea that innovation is necessary, which has also been raised by party officials. Thus, Beijing party secretary, Liu Qi, at a party meeting stated that 'Beijing will expand the orderly participation of Beijing residents in politics and the people's right to know' but he added the phrase 'we will transform the will of the party into the will and action of all Beijing residents'. Little thought seems to have been given to what might happen if the residents are not unanimous in their views or do not find the party's will acceptable. It has also been suggested that the party would experiment with a tripartite division of powers in Shenzhen, and the party secretary of Fujian, Song Defu, advocated the expansion of grass roots democracy beginning with community self-rule (Wang Dan, in *Taipei Times*, 2 January 2003).

Party leaders in Shenzhen have been ruminating for some time on how they might position themselves as political reform leaders to build on their reputation as economic reform trail blazers (Interviews in Shenzhen, September 2001). Proposed reforms to go into effect are the first serious attempts to limit the party's direct control over government institutions since Zhao Ziyang raised the issue in 1987. Shenzhen Mayor, Yu Youjun, felt that political reform was necessary to fulfil WTO commitments and to continue to encourage foreign investment. He noted that the party's role would be restricted to setting overall economic strategy and outlining other policies and that it would be forbidden from 'going over the heads of the government' to interfere in executive work (*Financial Times*, 13 January 2003). However, the intent is to make the system more efficient and to strengthen the party's capacity to rule rather than an attempt to liberalize the system.

With respect to cadre appointment and selection Jiang noted that 'Party members and ordinary people should have more right to know, participate, to choose and supervise'. This will encourage local experimentation with finding ways to canvass public opinion about local leaders that fall within the law. Whether this might lead to raising the level of direct elections from village head to that of the township is more contentious. Experimentation is more likely to be in line with the comments of Liu Qi noted above, to enhance the management of urban communities. Here there have been experiments to introduce village-style elections to their urban equivalents. This will be accompanied by ways to use public feedback to check on the level of cred-ibility of party officials. In this respect, one of the most dramatic initiatives was that launched by Zeng Qinghong in August 2002. It has been reported that for an official to become village party secretary they must first be elected as the village head (*Financial Times*, 13 January 2003). Elections for village heads are an established part of the political process but there have been many cases of clashes with non-elected party heads who outrank them. This step seeks to provide legitimacy to local party leaders, but it may well lead to the fusion of party and administrative power once again at the village level.

In the context of innovation, there are two interesting quotes in Jiang's report on the 'Three Represents':

> Keeping pace with the times means that all the theory and the work of the party must conform to the time and follow the law of development and display great creativity.

Innovation sustains the progress of a nation. Innovation requires emancipating our minds, seeking truth from facts and keeping pace with the times. There is no limit to practice nor innovation.

This theme was picked up by *Xinhua* news agency in a guest commentary (12 December 2002) that claimed that there were 'no limits to practical action, and there are no limits to innovation' and called for ideas and understanding to be liberated from the restraints of anachronistic ideas, methods and systems. This lays the ground for more widespread innovation, with administrative reform at the local level that will enhance accountability and transparency.

Beginning a process of serious political reform would have a number of benefits and would facilitate dealing with a number of problems. First, it could help strengthen the legitimacy of CCP rule. Legitimacy is currently based on the capacity to deliver the economic goods and the leadership is casting around for other sources. Thus, we see the strident appeals to nationalism and patriotism and the fascination with neo-Confucianism. A more democratic system would provide a residual legitimacy that might help the regime negotiate the difficult transition ahead.

Those who have taken power at the Sixteenth Party Congress will not be able to rely on traditional CCP methods for controlling the country, and will be under considerable pressure to find new ways to manage the Chinese polity. It is clear that the forces of globalization will require a considerable shift in the way the CCP governs the system and will require political reform that not only seeks to make the system more transparent but also more accountable. They will have to deal with a much more fluid domestic and international political order, where many of the key decisions affecting China will be taken by international organizations that will not respect the CCP's outdated notion of sovereignty. Given its record to date, this will be a significant hurdle for the current leaders to overcome.

Bold initiatives are unlikely and the politics of muddling through, which has served well in the economic realm, will probably persist for the next five years. An essentially technocratic approach will prevail while the leadership tries to maintain an authoritarian political structure combined with growing economic liberalization. Minimal reform is likely in the political system with a continued focus on strengthening the legal system and building capacity and skills within public administration.

Whether this politics of muddling through and administrative professionalization will be sufficient for the next period is debatable, and the leadership may be pressured to take a more dynamic approach. Certainly many reform ideas have been raised in the press, and it seems as though Hu Jintao is serious about creating greater accountability within the party at least. The ability to deal with the challenges of governance will attest to whether the CCP can retain its leadership over China's development in the twenty-first century.

Further Reading

Only works that are in English are cited below and the references are for book-length works except when no suitable monograph exists.

With China changing so fast it is difficult to keep up with events. There are three key journals that will help keep readers abreast of developments: *The China Quarterly, The China Journal* and *China Information*. Two other very good journals are *China Perspectives* and the *Journal of Contemporary China*. For economics, see *China Economic Review*. English-language sources from China include the weekly *Beijing Review* and the newspaper *China Daily*. The *China Daily* has a website (http://www.chinadaily.com.cn) and the official Chinese news agency *Xinhua* has an English-language site (http://www.xinhua.org) as does the *People's Daily* (http://english.peoplesdaily.com.cn). Other useful websites are: http://chinanewsonline.com (for economic and financial information), http://www.cnd.org (for general information) and http://china.scmp.com (Hong Kong's main English-language daily that has extensive China coverage).

1 Introduction

A great visual introduction to the diversity of China is Benewick and Donald (1999), while an interesting set of essays that take us behind the headlines is Weston and Jensen (2000). Useful general introductions are provided by Hook (1991a) and Mackerras and Yorke (1991), and a reference for the politics of China is Mackerras with McMillen and Watson (1998). Hinton (1980, 1986) provides 7 volumes of documents covering domestic and foreign relations for the period 1949–1984. The changing geography of China caused by reforms is handled well in Cannon and Jenkins (1990) and Leeming (1993). The three best introductions to the environment in China are Edmonds (1994, 1998) and Smil (1993). The legacy of Mao's policies on the environment is covered in Shapiro (2001). The question of China's ethnic minorities is covered in Dillon (1999), Gladney (1996), Heberer (1989) and Mackerras (1994). Belief is dealt with for China's Catholics in Madsen (1998) and for local ritual see Ahern (1981) and Dean (1993). The diversity of Chinese thinking and writing can be glimpsed through the translations in Barmé and Minford (1988) and Barmé and Jaivin (1992). The vibrancy of contemporary Chinese rock culture is covered in Jones (1992) and cultural issues are explored in Zha (1995). Dutton (1998) offers a fascinating view of life in China. How reforms have affected women is covered thoughtfully in Gilmartin *et al.* (1994), Jacka (1997) and Lee (1998). Honig and Hershatter (1988) provide a very personal view of the challenges faced by women.

2 China's Changing Road to Development: Political History, 1949–78

Superb introductions that navigate the reader through the complexity of China's history from imperial days down to the reforms are Spence (1990) and Fairbank and Goldman (1998). CCP history before 1949 is documented in Saich (1996) and readers should look at the debate on the nature of the CCP revolution contained in Johnson

(1962), essentially a product of nationalism, Selden (1971, 1995), a product of socio-economic revolution and Bianco (1971), a nationalist catalyst but the result of deeper social trends.

Selden (1979) provides an excellent documentary collection for the period together with an interesting analysis. The essays in MacFarquhar and Fairbank (1987) provide a state-of-the-art overview of the development of the PRC until 1965, as do the essays in Cheek and Saich (1997). Elite politics from 1949 to 1965 is analysed in masterful fashion in MacFarquhar's trilogy (1974, 1983 and 1997). The Great Leap Forward (GLF) is covered from an institutional perspective by Bachman (1991) whose findings are contested by Teiwes with Sun (1999), and the resultant famine is detailed in Becker (1996). Yang Dali (1996) takes the GLF as his starting point but follows with an analysis of state, rural society and institutional change down to the reform era. The politics of the early 1960s is covered in Baum (1975). Amazingly no outstanding single book exists on the Cultural Revolution but there are a number of works worth looking at, including Dittmer (1998), the essays in MacFarquhar and Fairbank (1991), White (1989) and Yan and Gao (1996). A fascinating documentary collection is Schoenhals (1996). The Lin Biao affair is well covered by Jin (1999) and Teiwes and Sun (1996).

3   China Under Reform, 1978–2003

The best introduction to the politics of the Deng Xiaoping era is Baum (1994). There are many good books covering the reform period and readers are advised to look at Benewick and Wingrove (1995), Dassù and Saich (1992), Harding (1987) and White (1991, 1993). The essays in Goldman and MacFarquhar (1999) provide the best, most recent overview of the reforms. Goldman (1994) provides an interesting introduction to political reform during the period. Wong and Zheng (2002) provide a more up-to-date review. The changing nature of ideology is covered in Brugger and Kelly (1990), Sun (1995) and Chan (2003). Key documents concerning the student-led demonstrations of 1989 can be found in Han (1990), Nathan and Link (2001) and Oksenberg, Sullivan and Lambert (1990), analysis in Calhoun (1994) and Saich (1990), and the impact on the provinces in Unger (1991). Fewsmith (1994) provides a fine overview of political debates about economic reform, Fewsmith (2001b) covers elite politics and the next generation of leaders is thoroughly analyzed in Li (2001).

Gittings (1996) and Schell (1988, 1994) chronicle how reforms have affected daily lives and Croll (1994) provides a fascinating glimpse of reform and rural China. Schell and Shambaugh (1999) provide a useful collection of documents for the entire reform era as does Burns and Rosen (1986) for the earlier period.

4   The Chinese Communist Party

There is no comprehensive review of the CCP that would compare with some of those written about the Soviet Communist Party. A general history of the CCP is provided by Uhalley (1988) while Lieberthal (1995) provides an excellent introduction to the way China is governed. Schurmann's work (1968) remains a classic analysis of the interrelationship of the role of ideology and organization in China, as does Barnett (1967) on cadres and the bureaucracy. The early period of CCP rule is thoroughly documented in Guillermaz (1976). Burns (1989) provides a thorough analysis of the party's *nomenklatura* system. The question of changing party–state relations is handled in Zheng (1997).

5   The Central Governing Apparatus

To understand the nature of the state as it has evolved historically and the implications for contemporary China readers would be well advised to start with Schram (1985, 1987) and the essays in Brødsgaard and Strand (1998). The question of organization in China up until the reforms is handled well by Harding (1981). Administrative reform is dealt with in Cabestan (1992). The changing role of the NPC and the politics of law-making are well covered in O'Brien (1990) and Tanner (1999). The most comprehensive overviews of legal developments under reform are Lubman (1999) and Peerenboom (2002). Useful collections of essays are Potter (1994) and Lubman (1996). Potter (2001) interestingly handles the domestic and international interplay. The most extensive analysis of human rights in China is Kent (1993), while detailed reports on various aspects of rights in China are published by Amnesty International, Human Rights in China and Human Rights Watch.

Two excellent accounts of the PLA under Mao are Gittings (1967) and Joffe (1965) and these should be supplemented by Joffe (1987) for the later period. Excellent accounts of recent developments are Mulvenon and Yang (1999) and Shambaugh (1996a, 2002).

6   Governance Beyond the Centre

Reforms have led to a revival of interest in the province as a unit of study. Detailed analyses are contained in Goodman (1997), Hendrischke and Feng (1999) and Fitzgerald (2002), while the economic dimensions are covered in Cheung, Chung and Lin (1998). Vogel (1989) details the changes that reform has brought to the province of Guangdong, while White (1998) looks primarily at Shanghai. Regional inequality is thoroughly analysed by Wang and Hu (1999).

There is a rapidly growing literature on how the reforms have affected the nature of the local state in China, and Oi (1989b, 1999) has been the major proponent of local state corporatism, while together with Walder (1999) she has explored the connection of property rights to reform. Blecher and Shue (1996) have been attracted to notions of the entrepreneurial and developmental state. Looking at developments in real estate in Tianjin Duckett (1998) also proposes the notion of an entrepreneurial state. Other good studies of the changing nature of the local state are Chan, Madsen and Unger (1992), Friedman *et al.* (1991), Ruf (1998), Walder (1998b) and Wank (1999).

7   Political Participation and Protest

Liu (1996) covers the politics of mass mobilization under Mao while Whyte (1974) explains the important role of small groups and political ritual. Burns (1988) provides a detailed review of political participation in rural China. Seymour (1987) provides the most extensive analysis of China's other political parties while changes in the unions are covered in Leung (1988). Nathan (1986) explores the concept of democracy in Chinese political culture. Goldman with Cheek and Hamrin (1987) and Hamrin and Cheek (1986) look at the changing role of intellectuals in China. Two good works on how reform has affected urban China are Davis *et al.* (1995) and Tang and Parish (2000), while Shi (1997) has provided a fascinating review of participation in Beijing. There is no single volume on the village election programme in China but important articles are Epstein (1997), O'Brien and Li (2000) and Pastor and Tan (2000). The implications of the reforms for democratization are debated in articles by McCormick (1994) and White (1994).

In addition to the works on the 1989 demonstrations a number of other works are important for understanding protest in China. Benton and Hunter (1995) translate and introduce significant documents on China's struggle for democracy from 1942 to 1989. Goldman (1967, 1981) looks at the turbulent relationship that intellectuals have had with the CCP. Moody (1977) analyses dissent and opposition under Mao. Perry and Selden (2000) edit a set of essays that tackle change and resistance in China. Bernstein and Lü (2003) look at peasant burdens and resistance.

8   The Chinese State and Society

The essays of Tsou (1986) provide some of the most perceptive analysis of the nature of the Chinese state under Mao, while Womack (1991) provides a set of essays that relate contemporary state–society relations to longer-term historical trends. Shue (1988) provides a sophisticated analysis of the nature of the relationship while Walder (1986) provides the classic account of communist neo-traditionalism and workplace dependency under Mao. Nee and Mozingo (1983) contains an interesting set of essays on the nature of state power before and after Mao.

In addition to the detailed monographs on the local state mentioned above, there have been a number of attempts to assess the nature of changing state–society relations and the consequences. The most interesting include Brook and Frolic (1997), Hook (1991b), Meisner (1996), McCormick and Unger (1996), Walder (1995b) and White, Howell and Shang (1996).

9   Economic Policy

Three of the most important works dealing with policy-making and implementation in China are Lampton (1987), Lieberthal and Lampton (1992) and Lieberthal and Oksenberg (1988). Riskin (1987) provides a good overview of economic development from 1949 to 1985, Ash and Kueh (1992) provide a good introduction to the progress of reforms, while Naughton (1995) shows how the Chinese economy gradually outgrew the plan. The World Bank series (1997a–1997g) provides important analysis of various sectors of China's economic and social reforms. Howe, Kueh and Ash (2003) provide a good overview of reform and translations of interesting articles.

Huang Yiping (1998) focuses on the institutional dimension of agricultural reform and Unger (2002) has a stimulating set of essays on rural transformation. Zweig (1989) provides the best view of agrarian radicalism in the Cultural Revolution and Zweig (1997) shows the role of farmers in restructuring rural production under the reforms, a theme also central to the work of Zhou (1996). Lardy (1983) provides a useful review of agriculture in China's general development. Byrd and Lin (1990) provide the most complete account of the initial success of China's rural industry.

The industrial sector development under Mao is covered in Andors (1977), while Lee (1987) brings the story up to the mid-1980s. The World Bank (1996b) outlines the challenges of the mid-1990s. Steinfeld (1998) provides the best analysis to date of the problems of reforming the state-owned sector of the economy. Lardy (1998b) provides a penetrating analysis of the problems confronting the financial and banking systems. The development of the private sector of the economy is covered well in Guthrie (1999) and the private entrepreneurs are analysed in Dickson (2003).

10   Social Policy

Dixon (1981) provides a good introduction to CCP thinking about welfare and the situation at the start of the reforms. Chan and Chow (1992) provide a view of perceptions of welfare and Chan (1993) looks in detail at the provision of the community-based welfare system in Guangzhou. Good analysis of the problems confronting welfare reform is provided in White and Shang (1998) and Wong (1998). Davis-Friedmann (1983) covers the policy towards the elderly, while Davis and Harrell (1993) look at how reforms have affected families in urban and rural China. Family planning is the subject of Milwertz (1997) and Sharping (2003). A controversial account of rural China that covers the coercive aspects of family planning is Mosher (1983).

UNDP (1998) covers important issues of the social transition including inequality and poverty alleviation. Riskin, Zhao and Li (2001) contains important information on inequality in China. In addition to the World Bank (1997a–1997g) series one should also consult World Bank (1990) on social security transition and the problems of ageing in World Bank (1994). The multifaceted nature of the urban workplace is explored in the essays in Lü and Perry (1997). The problem of reforming the rural healthcare system is well covered in IDS (1997), while Zhu and Jiang (1996) provide a frank assessment of China's public works programme and its impact on poverty alleviation. The two most important analyses of rural poverty are Nyberg and Rozelle (1999) and World Bank (2000).

A number of works have appeared concerning the question of migration, and among the best are Pieke and Mallee (1999), Solinger (1999) and West and Zhao (2000).

11 Foreign Policy

Camilleri (1980) and Gittings (1974) provide sophisticated analysis of Chinese foreign policy under Mao and how China saw the world. Excellent works that provide a general orientation are Garver (1993), Robinson and Shambaugh (1994) and Lampton (2001b). Economy and Oksenberg (1999) provide excellent reading on the challenges for China and the world as it becomes more of an international player, and Jacobson and Oksenberg (1990) look at China's integration with international economic institutions. Whether this is a threat to the United States and the West is argued in Bernstein and Munro (1997, most probably), Gertz (2000, most certainly) and Nathan and Ross (1997, not necessarily). Johnston and Ross (1999) provide an interesting set of essays on engaging China. Three extremely thoughtful books on the US–China relationship are Harding (1992), Lampton (2001a) and Vogel (1997). Dittmer (1992) has turned his hand to a thoughtful analysis of Sino-Soviet relations. Yahuda (1996) provides an excellent introduction to the Asia-Pacific region within which China has to operate, while Mandelbaum (1995) contains essays looking at the policies of the great powers in the Asia-Pacific.

The open-door policy is well-covered in Howell (1993). Lardy (1992) covers the important role that foreign trade has played in China's reforms. Pearson (1991) analyses the attempts by China to control foreign investment while Huang (2003) looks at the role that FDI more broadly has played in China's development. Zweig (2002) provides an excellent account of the internationalization of China's reforms.

12 Challenges in the Twenty-First Century

Corruption and its threat to CCP rule is the topic of Lü (2000), an earlier analysis is Gong (1994). How the media has changed is the topic of Lynch (1999), and Foster (2000) and Hughes and Wacker (2003) cover the development of the Internet in China. A doomsday scenario for China is provided in Chang (2001) while a more optimistic picture is painted in Brahm (2001).

Bibliography

Ahern, E. M. (1981) *Chinese Ritual and Politics* (Cambridge: Cambridge University Press).

Andors, S. (1977) *China's Industrial Revolution: Politics, Planning, and Management, 1949 to the Present* (New York: Pantheon).

Apter, D. and Saich, T. (1994) *Revolutionary Discourse in Mao's Republic* (Cambridge, MA: Harvard University Press).

Ash, R. F. and Kueh, Y. Y. (eds) (1992) 'The Chinese Economy in the 1990s', Special Issue of *The China Quarterly*, 131 (September).

Aubert, C. (1997–8) 'The Grain Trade Reforms in China: An Unfinished Story of State vs. Peasant Interest', *China Information*, 12(3).

Bachman, D. (1991) *Bureaucracy, Economy, and Leadership in China: The Institutional Origins of the Great Leap Forward* (New York: Cambridge University Press).

Barmé, G. and Jaivin, L. (eds) (1992) *New Ghosts, Old Dreams: Chinese Rebel Voices* (New York: Times Books).

Barmé, G. and Minford, J. (eds) (1988) *Seeds of Fire: Chinese Voices of Conscience* (New York: Hill & Wang).

Barnett, A. D. with a contribution by Vogel, E. (1967) *Cadres, Bureaucracy, and Political Power in Communist China* (New York: Columbia University Press).

Baum, R. (1975) *Prelude to Revolution: Mao, the Party, and the Peasant Question, 1962–1966* (New York: Columbia University Press).

Baum, R. (1994) *Burying Mao: Chinese Politics in the Age of Deng Xiaoping* (Princeton, NJ: Princeton University Press).

Baum, R. (1998) 'The Fifteenth National Party Congress: Jiang Takes Command?', *The China Quarterly*, 153 (January).

Baum, R. (2000) 'Jiang Takes Command: The Fifteenth National Party Congress and Beyond', in Hung-Mao Tien and Yun-Han Chu (eds), *China Under Jiang Zemin* (Boulder, CO: Lynne Rienner).

Baum, R. and Shevchenko, A. (1999) 'The "State of the State" ', in M. Goldman and R. MacFarquhar (eds), *The Paradox of China's Post-Mao Reforms* (Cambridge, MA: Harvard University Press).

Becker, J. (1996) *Hungry Ghosts: Mao's Secret Famine* (New York: The Free Press).

Benewick, R. and Donald, S. (1999) *The State of China Atlas* (London: Penguin).

Benewick, R. and Wingrove, P. (eds) (1995) *China in the 1990s* (Basingstoke: Macmillan).

Benton, G. and Hunter, A. (eds) (1995) *Wild Lily, Prairie Fire: China's Road to Democracy, Yan'an to Tian'anmen, 1942–1989* (Princeton, NJ: Princeton University Press).

Bernstein, R. and Munro, R. H. (1997) *The Coming Conflict with China* (New York: A. A. Knopf).

Bernstein, T. P. and Lü, Xiaobo (2000) 'Taxation Without Representation: Peasants, the Central and the Local States in Reform China', *The China Quarterly*, 163 (September).

Bernstein, T. P. and Lü, Xiaobo (2003) *Taxation Without Representation in Contemporary Rural China* (Cambridge: Cambridge University Press).

Bianco, L. (1971) *Origins of the Chinese Revolution, 1915–1949* (Stanford: Stanford University Press).

Bird, R. and Wallich, C. (1993) 'Fiscal Decentralization and Intergovernmental Relations in Transition Economies', in Policy Research Department Working Paper WPS 1122 (Washington, DC: World Bank).

Blecher, M. (1997) *China Against the Tides: Restructuring Through Revolution, Radicalism, and Reform* (London: Pinter/Cassell).

Blecher, M. (2002) 'Hegemony and Workers' Politics in China', *The China Quarterly*, 170 (June).

Blecher, M. and Shue, V. (1996) *Tethered Deer: Government and Economy in a Chinese County* (Stanford: Stanford University Press).

Bloom, G. *et al.* (1995) 'Financing Health Services in Poor Rural Areas: Adapting to Economic and Institutional Reform', *IDS Research Report*, 30 (Brighton).

Blum, S. D. (2000) 'China's Many Faces: Ethnic, Cultural, and Religious Pluralism', in T. B. Weston and L. M. Jensen (eds), *China Beyond the Headlines* (Lanham, MD: Rowman & Littlefield).

Boone, P., Gomulka, S. and Layard, R. (eds) (1998) *Emerging from Communism: Lessons from Russia, China, and Eastern Europe* (Cambridge, MA: MIT Press).

Bottelier, P. (2000) 'WTO and the Reform of China's State Banks', *China Economic Outlook*.

Brahm, L. J. (2001) *China's Century. The Awakening of the Next Economic Powerhouse* (New York: John Wiley).

Breslin, S. (1995) 'Centre and Province in China', in R. Benewick and P. Wingrove (eds), *China in the 1990s* (Basingstoke: Macmillan).

Brødsgaard, K. E. and Strand, D. (eds) (1998) *Reconstructing Twentieth-Century China: State Control, Civil Society, and National Identity* (Oxford: Clarendon Press).

Brook, T. (1997) 'Auto-Organization in Chinese Society', in T. Brook and B. M. Frolic (eds), *Civil Society in China* (Armonk, NY: M. E. Sharpe).

Brook, T. and Frolic, B. M. (eds) (1997) *Civil Society in China* (Armonk, NY: M. E. Sharpe).

Brown, L. R. (1995) *Who Will Feed China? Wake-Up Call for a Small Planet* (New York: W. W. Norton).

Brugger, B. and Kelly, D. (1990) *Chinese Marxism in the Post-Mao Era* (Stanford: Stanford University Press).

Burns, J. P. (1988) *Political Participation in Rural China* (Berkeley: University of California Press).

Burns, J. P. (ed.) (1989) *The Chinese Communist Party's Nomenklatura System: A Documentary Study of Party Control of Leadership Selection, 1979–1984* (Armonk, NY: M. E. Sharpe).

Burns, J. P. and Rosen, S. (eds) (1986) *Policy Conflicts in Post-Mao China: A Documentary Survey with Analysis* (Armonk, NY: M. E. Sharpe).

Byrd, W. A. and Lin, Q. (eds) (1990) *China's Rural Industry: Structure, Development, and Reform* (New York: Oxford University Press).

Cabestan, J.-P. (1992) *L'administration chinoise après Mao: les réformes de l'ère Deng Xiaoping et leurs limites* (Paris: Editions du Centre national de la recherche scientifique).

Cabestan, J.-P. (2000) 'The Relationship Between the National People's Congress and the State Council in the People's Republic of China: A Few Checks but No Balances', *French Centre for Research on Contemporary China*, Working Paper 1.

Cailliez, C. (1998) 'The Collapse of the Rural Health System', *China Perspectives*, 18 (July–August).

Calhoun, C. J. (1994) *Neither Gods nor Emperors: Students and the Struggle for Democracy in China* (Berkeley: University of California Press).

Camilleri, J. (1980) *Chinese Foreign Policy: The Maoist Era and its Aftermath* (Seattle: University of Washington Press).

Cannon, T. and Jenkins, A. (eds) (1990) *The Geography of Contemporary China: The Impact of Deng Xiaoping's Decade* (London: Routledge).

Chan, A. (1993) 'Revolution or Corporatism? Workers and Trade Unions in Post-Mao China', *The Australian Journal of Chinese Affairs*, 29 (January).

Chan A. (2003) *Chinese Marxism* (New York: Continuum).

Chan, A., Madsen, R. and Unger, J. (1992) *Chen Village under Mao and Deng: The Recent History of a Peasant Community in Mao's China* (Berkeley: University of California Press).

Chan, C. L. W. (1993) *The Myth of Neighbourhood Mutual Help: The Contemporary Chinese Community-Based Welfare System in Guangzhou* (Hong Kong: Hong Kong University Press).

Chan, C. L. W. and Chow, N. W. S. (1992) *More Welfare after Economic Reform? Welfare Development in the People's Republic of China* (Hong Kong: Department of Social Work and Social Administration, University of Hong Kong).

Chang, G. C. (2001) *The Coming Collapse of China* (New York: Random House).

Charles, D. A. (1961) 'The Dismissal of Marshal Feng Teh-huai', *The China Quarterly*, 8 (October–December).

Cheek, T. and Saich, T. (eds) (1997) *New Perspectives on State Socialism in China* (Armonk, NY: M. E. Sharpe).

Cheng, Tiejun and Selden, M. (1997) 'The Construction of Spatial Hierarchies: China's *Hukou* and *Danwei* Systems', in T. Cheek and T. Saich (eds), *New Perspectives on State Socialism in China* (Armonk, NY: M. E. Sharpe).

Cheung, P. T. Y. (1998) 'Introduction: Provincial Leadership and Economic Reform in Post-Mao China', in P. T. Y. Cheung, Jae Ho Chung and Zhimin Lin (eds), *Provincial Strategies of Economic Reform in Post-Mao China: Leadership, Politics, and Implementation* (Armonk, NY: M. E. Sharpe).

Cheung, P. T. Y., Chung, Jae Ho and Lin, Zhimin (eds) (1998) *Provincial Strategies of Economic Reform in Post-Mao China: Leadership, Politics, and Implementation* (Armonk, NY: M. E. Sharpe).

China Labour Statistical Yearbook 1998 (1998) (Beijing: China Statistical Publishing House).

China Statistical Abstract 2000 (2000) (Beijing: China Statistical Publishing House).

China Statistical Yearbook 1999 and 2002 (1999), (2002) (Beijing: China Statistical Publishing House).

Chow, Tse-tsung (1960) *The May Fourth Movement: Intellectual Revolution in Modern China* (Cambridge, MA: Harvard University Press).

Christensen, P. and Delman, J. (1981) 'A Theory of Transitional Society: Mao Zedong and the Mao School', *Bulletin of Concerned Asian Scholars*, 13(2).

Chung, Jae Ho (1998) 'Appendix: Study of Provincial Politics and Development in the Post-Mao Reform Era: Issues, Approaches, and Sources', in P. T. Y. Cheung, Jae Ho Chung and Zhimin Lin (eds), *Provincial Strategies of Economic Reform in Post-Mao China: Leadership, Politics, and Implementation* (Armonk, NY: M. E. Sharpe).

Chung, Jae Ho (2000) 'Regional Disparities, Policy Choices and State Capacity in China', *China Perspectives*, 31 (September–October).

Clarke, D. C. (1995) 'Justice and the Legal System in China', in R. Benewick and P. Wingrove (eds), *China in the 1990s* (Basingstoke: Macmillan).

Croll, E. J. (1984) 'Women's Rights and New Political Campaigns in China Today', Working Paper 1, Sub-Series on Women's History and Development.

Croll, E. (1994) *From Heaven to Earth: Images and Experiences of Development in China* (London: Routledge).

Dassù, M. and Saich, T. (eds) (1992) *The Reform Decade in China: From Hope to Dismay* (London: Kegal Paul International).

Datta, P. (1996) 'Committees of One Billion', in Division of Rural Work, Department of Basic-Level Governance, Ministry of Civil Affairs, *Village Elections: Democracy in Rural China, Commentaries* (Beijing: Ministry of Civil Affairs).

Davis, D. S. and Harrell, S. (eds) (1993) *Chinese Families in the Post-Mao Era* (Berkeley: University of California Press).

Davis, D. S. *et al.* (eds) (1995) *Urban Spaces in Contemporary China: The Potential for Autonomy and Community in Post-Mao China* (New York: Cambridge University Press).

Davis-Friedmann, D. (1983) *Long Lives: Chinese Elderly and the Communist Revolution* (Cambridge, MA: Harvard University Press).

Dean, K. (1993) *Taoist Ritual and Popular Cults in Southeast China* (Princeton, NJ: Princeton University Press).

Dearlove, J. (1995) 'Village Politics', in R. Benewick and P. Wingrove (eds), *China in the 1990s* (Basingstoke: Macmillan).

Deng, G. (2002) 'New Environment for Development of NGOs in China', in NGO Research Center, Tsinghua (ed.), *The 500 NGOs in China* (Beijing: UN Center for Regional Development).

Deng, Xiaoping (1984) *Selected Works of Deng Xiaoping (1975–1982)* (Beijing: Foreign Languages Press).

Deng, Xiaoping (1994) *Selected Works of Deng Xiaoping: Volume III (1982–1992)* (Beijing: Foreign Languages Press).

Deng, Zhenglai and Jing, Yuejing (1992) 'Jiangou Zhongguo de shimin shehui' [Building Civil Society in China], *Zhongguo shehui kexue jikan* [*Chinese Social Sciences Quarterly*] (Hong Kong), 1 (November).

Dickson, B. (2003) *Red Capitalists in China. The Party, Private Entrepreneurs, and Prospects for Political Change* (Cambridge: Cambridge University Press)

Dillon, M. (1999) *China's Muslim Hui Community: Migration, Settlement and Sects* (Surrey: Curzon Press).

Ding, X. L. (1994) *The Decline of Communism in China: Legitimacy Crisis, 1977–1989* (New York: Cambridge University Press).

Ding, X. L. (2000) 'The Illegal Asset Stripping of Chinese Firms', *The China Journal*, 43 (January).

Ding, Yuanzhu (2003) 'Zhongguo feiyingli bumen de fazhan he gaige' (The Reform and Development of Chinese Not-for Profits) in Ru Xin *et al.* (eds), *2003 nian: Zhongguo shehui xingshi fenxi yuce* [2003: Circumstances and Analysis of Chinese Society] (Beijing: Social Sciences Documentation Publishing House).

Dittmer, L. (1992) *Sino-Soviet Normalization and Its International Implications, 1945–1990* (Seattle: University of Washington Press).

Dittmer, L. (1995) 'Chinese Informal Politics', *The China Journal*, 34 (July).

Dittmer, L. (1998) *Liu Shaoqi and the Chinese Cultural Revolution* (Armonk, NY: M. E. Sharpe), rev. edn.

Dittmer, L., Fukui, H. and Lee, P. N. S. (eds) (2000) *Informal Politics in East Asia* (New York: Cambridge University Press).

Dixon, J. (1981) *The Chinese Welfare System, 1949–1979* (New York: Praeger).

Dorfman, M. C. and Sin, Y. (2000) 'China's Social Security Reform, Technical Analysis of Strategic Options', *Human Development Network* (World Bank, December).

Du Ying (2000) 'Guanyu nongcun yiliao weisheng tizhi gaige de jidian kanfa' [Some Ideas on the Reform of the Rural Medical Health System], in Economics Research Department, Ministry of Public Health and the Institute of Development Studies, *Zhongguo nongcun weisheng gaige yu fazhan guoji yantaohui* [International Conference on China's Rural Health Reform and Development] (Beijing).

Duckett, J. (1998) *The Entrepreneurial State in China: Real Estate and Commerce Departments in Reform Era Tianjin* (London: Routledge).

Duckett, J. (2001) 'Bureaucrats in Business, Chinese-style: The Lessons of Market Reform and State Entrepreneurialism in the People's Republic of China', *World Development*, 29(1).

Dunn, S. (1997) 'Taking a Green Leap Forward', *The Amicus Journal*, 18(4).

Dutton, M. (1998) *Streetlife China* (Cambridge: Cambridge University Press).

Eberstadt, N. (1988) *The Poverty of Communism* (New Brunswick, NJ: Transaction Books).

Economy, E. and Oksenberg, M. (eds) (1999) *China Joins the World: Progress and Prospects* (New York: Council on Foreign Relations Press).

Edmonds, R. L. (1994) *Patterns of China's Lost Harmony: A Survey of the Country's Environmental Degradation and Protection* (London: Routledge).

Edmonds, R. L. (1998) 'China's Environment', Special Issue of *The China Quarterly*, 156 (December).

Epstein, A. B. (1997) 'Village Elections in China: Experimenting with Democracy', in Joint Economic Committee, Congress of the United States, *China's Economic Future: Challenges to US Policy* (Armonk, NY: M. E. Sharpe).

Evans, P. B. (1995) *Embedded Autonomy: States and Industrial Transformation* (Princeton, NJ: Princeton University Press).

Fairbank, J. K. and Goldman, M. (1998) *China: A New History* (Cambridge, MA: Harvard University Press).

Falkenheim, V. C. (1972) 'Peking and the Provinces: Continuing Central Predominance', *Problems of Communism*, 21(4).

Fewsmith, J. (1994) *Dilemmas of Reform in China: Political Conflict and Economic Debate* (Armonk, NY: M. E. Sharpe, 1994).

Fewsmith, J. (2001a) *China Since Tiananmen: The Politics of Transition* (Cambridge: Cambridge University Press).

Fewsmith, J. (2001b) 'The Political and Social Implications of China's WTO Membership', *The China Quarterly*, 167 (September).

Fewsmith, J. (2003) 'The Sixteenth National Party Congress: The Succession that Didn't Happen', *The China Quarterly*, 173 (March).

Fitzgerald, J. (ed.) (2002) *Rethinking China's Provinces* (London and New York: Routledge).

Foster, W. (2000) *The Diffusion of the Internet in China* (Stanford: ISAC).

Friedman, E., Pickowicz, P. G., Selden, M. with Johnson, K. A. (1991) *Chinese Village, Socialist State* (New Haven: Yale University Press).

Frolic, B. M. (1997) 'State-Led Civil Society', in T. Brook and B. M. Frolic (eds), *Civil Society in China* (Armonk, NY: M. E. Sharpe).

Fu, Jun (2000) *Institutions and Investments: Foreign Direct Investment in China during an Era of Reforms* (Ann Arbor: University of Michigan Press).

Garver, J. W. (1993) *Foreign Relations of the People's Republic of China* (Englewood Cliffs, NJ: Prentice-Hall).

George, V. and Manning, N. (1980) *Socialism, Social Welfare, and the Soviet Union* (London: Routledge & Kegan Paul).

Gertz, B. (2000) *The China Threat: How the People's Republic Targets America* (Washington, DC: Regnery).

Gilmartin, C. K. *et al.* (eds) (1994) *Engendering China: Women, Culture, and the State* (Cambridge, MA: Harvard University Press).

Gittings, J. (1967) *The Role of the Chinese Army* (London: Oxford University Press).

Gittings, J. (1974) *The World and China, 1922–1972* (New York: Harper & Row).

Gittings, J. (1996) *Real China: From Cannibalism to Karaoke* (New York: Simon & Schuster).

Gladney, D. C. (1996) *Muslim Chinese: Ethnic Nationalism in the People's Republic* (Cambridge, MA: Harvard University Press), 2nd edn.

Gold, T. B. (1990) 'Party-State Versus Society in China', in J. K. Kallgren (ed.), *Building a Nation-State: China after Forty Years* (Berkeley: Institute of East Asian Studies, Center for Chinese Studies, University of California).

Goldman, M. (1967) *Literary Dissent in Communist China* (Cambridge, MA: Harvard University Press).

Goldman, M. (1981) *China's Intellectuals: Advise and Dissent* (Cambridge, MA: Harvard University Press).

Goldman, M. (1994) *Sowing the Seeds of Democracy in China: Political Reform in the Deng Xiaoping Era* (Cambridge, MA: Harvard University Press).

Goldman, M. with Cheek, T. and Hamrin, C. L. (eds) (1987) *China's Intellectuals and the State: In Search of a New Relationship* (Cambridge, MA: Council on East Asian Studies, Harvard University Press).

Goldman, M. and MacFarquhar, R. (eds) (1999) *The Paradox of China's Post-Mao Reforms* (Cambridge, MA: Harvard University Press).

Goldstein, L. J. (2001) 'Return to Zhenbao Island: Who Started Shooting and Why it Matters', *The China Quarterly*, 168 (December).

Gong, Ting (1994) *The Politics of Corruption in Contemporary China: An Analysis of Policy Outcomes* (Westport, CT: Praeger).

Goodman, D. S. G. (1979) 'Changes in Leadership Personnel after September 1976', in J. Domes (ed.), *Chinese Politics after Mao* (Cardiff: University College).

Goodman, D. S. G. (1980) 'The Provincial Party First Secretary in the People's Republic of China, 1949–1978: A Profile', *British Journal of Political Science*, 10(1).

Goodman, D. S. G. (1981) *Beijing Street Voices: The Poetry and Politics of China's Democracy Movement* (London: Marion Boyars).

Goodman, D. S. G. (1986) *Centre and Province in the People's Republic of China: Sichuan and Guizhou, 1955–1965* (New York: Cambridge University Press).

Goodman, D. S. G. (1994) 'JinJiLuYu in the Sino-Japanese War: The Border Region and the Border Region Government', *The China Quarterly*, 140 (December).

Goodman, D. S. G. (ed.) (1997) *China's Provinces in Reform: Class, Community and Political Culture* (New York: Routledge).

Graham, C. (1997) 'From Safety Nets to Social Policy: Lessons for the Transition Economies from the Developing Countries', in J. M. Nelson, C. Tilly and L. Walker (eds), *Transforming Post-Communist Political Economies* (Washington, DC: National Academy Press).

Grindle, M. S. and Thomas, J. W. (1991) *Public Choices and Policy Change: The Political Economy of Reform in Developing Countries* (Baltimore: Johns Hopkins University Press).

Grunfeld, A. T. (1985) 'In Search of Equality: Relations between China's Ethnic Minorities and the Majority Han', *Bulletin of Concerned Asian Scholars*, 17(1).

Gu, E. X. (2001) 'Market Transition and the Transformation of the Health Care System in China', *Policy Studies*, 22(3/4).

Guillermaz, J. (1976) *The Chinese Communist Party in Power, 1949–1976* (Boulder, CO: Westview Press, 1976).

Guo, Wei (1998) 'Jiakuai xianxiang jigou gaige, cong yuantou shang jianqing nongmin fudan' [Speed Up Organizational Structure Reform at the County and Township Level and Reduce the Farmers' Burdens from the Very Beginning], *Liaowang* [*Outlook Weekly*], 43 (26 October).

Guo, Xiaolin (1999) 'The Role of Local Government in Creating Property Rights: A Comparison of Two Townships in Northwest Yunnan', in J. C. Oi and A. G. Walder (eds), *Property Rights and Economic Reform in China* (Stanford: Stanford University Press).

Guthrie, D. (1999) *Dragon in a Three-Piece Suit: The Emergence of Capitalism in China* (Princeton, NJ: Princeton University Press).

Hamrin, C. L. (1992) 'The Party Leadership System', in K. G. Lieberthal and D. M. Lampton (eds), *Bureaucracy, Politics, and Decision Making in Post-Mao China* (Berkeley: University of California Press).

Hamrin, C. L. and Cheek, T. C. (eds) (1986) *China's Establishment Intellectuals* (Armonk, NY: M. E. Sharpe).

Han, Minzhu (ed.) (1990) *Cries for Democracy: Writings and Speeches from the 1989 Chinese Democracy Movement* (Princeton, NJ: Princeton University Press).

Harding, H. (1981) *Organizing China: The Problem of Bureaucracy, 1949–1976* (Stanford: Stanford University Press).

Harding, H. (1987) *China's Second Revolution: Reform after Mao* (Washington, DC: Brookings Institution Press).

Harding, H. (1992) *A Fragile Relationship: The United States and China since 1972* (Washington, DC: Brookings Institution Press).

Harding, H. (1997) 'Breaking the Impasse over Human Rights', in E. F. Vogel (ed.), *Living with China: US/China Relations in the Twenty-First Century* (New York: W. W. Norton).

Harkness, J. (1998) 'Recent Trends in Forestry and Conservation of Biodiversity in China', *The China Quarterly*, 156 (December).

Hartford, K. (1985) 'Socialist Agriculture is Dead: Long Live Socialist Agriculture! Organizational Transformation in Rural China', in E. J. Perry and C. Wong (eds), *The Political Economy of Reform in Post-Mao China* (Cambridge, MA: Harvard University Press).

Hartford, K. (1990) 'The Political Economy Behind Beijing Spring', in T. Saich (ed.), *The Chinese People's Movement: Perspectives on Spring 1989* (Armonk, NY: M. E. Sharpe).

He, Baogang (2002) 'From Village to Township: Will China Move Elections One Level Up?', *East Asian Institute Background Brief*, 126.

He Qinglian (1998) *Xiandaihua de xianjing: Dangdai Zhongguo de jingji shehui wenti* [*The Pitfalls of Modernization: Social and Economic Problems in Contemporary China*] (Beijing: Jinri Zhongguo chubanshe).

Heberer, T. (1989) *China and its National Minorities: Autonomy or Assimilation?* (Armonk, NY: M. E. Sharpe).

Hendrischke, H. and Feng, Chongyi (eds) (1999) *The Political Economy of China's Provinces: Comparative and Competitive Advantage* (New York: Routledge).

Hinton, H. C. (ed.) (1980) *The People's Republic of China, 1949–1979: A Documentary Survey* (Wilmington, DE: Scholarly Resources), 5 vols.

Hinton, H. C. (ed.) (1986) *The People's Republic of China, 1979–1984: A Documentary Survey* (Wilmington, DE: Scholarly Resources), 2 vols.

Hinton, H. C. (1994) 'China as an Asian Power', in T. W. Robinson and D. Shambaugh (eds), *Chinese Foreign Policy: Theory and Practice* (Oxford: Clarendon Press).

Honig, E. and Hershatter, G. (1988) *Personal Voices: Chinese Women in the 1980s* (Stanford: Stanford University Press).

Hook, B. (ed.) (1991a) *The Cambridge Encyclopedia of China* (Cambridge: Cambridge University Press), 2nd edn.

Hook, B. (ed.) (1991b) 'The Individual and the State in China', Special Issue of *The China Quarterly*, 127 (September).

Howe, C., Kueh, Y. Y. and Ash, R. (2003) *China's Economic Reforms: A Study with Documents* (London and New York: RoutledgeCurzon).

Howell, J. (1993) *China Opens Its Doors: The Politics of Economic Transition* (Boulder, CO: Lynne Rienner).
Hu, Shanlian and Jiang, Minghe (1998) 'The People's Republic of China', in D. H. Brooks and Myo Thant (eds), *Social Sector Issues in Transitional Economies of Asia* (Oxford: Oxford University Press).
Hu, Sheng (1982) 'On the Revision of the Constitution', *Beijing Review*, 18 (3 May).
Hu, Shikai (1993) 'Representation Without Democratization: The "Signature" Incident and China's National People's Congress', *Journal of Contemporary China*, 2(1).
Hua, Guofeng (1977) 'Political Report to the Eleventh National Congress of the Communist Party of China', in *The Eleventh National Congress of the Communist Party of China* (Peking: Foreign Languages Press).
Huang, Yasheng (1995a) 'Why China will not Collapse', *Foreign Policy*, 99 (Summer).
Huang, Yasheng (1995b) 'Administrative Monitoring in China', *The China Quarterly*, 143 (September).
Huang, Yasheng (1996a) *Inflation and Investment Controls in China: The Political Economy of Central–Local Relations during the Reform Era* (New York: Cambridge University Press).
Huang, Yasheng (1996b) 'Central–Local Relations in China during the Reform Era: The Economic and Institutional Dimensions', *World Development*, 24(4).
Huang, Yasheng (1998) *FDI in China: An Asian Perspective* (Singapore: Institute of Southeast Asian Studies).
Huang, Yasheng (2000) 'Why is There So Much Demand for Foreign Direct Investment in China? An Institutional and Policy Perspective', in Chung Ming Lau and Jianfa Shen (eds), *China Review 2000* (Hong Kong: The Chinese University Press).
Huang, Yasheng (2001) 'Fiscal Reforms and Political Institutions', *Problems of Post-Communism*, 48(1).
Huang, Yasheng (2003) *Selling China: Foreign Direct Investment During the Reform Era* (New York: Cambridge University Press).
Huang, Y., Saich, T. and Steinfeld, E. (eds.) (forthcoming) *Financial Reform in China* (Cambridge, MA: Harvard University Press).
Huang, Yiping (1998) *Agricultural Reform in China: Getting Institutions Right* (New York: Cambridge University Press).
Huchet, J.-F. (1999) 'Concentration and the Emergence of Corporate Groups in Chinese Industry', *China Perspectives*, 23 (May–June).
Huchet, J.-F. (2000) 'The Hidden Aspect of Public Sector Reforms in China. State and Collective SMEs in Urban Areas', *China Perspectives*, 32 (November–December).
Hughes, C. R. and Wacker, G. (2003) *China and the Internet. Politics of the Digital Leap Forward* (London and New York: Routledge Curzon).
Hughes, N. C. (1998) 'Smashing the Iron Rice Bowl', *Foreign Affairs*, 77(4).
Hussein, A. *et al.* (2002), *Urban Poverty in the PRC*, Asian Development Bank, Project No. TAR PRC 33448.
Institute of Development Studies (IDS) (1997) *Health in Transition: Reforming China's Rural Health Services* (Sussex: Institute of Development Studies).
Jacka, T. (1997) *Women's Work in Rural China: Change and Continuity in an Era of Reform* (London: Cambridge University Press).
Jacobson, H. K. and Oksenberg, M. (1990) *China's Participation in the IMF, the World Bank, and GATT: Toward a Global Economic Order* (Ann Arbor: University of Michigan Press).
Jenner, W. J. F. (1992) *The Tyranny of History: The Roots of China's Crisis* (London: Allen Lane).
Jiang, Zemin (1991) 'Beijing Rally Marks CPC Anniversary: Jiang Zemin Speech', in *FBIS-CHI-91–129S*, 5 July.

Jiang, Zemin (1997) 'Hold High the Great Banner of Deng Xiaoping Theory for an All-Round Advancement of the Cause of Building Socialism with Chinese Characteristics into the 21st Century', *Beijing Review*, 40(40) (6–12 October).

Jiang Zemin (2002) Report to the Sixteenth Party Congress at http://www.16comgress.org.cn/english/features/49007.htm

Jin, Qiu (1999) *The Culture of Power: The Lin Biao Incident in the Cultural Revolution* (Stanford: Stanford University Press).

Joffe, E. (1965) *Party and Army: Professionalism and Political Control in the Chinese Officer Corps, 1949–1964* (Cambridge, MA: East Asian Research Centre, Harvard University Press).

Joffe, E. (1987) *The Chinese Army after Mao* (Cambridge, MA: Harvard University Press).

Joffe, E. (1997) 'Ruling China After Deng', *Journal of East Asian Affairs* (Winter–Spring).

Johnson, C. A. (1962) *Peasant Nationalism and Communist Power: The Emergence of Revolutionary China* (Stanford: Stanford University Press).

Johnson, D. (1999) 'China's Reforms – Some Unfinished Business', unpublished paper (November).

Johnston, A. (2003) 'Is China a Status Quo Power?', *International Security*, 27(4).

Johnston, A. and Ross, R. S. (eds) (1999) *Engaging China: The Management of an Emerging Power* (New York: Routledge).

Jones, A. F. (1992) *Like a Knife: Ideology and Genre in Contemporary Chinese Popular Music* (Ithaca, NY: East Asia Program, Cornell University).

Jowitt, K. (1975) 'Inclusion and Mobilization in European Leninist Regimes', *World Politics*, 28(1).

Ke, Bingsheng (2001) 'China's WTO Entry and its Impact on the Agricultural Sector', paper delivered at the conference 'Financial Sector Reform in China', Kennedy School of Government, Harvard University.

Keating, P. (1994) 'The Ecological Origins of the Yan'an Way', *The Australian Journal of Chinese Affairs*, 32 (July).

Kelliher, D. (1997) 'The Chinese Debate over Village Self-Government', *The China Journal*, 37 (January).

Kelly, D. (1991) 'Chinese Marxism since Tiananmen: Between Evaporation and Dismemberment', in D. S. G. Goodman and G. Segal (eds), *China in the Nineties: Crisis Management and Beyond* (Oxford: Clarendon Press).

Kelly, D. (ed.) (1996) 'Realistic Responses and Strategic Options: An Alternative CCP Ideology and Its Critics', *Chinese Law and Government*, 20(2).

Kennedy School of Government (1999) 'Pension Reform in China: Weighing the Alternatives', Case Program 1547.0.

Kent, A. (1993) *Between Freedom and Subsistence: China and Human Rights* (Hong Kong: Oxford University Press).

Khan, A. R. (n.d.) *Poverty in China in the Period of Globalization: New Evidence on Trends and Patterns* (Geneva: ILO).

Khan, A. R. and Riskin, C. (1998) 'Income and Inequality in China: Composition, Distribution and Growth of Household Income, 1988 to 1995', *The China Quarterly*, 154 (June).

Kim, S. S. (1999) 'China and the United Nations', in E. Economy and M. Oksenberg (eds), *China Joins the World: Progress and Prospects* (New York: Council on Foreign Relations Press).

Knup, E. (n.d.) 'Environmental NGOs in China: An Overview', *China Environment Series* (Washington, DC: Woodrow Wilson Center).

Kornai, J. (1992) *The Socialist System: The Political Economy of Communism* (Princeton, NJ: Princeton University Press).

Kornai, J. (1997) 'Reform of the Welfare Sector in the Post-Communist Countries: A Normative Approach', in J. M. Nelson, C. Tilly and L. Walker (eds), *Transforming Post-Communist Political Economies* (Washington, DC: National Academy Press).

Kornai, J. (2000) 'Ten Years After "The Road to a Free Economy": the Author's Self-Evaluation', paper presented at the World Bank Annual Conference and Development Economics (April).

Kung, James Kai-sing and Liu, Shouying (1997) 'Farmers' Preferences regarding Ownership and Land Tenure in Post-Mao China: Unexpected Evidence from Eight Counties', *The China Journal*, 38 (July).

Lam, W. W.-L. (1999) *The Era of Jiang Zemin* (New York: Prentice-Hall).

Lampton, D. M. (ed.) (1987) *Policy Implementation in Post-Mao China* (Berkeley: University of California Press).

Lampton, D. M. (1992) 'A Plum for a Peach: Bargaining, Interest, and Bureaucratic Politics in China', in K. G. Lieberthal and D. M. Lampton (eds), *Bureaucracy, Politics, and Decision Making in Post-Mao China* (Berkeley: University of California Press).

Lampton, D. M. (2001a) *Same Bed, Different Dreams: Managing US–China Relations, 1989–2000* (Berkeley: University of California Press).

Lampton, D. M. (ed.) (2001b) *The Making of Chinese Foreign and Security Policy in the Era of Reform* (Stanford: Stanford University Press).

Lane, K. (1998) 'One Step Behind: Shaanxi in Reform, 1978–1995', in P. T. Y. Cheung, Jae Ho Chung and Zhimin Lin (eds), *Provincial Strategies of Economic Reform in Post-Mao China: Leadership, Politics, and Implementation* (Armonk, NY: M. E. Sharpe).

Lardy, N. R. (1983) *Agriculture in China's Modern Economic Development* (New York: Cambridge University Press).

Lardy, N. R. (1992) *Foreign Trade and Economic Reform in China, 1978–1990* (New York: Cambridge University Press).

Lardy, N. R. (1998a) 'China and the Asian Contagion', *Foreign Affairs*, 77(4).

Lardy, N. R. (1998b) *China's Unfinished Economic Revolution* (Washington, DC: Brookings Institution Press).

Lawrence, S. V. (1994) 'Democracy, Chinese Style', *The Australian Journal of Chinese Affairs*, no. 32 (July).

Lawyers' Committee for Human Rights (1996) *Opening to Reform? An Analysis of China's Revised Criminal Procedure Law* (New York: Lawyers' Committee for Human Rights).

Lee, Ching Kwan (1998) *Gender and the South China Miracle: Two Worlds of Factory Women* (Berkeley: University of California Press).

Lee, Ching Kwan (2000) 'Pathways of Labour Insurgency', in E. J. Perry and M. Selden (eds), *Chinese Society: Change, Conflict and Resistance* (New York: Routledge).

Lee, P. N. S. (1987) *Industrial Management and Economic Reform in China, 1949–1984* (New York: Oxford University Press).

Leeming, F. (1993) *The Changing Geography of China* (Oxford: Blackwell).

Leung, J. C. B. (1995) 'Social Welfare Reforms', in R. Benewick and P. Wingrove (eds), *China in the 1990s* (Basingstoke: Macmillan – now Palgrave Macmillan).

Leung, Wing-yue (1988) *Smashing the Iron Rice Pot: Workers and Unions in China's Market Socialism* (Hong Kong: Asia Monitor Centre).

Li, Cheng (2001) *China's Leaders: The New Generation* (Lanham, MD: Rowman & Littlefield).

Li, Cheng (2003) 'A Landslide Victory for Provincial Leaders', *China Leadership Monitor*, 5.

Li, Fan *et al.* (2000) *Chuangxin yu fazhan–xiangzhenzhang xuanju zhidu gaige* [Innovation and Reform: Reform of the System for Election of Township and Town Heads] (Beijing: Dongfang chubanshe).

Li, Lianjiang (2002) 'The Politics of Introducing Direct Township Elections in China', *The China Quarterly*, 171 (September).

Li, Wei and Pye, L. W. (1992) 'The Ubiquitous Role of the *Mishu* in Chinese Politics', *The China Quarterly*, 132 (December).

Li Xiguang *et al.* (1996) *Yaomohua Zhongguo de beihou* [*Behind the Scenes of Demonizing China*] (Beijing: Zhongguo shehui kexue chubanshe).

Li, Xueju, Wang, Zhenyao and Tang Jinsu (eds) (1994) *Zhongguo xiangzhen zhengquan de xianzhuang yu gaige* [*The Present Situation and Reform of Power in Chinese Villages and Towns*] (Beijing: Zhongguo shehui chubanshe).

Li, Yongping (1992) 'Sex Ratios of Infants and Relations with Socioeconomic Variables: The Results of China's 1990 Census and Implications', unpublished paper.

Li, Zhisui, with editorial assistance of A. F. Thurston (1994) *The Private Life of Chairman Mao: The Memoirs of Mao's Personal Physician* (New York: Random House).

Lieberthal, K. G. (1992) 'Introduction: The "Fragmented Authoritarianism" Model and Its Limitations', in K. G. Lieberthal and D. M. Lampton (eds), *Bureaucracy, Politics, and Decision Making in Post-Mao China* (Berkeley: University of California Press).

Lieberthal, K. (1995) *Governing China: From Revolution through Reform* (New York: W. W. Norton).

Lieberthal, K. and Lampton, D. M. (eds) (1992) *Bureaucracy, Politics, and Decision Making in Post-Mao China* (Berkeley: University of California Press).

Lieberthal, K. and Oksenberg, M. (1988) *Policymaking in China: Leaders, Structures, and Processes* (Princeton, NJ: Princeton University Press).

Lin Jun (2001) 'Recent Developments of Tax System Reforms in China: Challenges and Responses', *The International Tax Journal* (Winter).

Lin, Zhimin (1998) 'Conclusion – Provincial Leadership and Reform: Lessons and Implications for Chinese Politics', in P. T. Y. Cheung, Jae Ho Chung and Zhimin Lin (eds), *Provincial Strategies of Economic Reform in Post-Mao China: Leadership, Politics, and Implementation* (Armonk, NY: M. E. Sharpe).

Lippit, V. (1975) 'The Great Leap Forward Reconsidered', *Modern China*, 1(1).

Liu, A. P. L. (1996) *Mass Politics in the People's Republic: State and Society in Contemporary China* (Boulder, CO: Westview Press).

Liu, Jun and Lin, Li (1989) *Xinquanwei zhuyi: dui gaige lilun gangling de lunzheng* [*Neo-Authoritarianism: A Debate on the Theoretical Programme of Reform*] (Beijing: Beijing jingji xueyuan chubanshe).

Lohmar, B., Rozelle, S. and Zhao, C. (2000) 'The Rise of Rural-to-Rural Labor Markets in China', *UC Davis Agricultural and Resource Economics*, Working Paper No. 00-020.

Lu, Mai (1999) 'China's Urgent Challenge – To Provide Public Goods in a Market Environment', unpublished paper.

Lü, Xiaobo (2000) *Cadres and Corruption: The Organizational Involution of the Chinese Communist Party* (Stanford: Stanford University Press).

Lü, Xiaobo and Perry, E. J. (eds) (1997) *Danwei: The Changing Chinese Workplace in Historical and Comparative Perspective* (Armonk, NY: M. E. Sharpe).

Lu, Yun (1990) 'Democratic Party Leader on Multi-Party Co-operation', *Beijing Review*, 33(2) (8–14 January).

Lubman, S. (ed.) (1996) *China's Legal Reforms* (Oxford: Oxford University Press).

Lubman, S. B. (1999) *Bird in a Cage: Legal Reform in China after Mao* (Stanford: Stanford University Press).

Lynch, D. C. (1999) *After the Propaganda State: Media, Politics, and 'Thought Work' in Reformed China* (Stanford: Stanford University Press).

Ma, Guonan and Fung, B. S. C. (2002) 'China's Asset Management Corporations', *Bank for International Settlements*, Working Paper 115 (August).

Ma, Jun and Fan Zhai (2001) 'Financing China's Pension Reform', paper delivered to the conference 'Financial Sector Reform in China', Kennedy School of Government, Harvard University.

MacFarquhar, R. (1974) *The Origins of the Cultural Revolution 1: Contradictions among the People, 1956–1957* (London: Oxford University Press).

MacFarquhar, R. (1983) *The Origins of the Cultural Revolution 2: The Great Leap Forward, 1958–1960* (London: Oxford University Press).

MacFarquhar, R. (1997) *The Origins of the Cultural Revolution 3: The Coming of the Cataclysm, 1961–1966* (London: Oxford University Press).

MacFarquhar, R. and Fairbank, J. K. (eds) (1987) *The Cambridge History of China, 14: The People's Republic, Part 1: The Emergence of Revolutionary China, 1949–1965* (Cambridge: Cambridge University Press).

MacFarquhar, R. and Fairbank, J. K. (eds) (1991) *The Cambridge History of China, 15: The People's Republic, Part 2: Revolutions within the Chinese Revolution, 1966–1982* (Cambridge: Cambridge University Press).

Mackerras, C. (1994) *China's Minorities: Integration and Modernization in the Twentieth Century* (Hong Kong: Oxford University Press).

Mackerras, C., with McMillen, D. H. and Watson, A. (eds) (1998) *Dictionary of the Politics of the People's Republic of China* (London: Routledge).

Mackerras, C. and Yorke, A. (1991) *The Cambridge Handbook of Contemporary China* (Cambridge: Cambridge University Press).

Madsen, R. (1998) *China's Catholics: Tragedy and Hope in an Emerging Civil Society* (Berkeley: University of California Press).

Mandelbaum, M. (ed.) (1995) *The Strategic Quadrangle: Russia, China, Japan, and the United States in East Asia* (New York: Council on Foreign Relations Press).

Mao, Zedong ([1943] 1965) 'Some Questions Concerning Methods of Leadership', in *Selected Works of Mao Tse-Tung*, 3 (Peking: Foreign Languages Press).

McCormick, B. L. (1994) 'Democracy or Dictatorship? A Response to Gordon White', *The Australian Journal of Chinese Affairs*, 31 (January).

McCormick, B. L. and Unger, J. (eds) (1996) *China after Socialism: In the Footsteps of Eastern Europe or East Asia?* (Armonk, NY: M. E. Sharpe).

Meisner, M. J. (1996) *The Deng Xiaoping Era: An Inquiry into the Fate of Chinese Socialism, 1978–1984* (New York: Hill & Wang).

Merquior, J. G. (1993) 'A Panoramic View of the Rebirth of Liberalism', *World Development*, 20(8).

Meng, Q. and Hu, A. (2000) 'Xiaochu jiankang pinkun ying chengwei nongcun weisheng gaige yu fazhan de youxian zhanlüe' [Eliminating Health Poverty Ought to be a Top Strategic Priority in Rural Health Reform and Development], in Economics Research Department, Ministry of Public Health and the Institute of Development Studies, *Zhongguo nongcun weisheng yu fazhan guoji yantaohui* [International Conference on China's Rural Health Reform and Development] (Beijing).

Meng, Y. (2002) 'New Roles of NPOs and Partnership with Government and Business', in NGO Research Center, Tsinghua University (ed.), *The 500 NGOs in China* (Beijing: UN Center for Regional Development).

Milwertz, C. N. (1997) *Accepting Population Control: Urban Chinese Women and the One-Child Family Policy* (Surrey: Curzon Press).

Ministry of Agriculture (1999) 'Woguo nongye jiben jianshe zhong cunzai de wenti jiqi jianyi' [The Main Problems in China's Agricultural Capital Construction and Some Suggestions for Solving Them], *Zhongguo nongye jingji* [*Chinese Rural Economy*], 9.

Montinola, G., Qian, Yingyi and Weingast, B. (1995) 'Federalism, Chinese Style: The Political Basis for Economic Success in China', *World Politics*, 48(1).

Moody, P. R. (1977) *Opposition and Dissent in Contemporary China* (Stanford: Hoover Institution Press).

Mosher, S. W. (1983) *Broken Earth: The Rural Chinese* (New York: The Free Press).

Mulvenon, J. C. (1997) *Professionalization of the Senior Chinese Officer Corps: Trends and Implications* (Santa Monica, CA: Rand).

Mulvenon, J. C. (2002) 'The PLA and the Sixteenth Party Congress: Jiang Controls the Gun?', *China Leadership Monitor*, 5.

Mulvenon, J. C. and Yang, R. H. (eds) (1999) *The People's Liberation Army in the Information Age* (Santa Monica, CA: Rand).

Munro, R. (1988) 'Political Reform, Student Demonstrations and the Conservative Backlash', in R. Benewick and P. Wingrove (eds), *Reforming the Revolution: China in Transition* (Basingstoke: Macmillan).

Murphy, R. (2002) *How Migrant Labor is Changing Rural China* (Cambridge: Cambridge University Press).

Nathan, A. J. (1973) 'A Factionalism Model for CCP Politics', *The China Quarterly*, 53 (January–March).

Nathan, A. J. (1986) *Chinese Democracy* (Berkeley: University of California Press).

Nathan, A. J. (1994) 'Human Rights in Chinese Foreign Policy', *The China Quarterly*, 139 (September).

Nathan, A. J. (1999) 'China and the International Human Rights Regime', in E. Economy and M. Oksenberg (eds), *China Joins the World: Progress and Prospects* (New York: Council on Foreign Relations Press).

Nathan, A. J. and Link, P. (eds) (2001) *The Tiananmen Papers* (New York: Public Affairs).

Nathan, A. J. and Ross, R. S. (1997) *The Great Wall and the Empty Fortress: China's Search for Security* (New York: W. W. Norton).

Nathan, A. J. and Tsai, K. S. (1995) 'Factionalism: A New Institutionalist Restatement', *The China Journal*, 34 (July).

National Research Centre (1998) 'Evaluation of the Economic and Social Benefits of the Project Hope. A Summary of Basic Conclusions' (Beijing: unpublished mimeo).

Naughton, B. (1987) 'The Decline of Central Control over Investment in Post-Mao China', in D. M. Lampton (ed.), *Policy Implementation in Post-Mao China* (Berkeley: University of California Press).

Naughton, B. (1988) 'The Third Front: Defence Industrialization in the Chinese Interior', *China Quarterly*, 115 (September).

Naughton, B. (1992) 'The Chinese Economy: On the Road to Recovery?', in W. A. Joseph (ed.), *China Briefing, 1991* (Boulder, CO: Westview Press).

Naughton, B. (1995) *Growing Out of the Plan: Chinese Economic Reform, 1978–1993* (New York: Cambridge University Press).

Naughton, B. (1999) 'China's Transition in Economic Perspective?', in M. Goldman and R. MacFarquhar (eds), *The Paradox of China's Post-Mao Reforms* (Cambridge, MA: Harvard University Press).

Naughton, B. (2000) 'The Chinese Economy: Fifty Years into the Transformation', in T. White (ed.), *China Briefing, 2000: The Continuing Transformation* (Armonk, NY: M. E. Sharpe).

Nee, V. (1989) 'A Theory of Market Transition: From Redistribution to Markets in State Socialism', *American Sociological Review*, 54(5).

Nee, V. and Mozingo, D. (eds) (1983) *State and Society in Contemporary China* (Ithaca, NY: Cornell University Press).

Nelson, J. M. (1997) 'Social Costs, Social-Sector Reforms, and Politics in Post Communist Transformations', in J. M. Nelson, C. Tilly and L. Walker (eds), *Transforming Post-Communist Political Economies* (Washington, DC: National Academy Press).

Nevitt, C. E. (1996) 'Private Business Associations in China: Evidence of Civil Society or Local State Power?', *The China Journal*, 36 (July).

Nyberg, A. and Rozelle, S. (1999) *Accelerating China's Rural Transformation* (Washington, DC: World Bank).

O'Brien, K. (1990) *Reform without Liberalization: China's National People's Congress and the Politics of Institutional Change* (New York: Cambridge University Press).

O'Brien, K. J. (1994) 'Implementing Political Reform in China's Villages', *The Australian Journal of Chinese Affairs*, 32 (July).

O'Brien, K. J. and Li, Lianjiang (2000) 'Accommodating "Democracy" in a One-Party State: Introducing Village Elections in China', *The China Quarterly*, 162 (June).

OECD (2002) *China in the World Economy: The Domestic Policy Challenges* (Paris: OECD).

Ogden, S. *et al*. (eds) (1992) *China's Search for Democracy: The Student and Mass Movement of 1989* (Armonk, NY: M. E. Sharpe).

Oi, J. C. (1989a) 'Market Reforms and Corruption in Rural China', *Studies in Comparative Communism*, 22(2–3).

Oi, J. C. (1989b) *State and Peasant in Contemporary China: The Political Economy of Village Government* (Berkeley: University of California Press).

Oi, J. (1992) 'Fiscal Reform and the Economic Foundations of Local State Corporatism in China', *World Politics*, 45(1).

Oi, J. C. (1999) *Rural China Takes Off: Institutional Foundations of Economic Reform* (Berkeley: University of California Press).

Oi, J. C. and Walder, A. G. (eds) (1999) *Property Rights and Economic Reform in China* (Stanford: Stanford University Press).

Oksenberg, M. (1968) 'The Institutionalisation of the Chinese Communist Revolution: The Ladder of Success on the Eve of the Cultural Revolution', *The China Quarterly*, 36 (October–December).

Oksenberg, M., Sullivan, L. R. and Lambert, M. (eds) (1990) *Beijing Spring, 1989: Confrontation and Conflict: The Basic Documents* (Armonk, NY: M. E. Sharpe).

'On Questions of Party History – Resolution on Certain Questions in the History of Our Party Since the Founding of the People's Republic of China' (1981) *Beijing Review*, 27 (6 July).

Pairault, T. (1982) 'Industrial Strategy (January 1975 – June 1979): In Search of New Policies for Industrial Growth', in J. Gray and G. White (eds), *China's New Development Strategy* (London: Academic Press).

Park, A. *et al*. (1996) 'Distributional Consequences of Reforming Local Public Finance in China', *The China Quarterly*, 147 (September).

Park, A. and Ren (2001) 'Microfinance with Chinese Characteristics' *World Development*, 1.

Park, A. and Shen, Minggao (2000) 'Joint Liability Lending and the Rise and Fall of China's Township and Village Enterprises', unpublished paper.

Park, A., Wang, Sangui and Wu, Guobao (1999) 'Regional Poverty Targeting in China', Working Paper, Department of Economics, University of Michigan.

Parris, K. (1999) 'The Rise of Private Business Interests', in M. Goldman and R. MacFarquhar (eds), *The Paradox of China's Post-Mao Reforms* (Cambridge, MA: Harvard University Press).

Pastor, R. A. and Tan, Qingshan (2000) 'The Meaning of China's Village Elections', *The China Quarterly*, 162 (June).

Pearson, M. M. (1991) *Joint Ventures in the People's Republic of China: The Control of Foreign Direct Investment under Socialism* (Princeton, NJ: Princeton University Press).

Pearson, M. M. (1999) 'China's Integration into the International Trade and Investment Regime', in E. Economy and M. Oksenberg (eds), *China Joins the World: Progress and Prospects* (New York: Council on Foreign Relations Press).

Peerenboom, R. (2002) *China's Long March Toward Rule of Law* (Cambridge: Cambridge University Press).

Perry, E. J. (1995) 'Labour's Battle for Political Space: The Role of Worker Associations in Contemporary China', in D. S. Davis *et al.* (eds), *Urban Spaces in Contemporary China: The Potential for Autonomy and Community in Post-Mao China* (New York: Cambridge University Press).

Perry, E. J. (1997) 'Shanghai's Strike Wave of 1957', in T. Cheek and T. Saich (eds), *New Perspectives on State Socialism in China* (Armonk, NY: M. E. Sharpe).

Perry, E. J. (1999) 'Crime, Corruption, and Contention', in M. Goldman and R. MacFarquhar (eds), *The Paradox of China's Post-Mao Reforms* (Cambridge, MA: Harvard University Press).

Perry, E. and Selden, M. (eds) (2000) *Chinese Society: Change, Conflict, and Resistance* (New York: Routledge).

Pickowicz, P. G. (1989) 'Popular Cinema and Political Thought in Post-Mao China: Reflections on Official Pronouncements, Film, and the Film Audience', in P. Link, R. Madsen and P. G. Pickowicz (eds), *Unofficial China: Popular Culture and Thought in the People's Republic of China* (Boulder, CO: Westview Press).

Pieke, F. N. and Mallee, H. (eds) (1999) *Internal and International Migration: Chinese Perspectives* (Surrey: Curzon Press).

Polanyi, K. (1944) *The Great Transformation* (Boston: Beacon Press).

Potter, P. (ed.) (1994) *Domestic Law Reforms in Post-Mao China* (Armonk, NY: M. E. Sharpe).

Potter, P. B. (2001) *The Chinese Legal. Globalization and Local Legal Culture* (London and New York: RoutledgeCurzon).

Pye, L. (1981) *The Dynamics of Chinese Politics* (Cambridge, MA: Oelgeschlager, Gunn & Hain).

Pye, L. (1995) 'Factions and the Politics of *Guanxi*: Paradoxes in Chinese Administrative Behaviour', *The China Journal*, 34 (July).

Qian, Yingyi, Roland, G. and Lau, L. (1999) 'Reform without Losers: An Interpretation of China's Dual-Track Approach to Transition', *Journal of Political Economy*, 108(1).

Qindu Central Committee (1999) *Qindu gaige zhilu* [*Qindu's Road of Reform*] (Xianyang: Zhonggong Xianyang Qindu quwei yanjiushi).

Rawksi, T. G. (1999) 'Reforming China's Economy: What Have We Learned?', *The China Journal*, 41 (January).

Read, B. L. (2000) 'Revitalizing the State's Urban "Nerve Tips" ', *The China Quarterly*, 163 (September).

Riskin, C. (1987) *China's Political Economy: The Quest for Development since 1949* (Oxford: Oxford University Press).

Riskin, C., Zhao, R. and Li, Shi (eds) (2001) *China's Retreat from Equality: Income Distribution and Economic Transition* (Armonk, NY: ME. Sharpe).

Roberts, M. (trans) and Levy, R. (annot.) (1977) *A Critique of Soviet Economics by Mao Tsetung* (New York: Monthly Review Press).

Robinson, T. W. and Shambaugh, D. (eds) (1994) *Chinese Foreign Policy: Theory and Practice* (Oxford: Clarendon Press).

Rodrik, D. (1999) 'Institutions for High-Quality Growth: What They Are and How to Acquire Them', unpublished paper.

Rong, J. *et al.* (eds) (1998) *Cong yalixing tizhi xiang minzhu hezuo tizhi de zhuanbian* [*The Transformation from a Pressurized System to a Democratic Cooperative System*] (Beijing: Zhongyang bianyi chubanshe).

Rozelle, S. *et al.* (1998) Targeted Poverty Investments and Economic Growth in China', *World Development*, 26(12).

Ruf, G. A. (1998) *Cadres and Kin: Making a Socialist Village in West China, 1921–1991* (Stanford: Stanford University Press).

Sachs, J. and Woo, Wing Thye (1994) 'Structural Factors in the Economic Reforms of China, Eastern Europe and the Former Soviet Union: Discussion', *Economic Policy*, 18 (April).

Sachs, J., Woo, Wing Thye and Yang, Xiaokai (2000) 'Economic Reforms and Constitutional Transition', Centre for International Development, Harvard University, Working Paper 43.

Saich, T. (1983a) 'The Fourth Constitution of the People's Republic of China', *Review of Socialist Law*, 9(2).

Saich, T. (1983b) 'Party and State Reforms in the People's Republic of China', *Third World Quarterly*, 5(3).

Saich, T. (1983c) 'Party Re-Building Since Mao: A Question of Style?', *World Development*, vol. II, no. 8 (August).

Saich, T. (1984) 'Workers in the Workers' State: Urban Workers in the PRC', in D. S. G. Goodman (ed.), *Groups and Politics in the People's Republic of China* (Cardiff: University College).

Saich, T. (1989a) *China's Science Policy in the 80s* (Manchester: Manchester University Press).

Saich, T. (1989b) 'The Chinese Communist Party at the Thirteenth National Congress: Policies and Prospects for Reform', in King-yuh Chang (ed.), *Political and Social Changes in Taiwan and Mainland China* (Taipei: Institute of International Relations).

Saich, T. (ed.) (1990) *The Chinese People's Movement: Perspectives on Spring 1989* (Armonk, NY: M. E. Sharpe).

Saich, T. (1992) 'The Fourteenth Party Congress: A Programme for Authoritarian Rule', *The China Quarterly*, 132 (December).

Saich, T. (1993) 'Peaceful Evolution with Chinese Characteristics', in W. A. Joseph (ed.), *China Briefing, 1992* (Boulder, CO: Westview Press).

Saich, T. (1994a) 'Introduction: The Chinese Communist Party and the Anti-Japanese War Base Areas', *The China Quarterly*, 140 (December).

Saich, T. (1994b) 'The Fourteenth Party Congress: A Programme for Authoritarian Rule', *The China Quarterly*, 132 (December).

Saich, T. (1994c) 'Discos and Dictatorship: Party-State and Society. Relations in the People's Republic of China', in J. N. Wasserstrom and E. J. Perry (eds), *Popular Protest and Political Culture in Modern China* (Boulder, CO: Westview Press), 2nd ed.

Saich, T. (1994d) 'The Search for Civil Society and Democracy in China', *Current History*, 83(584).

Saich, T. (1995) 'Writing or Rewriting History? The Construction of the Maoist Resolution on Party History', in T. Saich and H. van de Ven (eds), *New Perspectives on the Chinese Communist Revolution* (Armonk, NY: M. E. Sharpe).

Saich, T. (ed.) (1996) *The Rise to Power of the Chinese Communist Party: Documents and Analysis* (Armonk, NY: M. E. Sharpe).

Saich, T. (2000a) 'Negotiating the State: The Development of Social Organizations in China', *The China Quarterly*, 161 (March).

Saich, T. (2000b) 'Globalization, Governance, and the Authoritarian Westphalian State: The Case of China', in J. S. Nye and J. D. Donahue (eds), *Governance in a Globalizing World* (Washington, DC: Brookings Institution Press).

Saich, T. (2002) 'China's WTO Gamble. Some Political and Social Questions', *Harvard Asia Pacific Review* (Spring).

Saich, T. (2003) 'Reform and the Role of the State in China', in R. Benewick *et al.* (eds), *Asian Politics in Development. Essays in Honour of Gordon White* (London: Frank Cass).

Saich, T and X. Yang (2003) 'Selecting within the Rules: "Open Recommendation and Selection" and Institutional Innovation in China', *Pacific Affairs* (Summer).

Sargeson, S. and Zhang, Jian (1999) 'Re-assessing the Role of the Local State: A Case Study of Local Government Interventions in Property Rights Reform in a Hangzhou District', *The China Journal*, 42 (July).

Sautman, B. (1992) 'Sirens of the Strongman: Neo-Authoritarianism in Recent Chinese History', *The China Quarterly*, 129 (March).

Schell, O. (1988) *Discos and Democracy: China in the Throes of Reform* (New York: Pantheon Books).

Schell, O. (1994) *Mandate of Heaven: A New Generation of Entrepreneurs, Dissidents, Bohemians, and Technocrats Lays Claim to China's Future* (New York: Simon & Schuster).

Schell, O. and Shambaugh, D. (eds) (1999) *The China Reader: The Reform Era* (New York: Vintage Books).

Schoenhals, M. (ed.) (1996) *China's Cultural Revolution, 1966–1969: Not a Dinner Party* (Armonk, NY: M. E. Sharpe).

Schram, S. R. (ed.) (1974) *Mao Tse-Tung Unrehearsed: Talks and Letters, 1966–71* (Harmondsworth: Penguin).

Schram, S. (ed.) (1985) *The Scope of State Power in China* (New York: The Chinese University Press and St Martin's Press).

Schram, S. (ed.) (1987) *Foundations and Limits of State Power in China* (Hong Kong: The Chinese University Press).

Schurmann, F. (1968) *Ideology and Organization in Communist China* (Berkeley: University of California Press).

Scott, J. C. (1985) *Weapons of the Weak: Everyday Forms of Peasant Resistance* (New Haven: Yale University Press).

Segal, G. (1994) 'China's Changing Shape', *Foreign Affairs*, 73(3).

Selden, M. (1971) *The Yenan Way in Revolutionary China* (Cambridge, MA: Harvard University Press).

Selden, M. (ed.) (1979) *The People's Republic of China: A Documentary History of Revolutionary Change* (New York: Monthly Review Press).

Selden, M. (1995) *China in Revolution: The Yenan Way Revisited* (Armonk, NY: M. E. Sharpe).

Seymour, J. D. (ed.) (1980) *The Fifth Modernization: China's Human Rights Movement, 1978* (Standfordville, NY: Human Rights Publishing Group).

Seymour, J. D. (1987) *China's Satellite Parties* (Armonk, NY: M. E. Sharpe).

Seymour, James D. (1991) 'China's Minor Parties and the Crisis of 1989', *China Information*, 5(4).

Shambaugh, D. (1991) 'The Soldier and the State in China: The Political Work System in the People's Liberation Army', *The China Quarterly*, 127 (September).

Shambaugh, D. (ed.) (1996a) 'China's Military in Transition', Special Issue of *The China Quarterly*, 146 (June).

Shambaugh, D. (1996b) 'China's Military in Transition: Politics, Professionalism, Procurement and Power Projection', *The China Quarterly*, 146 (June).

Shambaugh, D. (1997) 'Building the Party-State in China, 1949–1965: Bringing the Soldier Back In', in T. Cheek and T. Saich (eds), *New Perspectives on State Socialism in China* (Armonk, NY: M. E. Sharpe).

Shambaugh, D. (2002) *Modernizing China's Military. Progress, Problems, and Prospects* (Berkeley and Los Angeles: University of California Press).

Shao, Wenguang (1998) 'China: Reforms and the Impact for Globalization', unpublished manuscript.

Shapiro, J. (2001) *Mao's War Against Nature: Politics and the Environment in Revolutionary China* (New York: Cambridge University Press).

Scharping, T. (2003) *Birth Control in China 1949–2000. Population Policy and Demographic Development* (London and New York: Routledge Curzon).

Shi, Tianjian (1997) *Political Participation in Beijing* (Cambridge, MA: Harvard University Press).

Shirk, S. L. (1990) ' "Playing to the Provinces": Deng Xiaoping's Political Strategy of Economic Reform', *Studies in Comparative Communism*, 23(3–4).

Shue, V. (1988) *The Reach of the State: Sketches of the Chinese Body Politic* (Stanford: Stanford University Press).

Skinner, G. W. (1964–65) 'Marketing and Social Structure in Rural China (parts 1–3)', *Journal of Asian Studies*, 24(1–3).

Smil, V. (1993) *China's Environmental Crisis: An Inquiry into the Limits of National Development* (Armonk, NY: M. E. Sharpe).

Smil, V. (1995) 'Who Will Feed China?', *The China Quarterly*, 143 (September).

Smil, V. (1998) 'China's Energy and Resource Uses: Continuity and Change', *The China Quarterly*, 156 (December).

Snow, E. (1972) *The Long Revolution* (New York: Random House).

Solinger, D. J. (1999) *Contesting Citizenship in Urban China: Peasant Migrants, the State, and the Logic of the Market* (Berkeley: University of California Press).

Song, Qiang *et al.* (1996) *Zhongguo keyi shuo bu* [*The China That Can Say No*] (Beijing: Zhonghua gongshang lianhe chubanshe).

Spence, J. D. (1990) *The Search for Modern China* (London: Hutchinson).

Spence, J. D. (1996) *God's Chinese Son: The Taiping Heavenly Kingdom of Hong Xiuquan* (New York: W. W. Norton).

State Council (2001) 'The Development-Oriented Poverty Reduction Program for Rural China', *Xinhua* News Agency (15 October).

Steinfeld, E. S. (1998) *Forging Reform in China: The Fate of State-owned Industry* (New York: Cambridge University Press).

Steinfeld, E. S. (2000) 'Free Lunch or Last Supper? China's Debt-Equity Swaps in Context', *The China Business Review*, 27(4).

Stiglitz, J. (1999) 'Quis Custodiet Ipsos Custodes?', *Challenge*, 42(6).

Sullivan, L. R. (1990) 'The Emergence of Civil Society in China, Spring 1989', in T. Saich (ed.), *The Chinese People's Movement: Perspectives on Spring 1989* (Armonk, NY: M. E. Sharpe).

Sun, Yan (1995) *The Chinese Reassessment of Socialism, 1976–1992* (Princeton, NJ: Princeton University Press).

Swaine, M. D. and Johnston, A. I. (1999) 'China and Arms Control Institutions', in E. Economy and M. Oksenberg (eds), *China Joins the World: Progress and Prospects* (New York: Council on Foreign Relations Press).

Tang, Wenfang and Parish, W. L. (2000) *Chinese Urban Life under Reform: The Changing Social Contract* (Cambridge: Cambridge University Press).

Tanner, M. S. (1994) 'The Erosion of Communist Party Control over Lawmaking in China', *The China Quarterly*, 138 (June).

Tanner, M. S. (1999) *The Politics of Lawmaking in Post-Mao China: Institutions, Processes, and Democratic Prospects* (New York: Oxford University Press).

Teiwes, F. (1987) 'Establishment and Consolidation of the New Regime', in R. MacFarquhar and J. K. Fairbank (eds), *The Cambridge History of China, 14: The People's Republic, Part I: The Emergence of Revolutionary China, 1949–1965* (Cambridge: Cambridge University Press).

Teiwes, F. C. (1990) *Politics at Mao's Court: Gao Gang and Party Factionalism in the Early 1950s* (Armonk, NY: M. E. Sharpe).

Teiwes, F. C. (1993) *Politics and Purges in China: Rectification and the Decline of Party Norms, 1950–1965* (Armonk, NY: M. E. Sharpe), 2nd edn.

Teiwes, F. C. and Sun, W. (1996) *The Tragedy of Lin Biao: Riding the Tiger during the Cultural Revolution, 1966–1971* (Honolulu: University of Hawai'i Press).

Teiwes, F. C. with Sun, W. (1997) 'The Politics of an "Un-Maoist" Interlude: The Case of Opposing Rash Advance, 1956–1957', in T. Cheek and T. Saich (eds), *New Perspectives on State Socialism in China* (Armonk, NY: M. E. Sharpe).

Teiwes, F. C. with Sun, W. (1999) *China's Road to Disaster: Mao, Central Politicians, and Provincial Leaders in the Unfolding of the Great Leap Forward, 1955–1959* (Armonk, NY: M. E. Sharpe).

Tomba, Luigi (2001) *Paradoxes of Labour Reform: Chinese Labour Theory and Practice from Socialism to the Market* (Surrey: Curzon Press).

Tsou, Tang (1983) 'Back from the Brink of Revolutionary – "Feudal Totalitarianism"', in V. Nee and D. Mozingo (eds), *State and Society in Contemporary China* (Ithaca: Cornell University Press).

Tsou, Tang (1986) *The Cultural Revolution and Post-Mao Reforms: A Historical Perspective* (Chicago: University of Chicago Press).

Tucker, N. B. (2000) 'Dangerous Liaisons: China, Taiwan, Hong Kong, and the United States at the Turn of the Century', in T. White (ed.), *China Briefing, 2000: The Continuing Transformation* (Armonk, NY: M. E. Sharpe).

Uhalley, S., Jr (1988) *A History of the Chinese Communist Party* (Stanford: Hoover Institution Press).

Unger, J. (1985–6) 'The Decollectivization of the Chinese Countryside: A Survey of Twenty-eight Villages', *Pacific Affairs*, 58(4).

Unger, J. (1987) 'The Struggle to Dictate China's Administration: The Conflict of Branches vs. Areas vs. Reform', *The Australian Journal of Chinese Affairs*, 18 (July).

Unger, J. (ed.) (1991) *The Pro-democracy Protests in China: Reports from the Provinces* (Armonk, NY: M. E. Sharpe).

Unger, J. (2002) *The Transformation of Rural China* (New York: M. E. Sharpe).

Unger, J. and Chan, A. (1995) 'China, Corporatism, and the East Asian Model', *The Australian Journal of Chinese Affairs*, 33 (January).

Unger, J. and Chan, A. (1999) 'Inheritors of the Boom: Private Enterprise and the Role of Local Government in a Rural South China Township', *The China Journal*, 42 (July).

United Nations Development Programme (UNDP) (1998) *China: Human Development Report: Human Development and Poverty Alleviation 1997* (Beijing: UNDP).

United Nations Development Programme (UNDP) and International Labour Organization (ILO) (2002) *An Integrated Approach to Reducing Poverty in China* (Beijing).

Van Ness, P. and Raichur, S. (1983) 'Dilemmas of Socialist Development: An Analysis of Strategic Lines in China, 1949–1981', *Bulletin of Concerned Asian Scholars*, 15(1).

Vogel, E. F. (1989) *One Step Ahead in China: Guangdong under Reform* (Cambridge, MA: Harvard University Press).

Vogel, E. F. (ed.) (1997) *Living with China: US/China Relations in the Twenty-First Century* (New York. W. W. Norton).

Walder, A. (1982) 'Some Ironies of the Maoist Legacy in Industry', in M. Selden and V. Lippit (eds), *The Transition to Socialism in China* (Armonk, NY: M. E. Sharpe).

Walder, A. G. (1986) *Communist Neo-Traditionalism: Work and Authority in Chinese Industry* (Berkeley: University of California Press).

Walder, A. G. (1994) 'The Decline of Communist Power: Elements of a Theory of Institutional Change', *Theory and Society*, 23(2).

Walder, A. G. (1995a) 'Local Governments as Industrial Firms: An Organizational Analysis of China's Transitional Economy', *The American Journal of Sociology*, 101(2).

Walder, A. G. (ed.) (1995b) *The Waning of the Communist State: Economic Origins of Political Decline in China and Hungary* (Berkeley: University of California Press).

Walder, A. G. (1998a) 'The County Government as an Industrial Corporation', in A. G. Walder (ed.), *Zouping in Transition: The Process of Reform in Rural North China* (Cambridge, MA: Harvard University Press).

Walder, A. G. (ed.) (1998b) *Zouping in Transition: The Process of Reform in Rural North China* (Cambridge, MA: Harvard University Press).

Wang, Shaoguang (1995) 'The Rise of the Regions: Fiscal Reform and the Decline of Central State Capacity in China', in A. G. Walder (ed.), *The Waning of the Communist State: Economic Origins of Political Decline in China and Hungary* (Berkeley: University of California Press).

Wang, Shaoguang and Hu, Angang (1999) *The Political Economy of Uneven Development: The Case of China* (Armonk, NY: M. E. Sharpe).

Wang, Xin (forthcoming) 'China's Pension System Reform and Capital Market Development', in Yasheng Huang *et al.* (eds), *Financial Reform in China*.

Wang, Y. *et al.* (2001) 'Implicit Pension Debt, Transitional Cost, Options and Impact of China's Pension Reform', World Bank Working Paper 2555.

Wang, Zhenyao (1996) 'Village Committees: The Foundation of the Chinese Democratization', in Division of Rural Work, Department of Basic-Level Governance, Ministry of Civil Affairs, *Village Elections: Democracy in Rural China, Commentaries* (Beijing: Ministry of Civil Affairs).

Wank, D. L. (1998) 'Political Sociology and Contemporary China: State–Society Images in American China Studies', *Journal of Contemporary China*, 7(18).

Wank, D. L. (1999) *Commodifying Communism: Business, Trust, and Politics in a Chinese City* (Cambridge: Cambridge University Press).

Watson, A. (1984) 'Agriculture Looks for "Shoes that Fit": The Production Responsibility System and Its Implications', in N. Maxwell and B. McFarlane (eds), *China's Changed Road to Development* (Oxford: Pergamon).

Watson, A., Findlay, C. and Du, Yintang (1989) 'Who Won the "Wool War"? A Case Study of Rural Product Marketing in China', *The China Quarterly*, 118 (June).

Watson, J. L. (1992) 'The Renegotiation of Chinese Cultural Identity in the Post-Mao Era', in J. N. Wasserstrom and E. J. Perry (eds), *Popular Protest and Political Culture in Modern China* (Boulder, CO: Westview Press).

Wedeman, A. (2000) 'Budgets, Extra-Budgets, and Small Treasuries: Illegal Monies and Local Autonomy in China', *Journal of Contemporary China*, 9(25).

Wei, Jingsheng (1997) *The Courage to Stand Alone: Letters from Prison and Other Writings* (New York: Viking).

Wen, Hui (2002) *Shanghai Baby* (London: Robinson).

West, L. and Zhao, Yaohui (eds) (2000) *Rural Labour Flows in China* (Berkeley: Institute of East Asian Studies, University of California).

Weston, T. B. and Jensen, L. M. (eds), (2000) *China Beyond the Headlines* (Lanham, MD: Rowman & Littlefield).

White, G. (1982) 'Introduction: The New Course in Chinese Development Strategy: Context, Problems and Prospects', in J. Gray and G. White (eds), *China's New Development Strategy* (London: Academic Press).

White, G. (1983) 'Chinese Development Strategy after Mao', in G. White, R. Murray and C. White (eds), *Revolutionary Socialist Development in the Third World* (Lexington: University Press of Kentucky).

White, G. (ed.) (1991) *The Chinese State in the Era of Economic Reform: The Road to Crisis* (Armonk, NY: M. E. Sharpe).

White, G. (1993) *Riding the Tiger: The Politics of Economic Reform in Post-Mao China* (Stanford: Stanford University Press).

White, G. (1994) 'Democratization and Economic Reform in China', *The Australian Journal of Chinese Affairs*, 31 (January).

White, G., Howell, J. and Shang, Xiaoyuan (1996) *In Search of Civil Society: Market Reform and Social Change in Contemporary China* (Oxford: Clarendon Press).

White, G. and Shang, Xiaoyuan (eds) (1998) *Issues and Answers: Reforming the Chinese Social Security System* (Brighton, Sussex: Institute of Development Studies).

White, L. T. III (1989) *Policies of Chaos: The Organizational Causes of Violence in China's Cultural Revolution* (Princeton, NJ: Princeton University Press).

White, L. T. III (1998) *Unstately Power* (Armonk, NY: M. E. Sharpe), 2 vols.

White, S. *et al.* (1990) *Communist and Postcommunist Political Systems: An Introduction* (Basingstoke: Macmillan), 3rd edn.

White, T. (1987) 'Implementing the One-Child-Per-Couple Population Program in Rural China: National Goals and Local Politics', in D. M. Lampton (ed.), *Policy Implementation in Post-Mao China* (Berkeley: University of California Press).

Whyte, M. K. (1974) *Small Groups and Political Rituals in China* (Berkeley: University of California Press).

Whyte, M. K. (1991) 'State and Society in the Mao Era', in K. Lieberthal *et al.* (eds), *Perspectives on Modern China: Four Anniversaries* (Armonk, NY: M. E. Sharpe).

Whyte, M. K. (1992) 'Urban China: A Civil Society in the Making?', in A. L. Rosenbaum (ed.), *State and Society in China: The Consequences of Reform* (Boulder, CO: Westview Press).

Whyte, M. K. (1996) 'City Versus Countryside in China's Development', *Problems of Post-Communism*, 43(1).

Witke, R. (1977) *Comrade Chiang Ching* (Boston: Little, Brown).

Wittfogel, K. (1957) *Oriental Despotism: A Comparative Study of Total Power* (New Haven: Yale University Press).

Womack, B. (1982) 'The 1980 County-level Elections in China: Experiment in Democratic Modernization', *Asian Survey*, 22(3).

Womack, B. (ed.) (1991) *Contemporary Chinese Politics in Historical Perspective* (Cambridge: Cambridge University Press).

Wong, C. P. W. (1988) 'Interpreting Rural Industrial Growth in the Post-Mao Period', *Modern China*, 14(1).

Wong, C. P. W. (2000a) 'Central–Local Relations Revisited', *China Perspectives*, 31 (September–October).

Wong, C. P. W. (2000b) Presentation at the workshop 'Mapping the Local State in Reform Era China', Los Angeles, 8–9 June.

Wong, C., Heady, C. and Woo, W. T. (1995) *Fiscal Management and Economic Reform in the People's Republic of China* (New York: Oxford University Press).

Wong, J. and S. Chan (2002) 'Why China's Economy Can Sustain High Performance: An Analysis of its Sources of Growth', *East Asian Institute Background Brief*, 138 (November).

Wong J. and Yongnian Zheng (2002) *China's Post-Jiang Leadership Succession: Problems and Perspectives* (Singapore: World Scientific Publishing).

Wong, L. (1998) *Marginalization and Social Welfare in China* (London: Routledge).

Wong, L. and N. Flynn (2001) *The Market in Chinese Social Policy* (Basingstoke: Palgrave).

Woo, Wing Thye (1999) 'The Real Reasons for China's Growth', *The China Journal*, 41 (January).

Woo, Wing Thye (2001) 'Recent Claims of China's Economic Exceptionalism. Reflections Inspired by WTO Accession', *China Economic Review*, 12.

Woo, Wing Thye (n.d.) 'Some Unorthodox Thoughts on China's Unorthodox Financial Sector', unpublished paper.

World Bank (1990) *China: Reforming Social Security in a Socialist Economy* (Washington, DC: World Bank).

World Bank (1994) *Averting the Old Age Crisis: Policies to Protect the Old and Promote Growth* (New York: Oxford University Press).

World Bank (1996a) *China Pension System Reform* (Beijing: Resident Mission in China, World Bank).

World Bank (1996b) *Country Report: China* (Washington, DC: The World Bank).

World Bank (1997a) *At China's Table: Food Security Options* (Washington, DC: World Bank).

World Bank (1997b) *China's Management of Enterprise Assets: The State as Shareholder* (Washington, DC: World Bank).

World Bank (1997c) *Financing Health Care: Issues and Options for China* (Washington, DC: World Bank).

World Bank (1997d) *Old Age Security: Pension Reform in China* (Washington, DC: World Bank).

World Bank (1997e) *Sharing Rising Incomes: Disparities in China* (Washington, DC: World Bank).

World Bank (1997f) *China Engaged: Integration With the Global Economy* (Washington, DC: World Bank).

World Bank (1997g) *Clear Water, Blue Skies: China's Environment in the New Century* (Washington, DC: World Bank).

World Bank (2000) *China: Overcoming Rural Poverty* (Washington, DC: World Bank).

World Bank (2001) *World Development Report 2000–2001: Attacking Poverty* (Washington, DC: World Bank).

World Health Organization (2000) *World Health Report: Report of the Director-General 2000* (Geneva: World Health Organization).

Wu, Fei (1997), 'Zhongguo nongcun shehui de zongjiao – Huabei mouxiang nongcun tianzhujiao huodong kaocha [Religion in Rural Society – Investigation into Catholic Activities in a Certain County in Huabei], *Zhanlüe yu guanli* [*Strategy and Management*], 4.

Xiang, Biao (1996) 'How to Create a Visible "Non-State Space" Through Migration and Marketized Traditional Networks: An Account of a Migrant Community in China', paper delivered to the International Conference on Chinese Rural Labour Force Migration (Beijing).

Xu, Jianchu and Pei, Shengji (1997) 'People, Policy, Protection and Poverty: Transboundary Biodiversity Maintenance and Conservation In-between China, Vietnam and Myanmar' (Yunnan: Unpublished paper).

Xu, Xiangqian (1979) 'Strive for the Realization of the Modernization of National Defence', *Red Flag*, 10.

Xu, Yong (1997) 'Use Village Self-Governance to Promote the Administration of Village Level Public Finances', paper delivered to the Conference to Mark the Tenth Anniversary of the Organic Law on Village Self-Governance (Beijing).

Xue, Muqiao ([1980] 1982) 'Economic Work Must Grasp the Objective Laws of Development', in Bogdan Szajkowski (ed.), *Documents in Communist Affairs 1980* (Basingstoke: Macmillan – Palgrave).

Yahuda, M. (1996) *The International Politics of the Asia-Pacific: 1945–1995* (London: Routledge).

Yan, Jiaqi and Gao, Gao (1996) *Turbulent Decade: A History of the Cultural Revolution* (Honolulu: University of Hawai'i Press).

Yang, Dali (1994) 'Reform and the Restructuring of Central–Local Relations', in D. S. G. Goodman and G. Segal (eds), *China Deconstructs: Politics, Trade and Regionalism* (New York: Routledge).

Yang, Dali L. (1996) *Calamity and Reform in China: State, Rural Society, and Institutional Change since the Great Leap Famine* (Stanford: Stanford University Press).

Yang, Dali (1997) 'Surviving the Great Leap Famine: The Struggle over Rural Policy, 1958–1962', in T. Cheek and T. Saich (eds), *New Perspectives on State Socialism in China* (Armonk, NY: M. E. Sharpe).

Yang, Zhong (1996) 'Withering Governmental Power in China?', *Communist and Post-Communist Studies*, 29(4).

Yao, Wen-yuan (1975) 'On the Social Basis of the Lin Piao Anti-Party Clique', *Peking Review*, 18(10) (7 March).

Yeung, Godfrey kwok-yung (1995) 'The People's Liberation Army and the Market Economy', in R. Benewick and P. Wingrove (eds), *China in the 1990s* (Basingstoke: Macmillan – now Palgrave Macmillan).

Yu Shaoliang, Sun, Jie and Jiang, Zuoping (2000) 'Zhifu zengshou, jiekai nongmin "xinjie"' [Get Rich, Make Harvest, and Relax the Farmers' Minds], *Liaowang* [*Outlook Weekly*], 26 (26 June).

Yu, Wei and Ren, Minghui (1997) 'The Important Issue of Enterprise Reform: Health-care Insurance System', in G. J. Wen and D. Xu (eds), *The Reformability of China's State Sector* (River Edge, NJ: World Scientific Press).

Yusuf, S. (2000) 'The East Asian Miracle', in J. E. Stiglitz and S. Yusuf (eds), *Rethinking the East Asian Miracle* (New York: Oxford University Press).

Zeng, Yi *et al.* (1993) 'Causes and Implications of the Recent Increase in the Reported Sex Ratio at Birth in China', *Population and Development Review*, 19(2).

Zha, Jianying (1995) *China Pop: How Soap Operas, Tabloids, and Bestsellers are Transforming a Culture* (New York: New Press).

Zhang, Chunqiao [Chang Chun-chiao] (1975) 'On Exercising All-Round Dictatorship over the Bourgeoisie', *Peking Review*, 18(14) (4 April).

Zhang, Houan and Xu, Yong (1995) *Zhongguo nongcun zhengzhi wending yu fazhan* [*The Stabilization and Development of Chinese Village Politics*] (Wuhan: Wuhan chubanshe).

Zhang, Le-Yin (1999) 'Chinese Central-Provincial Fiscal Relationships, Budgetary Decline and the Impact of the 1994 Fiscal Reform: An Evaluation', *The China Quarterly*, 157 (March).

Zhang, Renshou (1995) 'Yanhai nongcun jingji fazhan moshi yu quyu wenhua bijiao yanjiu [Comparative Study of the Economic Development Pattern and Regional Culture in the Rural Coastal Area], *Jingji shehui tizhi bijiao yanjiu* [*Comparative Economic and Social Systems*], 2.

Zhang, Xiaoshan (1999) 'Who Will Take Care of the Rural Elderly and Sick People: The Current Situation of the Social Security Reform in China', in *Social Sciences: Chinese Academy of Social Sciences Forum* (Beijing: Foreign Languages Press).

Zhang Yi, 'Jingzhong: woguo nuer chusheng xinbie zai chixu shangsheng' (Warning: An Imbalance of Sex Ratio in China), in Ru Xin *et al.* (eds), *2003 nian: Zhongguo shehui xingshi fenxi yuce* (*2003: Circumstances and Analysis of Chinese Society*) (Beijing: Social Sciences Documentation Publishing House).

Zhao, Suisheng (1997) 'Political Reform and Changing One-Party Rule in Deng's China', *Problems of Post-Communism*, 44(5).

Zhao, Yaohui and Xu, Jianguo (1999) 'Alternative Transition Paths in the Chinese Urban Pension System', *China Centre for Economic Research*, Working Paper.

Zhao, Ziyang (1987) 'Advance Along the Road of Socialism with Chinese Characteristics', *Beijing Review*, 30(45) (9–15 November).

Zheng, Shiping (1997) *Party vs. State in Post-1949 China: The Institutional Dilemma* (Cambridge: Cambridge University Press).

Zheng, Yong-Nian (1994) 'Perforated Sovereignty: Provincial Dynamism and China's Foreign Trade', *The Pacific Review*, 7(3).

Zheng, Yong-Nian and Lye, Liang Fook (2002) 'Succession Politics, Power Distribution and Legacies: China After the 16th Party Congress', *East Asian Institute Background Brief*, 142.

Zhong, N. (2001) 'An Evolving Rehabilitation Service Delivery System in the People's Republic of China', *Journal of Rehabilitation* (July–September).

Zhou, Kate Xiao (1996) *How the Farmers Changed China: Power of the People* (Boulder, CO: Westview Press).

Zhu, Chuzhu *et al.* (1997) *The Dual Effects of the Family Planning Programme on Chinese Women* (Xi'an: Xi'an Jiaotong University Press).

Zhu, Ling (2000) 'Shei lai wei nongmin kanbing chiyao tigong shehui baozhang' [Who can Provide the Farmers with Medical Services], *Liaowang* [*Outlook Weekly*], 16 (17 April).

Zhu, Ling and Jiang, Zhongyi (1996) *Public Works and Poverty Alleviation* (New York: Nova Science).

Zhu, Rongji (2003) 'Government Work Report, Delivered at First Session of Tenth NPC (March)' *FBIS-CHI*-2003-0319.

Zweig, D. (1989) *Agrarian Radicalism in China, 1968–1981* (Cambridge, MA: Harvard University Press).

Zweig, D. (1997) *Freeing China's Farmers: Rural Restructuring in the Reform Era* (Armonk, NY: M. E. Sharpe).

Zweig, D. (2002) *Internationalizing China. Domestic Interests and Global Linkages* (Ithaca, NY: Cornell University Press).

Index